Territorial Integrity in a Globalizing World

Abdelhamid El Ouali

Territorial Integrity in a Globalizing World

International Law and States' Quest for Survival

Springer

Prof. Abdelhamid El Ouali
University Hassan II
Faculty of Law
Department of Political Sciences
Route d'Eljadida 9
20190 Casablanca
Morocco
hamid.elouali@gmail.com

ISBN 978-3-642-44770-9 ISBN 978-3-642-22869-8 (eBook)
DOI 10.1007/978-3-642-22869-8
Springer Heidelberg Dordrecht London New York

Printed on acid-free paper

Springer is part of Springer Science+Business Media (www.springer.com)

For Soumaya,
Mehdi,
Sara and
Nacer

"All societies face the problem of how to survive in the face of uncertainty, the never-ending challenges, dilemmas and crises"

Douglass C. North, John Joseph Wallis and Barry R.Weingast "Violence and Social Orders. A Conceptual Framework for Interpreting Recorded Human History", Cambridge University Press, 2009,133

Contents

Introduction

Territorial integrity has in the past decades been facing tremendous challenges. Self-determination claims have dramatically increased and led very often to civil wars. Some states have even been disintegrated. External interventions have put severe stress on territorial sovereignty. Old doctrines such as humanitarian intervention have been revived by some global and regional powers in order to achieve their own political goals. Last but not least, globalization has weakened the states to the extent that some have started to lose their congruence with their own nations, which has in fact led to the emergence of ethnonationalism and the radicalization of nationalistic movements claiming purely and simply their own independence. In all these situations, International Law has not been of great help to the states in order to meet these challenges. It was so because International Law does not provide for any particular protection to territorial integrity, although the latter is a cornerstone of that law.

We know that one of the recurrent interrogations about International Law is related to its primitive character which makes of it a fragile, uncertain and ineffective instrument in establishing durable peace and cooperation between states and peoples. Many explanations have been given to the primitive nature of International Law, but the most largely shared one is the decentralized character of International Law which has allegedly durably acted as a major obstacle to the emergence of a central authority. In fact, no system can exist without at least a minimum of central authority. Now, contrary to the conventionally shared perception, authority has never been absent from the international system, but it has a Janus faces or a twofold character, a formal one as authority belongs individually to every single state in the form of the traditional de jure principle of sovereignty and an effective by oligopolistic one which is a de facto collective absolute sovereignty held by a limited number of powerful states. It is that dual character of sovereignty which has made the functioning of the international system dependent on a recurrent remodeling of the configuration of forces. Being ultimately based on the unequal sharing of force, International Law has obviously mainly functioned at the detriment of the weakest states which constitute the bulk of the international society and whose sovereignty has been very often a pure "hypocrisy".[1] But the greatest hypocrisy of the Westphalian states' system has been to declare, on the one hand, that all the states are equally sovereign polities, and to continue, on the other hand, making of force the only one factor which can guarantee the existence of states, while knowing that the dissemination of force within the international system is disproportionate. All over the long human history, the states have been able to exist as political entities because their first function was to ensure the protection of their citizens. The famous legitimate monopoly of violence has no other justification or foundation than states' duty to protect every individual member of their own societies. Hence, the most serious weakness of International Law and which makes of it a primitive law lies in the fact that the latter does not possess a similar system by which it can protect the right of the existence of the states, that is their territorial integrity.

The issue of ensuring states' protection is all the more crucial as the main problem the states have been durably confronted with since their emergence thousands years ago has been their possible own disintegration. Being the result of internal as well as external factors, states' territorial integrity has been consequently under permanent threat of internal and external character.

The internal threat was, one can say, inscribed in state's own gens as the state has emerged out of the division of the society not only in classes but also in ethnicities. The latter division has durably been the most dangerous threat to state's existence. The state has addressed such division by constantly adapting its territoriality to changing social contexts. Indeed, one of the major characters of territoriality is its flexibility which indeed helps the state to adjust to changing local configurations of power. States collapsed in particular when they were no longer able to adjust to the rise of new internal situations and convince every segment of their populations that their "raison d'être" is to ensure their protection and well being. For millennia, International Law has been kept away from the internal dimension of territoriality. But, when it started to be involved in this issue, it was in order to render the state more fragile and facilitate its eventual disintegration as a result of the transformation of territorial integrity. Indeed, the latter has witnessed a major transformation in so far as it has started, further to the emergence at the end of the eighteenth century of popular sovereignty, that is self-determination, to integrate a potential of self-disintegration. It is that potential of self-destruction that has pushed early European nation-states, first, to constantly work on the homogenization of their societies, second, to accept to enlarge the civil and political rights of their citizens and, third, to consent to the welfare state. It is also that potential of self-destruction which has been exploited by powerful states to expand their hegemony and influence abroad by, under the guise of the right to self-determination, disintegrating rival empires and states and creating new polities. It is that potential which has been behind the "deep tectonic movement"[2] stretching across more than two

[1]Krassner (1999).

[2]Anderson (1992, p. 193).

centuries which has witnessed, from one hand, the "disintegration of the great polytechnic, polyglot, and often polyreligious monarchical empires"[3] built up so painfully in medieval and early modern times and, from another hand, the creation of many new states. Illustrative of this phenomenon is the dramatic increase in the number of the states which rose up from 23 states in 1826 to more than 195 today! Furthermore, territorial integrity's potential for self-destruction has been aggravated by the exacerbation of ethnic conflicts which has almost systematically resulted from the implementation of the right to self-determination and the very frequently fractured states to which that right has given rise. "It is the very process of the formation of a sovereign civil state", notes Clifford Geertz,[4] "that, among other things, stimulates elements of parochialism, communalism, racialism, and so on, because it introduces into society a valuable new prize over which to fight and a frightening new force with which to contend". Lastly, territorial integrity has been weakened by globalization as the latter plays a compounding role in the increasing disjuncture between the state and the nation. However, the crisis of territoriality seems to be pushing today towards the rise of a new paradigm where self-determination is increasingly requested to preserve state's territorial integrity through the implementation of democracy. A new understanding of self-determination is indeed being advanced thanks to which state's territorial integrity can be protected from internal threat but only if the concerned state can testify that it is a real democratic state that represents its whole population.

As to the external threat, it was also almost congenial to the state. State's power has its own dynamic which is to expand as far as it can even if such a move requires the conquest of new communities. The expansion of power has very often led not only to the conquest of new territories but also to the creation of new states. In fact, most of the pre-modern states had come into existence not as pristine but as secondary states mainly as a result of territorial conquests. International Law made its first appearance when it recognized state's right to use force in order to preserve its own existence. But, it authorized also the state to conquer other territories, that is to destroy other states and annex their territories. Such situation has, as is well known, completely changed with the creation of the United Nations, whose Charter has prohibited the use of force between states. However, the UN Charter did not put in place a system guaranteeing state's territorial integrity by the international community. Indeed, the UN Charter did not even consider establishing a system similar to the one created by the famous Article 10 of the League of Nations' Covenant. True, that Article had lost its credibility as the international community had never been able to make use of it. This may be considered as the biggest failure of the international community in establishing an international order guaranteeing the right of the existence of its members. It is that failure which makes of International Law a primitive law. In internal law, the right of individuals to existence and security is protected by the state. This is the "raison d'être" of the

---

[3]Idem.

[4]Geertz (1963, p. 120).

state. It is that raison d'être which justifies state's legitimate monopoly of violence. The biggest ambiguity of International Law is that it has proclaimed the prohibition of the use of force, but it has never been able to complement such prohibition by establishing a system guaranteeing territorial integrity, that is the existence of the states. True, the UN Charter has established a system of collective security, but the implementation of such system has very often been blocked and neutralized by the rivalry between powerful states.

In the past decades, many states have disintegrated and disappeared from the world map. Although external factors have played a key role in such disintegration, the international community has remained indifferent to a situation affecting some of its own members. Such a reaction reflects if any the biggest flaw of International Law: the lack of any obligation to protect the existence of the states members of the international community. Astonishingly, International Law has shown its limits even when confronted with the issue of fixing the international borders of the new states which emerged from the collapse of Yugoslavia and the Soviet Union.

However, while the famous Article 10 of the League of Nations' Covenant had never been implemented by the international community, it gave rise in states' practice to the obligation of non-recognition of territorial changes made by force. This has so far been the only major progress made by International Law in protecting territorial integrity although the latter is a fundamental principle if not the founding principle of that law.

The tremendous challenge to which states' territorial integrity has been faced with in the past decades requires therefore a rethinking of that major principle of International Law. Unfortunately, the doctrine has given little attention to the principle of territorial integrity, although it does consider territory of paramount importance for states' existence as well as International Law's formation. Focusing more on territory than on territorial integrity, the legal doctrine has been aware of the crucial importance of the former to the formation of International Law. Hence, it has been pertinently said that "if sovereignty had not been associated with the proprietorship of a limited portion of the earth, had not, in other words, become territorial, three parts of the Grotian theory, would have been incapable of application".[5] It has also been admitted that territory is "perhaps the most fundamental concept of International law".[6] Likewise, some authors have, when dealing with the concept of state's territorial sovereignty, admitted that the latter was a major principle from which are drawn many other International Law principles. Thus, according to Judge M. Huber, territorial sovereignty is "the point of departure in settling most questions that concern international relations".[7] Likewise, Malcolm N. Shaw is of the opinion that "The concept of territorial sovereignty is concerned with the nature of authority exercised by the state over its territory. The ideas of territory and sovereignty are closely linked in international law, since the concept of

[5]Maine ("Ancient Law", 1861, 61) quoted by Shaw (2005, p. 15).

[6]"International Law", London, Stevens, 1970, vol. 1, 2nd edition, p. 403.

[7]Palmas Island Case, 1928, 2 United Nations Reports of International Arbitration Awards, 829.

territory itself is concerned with those geographical areas over which sovereignty or sovereign rights may be exercised. Territorial sovereignty is, therefore, centered upon the rights and powers coincident upon territory in the geographical sense. As such it has provided the basis for modern international law".[8] But in fact, territorial sovereignty is nothing other than the legal expression of the phenomenon of the territoriality whose legal institutionalization has given rise to the principle of territorial integrity.

The rise of the principle of territorial integrity can be associated with the emergence of the state phenomenon thousands years ago. It has its origin in the phenomenon of territoriality. The latter has been, further to the emergence of the state, subjected to a process of institutionalization and broadening of its meaning and scope to the extent that it became consubstantial to the territorial sovereign right of the existence of the state. That process has led not only to the legalization of territoriality but also to the creation of major principles of International Law the objective of which was to protect the right of existence of the state. The latter, as modern anthropology has rightly shown, is not a phenomena which would have emerged primarily in Europe starting from the sixteenth century. The state is rather a very old and universal institution, but its form can differ from one historical context to another. The determination of the process which has led to the emergence of the principle of territorial integrity requires therefore a deep exploration of the conditions which have led to the emergence of the state itself. Such task is not easy as there is no institutional memory of the issue since International Law has been formalized or codified only starting from the seventeenth century and more systematically all along the nineteenth century. Hence there is a compelling need for a journey deep in the very old past of political collectivities. However in order to do so , one has to depart from mainstream international lawyers' scholastic routine which in this case consists in " not touching upon within the framework of a given science a question the solution of which pertains to another branch of science".[9] One cannot either count a lot here on political scientists as from their perspective "inquiry into the circumstances surrounding the origin of state belongs largely to the realm of theory and speculation".[10] Consequently one has to mainly solicit various scientific disciplines including anthropology. However, if an interdisciplinary approach can help us understand all the human, political and historical elements which have played a decisive role in the emergence of the state entity and consequently the principle of territorial integrity, it goes without saying that it is only the positive International Law which will be the ultimate logical guide and the only relevant criteria in the final formulation of a definition and consequently an understanding of the principle of territorial integrity.

Therefore, the present analysis aims, first, at rethinking the principle of territorial integrity as the cornerstone of the legal structure of the statehood and International

---

[8]"Territory in International Law", op.cit., p. 15.

[9]de Libera (2000).

[10]Garner (1910, p. 86).

Law as well. It aims, second, at showing that International Law does not provide for an appropriate protection of the principle of territorial integrity, that is the protection of the right of the existence of the states. It is that lack of protection of territorial integrity which has made the use of force the ultimate means for every state to ensure its own survival. This has been a durable rule in international relations since the emergence of early states thousands years ago. Such rule has not been abrogated by the UN Charter as the latter has made of self-defense an exception to the prohibition of the use of force. More gravely, it was that lack of international protection that has aggravated the difference between strong and weak states whose survival is very often dependent upon the "monnayable" protection that the former can provide to the latter. It is also not a surprise that military interventions within weak states' territories have continued to flourish despite the general prohibition of force. It is true that the United Nations have in the past decades devoted tremendous efforts to strengthen the prohibition of the use of force. However, this has not prevented powerful states from trying to circumvent that prohibition through the exhumation under a new packaging of old doctrines such as the so-called doctrine of humanitarian intervention. Hence, one of the key ideas which will be argued in this study is that peace and stability cannot become a reality in international relations unless an adequate protection is guaranteed by the international community to every state whether weak or strong. It is believed that it is time for the international community to bring back to reality Woodrow Wilson's dream of guaranteeing the territorial integrity of every recognized state which has adopted a democratic regime and shown great respect of human rights as this can dramatically help in making peace and stability prevail between nations.

Peace and stability require also putting an end to the manipulation of self-determination. But one of the findings of this book is that we are presently witnessing a shift towards a new paradigm where democratic self-determination is replacing self-determination/independence, hence dramatically reducing the occasions for such manipulation and therefore making an end, in particular through the implementation of territorial autonomy, to the emergence of non-viable states which have become in the past years serious sources of international insecurity.

Thus, a comprehensive and profound rethinking of the principle of territorial integrity is needed before showing how International Law remains powerless in helping states to address the increasing external and internal challenges that territorial integrity, that is states' right of the existence, is being faced with.

References

Anderson B (1992) The new world disorder. New Left Rev

de Libera A (2000) Archéologie et reconstruction. Sur la méthode en histoire de la philosophie médiévale. In: Un siècle de philosophie 1900–2000. Gallimard, folio/essais

Garner JW (1910) A treatise on the origin, nature, functions, and organization of the state. American Book Company

Geertz C (1963) The integrative revolution: primordial sentiments and civil politics in the new states. In: Geertz C (ed) Old societies and new states: the quest for modernity in Asia and Africa. Free Press, New York
Krassner SD (1999) Sovereignty: organized hypocrisy. Princeton University Press, Princeton
Shaw MN (2005) Territory in international law. In: Shaw MS (ed) Title to territory. Ashgate, Aldershot

Part I
Rethinking Territorial Integrity

It is generally agreed that the principle of territorial integrity is a positive norm of a paramount importance in the contemporary international society.[1] The principle of territorial integrity has been sanctioned by key international instruments, legal or political ones: treaties, old[2] or new,[3] fundamental charters, universal[4] or regional,[5] international jurisprudence,[6] International Organizations resolutions,[7] political declarations,[8] etc… However, contemporary International law does not paradoxically seem to explicitly offer any definition of the principle of territorial integrity. Yet the invocation of the principle is a bit of a ritual. But curiously that invocation is systematically made in a negative way. Thus we frequently come across statements that the principle of territorial integrity forbids "violation of a territory", "intervention against foreign territories", "use of force against a territory", "dismemberment of a territory", etc. This is no surprise as territorial integrity has been commonly approached in a very particular way.

In fact, the international community has traditionally approached the principle of territorial integrity in an indirect manner. Thus, with the exception of the Covenant of the League of Nations which has, thanks to the tremendous efforts deployed by President Woodrow Wilson, attached special importance to the principle of

---

[1] Dinh (1980, p. 356).

[2] See for instance, the clause on respect of the territorial integrity inserted in some treaties signed between Greek cities and mentioned by Ténékides (1956, p. 499).

[3] With regard to Morocco, for instance, see the preamble of the 1906 Algeciras Act or the 3 October 1904 French-Spanish declaration related to its territorial integrity.

[4] Art. 2.4 of the United Nations Charter.

[5] Art. 1 and 9 of the 1948 Bogota Charter; Art. 3.3 of the OAU Charter.

[6] ICJ, The Corfou Detroit case, ICJ Rep.,1949, 35.

[7] Para 6 of the 1514 (XV) resolution dated 14 December 1960, Declaration on the Granting of Independence to Colonial Countries and People; the 1970 Declaration on Principles of International Law Concerning Friendly Relations and Cooperation between States.

[8] The territorial integrity principle is one of the principles of pacific coexistence adopted by the Bandung Conference. See also the Helsinki Final Act.

territorial integrity, the latter has been intertwined with other principles such as the prohibition of the use of force (the famous art. 2.4 of the UN Charter) and self-determination (in particular the 1960 UN General Assembly Declaration on the Granting of Independence to Colonial Countries and Peoples and the 1970 Declaration on Principles of International Law Concerning Friendly Relations and Co-operation among States). These principles have overshadowed the principle of territorial integrity to the extent that almost no mention of it can be found in the related travaux préparatoires, particularly those which have led to the adoption of the UN Charter.

Contemporary International Law doctrine has also shown very little attention to the principle of territorial integrity.[9] A reified approach of the state and the territory has condemned that doctrine to at best have a truncated interpretation of the principle of territorial integrity or at worst to confuse the latter with other principles such as the principle of the final and stable character of the borders or more gravely the principle of the sanctity of borders.

It is generally rightly said that the principle of territorial integrity prohibits dismemberment of states, violation or use of force against their territory, intervention and interference in internal affairs, etc. But the principle of territorial integrity is more than that. In fact in essence the principle of territorial integrity is intimately linked to the state as a legal entity the main objective of which is to ensure its perennial existence within a specific territory whose borders have been established in accordance with International Law. The principle of territorial integrity is as such at the core of the state system. Its emergence as a legal principle is associated with the emergence of the state system itself. Furthermore, it has a constitutive character in so far as it has right from its inception not only given to the state its legal armature but has also generated other major international principles such as the principle of sovereignty, the principle of the exclusivity of state's jurisdiction and the principle of non-interference in internal affairs. Territorial integrity has also, as set out in the second part of this book, given rise to legal principles which are directly related to territory such as the necessary consent of the state when delimiting its territory, a principle which has been obviously called into question by the proponents of the uti possidetis or recently by the Security Council in some few instances, the most important being the unilateral delimitation of the Iraqi borders. Territory integrity has also given rise to the principle of the necessary consent of the state to territorial changes in compliance with the requirement of Constitutional law. Such requirement, which has been extensively discussed by traditional doctrine, has gained prominence in the past decades further to the development of self-determination and democracy.

[9] The same can also be said about non legal scholars. Thus J.G. Ruggie, for instance, though he regretfully notes that "It is truly astonishing that the concept of territoriality has been so little studied by students of International politics; its neglect is akin to never looking at the ground that one is walking on", he also neglects to define the notion of territoriality, although the latter is central in his study. Ruggie (1993, p. 174).

In fact, the principle of territorial integrity is nothing other than the territorial sovereign right to the existence of the state. However, such a right has been put under stress since the emergence of the state thousands years ago. It is so because the state has an inherent drive to disintegration. Meanwhile, the state has been able to remain the main form of social organization as it has shown a great ability to survive despite changing political and socio-economic situations and the transformation of human societies and their increasing complexity.

The present part will attempt to show, first, that the principle of territorial integrity is nothing other than the right to existence of the state, and, second, that the latter has been able to survive over thousands of years as the main form of social organization as a result of its great ability to adapt, thanks to what can be called the flexibility of territoriality, to changing historical contexts and situations.

References

Dinh NQ (1980) Droit international public, 2nd edn. L.G.D.J, Paris
Ruggie JG (1993) Territoriality and beyond: problematizing modernity in international relations. Int Organ 47(1)
Ténékides G (1956) Droit International et communautés dans la Grèce anciènne. RCADI II

Chapter 1
The State's Sovereign Right to Existence

Modern International Law doctrine has a reified approach to territorial integrity. This has led to the perception that territorial integrity is the completeness/unity of state territory. Such an approach has proven to be irrelevant in understanding the real nature, content and legal consequences of territorial integrity. Amazingly International legal and political scholars as well as political geography specialists have never enquired about the link between territorial integrity and territoriality. In fact, territorial integrity is in essence the elaborated and sophisticated legal expression of territoriality. It is intimately linked to the state as a legal entity the main objective of which is to ensure its perennial existence within a specific territory whose borders have been established in accordance with International Law. Therefore, a new approach is needed in order to better understand territorial integrity, a principle that can be considered as the cornerstone of International Law.

1.1 The Need for a New Approach to Territorial Integrity

Territorial integrity is fundamentally the result of the institutionalization or legalization of territoriality. Before showing that, there is first, a need to de-reify the legal approach to territorial integrity.

1.1.1 The De-Reification of the Legal Approach of Territorial Integrity

Contemporary legal doctrine has devoted no particular attention to the principle of territorial integrity. It appears to have confined itself to a reified approach regarding the question of the state, territory and borders. Though it sees the territory as "an

A. El Ouali, *Territorial Integrity in a Globalizing World*,
DOI 10.1007/978-3-642-22869-8_1, © Springer-Verlag Berlin Heidelberg 2012

important chapter of International Law and the general theory of state",[1] the doctrine has mainly focused on the material elements that constitute the state, the legal nature of territory, the competences and the exclusive jurisdiction that the states are entitled to exert over their own territory, and so forth.[2]

It is certainly the above approach that has led to the common opinion that territorial integrity reflects the completeness, entirety/totality or unity of the state territory. Thus, it has been said that the expression territorial integrity indicates that "a state has remained and must remain *intact*, that it has not been subject and must not be subject to any dismemberment",[3] that territorial integrity is "the character attached to the territory of every state, which should not be subjected to any kind of grip aiming at subtracting it, durably or momentarily, from the authority of the state"[4] or that "the notion of territorial integrity refers to the material elements of the state, namely the physical and demographic resources that lie within its territory (land, sea and airspace) and are delimited by the state's frontiers and boundaries."[5]

The tendency of the International Law doctrine to focus on the competencies exerted by states over their territories, which is usually called "territorial sovereignty", has pushed Malcolm M. Shaw to base his own judgment on the latter and then in a very rapid manner define territorial integrity.[6] Shaw's attempt deserves to be mentioned as it is extremely difficult, as I have said earlier, to find a contemporary author showing interest in the definition of the principle of territorial integrity. The author starts by recalling the importance of the territorial sovereignty by stating: "The territorial definition of states is a matter of the first importance within the international political system. It expresses in spatial terms the dimensions and sphere of application of *authority* (emphasis added) of states and provides the essential framework for the operation of an international order that is founded upon strict territorial division. In terms of International Law specifically, the territorial delineation raises and determines issues ranging from the nationality of

[1] Barberis (1999, p. 132).

[2] See, for instance, Schoenborn (1929, pp. 85–189), Delbez (1932, pp. 705–738), Dembinski (1975, pp. 71–96), Shaw (1982, pp. 69–91); for other bibliographical references, see Barberis (1999, p. 132 and seq.).

[3] Translation of "un Etat reste, est resté ou doit rester *entier*, ne subit, n'a subi ou ne doit subir aucun démembrement", "Dictionnaire de la Terminologie du Droit International" (J. Basdevant) publié sous le patronage de l'Académie du Droit International, Sirey, Paris, 1960, p. 340.

[4] "Dictionnaire de Droit International Public" sous la direction de J. Salmon, Bruylant, Bruxelles, 2001, p. 592.

[5] "Encyclopedia of Public International Law", published under the auspices of the Max Planck Institute for Comparative Public law and International Law under the direction of R. Bernhardt, Elsevier, North-Holland, 2000, p. 813.

[6] A total confusion between territorial integrity and territorial sovereignty is made by Korva Gombe Adar who peremptorily states that "The term "territorial integrity is used here to refer to the power of a sovereign state to exercise supreme authority over all persons and things within its territory" (Adar 1986, p. 425).

inhabitants to the applications of particular norms and it is the essential framework within which the vital interests of states are expressed and with regard to which they interact and collide. Many of the fundamental norms of both classical and modern international law are predicated upon, and defend, such spatial division ... the territorial definition of states is the spatial context for the application of state competence...." And then jumps to say that: "the principle of territorial integrity sustains the territorial definition of sovereign independent states ... (it) protects the territorial definition of independent states."[7]

Similar remark can be made with regard to Marcello G. Kohen's approach of the principle of territorial integrity which is in his opinion related to the respect of the exercise of the prerogatives of the sovereign state on its territory. But he adds that the principle of territorial integrity is also related to the inviolability of the state territory and the guaranty against any dismemberment of the same state territory.[8] However by adding these two elements, the author creates some confusion between the essence of the principle and its legal implications.

In reality, territorial sovereignty is one of the elements involved in the definition of the principle of territorial integrity. If seen in isolation, territorial sovereignty means nothing more than the competencies exerted by a state over, or within, its territory. Many crucial elements are ignored, including territory itself. Moreover, territorial integrity is a major concept which stands by itself and is not an auxiliary of any other principle.

Yet the confusion does not stop there, as some lawyers do liken the principle of territorial integrity to the principle of stability of territories and borders.[9] Others, more categorically, are of the opinion that the principle of territorial integrity is nothing other than the principle of *uti possidetis*.[10] Furthermore, still others liken the proscription of the use of force against territorial integrity with the latter.[11]

In essence territorial integrity is intimately linked to the state as a legal entity the main objective of which is to ensure its perennial existence within a territory that is limited by international borders duly recognized by International Law. On the contrary stability of territories or borders is the form which the latter can take as a result of their establishment in accordance with International Law. With regard to

---

[7] Shaw (1997, pp. 76 and 124).

[8] Kohen (1997, pp. 369–377).

[9] See for instance Shaw (1997, p. 151). See also Lalonde (2002, p. 143), who, although rightly adheres to the opinion that "the territorial principle is the foundation stone upon which rests the entire legal order", confines the same principle to a simple "manifestation" amongst others of the doctrine of stability of boundaries.

[10] See, for instance, Borella (1964, p. 29), Bedjaoui (1972, p. 95), Yakemtchouk (1975, p. 51), Bipoum-Woom (1970, pp. 127–128), Touval (1972, p. 90 and seq.), Antonopoulos (1996, pp. 34–35), Nesi (1998, p. 9), Kohen (1997, p. 453), Sanchez-Rodriguez (1997), Shaw (1999, p. 499). Similar confusion is also made by the I.C.J. See Burkina Fasso-Mali case, ICJ Reports, 1986, 554 at 565 para 22; Case Concerning the Territorial Dispute (Libya-Tchad), ICJ Reports, 1994, 6, at 38 para 75.

[11] See in particular Zacher (2001, p. 215).

the uti possidetis, as we will see later on, it is only a way among others to settle territorial disputes and, what is more cofusing, a means which is very controversial. As to the assimilation between the proscription of the use of force against territorial integrity and the latter, it actually consists of confusion between the instrument to protect a norm and the norm itself.

The principle of territorial integrity refers not only to the materiality of territory (i.e. its unity and completeness) but also to an immaterial element, which is the right to the existence of state within a given territory, the borders of which are well defined and recognized by International Law. Astonishingly enough, the classical doctrine of International Law has explicitly highlighted this matter. Moreover, it has conceived the right of the territorial existence of state as the supreme right from which all the other rights derive. Thus, reflecting the state of the classical doctrine of International Law in the nineteenth century which shared the opinion that the right to territorial existence of the state was the supreme right, H. Bonfils was able to recall that:

> "In fact, there is for the states, natural and necessary persons, *only one primary right, only one fundamental right*, the right to existence. From this really crucial and essential right, derive, as necessary corollaries, linked one to another by way of successive deductions, links of the same chain, all the other rights considered as *essentials, innate, absolute, permanent and fundamental*. From the right to existence derives the right to *conservation* and *freedom*. The right of conservation implies the right of *perfectibility, defense, and security*. From the right to freedom are inferred the right to *sovereignty and independence*, etc... But under these diverse denominations, it is the *same* right which moves and makes itself felt and which is the only fundamental right, the right to *existence*. The others, ineluctable consequences, partake of the character of absolutism and permanence of the paramount right, of which they are only emanations and developments (italics are emphasis made by the author)."[12]

Wheaton, one of the most influential writers in the classical period, wrote also that "One of the absolute international rights of states, one of the most essential and important, and that which lies at the foundation of all the rest, is the right of self-preservation. It is not only a right with respect to other state, but a duty with respect to its own members, and the most solemn and important duty which the states owes

[12] Our translation of: "En réalité, il n'y a pour les Etats, personnes naturelles et nécessaires, *qu'un seul droit primordial*, un *seul droit fondamental,* le droit à l'existence. De ce droit réellement primordial et essentiel, découlent, comme corollaires nécessaires, se rattachant les uns aux autres par voie de déductions successives, comme les chainons d'une unique chaine, tous les autres droits classés comme *essentiels, innés, absolus, permanents, fondamentaux*. Du droit à l'existence découlent le droit de *conservation* et celui de *liberté*. Le droit de conservation engendre le droit de *perfectibilité*, de *défense, de sûreté*. Du droit à la liberté se déduisent le droit de *souveraineté* et celui d'*indépendance,* etc.

Mais sous ces diverses dénominations, c'est un *même* droit qui se meut et s'exerce, le seul droit fondamental, le droit a l'*existence*. Les autres, inéluctables conséquences, participent au caractère d'absolutisme et de permanence du droit primordial, dont ils ne sont que des émanations et des développements", Rousseau (1912, p. 142).

to them. The right necessarily involves all other incidental rights, which are essential as means to give effect to the principle end".[13]

Among many authors of the same period, Amos S. Hershey has also indicated that:

> "There exist certain essential or fundamental rights and duties of states which underlay the positive rules and customs of International Law. These rights (to which are attached corresponding duties) are usually described as primary, inherent, absolute, fundamental, essential, permanent, etc... The most important of these fundamental rights of states is that of existence, which involves the rights of self-preservation and defense. To this right there is attached the corresponding duty of respecting the existence of other states."[14]

Similarly, the American Institute of International Law adopted, at its first session held in 1916, a "Declaration on the Rights and Duties of Nations" in which it highlighted in its first paragraph that: "Every nation has the right to exist, and to protect and conserve its existence; but this right neither implies the right nor justifies the act of the state to protect itself or to conserve its existence by the commission of unlawful acts against innocent and unoffending states".[15] A similar statement can also be found in the Article 3 of the Convention on the Rights and Duties of States adopted by the Conference of American States held at Montevideo on 23 December 1933.

Writing in 1922, that is at a time when the expression "right to existence of the state" started to disappear from the International Law vocabulary to the benefit of the expression "territorial integrity", P. Fauchille was able to stress that the famous Article 10[16] of the Covenant of League of Nations did nothing else – when calling upon the states to respect and preserve the territorial integrity of the members of the League – but recalling the obligation to respect the right to the existence of the states.[17] But paradoxically, the semantic change has over time led some lawyers, as shown above, to adopt a reified approach of a concept which is crucial to International Law.

Paradoxically, although the right to existence of the states was expressly referred to by international scholars in the classical period that led to the foundation of modern International Law, the reference to that right started to disappear at the beginning of the twentieth century. One of the very few scholars representing the old tradition in International Law and who, to our knowledge, was one of the last international lawyers to recall the state of the positive law by referring to the comprehensive meaning of the principle of territorial integrity and its foundational role in contributing to the emergence of other principles of International Law was M. Sibert who did recall that:

---

[13] Phillipson (1916, p. 87).

[14] Hershey (1927, pp. 230–231).

[15] See on that Declaration Root (1916, pp. 211–221).

[16] On the crucial importance of Article 10 of the League Covenant, see Part Two Chapter IV, I, B.

[17] Fauchille (1922, p. 408).

> "The right to existence is a fundamental right, and maybe the only fundamental right (here a footnote referring to the principle of territorial integrity) from which derive, as necessary corollaries, all the other rights considered as fundamental ones. Thus, from the right to existence derives the right to conservation and freedom. The right to conservation generates in turn the right to perfectibility, to defense and to security. From the right to freedom is deduced the right to sovereignty or independence, which, in turn, implies, internally, the rights of legislation, jurisdiction and property, and externally, the rights to equality, mutual respect and freedom of commerce. Under these diverse denominations, it is the same right which manifests itself, the only fundamental right: the right to existence."[18]

Among present scholars, M. Walzer, ironically a non lawyer, has been among the very few authors who have been able to establish a link between the right of existence to the state and territorial integrity. Thus, he believes that the state's rights to territorial integrity and sovereignty are simply the collective form of individual rights to life and freedom[19] and that consequently "territorial integrity and political sovereignty can be defended in exactly the same way as individual life and liberty."[20]

Having a reified approach to International Law, some lawyers have attempted to refute the validity of the concept of the right of existence of the state in well defined and recognized borders. In their analysis, these lawyers conclude to the "impossible construction of the right to existence"[21] as the state is not eternal, it appears, vanishes and comes back to life again. This conclusion is not relevant as International Law takes into consideration the spatial as well as the temporal existence of the state. H. Kelsen has in this respect clearly shown that the state has not only spatial but also temporal existence, that time must be considered as an element of the state just as much as space and that "it is general International law which determines the spatial and temporal sphere of validity of the national legal orders, delimits them against each other, and thus makes it legally possible that states exist beside each other in space and follow each other in time."[22]

---

[18] Our translation of: "le droit à l'existence constitue un droit fondamental, et peut-être le seul droit fondamental (a footnote referring here to the principle of territorial integrity) d'où découlent, comme corollaires nécessaires tous les autres droits classés comme fondamentaux. Ainsi du droit à l'existence découlent le droit de conservation et celui de liberté. Le droit de conservation engendre à son tour le droit de perfectibilité, de défense, de sûreté. Du droit à la liberté se déduit le droit de souveraineté ou d'indépendance qui, à son tour, entraine avec lui, à l'intérieur, les droits de législation, de juridiction, de domaine, et à l'extérieur, ceux d'égalité, de respect mutuel, de libre commerce. Sous ces diverses dénominations et selon différentes manifestations, c'est un même droit qui s'exerce, le seul droit fondamental: le droit à l'existence", Sibert (1951, p. 230).

[19] Walzer (2006, pp. 53–55).

[20] Idem, p. 54.

[21] Scelle (1948, p. 92).

[22] Kelsen (1934/1989, p. 289).

Yet, the right of the existence to the state can be confirmed through a deconstruction[23] of the principle of territorial integrity. Hence, the deconstruction of the principle of territorial integrity requires fundamentally a critical demarche, even if it seems a priori iconoclast for a discipline like International Law which has remained prisoner of the straitjacket of old thinking, traditions and clichés. This demarche necessitates a variety of perspectives to determine and decompose the elements which constitute the principle of territorial integrity and critically analyze them one after another far from any pre-notions and non-objective considerations, and, secondly, to carry out a reconstruction of the global configuration of the principle in a way to reach a definition that reflects the present state of positive International Law.

Deconstruction of territorial integrity can be carried out through the analysis of the process by which it has, first, been produced and then institutionalized and legalized.

1.1.2 The Production of Territorial Integrity

One can theoretically imagine, from a historical perspective going back to the origin of humanity, that law had nothing to do with the creation of the first human collectivities stabilized in territories and enjoying distinct sovereignties. It is power alone in its extreme bareness, as shown by modern Political Anthropology,[24] that is the prime creator of the political collectivities as "no principle has presided over the distribution of territories between human beings, it is the historical fact, which has decided of their allocation to a group of human beings".[25] It is power alone, which is also the stabilizing factor of populations, potential nations, through "the individualization and the unification of the territory within borders."[26] However, power – by power it is meant here and in the following pages the custodian of the political might, king, emperor and so forth –, with its tendency

[23] Deconstruction is, as Derrida has clarified, an analysis which tries to find out how a thinking – or a belief, an institution, a tradition, a society, etc. – works or does not work, to find the tensions, the contradictions, the heterogeneity within its own corpus. See Caputo (1997, p. 9). That is why it is not a method or some tool that you apply to something from outside. It is so because "deconstruction does not affirm what *is*, does not fall down adoring before what is *present,* for the present is precisely what demands endless analysis, criticism, and deconstruction" (Idem, p. 40). Therefore deconstruction requires first "a work of excavation, elucidation, and shaking of the prevailing views" (Guy Petitdemange 2003, p. 423). It requires, secondly, a deep journey in the memory of thinking and institutions (Derrida used very often to say that "(he) likes nothing more than memory". See, for instance, "La signification de la parole donnée", Mémoires, p. 27). It requires, thirdly, the use in a very interactive manner of different scientific knowledge and disciplines.

[24] See Balandier (1999, p. 43).

[25] Vischer (1970, p. 227).

[26] Ibid., p. 222.

to the absolute,[27] creates its own "fetters"[28] or limits which deploy their effects within two distinct spheres: the external and the internal ones. It is by trying to locate and determine these constraints that one can carry out the deconstruction exercise and ultimately show, through a reconstruction process, how International Law does really conceive the principle of territorial integrity, its content and scope.

The idea that each community has its own territory has been the result of the dual factors of the transition to a sedentary lifestyle[29] and the imposition of spatial limits as the expression of the failure of the quest of absolute power. The notion of spatial limits has been central in the creation of a collective consciousness, as it has generated the attachment of the social group to a territory that it considers its own.

The process of identification to a territory is primarily linked to borders. It is so because the borders play a crucial role in the creation of the territory and the institutions and symbols which are attached to them.[30] The borders first establish distances[31] and then differences[32] between territories and by doing so, they also create unity[33] within the same territories.[34] "*Territoriality*", writes D. Retaille, "is mainly the experience of unity. The territory is made of anchors and landmarks shared by the members of the group, which characterize it and make it different from what constitutes outside, the space of uncertainty."[35] In turn unity generates the attachment of the social group to a territory which it considers its own.[36]

---

[27] "The sad fact, points out John J. Mearsheimer, is that international politics has always been a ruthless and dangerous business, an it is likely to remain that way. Although the intensity of their competition waxes and wanes, great powers fear each other and always compete with each other for power. The overriding of each state is to maximize its share of world power, which means gaining power at the expense of other states. But great power do not merely strive to be the strongest of all the great powers, although that is a well known outcome. Their ultimate aim is to be the hegemon – that is, the only great power in the system.... But the desire for more power does not go away, unless a state achieves the ultimate goal of hegemony. Since no state is likely to achieve global hegemony, however, the world is condemned to perpetual great-power competition" Mearsheimer (2001, p. 2). Likewise J. Barthelemy (1917, p. 358) has noted that "Le premier mobile de l'activité d'un Etat à l'extérieur est naturel, spontané et pour ainsi dire physiologique. C'est la tendance de croître. Le cidre, comme l'a dit Max Harden, étend ses puissantes ramures et étouffe les arbrisseaux modestes qui tentent de végéter après lui. Aussi la force d'un Etat s'exerce par une loi de nature, sans qu'on ait a mêler à la constatation de ce phénomène physique de croissance, des considérations de moralité ou de droit".

[28] Gilpin (1981, pp. 96–105).

[29] See Cukwurah (1967, p. 13).

[30] See Paasi (1996).

[31] See, for instance, Arbaret-Schulz et al. (2004).

[32] See Gottman (1952).

[33] See Retaille (1990, p. 34).

[34] One can then understand why the Arabic language does, when it refers to territorial integrity, does talk, as we see earlier, of the "unity of territory".

[35] Retaille (1990, p. 31).

[36] See Newman (2004, p. 4). See also Goemans (2004, p. 16).

By individualizing the territory, the border individualizes and unifies the political collectivity: primitive group, state, ancient or new.[37] First, territory which, with parental or national link, contributes to the establishment of solidarity and unity among the social group[38]; second, it is territory that can, in the long run, ensure the survival of the group.[39] The latter, from the primitive group to the modern state, then attains a political dimension and necessarily proclaims the sacred character of the territory and its borders.[40]

The existence of borders is inherent to human collectivities. Borders can even be seen as the reflection of a global phenomenon affecting all species, as their existence and development are both related to the emergence of complexity in living systems.[41] The driving force of species is first of all survival.[42] According to C. Raffestin "all the living generate one or many limits: to **exist** (highlight added) consists first of all in building and producing limits and thereby producing a territory from a portion of space".[43] The notion of border, contrary to what has been alleged by certain colonial ethnographers, has then been into existence throughout the history of humanity,[44] since human collectivities, prompted by the quest of power have found themselves in confrontation with one another. All over the earth spaces where the quest of power has triggered confrontation between human collectivities, the border, zonal or linear, blurred or precise, has been the mountain, the forest, the river, the desert, etc.

In human terms, the borders are the result of the territorialization process, during which dominating individuals or groups aim to extend their power over larger human groups. Successful territorialization leads to territoriality.[45] The latter term means,[46] according to ethology, the control by an animal or a group of animals of

[37] See Goemans (2004, p. 20).

[38] See Jones (1959, p. 242).

[39] See Michael Rienzi "Pan-European Genetic Interests. Ethno-States, Kinship Preservation, and the End of Politics", http://theoccidentalquarterly.com/vol3no1/mxr-genetic.html.

[40] See Guichonnet and Raffestin (1974, p. 116).

[41] Fromm (2004, pp. 150–151).

[42] Ibid.

[43] Raffestin (1990, p. 295).

[44] Idem, p. 15, and Person (1972).

[45] See Raffestin (1986, p. 182).

[46] Contradictory and conflicting interpretations of the notion of territoriality can be very frequently found in the writings of many scholars. Thus some authors see in it a **process**. See, for instance, Stack (1986, p. 19). Others see in it a **status** that reflects the control extended over a territory. See White (2000, p. 32). Others see in territoriality a **geographic area**. See Luke (1994, p. 1). See also in almost the same vein, Haigh (2004). Others see in it "**a territorial regime**". See Kahler (2004, p. 9). Echoing that opinion, Kal Raustiala sees in it "**a defining attribute of the Westphalian state**". See Kal Raustiala "The Evolution of Territoriality: International relations & American Law", same Workshop, 2. Giving a political coloration to territoriality, Christopher K. Ansell and Giuseppe Di Palma define it as "the consolidation of political authority into territorially defined, fixed, and mutually exclusive enclaves", www.si.unmich.edu/ICOS/AnsellPaper.pdf, 2. Others see in it an

a certain area and its defense against other members of its own or their species.[47] By extension, the term means the control of a given space – and its resources – by dominating human individuals or groups, after they have succeeded in neutralizing any internal or external competitors and its use "for political, social, and economic ends".[48]

However, in order to ensure its strength and longevity, the territoriality of human groups has to assume some legitimacy and if possible a legal character that it cannot obtain without the tacit or explicit consent of internal and external rivals. The "passage obligé" has then been to "produce territory" from space,[49] that is, the attachment of the dominated human collectivity to "its territory". This has been accomplished by convincing the collectivity that the *raison d'être* of the dominating power is to ensure its "survival" or further to the emergence of the concept of nation, to protect the "identity"[50] of the nascent nations. A successful production of territory will translate into territoriality in its broad sense, that is, the social representation of a human collectivity appropriating a space, identifying itself with it and proclaiming its readiness to defend it against intruders. In other terms, it is "a behavioral phenomenon associated with the organization of space into spheres of influences of clearly demarcated territories which are made distinctive and considered at least partially exclusive by their occupants or definers".[51]

Reflecting the appropriation by a human group of a geographical space with which it identifies itself, territoriality becomes consubstantial with the existence of the group.[52] Yet the new community thus created will have a legal status only when it is recognized by external rivals, namely the political organization from which it has sought to get its independence. Territoriality, when accepted by internal and external competitors, can then develop and give rise to territorial integrity which, once institutionalized, becomes the legal armature which structures a new entity:

---

epistemological and socio-structural principle as well as a ***symbolic reference*** **to territory which underlies the construction of collective identities** and a ***form of segmentary differentiation*** **of world society**". See Christoph K. Ansell and Giuseppe Di Palma "Territoriality and Modernization" www.uni.bielefed.de/soz/iw/pdf/albert_.pdf, 3.

[47] On animals and territoriality, see Ardey (1967).

[48] Agnew (2004, p. 1).

[49] Raffestin (1980, p. 130), Allies (1983, p. 10).

[50] Hence it is most likely the emergence of nationalism and its sophisticated language which will lead to the substitution of the notion of "identity" to the notion of "survival". See on the link between identity and security, Ryerson Christie "Homeland ad Defense and the Re/Territorialization of the State", www.cda-cdai.ca/Symposium/2002/Christie.htm. The author writes in this regard that "when the physical body of the state is attacked, our very identity is assaulted. In essence an attack on the soil of a country is an attack on the people", 6.

[51] Malmberg (1980, p. 10).

[52] It can, according to M. Chisholm and D. Smith, "take different forms in different geographical and historical circumstances, and its specific manifestations must be contextualized" Chisholm and Smith (1990, p. 3).

the state, the essence of which is that it is a coercive legal order.[53] H. Kelsen was able to capture that fundamental characteristic of the state when he did show that "if a power is established anywhere, in any manner, which is able to ensure permanent obedience to its coercive order among the individuals whose behavior this order regulates, then the community constituted by this coercive order is a state in the sense of International Law. The sphere in which this coercive order is permanently effective is the territory of the state, the individuals who live in the territory are the people of the state in the positive International Law".[54] We know that various definitions of the state have been offered by the doctrine, but these definitions are either inspired by ideological considerations[55] or are not workable.[56] That is why many authors prefer, inspired by the 1933 Montevideo Convention,[57] to enumerate the conditions (territory, population and government) which characterize the state. However, taking into consideration the above analysis of the concept of territoriality, one can define the state as a coercive legal order which exerts independent and exclusive power over a territorially based population in accordance with International Law.

Here then, we reach our first conclusion: every political collectivity, group or state exists as such when it extends its authority over a geographical space and makes of it its own territory, a territory the foundations and limits of which are established in accordance with International Law[58](Conclusion 1). But the process of legalization of territoriality does not stop there as the right to existence of the state within its own geographical space has generated a series of key international legal principles in order to ensure its own protection.

1.2 The Institutionalization of Territoriality

The institutionalization of territoriality was made possible by the emergence of key principles that constitute the legal armature of the state and consequently, the foundation of International Law. These principles emerged in order initially to enable the state to exert its sovereignty and ensure its own survival and, later on, to

---

[53] See Kelsen (1934/1978, p. 287).

[54] Kelsen (1941–1942, pp. 69–70).

[55] See Kelsen (1934/1978, p. 286).

[56] See Grant (1998–1999, p. 413).

[57] Which states that "The state as a person of International Law should posses the following qualifications: a) a permanent population; b) a defined territory; c) a government; and d) a capacity to enter into relations with other states" (Article 1).

[58] The American Institute of International Law's "Declaration of the Rights and Duties of Nations" adopted in its first session held in 1916 states that: "IV. Every nation has the right to territory within defined boundaries."

make of the people, further to the emergence of self-determination, the real holder of sovereignty.

1.2.1 The State's Right to Sovereignty

The "raison d'être" of sovereignty was from its inception to protect the society and the state. Yet, starting from the seventeenth century, it will incorporate a new function: the domination through equality under what can be called the dual sovereignty system.

1.2.1.1 The "Raison d'être" of Sovereignty

The major constraint to which power as defined above was internally confronted to has been to know how it can be accepted by the whole society after it has emerged insofar as force alone is not a determining factor. Thus from the beginning the necessity to justify its existence was a major concern for power. An important concept has then emerged and that has never stopped since then to legitimate power: the need to preserve the existence of the society and the idea that the state is the ultimate protector of the same society.

The struggle for power is a recurrent phenomenon in every state. It happens between the holders of power, or the latter and those who are subjected to it.[59] Force was used from the beginning of first political bodies as a decisive factor in the conquest of power or its consolidation. With regard to the latter situation, "Force and compulsion have", underlines J. W. Garner, "played an important part in the consolidation of states and in the formation of new state forms".[60] However, even when it reaches its highest point, power requires the adherence or consent of those who are subjected to it. The consent can be expressed either formally or tacitly through the routine apathy of the society or the sharing of some common and important values.[61] That is the reason why power has to constantly justify itself. Max Weber has noted that power never limits itself to obedience, but tries always to demand adherence from those it dominates.[62] Power does that by trying to convince the society that his main function is to fundamentally work for the maintenance and the conservation of the whole society.

The need for conservation is essential to any society. Leslie A. White recalls in this regard that "man is an animal and, like all other animals, is engaged in

[59] See G. Balandier (1999, p. 34 and seq.).

[60] Garner (1910, p. 120); See also Carré de Malberg (1962, p. 199).

[61] See Firth (1964, p. 143 and seq.).

[62] See the presentation made by Freund (1966), Collins (1988).

a life-and-death struggle for survival" and that "just as biological organisms behave in a manner the consequences of which tend to be security of existence and continuity of life, so do cultural systems (i.e. the human beings systems) behave in such a manner as to protect and sustain the human organisms within their embrace. And just as biological organisms develop means of greater control over their life process, so do cultural systems tend to develop more effective means of making life secure and perpetual for groups of human beings".[63] The same author notes also that human being have from the beginning established a link between their need for conservation and territory. He says that: "A group of primates confines itself to a certain locality instead of ever exploring new territory.... The reasons for this are fairly clear: Familiarity with one's surroundings breeds confidence and a sense of security. Strange terrain makes one apprehensive; no one knows what dangers might lurk there".[64]

Taking into consideration the need for conservation, some anthropologists have even come to define polity by its function of maintaining and conserving the society. S. F. Nadel is of the opinion that the political institutions are those which ensure the maintenance and the conservation of the largest group, which is the society.[65] From his part, Leslie A. White is of the opinion that "the WHY of society or social organization is (therefore) clear. It is a way of sustaining and perpetuating life"[66] or what it is very often referred to as the "integrity of a social system". In most of the societies, this is the business of what he calls the "State-Church" mechanism (i.e. the power in its multi-faced countenances) whose function "is the preservation of the integrity of the socio-cultural system of which it is a part. This means ... coordination and control of parts and regulation of the system as a whole.... The struggle between dominant and subordinate classes has been chronic and perennial in civil societies. The lower classes-the slaves, serfs, industrial proletariat-periodically try to better their lot by revolt and insurrection. If the social system is to be kept intact, if it is not to explode in violence and subside in anarchy, the relationship of subordination and superordination between classes must be maintained; in other words, the subordinate class must be kept in a condition of subjection and exploitation. It is the business of the state-church to see that this is done."[67]

The states' permanent quest for conservation and survival is also posited by major theoretical approaches to International Relations. "For millennia, shows Dustin Ells Howes, prominent political thinkers have suggested that the primary aim of political entities is survival.... From Aristotle to Machiavelli, and from Waltz to Wendt, Western thinking about states in large part turns on the notion that

[63] White (1959, respectively p. 77 and 78).

[64] Idem, p. 59.

[65] Nadel (1951, p. 141).

[66] White (1959, p. 208).

[67] Idem, pp. 313–314.

the central characteristic of successful state is it ability to preserve itself as discrete entity".[68] The states' quest for survival was so obvious to Kenneth Waltz that in his seminal "Theory of International Politics", he limited himself to say, though all his book is posited on it, that "I assume that states seek to ensure their survival. The assumption is a radical simplification made for the sake of constructing a theory".[69] For his part John J. Mearsheimer, sharing also the view that all states in the international system aim to guarantee their own survival, explains that "Because other states are potential threats, and because there is no higher authority to come to their rescue when they dial 911, states cannot depend on others for their own security. Each state tends to see itself as vulnerable and alone, and therefore it aims to provide for its own survival".[70] This rule applies to weak states as well as to great powers. Analyzing the behavior of the latter, he adds that "survival is the primary goal of great powers. Specifically, states seek to maintain their *territorial integrity* (italics added) and the autonomy of their domestic political order. Survival dominates other motives because, once a state is conquered, it is unlikely to be in position to pursue other aims.... States can and do pursue other goals, of course, but security is their most important objective".[71] Kenneth Waltz clarifies in this regard that "Only if survival is assured can states safely seek ... tranquility, profit, and power."[72]

It is also not a surprise that since the seventeenth century, many thinkers-Locke, Hobbes, Grotius, Pufendorf, Rousseau and others-have tried in different ways to justify the pre-eminence of the power, democratic or non-democratic, in the society due to its ability to protect and preserve the latter. This was done, as we know, through the doctrine of the existence of a social contract, supposed to exist at the origin of the creation of state, signed between the community and the power and the objective of which is to preserve the whole society from destruction. Thus, according to Hobbes, "The final cause, end, or design of men (who naturally love liberty and dominion over others) in the introduction of that restraint upon themselves in which we see them live in commonwealth is the *foresight of their own preservation* (italics added), and of a more contended life thereby; that is to say, of getting themselves out of from that miserable condition of war, which is necessarily consequent ... to the natural passions of men, when there is no visible power to keep them in awe, and tie them by fear of punishment to the performance of their covenants and observation of those laws of nature...".[73]

Though the doctrine of the passage from nature to society was a mere fiction, it remains important as it has eloquently underlined that the first concern of

[68] Howes (2003, p. 669 and 690).

[69] Waltz (1979, p. 91).

[70] Mearsheimer (2001, p. 33).

[71] Idem, p. 31.

[72] Waltz (1979, p. 126).

[73] Hobbes (1668/1994, p. 106).

individuals living altogether under either democratic or non-democratic regimes is the preservation and conservation of their societies. Its importance derives also from the fact that it is possible to draw from it a conceptualization of the content and scope of dominance that the power exercises over the society. Many authors have sustained in the nineteenth century that a state arises when emerges a right to dominance within a given society.[74] Indeed, the right to dominance is the major criteria for the existence of a state. P. Laband has written in this respect that "the right to dominance is the right to order free persons and communities to act or abstain in a given manner.... Every state, even the small, has a right to dominance. No other collectivity possesses such right".[75] But it was M. Weber who, echoing Hobbes, conceptualized state's dominance through his famous concept of the "legitimate monopoly of violence".[76] Yet that conceptualization is in fact nothing other than the political expression of sovereignty when it comes to its internal aspect, meaning "the original, supreme, and unlimited power of the state to impose its will upon all persons, associations, and things within its jurisdiction; in short, it is that quality of the state by virtue of which it may command and enforce obedience to the exclusion of all other wills."[77]

It is also nothing else but the exclusive jurisdiction that every state exercises within its territory. Thus, unsurprisingly, internal law and International Law sanction then the same principle. After all, we realize that Political Anthropology has shown that the phenomena of state and its existence and survival are determined by internal and external factors as well, while the power or the sovereign is at the meeting point between local and international environments.[78]

Therefore, one can conclude here that by recognizing the exclusive jurisdiction of states – as well as the right to self-defense as we will see later on –, International Law has, in fact, recognized nothing other than the states' right to preserve their existence. International Law does so through the general concept of sovereignty which simultaneously covers the internal and external spheres as logically "the internal sovereignty, which means a domination within the territory, presupposes the international sovereignty which rules out the dominating power of a third state,

[74] See Nys (1901, p. 621).

[75] Laband (1861/1900, Vol. 1, p. 119).

[76] He says in this respect that every state claims "the monopoly of the legitimate use of physical force within a given territory", "Politics as a vocation" in "From Max Weber: Essays in Sociology", trans. and ed. by H. H. Gerth and C. W. Mills (1958, p. 77).

[77] Garner (1910, p. 80). Carré de Malberg has also written in this regard that "la souveraineté, c'est le caractère suprême d'un pouvoir: suprême, en ce que ce pouvoir n'en admet aucun autre ni au-dessus de lui, ni en concurrence avec lui. Quand on dit que l'Etat est souverain, il faut entendre par là que, dans la sphère où son autorité est appelée à s'exercer, il détient une puissance qui ne relève d'aucun autre pouvoir et qui ne peut être égalée par aucun autre pouvoir" (1920, p. 70).

[78] Balandier (1999, p. 44).

and also that international sovereignty implies in order to be effective the internal sovereignty".[79] In different words, sovereignty is "the recognition by internal and external actors that the state has the exclusive authority to intervene coercively in activities within its territory".[80]

The principle of sovereignty is then inherent to the concept of the state. Its main function is to protect the right of existence of the state and by doing so to ensure that the principle of territorial integrity is respected by other states[81] (Conclusion 2). It has emerged concomitantly with the state phenomenon thousands years ago and in different cultural environments and not starting from the European seventeenth century. "In a word", summarizes F. H. Hinsley,[82] "the origin and history of the concept of sovereignty are closely linked with the nature, the origin and the history of the state" and "when a society is ruled by means of the state – which, as he extensively shows, has emerged thousands years ago – the concept of sovereignty is sooner or later unavoidable".[83] What has in fact emerged in Europe starting from the seventeenth century is a dual use of the concept of sovereignty.[84]

1.2.1.2 The Dual Sovereignty System

"All the most important concepts", has written Carl Schmitt "of the modern theory of the state are theological concept which have secularized".[85] One of these concepts has been sovereignty[86] whose origin has remained confusedly linked to Western European history and its religious particularities. Its analysis has consequently been blurred. It is not surprising in this regard that most if not all the analysis devoted to sovereignty did consist in a summary or a breviary of the thinking of famous Renaissance European authors and not the social realities which have given rise to it. Sovereignty, equality of states and the other related principles have never been analyzed as social concepts that have their origin, as we have seen above, in the dynamic of power at the internal and external levels and its material expression: territoriality.

[79] Beaud (1994, p. 17).

[80] Thompson (1995, p. 219).

[81] K. J. Holsti writes in this respect that "Sovereignty is a foundational institution of international relations because it is the critical component of the *birth, maintenance*, and *death* of states. Sovereignty helps create state; it helps maintain their integrity when under threat from within or without; and it helps guarantee their continuation and prevent their death", 2004, p. 113.

[82] Hinsley (1966, p. 3).

[83] Ibid., p. 17.

[84] See El Ouali (1993, p. 28 and seq.).

[85] Schmitt translated from German by Schlegel (1988, p. 46).

[86] See Fardella (1997, p. 118).

Certainly, the most powerful European states have initially declared first their independence from the Pope and the Emperor. But, these powerful states have later on also tried to claim each for itself the fundamental attribute of the emperor: the *imperium romanum*, i.e. the absolute sovereignty or the supreme power of Rome. This was one of the main hidden objectives of the Thirty Years War.[87] By declaring itself sovereign, each of the most nascent powerful states did in fact claim for itself the right to exercise its omnipotence not only over its own population but also over the other states. However, the war has made every powerful state realize that its claim to universal monarchy or empire was "defeated" by other identical claims.[88] The final outcome of the Thirty Years' War was then to persuade powerful states to agree on a compromise solution which, although it has never been formalized in an explicit manner, consists in establishing a dual sovereignty system characterized by two formulas, a privileged one operating between themselves and an identical one shared with all the other states including minor ones.

– With regard to the most powerful states, the formula was the equality of strength or the balance of power which reassured them against the possibility of the emergence of one state power which may jeopardize their own survival. While ensuring their preservation, such equality gave them also a privileged status, what might be called: the ***collective enjoyment of a de facto absolute sovereignty***, a kind of a joint *imperium romanum* allowing them to impose their will on the other states and then collectively dominate the whole international system. It was thanks to that co-sharing of international power that a global political system has emerged since then in so far as shown by George Modelski, "the units whose patterns of interaction structure the global polity are the global powers. These are the suppliers of order to the global system; they are those capable of acting, and those disposed to act, there; they organize and maintain coalitions and they have a presence in all parts of the world, habitually deploying forces of global reach. Their actions and reactions define the state of politics at the global level".[89] It was the balance of power which has made the holding of a collective de facto absolute sovereignty possible. The principle of balance of power was, it has been said,[90] solemnly sacred by the Westphalia treaties (1648) on the basis of equality itself. In fact the balance of power systems are as old as

[87] See Osiander (2001, p. 262).

[88] See Modelski (1971, p. 58 and seq.), Hall (1996, pp. 51–54).

[89] Modelski (1987, p. 9).

[90] Frantz von Liszt has written in this respect that: "the absolute equality of rights of the Christian states, without establishing a difference between them in reason of their religions or political regimes, from one hand, and the recognition of the community created by these Christian states, on the other hand, found their expression in one and same principle, "the European principle of balance of power" called also "co-sharing principle". In accordance with this principle, each state has the right, either alone or by allying itself with others, to preserve itself from the threatening strength of states seeking hegemony", translated by Gidel (1928, p. 18). See also Turrettine (1949).

Adam as prudence has traditionally thought the states that force should never be "thrown into one hand".[91] This why all the states tend, when their survival or independence is at stake, to form alliances against the actor or group of actors who may threaten such survival or independence.[92]

– With regard to all states, mighty or weak ones, the formula will consist in sovereignty itself conceived as the enjoyment by all states of an exclusive jurisdiction within their own territories and independence – i.e. the lack of subordination of one to another – in their mutual relations. However, as sovereignty was quickly felt as a possible source of disorder due to the discretionary power it gives to the states, an adjustment will be introduced in the system by establishing the equality of rights.

Thus, sovereignty has not been a European invention. What was invented by Europe was the introduction of a radical change in the exercise of sovereignty as the latter started, in the seventeenth century, to be exercised either individually or collectively by dominant powers. In the latter situation, what is new is the implicit incorporation of the element of *imperium* within the notion of sovereignty. It was that dual sovereignty system which has structured inter-states relations since Westphalia treaties, with long periods of order punctuated by short period of disorder as a result of the variation in the state of power prevailing between dominant states.[93] But most often dominance will be exercised through or under the guise of equality of rights, another major invention of Europe.

We know that the end of the Middle Ages period witnessed the emergence of capitalism and that one of the claims of the rising merchant bourgeoisie was the dismantlement of the hierarchical feudal system and the obstacles it has created to commerce within as well as between states. That is why equality of rights and freedom will be a major claim of the same bourgeoisie at the intra and inter-states levels, both spheres being in fact the components of the same *continuum* as "international trade requires indeed owners of goods who are free, without any hindrance in their movements, equals under the law in order to undertake the trade in accordance to an equal law for all. The passage from craft industry to manufactory requires, on the other hand, workers equally free from corporative hindrances and able to establish a contract with the owner of the factory for the hiring of their labor force on equal footing. The claim for lifting the feudal hindrances and the establishment of an equality of rights was then made first in the interest of industry and trade. But, it gradually expanded until it assumed a general character, going over even the limits of a particular state".[94]

However, what is very often ignored is that the balance of power system and equality have been mainly used, respectively at the political and economical levels,

[91] Hume (1744/1985, p. 337).

[92] Waltz (1979, p. 119).

[93] See the important contribution of Modelski (1987).

[94] Trumer (1933, pp. 86–87).

in order to reinforce the international position of the most powerful states at the detriment of the weakest ones[95] and to make of sovereignty a mere hypocrisy.[96] These are, in our views, the real factors which do fundamentally explain why "the polities of many weaker states have been persistently penetrated"[97] and why we may have a de facto or even a de jure "continuum between sovereignty and nonsovereignty".[98]

The European dual power system has allowed powerful states to establish their control and influence on the international system in order to impose their own views and interests. By doing so it has also helped to substantially stabilize the international system. That is why it has been endorsed by the UN Charter system which is based, on the one hand, on a the detention of the ***collective imperium*** by a small number of states, permanent members holding extraordinary powers within the Security Council and, on the other hand, on sovereign equality of all member states, holding a very symbolic and moral power within the General Assembly. Such a system functioned more or less properly only when a co-sharing of power among permanent member states was reached. This is why the international system has been unstable since 1989 with the emergence of quasi-unipolarity.[99] But the same system has become instable also due to globalization which has fragmented and weakened states sovereignty.[100]

Thus the legitimacy of the power is intimately associated with the need to preserve the existence of the society. From the beginning, International Law has endorsed that concern through the general concept of sovereignty, the ultimate objective of which is to protect the state and its existence. Yet, International Law has also clearly given its legitimacy to that objective by endorsing the state's right to survival.

1.2.2 The State's Right to Survival

The power of any political entity, tribal group, state or empire, has always been challenged in the ultimate stage of its spatial expansion, by another power of the

[95] El Ouali (1993, p. 31 and seq). See also on the use of the balance of power system to reach the same objective (Gulick 1967; Haslam 2002, p. 103 cont.).

[96] Krassner (1999).

[97] Krassner SD. Sovereignty. www.globalpolicy.org/nations/realism.htm, p. 1

[98] Rosenau (1995, p. 195).

[99] El Ouali (1993, p. 13 and seq.). According to Todd, the international system has become instable due to the weakness of USA, the dominating power (2002, p. 9 and seq.).

[100] Chapter 2, 2.2.3.

same type.[101] Thus, it is the impossibility of an indefinite expansion, that is a final victory, that led to the emergence of the International Law: inter-tribes/groups law,[102] inter-states Law, ancient[103] or modern. Stemming from the balance of power, the first function of International Law was to codify the use of force before establishing the law governing peace,[104] as the use of force was conceived as the ultimate means guaranteeing the existence of the state. Nicholas John Spykman recalls in this respect that "the international community does not guarantee the member states life, liberty, property, or the pursuit of happiness. Whatever the paper provisions of international conventions may have stipulated, each individual unit has continued to depend for its very existence, as well as for the enjoyment of its rights and the protection of its interests, on its strength or that of its protectors".[105] But, the perennial existence of the state has very often required – always in order to maintain the balance of power, real or imaginary – the disappearance or the dismemberment of other states. This was, among other issues, one of the fundamental characters of the European Public law which until the end of the first half of the twentieth century admitted, through its Law of War, that the state's borders can move with the soldier's boots or that state's territory can expand or shrink in an accordion movement.[106] This was also the situation of the non-European world until 1945. We know that the last date is crucial in International Relations as it was the first time that the international community has accepted the prohibition of the use of force against territorial integrity (Article 2.4).

However, has the prohibition of the use of force against territorial integrity actually resulted in the disappearance of force as the supreme way to guaranty the existence of the state? We know that this is not the case and that the UN Charter recognizes the right of every state in self-defense situation to safeguard its existence by the use of force (Article 51). Furthermore, International Law has also continued to accept, through the state of necessity principle, that the states can even violate their international obligations in order to protect themselves from any grave and imminent peril threatening one of their essential interests.

1.2.2.1 Self-Defense

Article 51 of the UN Charter states that:

> "Nothing in the present Charter shall impair the inherent right of individual or collective defense if any armed attacks occurs against a Member of the United Nations, until the

[101] See Baecheler (2002, p. 93 and seq).

[102] See Parkinson (1975, p. 16).

[103] See Bederman (2001, p. 16 and seq.), Altman (2008, pp. 1–33).

[104] See El Ouali (1982, p. 75 and seq.).

[105] Spykman (1942, p. 436).

[106] See Nys (1904, p. 401 contd.).

Security Council has taken measures necessary to maintain international peace and security. Measures taken by members in the exercise of this right of self-defense shall be immediately reported to the Security Council and shall not in any way affect the authority and responsibility of the Security Council under the present Charter to take at any time such action as it deems necessary in order to maintain or restore international peace and security."

Thus, the Charter law, like the ancient law, keeps the use of force as the ultimate means to guarantee the existence of the state. Commenting on Article 51 of the UN Charter, the International Court of Justice (ICJ) recognizes in this respect that "it cannot lose sight of the fundamental *right of every state to survival* (italics added), and then its right to self-defense, in accordance with Article 51 of the Charter, when its survival is at stake."[107] Likewise, Nico Krisch reminds us that "The right to self-defense, *as the remainder of the more encompassing right to self-preservation* (italics added) reflects the idea of an international order based on the power struggle of states that can *ensure survival* (my emphasis) only by their own strength."[108] What was in fact new in the mind of those who adopted the Charter was first of all that "the use of the self-defense in order to protect the right of state to territorial integrity cannot be equated to a return to the state of anarchy, prevailing before the Charter, as well as to the admission to the benefit of the members of the international community of a real right of self-help. The states do no longer enjoy a right to war authorizing them to settle all their territorial conflicts by force"[109] and then that "it is peace and not an indefensible status quo they wanted to protect by declaring their support to the principle of respecting and maintaining territorial integrity. It is aggression they have outlawed without prejudging the legitimate claims while reserving the use of ways of peaceful settlement."[110] It is worth mentioning in this regard that since then, as shown by Mark W Zacher,[111] the prohibition of the use of force to settle interstate territorial conflicts has become a reality and that most of the states have shown great respect to that principle.

Therefore, it can safely be said that International Law, whatever was its nature, ancient or modern, has always recognized the right of the political entities to preserve their existence ultimately through the use of force, but in fact under very strict legal conditions. These conditions have been established by the classical International Law according to which self-defense is justified only when it is immediate, necessary and proportional to the armed attack of the aggressor

[107] Legality of the Threat or the Use of Nuclear Weapons", Advisory Opinion of 8 July 1996, ICJ Reports 1996, para 96.

[108] "Summary: Self-Defense and Collective Security", www.mpiv-hd.mpg.de/de/hp/beitrsumm/beitr151.pdf, p. 405.

[109] Delivanis (1971, p. 125).

[110] de Visscher (1970, p. 222).

[111] Zacher (2001, pp. 215–250). See also Holsti (2004, pp. 73–111).

state.[112] Yet, further conditions were added by Article 51. First, the state resorting to self-defense must immediately report to the Security Council. Second, its action must be seen as a temporary reaction until the Security Council could meet and address the situation. In any case, the most fundamental condition which requires to be absolutely met is that, as has been rightly highlighted by the ICJ, "the exercise of the right of self-defense presupposes that an armed attack has occurred."[113] But today, there is an attempt to dramatically expand the concept of self-defense in order to justify a "preemptive" attack, that is to use force in situations "where a party uses force to quell any possibility of future attack by another state, even when there is no reason to believe that an attack is planned and where no prior attack has occurred".[114] However preemptive self-defense is clearly unlawful under International Law as it "is fundamentally at odds with the Charter's design. It is an exception that would overthrow the prohibition on the use of force in Article 2(4) and thus the very purpose of the UN".[115] Thus, Israel was unanimously condemned by the UN Security Council after its jets "preemptively" bombed the nuclear reactor under construction at Osirak in Iraq in 1981. Likewise the US invasion of Iraq in March 2003 based on the preemptive self-defense doctrine, also called "Bush Doctrine", has been severely criticized by many international scholars. Amy E. Eckert and Manooher Mofidi have written in this regard that "The text of Article 51 explicitly requires an "armed attack" as a pre-condition to the use of force... In the case of Iraq, evidence of armed attack by Iraq on America or American targets was not present. It is not clear how imminent this threat was: there was no evidence that Iraq was engaged in any kind of preparations for future attacks against the United States. There was no evidence of this purpose, and even if there were any, merely opposing a state has never been considered a viable threat to that state."[116]

Thus, International Law has constantly recognized the right of every state to protect its existence by the ultimate use of force (Conclusion 3). However, that right is not absolute, as it finds its limits in the right of the other states to equally protect their existence. States can have different positions in terms of power and influence, but they enjoy the same rights and duties. This is the keystone of the present international legal system that has been created since the adoption of the UN

---

[112] The formulation of these conditions has been made by the U.S. Secretary of State, Daniel Webster, in 1837 following the Caroline incident. See Moore (1906, p. 409, 412). However, these conditions seem to be increasingly confused since the attack of 11 September 2001 against the World Trade Center when the issue at stake is the use of self-defense against terrorism. See Antonio Cassese "Terrorism is also Disrupting Some Crucial Legal Categories of International Law", www.ejil.org/forum_WTC; Janos Boka "Forcible Measures Against International Terrorism and the Rule of Law", www.uni-miskolc.hu/uni/res/kozlemenyek/2002/boka.html.

[113] Military and Paramilitary Activities (Nicaragua v. U.S.), 27 June 1986, ICJ Reports 1986, at 120.

[114] O'Connell (2002).

[115] Idem, p. 13.

[116] Eckert and Mofidi (2004, p. 147).

Charter, based on the principle that "the existence of any state cannot be considered more important than the existence of any other state, and even less can it be considered more important than the existence of the whole international community".[117] Yet curiously enough, the issue of ultimately disregarding the right of a state to its survival has recently been raised, with respect to two situations.

The first, which is related to the threat or use of nuclear weapons, has been incidentally raised by the ICJ in its Advisory Opinion about the Legality of the Threat or Use of Nuclear Weapons and in which it declared that

> "in view of the current state of international law, and of the elements of fact at its disposal, the Court cannot conclude definitely whether the threat or use of nuclear weapons would be lawful or unlawful in an extreme circumstance of self-defense, in which the very survival of a state would be at stake."[118]

However, the President of the Court at that time, Judge Mohammed Bedjaoui, while recognizing that the state's right to survival is a fundamental law, similar in many respects to natural law, stressed in a separate declaration that

> "the use of nuclear weapons by a state in circumstances in which its survival is at stake risks in its turn endangering the survival of all mankind, precisely because of the inextricable link between terror and escalation in the use of such weapons. It would thus be quite foolhardy unhesitatingly to set the survival of a state above all other considerations, in particular above survival of mankind itself."[119]

The second situation is related to the allegedly increasing precedence given by the UN Security Council to the maintenance of international peace, to the detriment of the security or even the existence of states. Nico Krisch has written in this regard that

> "The UN Charter subordinates self-defense to collective security to a large degree, and that general international law indicates that the resulting power of the Security Council to restrict self-defense extends even to cases where the integrity or existence of the defending state is exposed to significant danger. This reflects the strength that interests of the international community as a whole have gained vis-à-vis interests of the individual states in international law."[120]

However, the same author has nuanced his position when he recognized that "to grant the Security Council such power (i.e. to give priority to international peace on individual state's security and existence) would, however, seem to run counter to the very foundations of the international order: the Council could then 'sacrifice' a state, or part of its territory, for the common good of peace, and this enters into conflict with the state-centric character of international law."[121] This would entail a

---

[117] Kohen (1999, p. 312).

[118] ICJ Reports 1996, para 105 E.

[119] Declaration, ICJ Reports 1996, op. cit., p. 273.

[120] Krisch (2001, p. 412).

[121] Idem, p. 410.

radical revision of the foundations of international legal order which have been made to protect the states and their right to existence. This is obviously not yet the case today, especially when we know that the existence of the peoples is intimately and fundamentally linked to their own states and territories, a situation which International Law still recognizes as it also recognizes and even tries to codify further concepts such as the concept of the "state of necessity" the raison d'être of which is to protect existence of the state.

1.2.2.2 State of Necessity

A grave and imminent peril threatening the existence or the independence of a state may provide an excuse to their breach of international obligations.[122] Thus, the state of necessity may be a circumstance precluding wrongfulness in terms of state responsibility.[123] More precisely, the state of necessity is related to a situation in which a state's "sole means of safeguarding an essential interest threatened by a grave and imminent peril is to adopt a conduct not in conformity with what is required of it by an international obligation to another state".[124] The state of necessity can be invoked in situations where there is "a danger threatening the existence of the state, its political survival or its economic survival as well".[125] The sate of necessity exists also in various domestic legal traditions where it is similarly believed that "the irresistible instinct of conservation transcends law. There is a law superior to all juridical systems, that is the survival of individual".[126]

Reference to necessity appeared thousands years ago in various domestic legal systems.[127] It can also be found in the earliest diplomatic relations between states.[128] Sustained attention will be given to it starting from the sixteenth century

[122] Thomas Jefferson has stated in this regard that "The laws of necessity, of self-preservation, of saving our country when in danger, are of higher obligation..." cited by Gregory A. Raymond "Necessity in Foreign Policy", note 12. See next footnote for full reference.

[123] On the state of necessity, see, among others, de Visscher (1917), Rodick (1928), Salmon (1984), Jagota (1985); Raymond (1998), Love (1999), Romano (1999), Boed (2000), Laursen (2004), Kalamatianou (2004), Heathcote (2005), and S. Heathcote "Est-ce que l'état de nécessité est un principe de droit international coutumier?", R.B.D.I., 2007/1, Christakis (2007).

[124] International Law Commission, YB.Int'l L. Com., 34, U.N.Doc. AICN.4/ Ser.A/1880/Add.l (Pt.2).

[125] Cahier (1985, p. 290).

[126] Hesse (2002, p. 131).

[127] Hesse (2002, p. 126 and seq.).

[128] de Visscher (1917, p. 74 and seq.); Rodick (1928, pp. 2–3).

with the emergence of the European states. A particular attention will be given to it by the then nascent realist theory one pillar of which has been since then the "reasons of state" creed. "Common to all realists, consciously or not", writes Jonathan Haslam,[129] "is the notion of Reasons of state: the belief that, where international relations are concerned, the interests of the state predominate over all other interests and values. . . . Reasons of state emerged to legitimize a new social formation, the state, against a universalist alternative: initially the Holy Roman Empire and universal church. The state's core claim to legitimacy lay in its role in assuring the security of the community within state frontiers". Similarly, attention will also start to be given to the state of necessity by the legal doctrine.

Thus, H. Grotius was of the opinion that if a person is "menaced by present force with danger of life not otherwise evitable, war is lawful, even to the slaying of the aggressor . . . as a matter of self-protection."[130] Likewise, S. Pufendorf agreed that a man who kills another one in self-defense situation may be excused "once the aggressor, showing clearly his desire to take my life, and equipped with the capacity and the weapons of his purpose, has gotten into the position where he can in fact hurt me, the space being also reckoned as that which is necessary, if I wish to attack him rather than to be attacked by him."[131] E. de Vattel was even clearer by stating that "When once a state has given proofs of injustice, rapacity, ambition, or an imperious thirst of rule, she becomes an object of suspicion to her neighbors, whose duty is to stand on their guard against her . . .. [O]n occasions where it is impossible or too dangerous to wait for an absolute certainty, we may justly act on a reasonable presumption. If a stranger levels a musket at me in the middle of a forest, I am not yet certain that he intends to kill me: but shall I, in order to be convinced of his design, allow him time to fire ? But presumption becomes nearly equivalent to certainty, if the prince who is on the point of rising to an enormous power has already given proof of imperious pride and insatiable ambition . . . (restraint in such a situation would deprive) mankind of the right to regulate their conduct by the dictates of prudence, and to act on the ground of probability?".[132] However, all these authors were of the opinion that the concerned state has to weigh the elements surrounding the circumstances including the fact to assess the possibility of avoiding the danger by peaceful means.

Meanwhile, some authors have seen in the state of necessity an "unsound and practically dangerous"[133] doctrine which can be liable to abuse. While noting that the right to self-preservation is a core element in the state of necessity, Gregory A.

[129] Haslam (2002, p. 17).

[130] Grotius (1625/1853, p. 206).

[131] Pufendorf (1672/1964, p. 264 cont.)

[132] de Vattel (1758/1852, p. 308).

[133] Hershey (1927, p. 232) who refers in particular to Pradier-Fodere and Westlake.

Raymond has pointed out that "regardless of the frequency with which national leaders rely on the argument from necessity during stressful times, such appeals create serious problems. In a crisis situation, national leaders tend to perceive their range of alternatives as more restricted than those of their opponents. Often a sense of resignation emerges as they feel swept up in the march of events. Under such circumstances, leaders generally become concerned with the timing of an expected conflict rather than with avoiding its occurrence. Once a situation is framed in terms of when action must be taken instead of whether it should occur, opportunities are transformed into necessities and pressure seems overwhelming if perceived military advantages appear to be evaporating".[134] The state of necessity has then been a controversial doctrine.

Some international tribunals have also noted the controversial character of the state of necessity doctrine. Thus, commenting on the International Law Commission draft Article 33 (now Article 25) on the state of necessity which, as we will see hereafter, authorizes a state faced with a situation of grave and imminent danger to take unlawful action invoking then a state of necessity, the arbitral tribunal has, in the second Rainbow Warrior case, stated that that Article was of "controversial character".[135] Likewise, the arbitral tribunal, in the case between the Libyan Arab Foreign Investment Company (LAFICO) and the Republic of Burundi, was of the opinion that the ILC draft was "a matter of debate in the doctrine".[136]

The doctrine of state of necessity has been invoked in different contexts: to excuse the violation of the territorial integrity of other states due to the necessity of war or to forestall harmful operations by an armed group or in pursuit of an armed band, to protect nationals abroad, to excuse the non fulfillment of financial obligations, to address environmental emergencies, etc.. The International Law Commission has recognized that these invocations were sometimes unfounded as they were a "camouflage" for attempts to dominate, occupy or annex a foreign territory.[137] However, though most of the International Law scholars have raised doubts on the legitimacy of the state of necessity doctrine and have recommended to severely restrict its application[138] or even to abolish it,[139] the state of necessity has continued to be invoked by many states as "the concept of 'state of necessity' is far too deeply rooted in the consciousness of the members of the international

[134] Raymond 10.

[135] Rainbow Warrior (New Zealand v. France), 82 ILR 1990, p. 499, 554.

[136] 96 ILR 1991, pp. 282, 318–319.

[137] 2 YB.Int'l L.Comm'n. 34,U.N.Doc.AICN.4/Ser.A/1980/Add.l (Pt.2), at 39, 40, 43, 44, 46, 151.

[138] For a review of that doctrine, see Laursen (2004, pp. 499–500 and 507–508).

[139] Judge Krylov has declared in this regard as a consequence of the adoption of the UN Charter "the so-called right of self-help, also known as the law of necessity (Notrecht) which used to be upheld by a number of German authors, can no longer be invoked. It must be regarded as obsolete", Dissenting Opinion, Corfu Channel Case, ICJ Reports 1949, p. 77.

community and of individual within states. If driven out of the door it would return through the window, if need be in other forms".[140]

Despite the concern and weariness expressed in the past about the legitimacy and relevancy of the state of necessity doctrine, attempts are presently being made in order to revive it. These attempts aim mainly to achieve two completely different objectives.

The first attempt aims at finding a legal justification to the preemptive use of force which cannot, as we have seen above, take place within the very strict self-defense framework as established by Article 51 of the UN Charter and interpreted by the ICJ. Andreas Laursen, who is one of the proponents of that revival, has recognized the importance of that revival for a big Power like USA when he writes that "the U.S. Administration's interpretation of self-defense, which includes pre-emptive attacks on terrorists, lacks support in current international law. In lieu of a reasonable self-defense argument, the necessity excuse may provide a legal basis for a forceful response to a single imminent attack against a large number of people".[141] John-Alex Romano is even of the opinion that the revival of the state of necessity should lead to the emergence of a new paradigm in relation to the use of force especially in order to preempt any possible use of Weapons of Mass Destruction (WMD) by terrorists. He writes in this regard that "the concept of state of necessity brings needed flexibility to the regime governing preemptive strikes against terrorists.... Invoking the right of self-defense under Article 51 would require a high level of state involvement in the terrorist activity. By contrast, the concept of a state of necessity is not dependent on the conduct of the state acted against, but rather turns on the imminence of the peril at hand. Thus, this approach would cover situations that do not give rise to a right of self-defense...".[142]

The second attempt aims at invoking the state of necessity as a legal justification to the nonpayment of their debts by those among the developing countries which cannot materially honor their financial commitments. The proponents of that approach sustain the existence of an international customary rule allowing the states not to pay their debts when they are faced with serious economic and financial crisis. They argue that that rule has been endorsed by several international judicial decisions[143] and that "the International Law Commission has recognized that appalling economic circumstances in developing countries may constitute 'an imminent and grave peril for the nation', therefore precluding any wrongfulness

[140] Roberto Ago, Addendum to Eight report on State responsibility, [1980] 2 YB Int Law Comm'n 51, 53 UN Doc. A/CN.4/318/ADDS.5-7.

[141] Laursen (2004, p. 524).

[142] Romano (1999, p. 31).

[143] See ATTAC France, "L'état de nécessité. La dette extérieure: mécanismes juridiques de non-paiement moratoire ou suspension de paiement", www.france.attac-org/a310 and 311; H. R. Diaz "La force majeure: la situation en Argentine, moratoire ou suspension de paiement", http://users.skynet.be/cadtm/.

when these countries do suspend the payment of their debts".[144] The ICJ has, in a recent decision, while keeping silent about the controversial character of the state of necessity doctrine, declared that it "considers ... that the state of necessity is a ground recognized by customary international law for precluding the wrongfulness of an act not in conformity with an international obligation."[145] Nevertheless, it admitted that "such ground for precluding wrongfulness can only be accepted on an exceptional basis"[146] agreeing then with the ILC that "the state of necessity can only be invoked under certain strictly defined conditions which must be cumulatively satisfied; the state concerned is not the sole judge of whether these conditions have been met".[147]

At the core of the state of necessity doctrine lies in fact a conflict between two rights: the right to conservation of a state, on one hand, and, on the other, the right of another state which might be affected by the application of the first right. Fundamentally, it is that contradiction that the ILC has tried to address in an equitable manner in its draft Article 25 which states that:

1. Necessity may not be invoked by a state as a ground for precluding the wrongfulness of an act not in conformity with an international obligation of that state unless the act is the only one way for the state to safeguard an essential interest against a grave and imminent peril; and does not seriously impair an essential interest of the state or the states towards which the obligation exists, or of the international community as a whole.
2. In any case, necessity may not be invoked by a state as a ground for precluding wrongfulness if:

   (a) The international obligation in question excludes the possibility of invoking necessity; or
   (b) The state has contributed to the situation of necessity.[148]

First of all, the relevant act that is not in conformity with an international obligation and that needs to be undertaken in a situation of imminent peril threatening an essential interest, must be the only available means to safeguard that interest. The ILC has pointed out in this regard that "the peril must not have been escapable by another means, even a more costly one, that could be adopted in compliance with international obligation."[149] Taking this remark into consideration, the ICJ has admitted, in the case related to 'The legal Consequences of the

---

[144] André and Dutry (1999, p. 80).

[145] Gabcikovo-Nagymaros (Hungary/Slovakia), ICJ Reports 1997, para 52. The same position has been adopted by the ICJ in its Advisory Opinion on the Legal Consequences of the Construction of a Wall in the Occupied Palestinian Territory, 9 July 2004, ICJ Reports 2004, para 140.

[146] Idem.

[147] Idem.

[148] Extract from the Report of the International Law Commission on the Work of its Fifty-third Session Regarding the Commission's Draft Articles on Responsibility of States for Internationally Wrongful Acts, U.N. GAOR Int'l L.Comm'n., 56th Sess., Supp. No 10.at ch.E1, U.N.Doc. A/56/10 (2001).

[149] Report on Work of the 32nd Session, [1980] 2 Y.B.Int Law Comm'n 33.

Construction of a Wall in the Occupied Palestinian Territory' that "In the light of the material before it, the Court is not convinced that the construction of the wall along the route chosen was the only means to safeguard the interest of Israel against the peril which it has invoked as justification for that construction."[150] With regard to the notion of "essential interest", while it noted that it would be pointless to lay down pre-established categories of interests, it has however given some indications on these interests by referring to the existence of the state, its political and economic survival, the survival of a sector of its population, the continuing normal functioning of the government institutions and administration, the preservation of environment, and so on.[151] The ILC also pointed out that the peril must be grave, imminent and representing a present danger. Later on it clarified further that the "peril has to be objectively established and not merely apprehended as possible".[152]

Second, the interest of the state or the states toward whom the international obligation exists, "must obviously be less important than the interest it is thereby sought to save,"[153] that is the interest of the state which is faced with an imminent threat. The same situation should also prevail with regard to any interest of the international community, when that interest is protected by an *erga omnes* obligation.[154]

Third, the excuse of necessity cannot be invoked when it is explicitly or implicitly excluded by the international obligation in question. Likewise, the excuse of necessity cannot be invoked when the state has itself contributed to the situation of necessity. This was the conclusion reached by the ICJ in the case concerning the Gabcikovo-Nagymaros project, where it denied to Hungary the right to rely upon the state of necessity "in order to justify its failure to comply with its treaty obligations, as it had helped, by act or omission to bring it about."[155]

Thus, International Law has constantly recognized the right of the states to preserve their existence through the ultimate use of self-defense and state of necessity (Conclusion 4). However, International Law has also started, further to the emergence of self-determination, to recognize the right of people to sovereignty.

1.2.3 The Right of People to Sovereignty: The Emergence of Self-Determination

We know that peoples have generally been kept in subjection, since the creation of early states thousands of years ago till the end of the eighteenth century when they

[150] ICJ Reports 2004, para 140.

[151] Addendum to Eight Report on State Responsibility by Roberto Ago, op. cit., at p. 14.

[152] Crawford (2002, p. 183).

[153] Essential Interest of the State in Addendum to Eight Report, op. cit. at p. 50.

[154] See Crawford (1999, p. 39).

[155] ICJ Reports 1997, para 57.

began to emerge as political actors and increasingly as legal bodies enjoying fundamental rights or even sovereignty.

Human history has been indeed a long parenthesis of domination and subjection of people within states borders, with few exceptions limited in terms of time duration and scope – these exceptions are knowingly related to the Athenian democracy[156] and more importantly to the Roman Republic which proclaimed the sovereignty of the people.[157]

Amazingly, human being history has started in most of primitive societies with a kind of system where the "distancing" (i.e. creating a distance) between people and their leaders was very tenuous, if not non-existent. Modern anthropology[158] and Marxist theory[159] have been able each in its own way to substantiate that phenomenon and to show that its was that distanciation that has given rise to the early states.

The territorial element was in fact at the origin of the distanciation between people and their leadership. Territory has, by supplanting kinship, unified people of different lineages within a global collectivity, but it has at the same time confined people in a situation of subjection to new entities or social classes within their own polities. Living in atomized societies where individuals have lost most of their old solidarities, people did exist as such only when they did occasionally revolt against the dominant power or when they were requested to defend the territory against a foreign threat. But the latter situation was also an occasion for the dominant power to strengthen its position vis-à-vis the whole society as "if an external threat becomes real, everybody may lose and everyone has an interest to transfer enough strength to a common center to repel the aggression".[160]

Then the primary basis of the strength of the power vis-à-vis the whole society was first of all the latter's attachment to territory. This attachment was strengthened whenever the collectivity was threatened by foreign forces in so far as "the transpolity transforms the polity in a collective actor opposed to other collective actors, a fact which reinforces the sense of identity shared by any member of each polity".[161] But the relationship between people and territory has never gone beyond the limit of the affect and the symbol. It is so because the real sovereign and owner of the territory is the king or the emperor who has the right to dispose of it, to transfer it to another Prince or to do whatever he wants with it.[162]

However, the power has not limited itself to the people's attachment to territory in order to strengthen its social basis. It has also used ideology mainly through religion in order to provide a sacred character to Power. Thus, dominant powers become "the

[156] See e.g. Dunn (2005, pp. 23–70).

[157] See Canovan (2005, pp. 11–16).

[158] See for instance Clastres (1974).

[159] See Engels (1902).

[160] Baecheler (2002, p. 62).

[161] Ibid. p. 161.

[162] This issue is analyzed by Barberis (1999).

parents, the counterparts and the mediators of gods."[163] Acquiring a supra-human status, Power implies then veneration from the whole society and at the same time "a fear of disobedience which has the character of a sacrilegious infringement."[164]

Attached to a territory which in the end is not their own, subjected to a power which has given to itself the face of God, the people were also subjected to inequality through social stratification and a hierarchical organization of the society.[165] This has been the fate of people from the first political collectivities until the end of European absolutism.

We know that the attention has started to be given to the situation of peoples, their rights, political and legal status only at the end of the eighteenth century when, inspired by the English revolution, the American and French revolutions proclaimed that the people (called also "nation") was the absolute sovereign, putting then an end to the subjection of peoples to the monarch and creating new political systems based on equality and freedom. The principle of popular sovereignty has, then, by freeing the people, led to the passage from the patriarchal state to the nation-state. One of the major consequences of this passage was the transformation of territorial integrity which has since then integrated popular sovereignty, that is, what today we commonly very often call self-determination.

The concept of "nation-state" implies that the people should no longer be seen as subject but rather as the real sovereign who, as such, constitutes the collective source of state's authority. However, if the English, American and French Revolutions have decisively contributed to the emergence of the people as the new sovereignty, the rise of the latter to such status is the result of a long but a discontinued process[166] which has started with the Roman Republic where the sovereign power exercised by the emperor was meant to derive from the Roman *populous,* constituted by the plebeians, a class of citizens inferior to the patricians but superior to the remaining populations of the empire.[167] Amazingly, the importance or at least the potential importance of the people has survived in the popular imagery after the collapse of the Roman Empire as "the language of *populous/ people* was kept alive for two millennia by the massive inheritance of the Roman history, law and literature, which was still a source of political wisdom of the founding fathers of the American Constitution".[168] Amazingly also, the concept of people was occasionally used by medieval monarchies, although the latter were theocratic, and this whenever they did face difficulties in maintaining their powers. The recourse to the concept of people was in this case conceived as an instrument in

---

[163] Balandier (1999, p. 117).

[164] Ibid. (my translation).

[165] See for instance Baechler (2002, p. 75 cont.) and Balandier (1999, p. 92 cont.).

[166] For an account of the historical process which has led to the adoption of the principle of popular sovereignty, see David (1996).

[167] Millar (1998, p. 124).

[168] Canovan (2005, p. 11).

reserve that can be used by kings in emergency situations in which they did sometimes claim that their authority draws its legitimacy from their own people.[169] The kings did so also in the later Middles Ages in order to free themselves from papal authority.[170] But the concept of people was equally used as an instrument in reserve by those who wanted to question the legitimacy of kings' authority. Thus, conceived as an instrument in reserve that can be used in difficult times when kings' legitimacy was called into question, the concept of the people as the final source of authority, while originally designed to legitimate absolute powers, turned out in the long run to provide a means for popular resistance.[171] Nevertheless, this has never meant that the kings were accountable to the people or that the latter did exert any kind of authority, although the situation has somehow started to change at the occasion of the religious struggles initiated in the sixteenth century by the Protestant Reformation. However, the resistance theory has paved the way to the serious questioning of the divine right of the kings and the adoption of the principle of popular sovereignty by the English, American and French Revolutions. The resistance theory has started to take place in the three countries mainly when the kings requested the old Parliament in England (also later on with regard the American colonies) or the Estates General in France, emanation of the gentry and landowners in the former case or the Church, the nobility and Third States in the later one, to consent to abnormal heavy taxes. It was since then that the English Parliament and the French Estates General have started to fight against their respective kings in order to preserve their right to levy taxes. But their fight against the kings has been gradually extended to questioning the divine right of the latter's powers and claiming their right to represent the people. But, as we will see hereafter and later on when analyzing the implementation of self-determination, the rise of popular sovereignty has not been since then an easy issue due to the difficulty to determine who the "people" is. "The sovereignty of the people", did note Edmund S. Morgan with profound insight, "is a much more complicated, one might say more fictional, fiction than the divine right of kings. A king, however dubious his divinity might seem, did not have to be imagined. He was a visible presence, wearing his crown and carrying his scepter. The people, on the other hand, are never visible as such. Before we ascribe sovereignty to the people we have to imagine that there is such a thing, something we personify as though it were a single body, capable of thinking, of acting, of making decisions and carrying them out, something quite apart from the government, superior to government, and able to alter or remove a government at will, a collective entity more powerful and less fallible than a king or than any group of individuals it singles to govern it".[172]

---

[169] See Canning (1996, pp. 8–9).

[170] Idem, pp. 157–158.

[171] See Canovan (2005, p. 14).

[172] Morgan (1988, p. 153).

In England, the rise of popular sovereignty has been the result of a lengthy process which started in the 1640s with the struggle of the Parliament against the King and continued with the civil War and its consequence the Revolution of 1688. It was during that long period that the protagonists of that struggle, the Parliament, the King and even the Army did claim each one for its own benefit that it was the sole representative of the people.[173] Thus, for instance, as noted by Edmund S. Morgan, "The House of Commons (representing the gentry and the landowners) in the 1640s apparently intended to speak for a sovereign but silent people much as the king has hitherto spoken for a sovereign but silent God."[174] In their struggles against each other, the protagonists did fight not only with their armies but also through doctrinal writings published by different authors well before the publication by J. Locke one year after the 1688 Revolution of his famous "Two Treaties of Government" in which a brilliant presentation of the principle of popular sovereignty was made.[175] True, the English Revolution has ended up with the agreement between the concerned protagonists that they should no longer claim for their own benefit that they are the unique representatives of the people and that there is only one people: the whole English people. But it will take, as in France after the 1789 Revolution, two centuries to see, further to the rise of the working class and the expansion of the universal suffrage, the notion of "people" being identified with the whole people and not only to the landowning gentlemen.[176] More struggles will indeed be needed in order to enable the whole people to be elevated to the status of the unique sovereign. These struggles will be fought on behalf of popular sovereignty as will happen later on for colonial peoples. But while, in Western countries the struggle on behalf of popular sovereignty was carried out in order to establish democracy, in colonial countries the same struggle will be fought in order to formally create new independent states but which will remain for most of them under the informal dependence of the former colonial powers and where democracy will be absent, with the exception of the United States of America where the whole process, i.e. the decolonization, the rise of popular sovereignty and democracy, will be simultaneously achieved.

Indeed, the United States of America's experience is unique in the history of colonial peoples as if the Americans have initially started by limiting themselves to requesting similar rights as those enjoyed by the Englishmen, they ended up very quickly by casting off the authority of England and then proclaiming on behalf of popular sovereignty that they constitute a separate and independent people. The American Revolution distinguished itself also from the English and French Revolutions in that it proclaimed from the beginning that the only legitimate representatives of people were persons who have been elected by the latter,

[173] On the process which has led to the rise in England of popular sovereignty, see the aforementioned and well documented study of Morgan (1988, pp. 17–121).

[174] Idem, p. 152.

[175] Idem, pp. 17–121.

[176] See Joyce (1994, p. 206).

although it will take some decades to see the whole segments of the people taking part in the election. Thus, contrary to the other colonial peoples, the American people were able from the beginning to settle at once the difficult issues of reaching independence and establishing democracy. "The novelty of the American experiment", notes Margaret Canovan,[177] "was that it reunited and developed both Roman traditions, calling on the people as constituent sovereign but at the same time as rulers". Moreover, the American Revolution was also able to establish throughout federalism a kind of popular sovereignty at the local level in contrast with French Revolution which has proclaimed that the Republic was "One and Indivisible".

In France, the rise of popular sovereignty was mainly meant to throw off royal authority. Abbé Sieyès,[178] who, inspired by the English Revolution, has tremendously contributed to theorizing the notion of popular sovereignty during the French Revolution, has made it clear that "The holder (of sovereignty) has changed. Sovereignty which used to belong to the King is transferred to the Nation, where according to Article 3 of the 1789 Human Rights and Citizen Declaration it essentially resides."[179] However the particularity of popular sovereignty is that the people does not exercise itself sovereignty. The French Revolution was in fact at the extreme opposite of Jean Jacques Rousseau conception's of popular sovereignty[180] according to which the people is the unique and direct holder of the legislative as well executive power within the society. Expressing a general feeling, Sieyès has made it clear that "France is not and cannot be a democracy."[181] It is so because the French revolutionaries were afraid that the acceptance of a direct democratic regime may lead to the monopolization of power by particular groups in the society or more dangerously to the fragmentation of the French society. They were in fact worried about a possible revival of the "composite state", called also "system of state" or "mosaic state",[182] which was the main form that characterized most of the European states at their beginning in the sixteenth century as they were divided in several autonomous entities sharing together sovereignty with the then nascent central government. In 1500, Europe included about 500 states having that form.[183] The absolutist states, which prevailed during the seventeenth and eighteenth centuries, were able, thanks to a prodigious process of unification and homogenization, to become unified states where sovereignty was retained by only one authority: the King. However, the French revolutionaries were under the

[177] Canovan 2005, p. 28.

[178] On the general thinking as well as the contribution of Sieyès to the adoption of the principle of popular sovereignty, see Bastid (1970), Forsyth (1987), Pasquino (1998), Urbinati (2006, pp. 138–161).

[179] Archives Parlementaires, Discours de Sieyès du 7 Septembre 1789, vol.8, p. 694.

[180] See the analysis made by Rosanvallon (2000, pp. 9–28).

[181] Archives Parlementaires de 1789 à 1860, vol. 8, p. 694.

[182] See Strayer (1963, pp. 23–25) and also his comprehensive analysis Strayer (1970).

[183] See Tilly (1975, p. 15).

impression that the collapse of the French absolutist state was about to lead to the fragmentation of France and then to the re-emergence of fragmented sovereignty. This was then the main reason why they were against direct democracy or any form of self-government at the local level within a federal state as was the case in the United States. Sieyès has translated the feeling of the new French elite by vigorously stating that:

> "France must not be an assemblage of little nations, governing themselves separately as democracies; it is not a collection of states; it is a single whole composed of integral parts; these parts must not enjoy separately a complete existence, because they are not merely united wholes, but parts forming one whole. The difference is immense; it is of a vital interest to us. All is lost if we allow ourselves to consider the municipalities that are being established, or the districts, or the provinces, as so many republics united solely by the ties of common force or protection. Instead of a general administration spreading from a common centre and falling in a uniform manner on the furthest reaches of the empire; instead of a legislation formed out of the citizens coming together in an ascending scale that reaches up to the National Assembly, the whole authorized interpreter of the general will; instead of this will that descends once again with all the weight of an irresistible force on the very wills that have concurred to form it. Instead of all this we will have nothing more than a kingdom bristling with every kind of barrier, a chaos of local customs, regulations and prohibitions."[184]

Thus, according to the French Revolutionaries, sovereignty should be exerted by the people's representatives.[185] The people have then replaced God as the source of authority while its representatives, who are in fact the new Kings, exert that authority on its behalf. The "tour de force" of the French Revolution was then to give power to the people and at the same time take it from it. Clermont-Tonnerre has honestly said commenting on the 1789 Revolution that "Proclaiming sovereign a nation and prohibiting it from exerting sovereignty was maybe the most ingenious political invention."[186]

Hence the people is a mere fiction. It does not exist per se. It does become a symbolic reality only when a state succeeds in establishing its authority over separate individuals and groups and reunify them in a single community. The people is therefore a mere fiction or abstraction symbolizing sovereignty in any given state, even when the latter is a non-democratic one.[187] However it is an extremely powerful fiction as it is on its behalf that, segments of the society will since then and gradually in different parts of the world claim popular sovereignty in order to create their own polity. The French Revolution is here at the antipode of the American Revolution which, by opting for a federal form of government, admitted that the people can be plural as it can be made of communities culturally and

[184] "Dire de l'Abbé Sieyès sur la question du veto royal", Imprimerie de l'Assemblée Nationale, 1789, the above quotation has been translated by Forsyth (1987, p. 137).

[185] Idem, p. 330.

[186] "Analyse raisonnée de la Constitution française décrétée par l'Assemblée Nationale", Paris, 1791, 123 cité par Rosanvallon (2000, p. 15).

[187] See Yack (2003, p. 34).

ethnically different. By declaring that the French Republic is "One and Indivisible" and therefore sacrificing self-government at the sub-national level, the French Revolutionaries would be at the origin of the idea that the nation and the state must be congruent, an idea, as noted by Lord Acton few decades following the French Revolution, that "grew into a condemnation of every state that included different races (i.e. different nationalities or culturally and ethnically different communities), and finally became the complete and consistent theory that the state and the nation must be co-extensive."[188]

The English, American and French Revolutions have, then, each one in its own way, proclaimed popular sovereignty. However, the latter, while based on the assumption that all men in a given state were equal in terms of power sharing, has been mainly used in a way to "making it possible for the few to govern the many."[189] But the manipulation of popular sovereign will not be limited to the states' internal sphere. It will also, as we will see later on, be extended to the international sphere by taking the form of external self-determination which functioned since the French Revolution as an ideological means to disintegrate foreign states.

Leaving the political aspect of the principle of popular sovereignty to one side, one can ask the following question: what has been the legal consequence of the rise of such principle on the state as a legal entity?

It has been admitted that no distinction can be made between state sovereignty and national sovereignty as the state is not separated from the nation which in fact it does represent and personify. "All those theories", R. Carré de Malberg has rightly clarified, "which separate the state and the nation are at variance with the principle of popular sovereignty as upheld by the French Revolution. The (French) Revolution, by proclaiming that sovereignty, that is the power that characterizes the state, lies essentially in the nation, has indeed implicitly consecrated that fundamental idea that in the French law the powers and the rights of the state are nothing other than the powers and the rights of the nation. Consequently, the state is not a juristic person that is distinct and opposed to the nation: on the contrary, when it is said that power of political nature belongs to the nation, one should infer from this that there is an identity between the nation and the state in the sense that the latter is only the personification of the former".[190]

We have seen earlier that the right to dominance is the major criteria for the existence of a state. Such right is nothing other than the expression of sovereignty which means the legitimate power of the state to impose its will upon all persons and things under its jurisdiction. We have seen also that such power has its foundation in the need to preserve and maintain the society. Now, while that foundation might be perceived more or less as a fiction under the patrimonial state, it was no longer the

---

[188] "Nationality"(1862) reproduced in Balakrishnan (1996, p. 28).

[189] Morgan (1988, p. 294).

[190] Carré de Malberg (1920, p. 13).

case under the nation-state as the latter is supposed to represent the people. Hence, modern state appears to be an association where a group of persons or members "are associated and organized into a unity of will for a common end",[191] which is their own preservation through the maintaining and preservation of the whole society. But the state is an association distinct from the other associations in that it holds the legitimate power of coercion.[192] It is, therefore, not a surprise that H. Kelsen, who intended to have cognition of the state free from ideology, metaphysics and mysticism, reached the conclusion, as did earlier M. Weber, that the state is a coercive order. "If the state", he did rightly note, "is comprehended as a social community, it can be constituted only by a normative order. Since a community[193] can be constituted only by *one* such order (and is, indeed, identical with the order), the normative order constituting the state can only be the relatively centralized coercive order which is the national legal order".[194] However, the main criticism that can be made of Kelsen's conception of the state is that it did not show any particular interest in the foundation of the state's coercive power. But, as we have seen above, this has not prevented him from indicating elsewhere that the state is meant to reflect, express and represent the will of the people.

The state can then be theoretically analyzed as a coercive legal order that has been given authority by its people to act on its behalf in order to preserve the whole society and promote the interests of its citizens in accordance with International Law principles.[195] Taking into consideration the principle of popular sovereignty, that is self-determination, the state can also be seen as the body, the instrument or the "apparatus"[196] that is primarily meant to enable the people to determine itself, politically, economically, socially and culturally in accordance with International Law principles. It is significant in this regard that both the 1966 Covenant on Civil and Political Rights and the Covenant on Economic, Social and Cultural Rights do talk about peoples and not states when they as well as many UN General Assembly resolutions state similarly that the peoples have the right of self-determination and that by virtue of that right they freely determine their political status and freely pursue their economic, social and cultural development. Therefore the main actor, though still behind the scene, is the people and not the state. This is a crucial

---

[191] MacIver (1964, p. 6).

[192] Idem, p. 15.

[193] Kelsen clarifies elsewhere that "The state is not its individuals; it is the specific union of individuals, and the union is the function of the order which regulates their mutual behavior" Kelsen (1942, p. 64).

[194] Kelsen (1934/1989, p. 287).

[195] Guggenheim wrote in this regard that "We cannot conceive of the state as an above individual general will, independent from individuals.... The state acts on behalf of a whole number of individuals that are attributed to it. The state uses organs that it itself designate et whose acts are imputed to the community of individuals and the legal order is the expression", (1953, pp. 172–173). See also Robert McCorquodale "Self-Determination: a Human Rights Approach", www.eleves.ens.fr/home/blondel/law.html.

[196] Roth (1999, p. 2).

element without which one cannot understand the contemporary legal meaning, scope and implications of territorial integrity.

One of the key conclusions to be drawn from the above is that the principle of territorial integrity will remain relevant only if it incorporates the idea that its fundamental goal is to protect the existence of the people. U. O. Umozurike has rightly stressed in this respect that "the ultimate purpose of territorial integrity is to safeguard the interests of the peoples of a territory. The concept of territorial integrity is … meaningful (only) so long as it continues to fulfill that purpose to all the sections of the people".[197]

1.3 Conclusion: Defining Territorial Integrity

We can now, with the elements gathered above, carry out the reconstruction of the principle in order to show what it is and what it is not. The latter issue will be the occasion in the next section to dispel the confusion increasingly made between the principle of territorial integrity and other principles including the uti possidetis principle.

In order to reconstruct the principle of territorial integrity, let's first recall the conclusions reached during the deconstruction process. These conclusions are as follows:

- Since the emergence of the first political entities, peoples have durably had a close link with their territory to the extent that not only their daily life but also their identity has been marked by this element more than by any other factor. Perceived as sacred, territory has always determined the existence and fate of peoples.
- The state is a coercive legal order that has been given authority by its people to act on its behalf in order to preserve the whole society and promote the interests of its citizens in accordance with International Law principles.
- The foundations and limits of states' territory are established in accordance with International Law.
- International Law recognizes that every state has the right to ensure its existence through the legitimate use of force.
- International Law recognizes that the ultimate role of sovereignty is to protect the existence of the state.
- International Law recognizes that every state enjoys an exclusive competence within the limits of its own territory in order to preserve itself and the whole society.

[197] Umozurike (1972, p. 236).

- International Law has, through the right to self-determination, promoted subjected populations to the legal status of "peoples" who enjoy fundamental human rights as well as the right to sovereignty on their own territories.

Taking into consideration the above conclusions, it is then possible to determine what the International Law means by "principle of territorial integrity". Here is the definition, which we believe reflects the present state of positive International Law:

> "The principle of territorial integrity is the principle that recognizes the sovereign existence of states within their own territory and their right to preserve that existence in accordance with International Law."

The suggested definition has the merit to be concise; still, it cannot be accepted either by those who are of the opinion, as we have seen at the very beginning of this chapter, that the concept of existence cannot be applied to states or by those who do consider that the legitimate sovereign is no longer the state but the people. They may then be at ease with the following definition:

> "The principle of territorial integrity of states is the principle that recognizes the sovereign existence of peoples represented by their legitimate governments within territories on which the latter are entitled to exert exclusive jurisdiction and the legal basis and limits of which are established in accordance to the International Law."

The second definition seems to be more in line with the progressive International Law which has the tendency, as we have seen and we will see later on when analyzing the emergence of the new paradigm related to the right to self-determination, to consider that the real sovereign is the people, though International Law is not yet echoed by the constitutional and effective national law of many states and that the government has to be the emanation of the same people through a democratic and representative political system. It goes without saying that this definition applies only to peoples who have already determined themselves and belong to an already existing state recognized as such by the international community and not to peoples who wish to create their own states.

Both definitions can be acceptable as the first one reflects the present state of International Law while the second one represents promising potential for the future in terms of development of human rights and democracy. More importantly, whatever definition one opts for, it remains, even if we put aside the issue of "people", that both of them are based on similar fundamental elements which are:

- The right to existence of states/peoples which is reflected by the term "existence."
- The right of states/peoples to have a "sovereign existence", which refers here to sovereignty both of its aspects, the international one, that is, independence and the internal one, that is, the exclusive jurisdiction of states.
- The right of the states to exist "within their own territory." The latter expression refers to the recognition by the International Law that the foundations and limits of a given territory require to be established in accordance with its relevant rules and principles.

- The right to preserve that existence in accordance with International Law principles is very clear and refers here to the right of the state to defend its existence by all means and ways authorized by International Law including ultimately the right of self-defense when all peaceful means have been exhausted. But the right to conserve its own existence does not imply that the state is entitled to exert that right by the commission of unlawful acts against innocent and non belligerent states. The state can exert that right only within the limits authorized by International Law.
- The implicit reference to the obligation of the international community to respect and protect the existence of the state through the recognition of sovereignty in its dual aspect, independence and exclusive jurisdiction.

Therefore, what ultimately defines the principle of territorial integrity is the territorial sovereign right to existence of the state. It is that right which the state, whatever was its nature, has been able to protect thanks to its ability to survive as the main form of social organization since its emergence thousands years ago.

References

Adar KG (1986) The principle of self-determination and territorial integrity make strange litigants in international relations: a recapitulation. Indian J Int Law 26(3/4)

Agnew J (2004) Sovereignty regimes: sovereignty and territory over time and space. Paper presented at the international workshop on "globalization, territoriality, and conflict". The Institute for International, Comparative, and Area Studies (IICAS) at the University of California, San Diego, January 2004

Allies P (1983) L'invention du territoire. Presses Universitaires de Grenoble, Grenoble

Altman A (2008) Tracing the earliest recorded concepts of international law. The Ancient Near East in the Old Babylonian Period (2003–1595 BCE). J Hist Int Law 10 and in the same journal, 2004, vol 6 and 2005, vol 7

André L, Dutry J (1999) La responsabilité internationale des Etats pour des situations d'extrême pauvreté. R.B.D.I.

Antonopoulos C (1996) The principle of Uti Possidetis Iuria in contemporary international law. RHDI, 29

Arbaret-Schulz C, Beyer A, Permay JL, Reitel B, Selimanovski C, Sohn C, Zander P (2004) La frontière, un objet spatial en mutation. Groupe Frontière, EspacesTemps.net, Textuel, 29.10.2004. http://espacestemps.net/document842.html

Ardey R (1967) The territorial imperative. Collins, London

Baecheler J (2002) Esquisse d'une histoire universelle. Fayard

Balakrishnan G (ed) (1996) Mapping the world. Verso, London

Balandier G (1999) Anthropologie politique, 4th edn. P.U.F, Paris

Barberis JA (1999) Les liens juridiques entre l'Etat et son territoire: Perspectives théoriques et évolution du Droit International. A.F.D.I. 132

Barthelemy J (1917) Démocratie et politique étrangère. Paris

Bastid P (1970) Sieyès et sa pensée. Hachette, Paris

Beaud O (1994) La puissance de l'Etat. P.U.F., Paris

Bederman DJ (2001) International law in antiquity. Cambridge University Press, Cambridge

Bedjaoui M (1972) Le règlement pacifique des différends africains. A.F.D.I. 95

Bipoum-Woom JM (1970) Le droit international africain. L.G.D.J, Paris

Boed R (2000) State of necessity as a justification for internationally wrongful conduct. Yale Human Rights Dev Law J 3:4. http://islandia.law.yale.edu/yhrdlj/vol3.html
Borella F (1964) Le régionalisme africain. A.F.D.I. 10
Bonfils H (1912) Manuel de Droit International public (droit des gens), 6th ed., Rousseau, Paris
Cahier P (1985) Cours de Droit International Public. R.C.A.D.I.
Canning J (1996) A history of medieval political thought 300–1450. Routledge, London
Canovan M (2005) The people. Polity, Cambridge
Caputo JD (ed) (1997) Deconstruction in a Nutshell. A conversation with Jacques Derrida. Fordham University Press, New York
Carré de Malberg R (1962) Contribution à la théorie générale de l'Etat. Editions du C.N.R.S., Paris (1st edn, 1920)
Chisholm M, Smith D (eds) (1990) Shared space: divided place. Unwin Hyman, London
Christakis T (ed) (2007) La nécessité en Droit International. Actes du Colloque de la Société Française pour le Droit International, A. Pédone, Paris
Clastres P (1974) La société contre l'Etat, recherches d'anthropologie politique. Editions de Minuit, Paris
Collins R (1988) Weberian sociological theory. Cambridge University Press, Cambridge
Crawford J (1999) Second report on state responsibility. Int'l L.Comm'n51st Sess., at 32, U.N. Doc.A/CN.4/498/Add.2
Crawford J (2002) The international law commission's articles on state responsibility: introduction text and commentary. Cambridge Univ. Press
Cukwurah AO (1967) The settlement of boundary disputes in international law. Manchester University Press, Manchester
David M (1996) La souveraineté du peuple. Presses Universitaires de France, Paris
Delbez L (1932) Le territoire dans ses rapports avec l'Etat. R.G.D.I.P.
Delivanis J (1971) La légitime défense en Droit International Public. L.G.D.J., Paris
Dembinski L (1975) Le territoire et le Développement du Droit International", A.S.D.I.
de Vattel E (1758/1852) Le droit des gens ou principes de la loi naturelle appliqué à la conduite et aux affaires des nations et des souverains. Paris, Librairie de Guillaumin et Cie
de Visscher C (1917) Les lois de la guerre et la théorie de la nécessité. R.G.D.I.P
de Vischer Ch (1970) Théories et réalités en Droit International Public, 4th edn. A. Pédone, Paris
Dunn J (2005) Setting the people free. The story of democracy. Atlantic Books, London
Eckert AE, Mofidi M (2004) Doctrine or Doctrinaire. The first strike doctrine and preemptive self-defence under international law. Tulane J. Int. Comp. Law 12
El Ouali A (1982) l "existence transhistorique du Droit International. Quelques notes pour une critique de l'idéologie juridique dominante", Revue Marocaine de Droit et d'Economie du Développent, No 1
El Ouali A (1993) Nouvel ordre international ou retour à l'idée d'inégalité des Etas? Les Editions Maghrebines, Casablanca
Engels F (1902) The origin of the family, private property and the state. C. H. Kerr & Company
Fauchille P (1922) Traité de Droit International Public, 8th ed, Librairie, Paris
Fardella F (1997) La dogme de la souveraineté de l'Etat. Un bilan. Archives de Philosophie du Droit, Sirey 41
Firth R (1964) Essays on social organization and values
Forsyth M (1987) Reason and revolution. The political thought of the Abbé Sieyes. Leicester University Press, Leicester
Freund J (1966) Sociologie de Max Weber. P.U.F.
Fromm J (2004) The emergence of complexity. Kassel University Press GmbH, Kassel
Garner JW (1910) A treatise on the origin, functions and organization of the state. New York Book Cie
Gilpin R (1981) War and change in world politics. Cambridge University Press, New York
Gottman J (1952) La politique des Etats et leur géographie. A. Colin, Paris

Goemans H (2004) On the homeland. In: Globalization, territoriality, and conflict conference. International workshop. The Institute for International, Comparative, and Areas Studies (IICAS), at the University of California, San Diego, January 2004. http://www.intlstudies.ucsd.edu/IICASConferences/Globalization2004.htm
Grant TD (1998–1999) Defining statehood: Montevideo convention and its discontents. Columbia J Transnational Law 37
Grotius H (1625/1853) De Jure Belli ac Pacis
Guggenheim P (1953) Traité de Droit International Public, Librairie de l'Université, Georg & Cie S.A, Geneva
Guichonnet P, Raffestin (1974) Géographie des frontières. P.U.F., Paris
Gulick E (1967) Europe's classical balance of power. Norton, New York, Chap. 9
Haigh SP (2004) Globalization and the sovereign state: authority and territoriality reconsidered. Paper presented to the first oceanic international studies conference. Australian National University, Canberra, 14–16 July 2004, 11
Hall JA (1996) International orders. Polity Press, Cambridge
Haslam J (2002) No virtue like necessity. realist thought in international relations since Machiavelli. Yale University Press
Heathcote S (2005) State of necessity in international law. Thesis, University of Geneva
Hershey AS (1927) The essentials of international public law and organization. The MacMillan Company, New York
Hesse P-J (2002) Un droit fondamental vieux de 3000 ans: l'état de nécessité. Jalons pour une histoire de la notion. Droits fondamentaux, No 2, January–December 2002
Hinsley FH (1966) Sovereignty. C.A. Watts & Co. Ltd., London
Hobbes T. (1994) Leviathan (1668), Hackett Publishing, Cambridge
Holsti KJ (2004) Taming the sovereigns. Institutional changes in international politics. Cambridge Studies in International Relations. Cambridge University Press, Cambridge
Howes DE (2003) When states chose to die: reassessing assumptions about what status want. Int Stud Quart 47
Hume D (1744/1985) Of the balance of power. In: Miller E (ed) Essays: moral, political and literary. Liberty Classics, Indianapolis
Jagota SP (1985) State responsibility: circumstances precluding wrongfulness. Neth YB Int Law 16
Jones SB (1959) Boundary concepts in the setting of place and time. Association of the American Geographers 3
Joyce P (1994) Democratic subjects: the self and the social in nineteenth-century England. Cambridge University Press, Cambridge
Kahler M (2004) Globalization, territoriality, and conflict: definitions and hypotheses. Paper presented at the international workshop on "globalization, territoriality, and conflict. The Institute for International, Comparative, and Area Studies (IICAS) at the University of California, San Diego, January 2004
Kalamatianou P (2004) L'état de nécessité sous l'angle du droit comparé et de la justice pénale internationale. Revue de D.I. et D. Comparé, No 2
Kelsen H (1941–1942) The pure theory of law and analytical jurisprudence. Harvard Law Rev 55
Kelsen H (1934/1989) Pure Theory of Law, translated by Knight M, Smith Gloucester P, Mass
Kohen MG (1997) Possession contestée et souveraineté territoriale. PUF, Paris
Kohen MG (1999) The notion of 'state survival' in international law. In: Laurence Boisson de Chazounes and Philippe Sands (eds) International law, the international court of justice and nuclear weapons. Cambridge University Press, Cambridge
Krassner SD (1999) Sovereignty: organized hypocrisy. Princeton University Press, Princeton
Krisch N (2001) Self-Defense and Collective Security, Summary, Springer, Berlin Heidelberg
Laband P (1861/1900) Le droit public de l'Empire allemande, translated by Gandilhon M, Paris, V.Girard and E.Briére
Lalonde S (2002) Determining boundaries in a conflicted world. The role of Uti Possidetis. McGill-Queen's University Press, Montreal
Laursen A (2004) The use of force and (the state of) necessity. Vanderbilt J Transn Law

von Liszt F (1927) Le Droit International. Exposé systématique, translated by Gidel G, (1928) A. Pédone, Paris
Luke TW (1994) Fixing identity, fabricating space: sovereignty and territoriality after the cold war. Paper presented at the annual meeting of the Association of American Geographers, March 27–April 2 1994
MacIver RM (1964) The modern state. Oxford University Press, London (1st edn, 1926)
Malmberg T (1980) Human territoriality: survey of behavioral territories in man with preliminary analysis and discussion of meaning. Mouton Publishers, The Hague
Mearsheimer JJ (2001) The tragedy of great power politics. W.W. Norton & Company, New York
Millar F (1998) The crowd in Rome in the late republic. University of Michigan, Michigan
Modelski G (1971) Principles of world politics. Collier-Macmillan limited, London
Modelski G (1987) Long cycles in world politics. University of Washington Press, Seattle
Moore JB (1906) A digest of international law, Washington D.C., US Government Printing Office
Morgan ES (1988) Inventing the people. The rise of popular sovereignty in England and America. W.W. Norton & Company, New York
Nadel SF (1951) The foundations of Social Anthropology, London, Cohen and West
Nesi G (1998) l' uti possidetis hors du contexte de la décolonisation: le cas de l'Europe. 44 A.F.D.I.
Newman D (2004) The resilience of territorial conflict in an era of globalization. In: Globalization, territoriality, and conflict conference. International workshop. The Institute for International, Comparative, and Areas Studies (IICAS), at the University of California, San Diego, January 2004. http://www.intlstudies.ucsd.edu/IICASConferences/Globalization2004.htm
Nys E (1901) L'Etat et la notion d'Etat. Revue de Droit Internationale et de Législation Comparée 35
Nys E (1904) L'acquisition du territoire et le Droit International. R.D.I.L.C.
O'Connell ME (2002) The myth of preemptive self-defense. The American Society of International Law, Task Force on Terrorism, August 2002. www.asil.org/taskforce/oconell.pdf, Note 10
Osiander A (2001) Sovereignty, international relations, and the Westphalian Myth. International Organization 55(2)
Paasi A (1996) Territories, boundaries and consciousness: the changing geographies of the Finnish–Russian Border. Wiley, Chichester
Parkinson F (1975) Pre-colonial international law. In: Mensah-Brown AK (ed) African international law legal history. U.N.T.A.R., New York
Pasquino P (1998) Sieyès et l'invention de la Constitution en France. Editions Odile Jacob, Paris
Person Y (1972) L'Afrique noire et ses frontières, R.F.E.P.A., August
Petitdemange G (2003) Philosophies & philosophes du XXe siècle. Seuil, Paris
Phillipson C (1916) Wheaton's Elements of International Law, revised by Phillipson C, London, Stevens & Sons, New York, Baker, Vooehis é Co.
Pufendorf S (1672, 1852) De Jurae Nature et Gentium
Raffestin C (1980) Pour une géographie du pouvoir. LITEC, Paris
Raffestin C (1986) Ecogenèse et territorialité. In: Auriac-Brunet (dir.) Espaces, jeux et enjeux, nouvelle encyclopédie des sciences et techniques. Fayard, Paris
Raffestin C (1990) La frontière comme représentation: discontinuité géographique et discontinuité idéologique. Relations Internationales 63, (my translation)
Raymond GA (1998) Necessity in Foreign Policy http://www.questia.com/PM.qst?action=print&docld=5001404161&pgNum=1
Retaille D (1990) L'impératif territorial. Relations Internationales 63
Rodick BC (1928) The doctrine of necessity in international law. Columbia University Press, New York
Romano J-A (1999) Combating terrorism and weapons of mass destruction: reviving the doctrine of a state of necessity. Georgetown Law J. www.findarticles.com/p/articles/mi_qa3805is_199904/ai_n8839027
Root E (1916) The declaration of the rights and duties of nations adopted by the American Institute of International Law. A.J.I.L.

Rosanvallon P (2000) La démocratie inachevée. Histoire de la souveraineté du peuple en France. Gallimard, Paris
Rosenau JN (1995) Sovereignty in a turbulent world. In: Gene M, Lyons GM, Mastanduno M (eds) Beyond Westphalia. State Sovereignty and International Intervention. The John Hopkins University Press, Baltimore/London
Roth BR (1999) Governmental illegitimacy in international law. Oxford University Press, Oxford
Salmon J (1984) Faut-il codifier l'état de nécessité en Droit International? In: Makarczyk J (ed) Essays in international law in honour of Judge Manfred Lachs
Sanchez-Rodriguez (1997) *L'uti possidetis* et le effectivités dans les contentieux territoriaux et frontaliers. R.C.A.D.I., vol 263
Scelle G (1948) *Manuel de Droit International Public. Domat Montchrestien*, Paris
Schmitt C (1922/1988) Théologie politique, translated from German by Schlegel J. Gallimard, Paris
Schoenborn W (1929) La nature juridique du territoire de l'Etat. R.C.A.D.I. II 30
Shaw MN (1982) Territory in international law. N.Y.B.I.L.
Shaw MN (1997) The Heritage of States: the Principle of Uti Possidetis Juris Today, BYIL 1996, 75
Shaw MN (1999) Peoples, territorialism and decolonisation. EJIL 3
Sibert M (1951) Traité de Droit International Public, Paris, Dalloz
Spykman NJ (1942) Frontiers, security, and international organization. Geogr Rev
Stack R (1986) Human territoriality. Its theory and history. Cambridge University Press, Cambridge
Strayer J (1963) The historical experience of nation-building in Europe. In: Deutch KW, Foltz WJ (eds) Nation-building. Atherton Press, New York
Strayer J (1970) On the medieval origins of the modern state. Princeton University Press, Princeton
Thompson EU (1995) State sovereignty in international relations: bridging the gap between theory and empirical research. Int Stud Quart 39(2)
Tilly C (1975) Reflections on the history of the European state-making. In: Tilly C (ed) The formation of national states in Western Europe. Princeton University Press, Princeton
Todd E (2002) Apres l'Empire. Essai sur la décomposition du système américain". Gallimard, Paris
Touval S (1972) The boundary politics of independent Africa. Harvard University Press
Trumer M (1933) Le matérialisme historique chez K. Marx et Fr. Engels. Paris, les Editions Domat-Montchrestien
Turrettine R (1949) La signification des traités de Westphalie dans le domaine du droit des gens. Imprimerie Genevoise, Genève
Umozurike UO (1972) Self-determination in international law, Hamden CT: Archon Books
Urbinati N (2006) Representative democracy. Principles & genealogy. The University of Chicago Press, Chicago
Vaughan L (1999) Precluding wrongfulness or responsibility: a plea for excuses. Eur J Int Law 10
Waltz KN (1979) Theory of international politics. Addison-Wesley, Reading McGraw-Hill, New York
Walzer M (2006) Just and unjust wars. A moral argument with historical illustrations, 4th edn. Basic Books, New York
Weber M (1958) From Max Weber: Essays in Sociology, translated and ed. by Gerth HH and Mills CW. Routledge and Kegan Paul, Boston
White GW (2000) Nationalism and territory: constructing group identity in Southern Europe. Rowman and Liilefield, Lanham (Maryland) & Oxford
White LA (1959) The Evolution of Culture. The development of Civilization to the Fall of Rome, McGraw-Hill
Yack B (2003) Nationalism, popular sovereignty, and the liberal democratic state. In: Paul TV, John Ikenberry G, Hall JA (eds) The nation-state in question. Princeton University Press, Princeton
Yakemtchouk R (1975) Les frontières africaines. R.G.D.I.P. 51
Zacher MW (2001) The territorial integrity norm: international boundaries and the use of force. Int Organization 55(2)

Chapter 2
The State's Ability to Ensure Its Own Survival

We know that a heightened debate has taken place in the past two decades on the state, its relevance and possible obsolescence, but the state is still alive. In reality states have very often been able to adjust to changes as one of the dominant characteristics of territoriality is its flexibility.[1] It is the latter which has enabled the state to remain as the main form of social organization, although the state has an inherent drive towards disintegration.

With regard to disintegration, it has been suggested that open systems do appear as such as a consequence of differentiation in a biological, physical and social environment which used to be homogeneous.[2] Differentiation in turn creates a split between elements which tend to integrate in the system and constitute its core or center and elements which tend to move away and try to remain uncontrolled at the periphery of the system. Human societies are also necessarily subjected to division and separation.[3] A center/periphery division does exist in every society as the latter is torn between order and disorder that are continuously against one another. Society does then supposexch seeks to impose its will on all the members of the society and various elements of disorder and disintegration. It is that fundamental division that can make possible the "production of what is social."[4] That is why, recalls J.Chevallier, society is subject to a double contradictory attraction: one of a centripetal character by which the core elements of the society tend to integrate in the whole system, and the other one of centrifugal character by which the peripheral elements of the society tend to move away from the system.[5]

[1] See Casimir (1992, pp. 16–20).

[2] See von Bertalanffy (1950, pp. 134–165).

[3] See Gauchet (1977, p. 5).

[4] Chevallier (1978, p. 5).

[5] Idem, p. 4. See also Shils (1975).

A. El Ouali, *Territorial Integrity in a Globalizing World*,
DOI 10.1007/978-3-642-22869-8_2,

States, since their emergence more than five thousands of years ago, have been subjected to disintegration.[6] This has been the result of a process of division between different segments of the society. However, states, which can be called traditional states, were, despite their inner congenital weakness, able to survive as a predominant form of the organization of the society until the sixteenth century. They did so because of their great sense of adaptability as they managed to compensate for the lack of effectiveness of their territoriality by mainly sharing power with local communities.

The prevention of states' disintegration has dramatically improved with the emergence of modern states in the sixteenth century as the latter were able, first, to display an unprecedented control over their territories and then to homogenize their societies further to the proclamation of popular sovereignty, i.e. self-determination, and the ensuing creation of nation-states. Effectiveness did associate itself with the modern state to the extent that it was elevated to the status of a crucial International Law principal which not only allows the establishment of a right[7] -to territory, for instance- but also enables a new state to be recognized as such by the other members of the international community.[8]

Today, states are again having difficulties in ensuring the effectiveness of their territoriality. These difficulties are the result of a profound crisis of territoriality which has its origin mainly in two factors: first, globalisation which exerts a destructive impact on the capacity of the state to maintain an acceptable level of congruence between itself and the nation, second, the failure to build states and even less nation-states in many Southern countries where the implementation of a particular conception of self-determination and the doctrine of the intangibility of borders, has exacerbated the social and ethnic divisions in an already deeply divided societies.

Many states have in the past decades, in order to ensure their survival, opted for sharing power with local communities. Thus, territorial autonomy is back again but this time legally reinforced by democratic self-determination. This is one of the dominant aspects of the arising postmodernity which forces the states to share their power at the supra and sub-national levels. Hence, the flexibility of territoriality has proved to be instrumental in the survival of states.

This chapter will analyse, first, the phenomenon of states' drive towards disintegration, before showing how states have been able to survive thanks to the flexibility of territoriality.

---

[6] By disintegration, it is meant here mainly the situation where a state loses its internal cohesion which fact might ultimately cause it to fragment into parts. Thus, a state may lose it internal cohesion and not fragment into parts. However, it is such loss of cohesion that renders a state very weak and sometimes a source of danger for other states. This issue is widely developed by Migdal (2001, pp. 135–169).

[7] See for a general synthesis Doehring (1984, pp. 70–74).

[8] de Visscher (1967, p. 36).

2.1 The States' Drive Towards Disintegration

Some scholars do believe that the state was built on an original division in the society between its powerful components, motivated by the domination over the whole society and its weakest components which tend to protect themselves from domination by seeking freedom and separation.[9] In fact, the emergence of early states has taken place in societies which used to be homogeneous. The latter, called also simple societies, were organized in small, autonomous and self-sufficient communities. They have been the only one form of organization of human societies for several hundred thousand if not million years.[10] Modern anthropology[11] has shown that these societies, where equality between all their members has been considered as a sacrosanct principle, have been organized in a way to prevent the emergence of any kind of division between their members. Obsessed by homogeneity, these societies have imagined complex systems by which the emergence of a separate power cannot take place. The latter was kept spread and located in the whole society in such a manner as to prevent its monopolization by any persons or bodies. Hence there was in these societies a technical impossibility for the accumulation of any political or economic power by any group of persons. "Leadership, recall Henri J.M. Claessen and Pieter van de Velde,[12] is of limited importance in the simpler societies. Leaders are sometimes hardly recognizable or function temporarily only. For a very long time, human beings lived in small, little differentiated communities of hunters, fishers, and gatherers. There was little use for much organization or coercion". The chiefs used to have only a symbolic role in these societies. They had no right to levy taxes or to exert any power of coercion. Their power, essentially of conciliatory and mediatory character, felt short of that of chief. It is true that the chiefs used to exert some leading role during hostilities against other communities, but that role disappeared once the hostilities were over. Hence, there was in these societies "no king in the tribe, but a chief who is not a head of state. What did that mean? Simply that the chief had no authority, no power of coercion, no means to issue an order."[13] The lack of a centralized authority has not pushed these societies to live in a situation of anarchy,[14] as these societies were egalitarian and democratic. Every adult male was considered, and considered himself, the equal of all others. But nobody was entitled to issue orders to others and exercise himself justice. All social relations, including rights and obligations, were defined by customary rules which "covered every aspect of life from sexual

[9] See, for instance, Lefort (1972).

[10] See Carneiro (1978, pp. 203–223).

[11] See in particular Clastres (1974, p. 161 cont.); Lapierrre (1977).

[12] Claessen et al. (1985, p. 247).

[13] Clastres (1974, p. 175). See also Sahlins (1968, p. 21).

[14] See in this respect Dole (1966).

mores to the division of inheritance"[15] and disputes were settled by the heads of the household in small communities and by the village council in larger communities. In sum, power in primitive societies was the power not of a chief or a group of leaders but "the power of society as a whole."[16]

It was the destruction of the original primitive system based on equality that has led to the emergence of complex societies in the form of states. It is generally agreed that it was the appearance of inequality and the consequent division in the primitive societies which have led to the emergence of early states. But the rise of the latter has been simultaneously accompanied by the emergence of ethnic communities which will, with the passing of time solidify and become "named human populations with shared ancestry myths, histories and cultures, having an association with a specific territory and a *sense of solidarity*."[17] Such a situation has created a permanent tension in the society and put the existence of the states under recurrent threat. Some authors do believe that the society was consequently condemned in order to be viable as any other system to continuously seek establishing a balance between the center and the periphery,[18] while other scholars do believe that the society has never been able to integrate the peripheral elements into a global homogeneous entity. These conflicting perceptions of human societies reflect also on the conception of the state which is perceived, by the first category of scholars, as a factor of integration of the different parts of the society, while the second category sees in it a coercive instrument whose aims is to address the conflict between these parts within an order which maintains a kind of domination of the center over the periphery. In fact, what can be noted is that the states have started by being heterogeneous entities, a fact which has constituted a permanent threat to their own survival, and that such heterogeneity has been deepened further at a later stage as a result of external factors, mainly wars of conquest.

2.1.1 The Concomitant and Correlative Birth of States and Ethnic Heterogeneity

Hence, while it is generally agreed that it was the appearance of inequality and the consequent division in the primitive societies which have led to the emergence of early states, there is a total lack of agreement among the doctrine on the reasons and the process which have given rise to these states. Hence, according to some scholars, the state had emerged in order to integrate the society, while others do

[15] van Creveld (1999, p. 4).
[16] Andriolo (1978, p. 193).
[17] Yoffee (2005, p. 32).
[18] See Parsons (1961, pp. 30–79).

believe that the state was created in order to maintain the nascent division in the society.

The idea that the creation of the state was meant to integrate the society finds its origin in the doctrine of social contract which is based more on a speculative and philosophical hypothesis than on empirical facts. We know that such doctrine, which has been developed in the seventeenth and eighteenth centuries, states that government is the result of a pact between all individuals in the society by which the latter have made an end to the "state of nature" and created the "civil state." Thomas Hobbes was the first to present the social contract doctrine. Form him, all men are by nature equally free. They are also pushed by human nature to compete for dominance. From this philosophical postulate, he deduces that in the state of nature "men live without a common power to keep them all in awe, they are in that condition which is called war, and such a war is of every man against man."[19] However, men would realize that the maintaining of such situation was self-destroying and the only solution left was "to erect such a common power as may be able to defend them from the invasion of foreigners and the injuries of another, and thereby to secure them in such sort as that their own industry, and by the fruits of the earth, they may nourish themselves and live contentedly, is to confer their power and strength upon one man, or upon one assembly of men. . ."[20] By doing so, men have given rise not only to the government but also to the state as when they agreed on the transfer of all their power to the newly created governmental body, they expressed that consent through "an act by which a multitude simultaneously transforms itself into unity,"[21] or, in Hobbes' own words: "This is more than consent or concord; it is a real unity of them all, in one and the same person."[22]

While the doctrine of social contract has been conceived by Hobbes with a view to legitimating the absolutist political system in England,[23] it will be used by John Locke in order to democratize that system. Hence, for John Locke, when the people gave their consent to the creation of the government, first, they have not abdicated their natural right as "a Rational Creature cannot be supposed, when free, to put himself into Subjection to another, for his own harm,"[24] second, they did not contract with the government but agreed between themselves to uphold their respective rights and liberties[25] and therefore to be entitled to change their government, while that eventuality is prohibited in Hobbes' system.[26] From another angle, while for Hobbes the integrating factor is war, for Locke, it is mainly economy and

[19] Hobbes (1994, p. 76).

[20] Idem, p. 109.

[21] Forsyth (1994, p. 39).

[22] Hobbes (1994, p. 109).

[23] See Hampton (1986, p. 3).

[24] Locke (1988, p. 164).

[25] Idem, pp. 87–96.

[26] Hobbes (1994, pp. 110–111).

in particular the need to protect private property. Both differ also with regard to the importance of the social contract doctrine. Hence, while Hobbes has build his thesis on the doctrine of social contract, Locke has expressed some doubt about the plausibility of the contract account,[27] echoing critics who already at that time "have ridiculed what they took to be its (the doctrine of social contract) absurd historical pretensions."[28] That is why he has simultaneously tried to develop a foundation of political authority through a kind of a rudimentary historical anthropology. For Locke, it was the development of natural economy and the problems which have ensued, in particular disputes between people that have led to the emergence of political authority but in a gradual manner throughout a long process and duration of time. That conception of the appearance of political power is manifestly in total contradiction with the doctrine of social contract which supposes that appearance to take place instantaneously and once for all and not in a gradual manner.

In the eighteenth century, many authors have started to criticize the doctrine of social contract for being an artificial conception of the foundation of political authority. Among these authors, the most critical was D. Hume for whom almost all governments have been founded originally, either on usurpation or conquest, or both, without any pretence of a fair consent, or voluntary subjection of the people. Hence, according to Hume, warfare was frequently at the origin of government whose efficiency in unifying the society, establishing order, protecting private property and providing services to the people has pushed the latter to consent later on to the authority of that government. So, people have made allegiance to the government only when they realized how important was its utility and the benefits they can draw from its existence and performance. "Government", stresses Hume, "binds us to obedience only on account of its public utility,"[29] that is its capacity to maintain peace and order and distribute justice to which all men are sensitive in order to ensure the maintenance of society and "the observation of these general and obvious interests is the source of all allegiance, and of that moral obligation which we attribute to it."[30] Some authors have been of the opinion that Hume must be considered as contractarian as he conceived the foundation of government as based on mutual advantages.[31] Whether we agree or not with such an opinion, it remains that Hume's political philosophy, although it rejected the doctrine of social contract, aimed as did the proponents of the latter, at suggesting a conception of the foundation of political authority with the view to holding disparate social forces together and reinforcing political obligation.

---

[27] See Waldrom (1994, pp. 51–72).

[28] Idem, p. 55.

[29] Hume (1963, pp. 474–475).

[30] Hume "Of the Origin of Government" in "Essays", idem (1963), p. 67.

[31] See Gauthier (1979, p. 3).

Hence, for the proponents of the doctrine of social contract, the state is the result of an agreement reached by the people in order to protect themselves and the society. Being the outcome of the deliberate decision of the people, the state can be only an integrative entity. We have seen that this doctrine has been fundamentally built on speculative and philosophic systems. Aware of such weakness, some scholars have started from mid of the nineteenth century to seek a scientific explanation to the emergence of the state and therefore to the foundation to the idea of integration. The most prominent among these scholars was H.Spencer.

H. Spencer has tried to develop a biological theory of evolution and to implement it to the study of society. Evolution is a continuous process by which an organism develops from a homogeneous and simple state to a more heterogeneous and complex one. However, the move from homogeneity to heterogeneity does not mean the passage from order to disorder as the natural inclination of every organism is to pursue its own preservation as well as the preservation of the whole organisms with which it does interact. Hence in his application of evolution to society, Spencer sees the latter as an organism: "Society undergoes continuous growth. As it grows, its parts become unlike: it exhibits increase of structure. The unlike parts simultaneously assume different activities of unlike kinds. These activities are not simply different, but their differences are so related as to make one other possible. The reciprocal aid, thus given, causes mutual dependence of the parts. And the mutually dependents parts, living by and for one another, form an aggregate constituted on the same general principle as is an individual organism."[32] However, in contradiction with the idea that all parts of the society do cooperate and live by and for one another in order to preserve themselves and the whole society, Spencer does sustain, in a kind of early social Darwinism, that the society is subject to natural selection which allows the "survival of the fittest."[33] Warfare is a major means in that selection. Warfare leads to the unification of different forces in society and, when successful, leads also to the formation of government and a military leadership in the society, and by doing so a further division of the society in classes. Warfare generates also economic benefits for different components of the society. The crucial role hence played by warfare in the transformation of the society into a political organization has been, as we have seen above, an idea defended by Hobbes and Hume, but it takes a prominent position in Spencer's system. However, warfare can lead also to the conquest of new territories and the domination of foreign populations which will be subject to an inferior status. As historically many states, as we will see hereafter, have in fact been the result of an amalgamation or a juxtaposition of a great variety of alien communities and ethnic groups, Spencer has difficulty in adapting his theory of social evolution to such a situation: "We must not expect to find in a rule coercively established by an invader the same traits as in a rule that has grown up from within. Societies formed by conquest maybe, and

---

[32] Spencer (1967, p. 8).

[33] Idem, p. 78.

frequently are, composed of two societies, which are to a large measure, if not entirely, alien, and in them there cannot arise a political force from the aggregate will. Under such conditions, the political head either derives his power exclusively from the feeling of the dominant class, or else, setting the diverse feeling originated in the upper and lower classes one against the other, is enabled so to make his individual will the chief factor."[34] It is difficult to imagine how such newly created society can function like a living organism in which various communities can interact and find equal interest in preserving the whole social system. Hence, Spencer has a major difficulty in showing that human societies have a tendency to spontaneously integrate. "Overall in Spencer's analysis", comments J.Haas, "recognition is given both to integration and conflict in the development of political institutions; but the conflict is externally derived, it does not develop endogenously. Class differences are present in the social system, arising out of the unequal distribution of wealth and power as well as out of conquest, but interclass relationships are symbiotic and not necessarily antagonistic."[35] Such inconsistency is the consequence of Spencer's conception of social evolution which is mainly of a philosophic character and "has nothing to do with biology."[36]

As to the doctrine which sustains that the formation of the state is meant to maintain the division in the society, it has started to take form only with the anthropologist Lewis Henry Morgan. The latter was the first author to develop an anthropologic approach to old societies and therefore improve our understanding of these societies. He did so thanks to the collection of an enormous quantity of data and factual materials and the analysis of the information hence collected on the basis of an objective approach instead of a self-conceived past. For Morgan, human societies have developed through three stages: savagery, barbarism and civilization. These societies have witnessed progresses from one stage to another thanks to technological inventions and discoveries. These progresses were mainly the domestication of animals, the invention of agriculture (barbaric stage), and the development of trade and of the art of writing (civilized stage). These progresses have in turn, by improving agricultural productivity, increasing wealth and giving rise to a division of labour, led to unprecedented developments of social character such as the emergence of the notions of private property, monogamous family, social classes and political organization, the latter being "founded upon territory, and upon property."[37] The approach adopted by Morgan in the analysis of the evolution of old societies and in particular the social transformations which have been at the origin of the passage from primitive matriarchal family to patriarchal family, and which reflected the first form of human exploitation and anticipated the emergence of classes and class antagonisms, has exerted an enormous influence on Friedrich

[34] Idem, p. 106.

[35] Haas (1962, p. 63).

[36] Mayr (1982, p. 385).

[37] Morgan (1963, p. 6).

Engels' own analysis of these societies and who admitted that "This rediscovery of the primitive matriarchal gens as the earlier stage of the patriarchal gens of civilized peoples has the same importance for anthropology as Darwin's theory of evolution has for biology and Marx's theory of surplus value for political economy."[38] This influence has been exerted in particular on Engels' "Origins of the Family, Private Property, and the State", first published in 1884.

For Engels, The state came then into being when a small minority took over the exercise of power from the whole community in order to protect its nascent privileges and private property. "The state arose", writes F. Engels, "in the thick of the fight between classes, it is normally the state of the most powerful, economically dominant class, which by its means becomes also the politically dominant class and so acquires new means of holding down and exploiting the oppressed class. The ancient state was, above all, the state of the slaves owners for holding down the slaves."[39] Hence, E. Mandel sums it up that,[40] at a certain point in the development of society, before it is divided into social classes, certain functions such as the right to bear arms or to administer justice are exercised collectively – by all adult members of the community. It is only as this society develops further, to the point where social classes appear, that these functions are taken away from the collectivity to be reserved to a minority who exercise these functions in a special way, i.e. through the creation of the state.

Contemporary doctrine has suggested different causal explanations of the origin and nature of the states. Among the suggested causes are hydraulic state,[41] warfare,[42] population growth and social circumscription,[43] etc. But, these interpretations have also been questioned.

Hence, the hydraulic state interpretation, according to which the management of large-scale hydraulic agriculture would have led to the establishment of a group of rulers and then to the rise of the state,[44] has been criticised as in many areas major-scale irrigation works have required the prior existence of the state. Hence, J. Germet has among others shown that in China, for example, "although the establishment of a system of regulation of water courses and irrigation, and the control of this

[38] Engels " The Origins of the Family, Private Property, and the State" (1884), Preface to the fourth edition (1891).

[39] Engels (1972, p. 31).

[40] Mandel "Marxist Theory of the State", Marxist Internet Archives (1969), www.angelfire.com/pr/red/mandel/.

[41] Wittfogel (1957).

[42] Spencer (1896).

[43] Carneiro (1977).

[44] According to K. Wittfogel, the state came into being "when an experimenting community of farmers or protofarmers finds large sources of moisture in a dry but potentially fertile area. . . . a number of farmers eager to conquer [agriculturally, not militarily] arid lowlands and plains are forced to invoke the organizational devices which – on the basis of premachine technology – offer the one chance of success: they must work in cooperation with their fellows and subordinate themselves to a directing authority.", Wittfogel (1957, p. 18).

system, may have affected the political constitution of the military states and imperial China, the fact remains that, historically, it was the pre-existing states structures and the large, well trained labour force provided by the armies that made great irrigation projects possible."[45] Furthermore, many states arose in areas where the irrigation was not of crucial importance.

With regard to the circumscription theory, it sees in the state a response to some agricultural, demographic and ecological specific constrains. Hence, according to R. Carneiro, in areas of circumscribed agricultural land (Nile, Tigris-Euphrates, Indus Valley, and the Valleys of Mexico and Peru) population pressure has led to warfare between autonomous villages in order to acquire land, which warfare resulted in the long run in the creation of chiefdoms, then of states and finally of empires. Circumscription theory provides an interesting explanation to the emergence of the state as it takes into consideration a variety of factors. However, the relevance of most of these factors has been questioned. First, R. Carneiro has himself recognized that circumscription is not a necessary factor to the emergence of the state. Second, the population pressure can lead, in a situation of circumscribed land, to a halt in the growth of population and not necessarily to war.[46] Furthermore, even a growth of population does not necessarily lead to war and then to the creation of a state.[47] Third, warfare has frequently prevailed between primitive societies, but has not necessarily led to the emergence of a body of rulers. R.L. Carneiro himself, though he holds that "warfare is surely a prime mover in the origin of the state", does recognize that "it cannot be the only factor. After all, wars have been fought in many parts of the world where the state never emerged."[48] War has obviously strongly helped in creating the state. R. Cohen has shown in this respect that "war helps make states, states make war, and therefore states are in part, and must always be, war machines."[49] War has also helped in expanding and generating a dynamic of creation of new states as when "interstate warfare occurs in a region through time, minimum state size must increase as well. The greater the offensive power of one state, the less likely is that smaller ones in the region can survive without becoming bigger. . .themselves."[50] Force helps also in maintaining the state as "coercive force. . .constitutes an essential ingredient in the internal operation of all large-scale societies."[51] Yet it remains that war does not necessarily lead to the creation

[45] Germet (1968, p. 92). Robert M. Adams was able to show with regard Mesopotamia that: "there is nothing to suggest that the rise of dynastic authority in southern Mesopotamia was linked to the administrative requirements of a major canal system.", Adams (1960, p. 281). See also Carneiro (1977, p. 738) and Gunawardana (1985, p. 220).

[46] See Cowgill (1975, p. 517).

[47] See Wright and Johnson (1975, p. 276).

[48] Carneiro (1977, p. 734).

[49] Cohen (1985, p. 282).

[50] Idem, p. 287.

[51] Trigger (1985, p. 52).

of states. "It is often evident, recalls Robert M. Schacht, "that some kind of (armed) conflict accompanied the evolution (meaning here creation) of the state, but correlation does not necessarily imply causation."[52]

As to the warfare and social circumscription theory, it recognizes that war is only an instrument, though a crucial one, which has helped in the formation of states. Warfare plays that role when a series of socio-ecological conditions are met. These conditions are the scarcity of agricultural land, the restricted availability of food resources and population pressure reflected by a high density of population in areas where cultivable land is limited. It is these conditions which force peoples to struggle for scarce land and food resources and then to engage in war in order to acquire new lands. Small communities are then subjugated by dominant groupings and become integrated into larger communities where arise a separate body of rulers who monopolize the power to issue and enforce law, organize labour, collect taxes and whenever needed to draft men for war. The state then emerges and its territorial limits are reached when it comes to be neutralized by other arising states with equal forces and strength. The warfare and social circumscription theory has also been questioned as there are some communities "whose population density reaches 400 persons per square mile, yet who have no kings, no chiefs, no social stratification, no ranking, and indeed, none of the trappings of civilization whatsoever."[53]

The difficulty to determine the causal factors in the emergence of the states has led many authors to focus on a group of prime movers variables. Hence, H.T. Wright observes that the formation of the state is the outcome of many factors such as managerial requirements and the conflict between emerging classes and polities.[54] Likewise E. Service emphasizes several conditions such as warfare, irrigating agriculture, population growth, etc.[55] Kent V. Frannery is also of the opinion that warfare, population pressure, the demands of large-scale trade, or any combination of socio-environmental conditions can provide an explanation of state origin.[56] Henry J.M. Claessen, after having previously focussed on a single factor,[57] has come to imagine a "Complex Interaction Model" in which different factors do contribute to state formation. These factors are "(1) the societal format (societal size, population distribution, infrastructure); (2) the set of economic factors (resources, technology, including magic and applied science, relations of production, which will generally include kinship system); and (3) the set of ideological factors (myths, religions and science; law and norms, including kinship ideology)."[58]

---

[52] Schacht (1988, p. 442).

[53] Flannery (1972, p. 406).

[54] Wright "Toward an Explanation of the Origin of the State", prepared for Sch. Am. Res. Symp. "Explanation of Prehistoric Organizational Change", 1970.

[55] Service (1975, pp. 266–289).

[56] Flannery (1972, p. 412).

[57] Claessen (1978, pp. 533–596).

[58] Claessen (1985, p. 255).

As we can see, the conditions of the state origin seem to be very controversial. However, a promising interpretation of these conditions has been recently suggested by Peter N. Peregrine, Carol R. Ember and Melvin Ember,[59] who, while considering a plurality of variables, recognize some pre-eminence to social conflict, a factor which appears to be everywhere the real precursor of states. This approach of state formation based on what can be called a "uni-multiple explanation" can be of crucial importance for us as it can help to not only apprehend the factors which have led to the emergence of the states but also to understand the impact of that emergence on the homogeneity of societies. Employing multivariate data for a large sample of archaeological cases and a variety of statistical methods, these authors have empirically come to the conclusion that the emergence of the state is the outcome of the following process:

- First, domesticated and ceramic technology are precursors of sedentary life which is "alone (a) precursor of both social inequality and increased population density."[60]
- Second, both social inequality and increased population density are the direct precursor to agriculture (the reliance on domesticated plants and animals).
- Third, the existence of a link between reliance on food production and the emergence of villages and as well the existence of a link between villages and the emergence of both towns and social classes, a fact which "appears to support social conflict theories, which predict that social differences increase with village life and lead to the emergence of social classes".[61]
- Fourth, social classes and towns are the precursors of states.

The states have since their emergence thousands of years ago – approximately 3700 BC in Mesopotamia and later on in Mesoamerica[62] – been faced with the threat of disintegration as a result of the shift from an egalitarian and homogeneous societies. Hence, the seeds of disintegration were concomitant to the creation of the states as the latter are the result of division of labour and social division to which the latter has given rise.[63] However, war of conquest has also, and even more frequently, contributed to states disintegration and the creation of new ones. Territorial expansion has therefore aggravated the fragmented character of state's population by incorporating new ethnic communities,[64] and then deepened the ethnic heterogeneity of states.

---

59 Peregrine et al. (2007, pp. 75–86).

60 Idem, p. 78.

61 Idem, p. 79.

62 See Wright (1977, p. 386 cont).

63 Most of the theories on the origin of the state do agree that the latter is the result of the division of the society, but they disagree on the nature of that division and the interpretation of the ways that have been used by the states to address it. See, for a general analysis of these theories, Haas (1962, pp. 19–85).

64 See Smith (1988).

2.1.2 The Deepening of Ethnic Heterogeneity

From the above analysis, it appears that the states have first emerged as a result of the division of society. It was from that moment that political power has emerged in the society. It was that power, which has been at the origin of the territorialization process which would lead, when successful, to the emergence of territoriality and then to the formation of early states. But the power has its own dynamic which is to expand as far as it can, even if such a move requires the conquest of new communities. However, the expansion of power has very often led not only to the conquest of new territories but also to the creation of new states. In fact, most of the pre-modern states had come into existence not as pristine but as secondary states. The distinction between pristine and secondary states has been first introduced by Morton H. Fried who has made it clear that by the term pristine state "it is meant a state that has developed *sui generic* out of purely local conditions. No previous state, with its accumulative pressures, can be discerned in the background of a pristine state. The secondary state, on the other hand, is pushed by one means or another toward a higher form of organization by an external power which has already been raised to statehood."[65]

Hence, while early states had their origin in social division, most of the states had later on evolved and expanded as a result of conquest. The process by which the latter has given rise to states has been well described by Franz Oppenheimer. Apparently inspired by Ibn Khaldun,[66] he is of the opinion that when pastoral nomads come into contact with sedentary peasantry, they at first resort to robbery and killing. Such a situation is followed by repeated wars between the large but weak masses of peasants and the small but compact and easily mobilized pastoral group (the herdsmen) who at the end is able to impose its power on the former. Later, the peasants, after thousands of unsuccessful attempts to revolt, accept their fate and cease every resistance, while the pastoral group realises that it is his self-interest to allow peasants to gain their livelihood and even to protect them from alien aggression against the establishment of a regular mode of domination and exploitation consisting in the appropriation of agricultural surplus. Such development is crucial in human history as "although this is the beginning of all slavery, subjugation, and exploitation, it is at the same time the genesis of a higher form of society (i.e. the state), that reaches out beyond the family based upon blood relationship. . .In this, we find (also) the germ of that magnificent process of amalgamation which, out of small hordes, has formed nations. . .The moment when first the conqueror spared his victim in order permanently to exploit him in productive work, was of incomparable historical importance. It gave birth to nation and state. . ."[67] But the paths toward

---

[65] Fried (2004, p. 300).

[66] "The Muqaddimah: An Introduction to History" (1377). See on this Becker and Smelo (1931, p. 67).

[67] Khaldun (2007, p. 34 and 35).

state formation develop further when the extraction of the surplus from the peasantry becomes permanent and takes the form of tribute and when the herdsmen under the leadership of their lords start settling in the neighbourhood of the dominant peasants, a factor of great importance as it leads to the "union on one strip of land of both ethnic groups,"[68] that is the notion of a common territory. Hence, whenever feasible, the crowds of lords becomes more or less permanently settled and preferably in strategically important places (camps, castles or towns) from where "they control their 'subjects', mainly for the purpose of gathering their tribute, paying no attention to them in other respects. They let them administer their affairs, carry on their religious worship, settle their disputes, and adjust their method of internal economy. Their autochthonous constitutions, their local officials, are, in fact, not interfered with."[69] Finally, the necessity of keeping the subjects in order and maintaining them at their full capacity for labour with the view to ensuring a regular extraction of the economic "surplus" will increasingly push the lords "to interfere, to allay difficulties, to punish, or to coerce obedience; and thus develop the habit of rule and the usages of government."[70] The state takes then its final form enabling then the initially opposed ethnic groups to "intermingle, unite, and amalgamate to unity, in customs and habits, in speech and worship."[71] However, it remains that the state is an unstable entity as, being the result of warlike robbery, it can be preserved only by a continuing territorial expansion until "a collision takes place on the edge of the 'sphere of interests' of another primitive state, which itself originated in precisely the same way."[72]

The theory that conquest has been the only way of state formation and the emergence of social classes has been perceived as "abundantly exemplified by facts"[73] and that it is of "great value in accounting for the genesis of many, if not all the states."[74] Meanwhile, Oppenheimer theory has also been criticized. Hence, while admitting that there is no doubt that conquest played a part in most if not all processes of state formation, L. Krader is of the opinion that "The conquest theory failed as a general theory of the origin of the state because it introduced only external factors and failed to take into account internal processes."[75] However, it has been established that most of the states if not all of them have, after the initial period of the formation of early states, emerged as a result of conquest. Hence, after having introduced the distinction between pristine and secondary states, Morton H.

[68] Idem, p. 37.

[69] Idem, p. 39.

[70] Idem, p. 41.

[71] Idem, p. 41.

[72] Idem, p. 57.

[73] Lowie "The Origin of the State", op.cit, (1927, p. 21).

[74] Becker and Smelo (1931, p. 79).

[75] Krader (1968, p. 45).

Fried[76] has shown that "the number of pristine states is strictly limited; several centuries, possibly two millennia, have elapsed since the last one emerged in Meso-America, and there seems to be no possibility that any further states of the pristine type will evolve."

The final outcome of the emergence of political power has then been to create the state from within the original egalitarian society and to make it expand externally by incorporating neighbouring communities. The state has consequently, from the beginning, been, first, socially divided as a consequence of the division of the society and, second, culturally and ethnically differentiated mainly by the incorporation of neighbouring communities as a result of territorial expansion. It has been argued that initially social inequality used to be higher than ethnic heterogeneity, but through time it was the latter that became prominent.[77] However, though the two elements of inequality and heterogeneity are interrelated, it is well established that the latter has been a determining factor in the emergence of a complex society made of "nearly decomposable systems."[78] Hence, according to Herbert A. Simon most complex systems, including human societies, are hierarchical in structure in that, first, they are divided into parts, and the parts into parts, and so on, like an elaborate collection of Chinese boxes and, second, that the components at each level are not independent of each other, but there is much denser and more rapid interaction within the components at any level than between components at that level. That is why such systems are said to be nearly decomposable. In his analysis of ancient states in light of the concept of the decomposability of complex systems, Joseph A. Tainter was able to clarify[79] that these states are at least partly built up of social units that are themselves potentially stable and independent, and indeed at one time may have been so. Thus, a newly established state may include formerly independent villages or ethnic groups, or an empire may incorporate previously established states. To the extent that these states, ethnic group, or villages retain the potential for independence and stability, the collapse process may result in reversion (decomposition) to these "building blocks" of complexity. It is not surprising therefore that the idea that ancient states have originally been made of previously independent local communities has been extensively confirmed by Marxist theory and modern anthropology.

Hence, according to the Marxist theory, the dismemberment of the primitive community has led to the emergence of early states within the framework of the Asiatic mode of production. We know that the concept of Asiatic mode of production is controversial as it contradicts the major postulates of the Marxist theory and the analysis made by Engels, in the *Origin of the Family, Private Property and the*

[76] Fried (2004, p. 300).

[77] See McGuire (1983).

[78] Simon (1965, p. 70).

[79] Tainter (1988, pp. 23–24).

State, of the historical conditions of the emergence of the early states.[80] However, some of the findings reached in the analysis of the Asiatic mode of production may help in understanding the nature of the political order of ancient states. Hence, it is agreed that the Asian mode of production was an order of rule by a despotic monarch over a large number of small, autarkic and autonomous communities and through the latter, the individuals and families who were their natural components. Such order of rule has emerged as a result of services rendered to the autonomous local communities. Hence, according to M.Godelier, the power has emerged and started to be exercised over a multitude of independent local communities when a minority was able to establish a permanent form of leadership against services rendered to these communities. He argues in this regard that "This power at first takes root in functions of common interest (religious, political, economic) and, without ceasing to be a functional power, gradually transforms itself into an exploitative one. The special advantages accruing to this minority, nominally as a result of services rendered to the communities, become obligations with no counterpart, that is exploitation. The land of these communities is often expropriated to become the ultimate property of the king, who personifies the higher community. We therefore have exploitation of man by man, and the appearance of an exploiting class without the existence of private ownership of land."[81]

One of the major characteristics of the Asiatic mode of production was that individuals and families could not stand up independently of their community, the reason being that as long as "the basic unit of production was the community itself, the independence of individuals and families vis-à-vis the community was extremely weak."[82] This is one of the reasons why early states have tried to establish their control mainly on local communities as "if one has control of the functions of the community, one can exercise rule over the members of the community, for whom an independent stand in relation to the community is impossible".[83] However, such control was, as we will see later on, very weak even though the states were able to dispossess the local communities from their right to the ownership of land[84] and simultaneously exert some important functions such as large-scales tasks (drainage, irrigation, etc.). Such control was also very weak as the main concern of the states was the appropriation of surplus labour through the collection of taxes, the latter being "a form of rent in that they represented the condition of possession and use of the land by state subjects."[85] In fact, very often the reality of power has remained within the local communities

---

[80] See Curie (1994, pp. 251–268).

[81] Godelier (1978, p. 240). See also Friedman and Rowlands (1977, pp. 201–276).

[82] Shiozawa (2007, p. 310).

[83] Idem, p. 314.

[84] See Hindless and Hirst (1975, p. 194).

[85] Idem.

who economically were "self-sufficient and self-reproducing"[86] and politically continued to enjoy a certain degree of autonomy, a system which allowed the local leadership, who was traditionally vested in powerful families, notables and religious chiefs, to play a mediatory role between their communities and central government as long as the latter's strength was not under threat. Hence, the ethnic heterogeneity of the society has remained intact and has even been reinforced whenever the state was able to expand its control over new territories.

The idea that ancient states have originally been made of previously independent local communities has also been confirmed by modern anthropology. This is in particular one of the major conclusions reached by Norman Yoffee in a recent, very enlightening and critical analysis of the nature and evolution of early states.[87] The central purpose of that analysis is to question the myth prevailing among neo-evolutionist scholars that early states, or what they have called the "archaic states", were very similar to one another: large territorial systems which evolved from chiefdoms and were ruled by totalitarian despots who controlled, or even monopolized, all means of production and the distribution of goods and services, and instituted and imposed true law and order on their subjects. Yoffee shows, first, that there is no unilinear evolution and stages in the development of human societies[88] and that in particular chiefdoms have not been a necessary trajectory prior to the formation of primary states. One of the main reasons why chiefdoms have very frequently not led to the emergence of states has been their tendency to break down due to the fact that they did not possess a permanent and specialized coercive authority. Most of the early states appeared in different parts of the world following a process which has witnessed, first, the appearance of settled villages that were modestly differentiated socially and depended on agriculture, second, the appearance as a result of circulation of goods, of interaction spheres and the growth of belief systems between autonomous villages by which the latter were culturally connected on a regional basis while keeping local ties of kinship, and, third, the transformation of those villages that were the centres of production and exchange and the seats of temples and regional worship which were located into cities and became nodal points for military protection from neighbours, distribution points for agricultural laborers and locations for water distribution to the countryside and, fourth, the appearance of the city-states where rulers governed many other cities and their associated countrysides and who later on extended their power over a large territorial region where people shared the same beliefs, a common culture, ways of writing, etc., while keeping their ethnic ties, local cultures and languages. However, city-states were hardly problem-solvers as local ethnic communities have very frequently shown resistance to the rulers in the cities. Analyzing such resistance in the political and cultural context of Mesopotamia but which is very often more or

[86] Idem.

[87] Yoffee (2005).

[88] See on the traditional unilinear evolutionary approach of human societies, Ginsberg (1957).

less similar to the ones experienced elsewhere in different parts of the world, Yoffee highlights that :

> "If the ideology of the state was an invention in the late Uruk period (Uruk period: 4000-3300 BC), however, it did not dissolve the many other, older forms of power in Mesopotamian society. Leaders of 'ethnic groups', whose means of social identification were created or reconfigured in the interactions with many other groups in the new states, were powerful figures in Mesopotamia. Indeed, the number of such groups and the amount of their effective control of land and people did not diminish over time in Mesopotamia in which political leadership was focused in cities. Such leaders could mobilize followers who lived both in cities and in the countryside, and so had effective means of seizing political power in times of the weakness of urban rulers and their followers. Mesopotamia had many identities, as citizens of cities and members of ethnic groups, of temple communities, and of occupational groups (especially visible in merchant associations). These identities were to a certain extent malleable, as Mesopotamians could privilege one aspect of their identities over others as circumstances dictate."[89]

Thomas Bargatzky has, among others, argued that it is time to do away with the notion of growing complexity[90] and this even so in the context of ancient states.[91] Hence, he does believe that in upward evolving systems, i.e. systems which grow through the development of successive suprasystems, subsystems initially possess attractive forces and are less easily disrupted during system's formative stages. They perform more effectively than the younger suprasystem. However, evolution upward may proceed to the point where the weak suprasystem becomes strong enough to overpower its subsystems. Applying his thesis to sociocultural systems, he suggests a distinction between Early State, a society where the relation between upward and downward evolution – i.e. the growth through the development of specialized subunits – has not become mature and the Mature State where a critical point is passed when the cohesive forces of the suprasystem and the subsystems are equally balanced and the suprasystem becomes dominant. While such opinion can be relevant when describing the evolution of modern states till the present stage of postmodernity where the state is again witnessing the resurgence and exacerbation of heterogeneity, it does by no means reflect the evolution of pre-modern states which, as we have seen above, have had the tendency to be subject inter alia to increasing heterogeneity. Bargatzky mentions, in favour of his thesis, the progress made by early Dynastic Ur (ca. 2600 BC to 2400 BC) in developing social indicators of the Mature State such as social stratification, or social classes, and bureaucracy. However, while it is true that the early Ur dynasty has developed a highly centralized bureaucratic system, this could not prevent the rapid unravelling of the fabric of that administration and even the collapse of the state of Ur and its replacement by a new state under the hegemony of a new ethnic group.[92] The major problem faced by the city-states in Mesopotamia as well in other parts of

[89] Idem, p. 214.

[90] See Bargatzky (1987, p. 28).

[91] Idem, pp. 30–31.

[92] See on the evolution of Ur dynasty Yoffee (2005, pp. 144–147).

the world was their incapacity to adjust to extremely difficult situations created by their own territorial expansion. In fact such incapacity was inherent to the ancient states whatever their form was, city-states, kingdoms or empires, as they were structurally fragile, a situation compounded by the lack of adequate means of communication and transport. States' structural weakness used to appear clearly in post-conquest situations where they have had to establish their own order over large territories whose inhabitants were *by nature* recalcitrant as they did belong to various ethnic groups, cultural identities and affiliations. "The point to note, observes Patricia Crone, is that even the monarchy as an *impersonal* institution rarely enjoyed power of a kind that could be described as absolute. The fact that the news travelled slowly, and troops even more so, invariably meant that considerable power had to be handed over to people on the spot, be they governors despatched from the centre, provincial magnates allied with it, or others. Only they could know what was going on locally and they could react fast. By the same token, of course, they had considerable freedom to abuse their position, notably by fleecing the local population for private gain or by building up power-bases with a view to secession or bids for the throne."[93]

In fact, a dialectic relationship does exist between the state and ethnicity. First, the emergence of the state and ethnicity are interconnected, as it was the creation of the former that has led to the appearance of the later. It is true that ethnicity may have its remote origin in kinship,[94] but it has started to exist as such only following the creation of the state and as means of a collective resistance and defence against the latter which was perceived as the emanation of a human community which used to enjoy the same status as the newly dominated communities. It is amazing to see in this regard Anthony D. Smith tracing the historical origin of ethnies back to 3000 BC, which is in all aspects connected to the evolution of the state since then, without establishing any link between the later and the emergence of ethnic groups in the society.[95] Second, while it is true that socially it is "the ethnic boundary that defines (an ethnic) group, not the cultural stuff that it encloses",[96] it remains that the existence of a political community is a precondition for ethnic group mobilization as "it is primarily the political community, no matter how artificially organized, that inspires the belief in common ethnicity."[97] Hence, if socially ethnicity is a social construct by which a community establishes a boundary with other local communities, politically it does emerge as such only when a group defines itself by reference to the dominating ethnic group within the society, especially in situations where the state has not been able to reach a kind of autonomy enabling it to behave independently from classes and ethnic groups. This was in particular the case of pre-modern societies where the principal source of political and

93 Crone (1989, p. 45).

94 See Van den Berghe (1978, pp. 401–411).

95 Smith (1998, pp. 42–46).

96 Barth (1969, p. 15).

97 Weber (1978, p. 389).

economic power was the control over land and "where the primary issues are not, in fact, allocation of states resources (which is the case in industrial societies), but control of local communities, which is an issue both within ethnic groups and between ethnic groups and external forces, including other ethnic groups and the state."[98] Third, ethnicity has evolved from a means to protect a community to an instrument in the struggle for power among elites which offers powerful capacity mobilization of the masses than social classes' conflicts.[99] Fourth, the evolution of ethnicity in any given society is correlatively linked to the evolution of the state. Hence, it is only when the state extends its domination over the whole society or reaches a high level of autonomy from the same society that ethnicity ceases to be attractive or has a difficulty to rise up. It is therefore not surprising that pre-modern states have never been able to prevent the emergence and the development of ethnicity. The only one exception was ancient Egypt where some form of ethnic congruence used to exist between the society and a single ethnicity as a consequence of the territorial configuration of that country where a "strong territorial configuration (in Egypt) was the result of evolutionary trends towards stratification in the ecologically uniform environment of the Nile valley, the concentration of the most important resources within Egypt's borders, and the excellent transport link by the Nile (which allowed quick intervention of the state in its remote parts of its territory)".[100]

The major challenge to which the state has continuously been confronted since its inception has then been how to keep together disparate human communities. Disintegration was a major concern to the extent that it has been argued that a polity cannot reach the status of a state only after having adopted effective anti-fission institutions.[101] Thus, the main function of politics has all the time been "to ensure the cohesion of the society, i.e. to keep together the multiple elements, the diverse sub-systems, which make up the social order...".[102] Attempts have therefore constantly been made by rulers not to leave uncontrolled the division of the society. But, states' policies have varied in this respect due to the flexibility of territoriality.

2.2 The Flexibility of Territoriality Across History: How to Make States Survive

Ancient and modern states have addressed differently the crucial problem raised by their inner drive towards disintegration. Thus, while traditional states have sought to prevent their own disintegration by sharing power with local communities

98 Brass (1985), p. 33.

99 See Bell (1975).

100 Yoffee (2005, pp. 47–48).

101 See Cohen (1981, pp. 87–88).

102 Chevallier (1978, p. 24).

through a de facto territorial autonomy, modern states have managed to ensure their survival by displaying an effective control over their territories and homogenizing their societies. However, today the states are again witnessing, as a result of globalization, an increasing vulnerability of their territoriality. Contrary to a largely shared opinion, globalization has not led to the obsolescence of the state, but it has weakened its territoriality and particularly its ability to maintain its congruence with the nation. In fact, globalization has been giving rise to a new type of state, the postmodern state, which in order to address the increasing vulnerability of its territoriality is forced to share its power with sub-states entities. Amazingly, postmodern state, like ancient state, has realized that its own survival requires sharing its power with sub-state entities through territorial autonomy.

2.2.1 The Premodern State: Inventing Territorial Autonomy

The initial division of the society has necessarily made of early states very fragile polities. Such state of affairs has been confirmed by recent studies of collapse in early complex societies. Glenn M. Scwartz has noted in this regard that "the more the workings of complex societies were exposed, the more apparent it became that these were not smoothly functioning machines that ran perfectly once their engines were turned on. Complex societies could be unstable phenomena, prone to episodes of fragility and collapse."[103]

The major challenge to which the state has not stopped being confronted to since its inception has then been how to keep together opposed classes and disparate human communities. F. Engels notes that the state, once its own emergence had led to the division of the society, was from its inception compelled to address such division which threatened its own existence:

> "Here was a society which by all its economic conditions of life had been forced to split itself into freemen and slaves, into the exploiting rich and the exploited poor; a society which not only could never again reconcile these contradictions, but was compelled always to intensify them.[104] ... (Such) society had involved itself in insoluble self-contradiction and is cleft into irreconcilable antagonisms, which it is powerless to exorcise. But in order that these antagonisms, classes with conflicting economic interests, shall not consume themselves and society in fruitless struggle, a power, apparently standing above the society, has become necessary to moderate the conflict and keep it within the bounds of 'order'; and this power arisen out of society, but placing itself above it and increasingly alienating itself from it, is the state."[105]

However, as we have seen above, early complex societies were not only divided in classes but also in cultural and ethnic local communities. In order to prevent the

[103] Schwartz (2006, p. 3).

[104] Engels (1972, p. 31).

[105] Idem, p. 229.

disintegration of early states, attempts have therefore been made by the emerging rulers not to leave uncontrolled the ethnic division of the society.[106] This was all the more crucial to the state's leadership that the latter used to belong to one of these ethnic communities and were therefore suspected to reflect the interest of their original ethnic community.

The control of social and ethnic division has required, first, the reinforcement of the nascent state. E. Service has well described the process by which the state has technically taken its final shape. This process starts by the institutionalization of the central leadership which in turn leads to the emergence of government, defined as a "bureaucracy (i.e. a hierarchy of offices) instituted to rule a populace by right of authority"[107] and whose power rests mainly on a legal system which has recognized the legitimacy of its monopoly of force. The government exerts such monopoly of force through a formalized judicial structure and a system of repressive laws. Characterized by an institutionalized authority, the state is socially fully differentiated and territorially bounded. According to E. Service, the government "is not necessarily or evidently a repressive body since a responsible control of violence equals peace,"[108] a position which is not surprising as he is of the opinion that the government "was a redistributive, and allocative system, not an acquisitive system".[109]

With regard to the physical use of force, it was not all the time a sufficient and available instrument enabling the state to establish its control over the society. Such situation has frequently compelled the states to accept that local communities organize themselves in a way to keep order between their members. "The physical force at the disposal of the administrative hierarchy, writes Bruce G. Trigger, was limited. As a result, governments preferred low-level groupings to be self-regulating whenever possible and deployed their own coercive power only when other means of regulation broke down or when the activities of subordinate groupings challenged or threatened their power."[110] However, such decentralization of physical force and the threat to use it, which were practiced at all levels of society have resulted in "the replacement within all social classes and most social groups, including the nuclear and the extended family, of a relatively egalitarian model of human relations by an explicitly hierarchical one."[111]

The control of social and ethnic division has also required to convince the whole society that the "raison d'être" of power is to protect that society. This has been made, first, through ideological instruments amongst which religion played a

---

[106] In North et al. remarkable work (2009), Douglass C. North, John Joseph Wallis and Barry R. Weingast have dealt with the issue of how states have over ages managed to survive, but they have neglected in their study the analysis of the crucial factor of the ethnic division of the society.

[107] Service (1975, p. 10).

[108] Idem, p. 307.

[109] Idem, p. xiii.

[110] Trigger (1985, pp. 52–53).

[111] Idem, p. 55.

crucial role. The latter has been present in every single society. It has even been argued in this regard that "human organization could not have come into existence, or persisted, in the absence of ultimate sacred propositions and the sanctification of discourse."[112] That is why every state has been keen to have its own religion the function of which was to "inculcate concepts of the proper social relationships between rulers and the ruled, create a sense of shared meaning between state authorities and their subjects, legitimize the actions of central authorities, and, in some sense, define the terms of social belongings and citizenship in society."[113] It has been made, second, by convincing the society that its own preservation was mainly dependent upon the state. Indeed, the latter was generally perceived as the main player which can maintain order which was necessary in order to ensure the smooth running of economy and therefore the subsistence of the whole members of the society. "In many early civilizations, highlights Bruce G.Trigger, high population densities made everyone dependent on intensive forms of food production. Food supplies could be seriously threatened if the state failed to maintain internal order or if its food shortage system collapsed. Many people also depended upon a well-ordered society to ensure the distribution of food and necessary raw materials. Hence, the collapse, or weakening, of the state could adversely affect the poor as much as, or even more than, the rich. The majority of people, therefore, had practical reasons to support the state, as long as the exploitation of the lower classes was maintained at customary and acceptable levels of government."[114] Furthermore, the power exerted by the state on the society was strengthened by the fact that the leadership, which has emerged as a result of social stratification, has started to establish an increased control of the production and procurement of basic resources. Indeed, the control of such resources has enabled the leadership to be in possession of economic power and therefore to use the latter as a means of gaining compliance of the population. In his analysis of major theories of state formation, J. Haas has concluded that the central feature of these theories is the development of a new economic power base by the society's leaders. Most of these theories were able to agree that, in early states, "the production or procurement of basic resources is centralized in the hands of the social leaders, and all members of the society no longer have equal access to those resources. It is this differential access that makes the new economic power base of the leaders in an emergent stratified society markedly different from the power base of leaders in prestratified societies. This critical difference lies in the ability of the state leaders to withhold basic resources as a coercive means of enforcing their demands on the society."[115]

The control of social and ethnic division has required, according to the proponents of the general systems theory, a constant adaptation of the state to its

[112] Rappaport (1971, p. 29).

[113] Kolata (2006).

[114] Trigger (1985, p. 52).

[115] Haas (1982, p. 175).

social environment. Adaptation does refer, clarifies Roy A. Rappaport, to "the processes by which organisms (amongst which human society can be considered as a living system) or groups of organisms maintain homeostasis in and among themselves in the face of both short-term environmental fluctuations and long-term changes in the composition and structure of their environment."[116] In order to carry out their control of social and ethnic division, the states have generally established a series of subsystems arranged hierarchically, from lowest and most specific to highest and more general and in which each subsystem is regulated by a control apparatus whose job is to maintain homeostasis and prevent any threat to the survival of the whole system.[117] It has been argued in this regard that the main function of politics has all the time been "to ensure the cohesion of the society, i.e. to keep together the multiple elements, the diverse sub-systems, which make up the social order..."[118]

In fact, ancient states have, in general, rarely been able to establish a close control of their societies and even less to homogenize them. "Early states", recalls Hendrik Spruyt,[119] "only tangentially affected their societies. Premodern states constituted capstone governments. Ruling elites were often integrated and dispersed through the area of control, but society consisted of multiple divided communities, differentiated along ethnic, religious, and linguistic lines. Horizontal elites (the capstone government) overlaid vertically segregated societies". Instead of vertical integration, what mobilized the states was rather horizontal integration, that is territorial expansion. Conquest was more important to the states than integration of local communities in a unified and homogeneous society. Furthermore, conquest itself has not meant the establishment of a close control on territories. Exerting their domination mainly through political-military power, states' highest priority, if not their obsession, was to annex the maximum of new territories even if that meant the establishment only of a symbolic link with those territories and the newly incorporated local communities who generally were able to continue enjoying territorial autonomy as well as cultural diversity. Hence, what mainly characterizes the traditional state is that "it does exert over its territory only a very imperfect and vague control, through very often allegiance than directly; it occupies the space by extending its suzerainty over the existing communities who keep their jurisdiction over their territory."[120] It is so because what is important for the state is to gather tribute and levy taxes and to enable the ruling classes to monopolize resources.

Homogenization of the society as well as adaptation to social environment was not therefore a major concern of the traditional states. Instead of vertical

[116] Idem, pp. 23–24.

[117] See Flannery (1972, p. 409 cont).

[118] Chevallier (1978, p. 24).

[119] Spruyt (2002, p. 131).

[120] Loschak (1978, p. 163).

integration, what mobilized the states was rather horizontal integration, that is territorial expansion. That is why, the number of the states has tended to decrease, especially during the "secondary state formation"[121] when territorial expansion led to the creation of large empires to the detriment of autonomous states. It has even been argued in this regard that since the inception of early states, the general trend has been an enlargement of the size of the states and a drastic decrease in their number.[122] In fact, the decrease in the number of the states has never been a steady trend as human history has witnessed a continuous movement of creation, destruction and re-creation of states. "The early political forms of civilization, clarifies David Wilkinson,[123] are states systems...; universal empires are distributed more toward the later epochs. But states systems may recur at any time in civilization's lifespan...Although they will ordinarily be displaced in due course by a universal state..., most states systems so abolished are in time re-established..., if only then to be re-abolished." It should also be added that the passage from autonomous states to empires has never meant unification and homogenization of conquered societies. On the contrary, obeying to the logic of indefinite territorial expansion, the empires are based on hierarchical relations but which allow the former independent states and communities to enjoy some degree of territorial autonomy as well as cultural diversity[124] which they do fully recover once empires fall and decompose into independent political units.[125]

The existence of a certain degree of territorial autonomy and cultural diversity has never meant that empires – as well as traditional states – did implement democratic policies toward conquered communities as the unchanged pattern of governance has, with few exceptions, been autocracy. Autocratic rule has been the common lot of humanity throughout nearly all of its written history. It is a rule with startlingly few exceptions. Territorial autonomy and cultural diversity have frequently prevailed as a result of the lack of an effective control of the state or the empire on their large territories due to weakness of transport and communication links. Likewise, as empires were mainly interested in the extraction of local resources,[126] they generally avoided to intervening overtly in local affairs as long

---

[121] See Price (1978, pp. 161–186).

[122] Carneiro (1978, pp. 205–223).

[123] Wilkinson "Kinematics of World Systems", paper presented at the Annual Meeting of the International Society for the Comparative Study of Civilization, Boone, North Carolina, June 1984, 9.

[124] Empire has been defined as "territorially expansive and incorporative kind of state, involving relationships in which one state exercise control over sociopolitical entities (e.g. states, chiefdoms, on-stratified societies), and of imperialism as the process of creating and maintaining empires. The diverse polities and communities that constitute an empire typically retain some degree of autonomy-in self-and centrally-defined cultural identity, and in some dimensions of political and economic decision making", Spinoli (1994, p. 160).

[125] See Taagepera (1978, pp. 108–127).

[126] "The acquisition of regularized revenues, writes Carla M. Spinoli, through tribute or taxes is both a major goal and a significant outcome of imperial expansion and consolidation", Spinoli (1994, p. 165).

as obligations of tribute were fulfilled. But, this has not prevented occasionally empires from seeking to establish dependencies among local communities through in particular the creation of ideological allegiances to the center, the appropriation of local religious beliefs, the incorporation of local elites in the imperial administration, the establishment of kin relations between imperial family and these elites, etc.[127]

The durability of ancient states has varied from one state to another. Some states disappeared very quickly, while others were able to survive for centuries. But it is a matter of fact that they have all ended up by passing away. States' death has drawn the attention of philosophers and historians since Greek antiquity. The general belief was that the state, like living organisms, first comes to life, then develops and then dies. This conception of the state and its final fate has influenced modern scholars such as Oswald Spengler[128] and Arnold Toynbee[129] in their famous broad and comprehensive analysis of the emergence, the development and the end of civilisations. However, no global analysis has ever been devoted to the phenomenon of the collapse of ancient states. Meanwhile, while a general theory of the collapse process of ancient states needs still to be done, attempts have been made to understand why some states have passed away. Different explanations have then been given to the collapse of the concerned states: natural disasters such as drought or cataclysmic floods, economic factors, depletion of vital resources, social contradictions, centrifugal forces, states' mismanagement or maladaptation, barbarian invasions, destruction and annexation by a foreign state, etc. Yet, most of these explanations did focus on triggering factors and not on the complex situation which has been very often behind the disintegration of ancient states.

It has been argued that most ancient states "did not work very well,"[130] were not smoothly functioning machines, and that consequently "nothing (was) more normal for an ancient state than for it to "collapse."[131] Indeed, the major causal factor behind the collapse of ancient states lies in the nature and social fabric of these states themselves that is their cultural and ethnic heterogeneity, and their inherent incapacity to handle it. Heterogeneity has, more than classes division, made the states to be constantly subject to a state of permanent tension, latent or manifest, between its core and periphery. This tension has its origin, as we have seen above, in the monopolization of power by a single ethnic group exerting its domination over various and disparate local communities who, in order to protect themselves, remained attached to their cultures and identities and kept alive a high sense of independence. The tension between the core and the periphery did prevail in all

[127] See Spinoli (1994, pp. 162–169).

[128] Spengler (1918–1922).

[129] Toynbee (1933–1954).

[130] Cowgill (1988, p. 253).

[131] Yoffee (2005, p. 38).

ancient states and translated into open struggles whenever these states have not been able to control their peripheries through local elites and address their needs.

Indeed, the ancient state suffered from inherent structural contradictions which made of it an extremely weak polity. Hence, while every city-state showed its capacity to keep its strength intact as long as its power basis was limited to a circumscribed territorial sphere, yet it started to integrate a structural weakness whenever it expanded beyond its natural geographical and human environment. Such weakness was an unavoidable fatality as the control of a newly conquered territory required the existence of rapid and efficient means of communication and transport, which was technically impossible to obtain. This has left ancient states with no other choice than to grant a kind of autonomy to the newly dominated communities within the framework not of unitary states but rather composite states which very often took the form of empires. Such has been the faith of the states since the emergence of early city-states in Mesopotamia about 3500 BC. Hence, the first Sumerian city-states, which were warlike and very often expansionary polities, have started by adopting very highly centralized systems in order to establish direct rule over their newly conquered territories, but they failed very quickly and even ended by collapsing as such control required what not a single state could possess at that time: quick communications and transport and rapid military interventions.[132] It was that incapacity to establish a direct control and rule of their newly conquered territories that pushed later on other emergent Sumerian city-states to share their power with local communities under an imperial structure setting then the model for all subsequent empires.

It is inaccurate to pretend that two sorts of states appear to have been associated with early civilizations: city-state and territorial states, the latter being defined as a polity where a "ruler governed a large region through a multileveled hierarchy of provincial and local administrators in a corresponding hierarchy of administrative centers."[133] In fact, with the exception of ancient Egypt which was initially a highly centralized unitary state before it expanded beyond its natural borders which fact had led to the weakening of the central government and the emergence of feudalities and a kind of regional autonomies and semi-independent polity,[134] most ancient states have taken the form of empires. States have not evolved in a linear way from city-states to territorial states and then finally to empires. What has marked ancient civilizations was the frequent and quick passage from city-states to empires. The durability of the latter has varied from one empire to another depending on the strength enjoyed by their cores and their capacity to handle their peripheries through the implementation of a variety of systems of local autonomies. That is why the analysis of the collapse of ancient states is very frequently nothing other than the analysis of the collapse of ancient empires.

---

[132] See the analysis of the collapse of ancient Mesopotamian States by Yoffee (2005, pp. 131–160).

[133] Trigger (2003, p. 93).

[134] See Tainter (1988, p. 8).

It has been argued by Alexander Motyl that many empires have shown remarkable staying powers. Motyl believes that "an ideally functioning imperial system should, logically and obviously, persist indefinitely", the reason being that "empires resemble giant machines consisting of interlocking, independent parts arranged in, to use Eisenstaedt's phrase, a 'very delicate balance', they should hum along so long as the parts fit and function."[135] According to Motyl, the key characteristic of the empire and what makes of it a viable, persistent and stable political structure is the fact that the core-periphery relations "resemble an incomplete wheel, with a hub and spokes but no rim."[136] However, the most striking aspect of such structure is not the hub and spokes which do exist in just about every political system, but the absence of a rim, i.e. of political and economic relations between and among the peripheral units or between and among them and nonimperial polities, a crucial fact which implies that most exchanges of resources, money, goods, information, and personnel can take place only via the core and may consequently prevent the peripheries from uniting and pulling their resources against the core and eventually restoring their own independence. The absence of a rim is, according to Motyl, a key factor in preserving empires. He insists to say in this regard that "Metropoles that command peripheries to interact significantly would in essence be withdrawing from empire. Empire ends, then, not when or because the core ceases to dominate the peripheries but when or because the peripheries implicated in such domination begin to interact with one another significantly."[137] It is true that the lack of a rim, or what is traditionally called the "colonial Pact", has played a key role in maintaining imperial domination, but in fact it never prevented the peripheries from obtaining their independence. Empires have very often collapsed when the flow of resources from the peripheries to the core and vice-versa was drastically reduced as a result of unbalanced and unfair relations between the core and its peripheries. Motyl recognizes incidentally such a fact but he unfortunately does not elaborate on it.

Analyzing empires systems well before Motyl, Shmuel N. Eisenstadt has also reached the conclusion that empires have "provided the most massive and enduring form of government man had known prior to the modern period."[138] But the reasons invoked by Eisenstadt as causal factors behind the relative persistence of empires are more plausible and acceptable that the ones given by Motyl. Eisenstadt does recognize that in empire systems, a kind of permanent tensions did prevail between the core and its peripheries. The reason behind that tension was that the peripheries were reluctant to surrender their independence and to accept to be subject to unfair extraction of resources needed by the cores. However, such tension was reduced and stability introduced in the system whenever the peripheries came to believe that

[135] Motyl (2001, p. 22).

[136] Idem, p. 16.

[137] Idem, p. 21.

[138] Eisenstadt (1969).

parts of the resources extracted by the cores did return to them in the form of services such as the provision of security, the settlement of disputes through the establishment of judiciary systems, the circulation of goods, etc. The tension was also reduced whenever the peripheries were allowed to handle their own affairs by enjoying effective autonomies. On the contrary, tension and instability prevailed whenever excessive resources were extracted from the peripheries, services have been reduced or cancelled and autonomies suppressed. These are the main factors which may lead to the collapse of an empire as they create a situation where the core can no longer secure the resources needed for the preservation of its own existence. However, empires were often keen to avoid such self-destructive eventuality. "Many traditional empires, observes K. Barkey, were political formations, systems of rule that lasted a long time mostly due to their flexibility and capacity to adapt and innovate. Longevity, resilience, and flexibility remain key features of empire that have been undertheorized".[139] One of the clearest expression of empires' sense of flexibility and adaptation in the face of diversity, crisis, and change and which has ensured their longevity was that the relations between their centers and peripheries were "regularly subject to negotiations over the degree of autonomy of intermediaries in return for military and fiscal compliance... To rule over vast expanses of territory, as well as to ensure military and administrative cooperation, imperial states negotiate and willingly relinquish some degree of autonomy. No matter how strong an empire is, it has to work with peripheries, local elites, and frontier groups to maintain compliance, resources, tribute, and military cooperation, and to ensure political coherence and durability."[140] Finally, what is then of an extreme importance to the persistence and durability of empires is the conviction of human communities in the peripheries that they draw benefits from their membership of those empires. This is the crucial factor which ultimately makes a state survive, whatever form it can take.

Joseph A. Tainter has pertinently drawn the attention that, whether one endorses a conflict or an integration model of society, or some synthesis of these, it is of extreme importance to inquire into the benefits that a population derives from its investment in complexity, that is by accepting to be part of a given state. However, based on the economic principle of diminishing returns, Tainter's analysis of the states' fate is marked by a kind of unavoidable fatality as he believes that "continued investment in sociopolitical complexity reaches a point where the benefits for such investment begin to decline, at first gradually, then with accelerated force. Thus, not only must a population allocate greater and greater amount of resources to maintaining an evolving society, but after a certain point, higher amounts of this investment will yield smaller increments of return"[141]which fact leads fatally to the collapse of the state when triggering factors, such as climatic

[139] Barkey (2008, p. 3).

[140] Idem, p. 9 and 10.

[141] Tainter (1988).

fluctuations or foreign incursions of invasions, do enter into play. It is in this situation that the option to decompose becomes attractive to certain components of a complex society and that "behavioural interdependence gives way to behavioural independence."[142] However, according to Tainter, such fatality does characterize the ancient and not modern states who have shown a greater ability to integrate their populations.

2.2.2 *The Modern State: Making Effective Its Territoriality*

The modern state did not emerge as a new political organization of the society simultaneously in different parts of the world. "The modern state", recalls B. Anderson,[143] "cannot be taken to mean that a single type of modern states came in a variety of shapes and sizes, and they arrived by different routes." The route described hereafter is the Western Europe one which was the first to witness the emergence of modern state. It was with the emergence of the modern state in Western Europe starting from the sixteenth century that state power over its own territory became effective. Effective territoriality indeed is a central character of modern state. It has made an end to the parcellisation of power which had resulted from the fall of the Roman Empire and prevailed under the feudal system.

Meanwhile, if territoriality has become effective in modern state, it remained absent in remnant traditional states, that is those states that continued to exist in other parts of the world and this very often until mid-twentieth century when the modernization of the states will become a universal phenomenon. However, it is surprise to note that the ICJ has, in its Opinion on Western Sahara, put into the same category the modern and traditional state. Such erroneous likening of two totally different categories of states reflects a profound ignorance of the nature of remnant traditional state.

Hence, two issues will be discussed hereafter, first, the effective power of the modern state over its territory, second, the erroneous likening of the remnant traditional state to the modern state: The ICJ' Opinion in Western Sahara case.

2.2.2.1 The Effective Power of the Modern State Over Its Territory

The fragmentation of power which resulted from the collapse of Rome has led to the emergence of a collection of small kingdoms themselves subdivided in small units enjoying a great deal of autonomous power within the feudal system. We know that what characterized the latter was the establishment of relations of vassalage and

142 Idem, p. 121.

143 Anderson (1986, p. 1).

reciprocal obligations between kings, lords and the peasantry. But what characterized most the feudal system was the extreme fragmentation of power as a result of the absence of centralized administration.[144] Such situation reflected necessarily on the various existing kingdoms which could not be formally perceived as states as they did not possess the capacity to establish any permanent government structure and organized and centralised administration. That is why these kingdoms could survive only through the delegation to local lords of the rights to raise taxes and dispense justice.[145]

According to J. Gottmann, the political structure of the European world has by the fifteenth century started to be based on territory as "the rise of an increasing number of...communities affirming their right to self-government and therefore some freedom from the lord of the 'open country' around them, required territorial delimitation, especially as the wealth and power of some cities grew."[146] In fact, the need for territorial delimitation was the result of the initiation of a very important process of territorialization by the most prominent and dynamic kings. Indeed, the kings have, starting from the twelfth century, gradually expanded their power as a result not of pre-conceived and "conscious power aggrandizement."[147] but as consequence of two major factors: the establishment of an alliance between some few kings and the nascent burghers, on one hand, and, on another hand, an unprecedented increase in military capacity.

With regard to the alliance between the monarchy and the bourgeoisie, it was accepted by the latter, though burdened by heavy taxation, as it saw in it a way to create a large economic and commercial free space from which it can extensively benefit. Hendrik Spruyt goes even further to argue that the emergence of the French state was the result of the affinity of interests between the monarchy and the bourgeoisie as "the analysis of royal taxation reveals how both monarchy and mercantile groups preferred regularized taxation which also allowed for urban negotiation. The development of centralized administration enabled the king to construct a bureaucracy on nonfeudal basis. Moreover, it offered the bourgeoisie and lesser nobility career opportunities and input into royal decision making."[148]

With regard to the increased military capacity, it was the result of unprecedented technological innovations as well as the transformation of the armed forces in more structured, regular and larger armies.[149]Its impact on the emergence of the first modern states has been so crucial that some authors have been brought to believe that "the modern state without the military revolution is unthinkable. The road from arquebus to absolutism, or from the maritime mortar to mercantilism, was a direct

144 Strayer (1965, pp. 29–30).

145 See Russel (1968, p. 204).

146 Gottmann "The Significance of Territory", op.cit, 1973, p. 36.

147 Mann (1986, p. 379).

148 Spruyt (1994, pp. 88–89).

149 See Samuel E. Finner "State-and Nation-Building in Europe: The Role of the Military" in C. Tilly (ed.) "The Formation of National States in Western Europe", 1975, pp. 84–163.

one."[150] Likewise, according to C. Tilly, it was "wars (that) made states."[151] The military revolution has, first, enabled the kings to collect more taxes.[152] It has also given them proper means to expand their territorial power base. It was from that time that the most powerful kings have launched territorialization processes which started from around one centre,[153] such as the Ile de France, and expanded in a series of piecemeal territorial acquisitions through conquest and dynastic marriages.[154] However, the need to raise more taxes in order to cover the heavy expenses engendered by the military revolution was conditioned not only by reinforcing the territorialization process, but also by the necessity to ensure the contiguity and unity of the royal territory within fixed borders. Hence, the later started from mid-thirteenth century to take a fixed form in order not only to separate the rising new political sovereignties but also to serve as a means for determining the limits of the fiscal space where taxes can be collected. But it was at the end of thirteenth century that the need to use the borders as a fiscal tool required the knowledge of the exact whereabouts of the borders. However, that knowledge did become effective only by the middle of the sixteenth century when maps became more accurate[155] and the states were able to make full use of it only in the eighteenth century when they managed to have the necessary administrative and materiel means to mark their respective borders.[156]It was from that time that the border ceased to be zonal and became well defined and clearly marked on the ground.[157]

However, the new concern of having fixed borders did not mean that the European borders were from that time stable and definitive. In fact, the European borders have continued to change according to changing circumstances until the Second World War. Indeed, states' power and strength have, during that period and more than ever in human history, continued to be measured in terms of the largeness of their territories. Consequently the highest concern of the arising states was the distribution of territories between them. Such situation has been admitted by classical International Law which recognized that "in time of war, borders' change and the move of an army within territory's enemy were a question of fact; sovereignty did move with the move of force."[158]

---

[150] Davies (1996, p. 519).

[151] Tilly (1985) and Tilly (1990).

[152] See Ardant (1975, pp. 164–243).

[153] Very often urban centers and cities used to be at the origin of the territorialization process as happened with early and traditional states. For a fresh look on the role of urban centers in the emergence of modern states, see Sassen (2008, pp. 41–72).

[154] See Anderson (1996a, p. 21).

[155] Idem.

[156] See Black (1997).

[157] See Febvre (1973).

[158] Nys (1904, pp. 401–402).

The military revolution has also led to a new situation where "armies no longer just fought battles; they increasingly came to represent the state they fought for."[159] Strengthened by the extraordinary new warfare capacities, the kings were able to pursue the territorialization process by establishing a direct control of their realms through the recovery of their right to raise taxes, administer justice and adopt uniform and impersonal systems of law inspired by Roman law.[160] Such control was also dictated by the expansion of capitalism and the ensuing increase in wealth and the complexity of economy.[161] The modern state was then able to take its almost final form and features which are mainly: a controlled and well-defined territory; a relatively centralized administration and bureaucracy; a monopoly over the concentrated means of physical coercion within its territory, etc.[162]

However, effective territoriality is not limited to the control of space as it does also extend to peoples. One of the major concerns of the nascent modern state was, therefore, to establish its control over people by the adoption of a systematic policy of unification and homogenization of the population.[163] This policy has started to be gradually implemented in the early stages of the long process which has led to the emergence of the first modern states.[164] Thus, a strong royal power would be built in countries such as England, France and Spain thanks to centuries of ruthless effort aiming at destroying local allegiances and loyalties. This has resulted already by 1300 in a new situation where "loyalty to the state was stronger than any other loyalty"[165] and by the sixteenth century in unrivalled cultural homogeneity.[166] But the new states would not stop there as they would all over the sixteenth, seventeenth and eighteenth centuries continue under the absolutist regimes destroying the still remaining local loyalties and institutions. However, it was mainly liberalism that has contributed the most to the unifying and homogenizing of the society.

The main reason behind the emergence of the modern state was to create the conditions and the institutional framework conducive to the capitalist accumulation. One of these conditions was to set up new foundations of the society in which rationality replaces God and inspires governance and all social, economic and intellectual activities and where integration should lead to the rationalization of the process of production through in particular the elimination of corporatist, social or ethnic particularisms.[167] While it continued like the traditional state to be a war machine and to seek territorial expansion, the modern state was based on the need

[159] Opello and Rosow (1999, p. 50).

[160] See Nys (1901, p. 604).

[161] See Hakli (1994, pp. 43–45); Murphy (1996, pp. 81–160).

[162] Tilly (1975, p. 27).

[163] See Hakli (1994, p. 48 et seq).

[164] See Geary (2003).

[165] Strayer (1970, p. 57).

[166] Tilly (1975, p. 18).

[167] See Touraine (1992, p. 21 et seq).

to unify and reshape the society in a way to adjust to the needs of the arising capitalism. Absolutism has pursued the implementation of that policy, but it was mainly liberalism which contributed most to the unifying and homogenizing of the society.

As we have seen in the first chapter, popular sovereignty has, by making an end to patrimonial state, given rise to the nation-state. The concept of nation was initially meant by its creators to play a catalysis role in the struggle against monarchical power and the feudal hierarchical organization of the society. According to E. Gellner[168]; the rise of the concept of nation reflects also the transition from agrarian society to industrial society. However, the concept of nation has never meant in the beginning the creation in Western Europe of new territorial entities, but only the reorganizing of the pre-existing states[169] from the social, political and economical aspects in order to allegedly enable peoples to enjoy freedom and democracy. In fact the concept was first and foremost an ideological element the objective of which was to strengthen the new socio-economic basis of the state vis-à-vis the whole society and the external environment as well.[170] That is why the only new creation has been the "nations". The latter have never been a granted reality for all the time.[171] Instead they have been retroactively built in the old European states where, as shown by Anne-Marie Thiesse, "their origins are not lost in the mists of time, in the dark and heroic ages described by the first chapters of national histories. The slow forming of territories at random of conquests and alliances is not either a genesis of nations: it is only the tumultuous history of principalities and kingdoms. The real birth of a nation is the moment when a handful of individuals declare that it exists and undertakes to prove it. The first examples are not anterior to the eighteenth century: no nation in the modern sense, that is, apolitical one, (existed) before that date."[172] The nation is in sum the creation of nationalism but initially within the limits of internationally recognized borders.[173]

---

[168] Gellner (1983, p. 40).

[169] On the pre-existence of these states which generally were "warfare states" before becoming "nations states", Giddens (1985, p. 112 cont).

[170] I. Wallerstein states in this regard "Why should the establishment of any sovereign state within the interstate system create a corresponding 'nation', a 'people'? States in this system have problems of cohesion. Once recognized as sovereign, the states frequently find themselves subsequently threatened by both internal disintegration and external aggression. To the extent that 'national' sentiment develops, these threats are lessened The governments in power have an interest in promoting this sentiment, as do all sorts of sub-groups within the state. Any group who sees advantage in using the state's legal powers to advance its interest against groups outside the state or in any sub-region of the state has an interest in promoting nationalist sentiments as a legitimation of its claims. States furthermore have an interest in administrative uniformity which increases the efficacity of their policies. Nationalism is the expression, the promoter, and the consequence of such state-level uniformities", Wallerstein (1991, pp. 81–82).

[171] See Margaret Canovan (2004, p. 20).

[172] Theisse (2001, p. 11).

[173] See Gellner (1983, pp. 55–56).

As a consequence of the above was thus the emergence of the famous "nation-state", a concept which therefore means, within the West European context, nothing other than the existence of the same old peoples in the same old states within the same territories and borders but under new legal and political regime.[174] The new regime mainly implies that the people should no longer be seen as subject but rather as the holder of sovereignty (popular sovereignty) and which as such constitutes the collective source of the state's authority.

The transfer of power from the King to the people has, though having been a bloody one as in France, taken place in West Europe countries where states, as we have seen above, have already been in place for centuries. These states have been able to culturally homogenize their societies to the extent that competition for power has come to take place within the same social class or between conflicting social classes but within the same political-cultural configuration. This was and still remains a unique situation as democracy and its political expression in the form of popular sovereignty had to be implemented in a context where very often the territorialization process has been completed and where consequently no fraction of the society, or what will be later on called society ethnic group, could pretend to decisively question its membership of that society. This ideal situation will not, with few exceptions, exist elsewhere where the territorialization process has still to be completed. The drama in which most of the new states will be caught will be then how to achieve the territorialization process and simultaneously declare their adherence to a political system in which the people is sacred as the real sovereign in situations many peoples claim simultaneously popular sovereignty. Hence, while the territorialization was a relatively easy process when it was conducted on behalf of a transcendental force such as God, it has become a problematic issue where multiple segments of the society pretend that they are the real sovereign and that consequently they should be allowed to enjoy their territorial sovereign right to existence. "Any state", A.Cobban has written, "which could not persuade its people to regard themselves as a single national community, and so become a nation-state, must lose its cohesion and its diverse elements fly apart."[175]

The notion of popular sovereignty has therefore played a disruptive role insofar as the recognition that the people extends through the state its exclusive sovereignty over a given territory has opened the door to nationalistic claims by national or ethnical groups who felt deprived from their traditional and ancestral connections with what they did consider as their own territory. The resentment of these groups was even bigger in situations where have still prevailed "injustices that flow from absolutism, feudal privileges, and other abuses of authority within states, but with all of the injustices that come from the history of conquest, royal marriages, sales of territory, and just plain bad luck that defines the boundaries of states and

[174] See Hobsbawn (1990, p. 42 cont).

[175] Cobban (1947, p. 6).

empires."[176] That is why central national power's constant policy has been to homogenize the society by neutralizing any kind of particularism stemming from religion, ethnicity, corporatism, etc. . .and by leveling or reducing any differences or heterogeneity in cultural or social practices.[177]

Nevertheless, the congruence of the nations and the states has never been complete even in the first Western democratic states where membership in the nation and the state was rarely coincidental and where the people has never been able to exert a full control of the state. Political and economical privileges based on class, ethnicity, race, etc., have continued to insidiously prevail overshadowed by a new ideological instrument: the myth of the nation-state. According to Joel S. Migdal, perhaps no myth was stronger that the one that designated political entities not simply as states but *nation-states*.[178] That is why also the attachment of the people to the nation-state has been strengthened in Western Europe only when the emergence of the industrial society has pushed the governments to support the empowerment of their populations favoring then an increased popular participation in politics[179] and developing civic nation-states intended to embrace all those living in the national territory. It is in fact only by the end of the nineteenth century that "the welfare, culture, and daily routine of ordinary Europeans came to depend as never before on which state they happened to reside in."[180] The germs of a new paradigm of socio-political relations then emerged as modern states have started to assume an additional function: the provision of welfare to their citizens.[181] The state legitimacy has since then depended on its capacity not only to establish order and provide security but also welfare to its own citizens.[182] The reinforcement of the welfare state following the adoption of the Fordist compromise in the aftermath of the Second World War will definitely lead to the consecration of what can be called the Weberian-Durkhemian paradigm,[183] a kind of new state contract by which the people consent to accept the liberal state against the provision not only of order and security but also social solidarity. This aggiornamento in socio-political relations was an exceptional moment in the history of the Western states

[176] Ibid, p. 44. See also Tilly (1975, p. 43).

[177] Bauman (1990, p. 157).

[178] Migdal (2004, p. 21). See also Mikesell (1983, p. 257).

[179] See Smith (1998).

[180] Tilly (1992, p. 115).

[181] The process through which the citizens have been granted since the emergence of the nation-state different rights including socio-economic rights (welfare state) has been analyzed by Marshall (1950); Merrien et al. (2005, p. 74).

[182] See Axtmann (1996, p. 133); Geary (2002, p. 202).

[183] We know that the sociologist, E. Durkheim, and the French solidarity school of thought have played at the end of the nineteenth century a very important role in promoting the role of the state in social solidarity in order to reduce the then increasing Marxist influence and neutralize any popular revolutionary movements.

as it has led to a new societal consensus in which "the congruence of the state and the nation has been the most complete.[184]

However, while Western states contributed to the construction of territorial sovereignty at home, they rather denied violently this very sovereignty abroad[185] or, in the less bad case, spurred, as we will see later on, the creation of subjected states through the manipulation of the principle of nationalities and later on self-determination. In peripheral states, the "imagining"[186] of new communities was not therefore a spontaneous process as the latter necessitated the combined and complementary interventions of the local elites- the famous "ethnic entrepreneurs", the "awakeners", etc -[187] as well as of external major powers,[188] mainly West Europeans. When successful, such process has frequently led to the emergence of weak states, recurrently subjected to a dynamic of territorialization and reterritorialization as recently shown, for instance, with the disintegration of the Yugoslavian Federation and the appearance of a multitude of precarious states where yet segments of the society continue seeking independence. Hence, the states in the center and the periphery have evolved in different manner. Such difference was even bigger before the general expansion of colonization at the end of the nineteenth century, which will bring to the peripheral states what they have never been able to achieve: the effectiveness of territoriality. This was undoubtedly one of the most important impacts of colonization. It is a surprise to note in this regard how the ICJ has, through an anachronistic approach to the effectiveness of territoriality, erroneously likened remnant traditional peripheral state to the modern state in its Opinion in Western Sahara case.

2.2.2.2 The Anachronistic Requirement That a Remnant Traditional State Should Meet the Effectiveness of Territoriality: The ICJ's Debatable Opinion in Western Sahara Case

As is well known, the UN General Assembly has on 13 December 1974 called upon the International Court of Justice within the framework of a consultation process, to clarify to the General Assembly what policy to pursue in order to accelerate the process of decolonising Western Sahara. This policy would be based on the response given to the question of whether the territory of Western Sahara was, at the time of its colonisation by Spain, a *terra nullius*, and if not, what legal ties this territory had to the Kingdom of Morocco and Mauritania.

[184] Bihr (2000, p. 39).
[185] Colas (2007, p. 21).
[186] Anderson (1983, p. 15).
[187] Conversi (1995, p. 421).
[188] See Akzin (1964, pp. 67–68).

By agreeing to ask for an advisory opinion on a territorial conflict between three states, the General Assembly has indirectly agreed to open up the way to the implementation, by the conflicting parties themselves, of any decolonisation process that these parties may judge to comply with the conclusions of the Court regarding the conflict which divided them. In fact, although there is no question that an advisory opinion would imply an obligation on the part of the international organisations, the states, or the Court which gave it, it is less clear when it is a question of an advisory opinion on a territorial dispute between two or more states. In such a situation, although it is permissible to maintain that this type of advisory opinion does not involve any obligation, even when the views of the states, the international organisations and the International Court had been divided in this respect since the creation of the Permanent Court of International Justice, it still constitutes at the very least a legal title in the hand of the conflicting parties.[189] It was certainly for this reason and this reason alone, that Spain, so as not to find itself in a legal situation which could definitively damage its own interests, if its claims to Western Sahara were rejected by the Court, tried to dissuade the Court, as it had done with the General Assembly too, to accept providing the advisory opinion. But the Court rejected this request, and responded favourably to the General Assembly's request, by finally announcing its opinion on 16 October 1975.

In its advisory opinion, as it was predictable given the nature of this particular case, the Court, after having tried in vain, though in a succinct and peremptory manner, to clarify that its role was merely to provide the General Assembly with legal points which will be useful to the latter when it will look once again at the decolonisation of Western Sahara, was forced to dedicate almost all of its response to the analysis of legal claims made by Morocco (and Mauritania), and thus to inevitably give the consultation process a contentious form. This obviously affected the content of the provision of the opinion in which the Court was compelled to make its conclusions based on the analysis of these legal claims. So it concluded on the one hand that the Sahara territory had not been a *terra nullius* and on the other that, before Spanish colonisation, legal ties did exist between Morocco and Mauritania separately and the territory of the Sahara. But before delivering these conclusions, the Court declared, in a terse and peremptory way, that it "has not found legal ties of such a nature as might affect the application of resolution 1514 (XV) in the decolonisation of Western Sahara and, in particular, of the principle of self-determination through the free and genuine expression of the will of the peoples of the Territory."[190] Such a statement was totally contradictory to the fundamental position of the Court: the recognition of legal ties between the Sahara and Morocco and Mauritania respectively. Believing that it was obliged to adopt a compromise stand in the affair,[191] it attempted to counterbalance its conclusion, by

---

[189] See El Ouali (1984, p. 107).

[190] Advisory Opinion on Western Sahara, Collection, 1975, para 162.

[191] Cf. Chapez (1976, p. 48); Vallée (1976, p. 47).

which it admitted the existence of legal ties, by stating that the right to self-determination should be applied rather than attempting to deduce the legal consequences of such a statement. This was pertinently referred to at the time by Judge Nagendra Singh, who declared that: "as the Court finds that there were certain legal ties in existence, it becomes necessary to proceed to assess them with the sole purpose of evaluating them to ascertain if they indicate a definite step in terms of the decolonisation process. In short the strength and efficacy of these ties though limited must still be held to be of such an order as to point in the direction of the possible options which could be afforded to the population in ascertaining the will of the people. These options, in accordance with resolution 1541 (XV) as well as 2625 (XXV), could be either integration with Morocco or with Mauritania or having free association with any one of them or for opting in favour of a sovereign independent status of the territory. Even if it is conceded that the procedures for decolonisation lie within the exclusive province of the General Assembly it is yet appropriate for a court to point out the relationship between the existence of the legal ties and the decolonisation process in order fully to enlighten the General Assembly. To do so is not to trespass on the prerogatives of the General Assembly but to fulfil the role as the principal judicial organ of the United Nations."[192]

Having abandoned its legal role, the Court gave a political opinion meant to upset nobody "in that the states involved could, taking one conclusion from the opinion rather than another, find reasons to be satisfied with it."[193] It is true that the Court went on to examine the relevance of these legal ties, but actually it did so in such a way as to reduce their scope in order to leave the door open to different interpretations of its opinion which would not contradict the idea of confirming the relevance of Morocco's legal claims, or the idea of resorting to the right to self-determination. It did so by asking whether Morocco had had effective control over the Sahara at the time of the Spanish colonisation and for the period immediately afterwards.[194] But by going down this route, it put to one side the principle of intertemporality,[195] which would have forced it to look at the effectiveness of the authority of the State of Morocco in the Sahara in reference to the principles of International Law which were applicable in the nineteenth century, not to modern European states,[196] but to traditional states like Morocco. From this point of view,

[192] Statement by Judge Nagendra Singh, ICJ Reports, 1975, 80.

[193] J. Chapez (1976, p. 46).

[194] Western Sahara Case, ICJ Reports, 1975, para 93.

[195] Regarding the principle of intertemporality, the Institute of International Law clarified that without an indication to the contrary, the temporal scope of application of public international law norm is determined in accordance with the general principle of law, according to which any fact, act and situation must be looked at in light of the rules of law which are in force at the time, Resolution of 11 August 1975, A.I.L.I., 1975, vol. 56, 536–541. On this principle, see too Elias (1980, p. 285 *et seq*).

[196] See the criticism made of this aspect of the Court's judgment, Flory (1975). Cf also Woolridge (1979, p. 112).

there is, as we have seen above, a significant difference between modern European states and traditional states, for while the effectiveness of the state authority is a major feature of the former, the same can certainly not be said for the latter. One should recall that one of the major conclusions reached above was that the traditional states, also called pre-industrial or pre-modern states, which had prevailed for millennia in different forms and with different scopes, in Europe too (until the end of the eighteenth century where composite states still prevailed[197]), mainly because of the absence of means of communication and quick transportation of troops, could never establish effective and continued control over its own territory.[198]And it was this difficulty of ensuring the continued effectiveness of its authority that forced the traditional state to always obtain a legal recognition of that authority from the populations or groups involved. This recognition could take different forms[199] in particular that of religious leadership, allegiance, treaty etc. Nevertheless, this did not stop the traditional state trying to defend its borders and exercising its authority within its territory, as its sovereign existence, like that of the modern state, depended on its ability to impose its territoriality, and make sure that it was respected. But the inability of the state to exercise effective and continued control over its territory forced it to delegate its power and only occasionally to mobilise the bulk of its army to tackle dissidents. This explains the frequent movement of emperors and kings, leading their troops to deal with the dissidents once and for all and raise taxes.[200] The frequent movement of the kings of Morocco within the Moroccan territory to deal with dissidence (*bled siba*), including the Sahara, were not at that time particular to traditional Morocco. It is strange that the Court and curiously Moroccan legal advisers as well[201] had considered that the basis of power in Morocco was unusual in that it left no place for the territorial aspect. That is, as we have seen earlier, one of the Eurocentric prejudices which, in order to discredit non-European states and legitimise their colonisation, resulted in leading people to believe that non-European polities did not possess a territorial foundation[202] let alone, any boundaries. This was indeed the world's view through the prism of the model of the territorial state of Westphalia, which was to be found behind the Court's statement that what was unusual about the state of Morocco was its intangible basis, attributed to religious ties and allegiance to the king. But there too, the religious dimension and allegiance to the king did not make traditional Morocco unique in the history of states, as they all, including the absolutist states prevalent in Western Europe in the sixteenth, seventeenth and eighteenth centuries, but sometimes in different forms, added up to the basis of power in society. As for the religious tie, that is a phenomenon which has

[197] Cf. Strayer (1963, pp. 23–25); Tilly(1990, pp. 39–40).

[198] See, among others, Mann (1984, p. 331 et seq.); Crone (1989, p. 38 et seq).

[199] Cf. Man (1984, p. 331).

[200] See, among others, Wesson (1967, pp. 27–28 and 153–154).

[201] See the explanations given by one of Morocco's legal advisers, Dupuy (1990, pp. 117–127).

[202] Cf. Ferguson and Mansbach (1996, pp. 401–402).

been a part of the state since its birth, thousands of years ago. It is one of the essential characteristics of the traditional state.[203] As for the tie of allegiance, it could also be said that in the traditional state, as recalled by Guntram H. Herb, political power was founded on personal allegiance between subjects and their governors, rather than on a precise territorial base. Laws were based on customs and traditions, and not on territorial codes. Moreover, concepts of universalising power, such as the divine authority of the Pope, defied the power of princes in their own territories.[204] But when the Court talked about what it called, from this point of view, the "peculiarity" of Morocco, it was to reduce the legal scope of the religious tie and the allegiance to the king of the populations of the Sahara. So, after having affirmed that "the Sherifian State at the time of the Spanish colonisation of Western Sahara was a State of a special character is certain. Its special character consisted in the fact that it was founded on the common religious bond of Islam existing among the peoples and on the allegiance of various tribes to the Sultan, through their caids or sheikhs, rather than on the notion of territory,"[205] it immediately declared that "common religious links have, of course, existed in many parts of the world without signifying a legal tie of sovereignty or subordination to a ruler,"[206] which, we have just seen, is historically untrue. By wrongly implying that the basis of the Moroccan State's power and sovereignty was unique, and by reducing the scope of the religious ties and allegiance to the king, the Court could freely demand that the latter be taken into account by stating that "such an allegiance (of the populations of the Sahara to the king), however, if it is to afford indications of the ruler's sovereignty, must clearly be real and manifested in acts evidencing acceptance of his political authority. Otherwise, there will be no genuine display or exercise of state authority. It follows that the special character of the Moroccan State and the special forms in which its exercise of sovereignty may, in consequence, have expressed itself, do not dispense the Court from appreciating whether at the relevant time Moroccan sovereignty was effectively exercised or displayed in Western Sahara."[207] But to prove the effectiveness of the authority of a traditional state

[203] Yale H. Ferguson and Richard W. Mansbach wrote that "Religion is an important source of legitimacy. Every empire has its principal god or pantheon, and every significant city polity its sponsoring deity or saint. One variant is charisma or revelation, illustrated by the Islamic community, especially during Muhammed's lifetime, and also by the Christian Pope. Mesopotamian kings and Mesoamerican rulers, too, played the role of special intermediary between their peoples and the gods. Patron deities, saints – or in the instance of Venice, the Apostle Saint Mark – were sacred conduits for city dwellers who had secular local rulers. Another variant of religion is the idea of divine right as a source of dynastic legitimacy. Unlike revelation, divine right does not require direct communication with gods but entails their sanction. The Chinese equivalent of the divine right claimed by the European kings was the Mandate of Heaven.", Ferguson and Mansbach (1996, p. 390).

[204] Herb (1999, p. 10).

[205] Western Sahara case, ICJ Reports, 1975, para 95.

[206] Idem.

[207] Idem.

like Morocco, as it was in the context of the nineteenth century, was not easy, even less so as at the time, as the Court should have realized, attacks by the European colonisers against the south and south-east of the Moroccan territory had severely weakened the ability of the Moroccan state to exercise its authority effectively, not only in Sahara, but also in other regions of Morocco.[208]

But let us suppose that the Court had no choice but to liken the traditional Moroccan state to a modern state, and so inevitably to call on the principle of effectiveness in order to analyse Morocco's claims over the Sahara, it still remains that even under these conditions it was obliged to take into account the difficulty Morocco had in continuously exercising its authority over the whole of the territory of the Sahara because of the unusual nature of the latter, which, being a desert region and far away, did not allow to exercise such authority effectively, given the material and logistical constraints at that time. In fact, the principle of the effectiveness of state authority cannot be expected to apply in the same way everywhere. This is why well-established international jurisprudence obliges the judge to take into account the characteristics of the territory, especially when these characteristics make it difficult to exercise effective and continued state authority. This is what came out of the decisions of the international judge in the cases of Eastern Greenland,[209] of the Rann of Kutch[210] and of Dubai/Sharjah[211] and, generally, of positive law which admits that "effective possession is the control of a state over a territory, exercised in such a way as to guarantee that the state alone can display the prerogative of public power, and carry out regularly and manifestly the state functions *which are physically possible in terms of the nature, the geographic situation and other characteristics of the territory, and the interests of the state*."[212] But there too, the Court clearly failed to take into account the

[208] See P. Reuter preface to R. Lazrak "*Le contentieux territorial entre le Maroc et l'Espagne*", op.cit., 1974, p. 7.

[209] In this matter, the PCIJ declared that It is impossible to look at the decisions made in matters concerning territorial sovereignty without observing that, in many cases, the tribunal did not demand numerous illustrations of the exercise of sovereign rights, as long as the other state involved has put forward a stronger claim. This is particularly true of the demands for sovereignty over the territories situated in poorly populated territories, or which are not occupied by permanent residents, Eastern Greenland case, PCIJ, Series A/B, No 53, 46.

[210] The Arbitral Tribunal declared that "Since the Rann until recently has been deemed incapable of permanent occupation, the requirement of possession cannot play the same important role in determining sovereign rights therein as it would have done otherwise. Therefore, special significance must be accorded to the display of other states activities…", Case concerning the Indo-Pakistan Western Boundary (Runn of Kutch), between India and Pakistan, 1968, R.S.A., vol. XVII, 563.

[211] In this matter where the arbitration award was pronounced, it is true, a long time after the Court's judgment on the Sahara question, the arbitral tribunal confirmed the previous jurisprudence by admitting that "this exercise (of state authority) may be very limited when it is a question of territories which are sparsely populated or have no permanent habitants", I.L.R., 1993, vol. 91, 624.

[212] Kohen (1997, p. 229).

particular characteristics of the Sahara territory.[213] Even more seriously, it did not take into account the fact that positive International Law also admits that the demand for the effectiveness of state authority must not be absolute as long as the state demanding confirmation of its sovereignty over a territory is not in competition with another state for this same sovereignty,[214] which was clearly the case in the question of the Sahara. Thus, resorting to one of the old clichés of colonial ideology, the Court, while recognising the existence of legal ties between Morocco and the Sahara, recommended self-determination, even though it was widely known at the time that the application of such a right was seen by its advocates to be beneficial to their neo-colonial project: the creation of an artificial state in the Sahara. One might ask why the Court did not also attempt to examine, before coming to its conclusions, this idea of recourse to the right to self-determination in light of the principle of effectiveness by asking whether the "Sahrawi people" corresponded to a tangible reality, and how it had suddenly arisen from the sands of the desert. But the Court stubbornly applied the principle of effectiveness where, according to positive International Law, this principle had no place. Acting in this way, the Court did not realise that its demand for the effective authority of Morocco in the Sahara could also have another grave consequence: the questioning of the existence of Morocco as a state![215] So this is how the authority and one can say even the existence of a very old state can suddenly disappear into the desert, while an unknown people arises as if by magic, from this same desert, in less than a decade! A curious conclusion, when we know that the Court's opinion has the same theme the whole way through: the extreme division of the tribes of the Sahara, which sets them against each other as well as shattering the idea of common authority. With hindsight, we can today ask whether, by refusing to analyse things as they were and expressing the law and nothing but the law, the Court was not in some way responsible for the long lasting nature of the Sahara conflict.

Hence, leaving aside the very questionable opinion of the ICJ in the Western Sahara case, in human history, it was the modern state which has been the only type of political organization that was able to make of the effectiveness of its territoriality a reality. This was made possible thanks to the own dynamic of capitalism and the deliberate policy of modern state to establish and maintain some congruence between themselves and their nations. But such congruence is being weakened today by the crisis of territoriality. The latter, having its origin mainly in

---

[213] Merely stating that "in the present instance, Western Sahara, if somewhat sparsely populated, was a territory across which socially and politically organized tribes were in constant movement and where armed incidents between these tribes were frequent" (92), while as we know, it had also recognized that there were legal connections between a large number of the tribes of the Sahara and Morocco.

[214] Cf. Kohen (1997, p. 226).

[215] M. Bennouna observed that "hoping to come to a conclusion on the relationships of allegiance and sovereignty, the Court questions the very existence of Morocco, as its power was exercised in similar ways in regions of Marrakech or Fez", Bennouna (1976, pp. 94–95).

globalization, is leading to the emergence of a new type of state, the post modern state, which has an increasing difficulty in maintaining its congruence with the nation. That is why, an increasing number of states have, like ancient states, opted for territorial autonomy in order to ensure their own survival.

2.2.3 The Postmodern State: Going Back to Territorial Autonomy in Order to Address the Crisis of Territoriality Produced by Globalization

The present crisis of state territoriality has its origin mainly in the impact of globalization.

We know that in the last twenty years or so, many commentators have sustained the idea that globalization has rendered the state obsolete.[216] In fact, globalization has not rendered the state obsolete; it has rather contributed to weaken the state by making the hyphen between the latter and the nation more problematic.

Triggered by the compression of time and space – i.e. intense and fast exchanges in the world of economics, commerce and information technologies – globalization, it was maintained, had led to deterritorialization,[217] a process by which territory had lost its main function which was to organize economic, social and political life. Deterritorialization had in turn affected territoriality[218] and thus led to the "debordering"[219] of states or even to the "retreat of the state"[220] as the later had lost its autonomy and ability to draw up and implement public policies, particularly on economic issues in favor of deterritorialized actors (market, multinationals, etc.). According to some writers, globalization had even led to the transfer of people's allegiance from the state to new entities such as the regions,[221] post-national players or what has been called "ethnoscapes",[222] a new type of diaspora (migrants, refugees, multinationals staff, international bureaucrats, etc.)

Globalization is not a new phenomenon. It has its distant origins in the world system that started to emerge in Europe in the sixteenth century.[223] Its principal characteristics first crystallized in the second half of the nineteenth century.[224]

---

[216] For a general presentation of this view and its critique, see e.g. Cohen (2006, pp. 1–17).

[217] See Rosecrance (1996, p. 4).

[218] See Badie(1995, p. 123); Agnew (2005a).

[219] Albert and Brock (1996, pp. 69–106).

[220] Strange (1996).

[221] Ohmae (1996).

[222] Apparadurai (1996, p. 3 et seq., 81, 165).

[223] See Wallerstein (2004).

[224] See P.Q. Hirst and G.F. Thompson (1999) Globalization in Question: The International Economy and the Possibility of Governance, Cambridge, Polity Press, 2nd ed., ch.2.

However, the First World War put an end to it. Amazingly, the global economy was more integrated then than it is today, except in the area of the world's financial markets.[225] This is because the current globalization has not resulted in the destruction of the national character of economies,[226] particularly in the most developed countries.[227] Hence, the state remains a major player in the field of economics and world politics.[228] This also explains why globalization has never been a spontaneous phenomenon but rather one driven by a financial and political process initiated by the major powers, mainly the United States, from the early 1970 in order to address the structural crisis that has started to affect their economies.[229]

It is true that globalization has given rise to various powers and authorities that are dispersed in complex networks.[230] But, these networks, although they operate across states' boundaries, get constituted within them.[231] Furthermore, the new powers and authorities do still rely on states' law, authority, police and military forces.[232] Amazingly, the power sharing arrangements that these networks tend to imply has led in some areas to the growth in powers and responsibilities of the states.[233] In parallel, the states, which remain the sole providers of security and welfare to their citizens, have expanded their control over their territories and societies to the extent that they have penetrated the lives of their citizens in respect of a variety of domains.[234] "The efficacity of territoriality", observes P.J. Taylor,[235] "is too apparent and the container is too full for the demise of the state not to be a long-term affair." One has then to recognize that while globalization has provoked a significant loss of State capacity to influence economic issues,[236] it has not rendered the later

---

[225] Idem. See also Sassen (1996, p. 40).

[226] R. Gilpin (2001, p. 10).

[227] Hirst and Thompson (2002, p. 253).

[228] Idem.

[229] See G. Arrighi "Globalization, State Sovereignty, and the 'Endless' Accumulation of Capital", fbc.binghamton.edu/gairvn97.htm; Gowan (1999, p. 4); Martin and Schuman (1997, p. 66 et seq).

[230] Keating (2001, p. 20).

[231] See Sassen (2008, p. 419).

[232] Van Staden and Vollaard (2002, p. 162).

[233] See Weiss (2003, p. 316).

[234] Smith (2007, p. 25).

[235] Taylor (1994, p. 157).

[236] In fact, the loss of state's capacity to influence economy is a reality more in Western countries than in other countries such as China which, on the contrary, has witnessed the rise of the "development state", a kind of a strong state devoted to promote economic growth and prosperity. Martin Jacques does recall in this respect that "The emergent Chinese model bears witness to a new kind of capitalism where the state is hyperactive and omnipresent in a range of different ways and forms: in providing assistance to private firms, in a galaxy of state-owned enterprises, in managing the process by which the renminbi slowly evolves towards fully considerable status and, above all, in being the architect of an economic strategy which has driven China's economic transformation" In: Taylor (2009, p. 185).

obsolete.[237] It is so because nation-states still posses considerable powers.[238] Instead, the state, "as a particular form of territorial political community, is here to stay."[239] The crucial role played by the states in addressing present crisis of globalization alone suffices to show that the state phenomenon has not become redundant. The crisis has also shown that it is the governments that ultimately influence and impact multinational corporations and global capital and not the contrary.

The weakening of the states has led in particular to the emergence of the regionalization phenomenon, both within and between individual states, meaning that new territorial configurations are now charged with protecting and consolidating the process of accumulating transnational capital.[240] Thus, it has been possible to initiate or increase cooperation and integration on a regional basis (EU, NAFA, ASEAN, and APEC) with the aim, on the one hand, of setting up scale economies in production, increasing and diversifying investment sources, creating huge consumer markets, etc.[241] and on the other, creating regional entities within states with a view to tapping investment and stimulating local economies.

The increasing sharing of power by states with supra and sub-states entities has been interpreted as paving the way for the emergence of a "post-Westphalian"[242] or even a "new mediaeval order"[243] in which authority is divided between a whole range of institutions – on the one hand, quasi-supranational/inter-regional and, on the other, national or regional/local. One of the consequences of such a situation has been "a growing split between state and nation as well as a denationalization of the state."[244] Thus, over the past three decades, globalization has been a contributing factor in making congruence between state and nation more difficult, even in long-established Western democracies. It has done so by weakening the very foundations of modern state, amongst which in particular democracy and the welfare state.

---

[237] See Michalet (2003, p. 37).

[238] L. Martell has written in this respect that "Theses of the decline of the nation-state have to take into account the considerable powers that nation-states have. This varies between nation-states. . .But powers that many nation-states have, to varying degrees, remain over: the ultimate resort to force, military action and the capacity to use it internally or externally; spending on welfare and social services, the levels these are set at, and the type of system and or services preferred; power over amounts of investment in education and health and choice of policies in these areas; powers to raise or lower rates of taxation; power over law and order and justice, what policies to implement in these areas, and how much and in what ways to invest in them; policies over culture and arts; not to mention a number of levels of macro- and micro- economic policy." In: Martell (2010, p. 209).

[239] Jovanovic and Hendrard (2008, p. 1).

[240] Cf. Bihr (2000, p. 61 et seq).

[241] See Gilpin (2001, p. 293).

[242] See Clarck (1997, p. 31).

[243] Anderson (1996b, p. 144). Cf also Ilgen (2003, p. 15).

[244] Bihr (2000, p. 60).

Certainly, democracy has made progress in the past decades as the majority of the states are today governed by elected governments.[245] Some authors have seen in this move the "Third Wave of Democracy"[246] or the prelude to "Democratic Century".[247] Others have even come to consider that "Today everyone is a democrat".[248] However, the drive towards democracy which took place at the end of the Cold War, in different parts of the world, has very often given rise to hybrid regimes where democratic institutions are in practice reduced to pure façade[249] mainly as a result of their manipulation by non elected or even elected tutelary authorities that limit elected officials' power to govern. But, democracy has witnessed not only an illusory expansion, but also a regression in terms of quality and substance, and this even in old Western democracies. Some authors have argued that globalization has spread the wealth and stimulated the rise of middle class and, by doing so, has led to the reinforcement of liberty and democratic institutions.[250] In fact, globalization has led to inequality between individuals.[251] Now, as noted by Craig Murphy, "Increasingly unequal incomes mean increasingly unequal market power. In a world in which we let the market do much of our collective business, increasingly unequal market power means increasingly less democracy".[252] Globalization has indeed provoked a "progressive effacing of democracy"[253] whose dysfunction prevents the people from actively participating in a political process[254] dominated by collective institutions whose credibility has been seriously undermined.[255] It is not therefore a surprise that it has been suggested that the old democracies would rather enter a "post-democratic"[256] stage as their governments are less and less accountable to their own citizens and electors but to unelected powers, increasingly from outside the country.

As to the welfare state, it has also started to witness a serious crisis since the 1970s.[257] Globalization plays a crucial role in this crisis as one of its consequences is that the social policies that characterize modern welfare states are perceived as a

---

[245] See Karatnycky (2005).

[246] Huntington (1991).

[247] Lipset and Lakin (2004).

[248] Giddens (1999).

[249] See Levitsky and Way (2010).

[250] See, e.g. Dollar and Kraay (2002, pp. 120–133).

[251] See Alderson and Nielson (2002, pp. 1255–1299).

[252] Murphy (2001, p. 350).

[253] Fitoussi (2004, p. 89).

[254] "The formal procedures", notes Muller K (2007) of party politics, voting, representation, division of power, legislation, etc. stay in place. In practice, democratic participation and parliamentarian decision-making become severely restricted, elections turn into a matter of marketing, opinion polls and video-politics, Muller (2007, p. 488). See also Habermas (1975, pp. 36–37).

[255] See Corneliau (2000, p. 166).

[256] See Crouch (2004).

[257] See Pierson (1997, p. 143).

fetter on the economy[258] or luxuries which the states can no longer afford in a world of intensely competitive markets.[259] Consequently, today many authors do believe that economic objectives can be reached only at the expense of social objectives[260] and that therefore the welfare state may be seen as "a past social order".[261] The evidence is that the welfare state is under threat from powerful global forces and interests.

Amongst the serious consequences of the retrenchment of the welfare state is the weakening of the congruence between the state and the nation. The welfare state has been one of the pillars of the modern state as does recall Dahram Ghai when writing that the welfare state "is one and at the same time a manifestation of a political community, an expression of social solidarity, and an attempt to eliminate destitution, reduce class differences and forge cohesive and stable communities. It has served as a defining element in national identity and citizenship"[262] On the contrary, Globalization has caused a breakdown in society and the cohesion of modern states. Jurgen Habermas has noted in this respect that "No matter how one looks at it, globalization of the economy destroys a historical constellation (i.e. the modern state) that made the welfare state compromise temporarily possible. Even if this compromise was never the ideal solution for a problem inherent within capitalism itself, it nevertheless held capitalism's social costs within tolerable limits".[263]

The "desocialization"[264] of the economy thus engendered by globalization makes society lose its central role in matters of cohesion and unification. More gravely, the society becomes a "risk society"[265] in which not only social protection fades away but also where unemployment is no longer marginal as "Those who depend upon wage or salary in full-time work represent only a minority of the economically active population; the majority earn their living in more precarious conditions."[266] Analyzing the newly emerging social stratification in United Kingdom, Will Hutton shows that "there is a bottom of 30% of unemployed and economically inactive who are marginalized; another 30% who, while in work, are in forms of unemployment that are structurally insecure; and there are only 40% who can count themselves as holding tenured jobs which allow them to regard their

[258] See Esping-Andersen (1998).
[259] See Mitchell D (2000).
[260] See Kwiek M (2007, p. 149).
[261] Esping-Andersen (1996, p. 9).
[262] Forward of Esping-Andersen (1996, p. vii).
[263] Habermas (2001, p. 52).
[264] Kwiek (2007, p. 151).
[265] See Beck (1999).
[266] Beck (2000, p. 1).

income prospects with certainty".[267] Liberating the global market from political and social control has then created massive unemployment, social exclusion, stagnation and a drop in income for the majority of the population, and also an increase in insecurity, etc.[268] It is not therefore a surprise that society tends to produce individuals who are "uncertain, multiple, fragmented and dispersed."[269] It is also not a surprise that globalization has led to the "return of social classes",[270] a fact which represents a serious threat to the internal cohesion of many developed countries. Even a country like the United States has suffered from the disrupting impact of globalization inasmuch as it has brought about a "growing polarization in incomes and wealth between the rich and the poor"[271] and the emergence of a "white superclass."[272]

Many states seem then to be losing their legitimacy as which means that they are then no longer able to offer either security or wellbeing to their citizens. They are also faced with the emergence of serious problems among the ethnic and minority groups within their population. The growing fragmentation in modern society is also demonstrated by the inability not only to integrate new migrants but also to deal with the reappearance of national sub-state feeling, such is the case in Catalonia, Quebec, Scotland, etc.[273]

Globalization does not then render territory obsolete nor does it call into question the concept of territoriality.[274] Indeed, many indicators demonstrate that territory still matters,[275] while territoriality remains "an organizing principle of social life"[276] allowing people to continue living together in spatially organized polities.[277] Thus, what we have been witnessing in the past decades is a weakening of the effectiveness of territoriality which forces the states to share their power with supra and sub national entities and not a loss of its specificity.[278] The error of many scholars was to confuse such weakening with a phenomenon that does not exist, that is the alleged obsolescence of territory, borders and therefore the state itself. What is also important to note is that it was that weakening of territoriality which has been leading to the acceleration of the phenomenon of states' proliferation and not their obsolescence.

---

[267] Hutton (2000, p. 337).

[268] Grader (1997, p. 360 et seq).

[269] Dubet and Marticelli (1998, p. 49).

[270] See Bouffartigue (2004).

[271] Agnew (2005, p. 360 et seq).

[272] Lind (1996, pp. 215–216).

[273] Cf. Tierney (2005, pp. 161–183).

[274] See for an opposite view Elkins (1995, p. 17).

[275] See Introduction of Burgess and Vollaard (2006, p. 7).

[276] Immerfall (1998, p. 7).

[277] See Kahler (2006, p. 1).

[278] See Rogers J. Hollingsworth (1998) "Territoriality in Modern Societies: The Spatial and Institutional Nestedness of National Economies" in S. Immerfall (ed.) "Territoriality in the Globalizing Society. One Place or None?", op.cit.,17–18.

Thus, what we are in fact currently seeing is a process of reterritorialization by which globalization dynamics "tends to prompt incidences of state collapse and novel forms of state formation in various situations."[279] There are newly emerging situations where the disintegration of certain states, like Belgium, is imagined by the populations concerned as very probable.[280] It is true that globalization deterritorializes states insofar as it weakens them, but by doing so it also contributes to their disintegration (either to a small extent or to their total fragmentation) and the creation of new states. O. Tuathail is right to point out in this connection that "it is not simply that there is no deterritorialization without re-territorialization, but that both are parts of the ongoing generalized process of re-territorialization."[281] The chain territorialization-territoriality-territorial integrity is then still active and alive more than ever. It will then continue disintegrating states and producing new ones. The potential for the proliferation of new states is dramatically huge.[282] On another hand, globalization has certainly led to a change in some roles and functions of the borders as they have "become more permeable and open to the transboundary movement of people, goods and information,"[283] but these changes are limited to a group of states, mainly those belonging to the European Union where some attempts aim, as we have seen above, to create a federal system. In reality, globalization has, instead of making the borders obsolete, reinforced them. Hence, with regard to the European states, while it is true that they have almost dismantled their borders in their mutual relations, they have also maintained and sometimes even reinforced the external borders of the European Union in matter related to migration, refugee movements, etc. With regard to the rest of the world, what we are witnessing in fact is an ambivalent move consisting in an increasing economic opening of the borders concomitant with a political closure of national spaces where sometimes even new walls and fences of separation are being erected.[284] Furthermore, one can say that the huge disparities created between people belonging to different nations in term of socio-economic development have awakened the attachment to the national territory, which fact reflects necessarily on borders which "still matter and they even become more significant, in a political and ideological sense, under the conditions of globalization."[285]

Today, territoriality is effective more than it has ever been in human history when it comes to state's control of its territory. But, it is less effective when related to the ability of the state in maintaining its congruence with the nation. The problem of congruence between state and nation seems therefore to be becoming a general

279 Doornbos (2006, p. 47).

280 See R. Deschamps "Le fédéralisme belge a-t-il de l'avenir?", www.cifop.be/doc/srepb/srepb090306.pd.

281 Tuathail (1999, p. 143).

282 See Bacheli et al. (2004, p. 1 cont).

283 Newman (2000, p. 17). See also for Dittgen (2000, pp. 49–68).

284 See Newman (2000, p. 18).

285 Dittgen (2001, p. 49).

phenomenon, although the intensity of this varies according to whether the countries involved are old or new. In the case of many new countries, globalization is bringing about an extremely difficult economic situation, illustrated notably by a dramatic drop in GNP and growing inequality – which has doubled[286] – between developed and undeveloped countries. On the political front, globalization is increasing the instability of these countries, certain of whom have become completely ungovernable. Even more serious is the fact that globalization has stimulated the "rebirth of ethnic nationalism"[287] and the emergence of fundamentalist religious movements.[288] But, as we have seen above, it has also become increasingly difficult for the state in old developed democracies to keep its congruence with the nation. This is one of the major reasons why today territorial autonomy is again regaining prominence.

Hence, the crisis of territoriality is such that the stability and future of many states seem increasingly preoccupying. This crisis seems also to represent the transition to a new era reflected by the concept of postmodernity and the tendency of power- sharing mainly through territorial autonomy, amazingly in the same way that used to be the case by premodern states.

In the context of this book, it is meant by post-modernity the present phenomenon of vulnerability of state territoriality which is the result of a material condition characterized by extreme social fragmentation and differentiation, the loss or weakening of class-consciousness[289] as well as "the disaggregation of the self and the decline of the affect,"[290] facts which push peoples to show a preference for local identities and politics at the detriment of national identity and the hyphen between the state and the nation. It is that vulnerability of territoriality which forces the state, with a view to ensuring its own survival, to share the exercising of certain of its competences with supra or sub-state entities. Hence defined, postmodernity has nothing to do with postmodernism which, though it accurately notes that the world has entered in the past decades a new era marked by pluralism, diversity, heterogeneousness and particularism,[291] mixes between reality and desirability by deliberately seeking to rethink concepts of sovereignty, identity and democracy in a way to detach them from state's territory[292] which is an ideological demarche that, as we have seen above, is not corroborated by facts.

To the extent that this chapter deals with the internal aspect of territoriality, we shall concentrate our attention solely on the sharing of state competences with sub-state entities.[293] Now, it is agreed today that one of the distinctive features of

[286] Cf. Freeman (2004, p. 47); Castel (2002, p. 19 et seq.); Agnew (2001, pp. 133–154); Milanovic (2005, p. 107).

[287] Smith (1995, p. 2).

[288] Genov (1997, p. 413).

[289] See Harvey (1990, p. 341).

[290] Jameson (1992, p. 22). See also Anderson (1998, pp. 81–82).

[291] See Boivret (1995, pp. 11, 13, 19, 27, 30).

[292] See, instance, Walker (1993, p. 155); Connolly (1991, p. 479).

[293] For an analysis of the external aspects of postmodernity, see Sorensen (2001).

postmodernity consists of pushing states to attach more importance to territorial democracy, notably in the form of territorial autonomy.[294] Hence, while the Westphalian territorial state strived for uniformity and homogeneity, the postmodern state tolerates multiple identities and sub-loyalties as pre-modern empires[295]used to do very frequently.

The revival of territorial autonomy[296] has started to take place decades ago within the European context when, in order to avoid disadvantaged regions falling further into poverty and missing out on the phenomenon of globalization, the European Commission has encouraged decentralization in disadvantaged economic regions in agreement with the countries concerned who saw in that process a means of promoting development in these regions. Thus, some regions, some of which have traditionally constituted the territorial base of stateless nations (Catalonia, Scotland, Wales, etc.), have benefitted from progressive decentralization (Spain, 1978; Belgium, 1980; Great-Britain, 1997-8, etc.) accompanied by financial aid from the European Regional Development Fund (since 1975) and the countries concerned.

The promotion of regional decentralization by states and the European Commission[297] falls at the origin within the framework of the traditional policy implemented in the old European democracies aiming at homogenizing their respective nations, but in which cracks were beginning to appear, notably in the poorer regions due to the dismantling of the Welfare State engendered by globalization.[298] Thus the objective of the European Union was to correct dysfunctions in the market and avoid possible demands for self-determination. But the policy of decentralization followed by the European Union, while successfully and effectively promoting the development of certain regions,[299] has given a number of these regions the opportunity to emerge as more or less autonomous players on the international scene thanks notably to their involvement in the economic globalization. This has reinforced the regional and even nationalist sentiments of certain regional communities, thus creating a new dynamic which could in the future, were the European Union to withdraw its regional aid, strengthen the potential to cause a split between nation and state in the countries concerned.

---

[294] See Chevalier (2004, p. 73).

[295] See Walzer (1997, p. 85); Maier (2007, pp. 80–82).

[296] Territorial autonomy can be defined as the enjoyment, by a human group, of legislative, executive and possibly judiciary powers granted by the state as part of the exercising of territorial democracy. This is because "territorial democracy" is central to the notion of territorial autonomy as it allows effective enjoyment of human rights by the members of ethnic communities. For other different definitions of territorial autonomy, see Hannum and Lillich (1980, p. 859); Lapidoth (2003, p. 267); Wolff and Weller (2005, p. 13).

[297] Such promotion was imputed to the revival of old notion of industrial district as an instrument to attract foreign investments. See Michalet (2002, p. 189 et seq).

[298] See Scott (1998, p. 7).

[299] See Auberni (2003, p. 305).

Outside Europe, countries like the United States and Canada have for long since strengthened their symmetrical federalism by adopting cultural pluralism, based on the respect and the enhancement of the cultural and ethnic identity of all sections of their societies. Other countries, often those moving towards democracy, have ended up putting in place structures of territorial autonomy to reorganize their societies in order to make them more viable.

Initiated decades ago by some Western democracies, the move towards sharing power with subnational entities has been expanded to different parts of the world to the extent that at present there are two dozen countries encompassing over 40 per cent of the World's population that exhibit the fundamental characteristics of a functioning federation[300] and in which there are more than 500 local governments.[301] The appeal of federation- meant here in its largest sense, that is the sharing of power between the state and local communities – has been increasing so strongly due to its success in allowing greater economic welfare, respect for the rights of local communities and quality of life that "the federal idea is now more popular internationally than at any time in history."[302]

The popularity acquired by autonomy has led the latter, recalls H.Hannum,[303] to be adopted or proposed as a solution in countries as diverse as Finland, Norway, Sweden, Belgium, Spain, Denmark, Hungary, Romania, Yugoslavia, Bosnia and Herzegovina, Italy, United Kingdom, Turkey, Iraq, India, China, Sri Lanka, Papua New Guinea, Cyprus, the Philippines, Bangladesh, Russia, Georgia, Azerbaijan, Sudan, Sudan, Senegal, Canada, United States, Mexico, Brazil, Nicaragua, Panama and one can add Western Sahara. Thus, one can safely say that we are seeing the emergence of a new paradigm where territorial autonomy helps the states, as it did with the ancient states, to address the tremendous difficulties they increasingly have in ensuring the effectiveness of their territoriality. But, today, territorial autonomy is no longer a *de facto* institution because, as we will see later on, it has become one of the expressions of self-determination[304] which is also undergoing a radical change as it does increasingly mean not so much independence as the right to democratic governance. That radical change or the passage from one paradigm to another will be analyzed in the third part of this book.

Thus, globalization has dramatically contributed to the weakening rather than to the obsolescence of the state. Such weakening makes the states even more fragile that International Law has not been of a great help in protecting their territorial integrity against external threat.

[300] See Watts (2008, p. 1).

[301] Colomer (2007, p. xi).

[302] Idem, p. 7.

[303] "Territorial Autonomy: Permanent Solution or Step toward Secession ?", www.indonesiamission-ny.org/issuebaru/Mission/empwr/paper_hurstHannum_1.pdf.

[304] On the link between territorial autonomy and self-determination, see Brownlie (1992, p. 6); Heintze (1998); Roy (2006, pp. 150–158).

References

Adams RM (1960) Early civilizations, subsistence and environment In: Kraeling CH and Adams RM (eds) City Invincible, University of Chicago Press, Chicago
Agnew J (2001) The new global economy: time-compression, geopolitics and global uneven development. J World Syst Res VII(2)
Agnew J (2005a) Sovereign regimes: territoriality and state authority in contemporary world politics. Ann Assoc Am Geogr 95(2)
Agnew J (2005) Hegemony. The New Shape of Global Power. Temple University Press, Philadelphia
Akzin B (1964) State and Nation, Hutchinson university Library, London
Albert M, Brock L (1996) Debordering the world of states: new spaces in international relations. New Polit Sci 35
Alderson AS, Nielson F (2002) Globalization and the great U-turn: income inequality trends in 16 OECD ccountries. Am J Soc 107(5)
Anderson B (1983) Imagined Communities: Reflections on the Origins and Spread of Nationalism, Verso, London
Anderson B (1986) The Modernity of the Modern States In: Anderson B (ed) The Rise of the Modern State, Humanities Press International, Atlantic Highlands
Anderson M (1996a) Frontiers. Territory and State Formation in the Modern World. Polity Press, Cambridge
Anderson J (1996b) The shifting stage of politics: new medieval and postmodern territorialities? Environ Plan D Soc Space 14
Anderson P (1998) The Origins of Postmodernity. Verso, London
Andriolo K (1978) "On power in Egalitarian societies". Dialect Anthropol 3(2)
Apparadurai A (1996) Modernity at Large: Cultural Dimensions of Globalization. University of Minnesota Press, Minneapolis
Ardant G (1975) Financial policy and economic infrastructure of modern states and nations. In: Tilly C (ed) The Formation of National States in Western Europe. Princeton University Press, Princeton
Auberni JAI (2003) Pour une Europe encourageant ses identités historiques et culturelles. In: Coadic RL (ed) Identités et démocratie: diversité culturelle et mondialisation. Repenser la démocratie. Presses Universitaires de Rennes, Rennes
Axtmann R (1996) Liberal Democracy into the Twenty-First century: Globalization, Integration and the Nation-State. Manchester University Press, Manchester
Bacheli T, Bartman B, Srebrnik H (2004) A new world of emerging states In: Bacheli T, Bartman B, Srebrnik H (eds) De Facto States. The Quest for Sovereignty. Routledge, London
Badie B (1995) La fin des Territoires. Fayard, Paris
Bargatzky T (1987) Upward evolution, suprasystem dominance and the mature state. In: Henri J, Claessen M, van de Velde P (eds) Early State Dynamics. E.J.Brill, Leiden
Barkey K (2008) Empire of Difference: The Ottomans in Comparative Perspective, Cambridge University Press, New York
Barth F (1969) Introduction. In: Barth F (ed) Ethnic Groups and Boundaries. The Social Organization of Culture Difference. Little Brown and Company, Boston
Bauman Z (1990) Modernity and ambivalence. In: Featherstone M (ed) Global Culture: Nationalism, Globalization and Modernity. SAGE Publications, London
Beck U (1999) World Risk Society, Polity Press, Cambridge
Beck U (2000) The Brave New World of Work, Polity Press, Cambridge
Becker H, Smelo L (1931) "Conflict theories of the origin of the state". Sociol Rev 23(2)
Bennouna M (1976) L'affaire du Sahara devant la Cour Internationale Justice. Essai d'analyse structurale de l'avis consultatif du 16 octobre 1975, Revue Juridique, Politique et Economique et du Maroc
Bihr A (2000) Le crépuscule des Etats-nations, Cahiers libres, Editions Page deux

Bell D (1975) Ethnicity and social change. In: Glazer N, Moynihan DP (eds) Beyond the Melting-pot. M.I.T. Press, Cambridge
Black J (1997) Maps and Politics. London, Reaktion, chap. 5
Boivret Y (1995) Le postmodernisme. Les Editions du Boréal, Montreal, QC
Bouffartigue P (ed) (2004) Le retour des classes sociales. Inégalités, dominations, conflits, La Dispute, série Etats des lieux, Paris
Brass PR (1985) Ethnic groups and the state. In: Brass PR (ed) Ethnic Groups and the State. Croom Helm, London
Brownlie I (1992) The rights of peoples in modern international law. In: Crawford J (ed) The Rights of Peoples. Oxford Clarendon Press, Oxford
Burgess M, Vollaard H (eds) (2006) State Territoriality and European Integration. Routledge, London
Canovan M (2004) Sleeping dogs, prowling cats and soaring doves: three paradoxes of nationhood. In: Seymour M (ed) The Fate of the Nation-State. McGill-Queen's University Press, Montreal
Carneiro RL (1977) "A Theory of the Origin of the State". Studies in Social Theory No 3. Institute for Humane Studies, Menlo Park, CA, pp 3–21, initially published in Science, 1970,169
Carneiro RL (1978) Political expansion as an expression of the principle of competitive exclusion. In: Cohen R, Service ER (eds) Origin of the State: The Anthropology of Political Evolution. Institute for the Study of Human Issues, Philadelphia
Casimir MJ (1992) The dimensions of territoriality: an introduction. Casimir MJ, Rao A (eds) Mobility and Territoriality. Social and Spatial Boundaries Among Foragers, Fishers, Pastoralits and Peripatetics. Berg, New York
Castel O (2002) Le Sud dans la mondialisation. Quelles alternatives? La Découverte, Paris
Chapez J (1976) L'avis consultatif de la Cour Internationale de Justice du 16 octobre 1975 dans l'affaire du Sahara occidental. RGDIP
Chevalier J (2004) L'Etat post-moderne, 2nd edn. L.G.D.J, Paris
Chevallier J (1978) Le modèle centre / périphérie dans l'analyse politique. In: "Centre, périphérie, territoire", Publications du Centre Universitaire de Recherches Administratives et Politiques de Picardie (C.U.R.A.P.P.). Presses Universitaires de France, Paris
Claessen HJM (1978) The early state: a structural approach In: Claessen HJM and Salnick P (eds) The Early State, The Hague, Mouton
Claessen HJM (1985) Sociopolitical evolution as complex interaction In: Claessen HJM, van de Velde P and Smith ME (eds) Development and Decline: The Evolution of Sociopolitical Organization
Claessen HJM, van De Velde P and Smith ME (1985) Sociopolitical evolution as complex interaction In: Claessen HJM, van De Velde P and Smith ME (eds) Development and Decline: The Evolution of Sociopolitical Organization, Bergin & Garvey Publishers, South Halley
Clarck I (1997) Globalization and Fragmentation. International Relations in the Twentieth Century. Oxford University Press, Oxford
Clastres P (1974) La société contre l'Etat. Editions de Minuit, Paris
Cobban A (1947) National Self-Determination,The University of Chicago Press, Chicago (first edition, 1944)
Cohen R (1981) Evolution, fission, and the early state. In: Claessen HJM, Skalnik P (eds) The Study of the State. Mouton Publishers, The Hague
Cohen R (1985) Warfare and state formation In: Claessen HJM, van de Velde P and Smith ME (eds) Development and Decline: The Evolution of Sociopolitical Organization
Cohen S (2006) The Resilience of the State. Democracy and the Challenge of Globalization. Hurst & Company, London
Colas A (2007) Empire. Polity Press, Cambridge
Colomer JM (2007) Great Empires, Small Nations. The Uncertain Future of the Sovereign State. Routledge, London
Connolly W (1991) Democracy and territoriality. Millenium 20(3)

Conversi D (1995) Reassessing Current Theories of Nationalism: Nationalism as Boundary Maintenance and Creation
Corneliau C (2000) Les impasses de la modernité. Critique de la marchandisation du monde. Seuil, Paris
Cowgill GL (1975) On causes and consequences of ancient and modern population. Am Anthropol 77
Cowgill GL (1988) Onward and upward with collapse. In: Yoffee N, Cowgill GL (eds) The Collapse of Ancient States and Civilizations. The University of Arizona Press, Tucson
Crone P (1989) Pre-Industrial Societies. Basil Blackwell, Oxford
Crouch C (2004) Post-Democracy, Polity, Cambridge
Curie K (1994) The Asiatic mode of production: problems of conceptualizing state and economy. Dialect Anthropol 8(4)
Davies N (1996) Europe: A History. Oxford University Press, Oxford
de Visscher C (1967) Les effectivités du Droit International Public. A.Pédone, Paris
Dittgen H (2000) The End of the Nation-State? Borders in the Age of Globalization In: M. Pratt and JA Brown (eds) Borderlands Under Stress. Kluwer Law, The Hague
Doehring K (1984) "Effectiveness", Encyclopedia of Public International Law, vol. 7. Max Plank Institute, Amsterdam
Dole G (1966) Anarchy without chaos: alternatives to political authority among the Kuikuru. In: Swartz M, Turner V, Tuden A (eds) Political Anthropology. Aldine, Chicago
Dollar D, Kraay A (2002) Spreading the Wealth, Foreign Affairs
Doornbos M (2006) Global Forces and State Restructuring. Dynamics of States Formation and Collapse. Palgrave Macmillan, London
Dubet F, Marticelli D (1998) Dans quelle société vivons-nous? Seuil, Paris
Dupuy R-J (1990) L'avis Consultatif de la Cour Internationale de Justice. In: La Marche verte (ouvrage colléctif). Plon, Paris
Eisenstadt SN (1969) The Political Systems of Empires: The Rise and Fall of the Historical Bureaucratic Societies, Free Press, New York
Elias TO (1980) The doctrine of intertemporal law. AJIL 74(2)
Elkins DJ (1995) Beyond Sovereignty: Territory and Political Economy in the Twenty-First Century. University of Toronto Press, Toronto
El Ouali A (1984) Effets juridiques de la sentence internationale. Contribution à l'étude de l'exécution des normes internationales. LGDJ, Paris
Engels F (1972) The Origin of the Family, Private Property, and the State (1884)In: Eleanor Burke Leakock (ed) International Publishers, New York
Esping-Andersen G (ed) (1996) Welfare states in transition. National Adaptations in Global Economics, SAGE Publications, London
Esping-Andersen G (1998) The Sustainability of Welfare States into the 21st Century. Paper prepared for presentation at the Fundacion Campalans, Barcelona, February 1998. www.fcampalans.cat/archivos/papers/113.pdf
Febvre L (1973) Frontière: the word and the concept. In: Burke P (ed) A New Kind of History: From the Writing of Febvre. Routledge, London
Ferguson YH, Mansbach RW (1996) Polities, Identities, and, Change. University of South Carolina Press, Columbia
Fitoussi JP (2004) La démocratie et le marché. Grasset, Paris
Flannery KV (1972) The cultural evolution of civilizations. Annu Rev Ecol Systematics 3
Flory M (1975) L'avis de la Cour Internationale de Justice sur le Sahara Occidental. AFDI:273
Forsyth M (1994) "Hobbes's contractarianism. A comparative analysis". Boucher D, Kelly P (eds) "The Social Contract from Hobbes to Rawls". Routledge, London
Freeman A (2004) The inequality of nations. In: Freeman A, Kagarlitsky B (eds) The Politics of Empire. Globalisation in Crisis. Pluto Press, London
Fried MH (2004) On the evolution of social stratification and the state (1960) In: McGree RJ and Warms RL (eds) Anthropological Theory. An Introduction History, McGraw Hill, New York

Friedman J, Rowlands M (1977) Notes towards an epigenetic model of the evolution of civilization. In: Friedman J, Rowlands M (eds) "The Evolution of Social Systems". Duckworth, London
Gauchet M (1977) "La dette du sens et les racines de l'Etat", Libre, vol 2. Petite Bibliothèque Payot, Paris
Gauthier D (1979) David Hume, Philosophical Review, vol. LXXXVIII
Geary J (2002) False Dawn. The Delusions of Global Capitalism, second edition. Granta Books, London
Geary PJ (2003) The Myth of Nations. The Medieval Origins of Europe. Princeton University Press, Princeton, Chap. 6
Gellner E (1983) Nations and Nationalism, Basil Blackwell, Oxford
Genov NB (1997) Four global trends: rise and limitations. Int Sociol 12(4)
Germet J (1968) Ancient China, from the Beginnings to the Empire, Faber & Faber, London
Giddens A (1985) The Nation-State and Violence. University of California Press, Berkeley
Giddens A (1999) BBC Reith Lectures, LSE, London, Lecture I
Gilpin R (2001) Global Political Economy. Understanding the International Economic Order. Princeton University Press, Princeton
Ginsberg M (1957) On the concept of evolution in sociology. In: Ginsberg M (ed) "Essays on Sociology and Social Philosophy", vol.1. William Heinman, London
Godelier M (1978) The concept of the asiatic mode of production and marxist models of social evolution In: Seddon D (ed) Relations of production: Marxist Approaches to Economic Anthropology, Franck Cass, London
Gowan P (1999) The Global Gamble: Washington bid for World Dominance, London and New York
Grader W (1997) One World. Ready or Not. The Manic Logic of Global Capitalism. Penguin Books, London
Gunawardana RALH (1985) Total power or shared power? A study of the hydraulic state and its transformations in Sri Lanka from the third to the ninth century A.D In: Claessen HJM, van de Velde P and Smith ME (eds) Development and Decline: The Evolution of Sociopolitical Organization
Haas E (1962) The Evolution of the Prehistoric State. Columbia University Press, New York
Haas J (1982) The Evolution of the Prehistoric State, Columbia University Press, New York
Habermas J (1975) Legitimation Crisis. Becon Press, Boston
Habermas J (2001) The Postnational Constellation. Political Essays, The MIT Press, Cambridge
Hakli J (1994) Territoriality and the rise of the modern state. Fennia 172
Hampton J (1986) Hobbes and the Social Contract Tradition. Cambridge University Press, Cambridge
Hannum H, Lillich RB (1980) The concept of autonomy in International Law. AJIL 74
Harvey D (1990) The Condition of Postmodernity: An Enquiry into the Origins of Cultural Change. Blackwell, Cambridge
Heintze H-J (1998) On the legal understanding of autonomy. In: Suksi M (ed) Autonomy: Applications and Implications. Kluwer Law International, The Hague
Herb GH (1999) National identity and territory In: Herb GH and Kaplan DH (eds) Nested Identities. Territory, Nationalism, Territory, and Scale, Rowan & Littlefield Publishers, New York, Oxford
Hindless B, Hirst PQ (1975) Pre-Capitalist Modes of Production. Routledge, London
Hirst P, Thompson G (2002) The future of globalization. Coop Confl J Nordic Int Stud Assoc 37(3)
Hobbes T (1994) Leviathan (1668) In: Edwin Curley (Ed), Hackett Publishing Company Inc., Indianapolis/Cambridge
Hobsbawn E (1990) Nations et Nationalisme depuis 1870, folio/histoire, Gallimard, transl.
Hume D (1963) Of Passive Obedience In: Essays: Moral, Political and Literary, Oxford University Press, Oxford (first published in 1741 and 1742)
Huntington SP (1991) The Third Wave. Democratization in the Late 20th Century, University of Oklahoma Press, Norman

Hutton W (2000) High-Risk Strategy. In: Pierson C, Castles FG (eds) The Welfare State Reader, Polity Press, Cambridge
Ilgen TL (eds) (2003) Reconfigured Sovereignty. Multi-Layered Governance in the Global Age. Ashgate, Burlington
Immerfall S (1998) Territory and territoriality in the globalizing society: an introduction. In: Immerfall S (ed) Territoriality in the Globalizing Society. One Place or None? Springer, Berlin
Jameson F (1992) Postmodernism, or, the Cultural Logic of Late Capitalism. Duke University Press, Durham
Jovanovic M, Hendrard K (2008) Sovereignty, statehood, and the diversity challenge. In: Jovanovic M, Hendrard K (eds) Sovereignty and Diversity. Eleven International Publishing, Utrecht
Kahler M (2006) Territoriality and conflict in an era of globalization. In: Kahler M, Walter BF (eds) Territoriality and Conflict in Era of Globalization. Cambridge University Press, Cambridge
Karatnycky A (2005) Civic power and electoral politics. In: Freedom in the World 2005, Freedom House, New York
Keating M (2001) Beyond Sovereignty. Plurinational Democracy in a post-Sovereign World, The Desjardins Lecture, McGill University
Khaldun I (2007) The State (1927), Black Rose Books, Montreal/New York/London (translated by John M. Gitterman)
Kohen MG (1997) Possession contestée et souveraineté territoriale. PUF, Paris
Kolata AL (2006) Before and after collapse. Reflections on the regeneration of social complexity. In: Schwartz GM, Nichols JJ (eds) After Collapse. The Regeneration of Complex Societies. The University of Arizona Press, Tucson
Krader L (1968) Formation of the State. Prentice-Hall, Englewood Cliffs
Kwiek M (2007) The Future of the Welfare State and Democracy: The Effects of Globalization from a European Perspective" In: Czerwinska-Schupp E (ed) Values and Norms in the Age of Globalization, op.cit.
Lapidoth R (2003) Autonomie, unité et démocratie. In: Coadic RL (ed) Identités et Démocratie: Diversité Culturelle et Mondialisation. Presse Universitaires de Rennes, Rennes
Lapierrre JW (1977) Vivre sans Etat? Essai sur le pouvoir et l'innovation sociale. Seuil, Paris
Lefort C (1972) Le travail de l'oeuvre de Machiavel. Gallimard, Paris
Lind M (1996) The next American nation. The New American Nationalism & The Fourth American Revolution. Free Press Paperbacks, New York
Lipset SM, Lakin JM (2004) The Democratic Century, University of Oklahoma Press, Norman
Locke J (1988) Two Treaties of Government (1690) In: Laslett P (ed), Cambridge University Press, Cambridge
Loschak D (1978) Espace et contrôle social In: Centre, périphérie, territoire, Presses Universitaires de France, Paris (Publications du Centre Universitaire de Recherches Administratives et Politiques de Picardie (C.U.R.A.P.P.))
Lowie RH (1927) The Origin of the State, Harcourt, Brace and Company, New York
Maier CS (2007) Being there: place, territory, and Identity. In: Benhabib S, Chapiro I, Petranovic D (eds) Identities, Affiliations, and Allegiances. Cambridge University Press, Cambridge
Mann M (1984) The autonomous power of the state: its origins, mechanisms and results. Eur J Sociol 25
Mann M (1986) Sources of Social Power, vol 1. Cambridge University Press, Cambridge
Marshall TH (1950) Citizenship and Social Class and Other Essays. Cambridge University Press, Cambridge
Martell L (2010) The Sociology of Globalization, Polity, Cambridge
Martin H-P and Schuman H (1997) Le piège de la mondialisation, translated from the German, Solin, Actes Sud, Paris

Mayr EW (1982) The Growth of Biological Thought: Diversity, Evolution, and Inheritance. Belknap Press, Cambridge
McGuire RH (1983) Breaking down cultural complexity: inequality and heterogeneity. In: Schiffer MB (ed) Advances in Archaeological Method and theory, vol 6. Academic Press, New York
Merrien F-X, Parchet R, Kernen A (2005) L'Etat Social. Une perspective Internationale. A.Colin, Paris
Michalet C-A (2002) Qu'est-ce que la Mondialisation? La Découverte, Paris
Michalet C-A (2003) Souveraineté nationale et mondialisation. In: Laroche J (ed) Mondialisation et Gouvernance Mondiale. P.U.F., Paris
Migdal JS (2001) State in Society. Studying How States and Societies Transform and Constitute One Another. Cambridge University Press, Cambridge
Migdal JS (2004) State Building and the Non-Nation-State, Journal of International Affairs 58(1)
Mikesell MW (1983) The myth of the nation state. J Geogr 82(6)
Milanovic B (2005) Worlds Apart. Measuring International and Global inequality. Princeton University Press, Princeton
Mitchell D (2000) Globalization and Social Cohesion: Risks and Responsibilities. In: The Year 2000 International Research Conference on Social Security, International Social Security Association (ISSA), Helsinki
Morgan LH (1963) Ancient Society, or Researches in the Lines of Human Progresses from Savagery, Through Barbarism to Civilization (1877) In: Leakock E, Peter Smith, Gloucester
Motyl A (2001) Imperial Ends; The Decay, Collapse, and Revival of Empires, Columbia University Press, New York
Muller K (2007) Globalization and democracy. progress and paradoxes. In: Czerwinska-Schupp E (ed) Values and Norms in the Age of Globalization, Peter Lang, Berlin
Murphy A (1996) The sovereign state system as political-territorial ideal: historical and contemporary considerations. In: Biersteker T, Weber C (eds) State Sovereignty as Social Construct. Cambridge University Press, Cambridge
Murphy C (2001) Political consequences of the new inequality. Int Stud Q 45
Newman D (2000) Boundaries, territoriality and postmodernity: towards shared or separate spaces? In: M. Pratt and JA Brown (eds) Borderlands Under Stress. Kluwer Law, The Hague
North DC, Wallis JJ and Weingast BR (2009) Violence and Social Orders. A Conceptual Framework for Interpreting Recorded Human History, Cambridge University Press, Cambridge
Nys E (1901) L'Etat et la notion d'Etat. RDLILC 35
Nys E (1904) L'acquisition du territoire en Droit International. RDILC 36
Ohmae K (1996) The End of the Nation State: The Rise of Regional Economy. Harper Collins, London
Opello WC, Rosow SJ (1999) The Nation-State and Global Order. A Historical Introduction to Contemporary Politics. Lynne Rienner Publishers, London
Parsons T (1961) "An outline of the social system". In: Parsons T, Shils E, Naegele KD, Pitts JR (eds) "Theories of Society", vol.1. The Free Press of Glenoe, New York
Peregrine PN, Ember CR and Ember M (2007) Modeling State Origins Using Cross-Cultural Datas, Cross-Cultural Research 41(1)
Pierson P (1997) The New politics of the welfare state. World Polit 48
Price BJ (1978) Secondary state formation: an explanatory model. In : Cohen R, Service ER (eds) Origins of the State: The Anthropology of Political Evolution. Institute of the Study of Human Issues, Philadelphia
Rappaport RA (1971) The sacred in human evolution. Ann Rev Ecol 2
Rosecrance R (1996) The Rise of the Virtual States. Foreign Affairs 75
Roy I (2006) Vers un 'droit de participation'des minorités à la 'vie de l'Etat'? Evolution dur Droit International et pratique des Etats. Wilson & Lafleur Ltée, Montréal
Russel JB (1968) Medieval Civilization. Wiley, New York

Sahlins MD (1968) Tribesmen. Prentice-Hall, Englewood Cliffs
Sassen S (1996) Losing Control? Sovereignty in an Age of Globalization. Columbia University Press, New York
Sassen S (2008) Territory, Authority, Rights. From Medieval to Global Assemblages. Princeton University Press, Princeton (updated edition)
Schacht RM (1988) Circumscription Theory, American Behavioral Scientist 31: 4
Scott AJ (1998) Regions and the World Economy: The Coming Shape of Global Production, Competition and Political Order. Oxford University Press, Oxford
Schwartz GM (2006) From Collapse to Regeneration In: Schwartz GM and Nichols JJ (eds) After Collapse. The Regeneration of Complex Societies, The University of Arizona Press
Service E (1975) Origins of the State and Civilization. The Process of Cultural Evolution, W.W. Norton & Company, New York
Shils EE (1975) Center and Periphery: Essays in Macrosociology. University of Chicago Press, Chicago
Shiozawa K (2007) Marx's View of Asian Society and his Asian Mode of Production, Developing Economies 41(3)
Simon HA (1965) The Architecture of Complexity: Yearbook of the Society of General Systems Research 10:13–76
Smith AD (1988) On the Ethnic Origin of Nations. Blackwell, Oxford
Smith AD (1995) Nations and Nationalism in a Global Era. Polity Press, Oxford
Smith AD (1998) Nationalism and Modernism. Routledge, London
Smith A (2007) Nation in decline? The erosion and persistence of modern national identities. In: Young M, Zuelow E, Strun A (eds) Nationalism in a Global Era. The Persistence of Nations. Routledge, London
Sorensen G (2001) Changes in Statehood. The Transformation of International Relations. Palgrave, Houndmills, Basingstoke
Spencer H (1967) The Evolution of Society, A selection from Principles of Sociology (1876–1896) In: Carneiro R, University of Chicago Press, Chicago
Spengler O (1918–1922) The Decline of the West, trans. By C. Atkinson, Alfred Knopf, New York
Spencer H (1896) The Principles of Sociology, vol II-I. D. Appleton and Company, New York
Spinoli CM (1994) The archeology of empires. Ann Rev Anthropol 23
Spruyt H (1994) The Sovereign State and Its Competitors. An Analysis of Systems Change, Princeton University Press, Princeton
Spruyt H (2002) The Origins, Development, and Possible Decline of the Modern State, Annu. Rev. Polit. Sci 5
Strange S (1996) The Retreat of the State. The Diffusion of Power in the World Economy. Cambridge University Press, Cambridge
Strayer J (1963) The historical experience of nation-building in Europe. In: Deutch KW, Foltz WJ (eds) Nation-Building. Artherton Press, New York
Strayer JR (1965) Feudalism. Van Nostrand, Princeton
Strayer JR (1970) On the Medieval Origins of the Modern State. Princeton University Press, Princeton
Taagepera R (1978) Size and duration of empires: systematics of size. Social Sci Res 7
Tainter JA (1988) The Collapse of Complex Societies. Cambridge University Press, Cambridge
Tuathail O (1999) Borderless Worlds? Problematizing Discourses of Deterritorialization, Geopolitics 4/2
Taylor PJ (1994) The State as Container: Territoriality in the Modern World-System, Progress in Human Geography 18
Taylor PJ (2009) When China Rules the World. The Rise of the Middle Kingdom and the End of the Western World, Allan Lane/Penguin Books, London
Thiesse A-M (2001) La création des identités nationales. Europe XVIII-XXe siècle, Seuil, Paris
Tierney S (2005) Reframing sovereignty? Sub-state national societies and contemporary challenges to the nation-state. ICLQ

Tilly C (1975) Reflections on the history of European state-making. In: Tilly C (ed) The Formation of National States in Western Europe. Princeton University Press, Princeton
Tilly C (1985) War making and state making as organized crime In: Evans P, Rueschemeyer D, and Skocpol T (eds) Bringing the State Back In, Cambridge University Press, Cambridge
Tilly C (1990) Coercion, Capital, and European States, AD 990–1990. Blackwell, Cambridge
Tilly C (1992) Coercion, Capital, and European States, AD 990-1992. Blackwell, Oxford
Touraine A (1992) Critique de la modernité. Fayard, Paris
Toynbee A (1933–1954) A Study of History, Oxford University Press, Oxford
Trigger BG (1985) Generalized coercion and inequality: the basis of state power in the early civilization In: Claessen HJM, van de Velde P and Smith ME (eds) Development and Decline: The Evolution of Sociopolitical Organization
Trigger BG (2003) Understanding Early Civilizations. A Comparative Study. Cambridge University Press, Cambridge
Vallée Ch (1976) L'affaire du Sahara occidental devant la Cour Internationale de Justice. Revue Maghreb 71
van Creveld M (1999) The Rise and Decline of the State. Cambridge University Press, New York
Van den Berghe P (1978) Race and Ethnicity: A Sociobiological Perspective, Ethnic and Racial Studies 4
Van Staden A, Vollaard H (2002) The erosion of state sovereignty: towards a post-territorial world. In: Kreijen G (ed) State, Sovereignty, and International Governance. Oxford University Press, Oxford
von Bertalanffy L (1950) An outline of general systems theory. Br J Philos Sci 1
Waldrom J (1994) "John Locke. Social contract versus political anthropology". Boucher D, Kelly P (eds) "The Social Contract from Hobbes to Rawls". Routledge, London
Walker RBJ (1993) Inside/Outside: International Relations as Political Theory. Cambridge University Press, Cambridge
Wallerstein I (1991) Geopolitics and Geoculture, Cambridge University Press, Cambridge
Wallerstein I (2004) World: System Analysis. An Introduction. Duke University Press, Durham
Walzer M (1997) On Toleration. Yale University Press, New Haven
Watts RL (2008) Comparing Federal Systems. McGill-Queen's University Press, Montreal
Weber M (1978) Economy and Society In: Roth G and Wittich C, University of California Press, Berkeley
Weiss L (2003) Is the state being 'Transformed' by globalization?. In: Weiss L States in the Global Economy. Bringing Domestic Institutions Back in. Cambridge University Press, Cambridge
Wesson RG (1967) The Imperial Order. University of California Press, Berkeley
Wittfogel K (1957) Oriental Despotism. Yale University Press, New Haven
Wolff S, Weller M (2005) Self-determination. A conceptual approach. In: Weller M, Wolff S (eds) Autonomy, Self-Government and Conflict Resolution. Innovative Approaches to Institutional Design in Divided Societies. Routledge, Oxon
Woolridge F (1979) The advisory opinion of the international court of justice in the western Sahara case. Anglo Am Law Rev 8
Wright HT (1977) Recent research on the origin of the state. Ann Rev Anthropol 6
Wright HT, Johnson G (1975) Population, exchange, and early state formation in Southwestern Iran. Am Anthropol 77
Yoffee N (2005) Myths of the Archaic State: Evolution of the Earliest Cities, States, and Civilizations. Cambridge University Press, Cambridge

Part II
The Protection of Territorial Integrity Against External Threat

States' territorial integrity has been all over human history subjected to external threats. The latter have affected states' territory as well as its territorial sovereignty.

Since their inception thousands a years ago, the main external threat to which the states have been subjected to has been war of conquest which has led either to the annexation of parts of their territories or very simply to their own disintegration. International Law, ancient as well as classical one, has been reluctant to prohibit war of conquest. It has even accepted territorial changes by the use of force. An important attempt was made at the end of the first World War, thanks to the efforts deployed by American President, Woodrow Wilson, with the view of prohibiting territorial changes by force and establishing an international system guaranteeing territorial integrity. However, the international community, while it has at that time accepted to endorse the idea that unilateral territorial changes should be prohibited and that an international system should be established in order to guaranty territorial integrity, was not able to make of that system , established by the famous article 10 of the Covenant, an effective instrument to achieve that goal. Amazingly, the UN Charter has abandoned the idea of establishing such a system and limited itself to a general statement prohibiting the use of force against territorial integrity (article 2.4). This has resulted in an ambiguous protection of territorial integrity. Indeed, the Charter has, while it did prohibit the use of force against territorial integrity, left the latter internationally unprotected. It is that ambiguous protection of territorial integrity which makes of International Law a primitive law. True, the latter has gradually since the early years of the League of Nations proclaimed that unilateral territorial changes cannot be recognized, but it has established no system by which it can prevent such changes or when they did happen to reestablish the status quo ante.

Enjoying a very relative if not a hypothetical protection of their territorial integrity, the states have also witnessed a steady weakening of their territorial sovereignty through the limitation or the loss of exercise of sovereign competences and the enjoyment of an exclusive jurisdiction within their own territories. However, the move towards such a weakening does not affect all states as suggested by a largely shared opinion. In fact, it mainly affects Southern states. Amazingly, instead of correcting such situation, International Law has frequently contributed to the weakening of state's territorial sovereignty.

Two important issues will, therefore, be successively discussed hereafter: the ambiguous character of the international protection of territorial integrity and the weakening of territorial sovereignty.

Chapter 3
The Ambiguous Protection of State Territory

As we have seen above, the institutionalization of territoriality integrity was made possible by the emergence of central principles such as sovereignty, the prohibition of the use of force, self-defense, state of necessity, etc. The rationale behind the emergence of these principles was to ensure the protection of territorial integrity. International Law has also given rise to other principles the objective of which is to preserve state's territorial integrity. This chapter will focus mainly on the principles that are directly related to the preservation of the integrity of state's territory.

Amazingly, what can be noted with regard to the protection of states' territory is the fact that International Law, while it has prohibited any unilateral territorial changes, has provided only a very weak protection for the states whose territory has been affected by such changes.

3.1 The Prohibition of Unilateral Territorial Changes

International Law has constantly stressed the importance of preserving the integrity of state's territory. It did so by admitting that no territorial change can take place without the mutual consent of the concerned states. An attempt has been made to introduce an exception to that cardinal principle through the promotion of the uti possidetis as a principle of International Law. However, such an attempt was not successful in making International Law accept the uti possidetis as an exception to the crucial principle of the necessary consent of the states concerned to any territorial changes.

3.1.1 The Principle of the Necessary Consent of the State to Territorial Changes

First, the necessary consent of the state to territorial changes is required in respect to any territorial delimitation. Second, International Law stresses that the consent of

A. El Ouali, *Territorial Integrity in a Globalizing World*,
DOI 10.1007/978-3-642-22869-8_3,

the state to any territorial changes be made in compliance with the requirement of Constitutional law. It is only when states' borders have been established as a result of state consent that they become final and stable.

3.1.1.1 The Consent of the State to the Delimitation of Its Territory

The first principle is that the delimitation of states territories is an act of sovereignty. The I.C.J. has recognized that: "the fixing of a frontier depends on the will of the sovereign states directly concerned."[1] A.O. Cukwurah recalls in this respect that "When neighboring states delimit their international boundaries, what in effect they proceed to do is to fix the limit of their sovereignty. They reciprocally recognize sovereignty on either side of the boundary line". He adds also that "inasmuch as the boundary of a state is prima facie evidence of the limits of its sovereignty, a fixed boundary will be relevant to the status of a state only as a corollary to its territorial integrity. The delimitation of international boundaries is itself an act of sovereignty."[2] Furthermore, the delimitation of territories is an act of sovereignty of the neighboring states and the neighboring states only.[3] From this very crucial principle, one can infer that third parties, irrespective of their position in International Relations, are not entitled, unless authorized to do so by the concerned parties, to interfere in any territorial disputes between the latter in order to impose on them any kind of settlement. This obligation applies even to international bodies such as the UN General Assembly, the UN Security Council and the International tribunals including the International Court of Justice. Those who have infringed that principle have been severely criticized.

Hence, with regard to the UN General Assembly, France, for instance, has recalled in a written statement in the Namibia Advisory Opinion case that:

> "Nowhere in the text setting forth the functions of the General assembly. . .can any mention be found of a competence enabling that organ to "decide" whether this or that territory belongs to this or that state. . .The General Assembly has behaved as if it considered itself invested with legislative power on a universal scale, one which empowers it not only to formulate binding legal rules for all, even if they add to the Charter or modify it, but also to attach a power of sanction to those rules. . .Thus, we are faced with a decision of the General assembly which was taken ultra vires."[4]

Similar criticism was addressed to the UN Security Council in relation to its resolution confirming the termination of South Africa mandate for Namibia. Hence, Judge Sir Gerald Fitzmaurice has in the aforementioned Namibia Advisory Opinion

[1] ICJ Reports, 1994, 4, 25.

[2] Cukwurah (1967, pp. 29, 31) of Chapter 1.

[3] See de Visscher (1967, pp. 102 and seq, 110).

[4] Legal Consequences for States of the Continued Presence of South Africa in Namibia (South West Africa) notwithstanding Security Council Resolution (1970, pp. 367–368).

made it clear in his dissenting opinion that "even when acting under Chapter VII of the Charter itself, the Security Council has no power to abrogate or alter territorial rights, whether of sovereignty or administration. Even a war time occupation of a country or territory cannot operate to do that. It must await the peace settlement. This is a principle of international law that is as well established as any there can be, and the Security Council is as much subject to it (for the United Nations is itself subject to international law) as any of its individual members are. The Security Council might, after making the necessary determination under Article 39 of the Charter, order occupation of a country or a peace of territory in order to restore peace and security, but it could not thereby, or as part of the operation, abrogate or alter territorial rights...It was to keep peace that the Security Council was set up not to change world order."[5] The Security Council has also been criticized when it endorsed on 27 May 1993 a recommendation made on 20 May 1993 by the Iraq–Kuwait Boundary Demarcation Commission to determine and fix some sectors of the border while its mandate was only to demarcate it in accordance with previous agreements signed by both countries.[6] Commenting on this, I. Brownlie was able to say that: "It is probable that the alignment as such was disputed and, therefore, the adoption of a particular alignment by the Security Council involved rather more than a "demarcation". If this is correct, then the Security Council adopted a role which is inappropriate and incompatible with general international law...It is one thing to effect a restoration of Kuwaiti sovereignty on the basis of the status quo prior to Iraq's invasion. It is another to impose a boundary in the absence either of bilateral negotiation and agreement or arbitration or reference to the International Court."[7]

The excès de pouvoir, i.e. the non respect by international tribunals of their terms of reference, has more frequently generated demands of nullity of their previous decisions. The claim of excess of power, recalls K.H. Kaikobad,[8] constitutes an exercise of jurisdiction in excess of, or inconsistent with, the range of powers vested in the tribunal or court by the arbitral treaty, special agreement, or terms of

[5] I.C.J. Rep. 1971, 294.

[6] A severe criticism of the excès de pouvoir of that Commission is made by Kaikobad (1999), p. 302 cont. Maurice Mendelson and Susan also severely criticized the Commission by noting that contrary to what was stipulated in previous agreements between Iraq and Kuwait: "en termes généraux, l'effet global des décisions de la Commission est que d'importantes portions de territoires et des installations qui relevaient antérieurement de l'Iraq n'en dépendent plus. En bref, prétendre que la Commission a été engagée dans une simple opération de démarcation de caractère technique constitue une simplification considérable, même s'il est vrai que la Commission n'a pas été chargée de procéder a une redistribution de territoire", "Les décisions de la Commission des Nations Unies de démarcation de la frontière entre l'Iraq et le Koweït", A.F.D.I., 1993, 229.

[7] Brownlie (1995, p. 224). See also Lamb (p. 361, seq).

[8] Kaikobad (1999, p. 29).

reference set by the concerned states. After having examined several cases in which claims of nullity were raised due to excess of power, the same author concludes that these cases establish that "a tribunal is obliged to interpret its jurisdiction strictly, as opposed to adopting an expansive view of its powers. This requirement applies just as much to a latter tribunal requested to pass upon the question of nullity, which means that the tribunal is obliged not to take a liberal approach at the expense of exceeding its powers. Moreover, where the tribunal is in doubt or where, even after a careful examination of the issues, the precise limits are unclear or there is no real clarification of the scope of its powers, there is a duty not to exercise jurisdiction in a way which would probably be beyond its powers."[9]

Therefore the making of a frontier by the concerned parties and by these parties alone is a sacrosanct principle of International Law. It is because it was so convinced by the crucial importance of that principle that the European Commission has, after it has beginning of the nineties suggested that the international frontiers of the Republics which have emerged as a result of the dismemberment of Yugoslavia will be the old internal/administrative limits of the latter, insisted on obtaining the agreement of all the concerned parties including those who have succeeded to the Yugoslavian Federation. This was not an easy issue as it necessitated, due to the conflicting interests prevailing at that time, "an intense political pressure in order to (convince) the F.R.Y. to *accept* a solution based on the maintaining of the internal limits."[10]

It is worth mentioning that though the European continent witnessed a series of territorial changes following the collapse of the Soviet Union and Yugoslavia, the 1975 Helsinki Final Act has continued to refer to the necessary agreement of the concerned parties to any border settlement by solemnly proclaiming that:

> "They (the states) consider that their frontiers can be modified, in accordance with *International Law*, by peaceful means and through *agreement* (italics added)."

3.1.1.2 The State's Consent to Territorial Changes in Compliance with the Requirement of Constitutional Law

States are free to transfer part of their territory to one another, but what matters "is that the cession takes place with the full consent of the Governments concerned. Unless anything to the contrary is expressly agreed, a cession becomes effective

---

[9] Idem, p. 319. One should also recall that in addition to the fact that tribunals are governed by the terms of reference given by the parties, their decisions should remain res inter alios acta vis-à-vis third parties. This is a mandatory principle which should be taken into consideration by international tribunals when enunciating their decisions. See El Ouali (1984, p. 82 cont.).

[10] Delcourt (1998/1, p. 96).

only with the actual transfer of sovereignty."[11] By full consent of the Governments, it is meant that any transfer of a territory cannot take place unless it is made in compliance with the requirements of Constitutional law. One of these requirements is the necessary consent of the population concerned. Usually, such consent is expressed either directly through a plebiscite or indirectly through approbation by people's representatives, that is mainly the Parliaments.

The necessary consent of the population concerned to the cession of any part of state's territory is an old idea which has emerged at the end of the Middle-Age. The necessity to comply with such requirement was sometimes made in the treaty itself. This was the case, for instance, with regard to the treaty signed between France and England in 1359 by which the former accepted to cede to the latter large parts of its territory. However, the said treaty was rejected by the Estates General.[12] It happened also that, when such a requirement was not stipulated in the treaty, the population concerned protested against the signing of that treaty and requested the rejection of any territorial cession.[13] However, with the emergence and the development of the absolutist states from the sixteenth to the eighteenth century, the consultation of the population becomes less frequent,[14] though the 1648 Treaties of Westphalia have given rise to the institution of "option" which gave a choice to the population concerned to remain within their state of origin of join the state which has benefited from the territorial cession.[15] During the absolutist era, the standard practice was indeed that the conclusion of treaties was exclusively vested in the Crowns[16] who often did not show any interest in consulting their populations about territorial changes affecting their own country. However, prior to the end of that period, an important transformation will be witnessed in the exercise of the treaty-making power as in some countries, a room will be left to the legislative power and that the final conclusion of treaties has started to be made on behalf not of the princes but of own their states. Writing in the mid of the eighteenth century, E. Vattel reflected that change when he stated that "Public Treaties can only be entered into by Supreme Authorities, by Sovereigns who contract in the name of the State...A Sovereign who possesses full and absolute Empire has doubtless the right to treat in the name of the state which he represents, and his undertakings are binding on the whole Nation. But all Leaders of People have not the power to make Public Treaties on their own authority: Some of them have to take advice of a Senate or of the Representatives of the Nation. It is in the fundamental Laws of each State that one sees which Authority is capable of contracting validly in the name of

[11] Schwarzenberger (2005, p. 260).

[12] See Solière (1901, p. 19).

[13] See the cases discussed by Giroud (1920, p. 8 et seq).

[14] Idem, p. 21.

[15] Idem, p. 11.

[16] See on this Haggenmacher (1992–1993, pp. 315–324).

the State.[17] But the emergence of the principle of popular sovereignty and its gradual expansion will make the situation clearer as democratic states would refuse to proceed to any territorial changes without the consultation of the population concerned. A principle will emerge since then according to which a territory cannot be transferred from one state to another or incorporated in it without the consent of the concerned people.[18]

According to the early theorists of International Law, the rationale behind the idea that the transfer of a territory from one state to another requires the consent of the people concerned lies in the original contract that unites these people. Hence, when these people joined together to create a state, they were anticipating that the latter will be eternal within its territorial components and that consequently no change can be made to any of these territorial components without their consent. Such explanation was then based on the supposed original contract which was made between multifarious people and which has led to the creation of a state that unified that whole people in a single human community within a territory that belongs to that community.[19] In fact, if we put aside theoretical speculations, the necessary consent of the people to any territorial change which might affect their territory finds its "raison d'être" in the identification of the people with that territory. Every human group which is organized within a given polity identifies itself, as we have seen above, with a territory that becomes consubstantial with its own existence. The attachment of the people to their own territory has also been reinforced by the emergence of popular sovereignty. Therefore, it can be said that the principle that no territorial change can take place without the consent of the people concerned finds its origin, first, in the attachment and identification of the people with their own territory and, second, in popular sovereignty or, in other words self-determination, which makes of the people, as we have seen above, the real holder of sovereignty on its territory. It is therefore not a surprise that most of the plebiscites which have taken place since the proclamation of self-determination were related to the transfer of territory from one state to another.[20]

The necessary consent of the people to any change affecting their territory has also been endorsed by International Law as the latter makes the validity of treaties dependent on the respect of constitutional law requirements. It is true that a controversy has for a long time opposed scholars on the question of the validity of treaties concluded in violation with internal constitutional law. Such violation may happen in particular when the head of the state proceeds to the ratification of a treaty without requesting, when required, prior authorization from the Parliament.

---

[17] Vattel (1758).

[18] See Wambaugh (1927, p. 153 et seq). See also Merle (1961).

[19] On the view point of the early doctrine of International Law represented by Grotius, Pufendorf, etc., see Giroud (1920, pp. 22–28).

[20] Hence, most of the 18 plebiscites which have been organized from 1791 to 1905, were related to the transfer of territories from state to another. See the thorough analysis carried out by Wambaugh (1920).

But the controversy over what is usually called the imperfect ratification has been finally settled by the Vienna Convention on the Law of Treaties in favour of an intermediary solution. In order to grasp the importance and scope of that compromise solution, it is worth recalling the doctrine's approach to the delicate question of the validity of the treaties concluded in violation of constitutional law. The doctrine[21] can in fact be divided in three schools: the "internationalist", the "constitutionalist" and the "intermediary" one.

According to the internationalist doctrine, when a state expresses its consent to be bound by a treaty in a manner which is inconsistent with its constitutional law, such non-compliance does not affect the validity of the treaty. It is so because, it is argued, International Law does not comprise any rule which makes of the respect of the constitutional rules related to the treaty-making power a condition to the international validity of the treaty. Such rule does not exist in International Law because the latter leaves to the states the competence to determine the organs and the procedure by which can be formed the state will to abide by a treaty. What matters to International Law is the external manifestation by which the consent of the state has been expressed by the organ entitled to do so, that is usually the head of the state. Hence, according to this school of thinking, any treaty ratified by the head of the state is binding regardless of constitutional restraints. In fact, the idea that the head of the state has been invested by International Law with a complete authority to bind the state has originally been sustained mainly in countries where absolutism had not given place to a constitutional regime.[22] It comes down, highlights C. Fairman, from the days of absolutism, when for public purposes the prince was the state.[23]

One of the most prominent authors belonging to the internationalist school was L. Bittner.[24] According to him, there is an international customary rule which establishes that the declaration made by the head of the state in the form of an act of ratification is alone sufficient to express the state's assent to be bound by a treaty. He deduced such rule from what he believed was a long standing practice of the Austrian-Hungarian Empire. Two elements concurred in this practice in confirming that conclusion. The first element was that the texts of the full powers have remained unchanged since the thirteenth century. These texts have continuously affirmed the promise to ratify the treaty signed by the plenipotentiaries and did

---

[21] On the doctrinal controversy, see Research in International Law, Harvard Law School (1935), Part III, Law of Treaties, Comment to article 21, 29 A.J.I.L., 1935, Supplement, 635 ff.; Fairman (1936, 30 A.J.I.L.). Wildhaber (1971).

[22] This doctrine has been developed in the second half of the 19th in Germany and then in Italy. See the extensive bibliography referred to by Fairman (1936, p. 440, note 2).

[23] Idem, p. 441.

[24] Bittner (1924). We refer here to the conception of L. Bittner as extensively presented by Freymond (1947, p. 91ff).

not mention the necessity of the parliamentary approbation, though the latter was stipulated in the new constitutions. The second element is the silence kept by the instruments of ratification on the issue whether the treaty has to be effectively approved by the Parliament. Taking these two elements into consideration, L. Bittner thought that he was able to draw the conclusion that even though the Parliaments have been associated to the treaty-making power, this has not reflected on the traditional idea that International Law does take into account only the acts emanating from the heads of the states, acts by which they manifestly express their intention to definitively bind their countries. But the main criticism to be made to L. Bittner is that he took into consideration the fact that the formulation of the full powers and sometimes the instruments of ratification has traditionally been kept unchanged while states' practice has dramatically changed in order inter alia to enable the Parliaments to authorize the Executive to ratify the treaties.

The conclusion reached by L. Bittner is shared by G.G. Fitzmaurice for whom "the ratification in the international and in the constitutional sense should be considered as two entirely distinct matters; and that, except in the cases where a treaty itself expressly provides that its entry into force is dependent on municipal 'ratification' or legislation, the failure to 'ratify' in the constitutional sense ought not to have any bearing or effect on the international validity of the treaty, the latter being dependent wholly on the international and not the constitutional acts of the states concerned."[25]

The internationalist doctrine has been severely criticized. It has, first, been criticized, for its formalistic character insofar as it gives pre-eminence to the 'declaration' of state's will instead of the latter's 'formation'. Second, it has been criticized for not taking into account the constitutional law which determines alone the modalities of the formation of state's will. Third, it has been criticized to grant too much importance to the head of the state, while the latter has seen its power reduced with the expansion of democratic regimes. That is why the institutional doctrine has been less supported than the constitutionalist doctrine.

With regard to the constitutionalist doctrine, the competence to bind a state by a treaty is determined by its fundamental laws and consequently any non-compliance with the latter affects the validity of the said treaty. Hence, a treaty ratified by the head of the state without, when required, the prior consent of the Parliament, is void and deprived of any legal effect in International Law. The constitutionalist doctrine is also very old. J.C. Bluntschli had in the second half of the nineteenth century already noted that "The head of the state cannot be considered as binding its state by a treaty when it ratifies the latter without, when required, requesting the

[25] B.Y.B.I.L. (1934, p. 130). See also Anzilotti (1929, p. 366).

contribution and the assent of representative bodies (Senate, Parliament, Federal Council, House of Representatives)."[26]

P. Chailley is certainly the author who has the most contributed to the theorization of the idea of the legal invalidity of the imperfect ratification. His well informed and elaborated argumentation deserves a particular attention.

First, P. Chailley shows, after a thorough analysis of contemporary Constitutions, that most of these declare invalid any treaty imperfectly ratified.[27] Such invalidity is of an international and not only internal character as the municipal law requirements have been established in accordance with positive International Law.

Second, P. Chailley shows that, contrary to the affirmation made by L. Bittner, there is no customary rule which gives to the head of the state an internationally unlimited competence to conclude treaties.[28] Bittner affirmation is not even true with regard the absolutist kings of the old regime whose powers have varied over ages. Thus, in France, these powers were legally limited by the famous "Fundamental Laws of the Kingdom." These Laws were seen as a written Constitution that nobody could offend and they used to be invoked, according to the circumstances, by the King against the Parliaments or vice-versa. Amongst these Laws, there was particularly the one that limited the power of the Kings in territorial matters and which required the consent of the Estates General. Hence, it was a decision of the latter which has declared null and void the Treaty of Madrid of 14 January 1526 by which François the First ceded to Charles Quint the region of Bourgogne, the reason being that the king of France was not entitled to act against the Fundamental Law which prohibited him from alienating whatever part of the French territory.

Third, Chailley shows that the thesis of the validity of the imperfect ratification is inconsistent[29] with the necessary character of the ratification.[30] We know that such character later has been acquired by ratification, following the emergence of the nation-state and democratic political systems, which has rendered it an obligatory act in order to make of the treaty a final and binding legal instrument, while it was previously considered within the patrimonial political system as a superfluous act in accordance with the mandate theory.[31] Indeed in the later

[26] Bluntschli (1869).

[27] Chailley (1932, pp. 172–180).

[28] Idem, pp. 180–185.

[29] Idem, pp. 188 et seq.

[30] On the necessary character of the ratification, see Grandall (1916, p. 63); Vexler (1921, p. 87); Basdevant (1928-I, p. 67); Dehousse (1935, pp. 93–94); Gergopoulos (1939, pp. 3–4); Nicolopoulos (1942); Jones (1946); Freymond (1947, p. 47); Nair (1961, p. 132).

[31] Starke (1977) recalls in this respect that "In theory, ratification is the approval by the head of the state or the Government of the signature appended to the treaty by the duly appointed plenipotentiaries. In modern practice, however, it has come to possess more significance that a simple act of confirmation, being deemed to represent the formal declaration by a state of its consent to be bound by a treaty".

system, treaties were meant to become binding from the moment of their signature by the plenipotentiaries who did have full powers to commit their princes and not following their ratification. It was further to that radical transformation that the ratification became a discretionary act that the states are free to carry out or reject without having to justify themselves. Taking this into consideration, Chailley criticizes the international doctrine for giving pre-eminence to the "declaration" of state's will to the detriment of its "formation". Such attitude could be acceptable within the framework of the mandate doctrine insofar as the role of the head of the state was limited to the confirmation of the signature of its plenipotentiaries by certifying its authenticity. But such attitude is no longer justifiable as, further to the emergence of the necessary character of the ratification, the role of the head of the state has been extended in order to encompass the participation in the process aiming at the final formation of the treaty. Consequently, observes Chailley, one should agree that it would be more appropriate to conclude that today International Law sees in the ratification not the act by which the internationally competent organ declares the will of the state, and therefore sufficient in itself to commit the state, but the act of an organ constitutionally competent in forming such a will.

Fourth, Chailley examines critically the arguments put forward by Bittner when the latter refuses to recognize any relevance to the constitutional rules that limit the powers of the head of the state on the pretext that the reservation in respect to the compliance with the constitutional law is rarely mentioned in the full powers, the final clauses of the treaties and the letters of ratification. With regard to the full powers, they generally do not reflect the profound change undergone by the ratification as, having yet a format remnant of the old past as if the mandate theory was still alive, they continue to encompass the reservation in respect to the promise of ratification, while the latter has become a discretionary act. It is amazing in this respect that the full powers continue to encompass the reservation in respect to the promise of ratification, while they keep silent on the reservation in respect to the compliance with constitution law and procedure.[32] Similar remark can be made in respect of the letters of ratification.[33] As for the final clauses of the treaties, if it happens that they do not often encompass the reservation in respect to the obligation to consult the parliament, when the later is required by the Constitution, it is because such clause has become superfluous. Such reservation is in fact tacitly agreed on by the states when they are required under their constitutional law to obtain the approbation of their parliament prior to any ratification.[34]

After having rigorously criticized Bittner's view marked, as we have seen, by enormous erroneous conclusions due to his exegetical and literal approach, Chailley carries out a thorough analysis of states' practice which led him to conclude that " it belongs to domestic law to determine the international

[32] Chailley (1932, p. 193).

[33] Idem, pp. 194–195.

[34] Idem, pp. 195–198.

competence of the authorities in charge of concluding conventions between states in accordance with either complex or simplified procedure, that is treaties strictly speaking or agreements in a simplified form."[35]

The constitutional doctrine has been adopted by many other scholars such as L. Oppenheim,[36] W. Schucking,[37] J. Mervyn Jones,[38] G. Nicolopoulos,[39] P. Freymond,[40] R. Carré de Malberg,[41] etc.

As for the intermediary doctrine, it has been sustained by few authors such as J. Basdevant,[42] Lord Mc Nair[43] and Ph. Cahier.[44] This doctrine aims at reaching a compromise solution by suggesting that the domestic constitutional requirements should be taken into consideration only when these requirements are well known to foreign states or when their violation has been manifest. Ph. Cahier does recognize that the intermediary doctrine is theoretically not satisfactory, but it has the merit to be pragmatic. However, although having the latter character, such doctrine will not exert a palpable impact on states' practice as did the two other opposed doctrines. But this will not prevent it from influencing in a very decisive manner the drafters of the Vienna Convention on the Law of Treaties.

In fact, states' practice provides only few precedents in respect of the issue of the validity of the treaties that are imperfectly ratified, the reason being that the states do generally prefer settling that issue through diplomatic means and channels. Nevertheless, states have occasionally requested international tribunals to settle their disputes on the validity of the treaties that are imperfectly ratified. This has led to the adoption of few jurisprudential decisions,[45] parts of which have been invoked either by the international doctrine or by the constitutional doctrine. After having conducted a fair and thorough analysis of states' practice and international jurisprudence, C. Fairman comes to the conclusion that "municipal limits on competence (to conclude treaties) are not without relevance in International Law."[46] Such conclusion will also be endorsed by the Vienna Convention on the Law of Treaties (VCLT), but only in the event of a manifest violation of municipal law.

Indeed, in the long process of the codification of the law of treaties within the International Law Commission, initially the most largely shared view was the one

---

[35] Idem, p. 215.

[36] Oppenheim (1955).

[37] Schuking (1930, p. 225).

[38] Jones (1946, pp. 150–151).

[39] Nicolopoulos (1942, p. 141).

[40] Freymond (1947, p. 103).

[41] Carre de Malberg (1920, p. 543).

[42] Basvedant (1926V).

[43] Nair (1961, pp. 63 et seq).

[44] Ph. Cahier (1971, p. 231).

[45] On the States' practice and international jurisprudence, see Fairman (1936, pp. 446–461); Wildhaber (1971, pp. 154–167).

[46] Fairman (1936, p. 454).

inspired by the constitutional doctrine. Thus, such a doctrine started by impregnating the reports of the first and the second Special Rapporteurs, that is the 1951 report of M. Brierly[47] and the 1953 report of Sir Hersh Lauterpacht.[48] Then, the third Rapporteur, Sir Gerald Fitzmaurice took the opposite view by giving pre-eminence to the internationalist doctrine.[49] And, finally, the fourth and last Rapporteur, Sir Humphrey Waldock suggested the adoption of a compromise solution inspired by the intermediary doctrine.[50] In his report, Waldock recognizes the validity of a treaty which has been concluded without due consideration to the constitutional requirements as the organ who has expressed the consent of the state is supposed to have acted within the limits of the powers that it apparently possesses in International Law. He believes that such view reflects the state of international practice and jurisprudence and that it would prevent the states from taking pretext of alleged non-compliance with constitutional requirements in order not to implement the treaties they have accepted. After several discussions and amendments at the ILC and during the Vienna Conference, Wadlock's view was finally accepted and incorporated in the VCLR as Art. 46 which reads as follows:

1. A state may not invoke the fact that its consent to be bound by a treaty has been expressed in violation of a provision of its internal law regarding competence to conclude treaties as invalidating its consent unless that violation was manifest and concerned a rule of its internal law of fundamental importance.
2. A violation is manifest if it would be objectively evident to any state conducting itself in the matter in accordance with normal practice and in good faith.

Art. 46 might, due to its vague and ambiguous formulation, generate some serious difficulties at the occasion of its implementation. Amongst these difficulties, there are three which can be mentioned here.

First, it can be asked whether the violation of domestic law should be limited to the rules of procedure related to the competence to conclude treaties or extended also to the rules of substance contained in the Constitution. One can reasonably sustain that the later should also be taken into consideration as it would be inconsistent that the validity of a treaty would be dependent on the compliance with rules of procedure and not with the rules of substance contained in the Constitution and which might be of much greater importance.[51] Besides, Waldock has himself envisaged in his different reports the issue of the rules of substance,[52] while the ILC has never expressed its intent to limit the scope to Art. 46 to procedural rules.

Second, we can ask the following question: what should be meant by "a rule of internal law of fundamental importance"? A reasonable interpretation indicates that

[47] Doc. A/CN.4/41.

[48] But it is true with some nuances, see A/CN 4/63.

[49] YILC, vol. II, 1958, 20.

[50] YILC, 1963, vol. II, 42.

[51] See on this Ph. Cahier, 242.

[52] YILC, 1963, vol. II, 42.

by the latter it should be meant the Constitutions, written or customary ones, as well as any other rules related to the treaty-making power, even when these rules are of ordinary character. Moreover, it is not necessary that such rules should be of a written character, especially when the treaty is related to the cession of part of the national territory. Indeed, in the latter matter, the mandatory obligation to consult the nation either through a referendum or through its representatives is so obvious and natural that it does not need to be expressed in a written manner. The provisions of the very few Constitutions which expressly refer to that obligation seem quite superfluous and redundant. Here in fact, both internal law as well as International Law have the same exigency: the necessary respect of popular sovereignty, that is self-determination. Therefore, the "apparent capacitation theory" by which Waldock does admit that the organ who has expressed the consent of the state is supposed to have acted within the limits of the powers that it "apparently possesses" in International Law, is not applicable to treaties related to the cession of part of the national territory. Indeed, the fact that a head of the state ratifies a treaty of this kind without requesting the prior consent of his people either through a referendum or the approbation of the Parliament is a flagrant and manifest violation of internal as well International Law which does not need any further enquiry about whether a given constitutional law comprises or not a rule requesting such consent. International Law cannot be consistent if it does simultaneously insist on the nullity of a treaty which conflicts with a norm of *jus cogens* (Art. 63–65), knowing that self-determination is one of the most obvious and unquestionable norm of *jus cogens*, and admit that the ratification of a treaty concerning the cession of a territory without the approbation of the people concerned is "within the powers that (the Executive) apparently possesses in International Law". The obvious and legitimate character of such conclusion was recalled by Judge Rezek when he wrote that:

> "I know of no legal order which authorizes a representative of a Government alone definitively to conclude and put into effect, on the basis of his sole authority, a treaty concerning a boundary, whether on land or at sea - and *ergo* the territory - of the state. I ask myself whether there is any part of the world where such a failure to respect the most basic formalities would be compatible with the complex and primordial nature of an international boundary treaty."[53]

Third, it can be asked what type of nullity affects the treaty concluded in violation of domestic law. In principle, such nullity should be of a relative character if one takes into consideration the fact that under Art. 46 the nullity can be invoked by the state whose internal law has been violated.[54] However, when the treaty in question concerns a cession of part of the national territory, the nullity of such treaty cannot by obliterated by the effect of time. In International law, it may sometimes happen that "a relative title grows into absolute title which is valid *erga omnes*"[55]

[53] I.C.J. Reports (2002, p. 491).

[54] See Ph. Cahier, 243.

[55] Schwarzenberger (2005, p. 263).

thanks in particular to the interplay of estoppel or tacit acquiescence. But it is difficult to accept that the estoppel and tacit acquiescence can be of any great relevance when the issue is related to the cession of a territory in violation of domestic law as the state, or more precisely the Executive concerned, cannot alienate a right that it does not possess. A treaty related to territorial cession concluded in violation of domestic law is *ab initio* void and null and such character can be obliterated only by obtaining the consent of the population concerned. It is true that "stability and predictability in the pattern of state behaviour are essential for the promotion of a viable international order,"[56] but stability and predictability of states' behaviour cannot be sustainable if they are based on an infringement of legality, justice and the sacrosanct people's democratic right to self-determination. Although being in favour of the internationalist doctrine, M. Fitzmaurice and O. Elias do recognize that "International Law. . .should not properly be seen to be compounding the hardships that may be caused to such population (i.e. the inhabitants of the territory concerned), while sanctioning the actions of non-representative governments. . .The stability of treaties is a fundamental consideration to be accorded the first importance, but there are other factors to be weighed in the balance, and there are good reasons why treaties involving disposition of territory should be subjected to a stricter procedure in modern international law."[57]

The International Court of Justice missed in 2002 the opportunity to contribute in determining the meaning and scope of Art. 46.The opportunity was given to it in the Case Concerning the Land and Maritime Boundary between Cameroon and Nigeria. One of the issues raised in this case was the validity of an agreement – The Maroua Declaration of 1 June 1975 – which was called into question by Nigeria on the account that it was not ratified by the Supreme Military Council after being signed by the Nigerian Head of State. Cameroon rejected Nigeria's argument and argued inter alia that the later has not shown that the constitution of Nigeria did require the agreement to be ratified by the Supreme Military Council and that, even if there was a violation of the internal law of Nigeria, the alleged violation was not "manifest", and did not concern a rule of internal law of fundamental importance, within the meaning of Art. 46, paragraph 1 of the VCLT. In its judgment, the Court paid no attention to the Nigerian constitutional law and decided in a peremptory manner that the Maroua Declaration was an agreement in a simplified form which did not as such require ratification,[58] that there is no general obligation for states to keep themselves informed of legislative and constitutional developments in other states[59] and that

[56] Sharma (1997, p. 210).

[57] Fitzmaurice and Elias (2005, p. 387).

[58] ICJ Report (2002, para 264).

[59] Idem, p. 266.

a limitation of the Head of the State's capacity to conclude treaties is not manifest in the sense of Art. 46 unless at least publicized.[60]

The conclusion reached by the Court that the Maroua Declaration has to be considered as binding and establishing a legal obligation on Nigeria is certainly valid as, in a constitutional system, such as the one which prevailed in Nigeria in the 1970s, where the Government was made of one block of power insofar as it was difficult to make any distinction in terms of competences, authority and decision-making powers between the Head of the State and the Supreme Military Council and that consequently Nigeria was not entitled to claim that the signing of that Declaration by the former had to be confirmed by the latter. But what is difficult to accept is the demarche adopted by the Court in reaching its decision as it may imply a literal and very strict reading of Art. 46 especially when the contentious issue is of a territorial character. Certainly in a monolithic political system where there is no place for any organ representing the people, a declaration signed by the Head of the State can reasonably be considered as an agreement in a simplified form. But it is doubtful that the Court would have reached a similar conclusion had it been in the presence of a political system where a Parliament represents the whole population and shares with the Executive the treaty-making power in matters including the disposition of national territory.

One can also understand why the Court has given some pre-eminence to Art. 7 paragraph 1 of the VCLT which provides that the Heads of the State are considered to represent their State "in virtue of their functions and without having to produce full powers" and that it has concluded that there was no manifest violation of the Constitution. But the Court would have had serious difficulties in giving such pre-eminence to Art. 7 paragraph 1 to the detriment of Art. 46 had it been confronted to a different constitutional situation where the treaty-making power belongs in common, in specified instances such as the disposal of part of the state's territory, to the Executive and the Legislative organs. In fact, Art. 7 paragraph 1 has not been conceived of as meaning that the Heads of the state do, on their own decision, express the consent of their state to a treaty of a non-simplified form, but to declare that the procedure related to the exercise of the treaty – making power has been completed and that the treaty concerned should be considered as final, otherwise Art. 46 should be seen as superfluous and redundant. With regard to the conclusion of treaties in a non-simplified form, the Head of the state performs two functions: the participation, on one hand, to the formation of a treaty in the same way as the Legislative, and on the other hand, the declaration that such formation has been effectuated.

The Court seems also to be right when it declares that there is no general obligation for states to keep themselves informed of legislative and constitutional developments in other states. However, usually the states keep themselves well informed on the treaty-making power process prevailing in the other states,

[60] Idem, p. 265.

especially those with whom they intend to have a regular and steady relationship. It is then naïve to say that states are not obliged to be familiar with the rules related to the treaty-making power of their partners. For every state, it is crucial to be informed on the scope and limits of the legal capacity of those with whom they intent to commit themselves through a given agreement and the collection of such information is not something difficult to obtain as it belongs to that kind of information which are well publicized.

The Court, which usually does not miss an occasion to elaborate on the right of self-determination, could have taken the opportunity given to it in order to explore the links between that right and the disposal of part of the national territory by the Executive without any prior consultation of the people concerned, either directly through a referendum or through the approbation of the Parliament.

There are then serious legal obstacles which cannot make of the decision in the Bakassi Peninsula case in relation to Art. 46 a dictum applicable to all other circumstances, especially those where the issue at stake is the disposal of part of the national territory. It is true that such disposal is a very sensitive issue and one of the major concerns of the international community is to preserve the stability of the relations between states. However, such stability is difficult to achieve if it is established in a way that gives pre-eminence to short term considerations to the detriment of long term ones and which alone can help establish final and stable solutions, especially in matters related to territory and borders.

3.1.1.3 The Consequence of the Consent of the State to Territorial Changes: The Final and Stable Character of Borders

The principle of the final and stable character of borders should, first, be distinguished from the ideology of the "security in the possession" conceived for the first time by Metternich, not to ensure the "repos" of Europe as he used to proclaim, but because "after having achieved plans meditated for a long time, triumphed over Napoleon and brought France back to its old territorial limits, he managed to sanction in Vienna the most essential views of Austria. Having got, in the sharing out of spoils, magnificent shares, he was aspiring only to keep what has been acquired after much struggles."[61] But the notion of "security in the possession" never became a legal norm for the simple reason that the European boundaries continued to change as in the past and that, later on, the European states, as the rest of the states belonging to the international community, have never accepted, when adhering to the League of Nations Pact or the UN Charter, as we will see later on, that the state of peace established by these two international instruments, was meant to accept the recognition of an unlawful territorial status-quo to the detriment of legitimate territorial claims.

---

[61] Dupuis (1909, p. 153).

When the states want to settle their border disputes, they must settle them by searching for a stable, permanent and final solution. Territorial stability is indeed a fundamental principle of International law which has established that "boundary regimes are to be considered with a maximum degree of continuity and a minimum of change."[62] Sir Jeffrey Jennings has rightfully recalled in this regard that "some other kinds of legal ordering need to be capable of a constant change to meet new needs of a developing society; but in a properly ordered society, territorial boundaries will be among the most stable of all the institutions."[63]

The principle of the final and stable character of borders has been consecrated by international jurisprudence. Hence, the International Court of Justice has shown its full adherence to that principle when it recalled in the Temple of Preah Vihear case that "when two countries establish a frontier between them, one of the primary objects is to achieve stability and finality. This is impossible if the line so established can, at any moment, and on the basis of a continuously available process, be called into question, and its rectification claimed, whenever any inaccuracy by reference to a clause in the parent treaty is discovered. Such a process could continue indefinitely, and finality would never be reached so long as possible errors still remained to be discovered. Such a frontier, so far from being stable, would be completely precarious."[64] The principle of the final and stable character of borders has also been endorsed by the two Vienna Conventions. Thus, the 1969 Convention on the Law of Treaties states in its Article 62 para 2 that: "A fundamental change of circumstances may not be invoked as a ground for terminating or withdrawing from a treaty if (the latter) establishes a boundary." Similarly, the 1978 Convention on Succession to Treaties states in its Article 11 that: "A succession of states does not as such affect: a) a boundary established by treaty; or b) obligations and rights established by a treaty and relating to the regime of a boundary."

In fact, the aforementioned jurisprudence or the two Vienna Conventions do only recall a constant behavior of states who, almost systematically, insist on declaring in the treaties settling their borders disputes or in the arbitrary *compromis* submitting the latter to the international tribunals that the solution they are seeking

---

[62] Kaikobad (1983, p. 136).

[63] Jennings (1963, p. 70).

[64] ICJ Reports, 1962, 34. This is an old jurisprudence (See for previous precedents Cukwurah, 1967, p. 123 cont., of Chapter 1. which has been confirmed by the ICJ in the Aegean Sea Continental Shelf Case, ICJ Reports, 1978, para 85, the Arbitral Tribunal in the Beagle Channel case, ILR, 1978, para 18, by the ICJ again in the Tunisia/Libya case, ICJ Reports, 1982, 18 , 66, the Arbitral Tribunal in the Dubai/Sharjah Boundary case, 91 ILR, 543, 578, and once again by the ICJ in the Territorial Dispute between Libya and Chad in which it has reiterated that "Once agreed, the boundary stands, for any other approach would vitiate the fundamental principle of the stability of boundaries, the importance of which has been repeatedly emphasized by the Court", ICJ Report, 1994, 2 at 38.

should be considered as stable and final.[65] Kaiyan Homi Kaikobad recalls in this respect that: "Generally speaking, States seek to deny to their adjacent entities a continuously available process whereunder they can call into question the status of an alignment settled on the basis of either an express settlement or the operation of a set of legally valid criteria. It is this need which has found expression in the rule of law which, in general terms, is to the effect that a boundary established in accordance with law attains a compelling degree of continuity and finality."[66]

It is worth noting that when the International Law proclaims that the solution of border dispute must be stable and final, it does not talk of any solution be it illegal or invalid but of a solution "where either of the states can establish its legal credentials."[67] The principle of the final and stable borders has a corollary principle which is the principle that boundary disputes are to be settled on the basis of legal titles accepted by International Law.[68] Territorial or borders conflicts materialize in general when at least two titles compete for the recognition of sovereignty over a territory or a portion of territory (i.e. a frontier) in so far as a "territorial or a border conflict is nothing other than a conflict between legal titles."[69] With regard to the notion of title it "relates to both the factual and legal conditions under which a territory is deemed to belong to one particular authority or another. In other words, it refers to the existence of those facts required under International Law to entail legal consequences of a change in the juridical status of a particular territory"[70] The legal settlement of territorial and border disputes lies then on a confrontation between legal titles.

Lastly even the final and stable character of the border may not be perpetual inasmuch as it remains above all the common work of the parties as a result of their consent, expressed either initially within the framework of a judicial process or subsequently within the framework of bilateral negotiation. A.O. Cukwurah stresses in this regard that "but finality in this sense does not convey the same meaning as "in perpetuity". After all, in signing such boundary treaties the parties do not constitute themselves insurers against further disagreement. In fact, one boundary settlement may well lead to a further disagreement. The term "finality", as applied here, rather expresses the consummation of an intention to secure a legal relationship with regard to a common boundary, which is acceptable to both parties ... Stability should follow from such settlement."[71]

---

[65] See the analysis of the principle made by Cukwurah (1967, p. 110 cont., of Chapter 1); Kaikobad (1983, p. 119 cont.); and Lalonde (2002, p. 138 cont).

[66] Kaikobad (1983, p. 119).

[67] K. H. Kaikobad, idem, p. 121.

[68] See Reuter (1975, p. 168).

[69] Distefano (1995, p. 345).

[70] Shaw (1999a, p. 334).

[71] Cukwurah (1967, p. 122) of Chapter 1. See also Abi-Saab (1990, p. 346, 349).

3.1.2 *The Non-consecration of the* **uti possidetis** *as an Exception to the Principle of the Necessary Consent of the State to Territorial Changes*

A number of scholars have blurred the analysis of the *uti possidetis* by mixing up the latter with the principle of territorial integrity and the stable and final character of borders. They have also overestimated its impact on the settlement of border conflicts. Thus the *uti possidetis* was sometimes simply confused with the principle of territorial integrity and the stable and final character of the borders.[72] Likewise, it has also been said that the *uti possidetis* has "largely governed the determination of the size and shape of the states of former Spanish Latin America beginning in the early 1800s..,"[73] that "the principle of *uti possidetis juris* was applied by common consent to their respective territories *by the new independent states* (italics added) that emerged as a result of the demise of the Spanish colonial empire in South and Central America in 1810 and 1821 respectively"[74] or that "it is safe to conclude ... that the principle of *uti possidetis juris* is espoused by the entirety of the African states"[75]or even more that "Implemented in all latitudes and in every era, it (*the uti possidetis*) has a universal scope,"[76] etc.

D. Bardonnet has recognized that "we cannot confuse (the *uti possidetis*) with the principle of intangibility of borders nor with the principle of territorial integrity."[77] However, such confusion between the three principles has never been submitted to a critical analysis. Only one author – J. de Pinto Campinos – has criticized that confusion but in a peremptory manner, while still confusing the principle of the intangibility of borders with the principle of territorial integrity. He writes "We believe that these principles do not merge. The principle of the intangibility of borders or of the integrity of territory is a universal principle which, as corollary of the maintaining of the international peace and security, does concern every state; on the contrary, the principle of *uti possidetis* is a principle which is primarily related to states which emerged from, first the Latino-American and, second Afro-Asiatic decolonization."[78] However, as we may notice, this has not prevented the author from also confusing the principle of intangibility of borders with the principle of territorial integrity.

---

[72] See, for, instance, Borella, (1964); Bedjaoui (1972, p. 95); Benouniche et al. (1973, p. 135); Yakemtchouk (1975, p. 51); Bipoum-Woom (1970, pp. 127–128); Touval (1972, p. 90 and seq). Similar confusion is also made by the I.C.J. See Burkina Fasso-Mali case, ICJ Reports, 1986, 554 at 565 para 22; Case Concerning the Territorial Dispute (Libya-Tchad), ICJ Reports,1994, 6, at 38 para 75.

[73] Ratner (1996, p. 590).

[74] Antonopoulos (1996/I, p. 31).

[75] Idem, p. 35.

[76] Sorel and Mehdi, pp. 13–14.

[77] Bardonnet (1981, p. 35 and seq.).

[78] de Pinto Campinos (1980).

We know that the *uti possidetis* was initially borrowed by some Latin American states from the Roman Law which used to stipulate that, pending the final judicial settlement of a claim related to the possession of an immovable property, the latter will temporarily remain in the possession of one of the parties till the judge decides, on the basis of a confrontation of the legal claims and titles, who is the legitimate owner of that property. However, the borrowing was accompanied by the substitution of a "permanent" status quo to the normal temporarily one.[79] This has been interpreted by some authors as "bestow(ing) an aura of historical legality to the expropriation of the lands of the indigenous peoples."[80]

The Latin American *uti possidetis* formula meant then that the former colonial Spanish administrative limits and the old Spanish-Portuguese border limits would constitute the international boundaries of the new Latin American states. But which former old limits? Here is the major difficulty to which the Latin American states were immediately confronted as very often the old Spanish and Portuguese borders as well the old administrative limits were left undetermined[81] or established in an imprecise manner,[82] or even when they were determined, they did not correspond to the situation prevailing in the two critical dates, 1810 and 1821, fixed by the concerned Latin American states.[83] The fundamental expression of this difficulty was to know what limits should be taken into consideration: the legal limits or the factual ones? or in other words which principle: the uti possidetis juris or the uti possidetis de facto? This difficulty came in fact from the ambiguity which is inherent to the principle and which has durably made of the latter a controversial principle.

The ambiguity which finally makes of the *uti possidetis* a controversial principle is very simple: either the principle of *uti possidetis* means the taking into account of legal titles, and then we are in presence of the situation governed since its earliest stages by the International Law when, as we have seen, two entities, groups or states, accept, within the framework of mutual relationships based on equality in time of peace, to make use of law in order to settle their territorial or boundary disputes, or, on the contrary, the principle of *uti possidetis* means the taking into account of a situation of fact, which may lead to the denial of a legitimate right to territorial claim. Paul de La Pradelle has well reflected the contradictory character of the *uti possidetis* by stressing that "presented.... under the *uti possidetis juris* formula, the American or "colonial" principle is vitiated from its inception. It lies on a contradictory statement: the *uti possidetis* refers to a title not to the possession

[79] See Edouardo Jimenez de Arechaga, pp. 449–450.

[80] Reisman (1995, p. 350).

[81] Ayala (1931, p. 441) has noted in this respect that several controversies had arisen between Spain and Portugal about the delimitation of their respective colonies and that these controversies were still pending when happened the emancipation of these colonies.

[82] The old Spanish administrative limits, recalls P. de la Pradelle (1928, p. 78, note 1), were very often virtual limits reported on rudimentary maps.

[83] See Ayala (1931, p. 443); Guichonnet and Raffestin (1974, p. 130 cont.).

fact. Presented under the *uti possidetis de facto* formula, it is formally a pleonasm and basically mixes up with the principle of occupation."[84]

The inconsistency of the *uti possidetis* has raised serious doubts on the legal character of that principle because it is fundamentally difficult to imagine that a conflict may exist in one and same norm. H. Kelsen has shown that "if a logical contradiction exist between two assertions, only the one or the other assertion can be true; if one is true, the other is false. But a norm is neither true nor false, but either valid or invalid."[85] Surprisingly the inconsistency lying at the core of the principle of uti possidetis has not prevented some international lawyers from sustaining that the uti possidetis has assumed the character of a customary norm sacred,[86] first, within the decolonization context at a regional level by the Latin-American states since the nineteenth century and then by the newly independent African states in the sixties and finally outside the decolonization context by the European States in the beginning of the nineties in their efforts to stabilize the situation created by the dismantlement of Yugoslavia. These lawyers do pretend also that the customary character of the uti possidetis has been confirmed by some international judicial decisions. Serious objections[87] have been made against this attempt to provide a legal and constraining character to a very controversial principle.

In reality the *uti possidetis* has never been sacred as a principle of law by the Latin American states as suggested by some authors.[88] On the contrary, most of the scholars see in it a discredited principle.[89] As any new analysis aiming at substantiating such character may be perceived as a mere redundancy, it would be sufficient to recall the following facts:

---

[84] My translation of "Présenté…sous la formule uti possidetis juris, le principe Américain ou 'colonial' est vicié dans son origine. Il repose sur une affirmation contradictoire: l'uti possidetis renvoie à un titre non au fait de la possession. Présenté…sous la formule uti possidetis de facto, il est dans la forme un pléonasme et se confond pour le fond avec le principe de l'occupation"(de la Pradelle, 1928, pp. 86–87).

[85] Kelsen (1934, p. 205).

[86] See, in addition to the authors mentioned above, Antonopoulos (1996, pp. 34–35); Nesi (1998, p. 9); Kohen (1997, p. 453); Sanchez-Rodriguez (1997); Shaw (1999b, p. 499).

[87] For a critical analysis of the uti possidetis and its alleged customary character, see in particular El Ouali (Dec 1984–Jan 1985, p. 13 and seq); Lalonde (2001, p. 13 and seq; 2002); Delcourt (1998/1, p. 70 and seq.); Corten (1999, p. 430); Klein, idem, p. 323.

[88] Some authors argue in this respect that the uti possidetis has been frequently referred to in treaties and Constitutions as well as in a constant practice of Latin-American states. See, for instance, Sanchez Rodriguez (1997, p. 200). From his part, Kohen (1997) adds jurisprudential precedents.

[89] Waldock (1948, p. 35) has recalled in this respect that: "The doctrine of the uti possidetis has proven to be so indefinite and ambiguous that it has become somewhat discredited as a criterion for settling boundary disputes between Latin American states", B.Y.B.I.L.,1948, 35. Similar remarks were made by de la Pradelle "La frontière", op.cit., 86; Ayala (1931, p. 440 cont.); Roggs (1940, p. 289).

- The Latin American states have **together** initially adopted the principle of *uti possidetis* with the view to simply protest against the occupation of the Falkland islands by England in 1833 by stating that there were no longer any terrae nullius in Latin America.[90]
- The same states have never adopted **together** the *uti possidetis* as a way of settling their boundary disputes.[91]
- Only few Latin American states have incorporated the principle of *uti possidetis* either in their constitutions[92]or in some treaties settling a boundary dispute[93] or in few arbitration *compromis*.[94]
- The same states have ended up abandoning the *uti possidetis* due to its ambiguity.[95]
- Some arbitration tribunals have ended up also by disregarding the *uti possidetis* though the application of the latter was made mandatory by their terms of reference,[96] or by mixing it with equity.[97]
- Not a single arbitration tribunal has ever *proprio motu*, in the silence of the compromis, taken a decision to apply the uti possidetis.[98]

---

[90] See P. de la Pradelle "La frontière", op.cit., 78. See also the Arbitral Award of the Swiss Federal Council about some border questions pending between Columbia and Venezuela, 22 March 1922, Berne, 5 cont.

[91] See Ayala (1931, p. 454).

[92] This was the case of Columbia and Venezuela.

[93] See Nelson (1973, p. 279 cont.).

[94] See P.de la Pradelle "La frontière", op.cit., 77.

[95] Idem, p. 86.

[96] See Fischer (1933, p. 421 cont.); P. de La Pradelle "La frontière", op.cit., p. 85.

[97] Bardonnet (1981, p. 64 cont.).

[98] Marcello G. Kohen does pretend that the ICJ Chamber has, in the El Salvador/Honduras case, decided on its own, in the silence of the *compromis,* to apply the uti possidetis juris ("L'uti possidetis revisité: l'arrêt du 11 Septembre 1992 dans l'affaire El Salvador/Honduras", RGDIP,1993, 958). In fact the two parties have not left the law applicable to their dispute indeterminate. On the contrary, they have requested the Chamber to apply "the rules of International Law applicable between the Parties". Among these rules, there was the uti possidetis juris to which the two parties have at different occasions in the past agreed that it should be applicable to their dispute. Therefore, it is on the basis – i.e. a mutual agreement between the two parties – and not on its own that the Chamber will declare that the uti possidetis juris will applied to the case. The Chamber clearly states in this respect that "Both Parties are agreed that the primary principle to be applied for the determination of the land frontier is the uti possidetis juris; even though this, unusually for case of this kind, is not expressly mentioned in the Article 5 of the Special Agreement (i.e. the *compromis*). For Honduras, the norm of International Law applicable to the dispute is simply the *uti possidetis juris*; El Salvador, relying on the terms of Article 26 of the General Treaty of Peace, strongly contests that this is the sole law applicable, and invokes, as well as the *uti possidetis juris*, what have been variously called "arguments of a human nature" and "effectivités", to be examined further on in this judgment", ICJ Chamber, 1992 Report, para 40. The Chamber could have also mentioned that the two parties have recommended, in their Memorials and counter-Memorials, the application of the uti possidetis to the case. It should be highlighted that the Chamber will not in its final decision limit itself to the sole application of the

- Most of the boundary disputes have been settled in accordance with the relevant principles and rules of International Law and not on the basis of the uti possidetis.[99]
- Most of the borders have been established on the basis of mutual concessions and not in accordance with the uti possidetis.[100]
- Most of the borders have today nothing in common with the administrative territorial limits inherited from the colonization.[101]
- The *uti possidetis* has generated more conflicts than it has settled.[102]
- Lastly, the only one important positive effect the *uti possidetis* has produced was the contribution to the development of arbitration and consequently to the rules related to titles to territories.[103]

With regard to the opinion that African states have clearly endorsed the uti possidetis as a regional legal principle,[104] it is not certain that it is totally exact. It is true that most of the African states seem to have, through the adoption of the Cairo Resolution by the Heads of States and Governments of the O.A.U. in 21 July 1964, recommended the implementation of the *uti possidetis* to boundary disputes. Assuming this resolution is formally obligatory – which in fact is not the case as no O.A.U.

---

uti possidetis juris. Marcello G. Kohen does himself recognize this fact when he notes that "La méthode suivie par la Chambre en vue de délimiter la frontière dans chacun des six secteurs. . .n'a pas été univoque. La Chambre a beau prétendre s'être servie de l'uti *possidetis juris* partout, la réalité est toute autre. Ainsi, pour le premier secteur de la frontière, le principe n'a pas été appliqué du tout. Les fondements de la délimitation fixée par la Chambre se trouvent dans l'acquiescement et dans une combinaison entre un accord non ratifié et la ligne de partage des eaux. Dans le deuxième, troisième, cinquième et sixième secteur l'uti *possidetis juris* fut appliqué, en se servant de preuves diverses, aussi bien antérieures que postérieures a la date de l'indépendance. Il en va de même dans le quatrième secteur, sauf pour une section de la frontière ou l'on applique *l'équité infra legem* en se servant d'un accord non ratifié de 1869, face a l'impossibilité de déterminer "la ligne de l'*uti possidetis juris* de 1821", op.cit., p. 960.

[99] See Ayala (1931, p. 442).

[100] See Guichonnet and Raffestin (1974, p. 134).

[101] See Foucher (1991, p. 195).

[102] See Cukwurah (1967, p. 134) of Chapter 1; Ayala (1931, p. 454).

[103] See the analysis made by Nelson (1973, p. 267 cont.).

[104] Commenting on the 1964 OAU Cairo Resolution (in which the African Heads of States declared that "all member states pledge themselves to respect the frontiers existing on their achievement of national independence") and the practice of the African states, I. Brownlie concludes that these are elements which constitute "a rule of regional customary law binding those states which have unilaterally declared their acceptance of the principle of the *status quo* as at time of independence", "African Boundaries. A legal and Diplomatic Encyclopedia", London, C. Hurst & Company, 1979, 55. Antonopoulos (1996/I, pp. 34–35) even went too far by pretending that "the objections to the 1964 Cairo resolution on the part of Morocco and Somalia have effectively been curbed. Morocco has abandoned her territorial claims against neighbouring states and the holding of a referendum in Western Sahara. Somalia has followed policies of reconciliation with the neighbours. It is safe to conclude, therefore, that the principle of *uti possidetis juris* is espoused by the *entirety* (italics added) of the African states.

organ enjoys a normative power[105] – it still remains that it lies in its substance on a fundamental contradiction. Indeed that Resolution states in particular that:

> "Recalling, besides, that all the member states have taken, in accordance with article VI of the Charter of the Organization of the African Unity, the commitment to scrupulously respect the principles stated in the article III of the said Charter…3. Respect for the sovereignty and territorial integrity of each state and for its inalienable right to independent existence.
>
> 1. Reaffirm solemnly the total respect by all the Member States of the O.A.U of the principles stated in the para 3 of the article III of the Charter of the said Organization.
> 2. Pledge solemnly the respect by all Member States of the borders existing at the time of their accession to independence."

As we can see from this Resolution, the African Heads of States and Governments assert their commitment to the principle of territorial integrity as well as to the respect of the borders existing at the moment of the accession to independence of the African states. But are the two principles compatible? This can be the case if the Resolution aims at adopting the *uti possidetis juris*, but it cannot certainly be the case if the Resolution aims at adopting of the uti possidetis de facto. Indeed, we are in the presence, in the first instance, of a mere tautology in so far as the principle of territorial integrity recognizes that every state has the right to make legitimate territorial claims, while, in the second instance, we are in presence of nothing more than the rejection of that right and the substitution to it of another right that no longer exists in International Law: the right of occupation and acquisition of foreign territories. According to some authors, it was the latter meaning of the principle which has been adopted within the African context.[106] If this is right, the Resolution is then in contradiction with the O.A.U. Charter [107]as well as with International Law as both of them do not accept the occupation as a mode of acquisition of territories belonging to sovereign foreign states.[108] Meanwhile, some lawyers have also claimed that the occupation may correspond to effectiveness, which is a recognized principle of International Law?[109] We know that the latter principle is relevant only in the absence of an objection from the concerned states.[110] Now, an objection has been clearly expressed in our case, either directly by the rejection of the *uti*

[105] See Ndeshyo, Algiers Seminar previously mentioned, 226–227; Borella (1974, p. 239 cont.). It is because knowing the difficulties created by the lack of obligatory character of that Resolution that the experts committee in charge of the draft revision of the Charter of the O.A.U has suggested to add to the Article 3 of the latter a para. 4: "Respect of the boundaries existing at the time of their accession to their national independence". See also Mjad (not dated, p. 92).

[106] Tran Van Minh (p. 335).

[107] One of its declared fundamental principles is to "eliminate all forms of colonialism form Africa" (Article 2 al 1d).

[108] It was so even prior to the adoption of the law of decolonization within the UN Charter framework. See Decenciere-Ferrandiere (1940, p. 295 cont.).

[109] See, for instance, Nabil (p. 14).

[110] See De Visscher (1967, p. 102 and seq). The same author recalls also that "the effectiveness does not alone prevent a state from complying with its international obligations and that an

possidetis de facto.[111] or indirectly due to the inability of the latter to reach the objectives which have been assigned to it: the prevention of territorial conflicts and the building of the nation-state. With regard to the incapacity to prevent territorial conflicts, it has been noted that since 1960 Africa has witnessed the outbreak of 34 territorial conflicts and that of all the territorial disputes brought before the International Court of Justice, 57% were African, and that many disputes never reached stages of peaceful international settlement.[112] As to the failure of the nation-building process, it is now also well established that in Africa, as noted by Randall Baker, a "whole slate of states that have no legitimacy among their own people, whose identity is, instead, to some older, ethnic or cultural tradition *within* the new state or – worse still – across its boundaries, and becomes, therefore, a challenge to the persistence of the empty shell of the 'nation'."[113] However, despite the objection made to the uti possidetis by some states, it has been argued that that principle "has prevailed in conflicts where a party rejected it : the weight of the political will of a great number of states has got the upper hand. Those, who objected to it. . .have bowed before a continental attitude, a kind of holy alliance, hostile to any objection. . ."[114]

In Asia, the whole continent has not also endorsed the *uti possidetis* or given any particular attention to it in so far as the Asian states, having no particular approach to boundary issues,[115] prefer to settle the latter in accordance with the traditional principle and rules of International Law.[116]

Some lawyers are of the opinion that Europe contributed in the past decade to the application of the *uti possidetis* beyond the colonial context and by doing so has made of it a universal principle.[117] They refer in this regard to the European County's contribution to the settlement of the territorial and borders problems created by the dismemberment of Yugoslavia.

First, it is worth recalling that Europe has never endorsed the *uti possidetis*. Europe or precisely Western Europe has been the source of modern International Law and has never expressed any desire or willingness to change or amend the

---

internationally illicit act cannot be considered as a valid title in International Law, idem, pp. 24–25.

[111] From the origin, Morocco and Somalia, but also later on Kenya (see Benouniche 1967, p. 112). Tanzania and Malawi (see Elliot (p. 202, note 24)), by Togo (see Jouve (p. 405), etc.).

[112] Englebert et al. (2002, p. 110). See also the inventory (which include at least 32 cases at the time of its publication) made by Waters (1969, p. 189 cont.). See also in the same publication Zartman (p. 89 cont.); Bouvier (1972, p. 695 cont.). According to J. Castellino and Allen (2003, p. 26).

[113] Baker (2000, p. 7).

[114] Benouniche (p. 115). See also Boujori-Flecher (1981, p. 811 cont.); Person (1977, p. 197 cont.).

[115] See Dutheil de La Rochère (p. 135).

[116] See the analysis of Guichonnet and Raffestin (1974, p. 134 cont.). Peremptory are in this regard the statements according to which the Asian states have also adopted the principle of uti possidetis. Examples of such statements, can be found in Tran Van Minh (p. 63); Pinho Campinas (p. 98); Antonopoulos (1996/I, p. 35).

[117] See, for instance, Shaw (1996, p. 496 cont.); Nesi (1998). For an opposite opinion, See Craven (1995, p. 389); Lalonde (2002, p. 172 cont.).

content of that International Law when dealing with territorial or boundary matters. Furthermore, most of Western Europe borders are stable and in the past decades no major territorial or boundary conflicts have taken place between the Western European states that would have led these states to revisit the issue. On the contrary, the few and minor disputes which have appeared, have been solved through negotiation or judicial process in accordance with the traditional rules and principles related to territorial claims.

Therefore, the decision of the European Community to recommend that the international borders of the Republics which emerged as a result of the disintegration of Yugoslavia should be the latter's old administrative internal limits, was not dictated by the necessity to abide by a legal obligation – embodied in the so-called principle of the *uti possidetis* – but by a mere political motivation aiming at making an end to a chaotic situation. The European Community has in order to achieve that objective convened on 27 August 1991 an International Conference on Peace for Yugoslavia within the framework of which an Arbitration Commission (called also Badinter Commission) was created and whose opinions were to be delivered in a consultative capacity.[118] The Arbitration Commission issued fifteen opinions including the famous opinion No 3 which stated that:

> "Except where otherwise agreed, the former boundaries become frontiers protected by International Law. This conclusion follows from the principle of respect for the territorial status quo and in particular, from the principle of *uti possidetis*. *Uti possidetis*, though initially applied in settling decolonization issues in America and Africa, is today recognized as a general principle, as stated by the International Court of Justice in its Judgment of 22 December 1986 in the case between *Burkina Faso* and *Mali* (*Frontier Dispute*, ICJ Reports 1986, 554 at 565) which states that: "Nevertheless, the principle is not a special rule which pertains solely to one specific system of International law. It is a general principle, which is logically connected with the phenomenon of the obtaining independence, wherever it occurs. Its obvious purpose is to prevent the independence and stability of new states being endangered by fratricidal struggles."[119]

The above application of the *uti possidetis* by the Arbitral Commission has been severely criticized. First, for applying that principle in a preemptive manner, that is, before the emergence of the new states and by doing so interfering in the internal affairs of the Socialist Federal Republic of Yugoslavia(SFRY) which was then still a recognized state by the international community. "Indeed", writes S. Lalonde, "as applied by the Badinter Commission, the uti possidetis principle is far from neutral. It ultimately legitimized certain secessionist endeavors (Slovenia, Croatia) while branding others as illegitimate (Serbs entities within Croatia and Bosnia-Herzegovina)."[120] She adds also that "An interpretation that provides for the application of an international legal principle such as uti possidetis juris to the internal borders of an existing sovereign state is clearly contrary to the founding

[118] See Craven (1995, p. 334).

[119] ILR 1993, 172.

[120] Lalonde (2002, pp. 193–94).

principle of modern international legal order as guaranteed by Article 2 of the United Nations Charter-namely, the principle of respect for the sovereignty and territorial integrity of states as well as the principle of non-intervention in the internal affairs of states."[121] Second, the Arbitral Commission has been blamed for intentionally refraining from reproducing the entire sentence of the Chamber in the aforementioned quotation and then omitting the last words of it which read that "Its obvious purpose is to prevent the independence and stability of new states being endangered by fratricidal struggles once the administrating powers have withdrawn" and which shows that the ICJ was of the opinion that the *uti possidetis* is related to the colonial context and as such cannot be limited to the Latin American continent.[122] Third, it can be added that the Arbitral Commission does base itself on very controversial judicial decisions, as we can see hereafter.

Finally, the proponents of the idea that the *uti possidetis* has acquired a customary character do refer to some international judicial decisions which allegedly would have confirmed that character.[123] Amongst these judicial decisions, the most frequently cited is the Frontier Dispute in which, though the Parties have agreed that their case should be adjudicated on the basis of the "intangibility principle" (i.e. the *uti possidetis* in the African vocabulary), the ICJ Chamber finds it advisable to elaborate on the *uti possidetis* in a visible effort to sustain its general customary character. Besides, the Chamber recognizes that by stating that "Although, there is no need, for the purpose of the present case, to show that this (that is uti possidetis) is a firmly established principle of International Law where decolonization is concerned, the Chamber nonetheless wishes to emphasize its general scope, in view of its exceptional importance for the African continent and for the Parties."[124] And then, after a debatable analysis, the Chamber came to the conclusion that "The fact that the new African states have respected the administrative boundaries and frontiers established by the colonial powers must be seen not as mere practice contributing to the gradual emergence of a principle of customary International Law, limited in its impact to the African continent as it had previously been to Spanish America, but as the application in Africa of a rule of general scope."[125] Assuming that the Chamber was able to establish that the African states have felt compelled to commit themselves by the *uti possidetis*, it remains, as we

[121] Idem, p. 190. Similar criticisms have been made by other authors. See, for instance, Antonopoulos (1996/I, pp. 83–84); Hannun (1993, p. 52); Levrat (1999, pp. 336–337).

[122] See Lalonde (2002, p. 190).

[123] They refer generally to the following cases: Dubai-Sharjah Border Arbitration, award of 19 October 1981, I.L.R., vol. 91, 544; Guinea-Guinea Bissau Maritime Delimitation Arbitration, Award of 14 February 1985, vol. 77, 635; Frontier Dispute (Burkina Faso/Republic of Mali), ICJ Chamber, ICJ Reports 1986, 554; Guinea Bissau v Senegal case, Award of 31 1989, I.L.R., vol. 83, 35; Land, Island, and Maritime Frontier Dispute (El Salvador/Honduras), ICJ Chamber, ICJ Reports 1992; Libya/Chad case, ICJ Reports 1994, 83.

[124] ICJ Reports 1986, 565.

[125] Idem, p. 566.

have seen earlier, that the meaning given to the latter in the African context is completely different from the one which prevailed in Latin America. We know that in the latter context, the *uti possidetis* assumed a de jure character, which meant that any boundary settlement has to be based on legal titles. On the contrary, in Africa, it was decided that the borders should be the facto borders existing at the time of the independence. There are then some "difficulties" with the Chamber interpretation or assimilation of the African situation to the Latin American one as there is a "critical difference between the African (de facto) *status quo* and the Latin American *uti possidetis juris* principle".[126] Besides, the interpretation given to the uti possidetis by the Chamber is inconsistent with the one given by the ICJ itself in the El Salvador/Honduras as the former states that "the principle of *uti possidetis* freezes the territorial title: it stops the clock but does not put back the hands,"[127] while the latter does rightfully recognize that the *uti possidetis* was "essentially a retrospective principle, investing as international boundaries administrative limits intended originally for quite other purposes."[128] In any case, it remains difficult to accept the allegations made by the Chamber that there is an uniform, constant and general practice with regard to the delimitation of the boundaries in Latin America as well in Africa and which could lead to the conclusion that the *uti possidetis* has assumed a regional or universal character.[129]

Anyhow and regardless of the opinion we may have on the legal character of the *uti possidetis* and its relevancy in settling boundary disputes, the most important conclusion to be drawn here is that the *uti possidetis* cannot be confused with the principle of territorial integrity as it is only a way among others to settle territorial and boundary disputes[130] – a way which does give precedence to legal titles when it is of de jure character or a way which does disregard the same titles when it is of a de facto character – while territorial integrity has a much broader sense and scope or more precisely is of a completely different nature as it reflects the sovereign existence of the states within territories the borders of which are recognized by International Law.

The problem with the *uti possidetis*, as noted by R. Higgins, is that it has come to "mean all things to all men."[131] That is why, the uti possidetis is sometimes confused with other principles such as the principle of territorial integrity. This cannot be accepted as "*uti possidetis* is *uti possidetis* and territorial integrity is territorial integrity. *Uti possidetis* is the principle…whereby states become independent within the colonial boundaries, forfeiting any historical claims they might aspire to regarding territories now held within the old colonial boundaries of others.

[126] Lalonde (2001, p. 81).

[127] ICJ Reports 1986, 568.

[128] ICJ Reports 1992, 388.

[129] See the very comprehensive and enlightening analysis made by Lalonde (2002, p. 20 cont.).

[130] It is, stresses Cukwurah (1967, p. 190), only a method of delimitation.

[131] Higgins (p. 34).

Territorial integrity, quite simply, is what is required by Article 2(4) of the Charter-that no force be used against the territory of an independent state, whether by bombardment, incursion or occupation. *Uti Possidetis* is to do with parallel moments of decolonization; territorial integrity is a basic Charter principle applicable to all states."[132]

Being distinct from the principle of territorial integrity, the *uti possidetis* cannot neither be used in a way to contravene to the principle of territorial integrity which is, as shown above, a founding principle from which derive most of the principles of International Law amongst which the principle which states that territorial and boundary claims should be based on legal titles and that any settlement of territorial and boundary disputes requires the agreement of the concerned states. Law and equity between peoples require, therefore, that in situations where the *uti possidetis* assumes a de facto character, the implementation of the latter be subjected to the agreement of the concerned states. The fixing of borders through the mutual agreement of the concerned states is a sacrosanct international norm. It is also dictated by the need to establish permanent and durable peace between states. Yet, peace may sometimes require overpassing the express will of the states. The wisest solution should then be to find a balance between law, equity and peace. Unfortunately, the international community has not so far been able to find that balance by establishing objective criteria which could lead to it. But, this is not a surprise as International Law provides only a limited protection to states' territory.

3.2 The Limited Protection of State's Territory

As a primitive law, International Law leaves to the states themselves to protect their territorial integrity. All efforts aiming at redressing such situation, by establishing an international guarantee to territorial integrity, have so far failed. The only significant progress witnessed in the past decades has been to prohibit unlawful territorial changes. However, the sanction to the breach of that prohibition is limited to the non-recognition of territorial changes made through force.

3.2.1 The Lack of an International Guarantee to Territorial Integrity

Woodrow Wilson, the American President, has at the beginning of the First World War thought of establishing an international system by which states' territorial integrity would be guaranteed. In autumn 1914, he was of the opinion that "all nations must be absorbed into some great association of nations whereby all shall

[132] Idem.

guarantee the integrity of each so that any one nation violating the agreement between all of them shall bring punishment on itself automatically."[133] Such a system was initially limited to the preservation of peace in the Americas. It appeared, first, in the Revised Plan of the Pan-American Pact where it was said that "The high contracting parties to this solemn Covenant and agreement hereby join one another in a common and mutual guarantee of territorial integrity and political independence under republican forms of government."[134] But the system of collective guarantee of territorial integrity was also meant to serve later on as a model for the European nations[135] and then to the whole world. President Wilson was clear on this when he declared on 27 May 1916 that:

> "We believe these fundamental things: First, that every people has a right to choose the sovereignty under which they shall live...Second, that the small states of the world have a right to enjoy the same respect for their sovereignty and their territorial integrity that great and powerful nations expect and insist upon. And, third, that the world has a right to be free from every disturbance of its peace that has its origin in aggression and disregard of the rights of people and nations...
>
> If it should ever be our privilege to suggest or initiate a movement for peace among the nations now at war, I am sure that the people of the United States would wish their Governments to move along these lines...A universal association of the nations to maintain the inviolate security of the highway of the seas for common and unhindered use of all the nations of the world, and to prevent any war begun either contrary to treaty covenants or without warning and full submission of the causes of the opinion of the world – a virtual guarantee of territorial integrity and political independence."[136]

We know that the entrance of the United States into World War I in the spring of 1917 led to the interruption of the negotiations aiming at establishing a common system of cooperation between North and South America. But this has encouraged President Wilson to pursue his objective of providing the whole world with a system of collective guarantee of territorial integrity. However, while the great ambition of President Wilson was to make an end to wars of conquest and establish an international order allowing for sanctions of any violation of territorial integrity,[137] major European countries were planning on the distribution of enemy territories in the event of victory. Secret treaties, signed by the Allies in the years 1915–1917, made plans for future annexations by envisaging the partition of the Ottoman Empire between Russia, Great Britain, France and Italy, and initiating vast accessions to independence of territories and transferring millions of foreigners to the rule of Italy, Romania, Japan, France, and Russia at the expense of the Austro-Hungarian and German Empires.[138] Meanwhile, a new situation has been created in 1917 as a result of the Russian revolution which proclaimed its full adherence to the

[133] Quoted by Charles (1928, p. 237).

[134] Idem, vol. I, p. 239.

[135] See Seymour (1928, pp. 214–215).

[136] Address before the American League to Enforce Peace.

[137] See Stevenson (1988, p. 171).

[138] See Koran (1996, p. 135).

right of self-determination and its firm condemnation of annexation. This appeared clearly in the announcement made on 10 April 1917 by the Russian provisional Government where it is said that "Free Russia does not aim at dominating other nations, at depriving them of their national patrimony, or at occupying by force foreign territories. . .Its object is to establish a durable peace on the basis of the rights of nations to decide their own destiny."[139] This appeared even more clearly in the "Decree on Peace" adopted by Lenin a day after the victory of the Bolshevik Revolution on 7 November 1917, and where a call was made for "an immediate peace without annexations" and condemnation was made of "any incorporation into a large or powerful state of a small or weak people without the precise, clear an voluntarily expressed concurrence and desire of that people."[140]

The new situation created by the adherence of Russia to self-determination and its condemnation of the wars of conquest strengthened further President Wilson's own stand in favour of these principles. In a speech made on 11 February 1918, President Wilson made it clear that:

> "There shall be no annexations, no contributions, no punitive damages. Peoples are not to be handed about from one sovereignty to another by an international conference or an understanding between rivals and antagonists.
>
> National aspirations must be respected: peoples may now be dominated and governed only by their consent.
>
> Peoples and provinces are not to be bartered about from sovereignty to sovereignty as if they were mere chattels and pawns in a game, even the great, now for ever discredited, of the Balance of Powers; but that every territorial settlement involved in this war must be made in the interest and for the benefit of the populations concerned, and not as part of any mere adjustment or compromise of claims amongst rival states."[141]

The new situation created by the Russian Revolution strengthened also President Wilson stand in favour of establishing an international system meant to guarantee states' territorial integrity. One can understand President Wilson discontent when the British government shared with him in May 1918 their own draft for the creation of a league of nations in which there was no mention of the collective guarantee of territorial integrity, which formed the core of his own conception of the League. "It is surprising – notes F.S.Northedge- that the British authorities, who were willing to satisfy practically all Wilson's other wishes in the matter of the League, should evidently not have foreseen his objections to any proposals which left out his own important requirement, the mutual exchange of territorial guarantees. After all, he had made it well known."[142] In fact, the British government has never liked the idea of establishing a collective system guaranteeing territorial integrity of all states as the major objective of Great Britain, the then greatest world power, was to protect its empire which was expected to increase with the peace settlement

---

[139] See Temperley (1920, p. 183).

[140] The document is published in Kennan (1960, p. 117).

[141] See text in Temperley (1920, pp. 437–439).

[142] Northedge (1986, p. 30).

and not to take any commitment with the view of guaranteeing territorial integrity of the many new states which were likely to come into existence as a result of war settlement. We understand also why President Wilson has again stressed on 8 July 1918 in his famous Fourteen Points not only the importance of self-determination but also that "A general association of nations must be formed under specific covenants for the purpose of affording mutual guarantees of political independence and territorial integrity to great and small states alike" (the last Point).

At the time when President Wilson made his speech of 8 July 1918, several drafts for the creation of a League of Nations were being prepared by major Allied governments, but the American draft was alone to insist on the need of establishing an international system meant to guarantee territorial integrity. A sketch of the first American draft was made on 16 July 1918 by Colonel E.M. House, close collaborator of President Wilson. Inspired by the Fourteen Points, Colonel House suggested a global system aiming at establishing a compromise between the preservation of territorial integrity and any future peaceful territorial changes which might be dictated by the implementation of self-determination. This system consisted in the following:

> "The Contracting Powers unite in several guarantees to each other of their territorial integrity and political independence subject, however, to such territorial modifications, if any, as may become necessary in the future by reason of changes in present racial conditions and aspirations, pursuant to the principle of self-determination, and as shall also be regarded by three fourth Delegates as necessary and proper for the welfare of the peoples concerned, recognizing also that all territorial changes involve equitable compensation and that the peace of the world is superior in importance and interest to question of boundary"(No. 20 of the draft).[143]

In a letter by which he transmitted his draft to President Wilson, Colonel House justified the need for having a flexible system meant to guarantee territorial integrity by saying that

> "No. 20 was written with the thought that it would not do to have territorial guarantees inflexible. It is quite conceivable that conditions might so change in the course of time as to make it a serious hardship for certain portions of one nation to continue under the government of that nation".[144]

Upon his arrival in Paris on December 1918 to attend the Peace Conference, President Wilson revised his draft for the establishment of the League of Nations, but kept unchanged the section related to the international guaranty of territorial integrity despite the recommendation made by David Hunter Miller, the US legal advisor, to delete the provisions related to possible peaceful territorial changes as such general provisions will, in his view, make "dissatisfaction permanent, will compel every Power to engage in propaganda and will legalize irredentist agitation in at least all of the Eastern Europe."[145] At that time, Secretary of State, Robert L. Lansing was also against the incorporation in the Covenant of a provision on an international guarantee

[143] See Miller (1928, p. 10).

[144] Idem, vol. I, p. 14.

[145] Idem, vol. II, p. 71.

to territorial integrity as such guarantee would be in contrast to American interests and to the Monroe Doctrine and that it would be most likely rejected by the Senate. His preference went to "negative guarantee" or "self-denying covenant" whereby the states take the commitment not to violate each other's territory, instead of an affirmative or positive guarantee which would oblige the states to wage war in order to protect other states.[146] But his opinion was neglected by President Wilson.

At the time when the American delegation was finalizing its drat, the British delegation was also expanding and fine tuning its own draft. More elaborated on many aspects than the American one,[147] the British draft endorsed President Wilson's idea with regard to the establishment of an international guaranty of territorial integrity. More importantly, it was also from that time that the two delegations worked together in order to amalgamate their two drafts. This initially led on 27 January 1919 to the Cecil-Miller draft which reflected an agreement on several substantial issues amongst which the guarantee of territory integrity. With regard to the latter, Article III of the Cecil-Miller draft stipulated that:

> "The High Contracting Powers undertake to respect and preserve as against external aggression the territorial integrity and existing political independence of all States members of the League.
>
> If at any time it should appear that any feature of the settlement made by this covenant and by the present treaties of peace no longer conforms to the requirements of the situation, the League shall take the matter under consideration and may recommend to the parties any modification which it may think necessary. If such recommendation is not accepted by the parties affected, the states, members of the League, shall cease to be under any obligation in respect of the subject matter of such recommendation.
>
> In considering any modification the League shall take into account changes in the present conditions and aspirations of peoples or present social and political relations, pursuant to the principle, which the High Contracting Powers accept without reservation, that governments derive their just powers from the consent of the governed."

As the American and British delegations were not able to reconcile all their divergences through the Cecil-Miller draft, another attempt was made in order to bridge the gap. This was achieved through the Hurst-Miller draft which was finalized on 2 February 1919 and will be the basis of discussion for the Peace Conference. However, the agreed draft was established to the detriment of Article III related to the international guarantee of territorial integrity which has been amputated from its second and third paragraphs which were meant to deal with future territorial readjustments that can be dictated by changing situations and the need to take into consideration the aspirations of peoples. The rationale behind the decision to omit these two paragraphs was to avoid antagonizing the states which acquired large new territories and were therefore not willing to accept any future territorial changes. The decision was also

[146] He suggested in this respect the following provision: "Each power signatory or adherent hereto severally covenants and guarantees that it will not violate the territorial integrity or impair the political independence of any other power signatory or adherent to this convention except when authorized so to do by a decree of the arbitral tribunal hereinafter referred to or by a three-fourths vote of the International Council of the League of Nations created by this convention" (Lansing 1921, p. 53).

[147] See the comparative analysis made by Morley (1932, pp. 31–76).

motivated by the need to prevent undesired implementation of self-determination. Commenting on the adoption of this decision, Robert Lansing, the then Secretary of States, wrote that:

> "It was generally believed that the elimination of the modifying clause from the President's original form of guaranty was chiefly due to the opposition of the statesmen who represented the British Empire in contradistinction to those who represented the self-governing British Dominions. It was also believed that this opposition was caused by unwillingness on their part to recognize or to apply as a right the principle of "self-determination" in arranging possible future changes of sovereignty over territories."[148]

Thus, truncated, Article III became Article VII in the Hurst-Miller draft. It was submitted as such to the Commission on the League of Nations which was nominated by the Peace Conference on 25 January in order to adopt the Covenant.

The Commission held its first meeting on 3 February 1919, but it was on 6 February that it started to discuss for adoption Article VII which will become the famous Article X. During the discussion, two amendments were suggested by the British delegation. The first amendment requested the omission of the expression "and preserve as against external aggression", while the second amendment suggested to add a paragraph related to treaties revision and which reads as follows:

> "Subject, however, to provision being made by the Body of Delegates (Assembly) for the periodic revision of treaties which have become obsolete and of international conditions the continuance of which may endanger the peace of the world"

But the two British amendments were not accepted due to the firm opposition shown by President Wilson. However, the latter did suggest in a conciliatory move a separate article where it was said that:

> "It shall be the right of the Body of Delegates (Assembly) from time to time to advise the reconsideration by the States, members of the League, of treaties which have become inapplicable, and of international conditions, the continuance of which may endanger the peace of the world."

The separate article, hence suggested by President Wilson, which endorsed the British amendment but reduced its importance by limiting the role of the Assembly to a strictly advisory role as to the reconsideration by the states themselves of treaties which have become inapplicable, will, after slight amendments, become Article 19 which reads as follows:

> "The Assembly may from time to time advise the reconsideration by the Members of the League of Treaties which have become inapplicable, and the consideration of international conditions whose continuance might endanger the peace of the world."

Lastly, on the suggestion of President Wilson, the Commission agreed to add the following sentence to Article 10:

> "In case of any such aggression the Executive Council shall advise the plan and the means by which this obligation shall be fulfilled."

---

[148] Lansing (1921, pp. 94–95).

While this addition was felt by President Wilson as merely clarifying the operation of the guarantee, it seriously conditioned the effectiveness of the guarantee "if not completely nullified"[149] it due to the fact that the Council could only "advise" and not "prescribe" and that it could act only with unanimity.[150] The irony is that Article 10 will be the main factor behind the refusal of the United States Senate to approve the ratification of the Covenant and permit the United States membership in the League of Nations. Indeed whatever President Wilson tried to do in order to convince the American Senate that Article 10 did not provide for stringent obligations and commitments for the United States of America,[151] the challenge was too high as it was deeply felt in many sectors of the American society that "Wilson's handiwork would overturn his country's traditional policy of isolation from international power politics outside the Western Hemisphere, and would commit the United States to maintain peace and order throughout the world. Any proposal such as this (i.e. Article 10) was sure to stir up opposition."[152]

However, the opposition to Article 10 developed not only in the United States, but also within the League of Nations after the latter had come to existence.

[149] Eagerton (1979, p. 132).

[150] In his commentary on this article, Sir Frederick Pollock clarifies that "Many Americans are afraid of the United States being compelled under this Article to do police work in Europe or Asia which may be foreign to American interests. They forget that the United States has a permanent place and voice in the Council, that nothing can be done without the unanimous advice of the Council, and that even then the Council has no compulsory power", "The League of Nations", London, Stevens and Sons limited, 1922, 134.

[151] President Wilson has, all along the exhausting campaign during which he had to fight for the ratification of the Covenant, tried to convince the Americans that Article 10 is made of a mere moral obligation and that it does not infringe on the Senate traditional competence to authorize war. His thinking is well summarized in his speech of 19 August 1919 to the members of the Foreign Relations Committee of the Senate in which he said in particular that: Article 10 is in no respect of doubtful meaning when read in the light of the Covenant as a whole. The Council of the League can only "advice upon" the means by which the obligations of the great Article are to be given effect to. Unless the United States is party to the policy or action in question, her own affirmative vote in the Council is necessary before any advice can be given, for a unanimous vote of the Council is required. If she is a party, the trouble is hers anyhow. And the unanimous vote of the Council is only advice in any case. Each Government is free to reject it if it pleases.

Nothing could have been made more clear to the Conference than the right of our Congress under our Constitution to exercise its independent judgment in all matters of peace and war. No attempt was made to question or limit that right. The United States will, indeed, undertake under Article 10 to 'respect and preserve as against external aggression the territorial integrity and existing political independence of all members of the League', and that engagement constitutes a very grave and solemn moral obligation. But it is a moral, not a legal , obligation, and leaves our Congress absolutely free to put its own interpretation upon it in all cases that call for action. It is binding in conscience only, not in law.

Article 10 seems to me to constitute the very backbone of the whole Covenant. Without it the League would be hardly more than an influential debating society. Senate Document No 76, 66th Congress, 1st Session.

[152] Cooper (2001, p. 11).

The leading actor in this was Canada which on 4 December 1920 requested the Assembly of the League of Nations to decide that "Article 10 of the Covenant of the League of Nations be and is hereby struck out." The main concern of the Canadians was that Article 10 might drag Canada into European's wars and that its hard-won autonomy as British Dominion might be affected. Moreover, Article 10 was perceived as an ambiguous article due to the lack of consistency between its French and English versions. Hence, while the English version stipulated that members of the League undertake to "preserve as against external aggression," the French version talked of "maintenir contre toute aggression extérieure", which is more energetic. Likewise, while the English version did say that "the Council shall advise upon the means," the French version provided that "le Conseil avise aux moyens", which means, in the first case, that the Council does only recommend while in the second it does decide.

Canada's request to strike out Article 10 has raised a long controversy which lasted about 4 years.[153] It will end up by a further weakening of Article 10. With regard to the issue of collective security, the League of Nations was divided between "maximalists" and "minimalists,"[154] that is between those, such as France, China, Persia and the newly created states in Central and Eastern Europe, who were in favour of an international guarantee to territorial integrity and those, such as Great Britain, the British dominions and the Nordic States, who were opposed to any kind of international protection. But as most of the member states of the League were maximalists, the idea of omitting Article 10 was rejected in favour of the adoption by the Assembly of an interpretative resolution somehow echoing a fallback position of Canada when it realized that it could not defeat that article. However, submitted on 25 September 1923 to the Assembly for adoption, the latter resolution was not adopted although it was voted by 29 votes against one vote and this in grounds of the unanimity rule. However, this has not prevented Canada from concluding that the interpretative resolution has been adopted by the Assembly using the arguments of Henri Rolin, the rapporteur for the First Committee, who declared that "Once an interpretation has been accepted unanimously, or by a large majority of delegates as being the sense in which we, in all good faith, read the Articles of the Covenant, it is certain that Canada will no longer have reason to fear any discussion on the subject, either in Canada or abroad. If this article were ever to be put into execution, Canada would, without fear of danger, be right in complying with the interpretation which we give today."[155] At any rate, whatever perception one can have on the effective endorsement or not by the Assembly of the suggested interpretative resolution, it remains that following the Assembly vote (unanimity minus one vote) the legal authority of Article 10 "could

[153] On this controversy, see Eastman (1946, pp. 59–68). Veatch (1975, pp. 72–90).

[154] The expressions "maximalists" and "minimalists" have used by Rappard (1940, p. 217) to describe the situation then prevailing within the League in his book "The Quest for Peace".

[155] League of Nations (24 September 1923, p. 76).

of course no longer be regarded as intact."[156] The interpretative resolution reads as follows:

1. It is in conformity with the spirit of Article 10 that in the event of the Council considering it to be its duty to recommend the application of military measures in consequence of an aggression, or danger or threat of aggression, the Council shall be bound to take account, more particularly, of the geographical situation and of the special situation of each state.
2. It is for the constitutional authorities of each Member to decide, in reference to the obligation of preserving the independence and the integrity of the territory of the Members, in what degree the Member is bound to assure the execution of this obligation by employment of its military forces.
3. The recommendation made by the Council shall be regarded as being of the highest importance and shall be taken into consideration by all the Members of the League with the desire to execute their engagement in good faith.

As it can be noted from the above, the interpretative text introduced two new elements in the reading of Article 10. The first one and by far the most important was that members of the League are under no obligation to engage in any act of war without the consent of their Parliaments. Such interpretation was in total opposition with the opinion of those states "who felt the need of immediate, certain, and quasi-automatic sanctions to prevent foreign invasion."[157] Instead, with the new interpretation, it was left to the members of the League to freely determine the limits and the conditions of their obligations and the manner in which these were to be carried out. As noted by R. Veatch, "the intent of the interpretation was clearly to emphasize the absence of any obligation on the part of League members to follow Council recommendations."[158] The second element was that the Council should in its recommendation take into consideration geographical and political conditions prevailing in each state, which fact meant that the Council was not free to take whatever recommendation it wanted to make.

Weakened by the absence of the United States from the League and by its restrictive and ambiguous interpretation by the Assembly, Article 10 missed also what law needs most: legitimacy. President Wilson' design of punishing violations of territorial integrity was certainly a great and unprecedented design.[159] But establishing an international system of guarantee to territorial integrity supposes that the territorial distribution and delimitations between states are just and fair. Now, legitimacy was missing from the beginning when it was clear that "they (the victorious powers) distributed those confiscated possessions among themselves, substantially in accordance with the pattern which they had agreed upon in secret treaties during the war and with the realities of military occupation which prevailed at the end of the war; they gave to the League the shadow of supervisory authority

[156] Rappard (1940, p. 219).

[157] Eastman (1946, pp. 66–67).

[158] Veatch (1975, pp. 85–86).

[159] See Stevenson (1988, p. 171).

over their administration of the newly-acquired colonies while retaining for themselves the substance of sovereign control; they ostensibly became agents of the League, albeit self-appointed agents, but in fact they created the League as an instrument of their purposes and, in particular, designed it to serve as an agency bestowing ideological legitimacy upon their colonial conquests."[160] Thus, while the victorious states have seen in Article 10 a means to keep the status quo, the vanquished have seen in it an illegitimate instrument meant to prevent them from claiming sovereignty over their lost territories.[161] As highlighted by John Foster Dulles, those nations which dominated the League conceived the league primarily as an instrumentality for perpetuating the status quo. They conceived of peace as the avoidance of all change and branded those seeking territorial changes as potential aggressors.[162]

Lastly, Article 10 was also weakened by the League's failure to halt the annexation of Manchuria by Japan in 1931–1933 and of Abyssinia by Italy in 1936. Such two annexations were a fatal blow to the Covenant and the whole idea of collective guarantee to territorial integrity.[163] It is not therefore a surprise that no suggestion has been made to incorporate in the UN Charter a provision related to a collective guarantee of territorial integrity. What we find in the Charter is simply a "negative guarantee" similar to the one which has been suggested by R. Lansing instead of the affirmative guarantee which was at the basis of President Wilson system. Thus, Article 2.4 stipulates that "All Members shall refrain in their international relations from the threat or use of force against the territorial integrity or political independence of any state, or in any manner inconsistent with the purposes of the United Nations". Initially, at San Francisco conference, major powers did not consider incorporating in Article 2.4 the expression "against the territorial integrity or political independence of any state". The latter was incorporated in the final text at the request of small states.[164] At any rate, Article 2.4 appears clearly extremely weak in comparison to Article 10 in that "the resulting obligation of the United Nations members is much more limited that of the League members while the former are obliged 'to respect', they are not obliged to 'preserve as against external aggression the political independence and territorial integrity of members."[165] However, the UN Charter has compensated such a weakness by providing for a stronger prohibition of use of force as a means to carry out territorial changes. But amazingly, it is Article 10 which will be at the origin of the emergence of the principle prohibiting territorial changes by force and its corollary principle of the non recognition of any territorial change which has been made by the use of force.

---

[160] Claude (1964, p. 323).

[161] See Bloomfield (1957, pp. 32–42); Henig (1973, pp. 58–62).

[162] "War, Peace and Change", New York, Harpers, 1939, pp. 81–82.

[163] See on this Northedge (1986, pp. 137–164, 221–255).

[164] See UNCIO, Documents, VI, 342–346.

[165] Goodrich et al. (1969, p. 45).

3.2.2 The Prohibition and Non-recognition of Territorial Changes Through the Use of Force

As we have seen earlier, conquest was admitted by classical International Law as a means of acquisition of title to territory. This was the result of the legality of war. Now, war has been, with the exception of self-defence, prohibited by International Law throughout a long process which started at the beginning of the twentieth century and ended up with the UN Charter, related declarations, resolutions and judicial decisions and customary law. R.Y. Jennings has well established the link between the prohibition of war and the consequent prohibition of conquest. He wrote in this regard that "The prohibition of the use of force or threat of force in international relations rests not only upon the Charter of the United nations and its antecedent instruments but has probably also become a part of the general customary international law. It seems therefore impossible any longer to concede that the successful seizure of another's territory by force, i.e. conquest, or subjugation, may be itself a lawful title to the territory."[166]

We know that the move towards the prohibition of the use of force started with the Hague Convention II of 16 October 1907 on the limitation of the employment of force for the recovery of contacts debts whose Article 1 restricted and made conditional the recourse to force for the recovery of contractual debts by providing that:

> "The contracting Powers agree not to have recourse to armed force for the recovery of contract debts claimed from the Government of one country by the Government of another country as being due to its nationals.
>
> This undertaking is, however, not applicable when the debtor state refuses or neglects to reply to an offer of arbitration, or, after accepting the offer, prevents any compromise from being agreed on, or, after the arbitration, fails to submit to the award."

The recourse to force was also made conditional by the Covenant of the League of Nations. This was the philosophy of Articles 12, 13 and 15 of the Covenant which set up a kind of moratorium and made conditional the recourse to force to certain procedures. Hence, Article 12 stipulated that the members of the League are required, in case of a dispute likely to lead to a rupture between them, to submit that dispute either to arbitration or judicial settlement or to inquiry by the Council, and

[166] Jennings (1963, p. 67). The move towards the declaration of the illegality of war as a means to acquire title over a territory is also recalled by H. Lauterpacht who wrote that: The recognition of the title by conquest was, prior to the Covenant of the League, the Charter of the United Nations, and the General Treaty for the Renunciation of War, the necessary result of the admissibility of the right of war as an instrument both for enforcing the law and for changing rights. . .The position has, it is submitted, undergone change as the result of the Covenant of the league of Nations, the Charter of the United Nations, and, in particular, of the General Treaty for the Renunciation of war. Insofar as these instruments prohibit war, they probably render invalid conquest on the part of the state which has resorted to war contrary to its obligations. An unlawful act can normally produce results beneficial to the law-breaker (Lauterpacht, 1955, p. 574).

agree not to resort to war until 3 months after the award or the judicial decision has been pronounced or the report been made by the Council. Article 13 required that League members submit their disputes to arbitration or judicial settlement, carry out the award or judicial decision that may be rendered and that they will not resort to war against a member of the League which complies therewith. Lastly, Article 15 stipulated that in case of a dispute, which has not been submitted to arbitration or a judicial settlement, is likely to lead to a rupture, League members are required to submit the matter to Council and that if a report made by the Council is unanimously agreed to by members other than the parties to the dispute, member states will not go to war with any party to the dispute which complies with the recommendations of the report. As we can see, resort to war by the League members was conditioned by prior submission of their disputes to arbitration, judicial settlement or to the Council and it was further prohibited during a 3 months period following the pronouncement of the award, the judicial decision or Council's report. Articles 12, 13 and 15 were of course to be read together with Article 10. Now, the latter, as we have seen above, obligates the states to respect and preserve each other's territorial integrity. It should then be interpreted as prohibiting any kind of violation of territorial integrity including war of annexation.

International doctrine has been almost unanimous to share the conclusion that Article 10 prohibited war of conquest. For instance, P. Baker was of the opinion that the "real meaning (of Article 10) is that it abolished the right of conquest. It is directed against the violent transfer of territory from one sovereignty to another without the consent of the Members of the League. This was the meaning which President Wilson gave when he explained that 'territorial integrity' means immunity, not from armed invasion, but from forcible annexation."[167] Similarly, commenting simultaneously on Article 10, H.A. Rolin, wrote that the undertaking to respect territorial integrity "was the first commitment taken contained in Article 10. Yet, it will be forgotten as all the time the discussions turned around the second commitment related to the guarantee...The 'respect' (of territorial integrity) required by Article 10 was not strictly speaking a new limitation to the right to wage war, but a limitation imposed to the effects of all wars, whether licit or not, and hereby indirectly, to the purpose of any war, that is the prohibition of forcible annexation, even when it is partial, of the territory of a foreign state."[168] Likewise, H. Lauterpacht has sustained that "The repudiation of the principle of conquest was one of the main features of President's Wilson's addresses in which he formulated the foundations of the coming international order. Article 10 of the Covenant of the League of Nations... which, to use President Wilson's expression, constitutes the backbone of the Covenant, is essentially a prohibition of acquisition of territory by force. The discussions within the Assembly of the League, the opinion of writers, and the plain meaning of the Article itself show that, at least so far as the members

[167] Munch (1923, p. 58).

[168] Munch (1923, pp. 469, 470).

of the League are concerned, the title of conquest has been abolished. It seems that even the aggressor state against whom the League proceeds with sanctions is safe from conquest."[169] Echoing H. Lauterpacht, M.H. McMahon has also stressed the fact that Article 10 has prohibited wars of conquest. He shared also the view that the intention to interdict wars of conquest and to prevent territorial cessions made under duress was clearly understood by President Wilson who has repeatedly declared, when suggesting the incorporation of Article 10 in the Covenant, that "The day of conquest and aggrandizement is gone by." This interpretation conforms with President Wilson's own views on conquest as inimical to the right to self-determination and to Doctrine of Monroe which is the very antithesis of conquest. This interpretation conforms also with the fact that "since force is the main element in the conception of conquest, members of the League of Nations are legally restrained in the resort to it as between themselves on territorial questions."[170] In his criticism of those authors who did argue that Article 10 could not provide for a prohibition of wars of conquest as it was itself a guarantee of conquests undertaken by the victorious powers in the war of 1914–1918, McMahon, while admitting that Article 10 did partly play that role, stressed to say that this article cannot from the legal point of view be presumed to include only such an interpretation as it was clearly meant from the beginning "that future territorial changes brought about by the members of the League are contrary to Article 10 if obtained by violence or force."[171]

However, most of the authors have admitted that the prohibition of wars of conquest by Article 10 allowed some few exceptions. According to McMahon, Article 10, as a legal bar to the acquisition of territory by right of conquest, is unquestionably a positive limitation affecting only states bound by the Covenant.[172] Likewise, John Fischer Williams was of the opinion that in the event of military measures taken against a Power which has wrongly resorted to war, further to a recommendation made by the Council in accordance to Article 16 of the Covenant, "such a covenant-breaking Power could not rely upon Article 10, should it appear reasonable or should it be desirable, in the interest of peace, order, and good government of the world, that it should suffer loss of territory."[173] Similarly, Alfred Zimmern shared also the view that when a state establishes its control over the territory of another state pursuant to an arbitral award or judgment of the Permanent Court of International Justice, "in such a case, it is argued, there is no a question of a *violent* change but merely of the securing of a legal right."[174]

[169] Lauterpacht (1927).

[170] McMahon (1940, p. 100).

[171] Idem, p. 103.

[172] Idem, p. 101.

[173] Williams (1934).

[174] Zimmern (1939, p. 280).

It is a matter of fact that while the international doctrine was of the opinion that a new principle was emerging from Article 10, that is the prohibition of territorial changes by force, the principle did not yet fully translate on the ground as many countries and peoples still continued to feel frustrated by the injustice and unfairness of an article which, in their eyes, endorsed foreign subjugation of their national territories. This is why some authors were convinced that a new state of affairs has emerged and that conquest was over. According to Charles Cheney Hyde, Article 10 expressed a determination to safeguard what has been won by the sword and that, the Covenant became, despite the hope of some who were responsible for it, an instrument that in effect registered respect for conquest and defence for the successes of the victor.[175] Hence, according to Hyde, "if conquest is to sink into desuetude, peoples must be fairly contended with the boundaries that limit the area which they occupy, and must remain untempted by revenge to look with covetous eyes upon those of neighbour..."[176] However, if it is true that conquest did not yet disappear at that time, it has started to lose its legitimacy and gradually its legal basis. A new understanding of how territorial changes may be dealt with was in fact emerging and in which the prohibition of wars of conquest and the non-recognition of territorial changes made by the use of force have started to increasingly play an important role. Such move was mainly strengthened by the adoption of multilateral treaties prohibiting recourse to force.

We know that the decisive turning-point in the prohibition of war was the signing in 27 August 1928 in Paris of the Kellogg-Briand Pact which provided for a general prohibition of war by stipulating that "The High Contracting Parties solemnly declare in the names of their respective peoples that they condemn recourse to war for the solution of international controversies and renounce it as an instrument of national policy in their relations with one another" (Article 1). Although, it did not expressly mention wars of conquest, the 1928 Pact was interpreted as prohibiting that kind of wars. The International Law Association has in a report adopted in September 1934 declared that "The signatory states are not entitled to recognize as acquired *de jure* any territorial or other advantages acquired *de facto* by means of a violation of the Pact."[177] However some authors, while agreeing that the 1928 Pact implicitly condemned wars of conquest, did still believe that the latter remained a valid title in the cases where a state is not bound by that Pact,[178] or when the territorial changes are the result of "a defensive war in the form of redress or indemnity to the victorious belligerent."[179] This doctrinal view did not take into consideration the fact that the prohibition of war by the 1928 was gradually translating into a general customary rule which therefore obligated all

[175] Hyde (1936, p. 472).

[176] Idem, p. 476.

[177] International Law Association (1935, pp. 67–68).

[178] See, for instance, Garner (1936, p. 669).

[179] McMahon (1940, p. 119).

states whether they were parties to the Pact or not. It disregarded the principle that a state cannot seek to redress an offence made to the Pact by a foreign state by committing itself an offence to International Law. Such a doctrinal view went also against the new trend which has started to give prominence to the emerging principle of non-recognition of territorial changes made by the use of force.

Conceived as an exception to the traditional discretionary character of recognition, the then arising principle of non-recognition of territorial changes made through the use of force finds its legal foundation in the *ex injuria jus non oritur* principle, that is the principle which states that an illegal act cannot create or give rise to a legal act or situation. It means concretely the refusal "to regard the sovereignty of the dispossessed power over the area in question as ended and the sovereignty of the dispossessing power as established."[180] In other words, the *ex injuria jus non oritur* principle implies the duty to refuse the recognition of the legality of territorial changes made by resort to force, "it penalizes - writes Krystina Marek[181] – the law breaker by denying to him the intended result of his law breaking, namely the validity of the situation brought about by him in an unlawful manner."[182]

The move to refuse the recognition of territorial changes made by the use of war has started to take place further to the refusal of the United States to recognize the new situation created by the invasion of Manchuria by Japan in 1931 and the creation of the puppet state of Manchukuo.[183] In a note addressed to Japan and China on 7 January 1932, the American Secretary of State, Henry Stimson made clear that the United States Government "does not intend to recognize any situation, treaty or agreement which may be brought about by means contrary to the covenants and obligations of the Pact of Paris of August 27, 1928, to which treaty, both China and Japan, as well as the United States, are parties."[184] The doctrine Stimson, thus formulated, was subsequently endorsed unanimously by the Assembly of the League of Nations in a Resolution adopted on 11 March 1932 in which it declared that: "It is incumbent upon the members of the League of Nations not to recognize any situation, treaty, or agreement which may be brought about by means contrary to the Covenant of the League or to the Pact of Paris."[185] However, it is true that a similar position was not clearly taken by the Assembly and the Council following the invasion of Ethiopia by Italy on 3 October 1935. Indeed, although it declared Italy to be the aggressor,[186] and took economic sanctions against it and

[180] Langer (1947, p. 100).

[181] Marek (1968, p. 558).

[182] Chen (1951, p. 430) writes also in this respect that "the doctrine of non-recognition as applied to acquisition of territory...deprives the conqueror of the more convenient mode of consolidating his title, which does not become valid until legalized".

[183] Such move has started to take place much earlier within the limited context of Latin American States. See on this, McMahon (1940, pp. 154–178); Koran (1996, pp. 234–238).

[184] A copy of the note is available in 26 AJIL 1932, 342.

[185] League of Nations, Official Journal, 1932, Special Supplement, No 101, 87–88.

[186] League of Nations, Document C.417.1935.VII.

permitted the Ethiopian delegate to keep his seat in the Assembly,[187] the League never clearly condemned the annexation of Ethiopia nor did it even accept to discuss a resolution initiated by Ethiopia and aiming at urging member states not to recognize that annexation.[188]

The tendency not to recognize territorial changes made by the use of force has developed mainly in the American continent where "the obligation not to recognize title by conquest has been generally accepted."[189] A number of declarations and treaties were adopted to that effect. The first declaration in this sense was made on 6 August 1932 by nineteen American states, including the United States, following the outbreak of the territorial conflict between Bolivia and Paraguay and in which it was stressed that:

> "They (the American States) will not recognize any territorial arrangement of this controversy which has not been obtained by peaceful means nor the validity of territorial acquisitions which may be obtained through occupation or conquest by force of arms."[190]

At the conventional level, the Anti-War Treaty on Non-Aggression and Conciliation signed by 21 American States on 10 October 1933 declared in its Article II:

> "that as between the High Contracting Parties, territorial questions must not be settled by violence, and that they will not recognize any territorial arrangement which is not obtained by pacific means, nor the validity of the occupation or acquisition of territories that may be brought about by force of arms."[191]

Likewise, the Convention on Rights and Duties, signed on 26 December 1933 at the Seventh Pan-American Conference stated in its Article 11 that:

> "The contracting states definitely establish as the rule of their conduct the precise obligation not to recognize territorial acquisitions or special arrangements which have been obtained by force whether this consists in the employment of arms, in threatening diplomatic representations, or in any other effective coercive measure. The territory of a state is inviolable and may not be the object of military occupation nor other measures of force imposed by another state directly or indirectly or for any motive whatever even temporarily."[192]

Several other declarations and treaties have reiterated the adherence of the American states to the principle of the non-recognition of territorial changes made by force. One of these legal instruments was the Charter of the Organization of American States (1948) which declares in its Article 17 that "No territorial acquisitions or special advantages obtained either by force or by other means shall be recognized."[193]

---

[187] See on this Spencer (1937).

[188] See Garner (1936, pp. 679, 682).

[189] Briggs (1940, p. 76).

[190] Quoted by Hyde (1936, p. 473).

[191] League of Nations Treaty Series, 163 (1935–1936), 393.

[192] League of Nations Treaty Series, 16 (1936), 19.

[193] United Nations Treaty Series, 119 (1952), 48.

The American states' tradition of not recognizing territorial changes made by the use of force was undoubtedly very unique as it gave rise to a regional customary rule, while elsewhere the duty to refuse the recognition of forceful territorial changes was of a conventional character as it was deduced from the 1928 Pact's prohibition of war. This situation will change with the general prohibition of the use of force stated by Art. 2 (4) of the UN Charter and the ensuing policy which will be implemented by the UN in dealing with territorial changes made by the use of force.

Art. 2 (4) has been perceived as "the corner stone of peace in the Charter"[194] as it provides that all member states shall refrain in their international relations from the threat or use of force against the territorial integrity or political independence of any state, or in any manner inconsistent with the purposes of the United Nations. It undoubtedly constitutes a tremendous improvement in comparison to Art. 1 of the Briand-Kellogg Pact. First, contrary to the latter, it prohibits the use of force and not only war. This makes a great difference as some states used to disguise military actions under the pretext that the latter were not acts of war. Second, it extends the prohibition to the threat of the use of force and not only to the actual recourse to force. Third, it is linked to a collective system of sanctions of the unlawful threat or use of force (Chapter VII).[195]

The prohibition to refrain from the threat or use force has been since then reiterated and strengthened by a great number of international legal instruments. Amongst the latter, the Declaration on Principles of International Law Concerning Friendly Relations and Cooperation adopted by the UN General Assembly on 24 October 1970,[196] which states that "Every state has the duty to refrain in its international relations from the threat or use of force against territorial integrity or political independence of any state, or in any other manner inconsistent with the purposes of the United Nations. Such a threat or use of force constitutes a violation of International Law and the Charter of the United Nations and shall never be employed as a means of settling international disputes". Such Declaration has generally been considered by the I.C.J. as an expression of customary International Law.[197] Some international lawyers have even seen in it a peremptory rule of customary international law.[198] The International Court of Justice has also, on its

[194] Waldock (1952, p. 492).

[195] Simma (2002, p. 117).

[196] G.A. Res.2625 (XXV).

[197] See Case Concerning Military and Paramilitary Activities in against Nicaragua, I.CCJ. Reports, 1986, para 188 and Legality of the Threat or Use of Force of Nuclear Weapons, I.C.J. Reports, 1996, para 70.

[198] Hence, for instance, Sette Camara is of the opinion that "The non-use of force as well as non-intervention-the latter as a corollary of equality of states and self-determination-are not only very cardinal principles of customary international law but could in addition be recognized as peremptory rules of customary international law which impose obligations on all states", Separate Opinion, Nicaragua Case, I.C.J. Rep., 1986, 199.

part, concluded to the existence in customary International Law of an *opinion juris* as to the binding character of the principle of the prohibition of the threat or the use of force by stating that "This *opinion juris* may, though with all due caution, be deduced from, *inter alia*, the attitude of the Parties and the attitude of States towards certain General Assembly resolutions, and particularly resolution 2625 (XXV)...The effect of consent to the text of such resolutions cannot be understood as merely that of a 'reiteration or elucidation' of the treaty commitment undertaken in the Charter. On the contrary, it may be understood as an acceptance of the validity of the rule or set of rules declared by the resolution. The principle of non-use of force, for example, may thus be regarded as a principle of customary International law...Further...the principle of the prohibition of the use of force ...is frequently referred to in statements by state representatives as being not only a principle of customary international law but also a fundamental or cardinal principle of such law."[199]

It is thus clear that today the prohibition of the use of force has been elevated to the status of a general customary rule. Such rule implies, as a corollary principle, that no territorial change can take place through the use of force. The correlation between the prohibition of the use of force and the prohibition of the acquisition of territory by force has been recalled by R.Y. Jennings who wrote that "To brand as illegal the use of force against 'territorial integrity' of a state, and yet at the same time to recognize a rape of another's territory by illegal force as being itself a root of a legal title to sovereignty over it, is surely to risk bringing the law into contempt. For it is not simply a question whether it is possible to allow a title which cannot be pleaded without incidentally exhibiting the illegality. Nor is it merely a question of the limits of the maxim *ex injuria jus non oritur*. The question is whether an international crime of the first order can itself be pleaded as title because its perpetuation has been attended with success."[200] Consequently, the Security Council has in its Resolution 242 (1967) further to the occupation of Arab territories by Israel stressed on the illegality of the acquisition of territory by force by declaring "the inadmissibility of the acquisition of territory by war." Similar resolutions will be adopted further to the declarations of annexation of Jerusalem (1980)[201] and the Golan Heights (1981)[202] made by Israel. These resolutions will be reaffirmed by the Security Council on different occasions. The Security Council also took the same position in it Resolution 662 (1990) where it stated that the annexation of Kuwait by Iraq "under any form or whatever pretext has no legal validity and is considered as null and void." The same principle has been recalled by the Declaration on Principles of International Law on Friendly Co-operation among States which states that "The territory of a state shall not be the object of acquisition by another state resulting from the threat or use of force."

---

[199] Case Concerning Military and Paramilitary Activities In and Against Nicaragua (Nicaragua v. United States of America), I.C.J. Rep., 1986, paras 188 and 190.

[200] Jennings (1963, p. 54).

[201] Resolution 476 (1980).

[202] Resolution 497 (1981).

Meanwhile, some few authors do believe that territorial changes including the acquisition of territory can take place in case of lawful use of force, as would be the case in a situation of self-defence. Thus, according to Rudolf L. Bindschedler, annexation is not totally prohibited by present International Law as "it is only the unauthorized use of force which confers no legal title. What is the situation in the case of a war of self-defence, permitted under Article 2(4) of the Charter, or in the case of military sanctions? Logically, a right of annexation should be acknowledged if the territory affected belongs to the aggressor."[203] More clearly, Sharon Korman states that "the notion that a state that acts in self-defence is entitled to acquire a portion of the territory of the aggressor …constitutes rather a just and fitting response to the crime of aggression, which provides the victim with the reassurance against future attacks to which it is clearly entitled."[204] These authors seem to forget that self-defence, as we have seen earlier, is justified only when it is immediate, necessary and proportional to the armed attack of the aggressor state. Therefore, self-defence can by no means lead to the acquisition of foreign territories. The state of law in this matter had been recalled by R.Y. Jennings who wrote that "Force used in self-defence…must be proportionate to the threat of immediate danger, and when the threat has been averted the plea of self-defence can no longer be available. It is true that it may not be easy to say when this point is reached and that to some extent at least it is a matter of judgment of the actor. But when all allowance is made for the 'rough jurisprudence of nations', it must still be said that it would be a curious law of self-defence that permitted the defender in the course of his defence to seize and keep the resources and territory of the attacker."[205] Furthermore, as we have also seen earlier, self-defence, as consecrated by the UN Charter, did not mean that the states are authorized to settle their territorial conflicts by force. Anyhow, peace and stability have never been reached through injustice. That is why contemporary International Law has been keen to prohibit wars of conquest. Furthermore, it has also consecrated the obligation of non-recognition of territorial changes through the use of war whether such use was a lawful or unlawful act.

The UN Charter does contain no provision related to the obligation of non-recognition of territorial changes through the use of force. But, here also such obligation can be inferred from the prohibition to use force as stated by Art. 2(4), as been the case with Art. 10 of the Covenant and Art. 1 of the Briand-Kellogg Pact. Meanwhile, the legal vacuum, if any, has been filled by the Declaration on Friendly Relations which states that "No territorial acquisition resulting from the threat or use of force shall be recognized as legal". The duty not to recognize any territorial acquisition through the use of force has also been confirmed by the General Assembly in the resolution related to the definition of aggression which declares

[203] Bernhardt (1982, pp. 21–22).

[204] Koran (1996, p. 203).

[205] Jennings (1963, p. 55).

that "No territorial acquisition or special advantage resulting from aggression is or shall be recognized as lawful."[206] It has been confirmed in a series of decisions of the Security Council and the I.C.J.

The Security Council has reaffirmed the duty of the states not to recognize any territorial change imposed by force at different occasions. Several resolutions have been taken to this end following Israel's annexation of Arab territories including East Jerusalem and Golan Heights.[207] Thus, for instance, with regard the annexation of Jerusalem by Israel, the Security Council, after reaffirming the inadmissibility of the acquisition of territory by force and condemned the 'basic law' by which Israel decided to annex Jerusalem for being a violation of International Law and requested that all legislative and administrative measures and actions taken by Israel in order to alter the status of Jerusalem are null and void and must be rescinded, states that it "decides not to recognize the 'basic law' and such other actions that, a result of this law, seek to alter the character and status of Jerusalem and calls upon: a) all Member States to accept this decision; b) Those States that have established diplomatic missions at Jerusalem to withdraw such missions from the Holy City."[208]

The Security Council also on 18 November 1983, after having deplored the declaration of the independence of Northern Cyprus following the Turkish military intervention, called on all states to refuse recognizing it. But the most striking example of a Security Council decision stating the duty of non-recognition of territorial change through force was the one taken following the invasion on 2 August 1990 of Kuwait by Iraq. Thus in a resolution adopted unanimously on 9 August 1990, the Security Council declared that it:

> "Decides that annexation of Kuwait by Iraq under any form and whatever pretext has no legal validity, and is considered null and void;
>
> Calls upon all States, international organizations and specialized agencies not to recognize that annexation and to refrain from any action or dealing that might be interpreted as an indirect recognition of the annexation."[209]

Moreover, The Security Council was, following the invasion of Kuwait, able under Chapter VII to authorize on 29 November 1990 member states to use military force in order to compel Iraq to withdraw its forces from Kuwait,[210] an

---

[206] Art. 5 (3) of UNGA Res.3314 (XXIX), Annex, UN GAOR, 29th Sess., Supp., No.31, UN Doc. A/9631 (1974).

[207] The call on states not to recognize such annexation is incorporated in the same resolutions previously mentioned and which stated that the acquisition of territory by force is inadmissible. See also Resolutions 252 (1968), 267 (1969), 446 (1979), 465 (1980).

[208] Resolution 478 (1980).

[209] Resolution 662 (1990).

[210] The Security Council declared that it "Authorizes Member States co-operating with the Government of Kuwait, unless Iraq on or before 15 January 1991 fully implements. . .the foregoing resolutions (in particular the one asking it to withdraw its presence from Kuwait), to use all necessary means to uphold and implement Security resolution 660 (1990) and all subsequent relevant resolutions and to restore international peace and security in the area. . .", Resolution 678 (1990).

unprecedented move which the League's Council has never been able to implement under Art. 10 though the latter requested states, as we have seen earlier, to preserve each other's territorial integrity. But, it is unlikely that the Security Council would in the future accept to play similar role as the context of the post-Cold War which favored cooperation between great powers was something exceptional in international relations, in addition to the very particular situation of Kuwait as oil producer.

With regard to the I.C.J., it has clearly endorsed the principle of non-recognition of territorial changes through the use of force in the Legal Consequences of the Construction of a Wall in the Occupied Territory case. Hence, after having recalled that the Security Council had on 22 November 1967 emphasized the inadmissibility of acquisition of territory by war and called for the withdrawal of Israel armed forces from the occupied territories, the Court and after having considered that the construction of the wall and its associated regime create a "fait accompli" on the ground that could well become permanent, in which case, and notwithstanding the formal characterization of the wall by Israel, it would be tantamount to *de facto* annexation, it declares that "the Court is of the view that all states are under an obligation not to recognize the illegal situation resulting from the construction of the wall in the Occupied Palestinian Territory, including and around East Jerusalem."[211]

Today there is no doubt that all states are under the obligation not to recognize territorial changes imposed by force. Inferred from the prohibition to use threat or force against territorial integrity, such obligation has become a customary rule of International law due to its consecration by different international legal instruments and the decisions taken in various instances by the Security Council and the International Court of Justice. The majority of writers do agree on the existence of that international customary rule. Hence, for instance, I. Brownlie is of the view that "The strength of the norm of illegality…and the existence of a coherent body of doctrine and practice on the legal status of resort to force lead to the conclusion that an obligation of non-recognition exists."[212] Likewise, Surya P.Sharma does agree that "there exists a duty of non-recognition in general international law, apart from the UN Charter and other conventional obligations. This is supported by the practices followed concerning collective non-recognition as well as those of individual cases."[213] However, few writers are sceptical as to the efficiency of the policy of non-recognition. According to Ti-Chiang Chen, it "is an illusion that non-recognition can be regarded as a substitute for other more vigorous measures in upholding the law."[214] The same opinion is shared by Sharon Korman, who writes that "unless there is some prospect of the wrongdoer being compelled to abandon his unlawful success…non-recognition becomes little more than a pious

[211] I.C.J.Rep. 2004, para 159.

[212] Brownlie (1963, pp. 418–419).

[213] Sharma (1997, p. 157).

[214] Chen (1951, p. 441).

fiction. . .Thus the effectiveness of the law against force and conquest depends in the long run not upon the denial of title to the conqueror, but on the effectiveness of procedures for reversing the aggression before it produces its fruits."[215]

Thus, the states are left without any protection of their territorial integrity, that is their right to existence. The only progress made by International Law in this matter has been the prohibition of the recognition of territorial changes made through the use of force. The states appear therefore as very weak polities which have no other choice than to count on their own means, or the support of their allies, in order to ensure their survival. Handicapped by the structural inability of International Law to protect the members of the international community, the states have also witnessed in the past decades a steady move towards the weakening of their territorial sovereignty.

References

Abi-Saab G (1990) La pérennité des frontières en Droit International. Relations Internationales, No 64, Winter

Antonopoulos C (1996/I) The principle of Uti Possidetis Juris in Contemporary International Law. RHDI 29:31

Anzilotti D (1929) Cours de Droit International, translated by G. Gidel, Sirey, Paris

Ayala E (1931) Le principe de l'uti possidetis et le reglement des questions territoriales en Amerique, R.D.I.

Baker R (2000) Challenges to the traditional concepts of sovereignty. Public Administration and Development 20:1–15

Bardonnet D (1981) Equite et frontieres terrestres. In: Le Droit International: Unite et diversite, Melanges P. Reuter, A Pedone, Paris

Basdevant J (1926V) La conclusion et la rédaction des traites et des instruments diplomatiques autres que les traites, R.C.A.D.I.:581

Basdevant J (1928-I) La conclusion et la rédaction des traités et des instruments internationaux. RCADI

Bedjaoui M (1972) Le règlement pacifique des différends africains. AFDI

Benouniche M (1967) Observations sur les frontieres en Afrique, memoire de D.E.S., Alger, Faculte de Droit et des Sciences Economiques

Benouniche M. Observations sur les frontieres en Afrique

Benouniche M, Assad O, Laraba A (1973) Expose introductif sur l'approche institutionnelle. In: Problèmes actuels de l'unité africaine, Faculté de droit et des sciences économiques et Institut d'études politiques de l'Université d'Alger, Alger, S.N.E.D.

Bernhardt R (ed) (1982) Annexation. In: Encyclopedia of Public International Law, vol 3

Bindschedler RL (1982) "Annexation", Encyclopedia of Public International Law, ed. R Bernhardt, vol. 3

Bipoum-Woom JM (1970) Le droit international africain. LGDJ, Paris

Bittner L (1924) Die Lehre von den völkerrechtlichen Vertragsurkunden, Berlin

Bloomfield LP (1957) Evolution or revolution? The United Nations and the Problem of Peaceful Territorial Change. Harvard University Press, Cambridge

[215] Koran (1996, pp. 245–246).

Bluntschli JC (1869) Le droit international codifie, translated by M.C. Lardy, Guillaumin, Paris, Article 404bis
Borella F (1964) Le regionalisme africain, A.F.D.I.
Borella F (1974) Le système juridique de L'O.U.A. AFDI
Boujori-Flecher D (1981) Heurs et malheurs de l'uti possidetis: l'intangibilité des frontières africaines. RJPIC
Bouvier P (1972) Un problème de sociologie politique:les frontières des Etats africains. Revue de l'Insitut de Sociologie
Briggs HW (1940) Non-recognition of title by conquest and limitations on the doctrine. Proceedings, American Society of International Law 34
Brownlie I (1963) International Law and the Use of Force by States. Clarendon Press, Oxford
Brownlie I (1995) International Law at the Fiftieth Anniversary of the United Nations, General Course on Public International Law, R.C.A.DI., vol 225
B.Y.B.L. (1934) Do Treaties Need Ratification?
Cahier. Ph. (year) Violation du droit interne et nullite des traites
Cahier Ph. (1971) La violation du droit interne relatif a la competence pour conclure des traites comme cause de nullite des traites, Rivista di Diritto Internazionale
Carre de Malberg R (1920) Contribution a la theorie generale de l'Etat, Sirey, Paris, vol 1
Castellino J, Allen S (2003) A Temporal Analysis. Adershot, Ashgate
Chailley P (1932) La nature juridique des traite internationaux selon le droit contemporain, Sirey, Paris
Charles PH (ed) (1928) Survey of American Foreign Relations. Published for the Council on Foreign Relations by Yale University Press, New Haven
Chen T-C (1951) The International Law of Recognition. With Special Reference to Practice in Great Britain and the United States. Stevens & Sons, London
Claude I (1964) Swords into Plowshares: The Problems and Progress of International Organization, 3rd edn. University of London Press, London
Cooper JM (2001) Breaking the Heart of the World. Woodrow Wilson and the Fight for the League of Nations. Cambridge University Press, Cambridge
Corten O (1999) Droit des peuples à disposer d'eux-mêmes et uti possidetis: deux faces d'une même médaille? In: Corten O et al (eds) Démembrements d'Etats et délimitations territoriales: l'uti possidetis en question(s). Bruylant, Bruxelles
Craven MCR (1995) The European Community Arbitration Commission on Yugoslavia. BYBIL:334
de Arechaga EJ (year) Boundaries in Latin America: Uti Possidetis Doctrine. In: 1 Encyclopedia of Public International Law
de la Pradelle P (1928) La frontiere. Etudes de Droit International, Paris, these
de Pinto Campinos (1980) L'actualite de "l'uti possidetis" in "La frontiere", S.F.D.I., Colloque de Poitiers de 1979, A. Pedone, Paris
de Visscher Ch (1967) Les effectivités du Droit International Public. A. Pédone, Paris
Dehousse F (1935) la ratification des traités. Essai sur les rapports des traités et du droit interne. Recueil Sirey, Paris
Delcourt B (1998/1) L'application de *l'uti possidetis Juris* au démembrement de la Yougoslavie: règle coutumière ou impératif politique? RBDI
Distefano G (1995) La notion de titre juridique et les différends territoriaux dans l'ordre international. RGDIP
Dupuis Ch (1909) le principe de l'équilibre et le Concert européen, de la paix de Westphalie à l'Acte d'Algésiras. Librairie Académique, Paris
Dutheil de la Rochere J. Les procedures de reglement des differends frontaliers
Eagerton GW (1979) Great Britain and the Creation of the League of Nations. Scolar Press, London
Eastman SM (1946) Canada at Geneva. An Historical Survey and Its Lessons. The Ryerson Press, Toronto

Elliot A (1975) Boundaries in Africa: A Legal and Historical Survey, in: A.K. Mensah-Brown (ed) "African International Legal History", United Nations Institute for Training and Research, New York
El Ouali A (Dec 1984–Jan 1985) L'uti possidetis ou le non-sens juridique du principe de base de l'O.U.A pour le reglement des differends territoriaux. Revue Francaise d'Etudes Politiques Africaines
El Ouali A (1984) Effets juridiques de la sentence internationale. Contribution a l'étude de l'exécution des normes internationales. L.G.D.J., Paris
Englebert P, Tarango S, Carter M (2002) Dismemberment and suffocation. A contribution to the debate on African boundaries. Comp Polit Stud 35(10)
Fairman C (1936) Competence to Bind the State to an International Agreement
Fischer FC (1933) The arbitration of the Guatemalan-Honduran Boundary. ADIM
Fitzmaurice M, Elias O (2005) Contemporary Issues in the Law of Treaties. Eleven International Publishing
Foucher M (1991) Fronts et frontieres, un tour du monde géopolitique. Fayard, Paris
Freymond P (1947) La ratification des traits et le problème des rapports entre le Droit International et le droit interne, Thesis, Lausanne
Garner JW (1936) Non-recognition of illegal territorial annexations and claims to sovereignty. AJIL 30
Gergopoulos C (1939) La ratification des traités et la collaboration du Parlement. L.G.D.J, Paris
Giroud J (1920) le plébiscite international. Etude historique et critique du droit des gens, Thesis, Paris
Goodrich LM, Hambro E, Simons AP (1969) Charter of the United Nations. Commentary and Documents, 3rd and revised edn. Columbia University Press, New York
Grandall SB (1916) Treaties, Their Making and Enforcement. J. Byrne and Cie, Washington, DC
Guichonnet P, Raffestin C (1974) Géographie de frontières. P.U.F, Paris
Haggenmacher P (1992–1993) Some hints on the European origins of legislative participation in the treaty-making function. Chicago-Kent Law Rev 68
Hannun H (1993) Self-determination, Yugoslavia, and Europe: old wine in new bottles? Transnat'l L & Contemp Probs:3
Henig RB (ed) (1973) The League of Nations. Oliver & Boyd, Edinburgh
Higgins R. Postmodern tribalism and the right to secession, Comments in Peoples and Minorities in International Law
Hyde CC (1936) Conquest Today. AJIL:30
ICJ Report (2002) Case Concerning the Land and Maritime Boundary Between Cameroon and Nigeria (Cameroon v. Nigeria: Equatorial Guinea intervening), Judgment of 10 October
International Law Association (1935) Report of the Thirty-Eight Conference Held at Budapest, September 1934, Eastern Press, London
Jennings J (1963) The Acquisition of Territory in International Law. University Press, Manchester
Jones JM (1946) Full Powers and Ratification. A Study in the Development of Treaty-Making Procedure. Cambridge University Press, Cambridge
Jouve E (year) Relations Internationales du Tiers Monde et droit des peuples
Kaikobad KH (1983) Some observations on the doctrine of continuity and finality of boundaries. BYBIL
Kaikobad KH (1999) The quality of justice: "Excès de Pouvoir" in the adjudication of territorial and boundary disputes. In: The Reality of International Law: Essays in Honor of Ian Brownlie. Oxford University Press, Oxford
Kelsen H (1934) In: Knight M (ed.) Pure Theory of Law. Peter Smith, Gloucester, 1989
Kennan GF (1960) Soviet Foreign Policy, 1917–1941. Greenwood Press, Westport
Klein P (year) Les glissements semantiques et fonctionnels de l'uti possidetis. In: Corten O (ed.) Demembrements d'Etats et delimitations territoriales
Kohen MG (1997) Possession contestée et souveraineté territoriale. PUF, Paris
Koran S (1996) The Right to Conquest. The Acquisition of Territory by Force in International Law and Practice. Clarendon Press, Oxford

Lalonde S (2001) Uti Possidetis: its colonial past revisited. Belgian Rev Int Law 34(1)
Lalonde S (2002) Determining Boundaries in a Conflicted World. The Role of Uti Possidetis. McGill-Queen's University Press, Montreal
Lamb S Legal limits to United Nations Security Council Powers. In: The Reality of International Law: Essays in Honor of Ian Brownlie. Oxford University Press, Oxford
Langer R (1947) Seizure of territory: the Stimson Doctrine and related principles in legal theory and diplomatic practice. Princeton University Press, Princeton
Lansing R (1921) The Peace Negotiations, A Personal Narrative. Houghton Mifflin Company, Boston/New York
Lauterpacht H (1927) Private Law Sources and Analogies of International Law. Longmans, Green, London
Lauterpacht H (1955) Oppenheim's international law, 8th edn. Longmans, Green, London
League of Nations (1923) Records of the Fourth Assembly, Plenary Meetings, Text of the Debates, 24 September
Levrat N (1999) La prise en considération de l'ordre juridique étatique dans la définition des frontières internationales. In: Corten O et al (eds) Démembrements d' Etats et délimitations territoriales: l'uti possidetis en question(s). E. Bruylant, Bruxelles
Marek K (1968) Identity and Continuity of States in Public International Law, Geneve, Librairie Droz, 2nd edn.
McMahon M (1940) Conquest and Modern International Law. The Legal Limitations on the Acquisition of Territory by onquest. The Catholic University of America Press, Washington, Kraus Reprint Co., Millwood, New York, 1975
Merle M (1961) Les plebiscites organises par les Nations Unies. A.F.D.I.
Miller DH (1928) Drafting of the Covenant, vol II. Putnam's, New York
Mjad A (not dated) L'etat des travaux portant sur la revision de la Charte d'Adis Abeba, memoire de D.E.S., Faculte de Droit de Casablanca, not dated
Morley F (1932) The Society of Nations. Its Organization and Constitutional Development. The Brookings Institution, Washington
Munch P (ed.) (year) The making of the covenant from the British Point of view. In: Les origines et l'oeuvre de la Societe des Nations, Copenhague, Gyldendalske Boghandel, vol 2
Munch P (ed.) (year) L'article 10 du Pacte de la Societe des Nations. In: Les origines et l'oeuvre de la Societe des Nations
Nabil B (year) Le principe de l'intangibilite des frontieres au Maghreb
Nair LM (1961) The Law of Treaties. Clarendon Press, London
Ndeshyo E (year) L'application des actes de l'O.U.A par les Etats membres
Nelson LDM (1973) The arbitration of boundary disputes in Latin America. NLLR
Nesi G (1998) L'uti possidetis hors du contexte de la décolonisation: le cas de l'Europe. AFDI 44
Nicolopoulos G (1942) L'acte de ratification et sa place dans la procédure diplomatique de la conclusion des traités, Thesis, Lyon
Northedge FS (1986) The League of Nations. Its Life and Times. Homes & Meier, New York
Oppenheim L (1955) International Law. Longmans, Green and Cie, 8th edn., vol 1
Person Y (1977) 'L'Etat contre l'identité. In: Les espaces du prince. P.U.F., Paris
Rappard W (1940) The Quest for Peace. Harvard University Press
Ratner SR (1996) Drawing a better line: Uti Possidetis and the borders of New States. AJIL (90), No 4
Reisman M (1995) Protecting indigenous rights in international adjudication. AJIL 89
Reuter P (1975) Droit International Public, 5th edn. PUF, Thémis, Paris
Roggs SW (1940) International Boundaries, a Study of Boundary Functions and Problems. Columbia University Press, New York
Sanchez-Rodriguez LI (1997) L'*uti possidetis* et le effectivités dans les contentieux territoriaux et frontaliers. RCADI:263
Schuking W (1930) Portee des regles du droit constitutionnel pour la conclusion et la ratification des traites internationaux, Annuaire de l'Institut de Droit International

Schwarzenberger G (2005) Title to Territory: Response to a Challenge. In: Shaw MN (ed) Title to Territory. Ashgate, Dartmouth
Security Council Resolution 276 (1970) Advisory Reading, vol I, 1971
Seymour C (1928) The Intimate Papers of Colonel House, vol 1. Houghton Mifflin, Boston
Sharma V (1997) Territorial Acquisition, Disputes and International Law. Martinus Nijhoff, The Hague
Shaw MN (1996) The heritage of states: the principle of *Uti Possidetis Juris* today. BYBIL
Shaw MN (1999a) International Law, 4th edn. Cambridge University Press, Cambridge
Shaw MN (1999b) Peoples, territorialism and decolonisation. EJIL 3
Simma B (ed) (2002) The Charter of the United Nations. A commentary, vol I. Oxford University Press, Oxford
Solière E (1901) le plébiscite dans l'annexion, Thesis, Paris
Sorel J-M, Mehdi R. L'uti possidetis entre la consecration juridique et la pratique: essai de reactualisation
Spencer JH (1937) The Italian-Ethiopian dispute and the League of Nations. AJIL:31
Starke JG (1977) An Introduction to International Law, 8th edn. Butterworths, London
Stevenson D (1988) The First World War and International Politics. Oxford University Press, Oxford
Temperley HWV (ed) (1920) A History of the Peace Conference of Paris, vol I. Hodder and Stoughton, London
Touval S (1972) The Boundary Politics of Independent Africa. Harvard University Press, Cambridge
Tran Van Minh. Les conflits, Encyclopedie juridique de l'Afrique, tome 1
Tran Van Minh. Remarques sur le principe de l'intangibilite des frontieres
Vattel E (1758) Le droit des gens ou principes de la loi naturelle appliques a la conduite et aux affaires des nations et des souverains, chapters 12, 14, paras translated by P. Haggenmacher
Veatch R (1975) Canada and the League of Nations. University of Toronto Press, Toronto
Vexler V (1921) De l'obligation de ratifier les traits régulièrement conclus. Librairie Arthur Rousseau, Paris
Waldock CHM (1948) Disputed Sovereignty in the Falkland Dependencies. B.Y.B.I.L.
Waldock CHM (1952) The regulation of the use of force by individual states in International Law. RCADI 81(II)
Wambaugh S (1920) A Monograph on Plebiscites. Oxford University Press, New York
Wambaugh S (1927) La pratique des plébiscites internationaux. RCADI, IV
Waters R (1969) In: Winstrand CG (ed) Africa Boundary Problems. The Scandinavian Institute of African Studies, Upssala
Wildhaber L (1971) Treaty-Making Power and Constitution: An International and Comparative Study. Bale, Hebing & Lichtenhahn
Williams JF (1934) Some Aspects of the Covenant of the League of Nations. Oxford University Press, Oxford
Yakemtchouk R (1975) Les frontières africaines. RGDIP
Zartman IW. The Foreign and Military Polities of African Boundary Problems
Zimmern A (1939) The League of Nations and the Rule of Law, pp. 1918–1935. Macmillan and Co. Limited, London

Chapter 4
The Weakening of States' Territorial Sovereignty

Territorial integrity is, as we have seen earlier, the institutionalization of territoriality, which means the control by the state of a given space and its population, after having succeeded to neutralize internal and external competitors, and its use for political, social, and economic ends to the benefit of the whole population. Translated in juridical terms, territoriality reflects the supreme authority or jurisdiction of the state to control all persons or property within its territorial domain.[1] It reflects in other words the liberty of action of a state within its borders which is the natural consequence of sovereignty insofar as "comprising the power of a state to exercise supreme authority over all persons and things within its territory, sovereignty involves *territorial* authority (dominium, territorial sovereignty)."[2] As a consequence of sovereignty, the state enjoys therefore the right to territorial sovereignty, or the right to domestic jurisdiction, that is the power of a sovereign to affect the rights of persons, whether by legislation, by executive decree, or by the judgment of a court.[3] Being the master within its own territory, every state has the right to opt for its own political system and form of government, adopt its constitution, enact law determining the rights and duties of its citizens, establish the rules and regulations related to social and economic activities, fix the conditions for the entry and residence in its territory of foreign citizens, etc. All states without any distinction do equally enjoy such right as, put by Lord Macmillan, "It is an essential attribute of the sovereignty of this realm, as of all sovereign independent states, that it should possess jurisdiction over all persons and things within its territorial limits and in all causes civil and criminal arising within these limits."[4]

However, today we do witness a weakening of states' territorial sovereignty. Such a weakening is a steady phenomenon, which affects mainly domestic

[1] See Fenwick (1965, p. 296).

[2] Jennings and Watts (1992, p. 382).

[3] See Beale (1923, p. 241).

[4] Quoted in Shearer (1994, p. 184)

A. El Ouali, *Territorial Integrity in a Globalizing World*,
DOI 10.1007/978-3-642-22869-8_4, © Springer-Verlag Berlin Heidelberg 2012

jurisdiction. The latter has indeed been subject in the past decades to an increasing contraction of its scope and magnitude. But the contraction of domestic jurisdiction is not a universal phenomenon as it affects mainly Southern states' territorial sovereignty. Such weakening of Southern states' territorial sovereignty has become even clearer and more apparent with the resurgence of the humanitarian intervention.

4.1 The Contraction of Domestic Jurisdiction

International Law has traditionally recognized that every state possesses an exclusive jurisdiction within its territory. Such principle was recalled by Max Huber in the Arbitral Award of 4 April 1928 in the *Island of Palmas Case* by stating that: "The development of national organisation of states during the last few centuries and, as a corollary, the development of international law, have established this principle of the exclusive competence of the state in regard to its own territory in such a way as to make it the point of departure in settling most questions that concern international relations...Territorial sovereignty, as has already been said, involves the exclusive right to display the activities of the a state."[5]

However, in displaying its right to exclusive jurisdiction, each state has to take into account the rights of foreign states as such right "has a corollary duty: the obligation to protect within the territory the rights of other states...Without manifesting its territorial sovereignty in a manner corresponding to circumstances, the state cannot fulfil this duty".[6] Hence, territorial sovereignty does not authorize a state to exert unlimited power within its territory in a way to disregard the rights of foreign states and their citizens which have traditionally recognized as such by International Law.[7] In return, as long as all individuals and all property within the territory of a state are under its dominium and sway, all "foreign individuals and

[5] UNRIAA, 1928, vol. II, p. 829.

[6] Idem.

[7] Thus it is recalled in Oppenheim's International Law that "Like independence, territorial supremacy does not give an unlimited liberty of action. Thus, every state has a right to demand that its merchant may pass through the territorial sea of other states. Foreign Heads of State and envoys, foreign warships, and foreign armed forces must be granted a certain degree of inviolability and exemption from local jurisdiction. Through the right of protection over citizens abroad, which is held by every state according to customary law, a state cannot treat foreign citizens passing through or residing on its territory arbitrarily according to discretion as it might treat its own nationals. A state, in spite of its territorial authority, may not alter the natural conditions of its own territory to the disadvantage of the natural conditions of the territory of a neighbouring state- for instance, to stop or divert or pollute the flow of a river which runs from its own into neighbouring territory...", Jennings and Watts (1992, p. 391).

property fall at once under the territorial sovereignty of a state when they cross its frontiers."[8]

However, although it is generally agreed that there is in principle a presumption in favour of state's jurisdiction within its own territory, this has not meant that the spheres of such jurisdiction have all the time been perceived as rigid and creating an obstacle to the development of International Law and the extension of its domain. The tendency to restrict the sphere of national jurisdiction is an old phenomenon,[9] but it has developed further as a result of increased interdependence between states as well as the expansion of the United Nations' competences to the detriment of member states. This can be shown through the analysis, first, of extraterritoriality, and second, the expansion of United Nations' competencies to the detriment of domestic jurisdiction.

4.1.1 *Extraterritoriality*

In fact, extraterritoriality has, over the past decades, developed in two divergent directions, one towards the extension abroad of powerful states' sovereignty to the detriment of weaker states, and the other towards the protection of human rights through universal jurisdiction. These new developments will be analyzed hereafter after recalling the principle of the presumption in favour of states' jurisdiction within their territory.

4.1.1.1 The Presumption in Favour of States' Jurisdiction Within Their Territory

By extraterritoriality, it is meant all exercises of jurisdiction that are not based on the territoriality principle.[10] Sovereignty involves, as we have seen above, that states enjoy full jurisdiction over their territories and the persons and property that are located within these territories. States exert legal authority on their territory

---

[8] Idem, p. 384.

[9] The move towards increased expansion of International Law domain at the detriment of national jurisdiction has been rightly recalled by Charles G. Fenwick when stating that domestic questions "are, in respect to their objects, the sum total of national interests minus the interests governed by International Law. In one sense, therefore, the scope of domestic questions is in inverse ratio to the scope of international law; the wider the latter the narrower the former, and vice versa. As international law has gradually brought one set of conflicting interests after another within its jurisdiction, it has to a corresponding degree restricted the control of the individual state over those interests and thus converted questions relating to them from national or domestic questions into international questions", Fenwick (1925, pp. 144–145).

[10] Higgins (1994, p. 73).

through prescriptive jurisdiction, that is the power to legislate or otherwise prescribe legal rules as well as through enforcement jurisdiction, that is the power to apply such rules through judicial or executive action.[11] It has traditionally been agreed that exceptions to the national jurisdiction can arise only as a result of an agreement, either tacit or express, of the state concerned.[12] It is so because there is a presumption in favour of the full sovereignty of a state over its territory unless a title or a rule can be shown under which International Law would restrict the sovereignty.[13] Such a major principle has been stated in the *Lotus case* with regard the two aspects of state authority, that is the prescriptive and enforcement jurisdictions.

The *Lotus case* was raised following a collision in 1926 on the high seas between the French steamer, the *Lotus*, and the Turkish steamer, the *Boz-Kourt*, which resulted in loss of life and the Turkish ship. Following the collision, the Lotus ship docked at Constantinople port for repair. But the officer of the watch of the French ship was arrested and prosecuted. France opposed the proceedings. Then the matter was submitted by both countries to the Permanent Court of International Justice which was requested to state whether International Law prevented the Turkish Government from prosecuting the French officer on the ground that no state is entitled to extend its law on the high seas to foreign ships. In its judgment, the Court began by recalling the principle of exclusive jurisdiction by stating that "the first and foremost restriction by international law upon a state is that – failing the existence of a permissive rule to the contrary – it may not exercise its power in any form in the territory of another state. In this sense jurisdiction is certainly territorial. It cannot be exercised by a state outside its territory except by virtue of a permissive rule derived from international custom or a convention."[14] After recalling that enforcement jurisdiction was strictly territorial, the Court stressed that a state can extend its jurisdiction to acts which have taken place abroad as long as International Law does not prohibit it from doing so. It states in this regard that "It does not, however, follow that international law prohibits a state from exercising jurisdiction in its own territory, in respect of any case which relates to acts which have taken place abroad, and in which it cannot rely on some permissive rule of international Law. Such a view would only be tenable if international law contained a general prohibition to states to extend the application of their laws and the jurisdiction of their courts to persons, property and acts outside their territory, and if, as an exception to this general proposition, it allowed states to do so in certain specific cases. But this is certainly not the case under international law as it stands at present. Far from laying down a general prohibition to the effect that states may not extend the application of their laws and the jurisdiction of their courts to

---

[11] See Ott (1987, p. 137).

[12] See O'Connell (1965, p. 656).

[13] de Lupis (1974, p. 21).

[14] Lotus case, Judgment No 9, 1927, P.C.I.J., Ser A, No 10, 18–19.

persons, property and acts outside their territory, it leaves them in this respect a wide measure of discretion which is only limited in certain cases by prohibitive rules; as regards other cases, every state remains free to adopt the principles which it regards as best and most suitable..."[15] The Court held consequently that Turkey had not violated International Law as long as the latter does not restrict the jurisdiction of a state over ships docking in its ports.

Two major conclusions have been drawn from the Lotus dictum. First, a state can give extraterritorial effects to its national rules when they are related to matters such as civil status and taxation which are meant to be applicable to their nationals abroad, but on the condition that the states where these rules are meant to produce their effects express no objection to their implementation. Second, a state cannot use coercion in a foreign state's territory in order to ensure the implementation of its national rules. What is important to note is that while the scope of the first principle can be read with some flexibility, this is not the case with regard to the second principle. Commenting on the applicability abroad of national criminal laws, R. Higgins recalls in this respect that "the nationality principle, by which states in certain circumstances make their criminal law applicable to nationals abroad, is an extraterritorial form of jurisdiction. International Law in principle tolerates this basis of jurisdiction, so long as its exercise is not excessive and so long as there is not attempt to enforce it within the territory of another state."[16]

As for the enforcement jurisdiction, it has become a customary principle of International Law. The American Law Institute has confirmed in this respect that "The state's law enforcement officers may exercise their functions in the territory of another state only with the consent of the other state, given by duly authorized officials of that state."[17] That is why it has been traditionally agreed that jurisdiction cannot, for instance, been exercised on abducted persons. The importance of this principle has been recalled by C.J. Gabbay when stating that "There is an inherent objection to (exercising jurisdiction over an abducted) both on grounds of public policy pertaining to the ethical norms and because it imperils and corrodes the peaceful coexistence and mutual respect of sovereign nations. For abduction is illegal under International Law, provided that the abductor was not acting on his own initiative and without the authority or connivance of his government. A contrary view would amount to a declaration that the ends justify the means, thereby encouraging states to become law-breakers in order to secure the conviction of a private individual."[18] Now, the US Supreme Court has been severely criticised[19] for not respecting the latter principle in the United States

[15] Idem, p. 19.

[16] Higgins (1994, p. 73).

[17] American Law Institute (1987, §432 (2)).

[18] Quoted by Dugard (2006, p. 233).

[19] See, e.g., Rayfuse (1993, p. 882); Glennon (1992, pp. 745–756).

v.Alvarez-Machain case in which it held that the forcible abduction of a Mexican national from his own country, Mexico, by US agents cannot constitute a valid objection to his trial in the United States.[20] In his dissenting opinion, Justice Stevens has drawn the attention that "most courts throughout the civilized world. . .will be deeply disturbed by the 'monstrous' decision"[21] hence taken by the Supreme Court. Similar criticism were made of the decision by which the District Court of Jerusalem held erroneously in the Government of Israel v.Eichmann case that "it is an established rule of law that a person standing for trial for an offense against the laws of the state may not oppose his being tried by reason of the illegality of his arrest, or by the means whereby he was brought (that is abduction) to the area of the state."[22]

With regard to prescriptive jurisdiction, it has been suggested that it can be implemented in different circumstances. The most frequently cited circumstances are the following[23]:

- An important element for the exercise of prescriptive jurisdiction is that a significant portion of an activity has taken place in the territory of the state which is at the origin of such type of jurisdiction. Such a conclusion stems from the territorial principle according to which logically a state should be able to claim jurisdiction only if the offense has been committed, in part or in whole, in its territory; it must prove that a constituent element of the offense concerned occurred in its territory.[24]
- A state may, in accordance with the nationality principle, exercise jurisdiction over its nationals, wherever they are located. This is particularly the case in matters of civil or criminal laws.[25]
- A state has, in accordance with the protective principle, "the right to punish acts committed outside its territory, even by aliens, when the acts constitute (inter alia) an attack against its territory."[26]
- A state may, according to the passive personality doctrine, assert criminal jurisdiction over foreigners with respect to crimes committed outside their territory against one of their nationals.[27]
- A state may have jurisdiction, according to the "effects doctrine" implemented by US courts, on "persons not within its allegiance, for conduct outside its borders that has consequences within its borders which the state reprehends."[28]

---

20 ILM, 1992, 31, 900.

21 Idem, pp. 917–918.

22 ILR 1961, 36, 18.

23 See, e.g., Oliver et al. (1994, pp. 135–194); Swords (2002, pp. 494–495).

24 See Akehurst (1972–1973, p. 152).

25 Idem, pp. 156–157.

26 Article 4 the 1931 Resolution of the Institute of International Law.

27 See the critical analysis made by Sahovic and Bishop (1968, pp. 368–372).

28 US v. Aluminum Co. of America case, 148F.443, 1945.

– A state may have jurisdiction, in accordance with universal jurisdiction, when the "offenses involved are against humanity as a whole. Because all states have a legal interest in the obligations that have been violated, they are classified as erga omnes."[29]

4.1.1.2 Extraterritoriality as a Means to Extend Abroad Powerful States' Sovereignty

In fact most of the aforementioned doctrines or principles underlying prescriptive jurisdiction have raised controversial debates with regard to their legal basis, content and scope.[30] It is so because extraterritoriality has always been an abnormal and unilateral way of extending powerful states' sovereignty to the detriment of weaker states. Legal equality has traditionally pushed states to accept to mutually restrict their authority either through agreements or through practical acts and behaviour, which if repeated can give rise in the long run to customary rules. On the contrary, extraterritoriality does not very often operate in a reciprocal way as it is the law of one state that is implemented in another state. Thus, the same powerful state which invokes extraterritoriality in a given situation may in another situation invoke the territoriality of its law in order to preserve its own interests. Analysing the US policy in this respect, Kal Raustiala has established that "the rules of legal spatiality reflect American power and interests rather than normative ideals. When claims of jurisdictional congruence benefit important US interests, the Congress, the president, and the judiciary will cling to, or revive, older territorial principle. When functional pressures demand more global approach, spatiality will be altered in favour of extraterritoriality. As US power has grown, and the scope of the US interests abroad has grown, the US has been increasingly willing and able to assert its law extraterritorially. Adherence to principles is allegedly a signal aspect of the legal process. But the underlying principles that appear to guide decisions about territoriality are difficult to reconcile with conventional principles of justice; rather, with few exceptions extraterritoriality has been asserted to benefit the US and spatial limits to the law have been used to limit the rights and powers of outsiders."[31]

Exterritoriality is mainly related to economic matters whereby powerful states seek to implement their laws within foreign countries territories. It is no a surprise that it has initially developed during the first globalization starting from the second half of the nineteenth century where it led to the emergence of the capitulations system. Imposed through unequal treaties by Western powerful countries to non-Western countries, the object of the capitulations system was to exempt foreigners

[29] Magnarella (1995a, p. 164).

[30] See on this Akehurst (1972–1973 p. 145 and seq.); Mann (1964 p. 1 and seq.); Sahovic and Bishop (1968 pp. 354–374).

[31] Raustiala (2004, p. 27).

from the civil and criminal jurisdiction of the local magistrates and tribunals, and make them subject only to the laws and authorities of their own country, thus creating a kind of extra-territoriality for all citizens of the contracting states resident in or visiting any part of the East where these treaties were obtained.[32] Certainly various motivations were behind the capitulations system, but it is agreed that the primary intention was to establish fundamental legal conditions for enhancing trade and economic intercourse by preventing uncertainty and risk and providing Western enterprises with substantive and procedural rights and privileges.[33] The same motivations are behind the recent development of the investment arbitration treaties which aim at the de-localization of the judicial procedures related to the settlement of economic disputes by establishing that investors can elect to arbitrate before either an ad hoc tribunal organized under the United Nations Commission on International Trade Law (UNCITRAL) Arbitration Rules or the Stockholm Chamber of Commerce or a tribunal organized through the World Bank's International Center for the Settlement of Investment Disputes.[34]

Exterritoriality policies have not been limited to the relations between Western powers and peripheral countries; it has also been at the origin of serious difficulties between powerful states, particularly since the Second World War when the United States emerged as a big economic power and set up policies aiming at extending its hegemony over world economy. Thus, since the 1940s, the United States has started to give extraterritorial effects to federal statues in a wide range of areas such as antitrust, securities, criminal law, intellectual property, etc.[35] Simultaneously, US federal courts, which are deferential to the government, also followed suit. Thus, for instance, the effects doctrine has started to be given prominence by the US courts starting from 1945 following the judicial decision taken in the US v. Aluminum Company of America (ALCOA).[36] The implementation of the effects doctrine arouse strong reactions outside the US which fact pushed the US courts to nuance its scope and effects by introducing "reasonableness" and accepting to take into consideration foreign nations' needs and interests. But by assuming a political role through what has been known as the "interests balancing", the US courts have been severely criticized abroad.[37] However, this has not prevented the US courts from continuing to provide their support to the executive branch's policy aiming at giving US domestic rule extraterritorial effects. It has been noted in this respect that by the beginning of the twenty-first century, US courts had applied dozens of statutory and constitutional provisions extraterritorially to resolve a wide range of

[32] See Halleck and Baker (1893, pp. 387–388).

[33] See Filder (2000, p. 387).

[34] See Franck (2009, p. 443).

[35] Raustiala (2004).

[36] US v. Aluminum Co. of America case, 148F.443, 1945.

[37] See, e.g., Maier (1983, p. 31).

disputes.[38] Foreign states have also shown their strong opposition to the extraterritorial effects given to federal statutes such as the famous Helms-Burton legislation adopted on 12 March 1996 which provided inter alia for sanctions against foreign companies found to be "trafficking" in relation to properties belonging to American citizens and expropriated by the Cuban revolutionary government, and the D'Amato Bill adopted on 5 August of the same year which prescribed sanctions against foreign companies making investments of 40,000 US dollars or more in oil or gas projects in Iran and Libya. These two statutes have led to severe criticism from many states and organizations. Thus, for instance, protesting against the unfair retroactive effect and the manifest political and discriminatory character against foreign companies of the Helms-Burton Act as well as it abusive interpretation of commercial acts as trafficking acts, the Organization of American States (OAS) has concluded that:

> The exercise of such jurisdiction over acts of 'trafficking in confiscated property' does not conform with the norms established by International Law for the exercise of jurisdiction in each of the following aspects:
> (a) A prescribing state does not have the right to exercise jurisdiction over acts of 'trafficking' abroad by aliens unless specific conditions are fulfilled which does not appear to be satisfied in this situation;
> (b) A prescribing state does not have the right to exercise jurisdiction over acts of 'trafficking' abroad by aliens under circumstances where neither the alien nor the conduct in question has any connection with its territory and where no apparent connection exists between such acts and the protection of its essential sovereign interests.[39]

The violation of the principle of territoriality of law by the American government has been at the origin of serious difficulties and tension with foreign countries in particular Western Europe countries. The latter have often reacted by adopting measures with the view of blocking the extraterritorial effects given by the United States to some of its federal statutes and judiciary decisions. The European Community has also shown its opposition to the US extraterritorial policies in respect in particular of European subsidiaries of US companies, goods and technology. Thus, it warned that "US claims to jurisdiction over European subsidiaries of US companies and over goods and technology of US origin located outside the US are contrary to the principles of International Law and can only lead to clashes of both of a political and legal nature. These subsidiaries, goods and technology must be subject to the laws of the country where they are located."[40] However, this will not prevent later on the European countries from also embracing extraterritoriality.[41]

---

[38] See Putmam (2009, p. 484).

[39] I.L.M., 1996, 35, 1329, Inter-American Juridical Committee Examining the US Helms-Burton Act, 27 August 1996.

[40] I.L.M, 1991, 30, 1487.

[41] See Raustiala (2004, p. 36 and seq).

Exterritoriality of law has been interpreted as an illustration of the current wave of globalization.[42] Certainly, the exterritorializing of law reflects the competition between powerful states whose economy is deeply globalized, but it cannot be perceived as a spontaneous movement generated by globalization. On the contrary, it is a perfect expression of the fact that globalization is the result of powerful states' unilateral policies in international economic relations. Reflecting fundamentally economic unilateralism, the exterritoriality of law leads not to global and homogenized rules that apply to all actors but to the aggressive assertion of national laws to the detriment of foreign interests. A move towards the globalization of legal norms is certainly on the rise, but in a totally different social environment; it is the one to which has led the universalization of human rights and the prodigious use of universal jurisdiction in order to secure their protection.

4.1.1.3 Extraterritoriality as a Means to Protect Human Rights: Universal Jurisdiction

The prevalence of a state centric-system as well as the principle of the territoriality of law have durably created serious obstacles to the enforcement of human rights despite the unprecedented development witnessed by the latter since the Second World War. However, the expansion of the universal jurisdiction in the past decades has opened a new perspective for the protection and enforcement of human rights. The latter enjoy today both moral and positive universality in that all states not only bear the duty to honour them, but also have the competence or authority to prosecute alleged violators and enforce penalties, regardless of the place of the violations or the nationalities of the victims or defendants.[43]

As is known, the principle of universal jurisdiction recognizes that all states have a responsibility or a legitimate interest to punish acts and offenses that are perceived as particularly heinous or harmful to mankind or which affect gravely the whole mankind, even when these acts or offenses have taken place abroad and have been committed by other persons than their own nationals.[44] In other words, universal jurisdiction refers to the competence of a state under International Law to prosecute an international crime when no other internationally recognized prescriptive link – chief among them territoriality, nationality, passive personality and the protective principle- exists at the time of the alleged commission of the offence.[45] Thus, when a state acts under the universal jurisdiction, it claims to exercise jurisdiction over

[42] See, for instance, Stern (1994, pp. 979–1003), Raustiala (2004, p. 3 and seq).

[43] See Magnarella (1995b, p. 160).

[44] See Stern (1999, p. 737); de la Pradelle (2000, p. 905); Ratner and Abrams (2001, p. 161); Slaughter (2004, p. 169); O'Keefe (2004).

[45] See O'Keefe (2009, pp. 811–812).

any offender irrespective of any question of nationality or place of commission of the offense, or of any link between the prosecuting state and the offender.[46]

Universal jurisdiction arose as an exception to the principle of the territoriality of law out of the need to criminalize offenses that affect gravely mankind. It is therefore inherently linked to the notion of international crimes which includes all violations of law affecting those legal interests in whose preservation humanity has a general interest and for which criminal protection is provided in a treaty or under customary law.[47] The idea that there are certain offenses which need to be considered as international crimes has emerged since the tenth century when many states came to see in the piracy a threat to a common value of the international community: the freedom of navigation on the high seas.[48] A number of offenses have since then been gradually included in the notion of international crimes such as slavery, war crimes, crimes against peace, crimes against humanity, genocide and torture.[49] Some authors have suggested that this list is not exhaustive and that whenever a crime rises to the level of *jus cogens,* its violation becomes liable to universal jurisdiction.[50]

David J. Scheffer has argued that "Everyone talks about universal jurisdiction, but almost no one practices it. It has been a mostly rhetorical exercise since World War Two...The evidence of state practice is sparse".[51] Certainly, the impact of universal jurisdiction has, during the first decades following World war Two, been limited to the sphere of academic circles than to states' practice. But, universal jurisdiction has started to expand since the 1970s. It is true that such move was initiated by multilateral treaties[52] and not through independent decisions taken *ex officio* by national judges in accordance to a customary rule. However, the adoption of these treaties was a recognition that the classical jurisdictional regime, where no international judicial and enforcement mechanism did exist, has become unable to effectively prosecute and punish international crimes.[53] It was not a surprise therefore that the new situation created by these multilateral treaties has in turn

---

[46] See Carnegie (1963, p. 405).

[47] See Jescheck (1985, pp. 332–333).

[48] On the origin of universal jurisdiction, see Guillaume (1992, pp. 23–36); Bassiouni (2004, pp. 42–43); Kraytman (1985, p. 2).

[49] See Princeton Project (2001, p. 29). See also American Law Institute (1987) §404, which refers to "certain offenses recognized by the community of nations as of universal concern, such as piracy, slave trade, attacks on or hijacking of aircraft, genocide, war crimes, and perhaps certain acts of terrorism".

[50] See Randall (1988, p. 831).

[51] Scheffer (2001, p. 233).

[52] See Biguma (1998).

[53] This was due in particular, notes M. Inazumi, to "the shortcoming of relying on territorial jurisdiction and on the extradition system based on the principle of reciprocity", Inazumi (2005, p. 81).

pushed, first, national legislations,[54] and then national courts[55] to try to feel the gap. It is also true that the number of prosecutions of gross human rights violations through universal jurisdiction was initially limited; however, this number has started to increase during the 1990s and more importantly during the first decade of the twenty-first century. Such a move was the consequence of the establishment of the international criminal courts which has boosted the progress of international humanitarian and criminal law and convinced states of the importance of recognizing the interest of the international community in ending impunity and accepting universal jurisdiction.[56] It has been noted in this regard that more cases of universal jurisdiction have been reported in the past decade than throughout the whole history of modern International Law.[57] Some authors have even come to believe that the expansion of universal jurisdiction has led to the emergence of a customary law that allows a permissive exercise of universal jurisdiction over genocide, crimes against humanity, and some war crimes, and may be evolving towards a mandatory one.[58] Even more important is the fact that there is today a growing determination that grave international crimes must not go unaddressed and that universal jurisdiction appears in this regard, as noted by S. Macedo, "as a potent weapon: it would cast all the world's courts as a net to catch alleged perpetrators of serious crimes under international law. It holds the promise of a system of global accountability – justice without borders – administered by the competent courts of all nations on behalf of humankind."[59]

Certainly, universal jurisdiction has sometimes been at the origin of serious difficulties between some states. Its implementation has been sometimes selective.[60] It has also not been always successful.[61] But, today, universal jurisdiction has become so important that it has been embraced by the international human rights movement as a means to promote accountability for gross human rights violations and that a veritable transnational advocacy network organizes and strategizes for its effective implementation.[62] Indeed, one of the consequence of the expansion of universal jurisdiction is the emergence of what has been called the "transnational human rights litigation"[63], which allows individuals to delocalize the judicial process by selecting all over the world the most appropriate and effective judicial forum which can address the violations of human rights from

[54] On the increasing number of national legislations that have provided for the exercise of universal jurisdiction, see Butler (2004, pp. 67–76).

[55] See Slaughter (2004, pp. 168–190).

[56] Idem, pp. 87–98; Bottini (2004, p. 504).

[57] Reydmans (2003, p. 1).

[58] Broomhall (2003, p. 112).

[59] Introduction of Macedo (2004, p. 4).

[60] See Cryer et al. (2010, pp. 61–62).

[61] See Kontorovitch (2007). See also Kissinger (2001, pp. 86–96); Dachy and Wajs (2003).

[62] Reydmans (2003, p. 1).

[63] See Koh (1994, p. 103); Aceves (2000, p. 41); Frydman (2009), vol.77.

which they have suffered. These fora are of course of national character, but they exist in states which have developed civil and criminal responses to violations of human rights regardless of where such violations have taken place. Moreover, the progress in involving domestic courts in addressing violations of human rights abroad has been such that the "forum convenience" is increasingly not limited to the courts of those states which have adopted the universal jurisdiction.[64] Thus, although pressures have been put on some states such as Belgium to give up universal jurisdiction, the latter has not only continued to develop elsewhere but has also inspired the imagination of new mechanisms in order to sue the violators of human rights.[65] This has led inter alia to the emergence of the forum shopping in order to pursue the enforcement of human rights in an open judicial environment, where spatial and geographical legal limitations do no longer exist. Such move has been possible thanks to the rise of transnational civil society[66] and advocacy networks[67] and the progress witnessed in the perception that many judges have of their functions which they do henceforth conceive as transcending the borders of their own countries. Indeed, it is thanks to the efforts of advocacy networks and national judges of democratic states that transnational human rights litigation is becoming a reality and that its scope has continued to expand not only spatially but also materially by comprising political and civil as well as social and economic rights.[68] The transnational human rights litigation is becoming so crucial that it can take precedence over the competence of the International Criminal Court as long as a case is being investigated or prosecuted by a national court. Being a fall-back forum, the International Criminal Court plays only a complementary role when a national court is unwilling or unable to genuinely carry out the investigation or prosecution role.[69]

In conclusion, it clearly appears that extraterritoriality, with the exception of the transnational human rights litigation, has been an instrument by which powerful powers seek to influence situations which are normally governed by foreign laws. But the interference of strong states in the national affairs of other states can also take place through the use of the powers they posses within international organizations fora. This has been the case within in particular the United Nations which have witnessed an extension of their competences to the detriment of domestic jurisdiction.

[64] See Frydman (2009, p. 75).

[65] Idem, p. 88.

[66] See Florini (2000).

[67] See Keck Sikkink (1998).

[68] See on this new development Hall (2002), vol.41; Balthazar (1998), vol.29.

[69] See Newton (2001; Bottini (2004), p. 546 et seq).

4.1.2 The Extension of United Nations' Competencies to the Detriment of Domestic Jurisdiction

The past decades have witnessed an expansion of the competences of the United Nations to the detriment of national competences. Such an expansion has been generally tolerated by members' states as long as it remained of a limited nature and scope, but it has raised strong criticism when it affected individual states in a manner that contravened major principles of International Law. This is what happened in particular when the Security Council committed excès of power.

4.1.2.1 The Relative Limitation of Domestic Jurisdiction

In general, the extension of the UN competences at the detriment of domestic jurisdiction has been of limited character. This can be illustrated, first, by the experience of the League of Nations before envisioning the experience of its successor, the United Nations.

We know that the Covenant did comprise a domestic jurisdiction clause which states in its Art.15 (8) that:

> "If the dispute between the parties is claimed by one of them, and is found by the Council, to arise out of a matter which by international law is solely within the domestic jurisdiction of that party, the Council shall so report, and shall make no recommendation as to its settlement."

It is significant that the domestic jurisdiction clause was incorporated in the Covenant at the request of President Wilson who wanted to reassure the American people that the League would not be allowed to intervene in US domestic affairs.[70] Similar feeling was shared within many other states where there was a fear that the League might give rise to a "super-state" or a "super sovereignty."[71] But the incorporation of the domestic jurisdiction clause in the Covenant has disappointed those who were in favour of the expansion of International Law.[72] Such fear and disappointment were both excessive as Art. 15 (8) was very limited in its scope as it was only meant to exclude the Council's involvement in the settlement of issues pertaining to domestic affairs. The domestic jurisdiction clause, despite its phrasing, has its origin in the reservations that used to be frequently made in treaties or other legal instruments in order to exclude from obligatory arbitration matters of

---

[70] Jones (1951, p. 222 et seq).

[71] Williams (1929, p. 477).

[72] James L. Brierly has written at that time that the incorporation in the Covenant of the domestic jurisdiction clause " as a new catchword . . .capable of proving as great hindrance to the orderly development of (International Law) as the somewhat idols of sovereignty, state equality, and the like have been in the past", Brierly (1925, p. 8).

domestic character.[73] Furthermore, the likelihood that the Council upholds its competence was very limited due to the voting system, which based on the unanimity rule, allowed every member of the Council to block the adoption of any decision which does not fit with its interest. Besides, during the years of existence of the League, the competence of the Council was raised in only three instances.[74]

However, although Art. 15 (8) has remained of little importance in the Council's experience, it contained the germs for an incommensurable expansion of the competences of future international organizations, particularly the United Nations, to the detriment of states' domestic jurisdiction. Such potential of development was contained in the phrase which gives authority to the Council to decide when a matter is according to International Law within the domestic jurisdiction of a state. Initially largely unnoticed, the importance of such phrase will be highlighted by the Permanent Court of International Justice in the Case of the *Nationality Decrees in Tunis and Morocco*. This case has at its origin in a dispute between France and Great Britain who opposed to the application to its subjects of French decrees issued in Tunis and Moroccan protectorates on the ground that such application was contrary to a treaty signed with France. When Great Britain requested the Council to take up the matter, France rejected the latter competence on the ground that the issue was a matter of its domestic jurisdiction. It was in this context that the Council decided to refer to the Permanent Court of International Justice, for its opinion, the question whether the dispute referred to it was or not by International Law solely a matter of domestic jurisdiction (Art. 15, paragraph 8, of the Covenant). In its response, the Court clarified that matters which are "solely within the domestic jurisdiction" seem rather to contemplate certain matters which, though they may very closely concern the interests of more than one state, are not, in principle, regulated by International Law. As regards such matters, each state is sole judge.[75] It then reached the conclusion that "The question whether a certain matter is or is not solely within the jurisdiction of a state is an essentially relative question; it depends upon the development of international relations".[76] Such a conclusion will later on open the door to the expansion of the competences of international bodies, especially within the United Nations as it stresses that there is no fixed and intangible borderlines between International and domestic domains, and that the boundary between them varies in accordance with the development of International Law. The Court dictum will be since then the leading pronouncement

[73] See on this Wilson (1929, pp. 68–93); Ulimubenshi (2003, pp. 27–34). Jackson H. Ralston has noted about the reservation related to what has been called "domestic questions" that "without e definition at least, the exclusion (of domestic questions) seems superfluous. By the very conditions of its existence, an international court (or arbiter) deals with international questions and not those which are domestic", Ralston (1919, p. 44).

[74] See Fincham (1948, p. 20 et seq).

[75] PCIJ, Series B, No 4, (7 February 1927), pp. 23–24.

[76] Idem, p. 24. It consequently reached the conclusion that in the present state of international law, questions of nationality are in principle within this reserved domain.

on the issue of the content and scope of "domestic jurisdiction" inter alia under the UN Charter. Another factor will also enter into play: the increased interdependence between states as "generally speaking, one can say that the matters left to domestic competence by customary international law. . .have now modified this position. The most significant aspect of the development of treaty law today is the tendency for treaty norms to invade all sectors of a state's domestic life."[77]

It was certainly the need to take into consideration the increased interpenetration between the states that has pushed the drafters of the UN Charter to provide the organs of the latter with larger competences than those which had been attributed to the League of Nations and to conceive of domestic jurisdiction's scope in a broader manner in order to counterbalance the expansion of that competences. This concern has been aptly expressed by the drafters of the UN Charter who made it clear that:

> "The Organization we are developing is assuming, under the present Charter, functions wider in their scope than those previously assumed by the League of Nations or other international bodies and even wider than those which were contemplated at Dumbarton Oaks, especially in the economic, social and cultural fields. The tendency to provide the United Nations with a broad jurisdiction is, therefore, relevant and founded. The necessity, on the other hand, to make sure that the United Nations under prevalent world conditions should not go beyond acceptable limits or exceed due limitation called for principle 8 (which will become later on Art. 2.7) as an instrument to determine the scope of the attribute of the Organization and to regulate its functioning in matters at issue."[78]

It should also be noted that at San Francisco some delegates have insisted on including the principle of non-interference of the future United Nations' organs in domestic affairs as they were afraid that the provisions of the UN Charter, in particular article 55, which are related to the promotion of human rights might be construed in such a way as to allow these organs to intervene in Member states' internal affairs.[79]

One of the first consequences of the new perception of the interpenetration of the newly arising international legal order and its relationship with states' legal order is that the clause on domestic jurisdiction was conceived not only to be a bar to the involvement of the UN in the settlement of conflicts related to domestic matters as used to be the case with the League of Nations but also to become a basic principle of the organisation meant to prevent the latter from intervening in all issues having a domestic character, with the exception of actions to be taken by the Security Council when they are related to the maintenance of peace and security. Likewise, it was also decided that the clause on domestic jurisdiction should apply to all UN organs and not only the Security Council as was the case with the Covenant. However, no legal mechanism has been adopted to ensure that the limits between national and UN areas of competences are preserved, which fact will lead to an

[77] Conforti (2005, p. 134).

[78] U.N.C.I.O., Supplement to Report of Rapporteur, Committee I/1, to Commission I, Doc.1070, I/1/34 (I) (d) (Documents, VI, 486).

[79] See Goodrich and Hambro (1946, p. 190).

uncontrolled expansion of the UN competences to the detriment of domestic jurisdiction and sometimes to abuses of powers particularly by the Security Council. Such abuses will be all the more facilitated that the terminology used is often vague and imprecise as is the case with the controversial word "intervene" which aggravated the difficulty in defining the respective competences of the states and the United Nations. Thus, Art.2 (7) of the UN Charter, probably the most controversial article of the UN Charter,[80] does state that:

> "Nothing contained in the present Charter shall authorize the United Nations to intervene in matters which are essentially within the domestic jurisdiction of any state or shall require the Members to submit such matters to settlement under the present Charter; but this principle shall not prejudice the application of enforcement measures under Chapter VII."[81]

However, the prospect that the expansion of such interpenetration may benefit international competences to the detriment of national competences has made the drafters of the UN Charter believe it necessary to protect the latter by broadening the scope of domestic jurisdiction through the substitution of the phrase "matters which are essentially within the domestic jurisdiction of any state" to the phrase "matters which by international law are solely within the domestic jurisdiction of the state concerned" contained in Art. 15 (8) of the Covenant. Such modification was criticised at that time as it was perceived as retrogression from the system of the League and a disparagement of International Law and its progressive development.[82] However, UN practice will very quickly show that such criticism and fear were not justified. Thus, L. Preuss was able to note few years after the adoption of the UN Charter that "If the purpose of the Sponsoring Governments was to safeguard the domestic domain by limiting the powers of the United Nations", they chose an unreliable instrument for accomplishing this aim. For Article 2(7), with its vague and elastic phraseology, was to prove in practice to be susceptible of an interpretation in a sense precisely opposite to that which was intended by the framers."[83]

Indeed, although Art. 2.7 has frequently been invoked by states, its application was very often rejected by UN organs to the extent that some scholars have raised the question whether the domestic jurisdiction clause still fulfils its original purpose, that is to protect the sovereignty of member states.[84] This led to the reduction of the sphere of domestic jurisdiction in different areas such as matters related to the Non-Self-Governing Territories and the implementation of self-determination in order to accelerate the decolonization process, human rights,

---

[80] Gilmour (1967a, p. 331).

[81] See on Art. 2 (7) Berthoud (1948); Vallindas (1948); Goodrich (1949); Howell (1954, p. 48); See Preuss (1949-I); Rajan (1958); Bindschedler (1963-I, p. 108); Ross (1964); Verdross (1965); Gilmour (1967b, c); Ermacora (1968-II, p. 124); Trindade (1976, p. 25); Watson (1977, p. 71); Jones (1979); Nolte (2002); Conforti (2005); Kawser (2006, pp. 175–197).

[82] See Preuss (1949-I, pp. 597–604).

[83] Idem, p. 604.

[84] Nolte (2002, p. 150).

refugees and displaced persons, maintenance of peace and security, etc. However such reduction has remained of general character and did very rarely affect individual states. It did not also affect sensitive issues such as the form of states, the system of government, the management and utilization of territory and the economy, etc. B. Conforti has shown, further to a thorough examination of the UN practice, that "the original meaning and basic concept of Article 2, para.7, still remained alive and vital, except for the formation of individual specific unwritten rules derogating from it, particularly of norms relating to the areas of human rights and decolonisation. Also for human rights, we held that their violation. . .came within the matters 'essentially' belonging to the so-called gross violations, that is severe and brutal violations, such as apartheid, genocide, torture and so on."[85] The idea that Art. 2 (7) has been increasingly eroded and emptied of substance[86] seems therefore exaggerated. However, there are situations where UN organs have taken actions that sometimes went beyond the usually tolerated limitation to domestic jurisdiction to the extent that serious doubts have been raised about the legality of such decisions. These actions have been taken particularly by the Security Council, which has been accused of excès of power.

4.1.2.2 The Excès of Power of the Security Council

We know that the primary responsibility of the Security Council is to maintain international peace and security. To this end, the Security Council determines, in accordance with Art. 39 of the UN Charter, whether a situation is a threat to peace and security and, if so, authorizes enforcement action, which can take the form of sanctions (Art. 41) or the use of force (Art. 42). However, since 1946, the role of the Security Council has been extended in order to cover issues, which in principle are not under its responsibility.

Human rights have been one of the issues to which the Security Council has extended its role. The view has very early prevailed that Art. 2.7 was inapplicable in cases related to human rights violations.[87] This is what happened in particular when the Security Council condemned, in the 1960s, 1970s and 1980s, apartheid and racism as a threat to international peace and security and consequently adopted sanctions against South Africa and Southern Rhodesia. This is what happened also when the Security Council condemned the repression of the Kurdish population by the Iraqi regime, which constituted, according to Resolution 688 (1991), a threat to international peace and security. The latter resolution has been perceived as ushering a new era in the protection of human rights. However, it did not displace the understanding that human rights issues properly reside within the domestic

---

[85] Conforti (2005, p. 141).

[86] See, for instance, Nolte (2002, p. 171).

[87] See White (2005, p. 91).

jurisdiction of states and therefore remain beyond the reach of the UNSC.[88] In this regard, many states, including some permanent members, have durably insisted to say, at the occasions of different interventions of the Security Council dealing with human rights violations, that these interventions are of an exceptional and unique character and should not therefore be meant to set up a precedent. The Security Council has itself until the end of the 1990s insisted that a link be established between an international concern and violations of human rights, that is the existence of a transboundary effect of the latter.[89] However, that link was absent in the Kosovo crisis, which was analyzed by the Security Council in its Resolution 1203 (1998) as intrinsically constituting a threat to international peace and security. Such has also been the case in respect of East Timor crisis, which has been considered by the Security Council in its Resolution 1264 (1999) as a threat to international peace and security on the basis of reports of "systematic, widespread and flagrant violations of international humanitarian and human rights law". These two crises have in fact inaugurated a new policy of the Security Council where violations of human rights can be considered *per se* and not necessarily in connection with an adverse effect exerted on neighbouring countries. This policy has been implemented to different crises such as those related to the Democratic Republic of Congo, Ivory Cost and Sudan. Yet, it has been noted that these crises have a common denominator: the Security Council has made its intervention against human rights violations dependent on the existence of an armed conflict.[90] However, as we will see later on, today there is a kind of general agreement, though more formal than real, that the Security Council extends its role, under the Responsibility to Protect, to human rights violations even when the latter take place in a situations that have no connection with armed conflicts.

The tendency of the Security Council since the end of the Cold War to increasingly resort to Chapter VII of the U.N. Charter as a basis for action in cases of gross violations of human rights has also been illustrated by the creation of the International Criminal Tribunal for Yugoslavia (ICTY) and the International Criminal tribunal for Rwanda (ICTR). Both of these tribunals have been created and their Statutes adopted by a mere resolutions of the Security Council and not by treaties reflecting, as it is legally required by International Law, the consent of the concerned states. With regard to the creation of the ICTY, the UN Secretary-General has argued that the usual conventional process for the establishing of that tribunal would not be appropriate as it could be time-consuming and risky by giving the possibility to some states to not ratify the treaty creating the tribunal.[91] From its part, the Security Council has justified, in its Resolution 827 (1993), the creation of

[88] McClean (2011, p. 28).

[89] Idem, pp. 28–29.

[90] See Chesterman (2001, pp. 546–548).

[91] Secretary-General Report on Aspects of Establishing an International Tribunal for the Prosecution of Persons Responsible for Serious Violations of International Humanitarian Law Committed in the Territory of Former Yugoslavia, U.N. SCOR. U.N. Doc.S/25704 (1993), para 20.

the ICTY by the need to "put an end to such crimes (that is grave breaches of the 1949 Geneva Conventions, violations of the rules or customs of war, genocide and crimes against humanity) and bring to justice the persons who are responsible for them" and by doing so "contribute to the restoration of peace". Many commentators have raised doubts whether the Security Council has the mandate to set up such tribunals.[92] However, although it was clear that the Security Council has no mandate to create international tribunals, the Appeal Chambers have, in the *Tadic case,*[93] admitted that the Security Council was entitled to set up a court on the basis of Art. 41, although the latter does not, either expressly or implicitly, provide the Security Council with the authority to create international tribunals.[94] Some authors do also share the view that the Security Council is empowered, under Chapter VII, to take measures to enforce its decisions either by imposing non-military sanctions or authorizing the use of force. The establishment of the Yugoslavia Court is one example of the many innovative measures that the Security Council has employed in enforcing its decisions after the Cold War, creating for the first time a direct link between accountability and peace.[95] In fact, if a great number of states have agreed to the creation of the ICTY, it was in order to exert a preventive and deterrent effect on conflict in former Yugoslavia. These states insisted also on the ad hoc and exceptional character of the ICTY whose duration in time and scope of jurisdiction were meant to be limited.[96] They also insisted that the creation of such tribunal should not been seen as a precedent.[97]

However, it happens that the Security Council itself committed violations of human rights at the very moment when its role has started to be largely extended to protect that rights. These violations took place on the occasion of the so-called "Global war on terror". As is well known, the Security Council, in reaction to 11 September events and invoking Chapter VII, adopted on 28 September 2001 Resolution 1373 by which it ordered states to prevent and suppress the financing of terrorist acts, to criminalize the willful provision or collection of funds by their nationals or in their territories with the intention that the funds should be used in order to carry out terrorist acts, to freeze funds and other financial assets or economic resources of persons or entities suspected to participate in or facilitate the commission of terrorist acts, to cooperate, particularly through bilateral and multilateral arrangements and agreements, to prevent and suppress terrorist attacks and take action against perpetrators of such acts, to become parties as soon as possible to the relevant international conventions and protocols relating to terrorism, to amend their domestic law in order to criminalize terrorism and its financing,

---

[92] See, e.g. with regard to the ICTY, Rubin (1994, pp. 7–17).

[93] Tadic ICTY A.Ch.2 October 1995, paras 44–45.

[94] A similar view has been expressed by Blakesley (1994, pp. 84–85).

[95] See Baroni (2000, p. 235).

[96] See Sharga and Zalick (1994, p. 361).

[97] See Birdsall (2006, p. 10).

to reinforce the control of their border in order to prevent any terrorist activities, etc. The Security Council established also the Counter Terrorist Committee (CTC), consisting of all of its members, and whose role is to monitor implementation of Resolution 1373.

Among the actions provided for by resolution 1373, there are measures, which directly impact on individual human rights and dangerously undermine the rule of law. This is the case in particular with regard to basic due process and property rights of those persons who have been blacklisted. Indeed, the way the blacklisting can be made leaves no possibility for a judicial supervision to ensure individual rights in accordance to a transparent process. Thus, a person can be blacklisted without being given the chance to defend itself or even to know the reasons why it has been blacklisted.[98] More gravely, once a person is placed on the blacklist, it becomes an international pariah who cannot inter alia dispose of its assets. Such has been the case, for instance, of the famous Kadi whose financial assets have for years been frozen, following his unfair placement on the blacklist. Requested to consider Kadi's claim for a release of his assets, he European Court of Justice held that the imposition of the restrictive measures laid down by the contested regulation in respect of this person, by including him in the list contained in Annex I to that regulation, constitutes an unjustified restriction of his right to property. The Court clarified that the contested regulation, in so far as it concerns Mr. Kadi, "was adopted without furnishing any guarantee enabling him to put his case to the competent authorities, in a situation in which the restriction of his property rights must be regarded as significant, having regard to the general application and actual continuation of the freezing measures affecting him".[99]

It has been noted that the procedure meant to establish the blacklist was fully non transparent to the extent that an ample room was left for placements that may not be motivated exclusively by a legitimate concern for security, but may be abused in order to put a pressure on political opponents or serve vested interests.[100] In fact the opacity of the blacklisting is such that many persons have been unjustly placed on the blacklist. Furthermore, the listing process has been used for political purposes in particular in non-democratic states where it served as an additional means to repress those who are opposed to the government. "The fundamental changes that have occurred since September 11", observes Kim Lane Schepple,[101] "both articulate a new relationship between international and domestic law and also mark the declining hegemony of constitutionalist ideas among political elites. The primary marker of these changes is the increased abilities of national executives to use the cover of international law to undermine domestic constitutions at home. While this has not happened in every country, it happened in a surprising range of states after

---

[98] See Hoffman (2008, pp. 546–548).

[99] Joined Cases C-402/05 P & C-415/05 P, Kadi and Al Barakat v. Council of the European Union, 3.C.M.L.R.41, para 370.

[100] Idem, p. 546.

[101] See Schepple (2006).

September 11, including many states that have little or nothing to do with the front lines of the *Global War on Terror*".

Hence, Resolution 1373 and the resolutions taken afterwards in the context of the war against terrorism, in particular Resolution 1540, have not only posed a serious threat to due process, civil liberties and property rights, but they have also given the opportunity to governments to expand their powers at the detriment of Parliaments and tribunals. But, such negative effects exerted on domestic constitutionalism could not have been possible without the challenge posed to International Law by these resolutions. It was in fact the manifest illegality of these measures that have ushered such serious threat to domestic constitutionalism. By legislating for the whole world in a matter which is beyond its competence, the Security Council has indirectly encouraged governments to also overpass their own competences at the domestic level. Indeed, the problem lies in its origin in the usurpation by the Security Council of constituent authority. It is so because there is no provision in the UN Charter, which confers to the Security Council the right to enact general legislation or to adopt a decision that could be understood as general lawmaking.[102] In this regard, it has been suggested[103] that no legal limitation exists which forbids the Security Council to use Chapter VII in a legislative capacity. The language of Art. 39 is interpreted to stand for the proposition that the Security Council can create law. In fact, the role of the Security Council is of executive character. It consists mainly in determining whether a situation constitutes a breach to peace and security. In performing such role, the Security Council does apply law and not create it. Such a conclusion can be drawn from a literal interpretation of the Charter,[104] which is silent about the legislative powers of Security Council.[105] It is also confirmed by the fact that nothing in the *travaux préparatoires* shows that the framers of the Charter did envision to provide the Security Council with a legislative role.[106] There is also no support, in the practice of the UN member states, for the deduction, on the basis of the concept of implied powers, of legislative powers of the Security Council.[107] Lastly, international practice since the adoption of Resolution 1373 has not provided its support to the idea that the Security Council can act as a world legislature as many states have expressed their opposition inter alia to Resolution 1540 which aimed at giving the Security Council legislative powers in its fight against terrorism. Hence, expressing a general feeling prevailing among the Non-Aligned-Movement, India has declared at that occasion that:

[102] See Marschik (2005, p. 460).

[103] Harper (1994, p. 14).

[104] See Nolte (2000, pp. 320–321).

[105] See Schachter (1995, p. 120); Bowett (1997, p. 80).

[106] See Arangio-Ruiz (2000, pp. 660–682).

[107] See Marschik (2005, pp. 463–464).

> "India is concerned at the increasing tendency of the Security Council in recent years to assume legislative and treaty-making powers on behalf of the international community, binding on all states, a function not envisaged in the Charter of the United Nations.
>
> India has taken note of the observation of cosponsors that the draft resolution contained in document S/2004/326 does not prescribe adherence to treaties to which a state is not party. India cannot accept any obligations arising from treaties that India has not signed or ratified. This position is consistent with the fundamental principles of international law and the law of treaties.
>
> India will not accept externally prescribed norms or standards, whatever their source, on matters within the jurisdiction of its Parliament, including national legislation, regulations or arrangements, which are not consistent with India's national interest or infringe on its sovereignty."[108]

As we have seen above, Art. 2.7 excludes by definition that the Security Council can exercise legislative powers in particular in matters which are of the domain of domestic jurisdiction. It is true, as we have seen above, that these powers have been extended to the protection of human rights in accordance with limited criteria. However, these powers have been extended with the view of protecting and not undermining or violating human rights. Now, in its war against terror, the Security Council went far beyond that criteria as it arrogated to itself the competence to enact abstract norms, directly binding on member states of the UN which are to be immediately effective and which undermine existing domestic constitutional provisions or norms that conflict these rules, thereby changing domestic constitutions.[109]

It has been argued[110] that the Security Council is an instrument of power and that its actions are cloaked in legality and that in the absence of effective accountability, the powers of the Security Council to make International Law would license a powerful minority to dominate the rest of the world in addition to undermining the very foundation of the UN Charter. This is one of the reasons why it is increasingly believed that a judicial review of the actions of the Security Council should be carried out. Such opportunity was given to the I.C.J. in the Lockerbie case, but it was unfortunately missed. The Lockerbie case has drawn particular attention as it did directly affect domestic jurisdiction.

The Lockerbie case has, as is know, its origin in the tragic explosion on 21 December 1988 of a Pan American Flight over Lockerbie in Scotland when it was en route from London to New York. About 3 years later, the United States and the British Governments have, after having announced that they have gathered conclusive evidences that the explosion was perpetrated by two Libyan agents, requested the Libyan Government to extradite[111] these two agents in order to stand a trial

---

[108] UN-Doc.S/2004/329, 28 April 2004.

[109] Cohen (2011, p. 34).

[110] Akram and Shah (2005, p. 455).

[111] The two Governments used in fact the term "surrender" which does not exist in International Law instead of "extradite" as they were aware that a request for "extradition" was not appropriate due to the circumstances of the case. Alfred P.Rubin has noted in this respect that "The demand for

either in Scotland or in Washington D.C. In response, Libya refused to grant extradition and decided to prosecute itself its two nationals in accordance with the Montréal Convention for the Suppression of Unlawful Acts against the Safety of Civil Aviation of 23 September 1971. It also offered to the American and British Governments to send observers to the trial or to request the International Court of Justice to determine which state has proper jurisdiction. The American and British Governments could have tested Libya and its ability to properly prosecute the accused offenders in accordance with the Montreal Convention requirements, but they rejected the Libyan offer and decided to request the Security Council to support their demand.[112] On 22 January, the Security Council, without carrying out its own investigations, adopted Resolution 731 by which it requested the Libyan Government to immediately provide a full and effective response to the US and British requests, amongst which particularly the extradition of the two Libyan nationals. Libya responded by arguing that it was not obliged, under International Law as well as the Montréal Convention for the Suppression of Unlawful Acts against the Safety of Civil Aviation of 23 September 1971, to extradite its nationals and suggested that a trial of the latter be conducted in a neutral country. It also filed on 3 March 1992 a claim with the ICJ by which it requested the later to declare that Libya had fully complied with all of its obligations under the Montreal Convention, that the American and the British Governments had breached a number of provisions of the Montreal Convention amongst which in particular Art. 7 which does incorporate the principle *aut dedere aut judicare*, which leaves states members with the choice between extradition and prosecution of an alleged offender[113] and that the American and British Governments were obliged to refrain from any use or threat of force against Libya and from all violations of its sovereignty and territorial integrity. In addition, Libya requested the ICJ to take provisional measures in order to protect it from unilateral action due to its refusal to extradite its two nationals. From its part, acting under Chapter VII of the Charter, the Security adopted on 31 March 1992 Resolution 748 by which it determined that Libya's "continued failure to respond fully and effectively to the requests in resolution 731 constituted a threat to international peace and security" and decided to apply sanctions against Libya including a ban on all flights to and from Libya. About a year and half later, the Security Council broadened the sanctions against

surrender by the United States and Great Britain presupposed a Libyan legal obligation to surrender the accused. It appears that by changing the word from extradition to surrender the United States and the United Kingdom thought that the complications of extradition law could be avoided. It is very hard to understand their logic in this. There is no known basis for asserting that general international law contains a 'surrender' obligation distinct from 'extradition' or the expulsion of undesirable aliens", Rubin (1993, p. 7).

[112] For more details on the position taken by the Libya and the US and the UK prior to the submission of the Lockerbie case to the Security Council, see Plachta (2001, pp. 125–129).

[113] See on this principle Wise (1998, pp. 15–29).

Libya by adding to the ban imports of oil equipment and all services related to aviation.[114]

The major issue raised by the Lockerbie case was whether a state is obliged under International Law to extradite its own nationals. Now, International Law has been all the time very clear on the matter by admitting that a state is not, in the absence of an agreement between the concerned parties, under any obligation to extradite its nationals. However, a State, who refuses to extradite one of its nationals, has the duty to prosecute him or her. That state of the matter has been endorsed by states' general practice, their national law and judiciary jurisprudence.[115] The United States and the United Kingdom have also, although in an indirect manner,[116] adhered to this principle. The choice between extradition and prosecution has been taken into consideration by the 1971 Montréal Convention for the Suppression of Unlawful Acts against the Safety of Civil Aviation with regard to all persons suspected to have committed an offense and found to be in the territory of one of the contracting states. Hence, the Montreal Convention states in its Art. 7 that "The Contracting State in the territory of which the alleged offender is found shall, if it does not extradite him, be obliged, without whatsoever and whether or not the offence was committed in its territory, to submit the case to its competent authorities for the purpose of prosecution. Those authorities shall take their decision in the same manner as in the case of any ordinary offence of a serious nature under the law of that state". The state holding the suspect is then free to decide whether to prosecute that person or proceed to his or her extradition. The Montreal Convention states also in its Art. 5 (2) that the contracting parties are entitled to establish jurisdiction over suspected offenders when they are present in their territory and allows them to exercise criminal jurisdiction over these individuals in accordance with their national law (Art. 5.3). Moreover, it is well established that a state enjoys, even when the conditions for the proper extradition of an individual are met, the sovereign right to refuse to grant that extradition.[117] Thus, at the time of

---

[114] Resolution 883 of 11November 1993.

[115] See, e.g., Saint-Aubin (1913, pp. 296–297).

[116] M. Bourquin writes in this regard that "According to a generally admitted rule, a state does not extradite its nationals. Formally prohibited by the national law of many countries (Germany, Austria, Belgium, Hungary, Netherlands, etc.), the extradition of nationals is equally not observed by those many states, such as France, who do not possess national rules prohibiting it. There is only two great powers (United States and United Kingdom) which do admit it. However, their doctrine on this issue has no practical consequence as these two states do accept the extradition only to the governments with whom they are contractually committed and that, with the idea of reciprocity, nationals are in fact prevented from extradition due to the fact that one of the contracting parties does not want to handover its nationals", Bourquin (1927-I, pp. 192–193). See also Chauvy (1981, pp. 44–45). With regard to recent US policy, M. Cherif Bassiouni has underlined that "The official policy of the United States in treaty negotiations has been, until lately, to prevent when possible the surrender of nationals, but this is no longer the case. The Secretary of State can always refuse to surrender a citizen of the United States unless there is an explicit treaty provision providing for reciprocity", Bassiouni (2002, p. 684).

[117] Bassiouni (2002, p. 108).

the submission of the Lockerbie issue to the Security Council, International Law was clear on the matter of the extradition by a state of its own nationals, although the situation has somehow started to change in the past decade further to the progress made in the repression of international crimes which in certain circumstances obliges a state to hand over its nationals to international tribunals for prosecution. It was not therefore a surprise that the demand of the extradition of the two Libyan nationals was perceived as "extraordinary in itself because International Law does not require a state to extradite its nationals in the absence of an affirmative agreement or a reciprocal arrangement."[118] The decision of the Security Council requesting the extradition of the two Libyan nationals was therefore clearly inconsistent with International Law. Instead, the Security Council could have at most required the parties concerned to enter into negotiations in accordance to Art. 33 of the UN Charter or more properly to advise them to submit their conflict to the ICJ in accordance with Art. 14 of the Montreal Convention which states that "Any dispute between two or more Contracting States concerning the interpretation or application of this Convention which cannot be settled through negotiation, shall, at the request of one of them, be submitted to arbitration. If within six months from the date of the request for arbitration the Parties are unable to agree on the organization of the arbitration, any one of those Parties may refer the dispute to the International Court of Justice by request in conformity with the Statute of the Court."

It is true that the Security Council enjoys some discretion when determining the existence of a threat to international peace and security,[119] but it is not appropriate to suggest that peace "is not necessarily identical with law"[120] or that it is not the Security Council's "job to keep the entire system working smoothly and lawfully"[121] as no social system can remain peaceful and sustainable without due regard to justice and rule of law. Very often, international conflicts do arise in reason of serious breaches of Law which affect the rights of a given state. Therefore, the Security Council, while it may as a political organ be forced to make use of political means in order to reach its goals which are to preserve or restore peace, it cannot, when doing so, commit itself a breach of law and affect the rights of a state established in accordance with International Law. International peace and security require above all the maintenance and prevalence of rule of law. Ignoring such a reality never helps establishing durable peace, but to the contrary creates recurrent

[118] Marcella (1999, p. 94). D.Marcella writes in this regard that "The Montreal Convention applies to the facts of this case (i.e., Lockerbie case)...Libya is a party to the Montreal Convention and is the state where the 'alleged offenders' are present. Consistent with the attendant obligations, Libya is not required to extradite the suspects, since extradition would be inconsistent with Libyan national law. However, because extradition is unavailable under Libyan law, Libya is obliged by the Convention to undertake the necessary steps to establish jurisdiction over the suspects, and to prosecute them in the Libyan national courts", Idem, p. 99.

[119] See Lowe et al. (2008, p. 35).

[120] Kelsen (1951, p. 294).

[121] Idem, p. 37.

conflicting situations. International peace and security require therefore that the Security Council comply with International Law and avoid perceiving itself, as it has been once alleged, as "a law unto itself."[122] It is not a surprise that the UN Charter requires that the Security Council is also bound "to act in accordance with the purposes and principles of the United Nations."[123] The invocation by the Security Council of the Chapter VII is then inappropriate when it construes Libya's refusal to handover the two suspected offenders to the United States and the United Kingdom as a "threat to peace". Indeed, it is very hard to see the relationship between the old atrocity (the bombing) and a current threat.[124] It is also extremely difficult to understand how the explosion of the Pan American Flight can be seen as an urgent threat to international peace and security when such explosion has taken place about 3 years before the Security Council has started to deal with the issue.[125]

The way the Security Council has handled the Lockerbie issue[126] has certainly reflected on its credibility and legitimacy, illustrated in particular by disrespect for its sanctions by an increasing number of states.[127] It has also eloquently underlined one of the major weaknesses of Art. 2 (7), that is the lack of a judicial review system of UN bodies' decisions which might affect areas of domestic jurisdiction. The submission of the Lockerbie case to the ICJ was an important occasion to clarify the matter. But the Court was not given that opportunity as the parties concerned have years later reached a compromise solution before it did have time to decide on the merits of the Lockerbie case.[128] Meanwhile, the Court has given an idea on its own thinking when it tried to justify its refusal to issue provisional measures by stating that the parties concerned are obliged to accept and carry out the decisions of the Security Council in accordance with Art. 25 of the Charter, including the decision

---

[122] Dulles (1950, p. 194).

[123] Art.24 (2) of the UN Charter.

[124] Rubin (1993, op.cit.,11).

[125] Case Concerning Questions of Interpretation and Application of the 1971 Montreal Convention Arising from the Aerial Incident of Lockerbie (Libyan Arab Jamahiriya v United States), Provisional Measures, ICJ Rep.1992, Dissenting Opinion, 153.

[126] Reflecting a largely shared feeling, Alfred P. Rubin wrote in this respect "that It is certainly within the legal authority of the Security Council to act irrationally and make 'decisions' that reflect its political balance in disregard of the substantive law, morality and facts. But the effect of acting without apparent reason was felt throughout the world in ways apparently not considered seriously by the Security Council members", Rubin (1993, p. 10).

[127] See Hurd (2007, pp. 137–170).

[128] The Court has on 27 February 1998 recognized its jurisdiction in the Lockerbie case. However, on 10 September 2003, the Lockerbie case will be removed from the role of the Court at the request of the three parties. This came as a result of the agreement reached between these parties on August 1998 that the two suspected Libyan nationals will be sued in Netherlands under Scottish law by Scottish judges and after the Security Council had on April 1999 suspended the application of sanctions against Libya.

contained in Resolution 748 and that, in accordance with Art. 103 of the Charter, the obligations of the Parties in that respect prevail over their obligations under any other international agreement, including the Montreal Convention and consequently that the rights claimed by Libya under the Montreal Convention cannot be regarded as appropriate for protection by the indication of provisional measures.[129] Although, the Court insisted to say the right of the parties to contest at the stage of the merits the relevance of these findings remains unaffected, it would have been difficult for the Court to change its mind at the stage of its final decision. This is probably why some judges have been keen to issue dissenting opinions in which they expressed serious doubts on the legality of the Security Council's decisions in the Lockerbie case and in particular its rejection of the principle recognized by International Law and the Montreal Convention which holds that a state has the right to refuse the extradition of its nationals.[130]

The Lockerbie case has triggered a lively debate on whether the International Court of Justice can review the legality of the Security Council's decisions.[131] Most of the scholars do share the view that the Court should play that role. In the absence of any indication either in the UN Charter or in the *travaux préparatoires* enabling the Court to exert its control on the legality on the Security Council's decisions, many scholars have tried to find a legal ground for that control. But, supposing that the Court possesses an inherent power to determine the legality of United Nations organs' decisions when exercising its judiciary role in the contentious as well as the advisory process, which is in fact legally very doubtful as in International Law the establishment of an international competence requires the express agreement of the states concerned,[132] it still remains that it is also very uncertain that the Court's environment would accept that it plays that crucial role. Indeed, there are serious constrains which may render the control by the Court of the legality of Security Council's decisions a very difficult task. These constrains are of legal and political character. Amongst the legal constrains, four are of crucial importance and are not easily surmountable in the present international context: the lack of a general compulsory jurisdiction, the lack of a legal system by which a grieved state may

[129] Case Concerning Questions of Interpretation and Application of the 1971 Montreal Convention Arising from the Aerial Incident at Lockerbie (Libyan Arab Jamahiriya v. United Kingdom), Provisional Measures, ICJ Rep., 1992; Case Concerning Questions of Interpretation and Application of the 1971 Montreal Convention Arising from the Aerial Incident at Lockerbie (Libyan Arab Jamahiriya v. United States), Provisional Measures, ICJ Rep., 1992.

[130] See the Dissenting Opinions of Judges Bedjaoui, Weeramantry, Ajibola, El-Kosheri and Ranjeva.

[131] See McWhinney (1992); Franck (1992, p. 86); Reisman (1993, p. 87); Macdonald (1931); Bedjaoui (1993, 1994); Gowland-Debbas (1994, p. 88); Brownlie (1994); Gill (1995); Alvarez (1996, p. 90); Bowett (1996); Akande (1997, p. 46); Dupuy (1997); Dochring (1997); Malanczuk (1999); Martenczuk (1999, p. 10); Quigley (2000, p. 35); De Wet (2004); Manusama (2006).

[132] See El Ouali (1984, pp. 132–137).

unilaterally address itself to the Court in order to question the legality of a Security Council's decision, the long and cumbersome procedure of the Court and the fact that the Security Council enjoys a discretionary power when requested to enforce a decision of the Court.[133] As to the political constraints, there is the likelihood that any state which is in disagreement with the Security Council might hamper and freeze the latter's decision process, which very often requires speedy action, by submitting a request to the Court for reviewing the legality of a given decision or planned resolution by the Security Council and then the very possible politicization of the Court which already does very often echo general political trends in the General Assembly and the reluctance of the permanent member states to see the Court establishing its control on the legality of the Security Council's decisions.[134] Hence, there are serious risks that a spontaneous emergence of a judicial control of the legality of Security Council's decision might be counterproductive and plunge the UN system in a chaotic situation. The error made by many scholars is to liken the UN system with states' national systems and specially those very rare systems where judges have been able to establish a judicial control of the legality of states' decisions. It is therefore suggested that the Court cannot legally decide on its own to start controlling the legality of Security Council's decisions. By doing so, the Court might be blamed for overstepping its own powers as did the Security Council in the Lockerbie case and other instances. It is believed that the only reasonable way to establish a judicial control on the United Nations' resolutions and decisions is to proceed through a general reform of the prevailing UN system. But, in the meantime, it is urgent that the Security Council shows some self-restraints by avoiding acting ultra vires. In this regard, the practice of the League's Council can be a source of inspiration of the Security Council as the former used to create committees of jurists independent from the UN system and states' influence and whose role was to enquire on the legality of the Council planned actions and decisions. By doing so and showing a greater respect for the rule of law,[135] the Security Council would undoubtedly regain some of the legitimacy that it has lost since the end of the Cold-war. However, the problem is that the Security Council has not only continued to commit excès of power, but it has also refrained from taking any action which could have prevented powerful states from directly intervening, on the pretext of the protection of human rights, in the internal affairs of weaker states in order to achieve national goals. This is what happened in particular at the occasion of the resurgence of humanitarian intervention.

---

[133] Idem, pp. 182–190.

[134] D. W. Bowett has rightly recalled in this respect that "It must be conceded that there are few signs that, at present, the members of the Security Council are not prepared to contemplate judicial review by the Court: the Western powers would see this s a hindrance and neither Russia or China display any great confidence in the Court", Bowett (1996, p. 191).

[135] Nigel and White (2002, p. 124).

4.2 The Resurgence of Humanitarian Intervention

Humanitarian intervention is the use of force across state borders by a state or a group of states, which allegedly aims at preventing or ending grave violations of the fundamental human rights leading to the suffering or death of civilians who are other than their own citizens, without the permission of the state within whose territory force is applied.[136] It is a controversial doctrine as it has since its inception in the nineteenth century constantly assumed a unilateral character. Indeed, humanitarian intervention has been used by powerful states against weaker states in order to achieve their own interests under the guise of redressing human rights violations. The doctrine of humanitarian intervention reflects the refusal of powerful states to adjust to important International Law norms such as the equality of states and the prohibition of the use of force. In fact, humanitarian intervention emerged as an instrument in the hegemonial approach of International law, when the latter has started to endorse the principle of the legal equality of states and the principle of the prohibition to use force in International Relations. That is why humanitarian intervention has never been endorsed by International Law. However, as massive human rights violations have taken place in different parts of the world in the past decades, there is a need for reconceptualizing humanitarian intervention in order to make of it an objective instrument in order to protect peoples who may be subjected to such violations.

4.2.1 Humanitarian Intervention: An Instrument in The Hegemonial Approach to International Law

There are two major subjective motives that have generally been behind the use of humanitarian intervention, first, the uneasiness of powerful states about accepting the extension of legal equality to new states from the periphery, and, second, the uneasiness about accepting the prohibition of the use of force as stipulated by the UN Charter.

4.2.1.1 The Reluctance to Abide by States' Equality

As we have seen above, the principle of territorial integrity has given rise to different principles amongst which the principle of equality. However, the principle of equality which has emerged in the European context starting from the eighteenth century as a complementary element to the principle of sovereignty, has initially

[136] See Holzgrefe (2003, p. 18). However J. L. Holzgrefe adds the "threat of using force", which is not accurate, as we cannot talk of intervention, and humanitarian intervention is a kind of intervention, without the use of force. See, for a classical definition which excludes the "threat of the use of force", Badescu (2011, p. 9).

been limited in its implementation to the Western countries, while the non Western countries were subjected to an unequal status.[137] Unable to enjoy equality, non Western countries have then been excluded from the benefit of International Law and subjected to a de facto situation characterized at best by the signing of temporary, precarious and unequal agreements with the Western countries and at worse by direct intervention or colonization. Such discrimination was legitimized by the perception that the world is divided between "civilized" and "barbarians"[138] and that only Europe personifies civilization. Reflecting the general feeling which was prevailing in the nineteenth century, A.Pillet has written that "Legal equality does not exist between civilized and non civilized states. The former constantly behave in their relations with the latter as superiors commissioned to put them whether they like it or not on the civilization track: on this account they take upon them certain rights of direction, control and administration that the latter do in no way possess against them."[139] Likewise, J.T. Delos has, endorsing as well the general opinion prevailing on the eve of the Second World War, written that "Legal equality is a myth or even a danger if it is not based on a certain real equality. One cannot therefore blame International Law for not extending to all peoples the norms which suit the needs of civilized states."[140]

However a breach was made in the European system in 1856 by the Congress of Paris which extended to Turkey "the benefits of Public Law and European Concert," that is the benefit of International Law or in other terms the enjoyment of legal equality in its relations with the European states. But such situation became very quickly embarrassing to the European powers insofar as the principle of equality and its corollary the principle of non-intervention in local affairs were perceived as an obstacle which may thwart their hegemonic ambitions in their relations with Turkey. Indeed, many European powers were, as we will see hereafter, interested in the disintegration of the Ottoman Empire, hence, the fabrication, as we will see later on, of the principle of nationalities and also of the doctrine of humanitarian intervention. It was then allegedly on the latter ground that the European powers have militarily intervened in the Ottoman Empire in particular in Syria (1860), Crete (1866), Bulgaria (1877), Armenia (1896) etc.,[141] before imposing to it, through the Treaty of Berlin of 13 July 1878, a permanent control on its domestic administration acts under the guise of "guaranteeing" the respect of human rights. Hence, it was clear that in these first cases of humanitarian intervention "the alleged humanitarian motives were...

[137] See Marchal (1931, p. 79).

[138] Hornung (1885, 1886).

[139] Pillet (1898, p. 70).

[140] Delos (1939, p. 252).

[141] These cases of humanitarian intervention have been analyzed by Rougier (1910, p. 472 cont.).

influenced or affected by the political interests of the intervening state"[142] and that obviously "no genuine case of humanitarian intervention has occurred."[143] Furthermore, these humanitarian motives, if any, were inspired by religious considerations. Hence, "The victims to be protected by intervention", notes M. Finnemore, "were Christians; there were no instances of European powers considereing intervention to protect non-Christians. Pogroms against Jews did not provoke intervention. Neither did Russian massacres of Turks in central Asia in the 1860s. Neither did mass killings in China during the Taiping Rebellion against the Manchus. Neither did mass killings by colonial rulers in their colonies. Neither did the massacre of Native Americans in the United States".[144]From his part, M. Levene has shown how the European public opinion has been so well manipulated that it was "knowledgeable" with news of repeated massacre and rape of thousands of Christians in the Ottoman Empire and totally oblivious to the possibly many more tens of thousands of Muslims in this area, not to say the millions thereafter who suffered waves of ethnic cleansing at the hands of Christian Bulgarians, Serbs and Greeks.[145]

It was in the aftermath of the multiple interventions against Turkey that the doctrine of humanitarian intervention was for the first time theoretically formulated. This was done by E.Arntz according to whom "when a government, though acting within the limits of its sovereign rights, violate the rights of humanity, either through measures opposed to the interests of other states or by excess of injustice or cruelties which profoundly offend our morals and civilization, the right to intervention is legitimate as, whatever respectable are the rights to sovereignty and independence of the states, there is something which is more respectable, it is the right of humanity or of the human society which should not be gravely offended."[146] However, it is worth mentioning that E.Arntz has stressed that an isolated state cannot intervene alone in order to redress the situation and that such right should be exerted on behalf of humanity by all the existing states or at least by a big number of civilized states which meet together in congress or through a tribunal in order to take a collective decision.[147]

Despite its implementation in other situations than the one related to the Ottoman Empire, humanitarian intervention was not accepted by the whole doctrine. Hence, for instance, J.S. Mill was of the opinion that those who suffer from internal oppression must free themselves by themselves.[148] W.E. Hall has also stressed that International Law has nothing to do with "tyrannical conduct of a government towards its subjects, massacres and brutality in a civil war, or religious persecution"

---

142 Fenwick (1945, p. 645).

143 Brownlie (1963a, p. 340). See also Vervey (1985, p. 399); Malanczuk (1993, p. 9).

144 Finnemore (2003, pp. 65–66).

145 Levene (2005, p. 225).

146 In Rolin-Jacquemyns (1876, p. 673).

147 Idem.

148 Mill (1867, pp. 153–178).

as there is no consensus on the matter.[149] Similarly L. Oppenheim was of the opinion that "whether there is really a rule of the Nations which admits such interventions may well be doubted."[150] From his part, F. Despagnet has vigorously condemned it by stating that "the intervention against a government which, in the exercise of its internal sovereignty, violate the laws of humanity, cannot (either) be accepted, for fear of giving rise to all kinds of abuses and, under the guise of safeguarding the interests of populations, to completely ruin the respect of states sovereignty...Who cannot (indeed) see how the use of this alleged moral duty (of intervention) is a fertile ground for abuses and serve as a means to completely destroy the independence of states, especially that it will in fact be used only by powerful governments against very weak states? A tyrannical government has only one dispenser of justice: it is the people to which it imposes itself and the lack of union or courage of this people to get rid of it finds its sanction in the maintaining of the tyrant which does oppress it."[151] Lastly, A.Rougier has come to the conclusion, after a very comprehensive and critical analysis of humanitarian intervention, that the latter has been designed in order to dominate and subject other peoples and not to make them enjoy human rights and fundamental liberties. He has highlighted in this respect that "Each time where a powerful state does intervene on behalf of humanity in the domestic jurisdiction of another state, it will do nothing else than opposing its conception of what is just to the conception of the latter, by sanctioning it, if needs be, by the use of force. Its action will tend in fact to incorporate a state in its political sphere of influence. It will ***control*** it in order to prepare itself to dominate it. The humanitarian intervention appears therefore to be an ingenious means to gradually undermine and weaken the independence of a state in order to make it tend towards half-sovereignty; it is for that reason that I have felt interesting to analyze it".[152]

Since its inception in the second half of the nineteenth century humanitarian intervention has never been motivated by primarily humanitarian considerations as it is a matter of a fact that in very few, if any, instances has the right been asserted under circumstances that appear more humanitarian that self-interested and power seeking.[153] That is why the status of humanitarian intervention has remained problematic and discredited in a legally horizontally organized inter-states system, especially in the twentieth century with the increasing emphasis not only on the inviolability of the domestic jurisdiction and the progress made in the prohibition of the use of force[154] (first in a relative manner by the Covenant of the League of Nations and the Kellogg-Briand Pact and then in a more categorical manner by the UN Charter), but also on the legal equality of all states including those which

---

149 Hall (1909, p. 284).

150 Oppenheim (1928, p. 271).

151 Despagnet (1905, pp. 215–216).

152 Rougier (1910, p. 526).

153 See Franck and Rodley (1973a, p. 290).

154 Chesterman (2001, p. 43).

emerged from decolonization and which have taken advantage of the rivalry between the two superpowers during the Cold War in order to expurgate from International Law colonial and discriminatory rules.

The doctrine of humanitarian intervention has then been initially designed by hegemonic states which were not comfortable with the first ever legal equal relations established with peripheral states. The same uneasiness is behind the resurrection of the doctrine of humanitarian intervention in the past decades and especially since the collapse of the Soviet Union and the end of the Cold War. We know that the UN Charter, with the exception of the privileged situation given to the five permanent members within the Security Council, is based on the principle of equality of the states.[155] Such equality has made International Law applicable to the relations between all states without any discrimination including those states which have emerged as a result of the decolonization process which has been strongly supported by the UN and the new super-powers that emerged at the end of the Second World War, that is USA and USSR.

A series of international instruments have stressed the attachment of the international community to the principle of the legal equality of the states. Hence, for instance, the UN General Assembly has in its 1970 Declaration on Principles of International Law Concerning Friendly Relations and Co-operation among States inter alia stressed that "All States enjoy sovereign equality. They have equal rights and duties and are equal members of the international community, notwithstanding differences of an economic, social, political or other nature."

Legal equality can of course be compromised by military or economic inequality. With regard to the latter, the newly independent states have inherited a situation of deep economic dependence in their relations with the ex-colonial powers. This inequality was facilitated by many rules of International Law created by powerful states. Hence the huge efforts engaged by the Third world countries during the 1960s, 1970s and 1980s in order to substitute to these rules new ones based on justice, fairness and equity. These efforts have led to the emergence of a new legal corpus, going from the proclamation of the permanent sovereignty over natural resources in 1962 to the adoption of the Charter on the economic rights and duties of the states in 1974. In fact, these efforts have not been confined to economic relations as they covered a whole set of issues such as the rules related to treaties, international responsibility, right to development, status and economic exploitation of oceans, etc...All these efforts were meant to provide the ex-colonial peoples with proper legal means in order to make the sovereignty of their countries a reality and to establish with the ex-colonial powers relations based on effective legal equality. It is the ruin of all these achievements that is behind the attempts aiming at the resurrection of the doctrine of humanitarian intervention.

In fact the attempts aiming at the resurrection of the doctrine of humanitarian intervention do only symbolize and reflect a kind of a global policy meant by some

---

155 See Padirac (1953, p. 161 cont.).

powerful states to revive colonial reflexes and practices by subjecting again peripheral states to a legal inequality,[156] in addition to economic inequality which has never disappeared from the scene. Powerful states tend, as shown by N. Krisch,[157] to use International Law as a means of regulation as well as of pacification and stabilization of their dominance, but when faced with the hurdles of equality and stability that International Law erects, they withdraw from it. Hence the calls today for the re-establishment, as in the old colonial times, of shared sovereignty and trusteeship on the many countries that suffer under failed, weak, incompetent, or abusive national authority structures as allegedly the latter cannot fix themselves. "In the future, writes S.Krasner, better domestic governance in badly governed, failed, and occupied polities will require the *transcendence of accepted rules* (italics added), including the creation of shared sovereignty in specific areas. In some cases, decent governance may require some new form of trusteeship, almost certainly de facto rather than de jure."[158] The same author does recommend that shared sovereignty would involve the engagement of external actors in some of the domestic authority structures of the target state for an indefinite period of time[159] and he cites in this regard the control established by major European powers on the Ottoman Empire during the last decades of the nineteenth century[160] as referred to above! Hence also the attempts aiming at reformulating the conditions related, as we will see herewith, to the interpretation of International Law or even its creation through in particular new ways of establishing international customary rules which do suit major Western powers and from the process of which the majority of states will be excluded. I. Brownlie has, with regard to the latter issue, critically analyzed these efforts by noting that:

> "The *modus operandi* for the formation of customary law supposes an equality of states and also a principle of majoritarianism. A certain amount of contracting out is possible but the generality of states are permitted by their conduct to develop customary rules.

---

[156] See El Ouali (1993).

[157] Kirsch (2005, p. 371). N. Krisch clarifies in this regard that "Despite the positive use great powers have always made of International law, and despite their successes in flexibilizing and shaping it, the standard structure of international legal rules has always posed obstacles to great power politics. The central obstacle...is the relatively egalitarian character of international law: the right of all to participate in law-making, and their equal subjection to universal norms", Krisch (2004, p. 27).

[158] Krasner (2004, p. 86). Similar views are expressed by Ignatieff (2003) pp. 306–314; Keohane (2003, p. 286 cont). The latter after having declared that "We have to accept that states are differentiated both in their capacities and in *legal status* (Italics added) : despite the legal fiction of sovereignty, states are not all equal. One person's double standard is another's recognition of reality" (p. 277) has concluded with regard to humanitarian intervention and its desired impact on the future legal status of those states that have been subjected to that intervention that " the political consolidation of gains from humanitarian intervention will depend on institutions that *limit and unbundled sovereignty* (italics added), permitting troubled societies to *exercise some, but not all, aspects of classic sovereignty*" (italics added), p. 278.

[159] Idem, p. 108.

[160] Idem, p. 109.

> This approach to International Law creates problems for those who hold that inequalities of power between states should be reflected in the way in which law is made and applied, and this involves what may be called the hegemonial approach to law-making. The hegemonial approach to international relations may be defined as an approach to the sources which facilitates the translation of the difference in power between states into specific advantages for the more powerful actor. The hegemonic approach to the sources involves the occasions when the powerful actor will obtain "legal approval" for its actions and minimizing the occasions when such approval may be conspicuously withheld."[161]

Similarly and after having carried out a critical analysis of the way in which International Law rules related to the interpretation of international conventions (mainly the UN Charter) and the formation of customary rules have been biased in order to justify the idea that humanitarian intervention has, in the past decades and within a very short timeframe, been endorsed by International Law, M. Byers and S. Chesterman do conclude that:

> "It is true that powerful states have always had a disproportionate influence on customary law-making, in large part because they have a broader range of interests and activities and consequently engage in more practice than other states. But paying less attention to some states is one thing: having a legal justification for doing so is another. It is possible that the legal principle of equality is not, quietly but resolutely, under attack. In the US literature, in particular, analyses and arguments concerning customary international law increasingly make reference to "leading" and "major" states or nations-words that suggest that some states matter more than others in a manner significant to the formation of a custom."[162]

Thus some major powers had, since the end of the Cold War, a difficulty to accept the extension of the principle of legal equality to the peripheral states. They have also the same difficulty with regard to the prohibition of the use of force.

4.2.1.2 The Reluctance to Abide by the Prohibition to Use Force

Powerful states have never been comfortable with the prohibition of the use of force as established by the UN Charter in its Art. 2 (4). "Within a few years of the United Nations' founding", recalls Tom J. Farer,[163] "states able to pursue ends(other than immediate self-defence) by means of the threat or use of force began signaling their taste to do so, preferably without openly violating the new normative dispensation." In fact powerful states have not stopped since then to make use of force in a way that reduces the scope of that article[164] and, as we have seen earlier, expands the concept of self-defence in order to justify "preemptive" attacks. The difficulty to adjust to the new situation created by the UN Charter can be attributed to the fact that International Law is most constraining for dominant states if it includes strict limitations on the use of force. It is in this area that dominance is usually most

[161] Brownlie (1995, p. 49).

[162] Byers and Chesterman (2003, p. 193).

[163] Farer (2003, p. 59).

[164] Gray (2000, p. 8).

pronounced and restrictions on military action affect powerful actors much more than weaker states that usually have little hope to prevail militarily anyway. Broader rights to use force, though in principle applicable to all states, usually benefit mainly the dominant ones…It is thus not surprising that dominant states have frequently challenged international legal constraints on the use of force.[165] The resurrection of the doctrine of humanitarian intervention can then be interpreted as mere an attempt aiming at giving powerful states an additional justification for their illegal use of force, which is all the more easy to "demonstrate" as it belongs to a domain – human rights – that is marked by self-evidence. J. Babic has convincingly shown that the presumption that "human rights" represent some of the universal values in fact indicates their specific ideological purpose: to create an atmosphere of self-evidence. In this context, self-evidence assumes the place of explication; that is the process of offering sufficiently good reasons for humanitarian intervention in some cases proves redundant. The appeal to self-evidence, a form of reasonless gratuitous acceptance, is by no means a novel scheme of political justification. As with doctrines based on divine revelation or validated by a sacred book, self-evidence functions as a form of reductionism absorbing all the reasons from a list supplied in advance.[166]

In 1945 at the San Francisco Conference, the French government suggested the endorsement of the doctrine of humanitarian intervention through an amendment of the draft Charter authorizing states to unilaterally intervene in another states whenever there is a clear violation of essential liberties and of human rights constituting a threat capable of compromising peace.[167] But, the French proposal was rejected. However, some authors have, in spite of that rejection, argued that humanitarian intervention does constitute an exception to the prohibition of the use of force established by Art. 2(4). Amongst these authors, some, exhuming the jus naturalism, invoke an alleged Just War old tradition authorizing the use of force in order to protect innocent people who are violently mistreated by their rulers, others such as legal realists do have a very particularly broad reading of Art. 2(4) and states' practice deducted from their particular understanding of International Law and Law in general.

Some modern jus naturalists do refer to moralists, theologians and philosophers writing before the emergence of modern International Law or those who have later on contributed to the first doctrinal formulation of the later. Hence, according to T. Nardin, these authors have in the sixteenth and seventeenth century Europe justified war as a way to uphold law and protect rights, of which self-defense was only one. Rulers, these moralists argued, have a right and sometimes a duty to enforce certain laws beyond their realms. Some of these belong to the "law of nations" and more importantly to "natural law", understood as comprising precepts that are binding on

[165] See Kirsch (2005, p. 394).

[166] Babic (2003, pp. 46–47).

[167] 12 UNCIO, Commission II, Committee 2, Doc.207, III/2/A/3, 10 May 1945, 179 at 191.

all rational beings and can be known by reason.[168] The moralists, philosophers and theologians who are referred to, have in fact chronologically tried, first, to justify war of religions,[169] and, second, the war of conquest of peripheral states and communities. Ironically theologians and Spanish scholastics such as Fransisco de Vitoria[170] and Bartolome de Las Casas[171] are frequently presented as staunch defenders of the Indians who were at that time commonly perceived as barbarians, deficient and primitive peoples and who as such warranted colonialism and appropriation of their lands. In fact their main concern was how to "humanly" justify Spanish colonialism of the Americas.[172] Thus, for instance, Vitoria has, in full opposition to the ferocious and predatory Spanish colonialists, found that the 'Indians' had rights of *dominion* and that, furthermore, they were basically human beings, even if ones with considerable shortcomings. These rights had, however, to adjust to the expansive natural rights of all people, including the Spanish, to travel, trade, 'sojourn', and, in the cause of Christianity, to proselytize. Such natural rights could not be aggressively asserted unless they were resisted. However, when resisted, theses rights could be asserted to the full extent of conquest and disposition. Now, Vitoria did consider the Indians as inherently resistant.[173]

Modern jusnaturalists do in fact mainly refer to H. Grotius. Heavily inspired by the work of the Spanish theologians and scholastics, H. Grotius has also, though having a secular conception of natural law, accepted a right of sovereigns to wage war for the purposes of punishment against foreign rulers who "excessively violate the law of nature or of nations in regard to any persons whatsoever."[174] But by doing so, H. Grotius has also neatly legitimated a great deal of European action against native peoples around the world.[175]

Amazingly most of the natural law theorists whose writings emerged following the first period of colonization and who were more inclined to opt for legal positivism have rejected intervention for whatsoever reason. Hence, C. Wolff has in this regard categorically rejected H. Grotius' thesis by stating that "Approval is not to be given to the opinion of Grotius, that kings and those who have a right equal to that of kings have the right to extract penalties from any who savagely violate the law of nature or of nations"[176] and that "the source of error is found in the fact that evil seems to him of such a nature that it can be punished and that it is quite in

[168] Nardin (2000, p. 2). See also George (1998, pp. 54–69); Fixdal and Smith (1998, pp. 283–312).

[169] See, for instance, Giovanni da Legnano (1447).

[170] de Vitoria (1557).

[171] de Las Casas (1552).

[172] See Scott (1934); Anghie (1999, 2005).

[173] See Fitzpatrick (2003, p. 448).

[174] Grotius (1646), para 40(4).

[175] See Tuck (1999, p. 103), n. 35.

[176] Wolff (1748), para 169.

harmony with reason that it may be punished by him who is not guilty of it."[177] Likewise, E. de Vattel, who was against intervention unless asked for by an oppressed people, was of the opinion that "did not Grotius perceive that in spite of all the precautions added in the following paragraphs, his views open the door to all the passions of zealots and fanatics, and gives to ambitious men pretexts without number ?"[178]

It is inappropriate to pretend that the doctrine of humanitarian intervention had been formulated well before the second half of the nineteenth century and that there is an old and enduring tradition which dates back to the Middle Ages[179] and which, according to T. Nardin, holds that armed intervention is morally justified when people are violently mistreated by their rulers, and is reflected in the widely-held opinion that states, acting unilaterally or collectively, are justified in enforcing respect for human rights.[180] The examples given by T. Nardin are mainly related to a very particular context where, as we have seen above, not only intervention but also colonization were authorized by International Law in the relations between Western and non Western countries. The doctrine of humanitarian intervention has been conversely formulated in order to justify intervention between legally equal states. Furthermore the attribution of the paternity of that doctrine to authors such as Francisco de Vitoria, Bartolome de Las Casas and Hugo Grotius is incongruous as their first concern was mainly the legitimation of colonization and colonial domination. Modern jus naturalism has therefore a wrong reading of history. This is dictated by the need to justify the use of force by new hegemonic powers. In the present international hegemonic system, the justification of the resurrection of humanitarian intervention through the use of the just war doctrine means the revival of the concept of the bellum justum, or just war, the normative criteria of which are defined by the party that conducts the war[181] and where the hegemonial power acts as judge in her own case.[182] The same can be said about legal realism in its very particular understanding of the UN Charter and International Law in general and which is equally meant to justify the hegemonic policies of some powerful states.

[177] Idem, para 636.

[178] de Vattel (1758, para 7).

[179] There are some authors who believe that the idea of humanitarian intervention goes back to Thucydides. See, for instance, Bass (2008, p. 4).

[180] Nardin (2000).

[181] See Kochler (2001, p. 19). He has also written that "Whatever may be the idealistic rhetoric by which military actions are justified, the system of norms ensuring the peaceful co-existence among nations-what has been known essentially as 'the international rule of law'- will not only be gradually undermined but will finally collapse if an equivalent to the old *jus ad bellum* is introduced in international relations" (p. 25).He adds that "The revival of the just war concept in the new imperial environment *rehabilitates* war as a means of foreign policy. The taboo placed on the non-use of force has quickly vanished under the pressures of "humanitarian realpolitik" (i.e. realpolitik in humanitarian clothes), p. 28.

[182] Idem, p. 19.

Legal realism does allegedly value an approach to International Law based on human dignity,[183] dictated in particular by the conviction that the human rights norms have today been elevated to an imperative level of International Law.[184] We know that legal realism aims at shifting attention away from legal positivism to policy-oriented constitutive approach.[185] Legal realism claims to have a sociological approach of law and believes that only the self-interests of the subjects of law do constitute the foundation of the obligatory force of law. Thus any formal text of law cannot belong to the realm of law unless it meets the expectations of the interested parties. Law itself emerges and exists as such only after its adaptation to practical circumstances and to the interests which come to be expressed therein. In sum, Law does not exist as such and become valid at the time of its enactment by the concerned authority but only *a posteriori* by its confirmation by practice. Thus legal realism does consider explicit and implicit agreements, formal texts, and state behavior as being in a condition of effervescent interaction, unceasingly creating, modifying, and replacing norms. Texts themselves are but one among a large number of means of ascertaining original intention. Moreover, realists postulate an accelerating contraction in the capacity and the authority of original intention to govern state behavior. For original intention has no intrinsic authority. The past is relevant only to the extent that it helps us to identity currently prevailing attitudes about the propriety of a government's acts and omissions.[186] Furthermore, in the domain of International Law, powerful states have a preeminent authority in determining in accordance with their own interests the real meaning and scope of a legal text. To legal realists, clarifies Tom J. Farer, powerful states will not be constrained by old texts in dusty books construed in ways that seriously compromise their interests. Rules acquire authority in the international system by prescribing in greater or lesser detail the behavior that, in a particular area of activity, optimally advances the shared interests of major states. Moreover where, because circumstances have changed or in any event the particular constellation of facts was not foreseen, application of a rule in accordance with its common or long-established meaning threatens highly valued interests of important state actors, the meaning will fail to control behavior.[187] We have elsewhere[188] severely criticized such approach which,when applied to international judgments and awards, ends up by transforming the latter in simple contingent facts that can

---

[183] See Suzuki (1974, pp. 36–37).

[184] See Reisman (2000, p. 15).

[185] See Laswell and McDougal (1992). On the application of legal realism to International Law, see McDougal (1953); McDougal et al. (1968); Rosental (1970).

[186] See Farer (1991, p. 186).

[187] Farer (2003, p. 63).

[188] See El Ouali (1984, p. 116 cont). in which we have carried out a critical analysis of the legal realism as applied by Reisman (1971 to international judgments and awards in his book "Nullity and Revision. The Review and Enforcement of International Judgments and Awards", New Haven and London, Yale University Press, 1971, p. 900).

unilaterally be modified by any concerned party as it may wish in accordance to its own interests.

Hence, according to legal realists, Art. 2(4) does not exist as a legal text clearly prohibiting the use of force whose scope is determined in accordance with the will of the founders of the UN Charter as reflected in particular by the *travaux préparatoires* or as interpreted by the International Court of Justice, but it does exist only as a fact which assumes a legal character when it starts to be implemented, readjusted and adapted in accordance with the interests of the concerned states, that is the most powerful states. Very astonishing are the erratic interpretations which have been given by legal realists to that article, other UN Charter articles related to the use of force and UN practice, depending then on the changing circumstances but in order to achieve the same objective: the justification of humanitarian intervention. One can observe in this regard how the argumentations of a legal realist such as M. Reisman have been in the past three decades changing throughout his various writings aiming at justifying humanitarian intervention. Thus, the latter has been justified on the basis, first, of a very restrictive reading of Art. 2(4),[189] then on the failure of the UN security system due to its blockage during the Cold War by the veto of permanent states[190] and today, while the same UN security system has started to function, on the lack of consensus on human rights between permanent members of the Security Council.[191] These frequent changes in the argumentation have been noted and assessed by other scholars.[192] Therefore there is no need here to dwell at length on that subject. It suffices to note that these changes do reflect the difficulty to justify a doctrine which has never been endorsed by International Law.

4.2.2 The Non-endorsement of Humanitarian Intervention by International Law

Humanitarian intervention does manifestly contravene the principle of non-intervention and the prohibition of the use of force. That is why it has never been endorsed by states' practice as a right of a customary character. International Law has never endorsed the doctrine of humanitarian intervention because the latter manifestly contravenes, first, the principle of non-intervention and, second, the prohibition of the use of force.

From the inception of the humanitarian intervention doctrine in the second half of nineteenth century, many international lawyers, as we have seen above,

[189] Reisman and McDougal (1973, p. 167, 177).

[190] Reisman (1990, p. 866, 875).

[191] Reisman (2000, p. 15).

[192] See Farer (2003, pp. 62–68).

expressed serious doubts about its legality. They did so because humanitarian intervention was manifestly at variance with the principle of non-intervention in foreign states' affairs.

Reflecting the right to the existence of the state, the principle of territorial integrity implies, as we have seen earlier, other principles that are essential in order to make of that right a tangible reality. Amongst these principles there is the principle of non-intervention in the affairs of another state. "A state", recalls H. Wheaton, "is declared to have the right to exist and to protect and conserve its existence; to be entitled to independence in the sense of freedom of development; to equality with other members of the Family of Nations; to territory within defined boundaries, and to exclusive jurisdiction thereover."[193] The principle of non-intervention is a corollary to these rights as a state cannot enjoy these rights and deny them to the other states. More particularly, nonintervention is the necessary condition for sovereignty. When a state intervenes in the internal or external affairs of another state, it aims to deny to the latter its right to protect its sovereign existence through the exercise of sovereignty. Intervention aims then to substitute the sovereignty of one state to the sovereignty of another state.[194] It is an act which stands out of law. "There is no right of intervention because", recalls P. Pradier-Fodere,[195] " there is no right against law; the law is the independence; the intervention is the violation of the independence. Intervention is at variance with the existence of an inter-states system. M. Finnemore has shown in this regard that if states freely intervened militarily in one another's affairs whenever some gain could be achieved, we would live in a very different world as it is precisely because states show some restraint that we live in a world of sovereign states at all. In this sense, nonintervention is the practice that constitutes the state and sovereignty as foundational institutions of contemporary politics. Intervention, conversely, sets their limits.[196] That is why nonintervention was unknown to the feudal system and that it has started to emerge as an important principle of International Law only after the strengthening of sovereign equality between Western states. This happened definitely at the start of the second half of the nineteenth century after its first half had witnessed the implementation of a systematic policy of intervention of the Holy Alliance in order to restore or impose the monarchist legitimacy but to which a first thrust has been directed outside Europe in 1823 by the Monroe Doctrine. Another important element has also contributed to the strengthening of the principle of nonintervention: the gradual limitation of the use of force, first vertically and then horizontally, that is that move which has pushed towards first a relative prohibition of the use of force between Western states and then at a later stage towards the extension of

---

193 Wheaton (1929, p. 150).

194 Nys (1912, p. 229).

195 Pradier-Fodere (1883, p. 547).

196 Finnemore (2003, pp. 7–8).

such prohibition in the relationship between the Western countries and the nascent peripheral states.

Hence, beginning from the mid of the nineteenth century, the Western inter-states system started to witness vertically a steady erosion of force's normative value as it was increasingly viewed as illegitimate. Since then "waging wars for the glory of one's country", notes M. Finnemore,[197] "is no longer honored or even respectable in contemporary politics. Force is viewed as legitimate only as a last resort, and only for defensive or humanitarian purposes". However, while nonintervention was, though slow in coming, being consecrated in the Western inter-states system, it was completely excluded from the relations between Western states and peripheral states.[198] On the contrary, it has dramatically developed, especially in Latin America where the newly acquired independences were severely compromised in particular under the guise to collect debts[199] as great powers have used force or threat to use force in order to achieve many-fold purposes which served inter alia, first, as a method to compel the payment of the pecuniary claims of their nationals whether arising out or not of contracts, or torts; second, as a means for securing compliance of the settlement agreements; and, third, as a pretext for territorial conquests, financial or political control, and other foreign policy purposes.[200]

While many Western authors were of the opinion that the use of force to collect debts owed to the nationals of Western countries was lawful,[201] this was contested by Latin American lawyers except in self-defense situations.[202] L. Drago, the Argentinean Minister of foreign affairs, has achieved celebrity when, after having been alarmed by the December 1902 blockade and bombardment of some Venezuelan ports by Germany, Great Britain and Italy, he claimed in a famous memorandum that military intervention to collect debts was not lawful amongst states that enjoy the same status based on legal sovereign equality and that such intervention brings back the newly independent Latin American states to the former status of colonies.[203] The 1907 Hague Second Peace Conference did not remain impervious to his criticism against intervention as, after very laborious

---

[197] Idem, p. 19.

[198] See Thomas (1985).

[199] See Borchard (1951).

[200] Olivares Marcos (2005, p. 95).

[201] See Oppenheim (1928, p. 267) and for a comprehensive presentation of the legal perceptions at the time, see Williams (1924).

[202] C. Calvo has written in this respect that "en Droit International strict, le recouvrement de créances et la poursuite de réclamations privées ne justifient pas 'de plano' l'intervention armée des gouvernements, et que, comme les Etats européens suivent invariablement cette règle dans leurs relations réciproques, il n'y a nul motif qu'ils ne se l'imposent pas aussi dans leurs rapports avec les nations du Nouveau Monde", Calvo (1886, pp. 350–351).

[203] Dated 29 December 1902. See the translation of the memorandum in AJIL 1907, Supplement No 1, 1–6. On this memorandum, see Drago (1907, pp. 692–726); Moulin (1907, pp. 417–472).

negotiations, it endorsed the Latin American states views that forcible intervention to collect debts was illegal through the adoption of the Convention (II) Respecting the Limitation of the Employment of Force for the Recovery of Contract Debts and which states in its Art. 1 that "The Contracting Powers agree not to have recourse to armed force for the recovery of contracts debts claimed from the Government of one country by the Government of another as being due to its nationals. This undertaking is, however, not applicable when the debtor state refuses or neglects to reply to an offer of arbitration, or, after accepting the offer, prevents any compromis from being agreed on or, after the arbitration, fails to submit to the award".

While military intervention has since then ceased to be used to collect debts,[204] it has continued to be used against peripheral states in order either to promote commercial interests or to establish governments favored by Western countries.[205] However this has not prevented, at least legally, the vertical and horizontal move towards further limitation of the use of force through the adoption, first, of Art. 10 of the Covenant of the League of Nations, then of the Kellogg-Briand Pact and finally the Art. 2 (4) of the UN Charter which generalized and universalized that prohibition. Although these major legal instruments do not mention intervention, they do in fact implicitly[206] refer to it as intervention supposes the use of force, an element which in addition makes its distinction from war very difficult in states' practice.[207] Besides, the ICJ has noted the existence of the element of coercion in the notion of intervention. Thus, recalling the constitutive elements of the principle of nonintervention, the Court was able to clarify that "the principle (of nonintervention) forbids all states or groups of states to intervene directly or indirectly in internal or external affairs of other states. A prohibited intervention must accordingly be one bearing on matters in which each state is permitted, by the principle of state sovereignty, to decide freely. One of these is the choice of a political, economical, social and cultural system, and the formulation of foreign policy. Intervention is wrongful when it uses methods of coercion in regard to such choices, which must remain free. The element of coercion, which defines, and indeed forms the very essence of prohibited intervention, is particularly obvious in the case of an intervention which uses force, whether in the direct form of military action, or in the indirect form of support for subversive or terrorist armed activities within another state."[208]

Corollary to the principles of sovereignty and equality of states, the principle of nonintervention has been recognized as one of the major principles of International Law.[209] It has been endorsed, as we have seen above, by classical International

[204] Olivares Marcos (2005, p. 101).

[205] Finnemore (2003, pp. 46–47).

[206] Kelsen (1951, p. 770).

[207] Idem, pp. 8–9.

[208] ICJ (1986, para 205).

[209] See Ch. Rousseau (1980, p. 35).

Law. It is on that ground that the ICJ has vigorously condemned intervention by stating that "the alleged right of intervention as the manifestation of a policy of force, such as has, in the past, given rise to most serious abuses and such as cannot, whatever be the present defects in international organization, find a place in International Law."[210] But the principle of nonintervention has also been endorsed by a large number of international legal instruments: regional agreements, resolutions of international Organizations, international jurisprudence, etc.[211]The UN General Assembly has adopted in this regard a series of resolutions reaffirming its attachment to the principle of nonintervention. Hence, it has, e.g., vigorously condemned intervention in its 1965 Declaration on the Inadmissibility of Intervention in the Domestic Affairs of States by proclaiming that "(no) state has the right to intervene, directly or indirectly, for any reason whatsoever, in the internal or external affairs of any other state. Consequently, armed intervention and all other forms of interference or attempted threats against the personality of the state or against its political, economic and cultural elements are condemned."[212]

Nonintervention is not an absolute principle as it allows for an exception when a formal request of intervention is made by the legitimate government.[213] But attempts have been made to add other exceptions to this one such as in the case of the protection of nationals abroad[214] and humanitarian intervention. With regard to the first situation, International Law does admit the right of every state to defend its nationals abroad, but it does not authorize it to use force. The concerned state can only make international claims within diplomatic or judicial frameworks. With regard to the second situation, humanitarian intervention is strictly prohibited by International Law. The status of law in the matter has been solemnly made clear by the 1981 Declaration on the Inadmissibility of Intervention and Interference in the Internal Affairs of State which has clearly stressed "The duty of a state to refrain from the exploitation and the distortion of human rights issue as a means of interference in the internal affairs of states, of exerting pressure on other states or creating distrust and disorder within and among states or groups of states."[215] The condemnation of humanitarian intervention is reinforced as we have noted above by the prohibition of the use of force. But some contemporary authors are still of the opinion that humanitarian intervention is an exception to the principle of the prohibition of use of force. This is a wrong reading of the present status of positive International Law.

We have already seen how jusnaturalism and legal realism sustain that humanitarian intervention is an exception to the prohibition of the use of force. Their arguments were based, in the first instance, on a wrong reading of the history of

---

[210] ICJ (1949).

[211] Idem, p. 38.

[212] General Assembly resolution 2131 (XX). See also General Assembly resolution 2625 (XXV) and resolution 36/103.

[213] See Charpentier (1961, p. 489 cont.); Bennouna (1974).

[214] See Schweisfurth (1980, p. 159 cont).

[215] General Assembly resolution 36/103.

International Law and the related facts and, in the second one, on a complete misrepresentation of the legal character and fundamental requisites of International Law itself. We have criticized these two schools of thought and therefore there is no need to dwell on the issue once again though we will occasionally refer to the writings of some legal realists who, when lacking arguments, they try to adhere to those presented by some classical authors and thereby to arguments of a legal character which constitute the only one perspective we are interested in this section.

Some legal positivists[216] have, even before the resurgence of the doctrine of humanitarian intervention since the end of the Cold War, been of the opinion of the existence of a customary right of humanitarian intervention which would have survived the general prohibition of force by Art. 2 (4) of the UN Charter. These authors invoke states' practice in the nineteenth and early twentieth centuries. In fact, as we have tried to show above, humanitarian intervention has not been endorsed at that time by International Law. It is so because, first, the then alleged humanitarian intervention instances did not have any genuine humanitarian character,[217] second, these cases were rare and not uniform,[218] third, the use of humanitarian intervention was erratic and dependent on the discretionary power of the intervening state, while it could have been urgent and necessary to prevent some dramatic and humanly unacceptable instances,[219] and fourth, humanitarian intervention was perceived as being in contradiction with the principles of sovereignty and equality of states and their corollary the principle of nonintervention and that therefore only a few number of states have consented to it or more exactly have made use of it in order to achieve their national goals. It is worth mentioning in this regard that even some proponents of humanitarian intervention are of the opinion that there is little or no evidence that the international community considered the right to humanitarian intervention as legally binding (*opinion juris sive necessitates*), a *sine qua non* of customary international law.[220] That is why many authors are of

[216] See Lauterpacht (1955, p. 312); Lillich (1967, p. 334); Fonteyne (1974, p. 203 and seq).; Sornarajah (1981, pp. 57–58); Bazyler (1987, p. 547 cont).

[217] A. Rougier has confessed in this regard that "Si l'Europe a mis la Turquie en tutelle (par le biais de l'intervention d'humanité), c'est moins dans l'intérêt des sujets ottomans que pour parer aux conflits d'intérêts de l'Angleterre, de l'Autriche, de la France et de la Russie autour de la mer Noire", Rougier (1910, p. 525). H. Scott Fairley has also shown in this regard that "The case for humanitarian intervention is essentially misdirected. A history of black intentions clothed in white has tainted most possible applications of the doctrine", Fairley (1980, p. 63). See also for a comprehensive and critical analysis, see Sean D. Murphy who has shown that the purposes of most of the humanitarian interventions were political and economic ones, Murphy (1996, pp. 33–64).

[218] Brownlie (1963b, p. 340).

[219] A proponent of humanitarian intervention such as J. L. Holzgrefe has recognized that "such right (of humanitarian intervention) was not invoked, let alone exercised, in the face of the greatest humanitarian catastrophes of the pre-Charter era, including the massacre of 1 million Armenians by the Turks (1914–1919); the forced starvation of 4 million Ukrainians by the Soviets (1930s); the massacre of thousands of Chinese by the Japanese (1931–1945); and the extermination of 6 million Jews by the Nazis (1939–1945)", Holzgrefe (2003, p. 45).

[220] Idem.

the opinion that the state practice before 1945 does not confirm a general acceptance of the humanitarian doctrine as customary right under International Law.[221]

Proponents of humanitarian intervention, not ready to resign themselves to the fact that the latter is not an exception to the principle of nonintervention, have continued to claim that it is a customary right despite the prohibition of the use of force by the UN Charter in 1945 and the non endorsement of such alleged customary right by the ensuing states' practice.

With regard to the alleged exception of humanitarian intervention to the prohibition of the use of force by the UN Charter, it is based on unusual interpretations of Art. 2(4) and in particular its phrases "use of force against territorial integrity or political independence of any state" and "or in any other manner inconsistent with the Purposes of the United Nations." Hence, according to J. Stone, the use of force is prohibited only when it is directed against the territorial integrity or political independence of any state.[222] Likewise M. Reisman and Myres S. McDougal are of the opinion that since a humanitarian intervention seeks neither a territorial change nor a challenge to the political independence of the state involved and is not only not consistent with the purposes of the United Nations but is rather in conformity with the most fundamental peremptory norms of the Charter, it is a distortion to argue that it is precluded by Art. 2(4).[223] In fact the two phrases were meant by the drafters of the Charter to reinforce the prohibition of the use of force and not to let open any potential loopholes in it. The US delegate at the San Francisco Conference expressed at that time a general feeling when he "made it clear that the intention of the authors of the original text was to state in the broadest terms an absolute all-inclusive prohibition; the phrase "or in any other manner" was designed to insure that there should be no loopholes."[224] Such interpretation of Art. 2(4) is consistent with the first fundamental purpose that has been behind the creation of the United Nations which was to "save succeeding generations from the scourge of war" (Preamble, para 1) and to "maintain international peace and security"(Art. 1.1). This purpose has a preeminence on all other purposes[225] including the protection of human rights[226] as the enjoyment of the

[221] See I. Brownlie (1973, pp. 220–221); Franck and Rodley (1973b, pp. 279–285); Beyerlin (1982, p. 212); Malanczuk (1993, pp. 7–11); Vervey (1998, p. 191).

[222] Reisman and McDougal (1958, p. 95).

[223] Reisman and McDougal (1973, p. 177). See also D'Amato (1987, pp. 57–73); Teson (1997, p. 151). A similar restrictive interpretation has been initially given by the United Kingdon in the Corfu Channel case when it argued that the minesweeping operation it conducted in Albanian waters "threatened neither the territorial integrity nor the political independence of Albania", 1948 ICJ Pleadings, Corfu Channel case, vol 3, 296.

[224] 6 UNCIO 335, Summary Report of Eleventh Meeting of Committee I/1,4 June 1945.

[225] P. Malanczuk does recall in this respect "that unilateral humanitarian intervention is illegal due to the prohibition of the use of force as the prevalent principle in the present international legal system in the interest on international peace and security", Malanczuk (1993, p. 30).

[226] "It is highly questionable, writes S. Chesterman, that the drafters regarded human rights as of equal importance to peace", Chesterman (2001, p. 52).

latter supposes first of all peace and security. Such an interpretation is also in conformity with the content and scope of the principle of nonintervention which prohibits any direct or indirect form of intervention and interference in the internal or external affairs of any state. Post World War Two International Law has clearly endorsed such interpretation through inter alia ICJ decisions[227] and UN General Assembly resolutions.[228] Most of international lawyers also adhere to it.[229]

With regard to the practice that has prevailed during the period 1945–1989, it has been extensively critically analyzed by other authors.[230] Although the instances of alleged humanitarian intervention have increased in comparison with the previous period and that new actors from the South have been involved in some of these instances, the same remarks can still be made : scarcity of these instances,[231] lack of genuine humanitarian character,[232] selective exercise of the supposed right of humanitarian intervention[233] and lack of opinion juris.[234] The latter fact has even

[227] The ICJ has, in reply to UK's claim that its forcible intervention in Albanian waters was only meant to recover evidence of the causes of the destruction of two British warships, stated that "it can only regard the alleged right of intervention as the manifestation of a policy of force such as has in the past given rise to most serious abuses and such as cannot find a place in international law. It is still less admissible in the particular form it would take here-it would be reserved for the most powerful states", ICJ Reports, 1949, 4 at 34.

[228] Among many other UN General Assembly's resolution, the 1970 Declaration on Friendly Relations has clarified that "No State or group of states has the right to intervene, *directly or indirectly*, for any reason whatever, in the internal or external affairs of any other state" and that "Every State has an inalienable right to choose its political, economic, social and cultural systems, without interference *in any form* by another state".

[229] See, e.g., Higgins (1963); Brownlie (1963b, p .267); Mrazek (1989, pp. 86–87); Randelzhofer (1994, pp. 117–118).

[230] See, e.g., Murphy (1996, p. 83 cont).; Chesterman (2001, pp. 63–86).

[231] See Newman (2009, pp. 28–37).

[232] Idem.

[233] J. L. Holzgrefe has once again noted that in that period of time "No state or regional organization, for example, intervened to prevent or end the massacre of several hundred thousand ethnic Chinese in Indonesia (mid-1960s); the killing and forced starvation of almost half a million Ibos in Nigeria (1966–1970); the slaughter and forced starvation of over a million black Christians by the Sudanese government (since late 1970s); the murder of tens of thousands of Hutus in Burundi (1972); the slaying of 100,000 East Timorese by the Indonesian government (1975–1999); the forced starvation of up to 1 million Ethiopians by their government (mid-1980s); the murder of 100,000 Kurds in Iraq (1988–1989); and the killings of tens of thousands Hutus in Burundi (since 1993), Holzgrefe (2003, pp. 46–47). From his part, Mohammed Ayoob has noted that what make humanitarian interventions suspect is the fact that they "are undertaken on a selective basis and the same criteria are not applied uniformly in every case, such interventions lose legitimacy and credibility in the eyes of many, if not most members of the international system", Holzgrefe (2002, p. 86). See also Pattison (2010, pp. 169–173).

[234] S. Chesterman has rightly concluded in this respect that "it seems clear that writers who claim that state practice provides evidence of a customary international law right of humanitarian intervention grossly overstate their case…State practice disclosed at most three 'best cases' of humanitarian intervention, but even these lack the necessary *opinio juris* that might transform the exception into the rule", Chesterman (2001, pp. 86–87).

been admitted by one of the concerned powerful states – which is the United Kingdom – when it did state that "in fact, the best case that can be made in support of humanitarian intervention is that it cannot be said to be unambiguously illegal,"[235] and that its doubtful benefits would be heavily outweighed by its costs in terms of respect for International Law.[236]

Despite the implicit rejection of humanitarian intervention by the UN Charter and its continuing and clear non endorsement by states' practice, proponents of such doctrine have taken advantage of the new situation created by the end of the Cold War in order to stress that International Law has finally and within a very short period of time given its blessing to it. Legal realists have, as we have noted earlier, been extremely vocal in supporting that view. But even some legal positivists have come to argue that states' attitudes have started showing some tolerance[237] towards humanitarian intervention which fact would suggest a "nascent trend".[238] They all of them invoke cases of intervention which have allegedly been validated by the UN Security Council. Supposing that the Security Council has been entrusted by the UN Charter with the authority to authorize the use of force in situations other than those related to the threat to international peace and security or that the UN practice has widened the notion of "threat to peace" in a way to incorporate serious violations of human rights, which is still a questionable issue, it remains that the Security Council has not so far given its blessing either directly or indirectly to interventions labeled as humanitarian ones. As we will see in the next section, the Security Council will do so only within the framework and safeguards of the new concept of the "Responsibility to Protect".

Hence, it has been said that the UN has acquiesced in silence[239] when US, British and French forces were sent in 1991 to Northern Iraq following the campaign of repression against the Kurdish population initiated by the Iraqi government. Security Council Resolution 688, which at that time authorized free access to refugees and displaced Kurds by international humanitarian organizations, has even been perceived as "a forerunner to authorizations for humanitarian intervention in subsequent cases."[240] However such an interpretation of Resolution 688 is not convincing. First, the Security Council has never authorized either explicitly or implicitly the use of force which has ensued nor the establishment of two no fly zones in Northern and Southern Iraq. This has been acknowledged by one of the three intervening states.[241] Second, the Security Council has authorized free

---

[235] Foreign and Commonwealth Office Paper "Is Intervention Ever Justified?" (internal document dated 1984 and released in 1986, Foreign Policy Document No.148), B.Y.B.I.L., 1986, 619.

[236] Idem.

[237] Franck (2003, p. 223).

[238] Murphy (2001, p. 6).

[239] Franck (2003, p. 220).

[240] Danish Institute of International Affairs (DUPI) (1999, p. 65).

[241] Anthony Aust, the Foreign and Commonwealth Office Legal Counsel has recognized in this respect that "Resolution 688, which applies not only to northern Iraq but to the whole of Iraq, was

access to refugees in a cross-border operation and not direct military intervention in the Iraqi territory in order to allegedly make an end to human rights violations.[242] Third, the intervention in Iraq has been vigorously condemned by two permanent members of the Security Council, China and Russia.

Likewise, it has also been said that the UN has acquiesced to the unilateral intervention of ECOWAS (Economic Community of West African States) in Liberia (1990–1992), which has been retroactively endorsed by the Security Council. It is true that the Security Council has a posteriori, through a series of resolutions, commended that intervention,[243] but the latter cannot be interpreted as a humanitarian intervention case because, first, it was requested by the legitimate government[244] and, second, its declared objective was to make an end to an internal conflict[245] and not to violations of human rights. Furthermore, serious doubts have been raised about the impartiality of ECOMOG (ECOWAS Cease-fire Monitoring Group), which has been accused of furthering Nigerian policy and taking part in the conflict itself.[246]

But the most cited case in favor of the consecration of humanitarian intervention is NATO's intervention in 1999 in Kosovo. As we know, the province of Kosovo had, since the abolition of its autonomous status in 1989, witnessed an escalation of tension and violation of human rights. In 1998, the Security Council declared that the situation prevailing at that time in Kosovo constituted a threat to international peace and security, but was not able to take any decision as to the use of force due to the firm opposition shown by Russia and China. In March 1999, NATO's forces launched massive air strikes against Yugoslavia in order to "halt the violence and bring an end to the humanitarian catastrophe now unfolding in Kosovo."[247] Unable to pass a resolution through the Security Council condemning that intervention, Russia succeeded in May 1999 to broker a cease-fire agreement whose main terms included the restoration of autonomy and the acceptance of an international military presence in Kosovo. The agreement was welcomed in June by the Security Council in its Resolution 1244 by which it took the necessary measures for its

not made under Chapter VII. Resolution 688 recognized that there was a severe humanitarian situation in Iraq and, in particular, northern Iraq; but the intervention in northern Iraq "Provide Comfort" was in fact, not especially mandated by the United nations, but the states taking action in northern Iraq did so in exercise of the customary international law principle of humanitarian principle", 63 B.Y.B.I.L.(1992), 827.

[242] The preamble of Resolution 688 does clearly refer to Security Council concern with regard to "the repression of the Iraqi civilian population in many parts of Iraq, including most recently in Kurdish populated areas, which led to massive flow of refugees towards and across international frontiers and to cross-border incursions, which threaten international peace and security in the region".

[243] See Gray (2000, pp. 218–224).

[244] Idem, p. 219.

[245] See Chesterman (2001, p. 135).

[246] Gray (2000, p. 220).

[247] NATO Press Release 1999 (040).

implementation on the ground after having invoked Chapter VII. This decision has been interpreted as a tacit acceptance[248] or a retroactive endorsement[249] by the Security Council of NATO's intervention. Such conclusions stem from a wrong reading of Resolution 1244 which did not retroactively legalize NATO's actions but only prospectively authorized foreign states to intervene in the FRY to maintain peace.[250] It also overshadows the lack of consensus among the permanent members of the Security Council, which has prevailed since the beginning of the conflict. Resolution 1244 cannot also be seen as setting up a precedent. This has been denied by key members of the NATO.[251] Such opinion is shared by many authors.[252] It is based on several considerations. First, the extent of the human rights violations in Kosovo which have allegedly justified NATO's intervention "was not massive and widespread."[253] Second, the intervention was motivated by NATO's self interest and geo-political reasons.[254] Third, NATO's intervention has provoked much more casualties and suffering among the civilian population than the atrocities it was supposed to halt.[255] Four, NATO's intervention has been indirectly condemned by UN General Assembly.[256]

One of the often-cited cases in favor of the consecration of humanitarian intervention is also the intervention of Australia military forces in order to make an end to the East Timor case. As is well known, the origin of the East Timor case lies in the request of the Timorese to seek independence from Indonesia. While the fight for independence has taken for decades a low profile, it has suddenly escalated in tension and attracted international attention. In order to calm down the situation,

---

[248] Pellet (2000, p. 42).

[249] Franck (2003, p. 225).

[250] See Charney (1999) law.vanderbilt.edu/journal/32-05/32.5.1 html.

[251] See Chesterman (2001, pp. 215–216).

[252] Simma (1999) has reflected a general view when he wrote that "The legal issues presented by the Kosovo crisis are particularly impressive proof that hard cases make bad law" in "NATO, the UN and the Use of Force: Legal Aspects".

[253] Charney (1999).

[254] See Domagala (2004, pp. 24–31).

[255] Idem, p. 16.

[256] In a resolution adopted in 1999, the General Assembly has declared that "The General Assembly... Reaffirming...that no state may use or encourage the use of economic, political or any other type of measures to coerce another state in order to obtain from it the subordination of the exercise of its sovereign rights...Deeply concerned that, despite the recommendations adopted on this question by the General Assembly...(unauthorized) coercive measures continue to be promulgated and implemented with all their extraterritorial effects...Rejects (unauthorized) coercive measures with all their extraterritorial effects as tools for political or economic pressure against any country". GA Res.54/172, UNGAOR, 54th sess., UN Doc.A/RES/54/172 (1999). Stronger condemnation has been made by the Ministers for Foreign Affairs of the Group of 77 in a Declaration adopted in 24 September 1999 and in which it has been inter alia said that "The Ministers...rejected the so-called right of humanitarian intervention, which has no basis in the UN Charter or in International Law". See also the Declaration of the Group of 77 Summit (133 states), Havana, Cuba, 10-14 April 2000.

the Indonesian government agreed in January 1999 to grant to East Timor territorial autonomy. A referendum was organized to this end in August 1999. However, the referendum, instead of leading to the endorsement of autonomy as expected by the government, has led the Timorese to choose independence. The announcement of the outcome of the referendum was followed by an outbreak of violence, mass atrocities, assassinations and destruction of infrastructure, orchestrated by pro-governmental Indonesian militias. The international community reacted swiftly as it condemned the severe repression of the Timorese population. However, at the Security Council, many states warned that unilateral action on the model of NATO's intervention was unacceptable.[257] They also insisted that no intervention would take place without Indonesia's consent. From its part, the Australian government announced that it was willing to lead a multinational force if four conditions were met: a mandate from the Security Council, the consent of the Indonesian government, a short-term mission with the aim of restoring security prior to the deployment of a UN force and a strong regional component of the force.[258] It was on that ground that the Security Council took its Resolution 1264 (1999), which authorized an Australian led multinational force (INTERFET) to take all necessary measures in order to make an end to violence and provide humanitarian assistance.

Lastly, it goes without saying that the 2003 British and American war against Iraq was manifestly not a case of humanitarian intervention as it was waged without the consent of the UN Security Council, its clear motives were also not of a humanitarian character,[259] and its beneficial effects were massively disproportionate to deaths amongst the Iraqi population and to the chaos and anarchy created in Iraq.[260]

Hence, it appears very clearly that the states' practice has not since the end of the Cold War endorsed the doctrine of humanitarian intervention as a customary rule of International Law.[261] Therefore one can safely conclude that states' practice has been constant since the nineteenth century in its rejection of humanitarian intervention. This does not mean that the international community has no right to intervene to halt massive violations of human rights. But, such right cannot be implemented unless a reconceptualization of humanitarian intervention is carried out in a way to

[257] See Hehir (2008, p. 55).

[258] Idem.

[259] See Roth (2004); Cottey (2008, p. 430).

[260] See Pattison (2010, p. 177).

[261] Though being of the opinion that states' practice since 1990 may be seen as evidence of a greater acceptance that humanitarian intervention may be morally justifiable in extreme cases, the Danish Institute of International Affairs has recognized that "In conclusion, state practice after the end of the Cold War(1990-1999) concerning humanitarian intervention is neither sufficiently substantial nor has there been sufficient acceptance in the international community to support the view that a right of humanitarian intervention without Security Council authorization has become part of customary international law", Dupi (1999, p. 93).

make of the latter an objective, impartial and fair instrument meant to prevent and halt massive human rights violations.

4.2.3 The Need for Reconceptualizing Humanitarian Intervention

As we have seen above, humanitarian intervention has been used as an ideological instrument by powerful states against weak states in order to achieve their self-interest under the guise of ensuring the protection of foreign peoples. In fact, powerful states have conceived of humanitarian intervention as a means to circumvent major International Law norms such as the equality of states and the prohibition of the use of force. That is why International Law has never endorsed humanitarian intervention. However, the occurrence of massive human rights violations in the past decades in different parts of the world have led to an increased interest in the humanitarian intervention in order to make of it an ultimate instrument in order to redress such violations. But such interest was conditioned by the need to reconceptualize humanitarian intervention[262] in a way to make of it an objective and impartial means for the protection of the peoples who may be subjected to massive human rights violations. But, how to reconceptualize humanitarian intervention when the latter has durably been associated with foreign domination? Sponsored by the government of Canada[263] in order to carry out such reconceptualization, the International Commission on Intervention and State Sovereignty (ICISS) found it necessary to look at the notion of humanitarian intervention through a new angle: the international community responsibility to protect people at risk. Gareth Evans, one of the key members of the ICISS has confessed that it was necessary "to invent a new way of talking about humanitarian intervention. We sought to turn the whole weary debate about the right to intervene on its head and to re-characterize it not as argument about any *right* at all but rather as a *responsibility* – one to protect people at grave risk – with the relevant perspective being not that of the prospective interveners but, more appropriately, of those needing support."[264]

The reconceptualizing of humanitarian intervention is the natural consequence of the tremendous changes witnessed in the past decades by human rights. One of these changes is that the protection of the latter has become a responsibility which resides with the states as well as the international community. With regard to the states, it is increasingly agreed today that sovereignty has a corollary principle: the

[262] See Ramsbotham and Woodhouse (1996), Lepard (2003).

[263] Thomas G. Weiss and Ramesh Thakur (2010 have noted about Canada's role in favour of R2P that "Within the First United Nations, the *norm champion* of R2P from start to finish was Canada, a country that is strongly committed to multilateralism and has a history of close engagement with the United Nations, political credibility in both North and South, and a proud tradition of successful initiatives" in "Global Governance and the UN. An Unfinished Journey", p. 319).

[264] Evans (2006, p. 708).

state's responsibility to protect and preserve the human rights of its own citizens. It was that new perception of sovereignty which pushed the UN Secretary-General Kofi Annan to note that "State sovereignty, in its most basic sense, is being redefined. . .States are now widely understood to be the instruments at the service of their peoples, and not vice-versa. At the same time, individual sovereignty – by which I mean the fundamental freedom of each individual, enshrined in the Charter of the UN and subsequent international treaties – has been enhanced by a renewed and spreading consciousness of the individual rights. When we need the Charter today, we are more than ever conscious that its aim is to protect individual human beings, not to protect those who abuse them".[265] The new understanding of sovereignty has, according to the ICISS, threefold significance. First, it implies that the state authorities are responsible for the functions of protecting the safety and lives of citizens and promotion of their welfare. Secondly, it suggests that the national political authorities are responsible to the citizens internally and to the international community through the UN. And thirdly, it means that the agents of state are responsible for their actions, that is to say they are accountable for their acts of commission and omission.[266] With regard to the international community, it has also increasingly agreed that it should take on its "responsibility to protect."[267] Such responsibility exists when it appears clearly that the states are unwilling or unable to protect their own citizens.[268] In fact the international responsibility to protect is a corollary of the states' obligation to respect human rights. Such an obligation has become today an erga omnes obligation.[269] It therefore necessarily reflects on states' sovereignty as "if humanitarian intervention is indeed an unacceptable assault on sovereignty", asks Kofi Annan,[270] "how should we respond to Rwanda, to a Srebrenica- to gross and systematic violations of human right that offend every precept of our common humanity?" States' accountability in respect of human rights does not certainly reflect on sovereignty in a way to make it obsolete. It means solely that the exercise of sovereignty is henceforth conditioned by states' duty to ensure the protection of the human rights of their own populations and that if a state fails, for one reason or another, to conform to that duty, the international community becomes necessarily accountable for ensuring that protection.[271] "After all", observes Tal Dingott Alkopher,[272] "existing concepts of the rights of the state did not vanish once human rights were placed on the agenda; they exist side by side in a very fragile balance, which can be disrupted anytime

[265] The Economist,18 September 1999.

[266] ICISS (2001, p. 11).

[267] Idem.

[268] Idem, p. viii.

[269] Charney (1999, p. 1232).

[270] Annan (2000, p. 48).

[271] An analysis of this issue through a broad historical perspective has been made by Anne Orford (2009, p. 999, 2011).

[272] Alkopher (2007, pp. 1–27).

that human rights undermine the traditional organizational structures of territorial sovereignty." However, Tal Dingott Alkopher is wrong when he believes that such fragile balance can be disrupted by powerful states on the guise their intervention is made on behalf of the international community.

A reconceptualizing of humanitarian intervention is also needed as the latter has generally aggravated than improved the situation in the targeted states. In fact, the way in which humanitarian intervention has been carried out has rarely, if not never, led to the improvement of human rights. Indeed, humanitarian intervention has generally made such an improvement very difficult to achieve. Burleigh Wilkins has well described the dilemma which can be caused by humanitarian intervention with regard to the improvement of human rights by raising the question "Might not humanitarian intervention yields just the opposite effect where the protection of human rights is concerned? There are two real possibilities. An oppressive government may be prompted to become even more oppressive in response to an intervention, with confidence that its supporters and even some of previous critics will 'rally round the flag'. Or, once intervention occurs, the leadership of an opposition group may become more militant and disrespectful of the rights of others, or the leadership may pass into the hands of a more militant faction with even less respect for human rights than the oppressive regime with which we started out".[273] Furthermore, humanitarian intervention has very often condemned the peoples on behalf of which it has been carried out to live in very precarious situations where not only human rights are violated, but where also the basic conditions for security, stability and social and economic wellbeing are severely missing.[274] Thus, for instance, the NATO's intervention in Kosovo in 1999 was clouded by allegations that the intervention generated more carnage than it averted.[275] It has also rendered uncertain the future of that territory.

There is therefore a need to reconceptualize humanitarian intervention not only from ethical, political, and legal points of view, but also in a way to make of it an instrument aiming at establishing conditions conducive to the promotion of democracy and human rights as well as the building of socio-economic infrastructures which can help in ensuring the wellbeing of the whole population. "The problem", observes Jerzy Zalado," is not only when, under which conditions, and in what way to intervene but also how to prevent humanitarian crises and how to maintain peace after a military conflict and rebuild democratic, stable social structures and an economic infrastructure. The concept of the responsibility to protect is threefold: the responsibility to prevent, the responsibility to react, and the responsibility to rebuild."[276] It is that holistic approach which has been adopted by the ICISS in its attempt to reconceptualize humanitarian intervention as it aims to meet four basic objectives:

[273] Wilkins (2003, p. 37).

[274] See Newman (2009, p. 138 and seq).

[275] See ICISS (2001, p. vii).

[276] Zajadlo (2005, p. 657).

- To establish clearer rules, procedures and criteria for determining whether, when and how to intervene;
- To establish the legitimacy of military intervention when necessary and after all other approaches have failed;
- To ensure that military intervention, when it occurs, is carried out only for the purposes proposed, is effective, and is undertaken with proper concern to minimize the human costs and institutional damage that will result; and
- To help eliminate, where possible, the causes of conflict while enhancing the prospects for durable and sustainable peace.[277]

But setting up clear objectives to humanitarian intervention is not sufficient in order to make of the latter a legitimate and credible instrument, as the international community has also to identify the authority that can authorize the use of force. This is by far the most delicate issue to settle as determining the international body that can be entitled to authorize the use of force is extremely difficult in a system characterized by the lack of central authority and the tendency of states to act in accordance with their own interests. However, there is a general consensus that such gap can be filled by the UN Security Council. Reflecting that consensus, the ICISS has agreed that it "is in absolutely no doubt that there is no better or more appropriate body than the Security Council to deal with military intervention issues for human protection purposes. It is the Security Council which should be making the hard decisions in the hard cases about overriding state sovereignty. And it is the Security Council which should be making the often even harder decisions to mobilize effective resources, including military resources, to rescue populations at risk when there is no serious opposition on sovereignty grounds. That was the overwhelming consensus we found in all our consultations around the world."[278] The ICISS agreed also that the Chapters VI and VII are the source of authority of the Security Council to deal with security threats of all types.[279] However, anticipating a possible impasse within the Security Council due to the use of the veto power by one of the permanent members,[280] the ICISS agreed that, in case the

[277] ICISS (2001, p. 11).

[278] Idem, p. 49.

[279] Idem, p. 48.

[280] ICIIS admitted in this regard that "An issue which we cannot avoid addressing, however, is that of the veto power enjoyed by the present Permanent Five. Many of our interlocutors regarded capricious use of the veto, or threat of its use, as likely to be the principal obstacle to effective international action in cases where quick and decisive action is needed to stop or avert a significant humanitarian crisis. As has been said, it is unconscionable that one veto can override the rest of humanity on matters of grave humanitarian concern. Of particular concern is the possibility that needed action will be held hostage to unrelated concerns of one or more of the permanent members – a situation that has too frequently occurred in the past", idem, p. 51.

Security Council fails to act,[281] the General Assembly[282] or regional or sub-regional organizations[283] could assume the responsibility to protect. But, convinced that the Security Council is the most appropriate body to assume the responsibility to protect, the ICISS recommended that a permanent member, in matters where its vital national interests were not claimed to be involved, would not use its veto to obstruct the passage of what would otherwise be a majority resolution. Aware also that permanent members might try to abdicate their responsibility to protect by having a limited reading of the circumstances which should lead to carry out that responsibility, the ICISS has broadened the grounds which should justify military intervention. Hence, according to the ICISS, military intervention for human protection purposes is justified in two broad sets of circumstances, namely in order to halt or avert large scale loss of life, actual or apprehended, with genocidal intent or not, which is the product either of deliberate state action, or state neglect or inability to act, or a failed state situation; or large scale "ethnic cleansing," actual or apprehended, whether carried out by killing, forced expulsion, acts of terror or rape.[284]

The general impression given by ICISS' understanding of the responsibility to protect is that it is based on the idea that there is a legal or at least a moral obligation of the Security Council to take action whenever there are serious breaches of human rights. But powerful states, including Western powers, have shown a reluctance to be obliged to intervene,[285] preferring to decide on a case-by-case basis and in accordance to their national interests. That is why they have tried, at the occasion of the 2005 World Summit, to undermine the obligation to intervene, which is the essence of the responsibility to protect as suggested by the ICISS. Hence, during the negotiations of the *Outcome Document* of the World Summit, a number of concessions were obtained by powerful states. Amongst these concessions, it was decided to drop the idea that permanent members should not use their veto power. It was also decided to replace the expression the "obligation" which was contained in the original draft by the expression the "responsibility" to use appropriate measures to protect the populations. Consequently, any enforcement action is to be taken by the Security Council on a "case-by-case basis", which means the recognition of a discretionary power to the Security Council whether or not to take action. It was also decided to disregard the criteria for military intervention which are related, as recommended by the ICISS, to just cause threshold of large scale loss of life or large

[281] Idem, pp. 52–54.

[282] On the basis of Art. 10, which gives a general responsibility to the UN General Assembly with regard to any matter within the scope of UN authority, and Art. 11, which gives the General Assembly a fallback responsibility with regard specifically to the maintenance of international peace and security – albeit only to make recommendations, not binding decisions, as well as General Assembly Resolution "Uniting for Peace".

[283] On the basis of Art. 52 of the UN Charter.

[284] Idem, p. 32.

[285] See Hehir (2008, p. 71).

scale ethnic cleansing, right intention, last resort, proportional means and reasonable prospects.[286] These criteria were obviously meant to strictly limit the use of force for human protection purposes. It was also decided to drastically limit the instances in which the Security Council could intervene and which are genocide, war crimes, crimes against humanity and ethnic cleansing. Commenting on these concessions, A. Bellamy has noted with regret that the responsibility to protect, as stated in the *Outcome Document*,[287] " has done little to increase the likelihood of preventing future Rwandas and Kosovo…in order to secure consensus, the concept's advocates have abandoned many of its central tenets, significantly reducing the likelihood of progress in the near future."[288] Bellamy was right as the experience has since then shown that no substantial progress has been made in order to deter massive and flagrant violations of human rights. Thus, the Security Council has remained passive, while flagrant and massive violations of human rights have continued to take place in different parts of the world.[289] The Security Council has so far accepted to make use of the Responsibility to Protect in only two instances, where its involvement was besides characterized by some hesitancy. These cases are related to Darfur and Libya.

Thus, the Security Council has so far not been able to definitely put an end to the suffering of the local population in Darfur, which has been subjected since 2003 to ethnic violence, massacre, displacement and famine.[290] The failure of the Security Council to restore peace, security and stability in Darfur was, first of all, the product of the irresolute behavior of Western great powers to make use of force in a prompt and decisive manner. It was also the product of the opposition of China and Russia to any action, which could set up a precedent. But, the reluctance of the Security Council to act in a way to make promptly an end to the suffering of the local population in Darfur was also facilitated by the indeterminacy and the weakness of the Responsibility to Protect as endorsed by the UN,[291] as we have seen above, although it was clear that, according to UN reports, the population was subjected to crimes against humanity and genocide.[292] Certainly, the Security has not been totality indifferent to the suffering of the population as it has taken several measures meant to restore peace and security. But, these measures, such as Security Council's resolutions calling for disarming militia, the referral of the Darfur crimes to the International Criminal Court, the adoption of sanctions, the deployment of a peace operation, etc., came often very late and consisted in hollow threats that have

[286] ICISS (2001, pp. 32–37).

[287] The Responsibility to Protect, as stated in the Outcome Document, has been further softened when it was endorsed by the Security Council through its Resolution 1674. See Strauss (2009, pp. 291–323).

[288] Bellamy (2006, p. 155). See also Welsh (2008, p. 558); McClean (2011, pp. 35–39).

[289] See Bellamy (2011, pp. 51–92).

[290] See de Vaal (2007, p. 1039).

[291] See Mepham (2006). Feinstein (2007) McClean (2011, pp. 36 and 38).

[292] See Bellamy (2009, p. 41); Krieg (2009, pp. 24–25); Badescu (June 2009).

little or no impact.[293] All these measures, although they were gradually implemented and seemed therefore to conform to the last resort principle recommended by ICISS, reflected in fact the indeterminacy of the Security Council's response as they were not taken timely, which fact contributed to lessen the pressure on the Sudanese government and allowed it to maneuver skillfully. "Over the 2004-2007 period", notes A. de Waal,[294] "the international community pursued a range of objectives for Darfur that included improving security and humanitarian access, supporting the CPA, obtaining justice at The Hague, seeking a negotiated peace, dispatching a UN force and punishing those standing in the way of these goals. The multiplicity of these goals impeded a clear and coherent strategy. Some actions demanded the impossible while others set unrealistic deadlines. Few were followed up. On the occasions that Khartoum met one demand, another was placed on the table. With an internally dysfunctional regime facing a confused and inconsistent international community, it is unsurprising that little progress was made." In fact, the attitude of the Security Council in the Darfur crisis has been nothing else than a kind of refusal to "buy-in" to the Responsibility to Protect.[295] Certainly, the complexity of the situation in Sudan has dissuaded the Security Council from taking timely and decisive measures to implement the Responsibility to Protect.[296] But, the indeterminacy of the obligations stipulated in the Responsibility to Protect has played an important role in allowing major powers to act at their discretion. The later has been aggravated by the deliberate undermining and delegitimizing of the Responsibility to Protect within the UN fora by China, Russia and many states in Africa, Asia and in the Arab world in order to prevent it from becoming a consolidated and an operational norm.[297] Such situation has led to a kind of skepticism among the doctrine. Hence, after noting that such indeterminacy makes it unlikely that the Responsibility to Protect will act in the near future as a catalyst for international action in response to genocide and mass atrocities, Alex J. Bellamy is of the opinion that "it seems reasonable to argue that the most prudent path is to view the principle (i.e. the Responsibility to Protect) as a policy agenda in need of implementation rather than as 'red flag' to galvanize the world into action. This view would certainly be consistent with the evidence thus far that RtoP (i.e., the Responsibility to protect) is best employed as a diplomatic tool, or prism, to guide efforts to stem the tide of mass atrocities, and that it has little utility in terms of generating additional international political will in response to such episodes."[298] Such skeptical view is understandable with regard to the indifferent attitude of the Security Council towards the implementation of the

[293] Anonymous (2007).

[294] de Vaal (2007, p. 1043).

[295] Evans (2006, p. 716).

[296] See Bellamy (2010, p. 153).

[297] See Evans (2008, pp. 288–289).

[298] Bellamy (2010, p. 166).

Responsibility to Protect to different crisis and particularly the Darfur crisis. It is not a surprise that the Responsibility to Protect in the Darfur crisis has been rated as an abject failure in that it failed to galvanize international action, or, worse, exacerbated the situation by distracting the relevant actors.[299] However, the present Arab Spring may give the Security Council the opportunity to correct its attitude, in particular in connection to the Libya crisis.

With regard to the Libya crisis, the Security Council has on 17 March 2011 adopted Resolution 1973[300] by which it authorized the use of force and the creation of a no-fly-zone in order to ensure the protection of the Libyan civilian population which has been subject to widespread and systematic attacks which may amount to crimes against humanity. This was the first time, following the emergence of the concept of the "Responsibility to protect", that the Security Council has clearly authorized a military intervention in order to ensure the protection of a civilian population. What is striking is that it was also the first time that the Security Council has made sure to obtain the agreement of all concerned actors, including regional organizations. It was also the first time ever that the concerned population requested Security Council's intervention. What can also be noticed is that the permanent members, who were opposed to the Security Council's intervention, have made no use of their veto power. However, these states as well as other states that were not in favor of a military intervention, have questioned the legitimacy and the scope of the action taken to this end by US led coalition. Some argued that no military action was authorized by the Security Council and that the only measure that could be taken was the creation of a no-fly-zone, while it was clearly stated in Resolution 1973 that the Security Council "authorizes Member States that have notified the Secretary-General, acting nationally or through regional organizations or arrangements, and acting in cooperation with the Secretary-General, to take all necessary measures (Which in the UN jargon includes the use of military forces), notwithstanding paragraph 9 of resolution 1970 (2011), to protect civilians and civilian populated areas under threat of attack in the Libyan Arab Jamahiriya, including Benghazi, while excluding a foreign occupation force of any form on any part of Libyan territory…". Others argued that the US led coalition exceeded its mandate by attacking Libyan military sites that have no direct link with the need to protect the civilian population, while it was clear that these sites were the host of the military command from which the attacks against the civilian population were planned. That campaign, launched by the (undeclared) opponents to the Resolution 1973, has had as effect to push the US led coalition to accept that the NATO take over, which was requested by those members of the Atlantic Alliance who were against the use of force against the Libyan regime. This has immediately reflected on the operations on the ground which have been weakened and sometimes even frozen. The Libyan regime took advantage of that situation in order to

[299] See Bellamy (2010, p. 153).

[300] S/RES/1973 (2011), 17 March 2011.

increase its repressive attacks against the civilian population by besieging and bombarding Libyan cities and towns. Thus, the Libyan people continue to be killed as the NATO' forces accept to intervene, occasionally and in a very symbolic manner, only when the suffering of these people comes to be strongly recalled by international media. By doing so, the NATO has shown that it has a wrong reading of the "Responsibility to protect" which aims at saving lives of people who are subjected to criminal attacks. What is amazing is that, instead of taking decisive and immediate action in order to make a quick end to the suffering of the Libyan people, the NATO has put on the same footing the Libyan's army attacks against the civilian population and the reaction of the civilian population in order to protect itself and has come to see in both these attacks and the defensive reaction of the population a mere conflict between two equals that needs to be treated politically. By taking over from the US led coalition, the NATO has taken the responsibility to protect the Libyan people. Its duty is therefore to fulfill that responsibility. But, the NATO has increasingly shown its reluctance to fulfill Resolution 1973 to the extent that France and the United Kingdom have ended up expressing their dissatisfaction.[301] Regrettably, that reluctance has not only prolonged the suffering of the Libyan people, but it has also encouraged other Arab regimes, notably in Syria and Yemen, to severely repress their peoples.

The continuing suffering of the Libyan people shows once again how it is extremely difficult to establish an international mechanism by which people can be protected from despotic and anti-democratic and repressive governments. The Arab Spring has given the opportunity to the international community to show that it can protect people from repression and genocide by making a good use of the "Responsibility to protect". This opportunity has been missed because of selfish interests of some powerful states. But how to take advantage of that opportunity when some of these states are against democracy even within their own territories! The Libyan test has shown, if any, that the concept of the "Responsibility to protect" needs, first of all, that all powerful states share the same values, the most important being democracy and human rights. Now, the discussion – which has taken place in the past decade in the Security Council, the General Assembly and UN human rights bodies in relation to Rwanda, Darfur, and other crisis – has indicated that "member states no longer share a common legal or ethic consensus on the basis of which they could rally behind collective action to halt or prevent mass atrocities under all circumstances. Discussions among member states in the General Assembly and in the Human Rights Council reflect a general trend of gradual withdrawal from international standards on human rights, democracy and the rule of law offering exceptional security or economic circumstances as justification. It has become increasingly difficult to agree on joint action in support of human rights and justice in extreme cases, overriding national sovereignty".[302] The Libyan test

[301] See Reuters, 12 April 2011.

[302] Strauss (2009, p. 321).

has also shown that the implementation of the "Responsibility to protect" requires the creation of safeguards and mechanisms aimed at preventing that such implementation be diverted from its humanitarian objectives. It has shown also that the NATO cannot be the appropriate instrument in order to implement the "Responsibility to protect".

At the time of writing (end of May 2011), NATO appears to have changed its attitude by increasing its attacks against Libyan military central command in an attempt to speed up the process towards a political solution meant to facilitate a democratic transition. Noting that the Libyan pro-democratic forces are making tremendous progress in order to achieve their goals, the opponents to the implementation of the Responsibility to Protect to the Libyan crisis have also started to change their negative attitude. It is therefore very likely that the Responsibility to Protect will achieve its goal in Libyan. This will be an unprecedented event that will undoubtedly reinforce the legitimacy of the Responsibility to Protect.

As we have seen above, humanitarian intervention has been conceived by powerful states in order to dominate weak states by circumventing the principle of legal equality and other major principles such as the prohibition of nonintervention and the prohibition of the use of force. But powerful states have also used self-determination in order to make other states disintegrate.

References

Aceves WJ (2000) Liberalism and international legal scholarship: the Pinochet case and the move towards a universal transnational law litigation. Harvard Int Law J

Akande D (1997) The international court of justice and the security council: is there room for judicial control of decisions of the political organs of the United nations? ICLQ

Akehurst M (1972–1973) Jurisdiction in international law. BYIL:46

Akram M, Shah SH (2005) The legislative powers of the United security council. In: Ronald St. John Macdonald and Douglas M Johnston (eds.) Towards World Constitutionalism. Issues in Legal Ordering of the World Community. Martinus Nijhoff Publishers, Leiden

Alkopher TD (2007) The role of rights in rights in the social construction of wars: from the crusades to humanitarian interventions. Millennium J Int Stud 36

Alvarez JE (1996) Judging the security council. AJIL

American Law Institute (1987) Restatement (Third) of the Foreign Relations Law of the United States. American Law Institute Publishers, Philadelphia

Anghie A (1999) Fransisco de Vitoria and the Colonial origins of International law. In: Darian-Smith E, Fitzpatrick P (eds) Laws of the Postcolonial. Michigan University Press, Ann Arbor

Anghie A (2005) Imperialism, Sovereignty and the Making of International Law. Cambridge University Press, Cambridge

Annan K (2000) We the Peoples. Millennium Report. United Nations, New York

Anonymous (2007) Ensuring a responsibility to protect: lessons from Darfur. http://www.wcl.american.edu/hrbrief/14/2anonymous.pdf

Arangio-Ruiz G (2000) On the council law making. Rivista di Diritto Internazionale 83

Babic J (2003) Foreign armed intervention: between justified aid and illegal violence. In: Jokic A, Wilkins B (eds) Humanitarian Intervention. Moral and Philosophical Issues. Broadview Press, Toronto

Badescu CG (2011) Humanitarian Intervention and the Responsibility to Protect. Security and Human Rights. Routledge, London

Badescu CG (June 2009) The responsibility to protect and the conflict in darfur: the big let-down. Security Dialogue 40(3)

Balthazar LG (1998) Governments sanctions and private initiatives: striking a new balance for U.S. enforcement of internationally recognized workers rights. Columbia Human Rights Law Rev 29

Baroni F (2000) The international criminal tribunal for the former Yugoslavia and its mission to restore peace. Pace Int Law Rev 12

Bass GJ (2008) Freedom's Battle. The Origins of Humanitarian Intervention. Alfred A. Knopf, New York

Bassiouni C (2002) International Extradition: United States Law and Practice. Oceana Publications, New York

Bassiouni C (2004) The history of universal jurisdiction and its place in international law. In: Macedo S (ed) Universal Jurisdiction: National Courts and the Prosecution of Serious Crimes Under International Law. University of Pennsylvania Press, Philadelphia

Bazyler MJ (1987) Re-examing the doctrine of humanitarian intervention in light of the atrocities in Kampuchea and Ethiopia. Stanford J Int Law 23

Beale JH (1923) The jurisdiction of a sovereign state. Harvard Law Rev 36

Bedjaoui M (1993) Du contrôle de la légalité des actes du Conseil de Sécurité. In Recueil d'études en l'honneur du Professeur François Rigaux, Brussels

Bedjaoui M (1994) The New World Order and the Security Council. Testing the Legality of Its Acts. Martinus Nijhoff Publishers, Dordrecht

Bellamy A (2006) Whither the responsibility to protect? Humanitarian intervention and the 2005 World Summit. Ethics Int Affair 20(2)

Bellamy AJ (2009) The responsibility to protect or Trojan horse? The crisis in darfur and humanitarian intervention after Iraq. Ethics Int Affairs 19(2)

Bellamy AJ (2010) The responsibility to protect-five years on. Ethics Int Affairs 24(2)

Bellamy AJ (2011) Global Politics and the Responsibility to Protect. From Words to Deeds. Routledge, London

Bennouna M (1974) Le consentement a lingerence militaire dans les conflits internes. LGDJ, Paris

Berthoud P (1948) La compétence nationale des Etats. L'Article 2, paragraphe 7 de la Charte de San Francisco. Thesis, Neuchâtel, Brougg

Beyerlin U (1982) Humanitarian intervention. In: Bernhardt R (ed) Encyclopedia of Public International Law, vol 3. North-Holland Publishing, Amsterdam

Biguma NF (1998) La reconnaissance conventionnelle de la compétence universelle des tribunaux internes à l'égard de certains crimes et délits. Thesis, Université Panthéon-Assas, Paris II

Bindschedler L (1963-I) La délimitation des compétences des Nations Unies. RCADI

Birdsall A (2006) The international criminal tribunal for the former Yugoslavia.- Towards a more just order? Peace Conflict Dev 8

Blakesley CL (1994) Obstacles to the creation of a permanent war crimes tribunal. Fletcher Forum World Affairs 18(2)

Borchard EM (1951) State Insolvency and Foreign Bondholders, vol 269. Yale University Press, New Haven

Bottini G (2004) Universal jurisdiction after the creation of the international criminal court. NY Univ J Int Law Politics 36(2–3)

Bourquin M (1927-I) Crimes et delits contre la surete des Etats etrangers. RCADI

Bowett DW (1996) The court role in relation to international organizations. In: Vaughan L, Fitzmaurice M (ed) Fifty Years of International Court of Justice. Essays in Honour of Sir Robert Jennings. Cambridge University Press, Cambridge

Bowett DW (1997) Judicial and political functions of the security council and the international court of justice. In: Changing the Constitution of the United Nations. The British Institute of International and Comparative Law, London

Brierly JL (1925) Matters of domestic jurisdiction. BYBIL
Broomhall B (2003) International Justice and the International Criminal Court: Between Sovereignty and the Rule of Law. Oxford University Press, Oxford
Brownlie I (1963a) International Law and the Use of Force by States. Clarendon Press, Oxford
Brownlie I (1963b) International Law and the Use of Force. Oxford University Press, Oxford
Brownlie I (1973) Humanitarian intervention. In: John Norton Moore (ed.) Law and Civil War in the Modern World. Johns Hopkins University Press, Baltimore
Brownlie I (1994) The decisions of political organs of the United Nations and the rule of law. In: Essays in Honour of Wang Tieya. Martinus Nijhoff Publishers, Dordrecht
Brownlie I (1995) International law at the Fiftieth Anniversary of the United Nations. 255 RCADI, I
Butler AH (2004) The growing support for universal jurisdiction in national legislation. In: Macedo S (ed) Universal jurisdiction: national courts and the prosecution of serious crimes under international law. University of Pennsylvania Press, Philadelphia
Byers M, Chesterman S (2003) Changing the rules about rules? Unilateral humanitarian intervention and the future of international law. In: Holzgrefe JL, Keohane RO (eds) Humanitarian intervention. Ethical, legal, and political dilemmas. Cambridge University Press, Cambridge
Calvo C (1886) Le Droit International Public theorique et pratique, vol 1. Guillaumin/Pedone, Paris
Carnegie R (1963) Jurisdiction over violations of the laws and customs of war. BYIL 39
Charney JI (1999) Commentary: anticipatory humanitarian intervention in Kosovo. Vanderbilt J Transnational Law 32(5)
Charpentier J (1961) Les effets du consentement sur l'intervention, Melanges Seferiades, vol 2
Chauvy Y (1981) L'extradition, Paris, Q.S.J. No. 1920
Chesterman S (2001) Just War or Just Peace? Humanitarian Intervention and International Law, vol. 140. Oxford University Press, Oxford
Cohen JL (2011) Security council activism in the age of the war on terror. Implications for human rights, democracy and constitutionalism. In: Peled Y, Lewin-Epstein N, Mundlak G, Cohen JL (eds) Democratic Citizenship and War. Routledge, London
Conforti B (2005) The Law and Practice of the United Nations. Martinus Nijhoff Publishers, Leiden
Cottey A (2008) Beyond humanitarian intervention: the new politics of peacekeeping and intervention. Contemporary Politics 14(4)
Cryer R, Friman H, Robinson D, Wilmshurst E (2010) An Introduction to International Criminal Law and Procedure. Cambridge University Press, Cambridge
D'Amato A (1987) International Law: Process and Prospect. Dobbs Ferry, New York
Dachy E, Wajs M (2003) Compétence universelle. Une loi contre la justice. Filipson édition, Bruxelles
Danish Institute of International Affairs (DUPI) (1999) Humanitarian intervention. Legal and political aspects. DUPI, Copenhagen
de la Pradelle G (2000) La compétence universelle. In: Asenco H, Décaux E, Pellet A (eds) Droit International Pénal. Pédone, Paris
de Las Casas B (1552) In Defense of the Indians. Transl. Stafford Poole. Northern Illinois University Press, DeKalb, 1992
de Lupis ID (1974) International Law and the Independent State. Gower, Aldershot
de Vaal A (2007) Darfur and the responsibility to protect. Int Affairs 83(6)
de Vattel E (1758) Le droit des gens ou principes de la loi naturelle appliquée a la conduite et aux affaires des nations et des souverains. Classics of International Law, trans. Fenwick. Carnegie Institution, Washington, 1916, II
de Vitoria F (1557) De Indis et jure belli relectiones. Classics of International Law. Carnegie Institution, Washington, 1917

Delos JT (1939) L'expansion coloniale dans la doctrine de Vitoria et les principes du droit moderne. In: Scott JB (ed) Vitoria et Suarez. Contribution des the´ologiens au Droit International moderne. A. Pedone, Paris
Despagnet F (1905) Cours de Droit International Public, 3rd edn. Librairie de la Societe du Recueil General des Lois et des Arrets, Paris
Dochring K (1997) Unlawful resolutions of the security council and their legal consequences. Max Planck Yearbook of United Nations, 1
Domagala A (2004) Humanitarian intervention: the Utopia of just war? The NATO intervention in Kosovo and the restraints of Humanitarian Intervention. Sussex European Institute. http://www.sussex.ac.uk/seid/documents/wp76.pdf
Drago L (1907) States loans in their relation to international policy. AJIL
Dugard J (2006) International law: a South African Perspective, 3rd edn. Juta & Co, Cap Town
Dulles JF (1950) War or peace. MacMillan, New York
Dupuy PM (1997) The constitutional dimensions of the charter of the United Nations revisited. Max Planck Yearbook of United Nations, 1
De Wet E (2004) The Chapter VII Powers of the United Nations Council. HART Publishing, Oxford
El Ouali A (1984) Effets juridiques de la sentence internationale. Contribution à l'étude de l'exécution des normes internationales. LGDJ, Paris
El Ouali A (1993) Nouvel ordre international ou retour à l'inégalité des Etats ? Approche globale de la nouvelle configuration stratégique, économique et juridique mondiale. Les Editions Maghrébines, Casablanca
Ermacora F (1968-II) Human rights and domestic jurisdiction (Article 2 (7) of the charter. RCADI
Evans G (2006) From Humanitarian Intervention to the Responsibility to Protect. Wisconsin Int Law J 24(3)
Evans G (2008) The responsibility to protect: an idea whose time has come. . .and gone? Int Affairs 22(3)
Fairley HS (1980) State actors, Humanitarian Intervention and International Law: reopening Pandora's box. Georgian J Int Comparative Law 10
Farer TJ (1991) An inquiry into the legitimacy of humanitarian intervention. In: Damrosch LF, Scheffer DJ (eds) Law and Force in the New International Order. Westview Press, Boulder
Farer TJ (2003) Humanitarian intervention before and after 9/11:legality and legitimacy. In: Holzgrefe JL, Keohane RO (eds) Humanitarian intervention. Ethical, legal, and political dilemmas. Cambridge University Press, Cambridge
Feinstein L (2007) Darfur and beyond. Council on Foreign Relations, New York
Fenwick CG (1925) The scope of domestic questions in international law. AJIL 19
Fenwick CG (1945) Intervention: individual and collective. AJIL 39
Fenwick CG (1965) International Law, 4th edn. Appleton-Century-Crofts, New York
Filder DP (2000) A Kinder, gentler system of Capitulations? International law, structural adjustment policies, and the standard of liberal, globalized civilization. Texas Int Law J 35(3)
Fincham CBH (1948) Domestic Jurisdiction: Exception to Domestic Jurisdiction as a Bar to Action by the League of Nations and the United Nations. A.W.Sijthoff, Leiden
Finnemore M (2003) The Purpose of Intervention. Changing Beliefs About the Use of Force. Cornell University Press, London
Fitzpatrick P (2003) 'Gods would be needed. . .': American Empire and the Rule of (international) Law. Leiden J Int Law 16
Fixdal M, Smith D (1998) Humanitarian intervention and just war. Mershon Int Studies Rev 42
Florini AM (ed) (2000) The Third Force: The Rise of Transnational Civil Society. Carnegie Endowment for International Peace, Washington
Fonteyne JPL (1974) The customary international law doctrine of humanitarian intervention: its current validity under the UN charter. California Int Law J 4
Franck TM (1992) The powers of appreciation: who is the ultimate guardian of UN legality? AJIL

Franck TM (2003) Interpretation and change in the law of humanitarian intervention. In: Holzgrefe JL, Keohane R (eds) Humanitarian intervention. Ethical, legal, and political dilemmas. Cambridge University Press, Cambridge
Franck SD (2009) Development and outcomes of investment treaty arbitration. Harvard Int Law J 50(2)
Franck T, Rodley N (1973a) After Bangladesh: The law of humanitarian intervention by military force. AJIL 67
Franck TM, Rodley NN (1973b) After Bangladesh: the law of humanitarian intervention by military force. AJIL 67
Frydman B (2009) Le contentieux transnational des droits de l'homme: Une analyse stratégique. Revue Trimestrielle de Droit Européen: 77
George RP (1998) Natural law and international order. In: Mapel DR, Nardin T (eds) International Society: Diverse Ethical Perspectives. Princeton University Press, Princeton
Gill TD (1995) Legal and some political limitations on the power of the UN security council to exercise its enforcement powers under chapter VII of the charter. Netherland Yearbook of International Law, vol. 26
Gilmour DR (1967a) The meaning of 'Intervene' within Article 2 (7) of the United Nations charter. An historical perspective. ICLQ 16
Gilmour DR (1967b) Article 2 (7) of the United Nations charter and the practice of the permanent members of the security council. Australian YIL: 3
Gilmour DR (1967c) The meaning of 'Intervene' within Article 2 (7) of the United Nations Charter. An historical perspective. ICLQ: 16
Giovanni da Legnano (1447) Tractatos de bello, de represaliis et de duello. Classics of International law, transl Brierly. Carnegie Institution, Washington, 1917
Glennon MJ (1992) State-sponsored abduction: a comment on United States v. Alvarez-Machain. AJIL 4
Goodrich LM (1949) The United Nations and domestic jurisdiction. Int Org: 1
Goodrich LM, Hambro E (1946) The Charter of the United Nations: Commentary and Documents, 1st edn. World Peace Foundation, Boston
Gowland-Debbas V (1994) The relationship between the International Court of Justice and the security council in the light of the Lockerbie Case. AJIL
Gray C (2000) International Law and the Use of Force. Oxford University Press, Oxford
Grotius H (1646) De jure belli ac pacis. Classics of International Law, trans. Kelsey, Clarendon Press, Oxford, 1927, II, xx
Guillaume G (1992) La compétence universelle, formes anciennes et nouvelles. In: Mélanges offerts à, G.Levasseur. Paris, Litec
Hall WE (1909) A Treatise on International Law, 6th edn. Oxford University Press, Oxford
Hall SM (2002) Multinational corporations' post-unocal liabilities for violations of international laws. George Washington Int Law Rev:41
Halleck HW, Baker GS (1893) Halleck's International Law, or, Rules Regulating the Intercourse of States in Peace and War, vol 1, 3rd edn. K. Paul, Trench, Trübner, London
Harper K (1994) Does the United Nations security council have the competence to act as court of Legislature. NY Univ J Int Law Politics 27(1)
Hehir A (2008) Humanitarian Intervention After Kosovo: Iraq, Darfur and the Record of Global Society. McMillan, Palgrave
Higgins R (1963) The Development of International Law Through the Political Organs of the United Nations. Oxford University Press, Oxford
Higgins R (1994) Problems and Process. International Law and How We Use It. Clarendon Press, Oxford
Hoffman J (2008) Terrorism blacklisting: putting european human guarantees to the test. Constellations 15(4)
Holzgrefe JL (2002) Humanitarian intervention and state sovereignty. Int J Human Rights 6(1)

Holzgrefe JL (2003) The Humanitarian Intervention Debate. In: Holzgrefe JL, Keohane R (eds) Humanitarian Intervention. Ethical, Legal, and Political Dilemmas. Cambridge University Press, Cambridge
Hornung J (1885, 1886) Civilisés et barbares. RDILC
Howell JM (1954) Domestic Jurisdiction in International Law. Proc Am Soc Int Law
Hurd I (2007) After Anarchy. Legitimacy and Power in the United Nations Security Council. Princeton University Press, Princeton
ICISS (2001) The Responsibility to Protect. The International Development Research Centre, Ottawa
ICJ (1949) Corfu channel case. ICJ Reports, 4
ICJ (1986) Case concerning military and paramilitary activities in and against Nicaragua (Merits). ICJ Reports
Ignatieff M (2003) State failure and nation-building. In: Holzgrefe JL, Keohane RO (eds) Humanitarian Intervention. Ethical, Legal, and Political Dilemmas. Cambridge University Press, Cambridge
Inazumi M (2005) Universal Jurisdiction in Modern International Law: Expansion of National Jurisdiction for Prosecuting Serious Crimes under International Law. Intersentia, Antwerp
Jennings R, Watts A (eds) (1992) Oppenheim's International Law, 9th edn. Longman, Harlow
Jescheck H (1985) International crimes. In: Bernhardt R (ed) Encyclopedia of Public International Law, vol 8. North-Holland, Amsterdam
Jones HH (1951) Domestic jurisdiction: from the covenant to the charter. Illinois Law Rev 46
Jones GJ (1979) The United Nations and the Domestic Jurisdiction of States: Interpretations and Applications of the Non-intervention Principle. University of Wales Press, Cardiff
Kawser A (2006) The Domestic Jurisdiction Clause in the United Nations Charter. A historical view. Singapore Yearbook of International Law 10
Keck Sikkink ME (1998) Activists Beyond Borders: Advocacy Networks in International Relations. Cornell University Press, Ithaca
Kelsen H (1951) The Law of the United Nations. Stevens and Sons, London
Keohane RO (2003) Political authority after intervention: gradations in sovereignty. In: Holzgrefe JL, Keohane RO (eds) Humanitarian Intervention. Ethical, Legal, and Political Dilemmas. Cambridge University Press, Cambridge
Krisch N (2004) Imperial International Law, Global Law and Justice, Global Law Working Paper 01/04, NYU School of Law
Kirsch N (2005) International law in times of Hegemony :unequal power and the shaping of the international legal order. Eur J Int Law 16(3)
Kissinger H (2001) The pitfalls of universal jurisdiction: risking judicial tyranny. Foreign Affairs 80(4)
Kochler H (2001) Humanitarian Intervention in the Context of Modern Power Politics. International Progress Organization, Vienna, Stud Int Relat XXV
Koh HH (1994) The 'Haïti Paradigm' in United States Human Rights Policy. Yale Law J
Kontorovitch E (2007) "The inefficiency of universal jurisdiction", Public international law and economics: the power of rational choice methodology in guiding the analysis and the design of public international law institutions (Symposium). Working Paper, University of St. Gallen Law School
Krasner S (2004) Sharing sovereignty. New institutions for collapsed and failing states. Int Security 29(2)
Kraytman YS (1985) Universal jurisdiction. Historical roots and modern implications. BSIS J Int Studies
Krieg A (2009) The responsibility to protect- how history could repeat itself in Darfur'. PICA, A Global Research Organization
Laswell HD, McDougal MS (1992) Jurisprudence for a Free Society: Studies in Law, Science and Policy, vol 1. Martinus/Nijhoff/Kluwer Academic Publishers, Hingham

Lauterpacht H (1955) in L. Oppenheim "Oppenheim's International Law", 8th edn. Longman, London
Lepard BD (2003) Rethinking Humanitarian Intervention: a fresh approach based on fundamental ethical principles in international law and world religions. University of Pennsylvania Press, Philadelphia
Levene M (2005) Genocide in the age of the nation-state. the rise of the West and the coming of genocide. Palgrave Macmillan, New York
Lillich RB (1967) Forcible self-help by states to protect human rights. Iowa Law Rev 53
Lowe V et al (eds) (2008) Introduction of "The United Nations Security Council and War. The Evolution of Thought and Practice since 1945. Oxford University Press, Oxford
Macdonald R (1931) Changing relations between the International Court of Justice and the Security Council of the United nations. The Canadian Yearbook of International Law
Macedo S (ed) (2004) Universal Jurisdiction: National Courts and the Prosecution of Serious crimes under International Law. University of Pennsylvania Press, Philadelphia
Magnarella PG (1995a) Universal Jurisdiction and Universal Human Rights: A Global Progression. J Third World Studies 12(2)
Magnarella PG (1995b) Universal jurisdiction and universal human rights: a global progression. J Third World Studies 7(2)
Maier H (1983) Interests balancing and extraterritorial jurisdiction. Am J Comparative Law
Malanczuk P (1993) Humanitarian Intervention and the Legitimacy of the Use of Force. Het Spinhuis, Amsterdam
Malanczuk P (1999) Reconsidering the relationship between the ICJ and the security council. In: Heere WP (ed) International Law and the Hague's 750th Anniversary. TMC Asser, The Hague
Mann A (1964) The doctrine of jurisdiction in international law. RCADI 1
Manusama K (2006) The United Nations Security Council in the Post-cold era. Applying the Principle of Legality. Martinus Nijhoff Publishers, Leiden
Marcella D (1999) Passport to justice: internationalising the political question doctrine for application in the world court. Harvard Int Law J 40
Marchal A (1931) La conception de l'économie nationale et des rapports internationaux chez les mercantilistes français et leurs contemporains. Sirey, Paris
Marschik A (2005) Legislative powers of the security council. In: Ronald St. John Macdonald and Douglas M. Johnston (eds) Towards World Constitutionalism. Issues in Legal Ordering of the World Community. Martinus Nijhoff Publishers, Leiden
Martenczuk B (1999) The security council, the international court of justice and judicial review: what lessons from Lockerbie? Eur J Int Law
McClean E (2011) The dilemma of intervention: human rights and the UN security council. In Odello M, Canvadoli S (eds) Emerging Areas of Human Rights in the 21st Century. Routledge, London
McDougal MS (1953) International law, power and policy: a contemporary conception. RCADI, vol 82
McDougal MS, Laswell HD, Reisman M (1968) Theories about international law: prologue to a configurative jurisprudence. Virginia J Int Law 8
McWhinney E (1992) The international court as emerging constitutional court and the co-ordinate UN institutions. Especially the security council: implications of the aerial incident at Lockerbie. The Canadian Yearbook of International Law
Mepham D (2006) Darfur: The Responsibility to Protect. Institute for Public Policy Research, London
Mill JS (1867) A Few Words on Non-intervention. Dissertations and Discussions, vol 3, 2nd edn. Longmans, London
Moulin HA (1907) La doctrine de Drago, RGDIP
Mrazek J (1989) Prohibition on the use and threat of force: self-defence and self-help in international law. Canadian Yearbook of International Law 27

Murphy SD (1996) Humanitarian intervention: the United Nations in an evolving world order. University of Pennsylvania Press, Philadelphia
Murphy SD (2001) Calibrating global expectations regarding humanitarian intervention. Harvard University Conference on "After Kosovo: humanitarian intervention at the crossroads, January 2001, 6
Nardin T (2000) The moral basis of humanitarian intervention. Symposium on the norms and ethics of humanitarian intervention, Center for Global Peace and Conflict Studies, University of California, Irvine, May 26, 2000
Newman M (2009) Humanitarian Intervention; Confronting the Contradictions. Columbia University Press, New York
Newton MA (2001) Comparative complementarity: domestic jurisdiction consistent with the Rome statute of the international criminal court. Military Law Rev 167
Nigel AR, White D (2002) The United Nations System: Towards International Justice. Lynne Rienner Publishers, Boulder
Nolte G (2000) The limits of the security council's powers and its functions in the international legal system: some reflections. In: Byers M (ed) The Role of Law in International Politics. Oxford University Press, Oxford
Nolte G (2002) Article 2 (7). In: Simma B et al (eds) The Charter of the United Nations. A Commentary, vol. 1, 2nd edn. Oxford University Press, Oxford
Nys E (1912) Le Droit International Public. Les principes, les théories, les faits, vol 2. M. Weissenbrush, Bruxelles, New edit.
O'Connell DP (1965) International Law, vol. 1. Stevens, London
O'Keefe R (2004) Universal jurisdiction. Clarifying the basic concept. J Int Criminal Justice 2(3)
O'Keefe R (2009) The grave breaches regime and universal jurisdiction. J Int Criminal Justice 7(4)
Olivares Marcos GA (2005) The legal practice of the recovery of states external debts, Thesis, these. Institut Universitaire de Hautes Etudes Internationalse, Geneva
Oliver CT et al (1994) The International Legal System. Foundation Press, New York
Oppenheim L (1928) International law. A treatise, vol 1, Peace, 4th edn. Longmans, London
Orford A (2009) Jurisdiction without jurisdiction: from the Holly Roman empire to the responsibility to protect. Michigan J Int Law 30
Orford A (2011) International Authority and the Responsibility to Protect. Cambridge University Press, Cambridge
Ott DH (1987) Public International Law and the Modern World. Pitman Publishing, London
Padirac R (1953) Légalité juridique des Etats et l'organisation internationale. L.G.D.J., Paris
Pattison J (2010) Humanitarian Intervention and the Responsibility to Protect. Who Should Intervene? Oxford University Press, Oxford
Pellet A (2000) State sovereignty and the protection of fundamental human rights: an international law perspective. Pugwash Occasional Papers 1
Pillet A (1898) Recherches sur les droits fondamentaux des Etats dans l'ordre des rapports internationaux et sur la solution des conflits quils font naıtre. RGDIP
Plachta M (2001) The Lockerbie case: the role of the security council in enforcing the principle *Aut Dedere Aut judicare*. Eur J Int Law 12(1)
Pradier-Fodere P (1883) Traite de Droit International Public europeen et americain suivant le progres de la science et de la pratique internationale, vol 1. G. Pédone-Lauriol, Paris
Preuss L (1949-I) Article 2, Paragraph 7 of the Charter of the United Nations and matters of domestic jurisdiction. RCADI:74
Princeton Project (2001) Principles on Universal Jurisdiction. Princeton, New Jersey
Putmam TL (2009) Courts without borders: domestic sources of U.S. extraterritoriality in the regulatory sphere. Int Org 63
Quigley J (2000) The United Nations security council: Promethean protector or helpless Hostage? Texas Int Law J
Rajan MS (1958) United Nations and Domestic Jurisdiction. Orient Longmans, Bombay

Ralston JH (1919) International Arbitration from Athens to Locarno. Stanford University Press, California
Ramsbotham O, Woodhouse T (1996) Humanitarian Intervention in Contemporary Conflict. Polity, Cambridge
Randall K (1988) Universal jurisdiction under international law. Texas Law Rev 66
Randelzhofer A (1994) Article 2(4). In: Simma B (ed) The Charter of the United Nations: A Commentary. Oxford University Press, Oxford
Ratner SR, Abrams JS (2001) Accountability for Human Rights Atrocities in International Law: Beyond the Nuremberg Legacy. Oxford University Press, New York
Raustiala K (2004) The evolution of territoriality: international relations and American law. In: Kahler M, Walter B (eds) Globalization, Territoriality and Conflict. Cambridge University Press, Cambridge
Rayfuse R (1993) International abduction and the united states supreme court: the law of the jungle reigns. ICLQ 42
Reisman M (1971) Nullity and Revision. The Review and Enforcement of International Judgments and Awards. Yale University Press, London
Reisman M (1990) Sovereignty and human rights in contemporary international law. 84 AJIL
Reisman WM (1993) The constitutional crisis in the United Nations. AJIL
Reisman M (2000) Unilateral action and the transformation of the world constitutive process: the special problem of humanitarian intervention. Eur J Int Law 11
Reisman M, McDougal MS (1958) Aggression and World Order: A Critique of United Nations' Theories of Aggression. Stevens, London
Reisman M, McDougal MS (1973) Humanitarian intervention to protect the Ibos. In: Lillich RB (ed) Humanitarian Intervention and the United Nations. University Press of Virginia, Charlottesville
Reydmans L (2003) Universal Jurisdiction. International and Municipal Perspectives. Oxford University Press, Oxford
Rolin-Jacquemyns G (1876) Note sur la théorie du droit d'intervention, à propos d'une lettre de M. Le Professeur Arntz. RDILC VIII
Rosental B (1970) Etude de l'oeuvre de Myres Smith McDougal en matiére de Droit International. LGDIP, Paris
Ross A (1964) *La notion de compétence nationale* dans la pratique des Nations Unies. In: Mélanges offerts à Henri Rolin. Pédone, Paris
Roth K (2004) War in Iraq: not a humanitarian intervention. http://www.unhcr.org/refworld/pdfid/402ba99f4.pdf
Rougier A (1910) La théorie del'intervention d'humanite. RGDIP
Rousseau Ch (1980) Droit International Public. Paris, Sirey 4
Rubin AP (1993) Libya, Lockerbie and the law. Diplomacy Statecraft 4(1)
Rubin AD (1994) An international criminal tribunal for former Yugoslavia? Pace Int Law Rev 6(1)
Sahovic M, Bishop WW (1968) The authority of the state: its range with respect to persons and places. In: Sorensen M (ed) Manual of Public International Law. Macmillan, London
Saint-Aubin J (1913) L'extradition et le droit extraditionnel théorique et pratique. A.Pédone, Paris
Schachter O (1995) Law-making in the United Nations. In: Nandasiri Jasentuliyana (ed) Perspectives on International Law. Kluwer Law International, The Hague
Scheffer DJ (2001) Symposium: universal jurisdiction. myths, realities and prospects: opening address. New Engl Law Rev 35
Schepple KL (2006) International State of Emergency: Challenges to Constitutionalism after September 11, paper was originally prepared for the Yale Legal Theory Workshop, 21 September 2006, Princeton University, 1, digitalcommons.law.umaryland.edu/schmooze. . ./49/ - United States
Schweisfurth T (1980) Operations to rescue nationals in third states involving the use of force in relation to the protection of human rights. GYIL

Scott JB (1934) The Spanish Origin of International Law: Fransisco de Vitoria and His Law of Nations. Clarendon Press, Oxford
Sharga D, Zalick R (1994) The international criminal tribunal for former Yugoslavia. EJIL 5
Shearer IA (1994) Starke's International Law, 11th edn. Butterworths, London
Simma B (1999) NATO, the UN and the use of force: legal aspects. Eur J Int Law. http://www.ejil.org/journal/Vol10/No1/abl.html
Slaughter A-M (2004) Defining the limits: universal jurisdiction and national courts. In: Macedo S (ed) Universal Jurisdiction: National Courts and the Prosecution of Serious Crimes Under International Law. University of Pensylvania Press, Philadelphia
Sornarajah M (1981) Internal colonialism and humanitarian intervention. Ga J Int Comp L
Stern B (1994) Vers la mondialisation juridiques. Les lois Helmes-Burton et d'Amato-Kennedy. RGDIP 4:979–1003
Stern B (1999) A propos de la compétence universelle. In: Yakpo E, Boumédra T (eds) Liber Amicorum Mohammed Bedjaoui. Kluwer Law International, The Hague
Strauss E (2009) A bird in the hand is worth two in the bush – on the assumed legal nature of the responsibility to protect. Global Respons Protect 1(3)
Suzuki E (1974) The New Haven school of international law: an invitation to a policy-oriented jurisprudence. Yale Stud in World Pub Order 1
Swords C (2002) Canadian practice in international law at the department of foreign affairs in 2001-2002: jurisdiction and territorial sovereignty, extraterritorial evidence gathering. Canadian Yearbook of International Law
Teson FR (1997) Humanitarian Intervention : An Inquiry into Law and Morality, 2nd edn. Transnational Publishers, Irvington-on-Hudson
Thomas C (1985) New States, Sovereignty and Intervention. Gover, VII cont
Trindade AAC (1976) The domestic jurisdiction of states in the practice of the United Nations and regional organizations. ICLQ
Tuck R (1999) The Rights of War and Peace: Political Thought and International Order from Grotius to Kant. Oxford University Press, Oxford
Ulimubenshi PC (2003) L'exception du domaine réservé dans la procedure de la Cour Internationale. Thesis, University of Geneva
Vallindas P (1948) The concept 'matters which are essentially within domestic jurisdiction' in Art.2 section 7 of the United Nations Charter. RHDI: 1
Verdross A (1965) La 'compétence nationale' dans le cadre de l'Organisation des Nations Unies et l'indépendance des Etats. RGDIP
Vervey VD (1985) Humanitarian intervention under international law. Netherlands ILR 32
Vervey WD (1998) Humanitarian intervention in the 1990s and beyond: an international law perspective. In: Pieterse JN (ed) World Orders in the Making: Humanitarian Intervention and Beyond. St. Martin's Press, New York
Watson JS (1977) Autointerpretation, competence, and the continuing validity of Article 2 (7) of the UN charter. AJIL
Weiss TG, Thakur R (2010) Global Governance and the UN. An Unfinished Journey. Indiana University Press, Bloomington
Welsh JM (2008) The security council and humanitarian intervention. In: Lowe V, Roberts A, Welsh J, Zaun D (eds) The United Nations Security Council and War: The Evolution of Thought and Practice since 1945. Oxford University Press, Oxford
Wheaton H (1929) Wheatons's Elements of International Law, vol I, 6th edn. Stevens and Sons, London
White ND (2005) The Law of International Organizations. Lynne Rienner, Boulder
Wilkins B (2003) Humanitarian Intervention: some doubts. In: Jokic A (ed) Humanitarian Intervention. Moral and Philosophical Issues. Broadview Press, Toronto
Williams JF (1924) International Law and International Financial Obligations Arising from Contract, vol 4. Bibliotheca Visseriana, Leyden

Williams JF (1929) Chapters on Current International Law and the League of Nations. Longmans, Green, New York

Wilson RR (1929) Reservations clauses in treaties of obligatory arbitration. AJIL 23

Wise EM (1998) Aut Dedere Aut judicare: the duty to prosecute or extradite. In: Cherif Bassiouni M (ed) International Criminal Law. Procedural and Enforcement Mechanisms, vol II, 2nd edn. Transnational Publishers, Irvington

Wolff C (1748) Jus gentium methodo scientifica pertractatum. Classics of International Law, Trans. Drake. Oxford University Press, Oxford, 1934

Zajadlo J (2005) Legality and legitimization of humanitarian intervention. New challenges in the age of the war on terrorism. Am Behav Sci 48(6)

Part III
Protection of Territorial Integrity Against Internal Threat

As we have seen above, internal threat has been a major concern for the state since its inception thousands of years ago. The state was born out of the division of the society in social classes. Such a division was deepened by territorial conquests which made of the state a mosaic of ethnic groups. The traditional state has never been able to cement these ethnic groups into a single and unified people as it did not very often possess the capacity to control its whole territory and, as an indirect consequence, its society. The traditional state invented different ways and means in order to adjust to that difficult situation. Thus, it was able to survive for millennia thanks to the delegation of power to local communities through a de facto territorial autonomy system.

A radical change will be introduced in the nature of the state thanks to modernity. The latter, by rationalizing the functioning of the state further to the emergence of capitalism, will indeed enable the state to establish an efficient control over its territory and population. It was from that time that the state has started implementing its policy of unifying and homogenizing its society. Such policy will be reinforced with the emergence of popular sovereignty which will push the state, through the creation of the nation-state formula, to seek establishing the congruence between itself and the nation. However, while it helped in reinforcing and integrating Western states, popular sovereignty will play elsewhere a disintegrative role.

Popular sovereignty will indeed play a dual and ambivalent role: integrating Western countries by establishing and reinforcing democracy and giving rise therefore to civic states, on one hand, and, on another hand, fragmenting non Western countries by disregarding democracy and encouraging the flourishing of particularisms, ethnicity and disintegrative behavior in foreign societies. These were, during the past two centuries, the two real functions of self-determination within what can be called the classical self-determination paradigm.

However, the self-determination classical paradigm has started recently to witness a profound change as democracy is being increasingly perceived as a universal value from which all the peoples over the world should benefit. The universal expansion of democracy against states' disintegration: this is the new philosophy which inspires the emerging self-determination paradigm. Thus, self-determination is back to its original and authentic meaning: promoting democracy for the benefit of all the peoples not only in the North but also in the rest of the world.

Crucial factors are behind the ongoing self-determination paradigmatic change. Among these factors, there is, as we have seen above, the general crisis of territoriality prompted not only by globalization, but also by the failure to build viable nation-states in most Southern countries, which finds, in the latter case, its origin mainly in disintegrative self-determination. The crisis of territoriality has pushed many countries in the North to realize that territorial autonomy can help their own states survive. The interest in autonomy has also witnessed a steady interest in many parts of the world where almost half of the population do live today, at varying degrees, under a federal system of government which leaves to the local communities the possibility to run their own affairs themselves. Furthermore, territorial autonomy is increasingly seen as a mere expression of self-determination at the local level. In fact, territorial autonomy is becoming a central component in the rising new self-determination paradigm.

Two important questions will therefore be discussed in this chapter. The first question aims at determining how the classical self-determination paradigm has functioned in order to make disintegrate peripheral states. The second question aims at determining how the arising new self-determination paradigm tends towards integrating all states through the promotion of democracy .

Chapter 5
The Self-Determination Classical Paradigm: Making Peripheral States Disintegrate

Deep social and historical forces have certainly contributed in shaping, beyond the traditional West European area, national consciousness. The French Revolution ideals of liberty and self-determination have also greatly influenced the process of nation-building elsewhere in Europe. Conversely, nationalism has also developed as a consequence of French revolution wars of annexation. It has developed further in reaction to Napoleon's wars of annexation which, carried out without any form of popular consultation, have provoked discontent among the populations concerned and then prompted a form of nationalism hostile to France. Ironically, after having encouraged the rise of the national spirit in Italy, in the German world, and beyond, in order to weaken the latter social and political basis, Napoleon armies were fought on behalf of nationalism as "nation after nation rose to expel the foreign oppressor from its territory or from its sphere of influence."[1] Likewise, it was the dismemberment of Poland by Russia, Austria and Prussia at the end of eighteenth century which has been at the origin of Polish nationalism.[2] Similarly, it was also the suppression of national aspirations of the Hungarians, Bohemians, northern Italians, Germans and Czech by the Austrian empire, and the national aspirations of the Greeks, Serbs, Croats, Slovenes, Bulgars, Romanians, Albanians, etc. by the Ottoman Empire which has reinforced these aspirations.

Certainly, revulsion against imperial domination has been a "pivotal motive-force of modern nationalism."[3] However, it still remains that, with the exception of Germany and to some extent Italy, no nation was able to emerge as such and be elevated to statehood without the self-interested assistance of a major external actor or actors. External assistance has initially been limited to circumscribed situations according to the state of forces in presence before it took a larger dimension and magnitude as a result of extraordinary events such as wars or major crises affecting

[1] Gastony (1992, p. 41).

[2] Idem, pp. 41–42.

[3] Idem, p. 42.

A. El Ouali, *Territorial Integrity in a Globalizing World*,
DOI 10.1007/978-3-642-22869-8_5, © Springer-Verlag Berlin Heidelberg 2012

a multinational state. Most of the new states have, since the French Revolution, emerged as a result, first, of global crisis as those which have affected the then existing empires, following World War I and World War II , or recently of the disintegration of USSR and Yugoslavia. But, there is no single case of state's creation which would have during this large period of time been the result of a strictly endogenous determinism. "In practice", recalls A. Roshwald, "as recent events in Eastern Europe and the Soviet Union, the trappings of political sovereignty often come within the reach of nationalists suddenly and unexpectedly, under extraordinary and short-lived circumstance arising from regional or global crisis rather than from strictly internal developments. If not grasped immediately, the opportunity to establish a separate polity may not occur for generations. But the attainment of political independence under such circumstances cannot be regarded as part of the ineluctable course of history, nor can the specific institutional and territorial forms that independence takes be seen as the inevitable outgrowth of an incremental process of social and political evolution".[4] Thus, self-determination never operates without the support of foreign countries which see in it an important instrument in their attempts to weaken rival states. "As a weapon in the field of ideological warfare" note R. Norland and S. Zaidi,[5] "self-determination was flexible and served on multiple fronts. Communist and Third World states used it to denounce western imperialism, focussing on Israel and apartheid South Africa once the period of decolonization was over; western powers used it to pressure and dismantle the Soviet Union and multi-ethnic states like Yugoslavia".

The history of self-determination as implemented abroad is therefore mainly the history of the manipulation of a noble principle in order to make foreign states disintegrate. Yet, the manipulation of self-determination has played a decisive role not only in disintegrating states, but also in creating very often non-viable ones and in prompting the emergence of recurrent ethnonationalism.

5.1 The Foreign Manipulation of Self-Determination

Self-determination has become over time so self-evident that talking about its manipulation might be seen as a blasphemy. It is probably because it has also seen in self-determination a natural thing that the doctrine has devoted no particular attention to the political conditions which have very often been behind its implementation in concrete situations. In reality, the manipulation of self-determination has been a recurrent phenomenon in international relations. First, it was amazingly the French Revolution which, while it has dramatically contributed to the emergence of self-determination in the form of popular sovereignty, has invented the

[4] Roshwald (2001, p. 2).

[5] Normand and Zaidi (2008, p. 233).

manipulation of such a principle. Second, it was that manipulation of self-determination which will later on inspire powerful states to use the latter as a destabilizing arm in their struggle with each other. Third, it was the dramatic increase in the manipulation of self-determination which will lead to the transmuting of the latter as it definitely became a means in substituting formal independence to democracy. Fourth, such a transformation in the understanding of self-determination was so profound that it deeply reflected on the institution of states' recognition which became more politicized than ever.

5.1.1 The Invention of the Manipulation of Self-Determination

The French Revolution has certainly offered a universal model of emancipation and preached a message of liberation for all human beings everywhere.[6] However, the French Revolution has also invented a new pattern of disintegrating states and subjecting them to foreign domination through the manipulation of self-determination.[7] First, it needs to be recalled, that at the time it proclaimed the right to self-determination, the French Revolution maintained and expanded its colonial presence abroad.[8] Second, the French Revolutionary wars were fought in order not to free foreign peoples as solemnly proclaimed, but to divert the attention of the French people from the contradictions affecting the Revolution which was out of breath[9] and simultaneously to weaken the nobility and the clergy. Third, the French Revolutionary wars ended up by transmuting from wars of liberation to wars of conquest and annexation. "French mobilization", writes M. Bukovansky, "was made possible by the unleashing of the idea of popular sovereignty and the revolutionary political dynamics that ensued. Without that principle, it would have been impossible to legitimate and execute the mass dispossession of nobility and clergy as constitutive orders of the state (as it was, the assault on the clergy in particular posed severe domestic problems), nor would it have been possible to mobilize such a large army... As the wars progressed, liberation of peoples and 'sister republics'

---

[6] See Schwartzmantel (1998, p. 55).

[7] P. Henry has noted with regret that "Ce n'est jamais, en effet, sans un serrement de cœur que l'historien se penche sur ces interminables guerres de la Révolution et de l'Empire, dont l'héroïsme et la gloire peuvent faire oublier les désastres, matériels et encore plus intellectuels et moraux, qui en furent la rançon. C'était un bien bel idéal, l'un des plus purs qu'eût conçus l'humanité, qui allait sombrer peu à peu devant le goût des conquêtes et devant les haines accumulées au cours de cette formidable mêlée des peuples", Henry (1937, p. 66).

[8] See Saintoyant (1930); Tarrade (1989).

[9] See Attar (1999, p. 132).

gave way to direct administration with the co-optation of local elites and, increasingly, annexation."[10]

It should be recalled that, according to the French Revolution of popular sovereignty, the people is a mere fiction. It does not exist per se. It does become a symbolic reality only when a state succeeds in establishing its authority over separate individuals and groups and reunify them in a single community. The people is nothing more than a mere fiction or abstraction symbolizing sovereignty in any given state, even when the latter is a non-democratic one.[11] However, it is an extremely powerful fiction as it is on its behalf that some segments of the society may claim popular sovereignty in order to create their own polity. This was well understood by the French revolutionaries who realized that they could annex some territories adjacent to France by manipulating the right of self-determination.

Certainly, the French Revolution contributed to the spread in Europe of the ideals of popular sovereignty, that is self-determination, and that the "(French) Revolutionaries took their own struggle to be exemplary for the world as a whole."[12] However, a year later after having proclaimed popular sovereignty, the French revolutionaries realized that if the concept of self-determination could be used internally in order to keep the unity of France, it could also be used externally with a view to annexing territories adjacent to France. When the 1791 French Constitution solemnly declared in its chapter VI that "The French nation shall renounce to wage war in order to make conquests and shall not use its forces against the freedom of any people", it in fact indirectly endorsed a practice initiated since 1790 by which the populations of some adjacent territories (Avignon, Alsace, Savoy, etc.) "freely" decided by "themselves" to be incorporated in France in accordance with a scenario which will be implemented afterwards in many parts of the world. R.Johannet did describe that scenario when reporting on the annexation of la Savoy in September 1792. He writes in this respect that:

> "The easy (military) campaign of Savoy...deserves a particular mention as it was in la Savoy that, for the second time, the Republic implemented the popular voting process in order to carry out annexation. At the start of the entry of Montesquiou (French general with his army) to Chamberry on September, the clubs (supporters of the annexation), that were disseminated all over the country, behaved exactly as they did in the Comtat. They clamoured for the incorporation (of la Savoy) into France and they themselves took care of the local voting process which was meant to nominate the delegates authorized to participate in the final vote. From its side, the Convention (The then French Parliament) addressed a declaration to the Savoyards saying that in case the incorporation was not to be accepted 'the French will respect your blindness and will take care only of their own safety'. To the vigorous action of the clubs, has noted M. Louis Dimier, the last historian of la Savoy, 'it was felt useful to add other precautionary measures. Twenty days prior to the vote, Montesquiou requested Paris to provide him with 19,000 soldiers to keep la Savoy under control; it was planned that 4000 soldiers had to establish their control of

[10] Bukovansky (1999, p. 210).

[11] See Yack (2003, p. 34).

[12] Keitner (2007, p. 92).

> Montmeillan, Chamberry and the access to the various valleys in order, he said, to strengthen the preponderance that we wish of the popular party (close to France)'...On the next 21 October, the assembly of the delegates proclaimed that out of 658 municipalities 583 requested the incorporation to France."[13]

Following the organization of these plebiscites, a request was made to the French National Assembly in order to endorse the vote by which the people of Avignon and the Comtat opted for their incorporation into France. But the National Assembly would hesitate during months before taking its final decision as it was confronted to a very delicate situation marked by a conflict between the respect of France's previous commitment and the newly arising principle of self-determination. Interestingly, during the debate, a particular question would be raised on what would be the position of the National Assembly in case one of the French provinces decided to separate from France. But a firm reaction came from Menou, who on behalf of the Diplomatic Committee, declared: "No, as no province does form today an independent state. Certainly, before the Revolution and the constitutional pact which recently united all parts of France, any single part was entitled to separate; it did have the right to do so as no pact existed between it and the other parts. But today, the French are united by a social pact to which they are all committed. No one can break this pact without the consent of the other co-associated parts, otherwise the whole society would dissolve."[14] However, despite the clarity of this stand which was made in conformity with positive International Law principles, the annexation of Avignon and the Comtat as a result of the manipulation of the right of self-determination was formalized in September 1791 by a the French National Assembly which declared that "The National Assembly declares that by virtue of the rights of France over the united states of Avignon and the Comtat Venaissin, and in accordance with the freely and solemnly expressed wish of the majority of the communes and citizens of these two territories to be incorporated into France, the said two united states of Avignon and the Comtat Venaissin are, from this moment on, an integral part of the French Empire."[15]

Certainly, the French Revolution did not initially deliberately opt for territorial expansionism, but the objectives of the wars it launched - which initially were meant to offer an outlet for internal unrest caused by increasing divisions and the deteriorating economic situation[16] - quickly changed as "wartime efforts to spread the French ideal soon shifted from a policy of *exemplarity* (leading by example) to outright interference and ultimate occupation".[17] Moreover, the French Revolutionaries came, in the course of action, to decide that France should re-establish its

[13] Johannet (1918, pp. 109–110).

[14] See on this debate which took place on 30 April 1791, Giroud (1920, pp. 33–40).

[15] Archives Parlementaires, vol. 30, p. 631.

[16] Kohn (1967, p. 49).

[17] Keitner (2007, p. 105).

so-called "natural frontiers" and that it should be surrounded by satellite states.[18] This naturally led to further annexations which were carried out despite strong resistance of the populations concerned. Thus, the Belgians, for instance, were on March 1793 forced, under the pressure of the French army and the revolutionary clubs, to vote for union with France. Similar pressure also led at the same time to the union with France of parts of the Rhineland.[19] Hence, the French Revolution, after it started by manipulating the right to self-determination, ended up by purely and simply violating it in an outright manner. "Embarking", observes Carlton J.H. Hayes with some bitterness, "upon the Great War of 1792 in order to make the world safe for liberty, equality, and the right of national self-determination, it was not before they were waging it primarily for the greater glory of France."[20]

One of the legacies of the French Revolution has therefore been the manipulation of self-determination referendum[21] as since then in Europe the "use of manipulated plebiscites by dictators from Napoleon to Hitler gave direct voting a bad name in many quarters until late in the twentieth century."[22] Ironically, it was in the name of self-determination that many peoples would also fight against French domination or occupation. H. Kohn observes in this regard that in the European continent "the idea that a tyrant must be expelled, the cult of liberty, the aspirations towards- nationhood one and indivisible, the longing for a new national cohesion and a new national spirit, the idea of a state rooted in popular consent and enthusiasm- all these concepts of the French Revolution... were eagerly learned from France. But the emphasis shifted: the tyrants to be expelled were French influence and French armies of occupation. The liberty worshipped was not so much individual freedom from authoritarian government as national freedom from foreign governments."[23] Nevertheless, the French Revolution will also inspire powerful states in their desire to make other states disintegrate by promoting the principle of nationalities whose main functions was to encourage the rise of national spirit and separatism in these states.

Therefore, the manipulation of self-determination has since its inception by the French Revolution been very frequently behind the destabilizing and fragmenting of rival states, the "freeing" of foreign peoples and whenever possible their subjection to an external power.

Self-determination had until the First World War taken the form of the principle of nationalities which "requests that the state and the nationality (i.e. the nation) coincide, it does not accept only one state, the national state (i.e. the nation-state), it

[18] See Dehaussy (1989, p. 96).

[19] Kohn (1967, pp. 56–57).

[20] Hayes (1948, p. 80).

[21] See Hauser (1916, p. 21).

[22] Canovan (2005, p. 108).

[23] Kohn (1967, p. 119).

requires borders which are made not of the courses of the rivers, the direction of the mountains, the whims of force or diplomatic conventions, but in accordance with races or rather nationalities."[24] The principle of nationalities was, first, applied in the Central and Eastern European regions in the nineteenth century with the view of disintegrating the Ottoman and the Austrian-Hungarian and Russian empires. This certainly led to the liberation of peoples through the creation of new territorial entities,[25] but at the same time it put the newly created state under the subjection of a new foreign domination.[26] It is not a surprise that in most of the then newly created states, the reign of power was not held by local populations as "the newly created nation-states were continually consecrated with the establishment of ruling dynasties and usually with members from outside the nations in question. . .The creation of dynasties (of foreign origin) for the new nation-states of Europe shows that the dynastic-imperialism was still a potent force, though the national idea was on the rise."[27] It is also not a surprise that Central and East European regions have played the role of a laboratory on how to create new states through a process in which nationalism has been instrumental in "inventing" nations. That process, which will be later on implemented elsewhere, has been profoundly associated to foreign involvement or intervention to the extent that "One of the consequences of the intellectual cosmopolitism", recalls Anne-Marie Thiesse, "was (at that time) to assist in the making of these new nations, whose intellectuals were not sufficiently equipped in order to construct alone their antiquities and language. These attempts to help building identities were carried with great zeal as they were echoing (foreign) geopolitical designs, the most important being to repel the Ottoman Empire from Southern Europe."[28] Fully aware of the crucial importance of the support which might be given by a great power, nationalist leaders had as a constant policy to convince external actors to be on their side. Yet the final result was that the search for allies only led to national liberation if, on the one hand, the cause of the nation in question coincided with the interests of one of the European Powers and on the other, managed to achieve something towards its goals by its own efforts. In the short run, all other attempts were in vain.[29] The process of national liberation had then from the beginning never been under the control of the sole nationalist leaders as the success of national revolts in the nineteenth century, when they did succeed, is not to be interpreted as the triumph of democratic virtue unaided by force. On the contrary, nations only achieved their independence when they had the

[24] Johannet (1918, p. 19).

[25] It will also, as we know, lead to the reunification of Italy and Germany.

[26] Thiesse (2001, p. 83 cont.)

[27] White (2004, p. 194 and 196). See also Mastny (1989, p. 12).

[28] Thiesse (2001, p. 83).

[29] See Niederhauser (1981, p. 115).

effective backing of a strong foreign military power. Where this was lacking, as it was to the Poles, national independence was not achieved.[30]

Thus, the principle of nationalities mainly served as means of disintegrating the Ottoman, Austrian-Hungarian and Russian empires. It has consequently been implemented only where the desire of freedom of the populations concerned has been backed by foreign great powers. However, in order to keep up the appearances, the forms were initially frequently respected. A great number of referenda were indeed organized in the first half of the nineteenth century[31] in order to enable the populations concerned to decide about their destiny at the occasion, it is true, very often of the transfer of territories than the creation of a new state. But, the transparency and integrity of many of these plebiscites have been questioned as "the wishes of the populations were represented generally, not through a direct vote, but by the election of an assembly, often on a narrow franchise. . .Doubtless, in most cases the true wishes of the populace were represented by the plebiscites, but it has to be admitted that it was democracy with a difference."[32] Indeed, while the plebiscites appeared very often as dictated by the theoretical necessity to show to the public opinion that the nationalist task was based on the free will of all the members of a nation, they were in fact carried out in a way to meet the political agenda of those who have designed them and not the interests of the peoples concerned.[33]

However, as mentioned above, most of the plebiscites were, with the exception of the reunification of Italy, limited to the transfer of sovereignty in minor territorial instances and not to the creation of new states. Very frequently used in the first half of the nineteenth century, the plebiscites would gradually become rare and almost insignificant when new states started to emerge in Central and Eastern Europe. Hence, at the time when they were needed in order to accompany the process of states' creation in accordance with self-determination, plebiscites would practically disappear until World War I when they will re-emerge but in a very limited and questionable manner. In fact, a kind of implicit rule prevailed from the beginning and which has made the creation of new states, although being systematically proclaimed on behalf of self-determination, the result not of popular votes through the organization of plebiscites, but of the manipulation of nationalism abroad by major powers. Yet the manipulation of nationalism, as the political expression of self-determination, is a complex process. It requires, first, a

[30] See Cobban (1969, 43).

[31] 18 plebiscites were organized from 1791 to 1905. See the thorough analysis made by Wambaugh (1920).

[32] Cobban (1969 pp. 44–45).

[33] See Giroud (1920 p. 67). See also Lieber (1877, pp. 139–145).

predisposition from the targeted states' constituent communities,[34] and, second, the imagining of new nationalities.

As to the predisposition of targeted states' constituent communities, many studies have clearly shown that only a very few numbers among the latter were willing to separate from their own states, that is the three empires: the Ottoman, Austro-Hungarian and Russian empires. Emil Niederhauser has, in his study about the rise of nationalism in Eastern Europe, reflected that situation when he wrote that "The recognition of the national minorities, granting them equal status within the framework of a great empire, thus maintaining the empire and perhaps even strengthening it, was already a very impressive demand. But their leaders went even further when they demanded full independence and sovereignty. A few, or a group, did indeed do so, but the people as a whole was yet far from actively supporting them. These demands were, after all, challenges to great empires, far more powerful and strong than the small nationality making demand, especially where the Ottoman Empire was concerned, let alone the Habsburg. Surely this demand was quite unrealistic".[35] But if most of the constituting parts of these empires have thus shown a reluctance to embark on claiming separation, it was also because, having been living for centuries within small communities marked by profound attachment to their local socio-cultural environment, they did not very often perceive themselves as belonging to larger communities with whom they would have shared affinities and linked their fate and common future. That is why nationalities had to be created from scratch by those ethnic entrepreneurs who did have an interest in the emergence of those nationalities. Thus, a kind of general rule would prevail since then and which requires that political leaders who wish to establish their right to lead, on the basis of the principle of self-determination must obviously appeal to a sentiment of group identity and loyalty. And where it does not already exist or is only latent, they may even have to create it.[36] But the problem was how to create new nationalities from small and various communities not only marked by localism but also profoundly intermingled together to the extent it was very often difficult to distinguish one from another? How to create "nations" in the Balkans, for instance, where "unfortunately, national questions were particularly complex. In many districts, notably Macedonian, Turks, Greeks, Bulgars, Serbs, Vlachs, Albanians, Circassians, Jews, Gagauz, Armenians, and others beside lived in a glorious *olla podrida*. No clear delimitation of national boundaries was possible; worse still, even national feeling was hopelessly

[34] The success of a national minority to reach statehood was in fact determined by, as noted by Raymond Pearson, "the inter-relation of three cardinal factors: the demographic size of nationalistic quality of the minority concerned; the availability and strength of support from existing Great Powers; and, perhaps, more important, the state of health of the multi-national empire in which the minority was located", Pearson (1983, p. 84).

[35] Niederhauser (1981, p. 104).

[36] See Mayall (1990, p. 43).

capricious. Centuries of mixed marriages have resulted in bilingual or polyglot families, whose national sentiments were further complicated by the Turkish habit of using religion as a determinant, so that it was never certain whether any given individual would classify himself by his religion, his language, his local habitation, or his traditional customs?"[37] Meanwhile such incommensurable difficulties have not prevented ethnic entrepreneurs from "creating" new nations in accordance with a process where manipulation has been the guiding principle and was not so difficult to achieve in a matter where, observes J.Habermas, "because national identities have been intentionally fabricated by the intellectual efforts of writers and historians, and because national consciousness has been spread through the modern mass media from the start, national sentiments can be more or less easily manipulated."[38]

The process through which nationalities were created in Central and Eastern Europe has been well analyzed by many scholars. According to Miroslav Hroch,[39] three structural phases can be distinguished in this process. The first phase started with the collection by historians and intellectuals of information about the history, language and customs of the potential national group. The second phase was marked by the emergence of activists who sought to win over as many of their ethnic group as possible to the project of creating a future nation and this by patriotic agitation in order to "awaken" national consciousness among them. The third phase was the final phase where the national programme was complemented through the emergence of a full social structure which comes into being as a result of mass movement. But such process of nation-building in Central and Eastern European in fact set time bombs and triggered wars, repression, expulsion, forced displacement of population, extermination and ethnic cleansing. Instead of generating peace, nationalism, which ensued from the nation-building process, became a force for war as "pacific peoples were easily transformed into crusading belligerents. Once the drumfire of propaganda began, the ordinary citizen was swept into the path of national hatred."[40] However, if the ensuing nationalism brought oppression and war, the main culprit is the paradox which characterizes self-determination because, as noted by Hans J. Morgenthau, "there are no inherent limits to the application of the principles of nationalism. If the peoples of Bulgaria, Greece, and Serbia could invoke these principles against Turkey, why could not the people of Macedonia invoke them against Bulgaria, Greece, and Serbia?. . .Thus yesterday's oppressed cannot help becoming the oppressors of today because they are afraid lest they be again oppressed tomorrow."[41]

---

[37] Macartney (1934, pp. 135–136).

[38] Habermas (1975, p. 288).

[39] Hroch (2000, pp. 78–97).

[40] Snyder (1968, p. 15).

[41] Morgenthau (1957, p. 485).

The model suggested by Hroch in order to describe the process of nation-building in Central and Eastern Europe, although intellectually attractive, keeps silent about the involvement of great powers in that process in order to manipulate self-determination and its political expression: nationalism.

5.1.2 The Emergence of Self-Determination as a Destabilizing Arm in the Struggle Between Major Powers

Following the early manipulation of nationalism by the French Revolution and the Napoleon armies, nationalism manipulation ceased momentarily to be implemented, at least in a large scale, as an instrument for the weakening of rival states. It was so because the Holy Alliance had, in accordance with its very conservative values and ideological foundations amongst which the necessity to give pre-eminence to the principle of the dynastic rule, seen in the principle of nationality a destabilizing and subversive force. Hence, Austria, Russia and Prussia, the newly dominating powers, made sure to intervene in the internal affairs of the other states whenever there was a need to maintain and reinforce the political and social status quo. Aiming at preventing any transfer of power from the traditional rulers to the peoples, the motto of the time was bluntly expressed by Metternich for whom "All governments have to fight the same enemy; these enemies are the men who would govern in their place."[42] However, the Holy Alliance has not been able to prevent the independence of Belgium (1827) and Greece (1830). While, the rise of Belgium as an independent state was dictated by power balancing considerations, the independence of Greece has been the outcome of a real revolution, a fact which will later on inspire other peoples to do the same. It will also give a signal to major powers that the Ottoman Empire was ripe for disintegration from within, that is through the implementation of the principle of nationalities.

Once closed the historic parentheses created by the Holy Alliance, the manipulation of nationalism by major great powers re-emerged, but in an extensive and systematic manner. It was indeed from that time that it has come into play as one of the most destabilizing arms in the struggle between major powers. Its success since then has come from the fact that it added an ideological element to the traditional weapons. State's power and strength have at that time and in fact more than ever in human history continued to be measured in terms of the largeness of its territory and that consequently the highest concern of dominating states was the distribution of territories between them. International Law did also admit at that time that in time of war, borders' change and the move of an army within territory's enemy were

---

[42] Quoted by Haas (1953, p. 157).

a question of fact and that consequently sovereignty did move with the move of force.[43] As to the French Revolution's early attempt to change that rule by making sure to legalize annexations through plebiscites, it has been, as we have seen above, annihilated by the same Revolution. Lastly, one of the most prominent principles prevailing at that time between major European powers was the balance of power principle.

The functioning of the balance of power relied on the distribution of territories between dominating powers. That is why wars ended very often by the partition of territories among the winning powers without taking into consideration the desire of the populations concerned.[44] Such partition was perceived, did note H. Brougham in the early nineteenth century, as "a natural, though a very alarming corruption of that very balancing system upon which we have relied so implicitly for protection from all such disasters. The balancing system ... secures us completely in ordinary times from the danger of universal dominion; but it affords no protection to the smaller states against the combination of two or three ambitious sovereigns, and even seems to facilitate the concentration of all power and authority into the usurping hands of a few great potentates. Such combinations are evidently the devices upon which the ambition of those who would formerly have conquered alone, have recently been driven by the prevalence of the system of balance; and they seem only to give that ambition a greater steadiness of direction and greater assurances of success."[45] Sustaining the balance of power was also frequently requiring not only the partition of weak states but also purely and simply the aggrandisement of major powers territories to the detriment of small states. "The ambition of great and powerful power states", did also recall H.Brougham, "seldom aims at the subjugation of a great and powerful antagonist; it is satisfied, in the beginning, with the easier acquisition of some pretty dominion; and their weaker neighbours are only protected by the jealousy which such an act of depredation would excite among the peers and equals of the spoiler."[46] Thus, it was on behalf of the balance of power that the European major powers carried out "the most iniquitous territorial conquests and the most criminal breaches of law against the other European sovereign states.[47] Moreover, the principle of the balance of power became very often synonymous with dividing up territories as the co-sharing system, which, at the origin, was perceived as one of the elements complementing the balance of power, took an increasing importance and gradually became the most important element. States stopped dividing territories in order to establish a balance of power or make it ideal. They limited themselves to balance the sharing out of territories. It can even been said that they did balance in order to share out

[43] See Nys (1904, pp. 401–402).

[44] See Henry (1937, p. 95).

[45] Brougham (1803, p. 16).

[46] Idem, p. 18.

[47] See Komantra (1940, p. 85).

territories."[48] But, the balance of power required also very often the weakening of major rival powers from within. It was that key role that nationalism was meant to play. The most targeted states were initially those states that used to take the form of empires, that is, at that time of the Ottoman, the Austro-Hungarian and the Russian empires. Hence, West European powers have since then durably implemented policies aiming at weakening these empires through the encouragement of nationalism in the later various constituent communities,[49] although these policies have been sometimes contravened by the exigency to keep the balance of power.[50] However, it was clearly meant that such nationalism should lead to the creation only of small, subjected and dispersed states.[51] Thus, when France brought its support to the Piedmont in its fight for independence, its objective was to weaken the Austrian Empire as well as the rising power of Prussia, but not to the extent of encouraging the creation of a unified Italy as it was planned that the latter should be no more than a weak confederation of small states.[52] Moreover, every single empire has also implemented similar policies against its other rival empires amongst which the most targeted was the Ottoman Empire which was perceived as the "Sick Man of Europe."[53] Thus, the general policy pursued by great powers was to use foreign nationalism as instruments of foreign policy with a plan to forcibly annex and destroy them when opportunities presented themselves.[54]

Inspired by the French Revolutionaries' policy aiming at promoting nationalist aspirations abroad in order to achieve their own political agenda, every great power has also sought to awaken or propagate similar aspirations within the territories under the control of a rival power. However, the most targeted powers would be the empires. Thus, simultaneously to their policies aiming at building their own colonial empires oversees, West European powers' constant policy has been to seek disintegrating the Ottoman, Austro-Hungarian and Russian empires. Amongst the most targeted were by order of priority, first, the Ottoman Empire, then the Habsburg Empire and then eventually the Russian Empire. This order of priority was dictated by the situation prevailing within the three empires. Such situation clearly indicated that the Ottoman Empire was in status of advanced decay and instability and that therefore the establishment of client states in place of the Ottoman authority

[48] R. Dupuis "Aperçu des relations internationales en Europe de Charlemagne à nos jours", R.C.A.D.I., II, 78. See also Dupuis (1909).

[49] See Thiesse (2001, p. 83 and seq.) See also Henry (1937, pp. 94–193).

[50] Hence, although dispossessed of some of its provinces on behalf of the principle of nationalities, the Ottoman Empire has been able to survive until the First World War thanks to the implementation balance of power system. See among others Frèchet (1991, p. 99 et seq.)

[51] The example of the French policy in this respect is discussed by Ollivier (1895, pp. 170–175).

[52] See Sem (1868, pp. 45–46).

[53] See Ergang (1954, pp. 316–323).

[54] See White (2004 p. 201).

was perceived as more attractive than the alternative options of propping up the empire or taking direct control of particular region of it. With regard to the Habsburg Empire, it was regarded as a stable unit, but that sooner or later it would face increasing difficulties in addressing nascent nationalist aspirations. With regard to the Russian Empire, it was seen as still strong enough to resist any attempt aiming at facilitating its disintegration and that consequently major European powers were not in a position to exploit internal tensions within the empire in a way that would undermine its stability and that the arising nationalist opposition had to concentrate upon developing internally effective movements.[55] Yet, the disintegration of these empires would be a lengthy process as the Ottoman and Austrian empires would disintegrate only following World War I and the Russia empire would survive in the form of the Russian Federation and even see its strength indirectly reinforced further to the creation of the USSR and would eventually be partly dismembered only after the collapse of the later at the end of the twentieth century. Besides, it was the resilience of these empires that had made the emergence of nationalism also a very lengthy process.

The emergence of national aspirations in Central/East European was, first, the consequence of the three empires' incapacity to adapt to modernisation as did West European states, the reason being that the rulers were reluctant to give up old values, modes of thought and governance including the principle of absolute monarchic authority. This is why Central/East European ethnonationalism has developed, first, in reaction to the inexistence of a deep and large modernizing process.[56] It developed also as a result of the dilemma in which were caught the three empires with regard to the policy to be adopted in order to address arising needs of multiethnic, multireligious and multilingual populations as, while they recognized the necessity to fully mobilize the energies of the society, yet heir dilemma was how to meet this challenge without undermining the dynastic, patrimonial principles that formed the basis of their political legitimacy. The multiple compositions of the Habsburg, Russian and Ottoman empires made this problem particularly daunting: any attempt to stimulate patriotic emotions among the masses almost necessarily involved an appeal to their ethno-cultural identity; yet unleashing such sentiments among any given segment of a highly diverse population could only serve to alienate all the other segments.[57] Meanwhile, the three empires did not suffer similarly from that dilemma as they did all develop over centuries different politics of ethnicity which consequently yielded different results.

Amazingly, it was only the Ottoman empire that made sure, as did all the empires all over human history, to delegate some kind of powers to the local communities, while the Austro-Hungarian and Russians empires acted differently,

[55] Breuilly (1994, p. 144).

[56] See Sugar (1999, p. 5).

[57] See Roshwald (2001, pp. 7–9).

the former adopting a centralization policy without seeking to homogenize and unify the twelve ethnic groups that lived within its territory, and the latter opting for a territorialization policy aiming at integrating most of the local communities.

Thus, the Ottoman Empire has, in order to counter-balance the weakness of its bureaucracy, granted a great amount of power to its provinces within a kind of a de facto autonomy system. It has also, through the *millets*[58] system, authorized the various non-Muslim religious minorities to self-regulate issues related to family laws, inheritance and religious and educational institutions. It was thanks to the millets system that he Jews and Christians were able to expand their educational systems considerably in the eighteenth and nineteenth centuries, so that in no time their communities were better educated and more modern than the Muslims and that from the mid-nineteenth century, reforms were introduced that started a process in the direction of civil equality for Jews and Christians in the Empire.[59] However, this has not prevented West European powers – and the Russian empire as well- to intervene under, as we have seen earlier, the cover of the doctrine of humanitarian intervention allegedly on behalf of these minorities but in fact in order to weaken further the Ottoman empire and therefore facilitate its disintegration. The Ottoman Empire introduced some reforms (*Tanzimats*) starting from the 1840 s in order to make its administration more efficient and modernize its political and economic system. These reforms failed due to the general situation of decay and corruption that the empire was undergoing.

With regard to the Austrian Empire, from the beginning it suffered from major weaknesses. First, the emergence of the empire was not the result of a traditional territorialization process, but the assemblage of different territories as a consequence of dynastic alliances and inheritance. Second, it inherited feudal institutions and powerful estates as well as provincial loyalties, which would in the nineteenth century constitute the basis for the development of separate nationalisms and ethnic affiliations. Third, its largest ethnic group, the Germans, represented less than 23% of the whole population which was made of various ethnic groups. Fourth, its geographical location at the centre of Europe, although it was an important geopolitical asset, made of the empire a territory surrounded by potential rivals and enemies. It was certainly that situation that pushed the Empire, in order to ensure its own survival, to traditionally base its foreign policy on the balance of power system to which Metternich has given one its most brilliant implementations. It was also that situation which pushed the empire to pursue a centralization policy in order to homogenize and unify its society made of about twelve ethnic groups and minorities. But the dilemma in which it was caught was that before the centralization process did come to maturity and yield the desired result, national aspirations had already started to emerge in different parts of Europe as a consequence of the promotion of the French Revolution ideals, a fact which made any attempt to

[58] See Braude and Lewis (1982).

[59] See Hanf (1991, p. 46).

unify the society a difficult and uncertain process. "In a sense, notes Peter F.Sugar, they (the Austrian emperors) lacked the necessary time to complete successfully the task of centralization, which took centuries to perform in France and England, because soon they had to face the problem posed by the first demands of the newly emerging ideal of popular sovereignty."[60] But the problem is that, while recognizing the importance of the need to adjust to that situation, the Austrian emperors stubbornly decided to resist it. Hence, the Austrian Empire continued to avoid initiating any policy which could have helped in resolving the emerging nationality problem. On the contrary, it will for a long time remain mainly based on an absolute monarchical system and did nothing to prevent the development of inequalities of power sharing between the different communities. That is why the conservatism and the autocratic policy of the Empire were met with practically a general resistance which ended up by the 1848–1849 Revolutions that took the form of nationalist uprising in different provinces. However, although these Revolutions have introduced the postulate of equality of rights of the nationalities, no tangible halt was made to arbitrariness and discrimination.[61] On the contrary, the monarchy has not stopped from changing alliances with certain nationalities to the detriment of other nationalities, which ultimately reflected negatively on the relations among the different nationalities.[62] It has also used several Hungarian minorities against those Hungarian nationalists who wanted to separate Hungary from Austria.[63] It has also continued strengthening its traditional centralization policy which deteriorated the situation further. It is true that some attempts have been made to grant considerable amount of autonomy to self-governing municipalities, but concrete experience has shown that the policies implemented by these municipalities in terms of respect of minority rights have tended to be not appropriate.[64] However, the Austrian Empire would come to reason after its severe military defeats in its wars against Piedmont-Sardaigne and France in 1859, which will leave the road free for the reunification of Italy, and Prussia in 1866 and will push it to accept one year later to grant autonomy to the vast territory under the control of the Magyars. The Hungarian kingdom benefited then from a large autonomy covering all aspects of governmental power with the exception of the military and foreign affairs which were kept with the Austria Empire. However, being very conservative, the Magyar government would from its part implement an assimilation policy within the large territories under its control denying then to most of its various minorities their cultural rights and their right to conduct their own affairs. Moreover, the Magyar government would

[60] "Government and Minorities in Austria-Hungary. Different Policies with the same Result" in Peter F. Sugar (ed.) "East European Nationalism, Politics and Religion", op.cit., IV, p. 4.

[61] See G. Stourzh "Problems of Conflict Resolution in a Multi-ethnic State : Lessons from the Austrian Historical Experience" in Uri Ra'anan (ed.) "State and Nation in Multi-ethnic Societies: The Break-Up of multinational States", op.cit., p. 69.

[62] Idem, p. 73.

[63] Balogh (1999, p. 40).

[64] Idem, p. 74.

impose on Austria the obligation not to implement within the latter's territory any devolution of power to its own ethnic groups. This would inevitably generate bitterness and resentment among the various ethnic groups - it is true, more in Hungary[65] than in Austria[66] where a lesser harsh ethnic policy was implemented- and prepare the ground for the disintegration of the Austro-Hungarian empire. The lack of a consciousness of integration and a common national belonging was such among the various minorities and ethnic groups that the introduction of constitutionalism and democracy in Austria in 1907 would lead to nothing other than an extreme polarization between these minorities and ethnic groups as all parties represented in the Reichsrat were based on ethnic and regional loyalties.[67] The Austro-Hungarian Empire was then ripe for disintegration. The final deathblow would be given to it by its foreign enemies on the occasion of World War I.

With regard to the Russian Empire, it was the result of a territorialization process made of conquests carried over a great span of time and not of an assemblage of territories as a consequence of dynastic marriages as did happen for the Austro-Hungarian Empire. That is why that, although it covered wide-spread territories and was made of an extremely diverse ethnic composition and remained until 1917 a patrimonial state, it was less ripe for disintegration than the other two empires. The territorialization process, which resulted in the creation of a homogeneous core territory under the control of a centralized administration and military apparatus, was all the more efficient in the Russian empire that it was accompanied by a multifaceted and pragmatic policy made of russification,[68] a sense of practical compromise - as concessions were made to the different ethnic groups and allowing them to retain their traditional powers and privileged, especially in the Western borderlands where local communities were authorized to retain self-governing institutions[69]- and integration of non-Russians in the spheres of economy, power and aristocracy. It is therefore no a surprise that for much of its history, the Russian empire effectively functioned as a multinational state, in which the narrow upper stratum of ethnic Russians controlled political and military power, but in which a number of other nationalities attained high overall standards of living and education, and filled vital economic and administrative niches.[70] The integration of the different ethnic groups was so advanced that the Russians, although being by far the largest group within the whole population (46%), could not be socially distinguished from the other ethnic groups. "In the Russian empire", notes D. Lieven, "there seldom

[65] See Jaszi (1961, p. 298) cont.

[66] Idem, p. 283 cont.

[67] See Roshwald (2001, p. 19).

[68] On the long historical process which has led to the formation of the Russian identity see, e.g., Prizel (1998, chapter 5).

[69] See Thaden (1984).

[70] See Roshwald (2001, p. 21).

existed the enormous gap between the wealth of colonist and native which was a mark of the maritime empires' overseas possessions."[71] It is true that some nationalities, such as the Caucasian Moslems, have been perceived as inassimilable and therefore kept in the margin of the system, but it still remains that "the Russian state on the eastern flank of Christianity's struggle with Islam on the whole showed less a crusading spirit and more pragmatism and tolerance in its treatment of subject Moslems."[72] It is true also that the Russian empire has at the end of the nineteenth century moved in the direction of legitimating itself through appeals to the Russian nationalism, but it did so in a context where most of the Russian population perceived Russia as a plausible nation.[73] However, if the Russian nation was a plausible eventuality, it was not yet a reality, a status that it could not reach as what was missing was the flow of power from chosen rulers to the people. The Russian empire had still to re-adjust and rearticulate its legitimacy in accordance with the founding principle without which a nation cannot exist: popular sovereignty. A re-foundation of the Russian state legitimacy was all the more needed that at the end of the nineteenth century, the Russian nationalism became increasingly an expression of the most conservative forces in the country, while non-Russian nationalism sought uneasy alliances with the supranational parties on the left.[74] Furthermore, the Russian nationalism started to be increasingly perceived as coalescent to the Russian domination over non-Russian nationalities. A benign reading held at that time that the Russian empire contained peoples living symbiotically rather than competitively, but, observes Ronald G. Sany, "even in this softer construction of empire, the benefactor nationality is understood to be superior to the colonialized peoples. Without much self-reflexivity, intellectuals and policymakers thought of ethnic Russians' national identity as that of a ruling nation within a great empire, an imperial nation with inherent attributes of superiority, like those of the British, that gave them the right, even duty, to rule over others. Rather than leading to a single, multinational civic nation in the Russian empire, some seized upon the discourse of the nation to perpetuate empire with its hierarchies and distinctions, its debilitating contradictions, and its ultimate reliance on force and violence to prevent non-ruling peoples from attaining a position of equality and participation in the polity."[75] Certainly, the 1905 Revolution has introduced some progress in the Russian archaic patrimonial system, but it has also intensified ideological fragmentation among the Russian elites. It has also increased political awareness and identity expectations among non Russians, but most nationalist elites in the Russian empire did not seriously contemplate outright political separatism; talk of cultural

[71] Lieven (1995, p. 618).

[72] Idem, p. 621.

[73] Idem, p. 623.

[74] See Sany (2000, p. 491).

[75] Idem, p. 491.

autonomy and the possible reconfiguration of the state along federal lines was the norm.[76]

The policy aiming at disintegrating the Ottoman, Austrian and Russian empires led gradually to the emergence of a number of small states before the final collapse of the empires as a result of the First World War. Such impact of the "nationalist imperialism"[77] has been severely condemned as it has "brought back (part of the humanity) to the early phase of the city and this in a counter movement with the whole evolution of modern times."[78] True, the principle of nationalities also created a dynamic of territorialization which led to the emergence of Italy and Germany, two much bigger and important states. It was for that reason that the principle of nationalities has been severely condemned[79] in France starting from the end of th1860s, where some authors have seen in it "the scourge of the century,"[80] although France was one of the most vigorous proponents of that principle. France was henceforth one the first powerful states to suffer from the after effects of proselytizing the principle of nationalities.

The policy aiming at disintegrating the Ottoman, Austrian and Russian empires through the manipulation of the principle of nationalities as well as the struggle on behalf on the same principle between these three empires has had also as a consequence that those national cultures that prevailed, suppressed those that did not.[81] But, the suppression of minorities' cultures and identities became in the second half of the nineteenth century almost a quasi general phenomenon from which even dominant Western countries were not spared as "west Spaniards were suppressing Basques, English were suppressing the Welsh, Scots and (less successfully) Irish, and further west still British Canadians were suppressing the French, etc."[82] Minorities were even more perceived as a threat menacing states' stability and cohesion when these minorities enjoyed the support of powerful foreign rival states. The result was, as noted Michael Howard, a spiral of suppression and conspiracy that would fatally contribute to the outbreak of the First World War.[83] However, the international community would not draw the necessary conclusions from the destabilizing character of the manipulation of self-determination. On the contrary, such manipulation would since then take such dramatic proportions that it would lead to the transmuting of self-determination which ceases to be a right to democracy in order to become simply an instrument for creating formal independent states.

---

[76] See Roshwald (2001, p. 27). See also Hauser (1916, p. 1).

[77] Le Fur (1921, p. 579).

[78] Idem.

[79] On this condemnation, see Johannet (1918, p. 183 and seq).

[80] Frédéric Le Play quoted by Johannet (1918, p. 183).

[81] See Howard (2007, p. 28).

[82] Idem.

[83] Idem.

5.1.3 The Transformation of Self-Determination: From Democracy to Dependent Independence

Another element entering in the formation of classical self-determination paradigm was the substitution of the formal independence to democracy and freedom. Indeed, self-determination will lose its fundamental raison d'être which was to promote democracy and freedom in order to become an instrument meant to disintegrate rival states and create new ones where the government was subjected to foreign powers and the people deprived from their right to democracy and freedom. It was that substitution which led to a radical transformation of self-determination as the later did lose its fundamental raison d'être which was to promote democracy and became a simple instrument aiming at creating new independent states in peripheral areas. Such transformation did not of course affect the situation of peoples in Western countries where popular sovereignty, that is self-determination, continued to play a crucial role in reinforcing the democratic basis of the state. That transformation has instead affected mainly peripheral peoples who were condemned to be subjected to local absolutism itself placed under the domination of foreign powers. The transformation of self-determination in an instrument aiming at creating new states has started to take place at the end of the First World War and will be further consolidated following the Second World War under the United Nations system.

Amazingly, in the course of the First World War, the Western European powers and the United States of America did have diametrically opposed conceptions as to the meaning and content of self-determination.

As to the European colonial powers, namely France, Great Britain and Italy, self-determination was perceived as a political instrument meant to disintegrate enemy states in order either to annex parts of their territories or to establish therein client states. As Great Britain was, due to its traditional balancing power policy in Europe, opposed to the French's project of an important territorial weakening of Germany[84] but was itself interested by the latter colonies, the targeted states were mainly the Austro-Hungarian and the Ottoman Empires. Besides, as the war was unexpectedly lasting in time and becoming a massive war, the West European powers started to increase their support for national projects and encourage separatist agitation in these two empires. Secret agreements were also signed with the view of achieving the planned disintegration of the Austro-Hungarian and the Ottoman Empires. Moreover, plans aiming at the disintegration of these empires through the manipulation of self-determination were made. Hence, it was clearly declared in August 1916 in a draft paper of the British Foreign Office entitled "Suggested Basis for a Territorial Settlement in Europe" that a future settlement "should give full scope to national aspirations as far as practicable. The principle of nationality should therefore be one of the governing factors in territorial arrangements after

[84] See Ergang (1954, pp. 401–402).

the war."[85] In fact, the application of self-determination to the Austrian-Hungarian Empire was meant, from Britain's point of view, to "provide a splendid moral justification for her cynical policy of rewarding Italy, Romania and Serbia as allies at the Habsburgs' expense."[86] Likewise, Great Britain and France adopted a Declaration on 7 November 1918 in which it was hypocritically stated that they were fighting "for the complete and definite emancipation of the peoples so long oppressed by the Turks and the establishment of national governments and administrations deriving their authority from the initiative and free choice of the indigenous populations."[87] However, the European powers were totally against the implementation of self-determination to their own colonies. Reflecting a general European consensus on this, J. Giroud wrote at that time that "The implementation of the principle of nationality seems to be faced with considerable difficulties when the populations concerned did not have a defined national character or a national will. Such situation is to be found mainly in the territories outside Europe and which are inhabited by non civilized populations. These populations, which may have from some aspects a very real originality, do not possess the necessary elements in order to form nations in the sense that we (The Europeans) give to these word. The states of advanced civilizations will continue occupying these territories in accordance with an ineluctable rule which pushes them to expand and establish themselves where the abundance of raw materials are not exploited and cannot be exploited by indigenous populations. . .The phenomenon of colonization is not in conflict with the right of nationalities: the conqueror does not indeed find in front of him nations and national consciousness."[88]

As to the United States' conception of self-determination, it has continued to associate the latter with democracy. This was particularly the philosophy of President Woodrow Wilson who, inspired by the Enlightenment and the original meaning of self-determination, wanted to make of democracy the basis for peace settlement. In a speech given to the US Senate on 18 December 1916, he stressed that "No peace can last, or ought to last, which does not recognize that the governments derive all their just powers from the consent of the governed, and that no right anywhere exists to hand peoples about from sovereignty to sovereignty as if they were property."[89] President Wilson reiterated his support to democratic self-determination in his famous Fourteen Points where he declared that "What we demand in this war. . .is that the world be made fit and safe to live in; and particularly that it is made safe for every peace-loving nation which, like our own, wishes to live its own life, *determine its own institutions* (italics added), be assured of justice and fair dealing. . .". What was therefore of a crucial importance to President Wilson was a general expansion of democracy and not the creation of new

---

[85] Quoted in George (1938, p. 32).

[86] Heater (1994, p. 30).

[87] Quoted in Dockrill and Goold (1981, p. 139).

[88] Giroud (1924, p. 42).

[89] Quoted in Scott (1918, p. 250).

states. "Self-determination to Wilson was", writes George W. White "the empowerment of individuals to vote for their leaders and express their political opinions, which he saw as having been sorely lacking in Europe, and as the root of conflict. Typical of an Enlightenment thinker, Wilson tended to accept current state boundaries while promoting democratic ideals".[90] President Wilson was consequently against separatism and the creation of new states. He instead recommended autonomy. This was, for instance, the solution he suggested for the Austro-Hungarian Empire. Thus, one can read in Point X of the Fourteen Points that "The peoples of Austria-Hungary, whose place among the nations we wish to see safeguarded and assured, should be accorded the free opportunity of autonomous development". Similar recommendation was made for Turkey as while "the Turkish portions of the present Ottoman Empire should be assured a secure sovereignty, the other nationalities which are now under Turkish rule should be assured an undoubted security of life and an absolutely unmolested opportunity of autonomous development..." (Point XII).

President Wilson's conception of self-determination was not welcomed by Great Britain and France who have seen in it a threat not only to their territorial war aims but also to their own colonial empires as the application of democracy would have necessarily implied that subjected peoples in the colonies should be involved in the running of their countries. Put under pressure by his allies, President Wilson would gradually change his mind. He would be further pushed in this direction following the overthrow of the Romanov regime in Russia and the proclamation by the Russian Provisional Government of its unequivocal adherence to self-determination, a stand which would be radicalized when the Bolshevik seized power in November 1917 and declared that self-determination should virtually be extended to the whole world including colonial territories and that its implementation should be conceived in a way to give the opportunity to the populations concerned to make a choice between different options including independence. In fact, the Bolshevik government, which made clear its conception in this regard in December 1917 on the occasion of the negotiations of Brest-Litovsk with the Central Powers, put forward different scenarios applicable to a variety of situations. These scenarios and situations consisted mainly in the following:

- National groups not enjoying political independence before the war, to be guaranteed an opportunity to decide freely by means of referendum whether to adhere to any given state or to be an independent state.
- In regard to territories inhabited by several nationalities, the right of minorities to be protected by special laws, guaranteeing them cultural national independence, and, as far as practicable, administrative autonomy.
- Colonial questions to be decided on (similar) lines...[91]

Finding himself diplomatically isolated and disappointed by the tergiversations of the Austro-Hungarian Empire with regard to his suggestion aiming at

[90] White (2004, p. 208).

[91] See Mayer (1970, pp. 296–297). On the political motivations aiming in fact at weakening Western states, see Krylov (1996, pp. 370–371).

implementing territorial autonomy and federalizing its political structure, President Wilson changed radically his conception of self-determination by giving preeminence to independence instead of democracy and its corollary at the substate level, that is territorial autonomy. Analyzing such radical move in President Wilson's understanding of self-determination, George W. White did note that "Woodrow Wilson slowly and awkwardly came to the realization that his term, *self-determination* meant national independence and the necessary creation of nations-states. . . Wilson's demand for self-determination moved from a vision of turning empires in federalized states to the practice of dismantling empires and erecting nation-states in their place".[92]

Ironically, President Wilson would be associated in the popular imagination with disintegrative self-determination while he did strongly believe, as we have seen earlier, in the necessity to stabilize states by guaranteeing their territorial integrity and promoting democratic self-determination. However, although he changed his mind about the meaning and content of self-determination, President Wilson tried before the start of the Peace Conference to collect, through a group of specialists, all necessary information which would help delineate in a proper and fair manner the boundaries of the states to be created. Very keen to preserve the integrity of the process aiming at creating these new states, President Wilson told that group: "Tell me what is right and I will fight for it. Give me a guaranteed position."[93] But, the President would fail here also to achieve his objective due to the lack of agreement with his allies on the situation to which self-determination should be applicable as well as to his own inconsistencies as he tended to favor certain ethnic groups to the detriment of others.[94] This has also resulted in the organization of only few plebiscites[95] as well as the emergence of most of the new states as a consequence not of self-determination but of political considerations amongst which the interests of the victorious powerful states.[96] In deed, self-determination did have only a minor impact if any in the reorganizing of the territories of the broken empires and the redrawing of the map of Central and Eastern Europe. President Wilson would himself later on recognize that "It was not within the privilege of the Conference of Peace to act upon the right of self-determination of any peoples except those which had been included in the territories of the defeated empires."[97]

Many of the new states were consequently handicapped by minorities' problems. It is true that shortly after the Paris Peace Conference, some international agreements were signed to protect national minorities in the states which had arisen from the ashes of war. These agreements guaranteed certain rights, including the

[92] White (2004, pp. 210 and 211).

[93] Quoted by Seymour (1951, p. 17).

[94] See Whelan (1994, p. 101).

[95] See Wambaugh (1933); Farly (1956).

[96] See Cobban (1969, pp. 74–75).

[97] Wilson (1927, p. 244).

right to nationality, the right to one's own language, the right to education in the mother tongue, the right of property, etc. These rights were to be protected by the Council of the League of Nations. But the Council was reluctant to exercise the role attributed to it, an attitude which would be condemned by those countries to which such a system was imposed upon them by the victorious nations who, for their part, did not take any similar international commitment in favor of the minorities living in their countries.

Lastly, President Wilson conceded to his European allies, and this even before the start of the Peace Conference, that the territories which formerly belonged to the German Empire or to Turkey outside European area are to be put under a mandates system,[98] offering then no perspective for the implementation of self-determination to these territories either in its democratic or independence forms.

Although self-determination has not played a major role in the redrawing of the map of Europe, the chaotic way in which it has been implemented and particularly its likening with independence has made many leaders feel worried about its possible destabilizing impact on states. Reflecting a largely shared feeling, Robert Lansing, the then Secretary of State has expressed his worry about the incalculable consequences of self-determination leading to independence when he wrote that:

> "When the President (Wilson) talks of 'self-determination' what unit has he in mind? Does he mean a race, a territorial area, or a community? Without a definite unit which is practical, application of this principle is dangerous to peace and stability...
>
> The more I think about the President's declaration as to the right of 'self-determination', the more convinced I am of the danger of putting such ideas into the minds of certain races. It is bound to be the basis of impossible demands on the Peace Conference and create trouble in many lands.
>
> What effect will it have on the Irish, the Indians, the Egyptians, and the nationalists among the Boers? Will it not breed discontent, disorder and rebellion? Will not the Mohammedans of Syria and possibly of Morocco and Tripoli rely on it? How can it be harmonized with Zionism, to which the President is practically committed?
>
> The phrase is simply loaded with dynamite. It will raise hopes which can never be realized. It will, I fear, cost thousands of lives. In the end it is bound to be discredited, to be called the dream of an idealist who failed to realize the danger until too late to check those who attempt to put the principle in force. What calamity that phrase was ever uttered! What misery it will cause!"[99]

Robert Lansing's observations were premonitory of the situation which would prevail since the end of the First World War until today and which has witnessed an unprecedented upsurge and exacerbation of nationalism and ethnic conflicts not only in the Balkans but also in different other regions of the world, including the developed ones. This is so because the erroneous likening of self-determination with independence has made of "ethnicity the ultimate measure of political

---

[98] See Porter (1922, pp. 563–583).

[99] Lansing (1921, pp. 97–98).

legitimacy, by holding that any self-differentiated people, simply because it *is* a people, has the right, should it so desire, to rule itself."[100]

The destructive consequences of self-determination-independence were certainly behind the move made by many states on the occasion of the drafting of the United Nations Charter in order to reestablish the preeminence of the original and authentic meaning of self-determination. However this attempt would fail as self-determination would for decades be more than ever likened with independence.

The right to self-determination was framed in very general terms in The UN Charter. Hence, it was stated in Article 1 that "the purposes of the United Nations are... to develop friendly relations among nations based on respect for the principle of equal rights and self-determination of peoples, and to take other appropriate measures to strengthen peace." Likewise, Article 55 declared that "With a view to the creation of conditions of stability and well-being which are necessary for peaceful and friendly relations of peoples, and to take other appropriate measures to strengthen peace."

Initially, the Dumbarton Oaks proposals which were at hand of the delegates gathered in April 1945 at San Francisco in order to establish the new organization, did not include any reference to self-determination. The reference to the latter was added at the request of the Soviet Union in order to serve as one of the major purposes and objectives of the United Nations. With the exception of Belgium, many states expressed their adherence to the USSR amendment. What is of great interest is that they insisted that the purpose of self-determination should be the reinforcement of peace and democracy and not the disintegration of states. Hence, for instance, the delegate of Colombia warned that "if it (i.e. self-determination) means self-government, the right of a country to provide its own government, yes, we would certainly like it to be included; but if it were to be interpreted, on the other hand, as connoting withdrawal, the *right of* withdrawal or secession, then we should regard that as tantamount to international anarchy, and we should not desire that it should be included in the text of the Charter."[101] Other delegates warned against possible manipulation of self-determination.[102] Reporting on the general debate which took place between the states on these issues, the Rapporteur of the Committee, in charge of the drafting of the article on self-determination, was able to state inter alia that "the principle (of self-determination) conformed to the purposes of the Charter only insofar as it implied the right of self-government of peoples and not the right of secession"[103] and that "an essential element of the principle (of self-determination) is free and genuine expression of the will of the people, which

[100] Connor (1972, p. 331).

[101] See the minutes of the debates at the First Committee of the First Commission of the San Francisco Conference, 15 May 1945,20, Library of the Palais des Nations, Geneva.

[102] See, for instance, the intervention of the Egyptian delegate, The minutes of the debates, idem. 14 May, 20; See also the report made by the Rapporteur, Idem, 15 May, 12.

[103] UNCIO, Vol. VI, p. 298.

avoids cases of the alleged expression of the popular will of the population, such as those used for their own ends (i.e. through manipulation) by Germany and Italy in later years."[104]

Thus, initially there was a quasi general consensus that self-determination meant self-government, i.e. democracy, and not secession and independence. Such quasi consensus was also shared by great powers which declared four years before in the Atlantic Charter that "they respect the right of all peoples to choose the form of government under which they will live; and they wish to see sovereign rights and self-government restored to those who have been forcibly deprived of them". The only difference which existed between states was about the right of independence of colonial peoples which was supported by the Soviet Union, China and third world countries, while colonial powers were obviously opposed to it. But, at the suggestion of the United States -who were suspected by its allies, the European colonial powers, to favor the consecration of the right to independence in order to dismantle their empires and bring into their orbit the states which would emerge from that dismantling- a compromise solution consisting in the creation of a trusteeship mechanism which will be responsible for giving effect to the right to self-government in accordance with the varying circumstances of each territory.[105]

However, the initial clarity in the understanding of the meaning and content of self-determination would be obscured following, first, the debate which took place within the United Nations in the 1950s on the occasion of the drafting of what will become later in 1966 the two Covenants on civil, political, social and economic rights and, then, the adoption in 1960 by the General Assembly of its famous resolution 1514 (XV) on the independence of colonial peoples.[106] In fact, what happened since then was a gradual focus on independence to the detriment of democracy.

World War II certainly raised high and legitimate expectations for independence among the colonial peoples. But, these expectations could have been reached simply through the proclamation of the right to independence of colonial peoples. But USSR and third world countries felt that it was important that such a right be embodied in the right of self-determination. This was also legitimate as a people cannot determine itself if it is still subject to colonization. However, the likening of the right of independence with self-determination has led gradually to the overshadowing of democracy in so far as the major component of the latter as most of the states which were behind such likening were against the establishment of democratic regimes in their own countries. In the debates which took place in early fifties in the Third Committee of the General Assembly and the Commission on Human Rights,[107] a group of states have tried to draw the attention that self-determination

[104] UNCIO, Vol. 6, p. 455.

[105] See Russell and Muther (1958, p. 808) cont.

[106] See the very enlightening study of Burke (2010), Chapter 2 "Transforming the End into Means": The Third World and the Right to Self-Determination.

[107] On these debates, see Cassese (1995, pp. 47–52) and Norland and Zaidi (2008, pp. 214–221).

cannot be limited only to independence and that it should extend also to democracy and more importantly that it is not a transitory right that peoples exercise once and for all when they obtain their independence. Thus, for India "Individual and political right could not be implemented if the people to whom they have been granted lived under a despotic regime. As has been recognized in Article 21, paragraph 3 (of the Universal Declaration of Human Rights), the will of the people should be the basis of the authority of the government."[108] Likewise, for the United States, "self-determination is a right which belongs to all peoples without any distinction; the United Nations should not. . .refer only to people which have never exercised the right of self-determination. . .(and not) peoples which have once exercised the right and had it snatched from them."[109] However, although in the beginning the majority of states, as noted by A.Cassese, "became increasingly adamant in their insistence that the article on self-determination in the Covenants on human right have a wider state (i.e. including democracy) and not merely the limited colonial situation,"[110] the desire to include the right of democracy and political participation in the Covenants on human rights would fail following the emergence of new states among third world countries which were not interested in democracy. Such a move will definitely open the door to the formation of the classical self-determination paradigm where democracy is overshadowed by formal independence. Resolution 1514 (XV) and its interpretation under the United Nations practice will play a major role in this direction.

It is frequently said that the famous Resolution 1514 (XV) adopted by the UN General Assembly on 14 December 1960 has consecrated self-determination. In fact the purpose of that resolution was, as indicated by its title, to grant independence to colonial countries and peoples and not to adopt an international legal instrument on self-determination. True, Resolution 1514 (XV) does contain a para 2 where it is said that "All peoples have the right to self-determination; by virtue of that right they freely determine their political status and freely pursue their economic, social and cultural development", but this para as well as para 6 related to the obligation to preserve states' territorial integrity are overwhelmed by the rest of the paras which are all devoted to the acceleration of the independence process. Para 5 reflects clearly the general motive behind the adoption of Resolution 1514 (XV) as it states that "immediate steps shall be taken in Trust and Non-Self-Governing or all other territories which have not yet attained independence, to transfer all powers to the peoples of those territories, without any conditions or reservations, in accordance with their freely expressed will and desire, without any distinction to race, creed or colour, in order to enable them to enjoy complete independence and freedom." It was certainly the United Nations' major concern to

---

[108] UN Doc. A/C.3/SR.310 para 14.

[109] General Assembly, Third Committee, Summary Records, General Assembly document A/C.3/SR.447, 18 November 1952, pp. 174–175.

[110] Cassese (1995, p. 49).

proceed at that time to the "speedy and unconditional ending of colonialism"[111] that has pushed it to neglect seeking to set the proper conditions enabling the future states to be viable political entities. At the time, the United Nations' hasty attitude was severely criticized. Thus, for instance, Brazil did draw the attention that "It is necessary that the peoples still under a colonial regime convince themselves that independence is not just a magic word followed by a flag, an anthem and diplomatic representation, but the effective political, economic and cultural mastery of the country's wealth and heritage, their utilization in the service of the whole population, and the practice of liberty through political institutions based on a representative regime with full freedom of opinion."[112] Pressured by USSR and many third world countries to hasten the decolonization process, the United Nations has likewise neglected the fact that decolonization could require different solutions as the colonization has not everywhere taken the same form. Hence, while the colonial powers have very often created political entities from scratch, it happened also that they annexed territories which belonged to independent states. Independence cannot, therefore be the right solution. That is why the United Nations will very quickly try to remedy such a defect. This will be done through Resolution 1541 (XV) which, adopted by the General Assembly on 15 December 1960, states that "A non-self-governing territory can be said to have reached a full measure of self-government by: a) emergence as a sovereign independent state, b) free association with an independent state, or c) integration with an independent state."[113] But resolution 1541 did not avail as the only solution which will be given to decolonization was independence. Furthermore, the independence was conceived, as it happened in Africa, within the artificial territorial limits created by colonial powers in order to delimit their respective colonial possessions. Hence, the right to self-determination-independence, interpreted in light of the discredited political principle of the uti possidetis, was meant to be applicable to every situation without any due consideration of the nature and the form taken by colonial domination.

Thus, it was on the occasion of the decolonization process that self-determination has lost its main meaning, i.e. that the governments derive their powers from the consent of their peoples, and became simply likened with the independence of colonial peoples. It was the emerging Third World countries that have been at the origin of such radical change. Amazingly, these countries have, in the beginning of the 1950s, in the course of the preparation within the United Nations of the human rights covenants draft (the future two 1966 Covenants), started of to be in favor of democratic self-determination. They have even convinced the Bandoeng

---

[111] Emerson (1964, p. 29).

[112] GAOR (1960) Plenary Meetings, 934th mtg., (A/PV.917), para. 20.

[113] The 1970 Declaration on Friendly Relations will enlarge the spectrum of possible solutions other than the independence by stating that "The establishment of sovereign and independent state, the free association or integration with an independent state or the emergence into any other political status freely determined by the people constitute modes of implementing the right of self-determination of that people".

Conference to endorse such conception. However, they have started to change their views at the end of the 1950s and particularly on the occasion of the adoption of Resolution 1514. Moreover, they became since then resolutely against the democratic conception of self-determination, especially when many liberation movements took power. After analyzing that process by which self-determination has been, thanks to the advocacy role of a number of emerging Third World countries, separated from democracy following the Second World War, Roland Burke was able to conclude that:

> "While the right to self-determination was a constant theme in Afro-Asian human rights rhetoric, its content was not fixed, being highly dynamic and subject to radical re-interpretation over time. Between the preparation of Article 1 of the human rights covenants in the early 1950s and the climate of 1966, the definition of the right to self-determination underwent a dramatic shift, which mirrored the broader trend away from individual rights, and toward state prerogatives in Afro-Asian bloc policy at the UN. Self-determination's metamorphosis mirrors the broader fate of democracy in the Third World, as the first wave of nationalist governments transformed into antidemocratic regimes."[114]

It was under the aegis of such non-democratic conception of self-determination that most colonial territories have in less than two decades become independent. This was certainly one of the greatest achievements of the United Nations. But, the United Nations carried the decolonization process in a way which sometimes deliberately ignored the reality on the ground as "when examining the position of the organization (i.e. the United Nations) in respect of colonial "peoples" will, we can observe, indeed, that it did not only presume that within these "peoples" existed a majority in favor of independence, it also did sometimes, imagine and even impose that will."[115]

It is generally well known that the United Nations way of implementing self-determination has led to the emergence of artificially created states whose populations were in virtually all cases not consulted by the United Nations on the territorial and human configuration of their future states. The International Court of Justice subsequently gave its blessing to this mechanical and grotesque application of the right to self-determination when it affirmed that this absence of consultation of the concerned populations did not lessen the validity of the right to self-determination.[116] Plebiscites and referenda were the exception at the time when the overriding rule was to tacitly agree that the populations concerned must continue living within the artificial delimitations imposed by the colonial powers, even when those delimitations were not ethnically and economically viable.[117]

It is significant to note that the ideology that self-determination meant necessarily automatic independence was so strong that the United Nations has never appropriated the right to organize itself referenda for self-determination of a

[114] Burke (2010, pp. 36–37).

[115] Guilhaudis (1976, pp. 67–107).

[116] Western Sahara Case (1975, p. 33).

[117] See, for instance, Person (1972, p. 18).

specific territory. This task has always been given to the state interested in the future of the territory in question, while the UN merely supervises and monitors the way the referendum is carried out. In this respect, M. Merle pointed out that the United Nations "have benefited from the support of the local authorities who have assumed responsibility for the legal and practical organization of the consultation process prescribed by the United Nations General Assembly," that "the role of the commissioner elected by the United Nations General Assembly and his staff was above all an observational one, justified by the need to give an account to the General Assembly of the conditions under which the consultation has taken place," and that, in practice, the involvement of the commissioner and of his deputies "has never been a substitute for the powers of the relevant (local) authorities to organize the referendum."[118] This was the case, not only for colonial territories, but also for those territories claimed by a state attempting to recuperate part of its territory despoiled by a third party power. This was well illustrated by the reclamation of West Irian in 1969 by Indonesia where, in compliance with an agreement made in 1962 with the UN, it fell to the former to organize the consultation process for the relevant inhabitants, under the supervision of the UN Special Representative of the Secretary-General.[119] Then in Namibia, it was the South African Administrator-General who took on the organization of elections to establish the independence of the Namibian territory, while the role of the United Nations Transition Assistance Group (UNTAG), under the authority of the UN Special Representative of the Secretary-General, was to supervise and monitor these elections.[120] The United Nations will start showing closer interest in the organization of the referenda only since the adoption of the 1990 Settlement Plan related to the case of Western Sahara. The United Nations' lack of proper experience in the organizing of referenda will constitute a serious handicap in its attempt to implement that Plan. It was no surprise that, at the start of the first difficulties in implementing the Settlement Plan that Boutros-Ghali, the then UN Secretary General, did confess on 28 February 1992 at a meeting of the Security Council that the United Nations has never been prepared to organize itself referenda. In fact, the United Nations' failure to so far settle the Saharan conflict is due to its initial insistence on applying the self-determination-independence scheme to a conflict which was related to the retrocession of part of the Morocco territory and not to an artificially created colony. But the United Nations has in the past decade started to realize that democratic self-determination and its expression at the substate level, i.e. territorial autonomy, can help settle definitively the issue in a fair and just manner.[121]

---

[118] "Les plébiscites organisés par les Nations Unies" AFDI 1961 p. 435 and 437. See also Vignes (1963, p. 297 et seq.)

[119] See Morand (1971, p. 513 et seq.)

[120] See Marc Aicardi de Saint Paul "les élections namibiennes (7-11 novembre 1989)", Afrique contemporaine, 1er trim., 1990, p. 64 et seq.

[121] See El Ouali (2008, pp. 127–145).

Thus, the dominant conception which prevailed within the United Nations since 1960 was that self-determination is nothing other than the right to independence.[122] Such conception was so dominant that it has exerted its effect outside the decolonization context by pushing many ethnic groups to claim independence very frequently through the use of violence. Hence, it has been shown that at the end of the twentieth century more than half of the wars were waged in order to impose separation on behalf of self-determination[123]and that 233 ethnic groups representing about 900 million people did claim independence on the same basis.[124] Such a dominant conception was tacitly meant to be applied only to peripheral states. Now, Northern countries would discover after 1989 further to the disintegration of the Soviet Union and Yugoslavia that that conception can also be implemented at their expense and create a destabilizing situation particularly in Europe.[125] Meanwhile, according to some authors, the implementation of self-determination-independence to non-colonial situations was legitimate as since 1960 none of the major international instruments nor states' practice have limited the implementation of self-determination to colonial confines.[126] But, the sudden break-up of the Soviet Union and Yugoslavia and the emergence of a great number of new states in Europe will be a crystallizing factor in pushing Northern countries, as we will see later, to change their conception of the content and meaning of self-determination.

Hence, the manipulation of self-determination has led to the transformation of the latter into an instrument of states' disintegration instead of a means meant to reinforce the states through the building of democracy. But such manipulation will also distort the meaning and role of states' recognition through the politicization of the latter.

5.1.4 The Politicization of State Recognition

At the start of the modern era, recognition was a necessary requirement in order for an entity to become a state and be a member of the small community encompassing the European states. The membership in that community was limited to the then so-called "civilized" states.[127] Recognition was implemented as such only within the European geographical area, but the latter will be gradually extended to other Western states countries. Originally, state recognition was not a circumstantial act. J. Lorimer recalls in this respect that "Any doctrine. . .which professes to regard it (i.e. recognition) as an act of courtesy, comity, or the like, the exercise of which may be jurally withheld – deprives international law of a permanent basis in nature,

[122] Guilhaudis (1976, p. 76 and seq.)

[123] See Wallensteen and Sollenberg (2000, vol. 37, p. 635).

[124] See Stremlan (1995, vol. 18, p. 33).

[125] See on this among others, Falk (1997, pp. 55–61).

[126] See Cass (1992, vol. 18, p. 33); McCorquodale (1994, vol. 43, pp. 860–861).

[127] See Lorimer (1983, p. 32).

and fails to bring it within the sphere of jurisprudence."[128] Thus, recognition[129] used to obey strict criteria which are in fact "identical with the requirements of statehood as laid down by international law, namely, the existence of an independent government exercising effective authority within a defined area."[130] However, the situation started to change when France recognized prematurely the United States, an act which was perceived by Great Britain to constitute an intervention in its internal affairs.[131] It was since then that state recognition has started to be politicized as "for the past two hundred years the criteria for acknowledgement of new states have been tied to the idea of self-determination of peoples. Indeed, recognition and self-determination have been two sides of the same coin. State recognition can be said to have (1) emerged over two centuries ago as a fully-fledged practice in response to the idea of self-determination of peoples and (2) altered with changes in its understanding that occurred since that time."[132] It was therefore self-determination which has made of state recognition a political and discretionary act "determined solely by considerations of convenience or national interests."[133] It was that transmutation in the understanding of state recognition which has made of the rules related to the latter nothing other than "legal vehicles for political choices."[134] Such transmutation will also exert its influence on part of the doctrine which, very often ignoring or neglecting the process that leads to the emergence of state territoriality, is of the opinion that recognition has nothing to do with the creation of states and that its role is solely to declare that a state exists. Such conception is not exact as we will see hereafter.

As we know, there are two theories related to the nature of state recognition, the declaratory and the constitutive one.[135] What distinguishes mainly the two theories is the impact of the recognition of state's existence.

Hence, according to the declaratory theory, an entity starts to exist as a state from the moment it satisfies the criteria of statehood. Ti-Chiang Chen declares in this respect that "whenever a state in fact exists, it is at once subject to international (meaning it starts to be a subject of International Law and having its own international personality), independently of the will of other states."[136] State recognition is, therefore, the mere acknowledgement that a new state exists as well as the readiness of the recognizing state that it is willing to enter into relations with it.

[128] Idem, p. 104.

[129] By the word "recognition", it is meant state recognition hereafter in the text.

[130] Lauterpacht (1947, p. 26).

[131] Idem, p. 95.

[132] Fabry (2008, p. 51).

[133] Menon (1994, p. 26).

[134] Worster (2009, p. 116).

[135] For a critical review of these two theories, see Grant (1999) and Worster (2009, pp. 119–144).

[136] Chen (1951, p. 14).

Consequently, recognition is an automatic act which excludes any discretionary consideration from the recognizing state. Thus, according to James l. Brierly, "The better view is that the granting of recognition to a new state is not a 'constitutive' act; it does not bring into legal existence a state which did not exist before. A state may exist without being recognized, and if it does exist in fact, then, whether or not it has been formally recognized by other states, it has a right to be treated as a state."[137]

The declaratory theory does not reflect the process by which states come into existence thanks in particular to recognition. More gravely, it can be used in order to facilitate the emergence as states of entities that do not meet the traditional state criteria. William Thomas Worster has noted in this respect that "even if the theory were not, in itself, objectionable on this ground and was followed unanimously by states, other difficulties with the theory include the selection of the criteria to apply, the instability and unpredictable nature of competing versions of criteria, the application of those criteria, the hypocrisy in applying different criteria to different states, and the legitimacy of some proposed criteria. These issues may lead one to wonder whether the declaratory theory constrains the discretion of states to an appreciable degree."[138]

With regard to the constitutive theory, recognition participates in the process of state creation. As noted by Oppenheim, "International Law does not say that a state is not in existence as long as it is not recognized, but it takes no notice of it before recognition. Through recognition only and exclusively a state becomes an international person and a subject of International Law."[139] Likewise, for H. Kelsen who has contributed most to the elaboration of the constitutive theory, "The legal act of recognition is the establishment of a fact; it is not the expression of a will. It is cognition rather than re-cognition. It has the same character as the establishment of a legally relevant fact by a court. Its effects is that the recognized community becomes in its relation with the recognizing states itself a state, i.e. a subject of rights and obligations stipulated by general international law. Before recognition, the unrecognized community does not legally exist *vis-à-vis* the recognizing states. Only by the act of recognition does it come legally into existence in relation to the recognizing state."[140] However, although the constitutive theory hence presented is more satisfactory than the declarative one, surprisingly Kelsen did not, as well as the other proponents of that theory, make any attempt to substantiate his thesis. In fact the legal basis of the constitutive theory is to be found in the objective conditions that lead to the creation of a new state.

---

137 Brierly (1963, p. 139).

138 Worster (2009, p. 119).

139 Oppenheim (1905, p. 110).

140 Kelsen (1941, p. 608).

It should be recalled that, as we have seen earlier,[141] the state is the result of a successful territorialization process which leads to territoriality, that is, the control of a given space by a dominating group after having succeeded to neutralize internal and external competitors, and consequently a community cannot emerge as a state unless it obtains the explicit or tacit recognition of its internal and external rivals. Thus, for instance, a community, which wants to detach itself from a given state and create its own state, has first to obtain the consent of the latter state. This is a mandatory rule of general International Law which is reflected by the prohibition of secession. This rule is further justified by the need to guarantee the stability of states as well as the stability of the international system. Recognition by the parent state is then a determining factor in the creation of the new state. It can be called a primary recognition as it has a constitutive character. The primary recognition should be distinguished from the secondary recognition which aims only at establishing political relations with the newly created state. The secondary recognition is made by external states once the primary recognition has been performed and led to the creation of the new state. Such recognition has therefore a declaratory character as it is made on the presumption that the whole process - the internal as well as the external one - leading to the creation of the new state, has been completed. Consequently, a premature recognition by an external state, that is, prior to the completion of the whole process of state creation, is merely an intervention in the internal affairs of the parent state. "Recognition of a community as a state", recalls H. Kelsen, "even though it does not fulfill the conditions laid down by international law, is a violation thereof. If, for instance, part of an existing state tries to separate itself by revolution, and another state recognizes this part of the state as a state before the conditions prescribed by international law are fulfilled, the recognizing state infringes upon the right of that state against which the revolutionary attempt at separation is directed. The question whether the right of a state has in fact been infringed by the act of recognition- a question which is disputed between this state and the recognizing state- is only a special application of the general principle concerning the question whether in a given case one state has violated the right of another state."[142] However, as we will see here below, the manipulation of self-determination has made of the external recognition an important political tool in the creation of new states although sometimes the latter did not satisfy the criteria of statehood.

The rules of state recognition, as established by general International Law, have traditionally taken into account the internal and external dimensions of the process of state creation.

As to the internal dimension in the process of state creation, it is related to determining whether territorialization has led to the emergence of a coercive and more or less centralized power that exerts an effective authority over a given territory.

[141] See first chapter.

[142] Kelsen (1941, p. 610).

The holding of power by the purported state entity should indeed lead to the emergence of an effective government, that is "a political organization by which relations in the community are regulated and through which the rules are upheld."[143] The requirement of the effectiveness of the newly emerging authority has been highlighted by the Committee of Jurists in the Aaland Islands case where it raised inter alia the issue whether Finland became a state in the following terms: "for a considerable time, the conditions required for the formation of a sovereign state did not exist. In the midst of revolution and anarchy, certain elements essential to the existence of a state, even some elements of facts, were lacking for a fairly considerable period. Political and social life were disorganized; the authorities were not strong enough to assert themselves; civil war was rife; further, the Diet, the legality of which had been disputed by a large section of the people, had been dispersed by the revolutionary party, and the Government had been chased from the capital and forcibly prevented from carrying out its duties... It is therefore difficult to say at what exact date the Finnish Republic, in the legal sense of the term, actually became a definitely constituted sovereign state. This certainty did not take place until a stable political organization had been created, and until the public authorities had become strong enough to assert themselves throughout the territories of the state, without the assistance of foreign troops. It would appear that it was in May 1918, that the civil war ended and that the foreign troops began to leave the country, so that from that time onwards it was possible to re-establish order and normal political and social life, little by little."[144]

The authority of the emerging power should be exerted over a given territory as "a group of people without a territory cannot establish a state."[145] Indeed, the possession of a territory is a necessary requirement of statehood as "without it there can be no stable and effective government."[146] International Law does not require that the borders of the arising state be from the outset clearly defined.[147] However, the territory of the arising state should have some consistency. The presiding principle in the matter has been recalled by the Polish-German Mixed Arbitral Tribunal when it did state that "whatever may be the importance of boundaries, one cannot go so far as to maintain that as long as this delimitation has not been legally effected, the state in question cannot be considered as having any territory whatever...In order to say that a state exists...it is enough that the territory has sufficient consistency, even though its boundaries have not yet been accurately delimited, and that the state actually exercises independent public authority over that territory."[148]

---

[143] Blix (1970, p. 633).

[144] League of Nations Official Journal, Special Supplement, 1920, no 3, pp. 8–9.

[145] Raic (2002, p. 60).

[146] Lauterpacht (1947, p. 30).

[147] Menon (1994, pp. 34–36).

[148] Deutsche Continental Gas-Gesellschaft v.Polish State, I.L.R., Vol. 5, p. 11.

With regard to the external dimension of the process of state creation, it is related to determining whether the territorialization process has succeeded to make of the newly emerging internal power an authority which is independent from any external authorities including the parent state. The new power has indeed to assert that it exerts the exclusivity of authority over a given territory. One can recall in this regard that Judge Max Huber has clarified in his famous arbitral award in the Island of Las Palmas that "Independence in regard to a portion of the globe is the right to exercise therein, in the exclusion of any other state, the functions of a state."[149] The newly arising power should be independent not only from the parent state but also from any other authority as "if a community, after having become detached from the parent state, were to become, legally or actually, a satellite of another state, it would not be fulfilling the primarily condition of independence and would not accordingly be entitled to recognition as a state."[150] D. Anzilotti has pertinently highlighted the distinction between an independent and dependent state by clarifying that "Independence…is really no more than the normal condition of states in international law; it may also be described as sovereignty (*suprema potestas*), or external sovereignty, by which it is meant that the state has over it no other authority than that of international law…The idea of dependence…implies a relation between a superior state and an inferior or subject state…;the relation between the state which can legally impose its will and the state which is legally compelled to submit to that will…It follows that the legal conception of independence has nothing to do with state's subordination to international law or with the numerous and constantly increasing states of *de facto* dependence which characterize the relation of one country to other countries. It also follows that the restrictions upon a state's liberty, whether arising out of ordinary international law or contractual engagements, do not as such in the least affect its independence. As long as these restrictions do not place the state under the legal authority of another state, the former remains an independent state however extensive and burdensome those obligations may be."[151]

These are then the main rules related to state recognition. However, these rules will be altered at the occasion of the manipulation of self-determination as secondary recognition will play the role of primary recognition and the criteria related to statehood will be put aside whenever needed. But such subversion of the rules related to state recognition will take place massively only after the launching of the decolonization process.

The rules related to state recognition will, for a long period after the emergence of self-determination at the end of the eighteenth century, show a great deal of resilience. Hence, France's premature recognition of the United States of America did not exert a great impact on the other European powers which preferred to

[149] 2 United Nations Reports of International Awards, p. 838.

[150] Lauterpacht (1947, p. 28).

[151] Separate Opinion, Customs Regime between Germany and Austria (Protocol of 19 March 1931), Advisory opinion, PCIJ? Ser.A/B, No 41, 45.

recognize the American state only once it has been recognized by the parent state, i.e. Great Britain. Likewise, the Latin American states were recognized only once they had given evidence that they did satisfy state's criteria. Thus, although they were, in contrast with their proclaimed neutrality,[152] supportive of the independence of the Latin American states – in which they had seen a weakening of rival European states and a potential for the emergence of satellite states – and they did not wait for the prior consent to the emergence of these states by the parent state, that is Spain, the United States did recognize these states only when it made sure that the latter did satisfy statehood criteria. Hence, the Secretary of State John Quincy Adams made clear that "In every question relating to the independence of a nation, two principles are involved; one of *right*, and the other of *fact*; the former exclusively depending upon the determination of the nation itself, and the latter resulting from the successful execution of that determination...The United States...yielded to an obligation of duty of the highest order by recognizing as independent states nations which, after deliberately asserting their right to that character have maintained and established it against all the resistance which had been or could be brought to oppose it...This recognition...*is the mere acknowledgement of existing facts* (italics added), with the view to the regular establishment, with the nations newly formed, of those relations, political, commercial, which is the moral obligation of civilized and Christian nations to entertain reciprocally, with one another."[153] But the US policy, which was shared by Great Britain, was opposed by European states amongst which some did even consider military intervention in order to re-establish Spain in its colonial possessions. The European powers will follow path only after the parenthesis created by the Holy Alliance and its policy of monarchical legitimacy and prohibition of territorial changes. However, while, as we have seen above, they would thanks to the manipulation of self-determination be behind the emergence of new states, they would insist that the latter be territorially, economically and culturally viable entities.[154]

Thus, the main elements which characterize state recognition policy following the emergence of self-determination were the increasing disregard of the prior consent or recognition of the new state by the parent state, the requirement that the peoples become free by their own efforts, that is without the assistance of any foreign intervention and the necessity for the new states to be viable states. According to M. Fabry, what conditioned most the recognition policy from 1815 to 1950, was the requirement of what he calls "a de facto statehood", that is the achievement of effective statehood by the concerned peoples. He writes in this

[152] As noted by Vincent (1974, 107 note 190).

[153] Quoted in Manning (1925, vol. 1, pp. 156–157).

[154] See E. Hobsbawn (1990, p. 65 et seq.).

respect that "Crafted by early nineteenth-century American and British foreign policymakers and normatively grounded in classical liberal thought, the *de facto* standard was premised on the belief that the peoples had a natural right to live under independent government of their choosing. As such, they had no right to be interfered with by third parties as they pursued their choice, but not any right to insist that third parties help them bring about its attainment. Self-determination was expressed through, and externally gauged by, self-achievement".[155] But state recognition will as a result of the decolonization movement launched at the end of the 1950s witnesses a radical change with the abandonment of the traditional criteria related to statehood.

As self-determination was from then on interpreted as the automatic right of independence of colonial peoples, it was felt that there was no need to check whether a given community did satisfy the traditional criteria of statehood. The mere admission of a given community to the United Nations would, it was thought, function as a collective recognition act by the international community.[156] As noted by John Dugard, "Evidence of independent statehood would present little difficulty, as this would be provided by admission to the United Nations."[157] All what was needed for a community to be member of the United Nations and then be recognized as a "state" was a decision of the Special Committee on Decolonization requesting independence as well as the colonial power agreement to that independence.[158] The profound alternation of recognition has not gone unnoticed at the time. Thus, Denys P. Myers did note that recognition "has become almost automatic…(it is) only a cordial cognitive act…(it) is characterized by instantaneous, sometimes even anticipatory, response to the fact of independence…In an international atmosphere conducive to independence, granting independence became an industry of the metropoles, and recognition as a result politically automatic."[159] On her part, R.Higgins did also note that "the traditional requirement of a stable and effective government in a territory claiming statehood runs counter to the developments in international law regarding a legal right of self-determination. It is often at variance with political reality: the anti-colonial pressures upon Western European states, and uneconomic costs for them remain by force in their colonial possessions, have caused these states in several cases to withdraw from

---

[155] Fabry (2008, p. 52).

[156] In total contrast with the League of Nations which required for admission that the applicant shows that it has (1) a de jure or de facto government, (2) a stable government, (3) a settled borders, (4) its country is fully self-governing, that is, enjoying effective independence and that (5) it has been able to implement its international obligations. See Malbone (1933, pp. 12–13).

[157] Dugard (1987, p. 65).

[158] Idem, p. 66.

[159] Myers (1961, p. 703, 706).

territories which they had previously governed before any adequate indigenous system of government had been formed."[160] Likewise, William V. O'Brien and Ulf H. Goebel have noted that "The inescapable conclusion seems to be that the basic principle in the recognition of new states has changed. Formerly, nations that had demonstrated their capacity to exist as sovereign independent states were recognized, unless they failed to meet some other criteria. Today, demonstration of the capacity to exist independently is not usually required of new states. The simple certification of the existence of a new state through an orderly transfer of sovereignty from metropolis states to former dependency is taken, in most instances, without question, as satisfactory evidence that a new state, actually exercising sovereign powers, has come into existence and eligible to recognition."[161] Hence, the final result of the collective recognition policy has been that "all members of the United Nations are accepted as states despite the fact that several probably would not have received widespread recognition by individual states had they been left to make a determination of statehood in accordance with the traditional criteria."[162]

Thus, mere admission to the United Nations was used in "indecent haste"[163] as a substitute to the compliance with the traditional statehood criteria of pseudo-states which failed to qualify with basic requirements such as independence and effective government. The hasty and accelerated move towards the creation of these states was dictated, on one hand, by the feeling, prevalent within the colonial powers as well as in the United States,[164] that "it was increasingly urgent to exchange colonial control for informal empire"[165] due to the threat then constituted by the Soviet Union to expand its influence to colonial countries, and, on the other hand, by the pressure exerted by client rulers and proto-nationalists to immediately benefit from the transfer of power in order to prevent its seizure by rival candidates.[166] The victims of this hasty and precipitous move towards decolonization were obviously the colonial peoples who lived since then for most of them under external and well as internal dependence through the creation of non-viable states which remained structurally linked to their respective metropoles. The other victim was the international community as many new states were not only a financial burden, but also have not stopped threatening international peace and security and sometimes be the host of terrorist movements. The other victim was also International Law which was turned upside down as since then "Contrary to traditional practice, statehood is

160 Higgins (1963, p. 23).

161 "United States Recognition Policy Towards the New Nations" in O'Brien (1965).

162 Dugard and Raic (2006, p. 99).

163 Idem, p. 208.

164 The United States did also have their own plans for global free trade since, as noted by Kimball (2000, p. xiii).

165 Roger and Robinson (1994, p. 485).

166 See Perham (1961, p. 64).

posited rather than real. It no longer depends on meeting certain qualitative criteria but has basically been conferred by the international community by means of recognition *and* a matter of right. Thus the statehood of quasi-states is positively juridical instead of being empirical."[167]

In the past decades, the most grotesque attempt to make of the admission of a pseudo-state to an international organization a substitute to the compliance with the traditional statehood criteria was the admission to the Organization of African Unity (OAU) of the so-called "Sahrawi Arab Democratic Republic" (SADR). The latter has been created by Algeria as a consequence of the failure of its alliance with Spain, which was meant to establish an artificial state in Western Sahara through the manipulation of self-determination.[168] Hence, not happy with the retrocession of Western Sahara by Spain to Morocco following the signing between the two countries on 14 November 1975 of the Madrid Accord, Algeria created SADR in order to challenge that retrocession. Taking advantage of the transitory period during which power was being transferred from Spain to Morocco, Algeria started, with the assistance of the Polisario, by, first, invading Western Sahara in order to transfer by force to its own territory thousands of Saharawis.[169] As the number of the Saharawis was very small, they brought also from the Sahel thousands of people[170] who were in search of food because of the drought which was at that time prevailing in the region. After their transfer to Algeria, the Saharawis and the Sahelians were altogether put in military camps in the region of Tindouf (Algerian territory) under the supervision of the Polisario militia and Algerian security forces. By doing so, Algeria wanted to create a refugee-like situation in order to get the sympathy of the international community and in particular of the United Nations High Commissioner of Refugees (HCR) who nevertheless has since then never been able to establish its direct control of the camps, limiting its role to providing humanitarian assistance through Polisario Red Crescent. But, Algeria wanted, before all, to make of the Saharawi and the Sahelian "refugees" the population of the SADR which is created on 28 February 1976, the same day when Western Sahara was definitely recuperated by Morocco.

But how to convince the international community to recognize the SADR, knowing that the later was established in the territory of a foreign country and made up of a population which has been transferred by force from its home place and put in military closed camps, which facts are severely prohibited by International Law? The solution was to manage to get the SADR be admitted to the OAU

[167] Kreijen (2002, p. 4).

[168] See El Ouali (2008, p. 77 et seq.)

[169] See Hodges (1987, pp. 287–288); Damis (1983, pp. 71–72).

[170] See on this issue J. Mercier "The Saharawis of Western Sahara", Minority Rights Group Report, No. 40, p. 11. This fact is recognized by S. Caratini, although she is a sympathizer of the Polisario. See her book "La prison du temps. Les mutations sociales à l'œuvre dans les camps de réfugiés sahraouis", Afrique Contemporaine, 2007, No. 221, vol. 1, p. 12.

where Algeria was very influent. Thus, despite its fictitious and illegal character, the SADR was accepted by the OAU as one of its members in flagrant violation of International Law rules as well as its own Charter.

The admission of the so-called SADR to the OAU was a blatant violation of International Law and of the Charter of the OAU in terms of three fundamental questions:

- The admission of the SADR to the OAU, by foreseeing the result of the consultation process for the referendum, a process that Algeria itself has been lobbying for since 1966, was firstly a total contradiction to the right to self-determination as a recognized right of a group of individuals to freely decide their destiny, and to choose the national and state political system under which it wanted to live. This decision also implied a contempt towards the group of individuals involved, who would find themselves deprived of their fundamental right to self-determination because, as pointed out by S. Talmon, "strictly speaking, after recognition of the SADR as a state, the question of self-determination of the Saharan people could no longer arise. However, if the Saharan people have not yet exercised their right to self-determination, recognition of the SADR as a state, which is in fact only one of four possibilities to be put to the people in the planned referendum, under UN auspices (these four possibilities, the author adds, were independence, autonomy of the Sahara under Moroccan sovereignty, creation of a federation, or preserving the status quo), preempts the outcome of that referendum and may be regarded as a disregard for the people's right to self-determination."[171] By acknowledging the so-called SADR, the OAU became not only judge and jury in the Sahara conflict, but was also putting itself in the place of the Sahrawi populations.
- The admission of the SADR to the OAU then constituted a blatant violation of the most fundamental principles of the notion of the state. This supposes, we know, the existence of three fundamental elements: a territory, a population, and an effective and sovereign power.[172] The SADR was only a state in name, as it had no territory, apart from Tindouf which was under the sovereignty of Algeria. Secondly, it had no population as such, apart from a minority of Sahrawi held, for the most part, against their will in Tindouf and a large number of economic refugees fleeing the drought prevalent at that time in the countries of the Sahel. Lastly, it had no effective and sovereign power over the territory and the population of the Sahara.

[171] "Who is a Legitimate Government in Exile? Towards Normative Criteria for Government Legitimacy in International Law" in Goodwin-Gill and Talmon (1999, pp. 508–509).

[172] See above. See also Crawford (1976–1977, pp. 93–182). The implementation of the criteria for statehood to the SADR by Pazzanita (1985, p. 141).

- Finally, the admission of the so-called SADR constituted a violation of the very Charter of the OAU,[173] in particular of its clause which demands that all member states must be independent and sovereign, and a disregard for the preliminary question put by Morocco about the interpretation of this clause and the determination of its scope in this specific case. The argument with which M. Bedjaoui tried to deny the existence of such a violation of the OAU Charter, by giving as an excuse the fact that "the Charter of the OAU did not indicate the specific criteria according to which an African state can be identified as 'independent and sovereign"[174], was not convincing, as the question of whether a state is independent or sovereign is determined by general International Law.[175] The determination of the independent and sovereign nature of a state is therefore a strictly legal one. As we have seen above, independence or sovereignty, both terms being synonymous, is the legal expression of the state territoriality, in other words, the effective control that a state can exercise in accordance with International Law over a given territory and that the independence in respect of a part of the world is the right to exercise the powers of the state therein, to the exclusion of any other state. It is surprising to see the same writer saying that "Nevertheless, the Charter [of the OAU] is not totally silent about the criteria for identifying 'the independent and sovereign state'. It has made it *an eminently political question which it has left up to the opinion of each of its member states. But the Charter has given itself general objectives, in particular the liberation of the continent. It would not be very close to the spirit of the Charter if the states lost sight of the Organization's objectives.*"[176] It is true that the states enjoy a discretionary power to recognize whatever entity they want to recognize, the only sanction being the loss of their credibility, but an inter-state organization, which proclaims its regard for international legality, can only admit sovereign state entities, that is to say entities which exercise effective power over a given territory, and in accordance with the relevant regulations of International Law. In this case, the so-called SADR had no control over any part of the Sahara. Moreover, it had been created in blatant violation of International Law, in that what was required by the international community at the time was first of all the application of the right to self-determination with a view to allowing the population concerned to decide whether they wanted to remain connected to the Moroccan state or create their own state. It is interesting to see that today writers who maintained at the time that the SADR constituted a state have changed their position to take into account the reality. So, for

[173] Cf. Bennouna (1980, pp. 193–198).

[174] "L'admission d'un nouveau membre à l'Organisation de l'Unité Africaine" in Mélanges offerts à Charles Chaumont, Le droit des peuples à disposer d'eux-mêmes. Méthodes d'analyse du Droit International, Paris, A. Pédone, 1984, p. 48.

[175] See Crawford (1979, p. 48 et seq.)

[176] "L'admission d'un nouveau membre à l'Organisation de l'Unité Africaine", op.cit., 48, italics added.

Gino Naldi, the statement that the SADR constitutes a state[177] can no longer be made today. He deserves to be cited at length when he discusses the factors which have led him to change his position. Hence, he writes in this respect that:

"The passage of time appears to have weakened rather than strengthened the SADR's claim to statehood. The completion of the wall defense has progressively allowed Morocco to establish effective control over most of the disputed territory, a situation that has persisted for some fifteen years. The SADR fails therefore to satisfy one of the primary requirements of sovereign statehood, that of exercising exclusive authority over the bulk of its territory. The ability of the SADR to conduct foreign relations appears to have diminished, or at best there does not to seem evidence of its having increased, notwithstanding the fact that it is a member of the African Union, the OAU's successor. The SADR has failed to convince the wider international community of its claim to statehood. Indeed, some states have withdrawn their recognition of the SADR. The UN, as has been seen, considers the situation as a question of decolonization. Even allowing for the fact that in these circumstances the criteria of statehood can be interpreted more flexibly, the SADR nevertheless seems to have significant obstacles to overcome. Accordingly, grounds exist for believing that the SADR may no longer meet the requirements of statehood, assuming it ever did."[178]

Retrospectively, what adds to the grotesque character of the admission to the OAU of the SADR is that today the latter is still a member of that organization while it is recognized by less than half of the members of the African Union, which has succeeded to the OAU.

Thus, the manipulation of state recognition effected under the guise of self-determination, but in fact with the view of achieving political ends, has led to the alteration of the natural process of state creation. Indeed, instead of being the result of a successful territorialization process, that is the expansion and establishment of an effective political authority over a given territory, the state becomes the result of an external act, that is state recognition, even when that state does not exist as such on the ground. Certainly the manipulation of state recognition has not been problematic as long as there has been a large consensus within the international community on the policy of freeing colonial peoples by the creation of new states. But, the manipulation of state recognition may lead to international tension or war when it is carried out by some states in order to make other states disintegrate. This is what happened in particular with regard to Yugoslavia. "State recognition policy", observes Raju G.C. Thomas, "proved to be an inventive method of destroying longstanding sovereign, independent states... Disintegration and war in the former Yugoslavia were caused mainly by the hasty and reckless Western policy of recognizing new states from an existing longstanding state. Indeed, the Western powers dismembered Yugoslavia through a new method of aggression: *diplomatic recognition.*"[179]

---

177 Naldi (1985, p. 448).

178 Naldi (2005, p. 33).

179 Thomas (1996).

The paradox is that some powerful states, after having taken advantage of the discretionary character of state recognition in order to create ex nihilo following the end of the Cold War new states without due consideration to statehood criteria,[180] want today to limit that discretion when it is used by other states in order to refuse to recognize as a state an entity which has been artificially created.[181] That is what happened in particular further to the creation by these same powerful states, through recognition of the Kosovo, of an entity that they want to see recognized as an independent state by reluctant states on "legal basis rather than political considerations"![182] State recognition would then function in two different ways: a political one, consisting in the creation out of the blue, by foreign states of a new state to the detriment of parent state and without any consideration to statehood criteria, and a legal one, which will operate once the structures of the new state have been established with the assistance of those same foreign powers. This ambivalent use of state recognition reflects the impasse to which the manipulation of self-determination has led today. It is no a surprise that the legality of the proclamation of Kosovo's unilateral independence has been referred to the ICJ for an advisory opinion[183] and that a "war of recognitions"[184] has ensued between concerned great powers through in particular the recognition of South Ossetia and Abkhazia. These two events, the referral to the International Court of the Kosovo's case and the problematic counter-recognition of the independence of South Ossetia and Abkhazia, show that the manipulation of self-determination, which was more or less easy to implement in the context of the decolonization, create serious difficulties when it aims at disintegrating longstanding states.

Unfortunately, the ICJ does not seem to have well understood, in its Advisory Opinion of the 22 July 2010 on the issue of "the Accordance with International Law of the unilateral declaration of independence in respect of Kosovo", that for the sake of international peace and security, time has come to reestablish consistency and clarity in the policy of state recognition.[185] Indeed, it was a surprise to see the Court endorsing in a very peremptory manner the idea "that general international law contains no applicable prohibition of declaration of independence"[186] by non-state local actors. As a justification to such curious stand, the Court limited itself to say that during the eighteen, nineteenth and early twentieth centuries, there were

---

[180] In the aftermath of the end of the Cold War, several new states have been recognized while they, notes Eckert, (2002, p. 33).

[181] This issue is discussed extensively by Worster (2009, pp. 145–171).

[182] Fierstein (2008, p. 441).

[183] G.A. Res. 63/619, U.N. Doc. A/63/619, 18 October 2008.

[184] Worster (2009, p. 117).

[185] ICJ Reports 2010.

[186] Advisory Opinion, of 22 July 2010 on the issue of the "Accordance with International Law of the unilateral declaration of independence in respect of Kosovo", ICJ Report 2010, para 84.

numerous instances of declarations of independence, often opposed by the state from which independence was being declared,[187] while, as we have seen above, these declarations have frequently raised opposition not only from the parent state but also from many foreign states, a fact which clearly shows that there was no general agreement of the acceptance by the international community of such kind of declarations. By doing so, the Court has given some legitimacy to the very controversial policy which has allowed non-state local actors and foreign states to create new states against the will of the parent state. One can consequently expect that secessionist movements will not miss the opportunity to see in the stand hence taken by the Court an encouragement to obtain separation from their parent states by proclaiming their independence. "As regards the legality of unilateral declarations of independence", warns Cedric Ryngaert, it is, *per analogiam* , not excluded that in practice a backlash will take place, and that state practice may have the effect of prohibiting unilateral declarations of independence. The Court's opinion indeed manifests itself as a veritable Pandora box. It serves as an incentive for declarations of independence by other regions, and is difficult to reconcile with the international community's striving for order and territorial stability".[188] Hence, the manipulation of self-determination may not see soon an end, although it does lead to incalculable and very often serious reverse effects.

5.2 The Effects of the Manipulation of Self-Determination

Amazingly, genocide has been one of the most serious effects of the manipulation of self-determination by powerful states. Hence, put under external pressure, the parent states, mainly the traditional empires, were brought to give up their tolerant ethnic policies and adopt very aggressive behavior towards their subject peoples. Such aggressive behavior has had sometimes particularly dire consequences for those who were perceived, correctly or incorrectly, as the protégés or proxies of those foreign powers – very frequently Western powers , as we have seen earlier – who have encouraged them to seek separation from their countries. Genocide was one of these dire consequences.[189] "Of course, one cannot charge", notes Mark Levene,[190] "the Western powers with direct responsibility for the various acts of genocide along our tectonic plate. Through their hegemonic position, combined with normal statist self-interest, they simply helped create and possibly accelerate conditions in which genocide was likely to be an outcome. By giving the Armenians, for instance, every incentive to see themselves as a separate nationality under Great Power Protection,

[187] Idem, para 79.

[188] Ryngaert (2010, p. 490). See also the analysis made by Falk (2011, pp. 56–58).

[189] See Levene (2005).

[190] Idem, p. 225.

they in effect poured a bucket of poison into Turkish-Armenian relations, yet without any intention of coming to the rescue when the Turks predictably overreacted".

But let us leave aside the impact of the manipulation of self-determination on the relations between the parent state and the local communities who seek separation and concentrate on successful manipulation. The main and immediate effect of a successful manipulation of self-determination is, as we have seen above, to make foreign states disintegrate. But it has also very frequently another effect which is to create states incapable to establish conditions conducive to their own integration. Thus, the manipulation of self-determination does, in addition to the disintegration of original states, create the conditions for furthering the disintegration of the nascent states. This is one of the main reasons why today, self-determination has fallen into disruption.

In fact, the manipulation of self-determination has led to the creation of fractured states which, in turn, has given rise to ethnonationalism which is a potential factor for making these states further disintegrate. The manipulation of self-determination triggers then a recurrent vicious circle generating continuously a situation of precariousness for the new states.

5.2.1 The Creation of Non Viable States

It is generally agreed that most of the states which have been created following the two World Wars thanks to the powerful idea of self-determination are extremely weak in terms of internal cohesion.[191] State's failure in Southern countries and particularly in Africa has also spurred in the past decade a heightened debate on whether the colonial boundaries share a responsibility in such failure.[192]

It is known that the colonial delimitations had been established by colonial powers with the aim of satisfying their own interests, and not those of the colonial peoples who often found themselves divided by borders which took no account of traditional territorial identities. Thus, the colonial action was endorsed within the United Nations under the guise of a particular conception of the right to self-determination where the opinion of the populations concerned was ignored for the benefit of a legal, ethnic and economic heresy, corresponding to what is commonly called the principle of the sanctity of borders, which acted as the arbitrary distributor of territories in order allegedly to spare the new states from pointless conflicts. Furthermore, and more gravely, such distribution of territories was carried out in a context where the effectiveness of authority over these territories was very often absent, which fact, totally at odds with the principle of

[191] Migdal (2001, p. 136).

[192] For a thorough discussion of this debate, see Englebert et al. (2002, pp. 1093–1118).

effectiveness of authority, has also been at the origin of the inherent weakness of the nascent states.[193]

Thus, self-determination-independence, read and interpreted in light of the controversial political principal of the sanctity of colonial borders, has led to the emergence of many states which "rest on shaky foundations as far as their inner unity is concerned."[194] Nevertheless, in the 1960s, a number of writers were of the opinion that modernization would lead to ethnic identity disappearing in the new countries. This was particularly the point of view of Karl Deutch for whom nationalism was meant to play a key role thanks notably to the mobilization of the peasant and rural population. The transition towards an industrial economy and the creation of the nation in these countries were to be achieved over a few generations.[195] But, as we know, the facts proved Deutsch wrong.[196] His ethnocentrism led him to confuse two very different things: the creation of the state and the formation of the nation. Whereas in the case of European countries, the nation was created by the state, in developing countries and those in Central and Eastern Europe, the construction of the state and the formation of the nation should be carried out simultaneously. In fact what we were witnessing in the majority of the new countries in the South was the appearance of neopatrimonial states dominated by military oligarchies and prominent clannish minorities, where the majority of the population was completely marginalized and excluded from power-sharing. In addition, these oligarchies were unable to ensure the wellbeing of the population and lay the base for both economic development and the nation-state. In reality, very few nations saw the light of day.[197] Quite the opposite, the military oligarchies deepened the ethnic divisions and created states whose main function was to capture the wealth of their countries. Thus, instead of integrating states, it was the predatory states which took hold in almost all the new countries in the South. Incapable of having a state mentality and developing national projects, the oligarchies inexorably pushed their countries towards a state of chaos where the population was not ensured even the minimum required from a state: the maintenance of security and public order. Thus, the obstacles to the creation of nation-states existed from the outset,

---

[193] See Kreijen (2002, pp. 46–107).

[194] Emerson (1964, p. 30).

[195] According to the following process: "Open or latent resistance to political amalgamation into a common national state; minimal integration to the point of passive compliance with the orders of such amalgamated government; deeper political integration to the point of active support for such common state but with continuing ethnic or cultural group cohesion and diversity; and finally, the coincidence of political amalgamation and integration with the assimilation of all groups to a common language and culture-these could be the main stages on the way from tribes to nation...How long might it take for tribes or other ethnic groups in a developing countries to pass through some such sequences of stages? We do not know, but European history offers at least few suggestions", "Nation-Building and National Development: Some Issues for Political Research" in Deutsch and Foltz (1963, pp. 7–8).

[196] For a systematic critic of Deutch theory, see Connor (1972, p. 331).

[197] See Horowitz (2000, p. 567).

particularly in Africa. "Many of these states that entered this non-functioning category," recalls R. Baker,[198] "are the by-products of the creation of spurious statehood as a result of the precipitated ending of the colonial era...The imperial epoch indulged in a reckless ordering of boundaries with cavalier disregard for ethnic or political realities on the ground. The end-product if this 'great game' is a whole slate of states that have no legitimacy among their people, whose identity is, instead, to some older, ethnic or cultural tradition within the new state or – worse still – across its boundaries, and becomes, therefore, a challenge to the persistence of the empty shell of the 'nation'...The historical and legitimate states are still there, of course, but they are tribal and are seen, irony of ironies, as a threat to the 'integrity' of the new chimerical nations. These same new 'nations' have been engaged in a spurious and largely empty process of 'nation building' where there is no nation to build."

Thus, being the product of the schematic and thoughtless application of the right to self-determination, numerous new states were unable to function as they could not establish any control over their territories or the populations in them.[199] The majority of these states are "quasi-states"[200] in that, although they have the formal appearance of a state, they are unable to fulfill the functions traditionally incumbent on the state.[201] Even more serious, the failure of these pseudo-states is such that they are not only unable to protect their own populations, who are forced to place themselves under the protection of warlords,[202] but they have also become a danger for the security of foreign states as they tend to generate violence, civil wars, organized crime and terrorism.[203] It is so because "states that are not in control of their own territory are potentially a danger due to the possibility of non-state actors using that territory for particular purposes... Territorial integrity must mean more than merely territorial preservation or inviolability."[204] Being unable to contain the monopoly of legitimate violence, a pre-condition for setting up states,[205] these quasi-states are stillborn states which "failed before they formed."[206] Thus it can easily be understood that, contrary to the claims of certain writers,[207] if the nation-state did not emerge in many Southern countries, it was not because it did not have an appropriate breeding ground but simply because they had never tried to cultivate it.

---

198 Baker (2004, pp. 6–7).

199 John G. Mason "Failing Nations: What US Response?", http://ww2.wpunj.edu/chss/polisci/faculty/mason/jmfailed.htm.

200 Jackson (1990, p. 21).

201 Rotberg (2002, pp. 85–96).

202 Rotberg (2003, pp. 5–6).

203 See Ben N. Dunlap "State Failure and the Use of Force in the Age of Global Terror", www.bc.edu/schools/aul/bibs/postconflict-htm.

204 Eiden (2006, p. 483).

205 Ignatieff (2003, p. 305).

206 Part of the title of the work by Anderson (2004, p. 1).

207 See, for example, Badie (1992).

Hence, the situation created by the wrong implementation of self-determination in many Southern countries is such that many foreign countries frequently see in the states that have "failed" an element of instability as much as an obstacle to the smooth running of globalization. As Richard Rosecrance and Arthur Stein observe, this is the main reason that explains why today "international opinion and Great powers' support for self-determination and the creation of new states have lessened. As governments have perforce embraced globalization, they have also become leery of dissidents who reject it. Even more significant, dissenters who use the methods of international terrorism to gain attention for their plight have thereby generally discredited themselves. Thus, the international climate of opinion and action has turned against axiomatic national self-rule for every dissident group."[208]

Consequently, a large number of new countries are threatened with implosion as a result of the resurgence of ethnic nationalism, which calls into question the principle of the intangibility of borders and the artificial state entities they set up.[209] Ethnonationalism is spurred on by the inability of the state to achieve proper territorialization and, in case the latter is by miracle established, its inability to "create" the nation, promote and maintain the homogeneity of society and give all citizens the wherewithal to realize their social and economic well-being. But the inability of the state to achieve proper territorialization and create a nation mainly finds its roots in self-determination/independence which has often given rise, as we have seen, to the emergence of artificial state entities dominated by oligarchies which have deepened the original divisions in society and turned the state into a private property. It is true that the inability of the state to achieve proper territorialization was also aggravated by the structural economic crisis in which many Southern states find themselves and which has its origin in the maintenance of economic dependence and the imposition since early 1980s of structural adjustment programmes. Thus, most of these countries are increasingly impoverished. The gap between them and rich countries has grown significantly due also to the difficulty they have in adapting to globalization, which, as we have seen above, weakens the state and makes it lose its congruence with the nation.

Thus, it is believed that Southern societies particularly in Africa will not make sustainable progress in building democratic systems and fostering economic development unless they acquire coherent, legitimate and effective states.[210] But fixing failed states[211] is not an easy task especially that the latter's societies are plagued by the rise of ethnonationalism.

[208] Rosecrance and Stein (2006, p. 5).

[209] See Parkinson (1993, p. 336).

[210] Joseph (2003, p. 159).

[211] See Ghani and Lockhart (2009).

5.2.2 The Rise of Ethnonationalism

As we have seen above, the principle of nationalities was applied first in the Central and Eastern European regions in the nineteenth century with the view of freeing peoples through the creation of new territorial entities but at the same time subjecting them to new foreign domination. That region has played the role of a laboratory for the creation of new states through a process in which nationalism has been instrumental in "inventing" nations. That process which will be implemented elsewhere requires, first, that "all communities larger than the primordial villages of face-to-face contact (and perhaps even these) are imagined,"[212] but only insofar as "certain objective preconditions for the formation of a nation exist."[213] However, all the nationalist movements did have a common denominator: the defining of the nation in terms of a given territory as the control of the latter was their final objective. D. Conversi has pointed out that "nationalism is a struggle over the definition of spatial boundaries, that is over the control of a particular land or soil"[214] and that therefore "nationalism must be seen as...an attempt to seize control of the state."[215] But territories, shows Sack, "are the results of strategies to affect, influence and control people, phenomena and relationship."[216] Meanwhile the control of a territory fundamentally requires attaching to it a collective identity. Now, the Self requires the existence and the opposition to the Other. The latter, shows I.B. Neumann, has "the status of an epistemological as well as an ontological necessity, without which there can be no thinking self."[217] The borders, as we have seen earlier, play a crucial role in the creation of the group identity. The identity in turn leads to the creation of the national homeland. However, clarifies J. Agnew, territories and homelands "are made out of places"[218] as the latter are "the structuring or mediating context in social relations."[219]

It is worth noting that when a secession process is successfully completed and brings to existence a state duly recognized by the international community, the newly established state will in turn develop its own nationalism with a view to strengthening its control and hegemony over the society. This phenomenon of repetition on a smaller scale of a general policy implemented by modern states, observes Nergis Canefe,[220] is best exhibited in new forms of national

---

[212] Anderson (1983, p. 15).

[213] See for instance Hroch (1985).

[214] Conversi (1995, pp. 553–584).

[215] Ibid, p. 4.

[216] Sack "Human Territoriality : Its Theory and History", op.cit., p. 19.

[217] Neumann (1996, p. 48).

[218] Agnew (1987, p. 1).

[219] Ibid, p. 70.

[220] Canefe "Sovereignty Without Nationalism? A Critical Assessment of Minority Rights Beyond the Sovereign Nation-State Model" in "The New World Order. Sovereignty, Human Rights, and the Self-Determination of Peoples", op.cit., p. 108.

historiography in which national history and identity will be closely linked to territory, the latter playing a crucial role in the new ideological configuration in so far as "the construction and maintenance of hegemony requires a single-handed mastery over territorial and spatial particulars. History becomes coterminous with territory, and historicity and cultural identity become endemic to territoriality. Consequently, what happens during the formation of counterhegemonic identity claims is that the same history is rewritten with a new cultural and territorial accent". In this regard it is well known that in Central and Eastern Europe, nationalism has led to the creation of ethnic nation-states, i.e. states dominated by one ethnic hegemonic group. This has led to the emergence of ethnonationalism as a defensive reaction from subjected minorities. In Southern countries, the idea to separate peoples on ethnic basis has also been used by colonial powers in order to strengthen their grip on the colonies. It was also, as we have seen above, encouraged, by the independent clan states which succeeded colonial powers. "It was the colonial powers, and the independent states succeeding them" , shows J.B. Bowen,[221] which declared that each and every person had an "ethnic identity" that determined his or her place within the colony or the postcolonial system. . .True, before the modern era, some Africans did consider themselves Hutu or Tutsi, Nuer or Zande, but these labels were not the main sources of everyday identity. A woman living in central Africa drew her identity from where she was born, from her lineage and in-laws, and from her wealth. Tribal or ethnic identity was rarely important in everyday life and could change as people moved over vast areas in pursuit of trade or new lands. Conflicts were more often within tribal categories than between them, as people fought over sources of water, farmland, or grazing rights."[222] Ethnies are then also social constructs made out of previously diverse cultural groupings and can be subjected to changes.[223] "It is clear", writes R.M.Williams,[224] "that present-day ethnic populations have been constructed over time by conquest, religious movements, migration, biological blending, acculturation, and absorption of ethnic-linguistic groups."[225] Their distinctiveness if any comes from the fact that ethnies are related to the belief in a common descent, the existence of ethnic boundaries[226] and their limited character in terms of space. However ethnonationalism is even less distinct from nationalism. T.H. Eriksen has shown in this regard that the proto-nations or what are often called ethnonationalist movements are "groups (that) have political leaders who claim that they are entitled to their own nation-state and should not be 'ruled by others'. These groups, short of

221 Bowen (1996, p. 4).

222 Bowen (1996, p. 4).

223 See the extensive doctrine referred to in this sense by Williams (1994), maxweber.hunter.cuny.edu/pub/eres/SOC217_PIMENTEL/ethnic conflicts.pdf, p. 5.

224 Idem.

225 Idem.

226 F. Barth has shown in this regard that "it is the ethnic boundary that defines the group, not the cultural staff that it encloses" in "Introduction" in Barth (1969, p. 15).

having a nation-state, may be said to have more substantial characteristics in common with nations than with either urban minorities or indigenous peoples. They are always territorially based; they are differentiated according to class and educational achievement, and they are large groups. In accordance with common terminology, these groups may be described as 'nations without states'"[227]The emergence of ethnonationalism which aims at creating a state from within, obeys therefore to the same process as nationalism whose objective is the creation of a state from scratch.[228] Hence it does not arise spontaneously from the existence of "primordial bonds" such as race, language, religion, etc.[229] It does not also result from pre-nationalistic sentiments or old myths as "Men become nationalists through genuine, objective, practical necessity, however obscurely recognized."[230] Nationalism emerges as such when an ethnic group, having such bonds and sentiments, has been mobilized by its own elites against a situation of discrimination and domination to which it has been subjected by its "own" state which, though it does pretend that it represents the whole society, has been put under the control of a dominant ethnic group seeking advantages for itself. R. Brass has reflected the complexity of that situation in which the elites of the dominated group play a key role in raising self-consciousness among that group. Such a situation supposes, first, a competition between the elites of the different ethnic groups about the control of the state and, through the latter, the control of economic resources. It supposes, second, that the state does implement a discrimination policy between the ethnic groups. It requires, third, that the interests of the elites of the dominated ethnic group are put under jeopardy. It is such threat to the major interests of those elites that will push the latter to distance itself from the state and mobilize the ethnic group to which it belongs and enter in conflict with that state in order to create its own polity. Brass then concludes in this regard that "Clearly, both types of conflicts-for control at the center and for control over local territories and communities-take on an added significance when elites in competition from different ethnic groups and/or use different languages. The ability to mobilize large number of people around symbols and values with a high emotional potential is a major, though unstable, resource that can be brought into the fray against the controllers of bureaucratic apparatuses, instruments of violence and land."[231]

Certainly the elites which foment a rebellion in order to create their own state are not often primarily motivated by a compassion for the ethnic group grievances

[227] Eriksen "Ethnicity and Nationalism. Anthropological Perspectives", op.cit., pp. 14–15.

[228] The emergence of nationalism and ethnicity do generally obey to the same process. See T.H. Eriksen "Ethnicity and Nationalism", op.cit., p. 99; C. Jaffrelot "For a Theory of Nationalism", op.cit.

[229] As suggested by Geertz (1963, p. 109).

[230] Gellner (1964, p. 160).

[231] "Ethnic Groups and the State" in Brass (1985, p. 28).

against the state or ideological considerations but by the desire for economic gains and privileges.[232] Likewise, ethnic identity and ideology are not the first motive of those who join an insurgency; "rather, everyone is a potential rebel, if the net (expected) economic benefits of rebellion are greater than the benefits of the status quo."[233] However, rebellion cannot be fomented out of the blue. It still supposes the existence of grievances of the whole ethnic community against the structural violence exerted against it by the state and which prevents it from enjoying a normal and decent livelihood. Structural violence does exist where "current institutional structures prevent or inhibit people from satisfying human development needs such as security, acceptance, or effective participation in a just and equitable manner."[234] But it does exist also when these structures create poverty and political and economic differences and inequities between ethnic groups.[235] T.R. Gurr, M. Woodward and T.H. Marshall[236] have suggested in this respect an eclectic and multivariate model that incorporates different factors which may explain the onset of ethnic warfare. These factors are: state's active and systematic discrimination against minority groups, the existence of medium to high ethnic diversity in large countries, partial democracy with factionalism, bordering states with major armed civil or ethnic conflict, any ethnic war or genocide in previous 15 years and large youth population. These factors do certainly facilitate the onset of ethnic wars, but it remains that the most determining factor is the state's failure to perform its normal socio-economic functions to the benefit of the people. The Collier-Hoeffer (CH) model has shown in this regard that political grievances are indeed less important than the socio-economic ones.[237] Hence the likelihood to mobilize the people against the state is greater when the latter fails to generate economic growth, ensure an increase of the GDP per capita, reduce unemployment and poverty and raise the schooling rates in particular secondary schools enrolment. That likelihood is even greater in case of ethnic dominance i.e. when a large ethnic group exerts its hegemony over the whole society. N. Sambanis[238] is of the opinion that the Northern Ireland issue is a case that clearly fits the CH dominance hypothesis. Hence land distribution at the time of British colonialism favored Protestants and only 14% of the land was given to Catholics. There was heavy ethnic competition in Ireland's burgeoning industry, creating similarly antagonistic ethnic relations in other countries where a rough identification of ethnic and professional affiliations

[232] Collier and Hoeffler (2001, p. 3).

[233] Sambanis (2003).

[234] Samarasinghe et al. (2001), http://www.certi.org/publications/Manuals/CVA.htm.

[235] Gurr (1993) and also "Peoples Versus States: Minorities at Risk in the New Century", Washington, D.C., United States Institute of Peace, 2000, chap. 3.

[236] "Forecasting Instability: Are Ethnic Wars and Muslim Countries Different?", globalpolicy.gmu.edu/pitf/PITF ethnicmuslim.pdf.

[237] Paul Collier and Anke Hoeffler (2001, p. 563) cont.

[238] Idem, pp. 27–28.

prevailed. These policies in Northern Ireland, he concludes, created a sense of economic grievance.

The potential for future disintegration of states due to ethnonationalism is huge. T.R.Gurr has indicated that "Nearly three-quarters of the 127 largest countries in the world had at least one politicized minority in 1990, 233 groups in 1990 had an estimated 915 million members, 17.3 percent of the global population."[239] Faced with such a destructive force as ethnationalism which threatens its existence, the state has not remained passive. It reacted by creating its own nationalism. Thus, while according to most of the nationalisms, the political organization should be ethnic in character in that it represents the interests of a particular ethnic group, the state in place has devoted its energy to convince the popular masses that it alone represents them.[240] It has done that, first, by claiming the monopoly to build the national identity.[241] It has, second, shifted allegiances from traditional authorities to its own authority.[242] To do that, it has imposed its own definition of national identity through assimilation/homogenization via institutions such as primary schools and military conscriptions. It also abolished all kinds of segmental relations generated by clans, tribes, feudalities, etc.[243] Some states went even further by using brutal methods such as displacement of reluctant ethnic groups or extermination and genocide or recently "ethnic cleansing."

The state-nations have then been since their inception caught between two antagonistic forces, one seeking disintegration and the other one conservation. Those who have been the most successful in overcoming that contradiction and peacefully integrate any potential ethnic centrifugal forces have been those who opted for the civic nation-states model, although amazingly the expansion of democracy-a democratic regime has been formally established in almost 50 per cent of the countries of the world-[244] has also made difficult the congruence between the state and the nation especially in ethnically divided societies where it has given to the dormant nationalistic claims the possibility to express themselves.[245] This was in particular the case of Central-Eastern Europe and former Soviet Union where democratic transition, and also hasty market reforms, have led not only to the resurgence of nationalistic demands but also to massive political, social and economic dislocations and consequently the fragmentation and weakening of the nascent states.[246] In Central-Eastern Europe, it has traditionally been particularly difficult to establish congruence between the state and the nation. The

[239] Gurr (1993, p. 10).

[240] T.H. Eriksen "Ethnicity and Nationalism", op.cit., pp. 59–60.

[241] Deloye (2003, p. 58).

[242] Strayer (1970, p. 22).

[243] Mauss (1969, vol. 3, p. 588).

[244] See Lane and Ersson (2003, p. 18).

[245] See Horowitz (1997, p. 451).

[246] See Bunce (1999); Verdey (1996, pp. 204–228).

historical drive has been towards ethnic differentiation rather than integration.[247] The presence in many countries of substantial ethnic minority populations has certainly not made the process easy. But the major handicap was the dominant mode of nation building which has generally given preeminence to the ethnic-states formula. The collapse of Yugoslavia and the USSR has more or less led to the revival of that formula through what R. Brubaker has called the "nationalizing state" in which the core nation is identified with the dominant ethnic group and where ethnic minorities are left with the option either to assimilate into the core nation or to be *dissimilated* i.e. marginalized in society.[248] In some situations, the minorities have not even been given that option as they were subjected to forced displacement or ethnic cleansing. It is likely that the marginalization and the eviction of the minorities from civic integration may leave the latter with no other alternative than "permanent irredentist pressures on the newly-formed state's majorities, with incendiary activities culminating in further territorial re-divisions or partitions-the eventual fate, no doubt, of Bosnia-Herzegovina, since the Dayton Peace Accords have legitimized the de facto decentralization and pseudo-partition of the country."[249] Some[250] have argued that a "Europeanization" process has started to take place in Central-Eastern Europe which, thanks to the strengthening of democracy, will in the long run lead to the adoption of the civic state formula or at least to the attenuation of the harshness of the present system. A drive towards that direction has started to materialize in some countries such as the Czech Republic, Hungary, Poland and Slovenia where the governments do implement and promote human and minority rights and provide minorities with guarantees of political participation and cultural autonomy.[251] It is likely that the movement towards building civic-states will reach its goal in these countries, especially further to the rise of self-determination postmodern paradigm which aims, through the development of democracy, at preventing states' disintegration.

References

Agnew J (1987) Place and Politics, Allen & Unvin, London

Anderson B (1983) Imagined communities: reflections on the origins and spread of nationalism. Verso, London

---

[247] Liebich (1991, p. 60).

[248] Brubaker (1996, 79) cont.

[249] T. Bahcheli, B. Bartmann and H. Srebrnick "A New World of Emerging States", Introduction of "De Facto States. The Quest for Sovereignty", op.cit., p. 2.

[250] See D.J. Smith "Framing the National Question in Central and Eastern Europe: A Quadratic Nexus?", www.ethnopolitics.org/ethnopolitics/archive/volume_II/issue_1/smith.pdf.

[251] See P. Kovacs "A Comparative Typology of Ethnic Relations in Central and Eastern Europe" Igi.osi.hu/publications/1998/21/5.HTML.

Anderson L (2004) Antiquated before they can ossify: states that fail before they form. J Int Affairs 58(1)
Attar F (1999) La Révolution française déclare la guerre à l'Europe. L'embrasement de l'Europe à la fin du 18e siècle. Editions Complexe, Paris
Badie B (1992) L'Etat importé. Essai sur l'occidentalisation de l'ordre politique. Flammarion, Paris
Baker R (2004) Challenges to Traditional Concepts of Sovereignty. Public Administration and Development 20
Balogh S (1999) Autonomy and the new world order. A solution to the nationality problem. Matthias Corvinus, Toronto
Barth F (ed) (1969) Ethnic groups and boundaries. The social organization of culture difference. Allen & Unwin/Bergen, London
Bennouna M (1980) L'admission d'un nouveau membre à l'Organisation de L'Unité Africaine. AFDI
Blix (1970) Contemporary Aspects of Recognition, 130 R.C.A.D.I., vol. II
Bowen JB (1996) The myth of global ethnic conflict. J Democracy 7. www.mtholyoke.edu/acd/intrel/bowen.htm
Brass P (1985) Ethnic groups and the state. Croom Helm, London
Braude B, Lewis B (1982) Christians and Jews in the Ottoman Empire. The functioning of a plural society. Holmes and Meier, New York
Breuilly J (1994) Nationalism and the state. The University of Chicago Press, Chicago
Brierly JL (1963) The Law of Nations: An Introduction to the International Law of Peace In: Humphrey Waldock (ed.), 6th ed., Clarendon Press, Oxford
Brougham H (1803) Gentz, Etat de l'Europe. Edinburgh Rev 3
Brubaker R (1996) Nationalism Reframed, Cambridge University Press, Cambridge
Bukovansky M (1999) The altered state and the state of nature – the French revolution and international politics. Rev Int Stud 25
Bunce V (1999) Subversive institutions: the design and the destruction of socialism and the state. Cambridge University Press, Cambridge
Burke R (2010) Decolonization and the evolution of international human rights. University of Pennsylvania Press, Philadelphia
Canovan M (2005) The people. Polity Press, Cambridge
Cass D (1992) Rethinking self-determination: a critical analysis of current international theories. Syracuse J Int Law Comm 18
Cassese A (1995) Self-determination of peoples. A legal reappraisal. Cambridge University Press, Cambridge
Chen T-C (1951) The International Law of Recognition, With Special Reference to Practice in Great Britain and the United States, Stevens & Sons Limited, London
Cobban A (1969) The nation state and national self-determination. The Fontana Library, London
Collier P, Hoeffler A (2001) Greed and grievance in civil war. World Bank Policy Research Working Paper No. 2355, October 2001
Connor W (1972) Nation-building or nation-destroying? World Polit 24
Conversi D (1995) Reassessing Current Theories of Nationalism. Nationalism as Boundary Maintenance and Creation, Nationalism and Ethnic Politics, 1(1):553–584, easyweb.easynet.co.uk/converse/reassessing.pdf, p. 7
Crawford J (1976–1977) The criteria for statehood in international law. BYBIL
Crawford J (1979) The creation of states in international law. Clarendon Press, Oxford
Damis J (1983) Conflict in Northwest Africa. The Western Sahara Dispute. Hoover Institution Press, Stanford
Dehaussy J (1989) La Révolution française et le droit des gens. In: "Révolution et Droit International. A. Pédone, Paris
Deloye Y (2003) Sociologie historique du politique. La Découverte, Paris
Dockrill ML, Goold JD (1981) Peace without promise. Batsford, London

Dugard J (1987) Recognition and the United Nations, Grotius Publications Limited, Cambridge
Dugard J, Raic D (2006) The role of recognition in the law and practice of secession. In: Kohen MG (ed) Secession. International law perspectives. Cambridge University Press, Cambridge
Dupuis Ch (1909) Le principe de l'équilibre et le Concert européen. De la paix de Westphalie à l'Acte d'Algesiras. Perrin et Cie, Paris
Eiden S (2006) Space of humanitarian exception. Geografika Annaler Human Geography 88B(4)
El Ouali A (2008) Saharan conflict. Towards territorial autonomy as a right to democratic self-determination. Stacey International, London
Emerson R (1964) Self-determination revisited in the era of decolonization. Occasional Papers in International Affairs, Center for International Affairs. Harvard University
Englebert P, Tarango S, Carter M (December 2002) Dismemberment and suffocation. A contribution to the debate on African boundaries. Comp Polit Stud 35
Ergang RR (1954) Europe since Waterloo. D.C.Health, Boston
Fabry M (2008) Secession and state recognition in international relations and law. In: Pavkovic A, Radan P (eds) On the way to statehood. Secession and globalization. Ashgate, Aldershot
Falk RA (1997) The right of self-determination under international law: the coherence of doctrine versus the incoherence of experience. In: Danspeckgruber W, Watts A (eds) Self-determination and self-administration; a sourcebook. Lynne Rienner, London
Falk R (2011) The Kosovo advisory opinion; conflict resolution and precedent. AJIL 105(1)
Farly LT (1956) Plebiscites and sovereignty – the crisis of political legitimacy. Westview Press, London
Fierstein D (2008) Kosovo's declaration of independence: an incident analysis of legality, policy and future implications. Boston Univ Int Law J 26(3)
Frèchet H (1991) Histoire de l'Europe au XIXe siècle. Ellipses, Paris
Gastony EB (1992) The ordeal of nationalism in Modern Europe, 1789-1945. The Edwin Mellen Press, Lewiston
Geertz C (1963) The integrative revolution. Primordial sentiments and civil politics in the new states. In: Geertz C (ed) Old societies and new states. The Free Press of Glencoe, London
Gellner E (1964) Thought and change. Weidenfeld & Nicolson, London
George L (1938) The Truth about Peace Treaties, vol 2. Gollancz, London
Ghani A, Lockhart C (2009) Fixing failed states. A framework from rebuilding a fractured world. Oxford University Press, Oxford
Giroud J (1920) Le plébiscite international. Etude historique et critique de droit des gens. Le Puy, Paris
Giroud J (1924) Le droit des nationalités. Sa valeur. Son application, R.G.D.I.P.
Goodwin-Gill GS, Talmon S (eds) (1999) The reality of international law. Essays in Honour of Ian Brownlie. Clarendon Press, Oxford
Grant TD (1999) The recognition of states: law and practice in debate and evolution. Praeger, London
Guilhaudis JF (1976) Le droit des peuples a disposer d'eux-mêmes. Presses Universitaires de Grenoble
Gurr TR (1993) Minorities at risk: a global view of ethnopolitical conflicts. U.S. Institute of Peace Press, Washington
Haas E (1953) Belgium and the balance of power: a critical examination of some balance power theories in the light of policy motivations of the major European States toward Belgium, 1830-1839. Columbia University, PhD
Habermas (1975) The European Nation-state-Its Achievements and Its Limits. On the Past and Future of Sovereignty and Citizenship in G. Balakrishnan Mapping the Nation
Hanf T (1991) Reducing conflict through cultural autonomy: Karl Renner's Contribution. In: Ra'anan U (ed) State and nation in multi-ethnic societies: the break-up of multinational states. Manchester University Press, Manchester
Hauser H (1916) Le principe des nationalités. Ses origines historiques. Librairie Félix Alcan, Paris

Heater D (1994) National self-determination. Woodrow Wilson and his Legacy. Macmillan, London
Henry P (1937) Le problème des nationalités. Librairie Armand Colin, Paris
Hayes CJH (1948) The Historical Evolution of Modern Nationalism, Macmillan, London
Higgins R (1963) The Development of International Law through the Political Organs of the United Nations, Oxford University Press, London
Hodges T (1987) Sahara occidental. Origines et enjeux d'une guerre du désert. Editions L'Harmattan, Paris
Horowitz D (1997) Self-determination: politics, philosophy, and law. In: Shapiro I, Kimlicka W (eds) Ethnicity and group rights, Nomos 39. New York University Press, New York
Horowitz DL (2000) Ethnic groups in conflict. University of California Press, Berkeley (1st edn, 1985)
Howard M (2007) Empires, nations and wars. Spellmount, Gloucestershire (1st edn, 1991)
Hroch M (1985) Social preconditions of national revival in europe: a comparative analysis of the social composition of patriotic groups among the smaller European Nations. Cambridge University Press, Cambridge
Hroch M (2000) From National Movement to the Fully-formed Nation : The Nation-building Process in Europe in: G. Balakrishman (ed.) Mapping the Nation, Verso, London/New York
Ignatieff M (2003) State failure and nation-building. In: Holzgrefe JL, Keohane RO (eds) Humanitarian intervention. Cambridge University Press, Cambridge
Jackson R (1990) Quasi-states: sovereignty, international relations, and the third world. Princeton University Press, Princeton
Jaszi O (1961) The dissolution of the habsburg monarchy. The Chicago University Press, Chicago
Johannet R (1918) Le principe des nationalités. Nouvelle Librairie Nationale, Paris
Joseph RA (2003) Africa: states in crisis. J Democracy 14(3)
Keitner CI (2007) The paradoxes of nationalism. The French Revolution and its meaning for contemporary nation building. State University of New York, New York
Kelsen H (1941) Recognition in International Law : Theoretical Observations, A.J.I.L., 35(4)
Kimball WF (2000) Revolutionary-era Americans condemned colonialism for its closed economic systems, since those closed doors threatened 'freedom' for the United States to grow and prosper in a world of empires. In: Ryan D, Pungong V (eds) The United States and decolonization. Power and freedom (Foreword). Macmillan, London
Kohn H (1967) Prelude to Nation-States. The French Revolution and German Experience, 1789-1815, D. Van Nostrand, Princeton
Komantra T (1940) Le développement du sentiment de solidarité dans la société des Etats. Rousseau et Cie, Paris
Kreijen G (2002) The transformation of sovereignty and African Independence: no shortcuts to statehood. In: Kreijen G (ed) State, sovereignty, and international governance. Oxford University Press, Oxford
Krylov M (1996) Self-determination from Marx to Mao. Ethnic Racial Stud 19
Lane J-E, Ersson S (2003) Democracy. A comparative approach. Routledge, London
Lansing R (1921) The Peace Negotiations: A Personal narrative, Houghton Mifflin, Boston
Lauterpacht H (1947) Recognition in international law. Cambridge University Press, Cambridge
Le Fur L (1921) Philosophie du Droit International. RGDIP
Levene M (2005) Genocide in the age of the nations -state. The rise of the west and the coming of genocide, vol II. I.B.Taurus, New York
Lieber F (1877) De la valeur des plébiscites en Droit International. RDILC
Liebich A (1991) Une mosaïque ethnique. Géopolitique
Lieven (1995) The Russian Empire and the Soviet Union as Imperial Polities, Journal of Contemporary History, 40(4)
Lorimer J (1983) The institutes of the law of nations, vol 1. William Blackwood and Sons, Edinburgh
Macartney CA (1934) National states and national minorities. Oxford University Press, London

Malbone GW (1933) The League of Nations and the recognition of states. University of California Press, Berkeley
Manning WR (ed) (1925) Diplomatic correspondence of the United States concerning the independence of Latin American Nations, vol 1. Oxford University Press, New York
Mastny V (1989) Eastern Europe and the west in the perspective of time. In: Griffith WE (ed) Central and Eastern Europe: the opening curtain? Westview Press, Boulder
Mauss M (1969) La nation in Œuvres. Minuit, Paris (1920), vol. 3
Mayall J (1990) Nationalism and international society. Cambridge University Press, Cambridge
Mayer AJ (1970) Wilson v. Lenin. Political origins of the new diplomacy 1917-1918. Random House, New York
McCorquodale R (1994) Self-determination: a human rights approach. ICLQ 43
Menon PK (1994) The law of recognition in international law. Basic principles. The Edwin Mellen Press, Lewiston
Migdal JS (2001) State in Society. Studying How States and Societies Transform and Constitute One Another
Morand J (1971) Autodétermination en Irian occidental et à Bahreïn. AFDI
Myers DP (1961) Contemporary Practice of the United States Relating to International Law, A.J.I. L., 55(3)
Naldi G (1985) Opinion expressed in "The Statehood of the Sahara Arab Democratic Republic", Indian Journal of International Law 25
Naldi G (2005) "Western Sahara: Suspended Statehood or Frustrated Self- Determination?", African Yearbook of International Law 13
Neumann IB (1996) Self and Other in International Relations, European Journal of International Relations 2
Niederhauser E (1981) The rise of nationality in Eastern Europe. Kner Printing House, Budapest
Norland R, Zaidi S (2008) Human Rights at the UN. The Political History of Universal Justice. Indiana University Press, Indianapolis
Normand R, Zaidi S (2008) Human Rights at the UN. The political history of universal justice. Indiana University Press, Indianapolis
Nys E (1904) L'acquisition du territoire en Droit International. RDILC 36
O'Brien WO (ed) (1965) The new nations in international law and diplomacy. Yearb World Polity III
Ollivier E (1895) L'empire libéral, vol. 1 "Du principe des nationalités. Garnier Frères, Paris
Oppenheim L (1905) International Law, 1st edn
Parkinson F (1993) Ethnicity and independent statehood. In: Jackson RH, James A (eds) States in a changing world. A contemporary analysis. Clarendon Press, Oxford
Pazzanita AG (1985) Seems to be of phantasmagorical character as the author believes, among other things, that the Frente POLISARIO (which has proclaimed SADR) controls about 75 to 80 per cent of the territory (of Sahara). See his article "Legal Aspects of Membership in the Membership in the Organization of African Unity: The Case of the Western Sahara", Case Western Reserve Journal of International Law 17
Pearson R (1983) National minorities in Eastern Europe: 1848-1945. Macmillan, London
Perham M (1961) The colonial reckoning. From the Reith Lectures, 1963
Person Y (1972) L'Afrique noire et ses frontie'res, R.F.E.P.A.
Porter PB (1922) Origin of the system of mandates under the League of Nations. Am Polit Sci Rev XVI
Prizel V (1998) National identity and foreign policy: Nationalism and Leadership in Poland, Russia and Ukraine. Cambridge University Press, Cambridge
Raic D (2002) Statehood and the law of self-determination. Kluwer Law International, The Hague
Roger VM, Robinson R (1994) The imperialism of decolonization. J Imperial Commonwealth History 22(3)
Rosecrance R and Stein A (2006) No More States? Globalization, National Self-Determination and Terrorism, Rowman & Littlefield Publishers, Inc. New York/Toronto/Plymouth

Roshwald A (2001) Ethnic nationalism and the fall of empires. Central Europe, Russia and the Middle East, 1914–1923. Routledge, London
Rotberg RI (2002) The new nature of nation-state failure. Washington Quart 25(3)
Rotberg RI (ed) (2003) State failure and the state weakness in a time of terror. Brookings Institution, Washington
Russell RB, Muther JE (1958) A history of the United Nations charter: the role of the United States 1940-45. Brookings Institution, Washington
Ryngaert C (2010) The ICJ's Advisory Opinion on Kosovo's Declaration of Independence: A Missed opportunity?. Netherlands International Law Review, 57(3)
Saintoyant J (1930) La colonisation française pendant la Révolution (1789-1799). La Renaissance du Livre, Paris
Samarasinghe S, Donaldson B, McGinn C (2001) Conflict vulnerability analysis. Issue, Tools & Responses", April 2001. http://www.certi.org/publications/Manuals/CVA.htm
Sambanis N (2003) Using case studies to expand the theory of civil war. CPR Working, Social Development Department of the Environmentally and Socially Sustainable Development Network of the World Bank, Paper No. 5, May 2003
Sany RG (2000) Nationalities in the Russian Empire. Russian Rev 59(4)
Schwartzmantel J (1998) The age of ideology. Political ideologies from the American revolution to postmodern times. New York University Press, New York
Scott JB (ed) (1918) President Wilson's Foreign Policy: Messages, Addresses, Papers. Oxford University Press, New York
Sem V (1868) Quelques Conséquences du principe des nationalités ou essai de critique politique. Librairie Internationale, Paris
Seymour C (1951) Geography, justice and politics at the Paris Conference of 1919. The American Geographic Society, New York
Snyder LL (1968) The new nationalism. Cornell University Press, Ithaca
Strayer JR (1970) Les origines médiévales de l'Etat moderne. Payot, Paris
Stremlan J (1995) Antidote to anarchy. Washington Quart 18
Sugar PF (1999) Ethnicity in Eastern Europe. In: Sugar PF (ed) East European nationalism, politics and religion, vol II. Ashgate, Aldershot
Tarrade J (ed) (1989) La révolution française et les colonies. Société Française d'Histoire d'Outre-mer, Paris
Thaden E (1984) Russia's western borderlands, 1710-1870. Princeton University Press, Princeton
Thiesse A-M (2001) La création des identités nationales. Europe XVIII-XXe siècle. Points/ Histoire, Paris
Thomas RGC (1996) Nationalism, Secession, and Conflict: Legacies from the Former Yugoslavia, paper presented at the 1st Annual Association for Study of Nationalities Convention, April 26–28, 1996
Verdey K (1996) What was socialism, and what comes next. Princeton University Press, Princeton
Vignes G (1963) les consultations populaires dans les territoires sous tutelle. RGDIP
Vincent RJ (1974) "In fact, it was a neutrality favorable to the rebel cause, so that nonbelligerency rather than neutrality was the accurate description of American policy. Spain could object to such a policy not only because the neutrality was not impartial but also because American recognition of the belligerency of the rebels (which was concurrent with the proclamation of Neutrality of September 1911) could be regarded as intervention in Spanish affairs", "Nonintervention and International Order", Princeton University Press, Princeton
Wallensteen P, Sollenberg M (2000) Armed conflicts, 1989-1999. J Peace Res 37
Wambaugh S (1933) Plebiscites since the World War, vol 1. Washington
Wambaugh S (1920) A monograph on plebiscites. Oxford University Press, New York
Whelan A (1994) Wilsonian self-determination and the versailles settlement. ICLQ 43
White GW (2004) Nation, state, and territory. origins, evolutions, and relationships, vol 1. Rowman and Littlefield, New York

Williams RM (1994) The sociology of ethnic conflicts: comparative international perspectives. Annu Rev Sociol 31

Wilson (1927) War and Peace, Vol. II, New York

Worster WT (2009) Law, politics and the conception of the state in state recognition theory. Boston Univ Int Law J 27(1)

Yack B (2003) Nationalism, popular sovereignty, and the liberal democratic state. In: Paul TV, John Ikenberry G, Hall JA (eds) The nation-state in question. Princeton University Press, Princeton

Chapter 6
The Self-Determination Postmodern Paradigm: Preventing States' Disintegration

The triggering factor in the shift to a new paradigm was the outbreak of virulent ethnonationalism in many different regions of the planet following the end of the Cold War. The most destructive ethnonationalism was the one that emerged following the disintegration of the Soviet Union and Yugoslavia as it has led not only to the rise of new states but also to a chain of infinite claims for statehood raised by communities living in these same states, a situation that made the developed world realize that they were not immune from the disintegrative impact of the confusion between self-determination and independence which they thought was confined to peripheral states. The whole world suddenly discovered also how strong was the ideology surrounding the idea of self-determination-independence as it extended beyond the traditional limits of the decolonization process. Worries were then expressed by officials on the risk that the violent outbreak of ethnonationalism might have for international stability. Thus, on 17 June 1992, Boutros Boutros-Ghali, the United Nations Secretary General, has warned that "If every ethnic, religious or linguistic group claimed statehood, there would be no limit to fragmentation; and peace, security and economic well-being for all would become even more difficult to achieve."[1] Likewise, the United States Secretary of State, Warren Christopher has drawn the attention that "If we don't find some way that the different ethnic groups can live together in a country, how many countries will we have? We'll have 5,000 countries rather than the hundred plus we now have."[2] The disillusion about self-determination rapidly and largely extended also to the international doctrine. Hence, in a very short time, as noted by R. Lapidoth "although hailed and acclaimed by many for about 40 years, since 1989, it (i.e. self-determination) has lost much of its glamour due to the various cases of use of force on ethnic

[1] "An Agenda for Peace", Report of the Secretary-General pursuant to the statement adopted by the Summit Meeting of the Security Council on 31 January 1992, A/47/277 - S/24111, para 17, 17 June 1992.

[2] Hearing at the senate, February 1993.

A. El Ouali, *Territorial Integrity in a Globalizing World*,
DOI 10.1007/978-3-642-22869-8_6, © Springer-Verlag Berlin Heidelberg 2012

grounds that the parties tried to justify by reference to the principle of self-determination."[3]

If the end of the Cold War was a triggering factor in favoring the paradigmatic shift from self-determination-independence to democratic self-determination, such shift was also the result of the structural factor which was (and is still) at play, that is the crisis to which state territoriality has been subjected to in the past decades. This crisis is, as we have seen earlier, widespread and affects, to varying degrees, states in both the northern and southern hemispheres.

For southern countries, the crisis can be traced back to a number of factors, in particular the right to self-determination-independence conception itself, which has very often, as we have seen above, given rise to unstable countries marked by an inability to ensure the well-being and safety of their citizens. But even more serious is the fact that these countries tend to become a source of insecurity for other countries, causing further problems – in particular, illegitimate violence and terrorism.

For countries in the northern hemisphere, the crisis is rooted in globalization whose main effect is to transform the principles of the organization of modern society and weaken the links between the state and the people, thus sabotaging the basic structure of national cohesion. Since this renders it less and less capable of fulfilling its traditional role as provider of economic and social well-being, the state goes through a post-modernization process by accepting to share its sovereignty with supra-state or sub-state bodies.[4]One of the distinctive features of postmodernity consists of encouraging established Western democracies to accord more importance to territorial democracy, notably in the form of territorial autonomy. "Everything happens," writes Jacques Chevalier,[5] "as if it had become necessary to administer to the people in every detail, taking account of every local peculiarity, so that the *principle of proximity* involves the appearance of a new model of relations between state and territory, emblematic of postmodernity. This movement tends to blur the traditional distinctions between the types of territory division: there tends to be an inevitable slide towards the forms of organization which are most favorable to local autonomy; and one is also simultaneously witnessing the diversification of territorial status."

The new paradigm which seems to be coming into being is that of the end of self-determination-independence and the switch to democratic self-determination. In this paradigm, territorial autonomy, conceived of as an expression of democratic self-determination at the substate level, plays a pivotal role. But there is also

[3] "Commentary" in W. Danspeckgruber and A. Watts (eds.) "Self-Determination and Self-Administration. A Sourcebook", op.cit. (1997), p. 67.

[4] In the context of this book, it is meant by post-modernity the phenomenon of vulnerability of state territoriality which finds its origin in globalization and which compels the state, with a view to ensuring its own survival, to share the exercising of certain of its competences with supra or sub-state entities. To the extent that this study deals with territorial autonomy, we shall concentrate our attention solely on the sharing of state competences with sub-states entities. For an analysis of the external aspects of postmodernity, see Sorensen (2001).

[5] Chevalier (2004, p. 73).

another element which enters into play: the tendency of the international community to make the preservation of territorial integrity dependent on states' compliance with democracy. In fact, these two factors combine together in order to make of democracy a crucial element without which states may have a tremendous difficulty to ensure their survival. They both constitute the two major components of the new paradigm which is on the rise. Taking this into consideration, self-determination is henceforth meant to fulfil two new functions: preserving territorial integrity through democracy and sharing power with local communities through territorial autonomy.

However, the evolution to which self-determination is being subjected to does not mean that the states are from now on immune from disintegration in so far as territorial autonomy possesses an ambivalent character as it can help the states integrate its diverse communities as it can also enable the latter to seek separation in order to create their own polities.

Self-determination is then increasingly becoming an instrument of states' integration rather than states' disintegration. Such a move has started to influence the approach adopted in order to settle certain conflicts. Among the later, the most important is the Western Sahara conflict not only because it is the oldest conflict, but also because the impact on it of the transition from one type of self-determination to another seems to be very profound.

Taking the above into consideration, three questions will be discussed hereafter: the new functions of self-determination, the ambivalent character of territorial autonomy and the impact of the current self-determination paradigm on the Western Sahara conflict.

6.1 The New Functions of Self-Determination

At the opposite of the classical self-determination paradigm, the new self-determination paradigm aims at protecting the right to existence of the states. That is why self-determination is meant to fulfil two new functions: preventing secession by making of democracy an imperative for every state, and sharing power with local communities through territorial autonomy.

6.1.1 Preventing Secession: The Democratic Imperative

It is generally agreed that under the current state of International Law, there is no right of secession, that is there is no rule which recognizes a territorial right to separation from a mother country.[6]

[6] See Hannum (1998a, p. 13; 1998b, p. 776); Suksi (2005, p. 200).

The United Nations has formally, in its implementation of the principle of self-determination, constantly stressed the necessity to have full respect of the principle of territorial integrity. This can inter alia be attributed to the fact that "In the Charter, the principle of self-determination was of a clearly subordinate status in relation both to the prohibition on the use of force and the right of territorial integrity (Article 2(4)) as well as to the general commitment to ensuring peace and security (e.g., Chapter VII) all of which were regarded as the foundational norms of the post-war international system."[7]

We find the insistence on the obligation to respect the principle of territorial integrity, first, in the General Assembly's 1960 Declaration on the Granting of Independence to Colonial Countries and Peoples which states that "any attempt aimed at the partial or total disruption of the national unity and the territorial integrity of a country is incompatible with the purposes and principles of the Charter of the United Nations."

The principle of self-determination, which was limited to colonial peoples only, has been implemented within the colonial territorial limits[8] with the understanding that this should not be seen as a rupture in the territorial integrity of the colonial states as, according to the United Nations, "the territory of a colony or other non-self-governing territory has under the Charter a status separate and distinct from the territory of the state administering it" (1970 Declaration on Principles of International Law concerning Friendly Relations).

Third, once the right of self-determination has been applied to a colonial territory, it cannot be implemented again within the same territory. Therefore, any claim to unilateral secession will categorically be disregarded and preeminence given to the principle of territorial integrity.[9]

The no-right-to-secession is in fact a general rule as it applies also to non-colonial territories.[10] The recognition that the principle of territorial integrity should prevail over that of self-determination is not new as already in 1920, the International Committee of Jurists, who was appointed to address the question of the Aalands Islands, was of the opinion that:

> "...in the absence of express provisions in international treaties, the right of disposing of national territory is essentially an attribute of every state. Positive International Law does not recognize the right of national groups, as such, to separate themselves from the state of which they form part by the simple expression of a wish, any more than it recognizes the right of other states to claim such a separation."[11]

---

[7] Simpson (1996, p. 39).

[8] On the difficult relationship between the self-determination principle and the maintaining of the former colonial boundaries (via the implementation of the uti possidetis), see Klabbers and Lefeber (1993, pp. 37–75).

[9] Crawford (1979, pp. 101–102).

[10] See the comprehensive analysis made by Christakis (1999, p. 141 cont.).

[11] League of Nations (1920, p. 5).

The same opinion was shared by the Commission of Rapporteurs in its report to the Council of the League of Nations in which it justified its rejection of the right of a minority to make secession by stating that:

> "To concede to minorities either of language or religion, or to any fractions of the population, the right of withdrawing from the community to which they belong, because it is their wish or their good pleasure, would be to destroy order and stability within states and to inaugurate anarchy in international life; it would be to uphold a theory incompatible with the very idea of the state as a territorial and polity entity."[12]

The United Nations has been uncompromising in the implementation of the no-right-to-secession rule. The Bangladesh case has sometimes been presented as a breach in the UN position with regard to secession. But in fact, Bangladesh has been admitted on 17 September 1974 as a member of the UN, and then indirectly recognized by the latter, only once it had been recognized by Pakistan on 2 February 1974. It is true that a number of new states emerged as such in the 1990s, in particular in Central-Eastern Europe and Central Asia, but they emerged only after the dissolution of USRR, Yugoslavia and Tchecolovaquia and not in reason of unilateral secessions which would have kept alive, though territorially reduced, the latter states.[13] It is also true that Yugoslavia was not dissolved insofar as Serbia and Montenegro had initially proclaimed that the Yugoslavian Federation continued to exist, but this did not prevent them from adopting on 27 April 1992 a new Constitution of the Federal Republic of Yugoslavia in which it was clearly stated that they were its sole components, which fact has here also constituted an indirect recognition of the Republics which seceded from the great Yugoslavia, and which inevitably facilitated one month later their admission to the UN. Likewise, the admission to the United Nations of Southern Sudan took place only when the later emerged as an independent state further to the referendum organized on 7 February 2011 in compliance with the Comprehensive Peace Plan (CPA) signed on 5 January 2005 between the Sudanese Government and the Sudan People's Liberation Movement. Hence, the membership of a seceding state to United Nations has so far been accepted only when the parent state has deliberately recognized the independence of that state. It was in accordance with that principle that the UN have refused to recognize unilateral secessions even if the latter have come to enjoy some effectiveness. This has been so far the case of the "Republic of North Cyprus" which has been recognized only by one state, Turkey and of Kosovo, although the later has been recognized by a great number of states.

Hence, no unilateral secession of non-colonial territories has been accepted by the international community and the states which emerged from that secession have not been admitted to the United Nations. The Supreme Court of Canada has, in its

---

[12] League of Nations (1921, p. 28).

[13] See Crawford (2000), para 26. The same author draws in this respect the attention " that it is necessary to distinguish unilateral secession of part of a state and the outright dissolution of the predecessor state as a whole. In the latter case there is, by definition, no predecessor state continuing in existence whose consent to any new arrangements can be sought", para 27.

opinion on 20 August 1998 on whether the Government of Quebec has the right to effect secession unilaterally, stated that to be legal, a secession would necessitate an amendment of the Constitution which would entail the negotiation of many issues of great complexity and difficulty, possibly including that of territorial boundaries. It added that the negotiation could take place only in the presence of a clear support for secession, expressed through a clear majority and a clear question. The position expressed by the Supreme Court of Canada is somehow relatively liberal as it has not rejected the right to secession but has linked its exercise to a number of conditions which, it is true, cannot be easily met. The other particularity of the opinion of the Court is that it has recognized that the right to self-determination can, in certain circumstances, be admitted outside the decolonization context. The Court has stated in this regard that "In summary, the international law right to self-determination only generates, at best, a right to external self-determination in situations of former colonies; where a people is oppressed, as for example under foreign military occupation; or where a definable group is denied meaningful access to government to pursue their political, economic, social and cultural development. In all three situations, the people in question are entitled to a right to external self-determination because they have been denied the ability to exert internally their right to self-determination."[14] The Canadian Court has in fact in this statement echoed a judicial as well as doctrinal trend which does argue that a right to secession can be exercised by national minorities when they are denied the right to be represented in the government and are subjected to grave and massive violations of human rights.

This new trend has its remote origin in one of the conclusions reached by the Commission of the Rapporteurs in the Aaland Islands case that "the separation of a minority from the state of which it forms a part and its incorporation in another state can only be considered as an altogether exceptional solution, a last resort when the state lacks either the will or the power to enact and apply just and effective guarantees."[15] But, the new trend is also a direct echo of the decision of the African Commission on Human Rights which has made conditional the preservation of territorial integrity by states' respect of human rights. Thus, it ruled that:

> "In the absence of concrete evidence of violations of human rights to the point that the territorial integrity of Zaire should be called into question and in the absence of evidence that the people of Katanga are denied the right to participate in government as guaranteed by Article 13 (1) of the African Charter, the Commission holds the view that Katanga is obliged to exercise a variant to self-determination that is compatible with the sovereignty and territorial integrity of Zaire...The quest for independence of Katanga therefore has no merit under the African Charter on Human and Peoples' Rights."[16]

---

[14] Opinion of the Supreme Court of Canada on the Reference Re Secession of Quebec (1998) 2S.C. R. 217, para. 138.

[15] Report presented to the Council of the League of Nations by the Commission of Rapporteurs, League of Nations (1921, p. 28).

[16] Katangese peoples Congress vs. Zaire, African Commission on Human and Peoples' Rights, Comm. No. 75/92, 1995, para 6.

There are also some authors who are of the opinion that the United Nations has started, since the end of the Cold War, to depart from its intransigent policy towards secession. Gerry J. Simpson argues in this respect that "There is little doubt. . .that the international community has become more sympathetic to secession or, at least, embryonic secession. The events that have taken place in Iraqi Kurdistan, the former U.S.S.R., Eritrea, and the Northern Balkans have consequences for customary international law that are difficult to gauge.This much is certain: there has been a detectable shift in emphasis away from an absolute, unconditional right to political sovereignty and territorial integrity towards more flexible, less statist positions."[17]

Generated mainly by the breakup of the territorial integrity of the Soviet Union and the Yugoslavian Federation, an intense debate has taken place in the past decade among international lawyers and diplomats over the right of self-determination in the non-colonialist context. It is true that this debate has created some uncertainty which in turn, it is believed, has "contributed to many human tragedies. . .by giving false hope to minority groups that they have rights to autonomy or independence against the states in which they are found, even absent a colonial context. . . (and) thus, one task of the international community should be to clarify the right of self-determination in non-colonial context. The clearer the law on the subject, the less likely groups will assert unfounded claims or engage in risky provocations. Reciprocally, legally supported claims of self-determination may deter egregious actions by the mother state and will encourage other states to lend appropriate support to such lawful claims of self-determination."[18]

We have seen earlier that both the Covenant on Civil and Political Rights and the Covenant on Economic, Social and Cultural Rights do talk about Peoples and not States when they state similarly in their Article 1 that "1. All the peoples have the right to self-determination. By virtue of that right they freely determine their political status and freely pursue their economic, social and cultural development" and "2. All peoples may, for their own ends, freely dispose of their natural wealth and resources. . ." The Declaration on Principles of International Law does also state that "By virtue of the principle of equal rights and self-determination of peoples enshrined in the Charter. . .all peoples have the right to freely determine, without external interference, their political status and to pursue their economic, social and cultural development." By doing so, the two Covenants and the Declaration do also recognize that self-determination is not a one-off exercise[19] and that

---

[17] Simpson (1996, p. 55). This opinion is not shared many others like J. Crawford who stated in this respect "that it is necessary to distinguish unilateral secession of part of a state and the outright dissolution of the predecessor state as a whole. In the latter case there is, by definition, no predecessor state continuing in existence whose consent to any new arrangements can be sought", Crawford (2000, para 27).

[18] Jonathan I. Charney "Self-determination: Chechnya, Kosovo, and East Timor", law.vanderbilt.edu/journal/34-02/charney-html,2-3.

[19] Idem.

therefore it should not be limited to the colonial context only. However, the Declaration went even further as it subjected the sustainability of states' territorial integrity to their commitment to respect the rights of their peoples. The Declaration clearly states in this regard that:

> "Nothing in the forgoing paragraphs shall be construed as authorizing or encouraging any action which would dismember or impair, totally or in part, the territorial integrity or political unity of sovereign independent states conducting themselves in compliance with the principle of equal rights and self-determination of peoples as described above and thus possessed of a government representing the whole people belonging to the territory without distinction as to race, creed or colour."

The obligation of the states to respect the rights of their peoples as a necessary condition for the sustainability of territorial integrity has been confirmed by the Vienna Declaration and Programme of Action adopted by the World Conference on Human Rights of 25 June 1993 which, after having taken up the aforementioned statement of the Declaration on Friendly Relations, made a large reference to "a Government representing the whole people belonging to the territory without distinction of any kind" and not only as did the latter Declaration to "territory without distinction as to race, creed or colour."

The principle of territorial integrity is not an "end"[20] in itself. It has been designed, as we have seen earlier, to protect the existence of the state but beyond that it is the existence of the people which is meant, otherwise the principle would have no meaning and legitimacy. Contemporary International Law has also made of subjected populations "nations" and then elevated the latter to the status of "peoples" enjoying not only fundamental rights but also the right to sovereignty on their own territories. Therefore, the principle of territorial integrity can be relevant only if it does incorporate the idea that its fundamental goal is to protect the existence of the people. But the protection of the existence of people requires the respect of popular sovereignty, that is the right of people to self-determination which, as we have seen earlier, is nothing other than the right to democracy and self-government. While the right to democracy has been for more than two centuries limited to the Western countries, as an expression of popular sovereignty and therefore of self-determination, today there is a general move towards its universal implementation. Thus, universal instruments have started to establish a link between self-determination and democracy. Amongst these instruments, there is the 1948 Universal Declaration on Human Rights which proclaims in its Art. 21 (3) that "the will of the people shall be the basis of the authority of the government". Likewise, the 1966 International Covenant on Civil and Political Rights provides in its Article 25 that "Every citizen shall have the right and the opportunity, without any of the distinctions mentioned in article 2 and without unreasonable restrictions: (a) To take part in the conduct of public affairs, directly or through freely chosen representatives; (b) To vote and to be elected at genuine periodic elections which

---

[20] Simpson (1996, p. 54).

shall be by universal and equal suffrage and shall be held by secret ballot, guaranteeing the free expression of the will of the electors…". It is also important that an increasing number of universal and regional organizations have come to regard democracy as the only acceptable regime, that the whole world has witnessed extensive democratization in the aftermath of the end of the Cold War, and that democracy was becoming "protected by collective international processes."[21] Having all this in mind, we can therefore understand why the preservation of territorial integrity is increasingly made conditional on the full respect of peoples' right to democracy and self-government.

Taking into consideration the obligation of the state to protect the "internal" right of self-determination, that is the right for its people to freely chose its own political, economic, social and cultural status,[22] some lawyers have recently raised the question whether peoples should be authorized to claim secession when their fundamental rights are gravely violated by their government. Among these rights, there is in particular the right to have a government representing the whole people belonging to a territory.[23] That question can be all the more relevant when a minority, having a territorial basis, is systematically denied political, economic and social equality.[24] Convinced that state practice has started to support a broader application of the right to self-determination beyond strictly colonial confines, Robert McCorquodale is of the opinion that "After the recognition by the international community of the disintegration as unitary states of the Soviet Union and Yugoslavia, it could now be the case that any government which is oppressive to peoples within its territory may no longer be able to rely on the general interest of territorial integrity as a limitation on the right of self-determination" and that "It appears that only a government of a state which allows all its people to decide freely their political status and economic, social and cultural development has an

---

[21] Franck (1992).

[22] On the distinction between "external" which can lead to secession and "internal" self-determination which is related to the rights that peoples should be allowed to enjoy within the territorial limits of their states, see Casseese (1995, p. 72).

[23] Gerry Simpson argues in this regard that "The Declaration (on Friendly Relations) makes territorial integrity a rebuttable presumption that can only be invoked by states that act in accordance in accordance with the principle of self-determination…An assertion of the right of secession would be a remedy of the last resort for peoples or groups, an exercise of the ultimate collective human right as a means to secure basic individual human rights where devolutionary, democratic, and colonial models of self-determination have failed", "The Diffusion of Sovereignty : Self-Determination in the Post-Colonial Age", op.cit., 54. See also Cass (1992); Laing (1991–1992, pp. 246–248); Tomuschat (1993, pp. 2–8); Buchheit (1978, p. 220); Kirgis Jr (1998, 304 cont.); Nanda (1981, p. 251).

[24] This possibility has been accepted by the Supreme Court of Canada in its Decision on the Reference Re Secession of Quebec when it stated that "A right to secession only arises under the principle of self-determination of peoples at international law where "a people" is governed as part of a colonial empire; where "a people" is subject to alien subjugation, domination or exploitation; and possibly where "a people" is denied any meaningful exercise of its internal right to self-determination within the state of which it forms a part", (1998) 2S.C.R. 217 at para 154.

interest in territorial integrity which can possibly limit the exercise of a right of self-determination. So territorial integrity, as a limitation on the exercise of the right of self-determination, can apply only to those (minority of) states in which the government represents the whole population in accordance with the exercise of internal self-determination."[25] More categorically, Michael P. Sharef is of the opinion that International Law has already and largely started to endorse the right to secession as he states that "The modern trend, evidenced by the writing of numerous scholars, U.N. General Assembly resolutions, declarations of international conferences, judicial pronouncement, decisions of international tribunals, and some state practice support the right of non-colonial "people" to secede from an existing state when the group is collectively denied civil and political rights and is subject to egregious abuses."[26]

The opinion that the right to secession has been sanctioned by the Declaration on Principles of International Law and the 1993 Vienna Declaration when a minority is systematically denied political, economic and social equality has been criticized as "such a major change cannot be introduced by way of an ambiguous subordinate clause, especially when the principle of territorial integrity has always been accepted and proclaimed as a core principle of international law, and is indeed placed before the qualifying clause in the provision in question."[27] The two Declarations do in fact refer to colonial situations and apartheid. This is made clear by the wording of the two Declarations[28] and their negotiating history as reflected in the *travaux préparatoires*.[29] Moreover, even some of those who are proponents of the right to secession in case of systematic violation of the basic rights of the minorities do recognize that "there is considerable evidence that, in the new era of postmodern tribalism, whatever the meaning of the admittedly continuing right of self-determination, it has not been endowed by states in texts or practice with anything remotely like an internationally-valid *right*, accruing to every secession-minded people anywhere, to secede territorially, at will, from

[25] McCorquodale (1994). From his part, T.M. Franck does consider the persistent and egregious denial to a territorially based minority of political and social equality as a repression "coming within a somewhat stretched definition of colonialism. Such repression, even by an independent state not normally thought to be "imperial" would then give rise to a right of "decolonization". While this requires something akin to common law's legal fiction, the notion of decolonization applied to a post-imperial state is not a new invention. India first advanced such a theory of neocolonial liberation and right of secession on the occasion of its invasion of East Pakistan, an action leading to the independence of Bangladesh", Franck (1993, p. 14).

[26] Scharf (2003, pp. 381–382).

[27] Shaw (1997, p. 5). However, it should be recalled that the Vienna Declaration and Program of Action adopted in 1993 by the Un Conference on Human Rights has endorsed the idea initially formulated by the Declaration on Principles of International Law that the principle of territorial integrity has precedence on the principle of self-determination only as long as the government does represent the whole population. See Scharf (2003).

[28] Weller (2005, p. 11).

[29] See Corten (1999, p. 342).

established states that are members in good standing in the international community."[30] Besides, it is intellectually difficult to accept that such initiative could have been endorsed by those states that have been recurrently accused of being responsible of grave violations of human rights and that are manifestly unable to fulfill the required criteria of democratic and real representation of their citizens.[31] However, it has become clear today that those who still believe that the principle of territorial integrity is a sacrosanct principle that has precedence over self-determination, have started to concede that "developments in respect of the idea of internal self-determination and self-government are however occurring...But these developments are still tentative (*de lege ferenda*), and they do not affect the established rules and practices with respect to self-determination and the territorial integrity of states."[32]

It therefore clearly appears that the principle of territorial integrity is losing its sacrosanct character as the respect of peoples' right to democracy and self-government is increasingly perceived as a necessary condition without which such a principle can no longer be legally and politically relevant and consistent. But, this does not mean that secession has become the only alternative left when a state fails to secure the right of all the populations to democracy and self-government.

Certainly, there is really a new trend in International Law as the latter has started to recognize that a self-identified group has the right to secede when it is egregiously denied its political and civil rights. However, it still remains that International Law requires that such a group establishes that it constitutes a "people". This is the biggest obstacle that a group claiming the status of "people" can first be faced with. While it was, within the decolonization framework, already difficult to identify the "colonial people", though the latter was clearly meant to be a people subject to "alien subjugation, domination or exploitation"(Declaration on the Granting of Independence to Colonial Countries and Peoples), [33] it will be even more difficult to identify the "people" outside that framework. We know that the international community has never been able to agree on a definition of the "people", though the characteristics of the latter, as suggested by the UNESCO, are apparently not difficult to determine as they do consist mainly in: common historical tradition, religious or ethnic identity, cultural homogeneity, linguistic unity, religious or ideological affinity, territorial connection and common economic life.[34] Likewise, it is not theoretically difficult to draw an acceptable definition from these elements and find a common denominator to the suggested definition. "Commentators have sought", notes Javier Leon Diaz, "to melt the various definitions within the term "ethno-national" group, which is a politically self-conscious sub-national group that asserts plausible claims to a particular territory and shares racial, cultural, or historical characteristics that distinguishes

---

[30] Franck (1993, p. 16).

[31] See Christakis (1999, p. 298).

[32] Crawford (2000, p. 11).

[33] See "La notion de peuple en Droit International" in "Réalités du Droit International Contemporain", 3e rencontre de Reims, C.E.R.I., 1976, 117–278.

[34] See Scharf (2003, p. 380).

its members from the dominant population. In short, in order for a group to be entitled to the right of self-determination, it must possess a focus of identity sufficient for it to attain distinctiveness as a people. . .and demonstrate close connections to a particular territory."[35] However, what sometimes makes the claim of self-determination blurred is that it very often, and even systematically according to some authors, reflects a claim for territory under the guise of other considerations.[36]

Some authors attribute the lack of an acceptable definition of "people" to the fact that "nations and peoples, like genetic populations, are recent, contingent, and have been formed and reformed constantly throughout history."[37] While one may agree, as we have seen earlier, that the nations and peoples are a social phenomena marked by their own dynamic, it remains that in reality, the international community is not yet ready to bind its hands by a definition while the issue of the recognition of a people and therefore of a new state is a highly political one.[38] The matter is in fact left open to the interplay of power and influence, the power of a people to "impose itself" on the ground-a "people" does exist as such only *ex post facto*[39] – and by the will, influence, capacity and strength of supportive external actors.

Certainly, the contemporary practice "of lowering the standards for recognizing new states is a reflection of the inherent moral quality of statehood and of the general norm of self-determination and self-rule,"[40] but it is also a reflection of the globalization which leads to the fragmentation of states,[41] at least the weakest

[35] Javier Leon Diaz "Minority Rights. Status and Scope", http://www.javier-leon-diaz.com/docs/Minority_Status1.htm, 2.

[36] See Brilmayer (1991, p. 177).

[37] Kamenka (1988, p. 127).

[38] Robert McCorquodale writes in this regard that "In this aspect of the right state practice is not conclusive as recognition of a people as a "people" is ultimately a political decision, which may not accord with the legal position, and those entitled to the benefit of the protection of a right should not depend on the whims of governments", McCorquodale (1994, p. 6).

[39] Fernando R. Teson highlights in this respect that "Many international lawyers have understandably given up (to find a definition to "people") and have resorted to one of their favorite all-purpose tools: the principle of effectiveness which roughly holds that if a group fights and achieves its independence it must be recognized as such by other states, and then it becomes legally sovereign. An international lawyer confronted with a secessionist movement reasons as follows. If the secessionists win, then they form their own state, which third states must recognize because it is effective (i.e. the new government effectively exercises political power over the population in the territory), and the right of self-determination has been exercised. If the government wins, then there is no new state, third states ought to refrain from recognition because the rebels have no effective government, and the right of territorial integrity has been vindicated. As a consequence, if our imaginary lawyer is consulted *in advance* about the dispute he has to say that there are no preexisting principles and that the outcome can only be decided in the battlefield !", Teson (1998, p. 132).

[40] Holsti (2004, p. 49).

[41] Serge Sur has noted in this respect that "In recent years, the growth in the number of states formed through dissociation from already existing states has developed a new dynamic, in a new context and spirit. It could be said that international society has become a machine for destroying than producing states", Sur (1997, p. 3).

among them, as well as to the phenomenon of "glocalisation"[42] which may be the premise of new sub-territorial entities. While this new trend if any may be a chance for many forgotten peoples to recover their dignity, it may also seriously impact the stability, security and viability of the international system.[43]A reasonable solution would it not be to make of self-determination a really "Emerging Right to Democratic Governance"[44] and to simultaneously preserve the society from the "tyranny of the majority"[45] instead of adding difficulties to the peripheral multiethnic states? According to T.M. Franck, there are already signs towards a trend in that sense marked in particular by a practice where "the probable redefinition of self-determination does recognize an international legal right, not to secession but to democracy. In the transition from colonial to post-colonial contexts, the right (to

[42] Jean-François Baillard draws the attention in this regard that "L'un des grands apports de l'anthropologie postmoderne aura été de montrer comment la mondialisation sonne moins la "fin des territories" que leur réinvention à travers des effets de "glocalisation, c'est-a-dire de compactage des dimensions globale et locale, éventuellement (encore que non nécessairement) au détriment de l'intermédiation nationale", Baillard (2004, p. 189).

[43] "International stability", writes Stephane Dion, "is also a constant concern. Separatist movements are potential factors of disorder. If the international community is so clearly opposed to recognizing unilateral secession as an automatic right outside the colonial context, it is no doubt because a.) it would be very difficult to determine to whom that right should be granted.) because such an automatic right to secession would have dramatic consequences for the international community-with over 5,000 human groups each claiming a collective identity for itself in the world- and c.) because the creation of each new state would risk mobilizing, within that same state, minorities which would in turn stake their own claim for independence", Dion "Democratic Governance and the Principle of Territorial Integrity", op.cit., 4.

[44] Title of the article by Franck (1992, pp. 46–91). On the growing attention given by the doctrines to the right to democratic governance, see e.g. Fox and Roth (2000); Burchill (2006); Fabry (2009, pp. 721–741).

[45] One should indeed have in mind that "a mere right to democratic governance-laudable as it is – bears the risk of subjecting a people, which is a numerical minority, to the "tyranny of the majority. The interests of such numerical minority may therefore not be adequately protected by a proportion division of power", Klabbers and Lefeber (1993, p. 44). As insists to say H. Hannun "one person, one vote may not be sufficient", Hannum (1990, p. 471). Taking this into consideration, R. McCorquodale reasonably recommends that "Thus, instead of secession being the only option, peoples would be able to exercise their right to self-determination by such methods as the creation of a federation; guarantees of political power to defend or prompt group interest; the giving of special assurances (as with minority rights);providing for a specific recognized status to a group; or by "consociational democracy", McCorquodale (1994, p. 11). We know that the 1966 Covenant on Civil and Political Rights does ensure the protection of minorities rights (its Article 27 states that "In those states in which ethnic, religious or lo minorities exist, persons belonging to such minorities shall not be denied the right, in community with the other members of their group, to enjoy their own culture, to profess and practice their own religion, or to use their own language").These rights have been reiterated and expanded by the 1992 UN General Assembly Declaration on the Rights of Persons Belonging to National or Ethnic, Religious and Linguistic Minorities. Furthermore, there seems today, according to N. Lerner, a "agreement as to the need to take steps, nationally and internationally, to protect the rights, identity and preservation of ethnic, religious, and cultural groups, in order to ensure for all a basic list of rights.", "The Evolution of Minority Rights in International Law" in "Peoples and minorities in International law", op.cit. (1993), p. 100.

self-determination) is being reinterpreted in the practice of states to take on new vigor as the instrument for regional and global reinforcement of minimum standards of governmental legitimacy."[46] Amongst the signs to which T.M. Franck does allude, the most important is by far the issue of sharing of the power throughout territorial autonomy.

6.1.2 Power Sharing with Local Communities Through Territorial Autonomy

There is no generally accepted definition of territorial autonomy. It is so because there is no uniform model of autonomy. The content of territorial autonomy can vary from case to case depending on the relationship in terms of power struggle between the parties (i.e. the ethnic group concerned and the state to which it belongs), their negotiation skills and the degree of influence any external players might be able to exert in favor of one or another of these parties. Even so, a certain number of definitions of territorial autonomy have been put forward.

For instance, a fairly complex definition was suggested by Hannum and Lillich who see autonomy as referring to "independence of action on the internal or domestic level, as foreign affairs and defense normally are in the hands of the central or national government, but occasionally power to conclude international agreements concerning cultural or economic matters also may reside with the autonomous entity."[47]

A slightly clearer definition is put forward by Lapidoth who maintains that territorial autonomy means that "a sub-state entity has powers – often exclusive – of legislation, administration and, in certain cases, judiciary in specific areas".[48]

Finally, we should mention the definition advanced by S. Wolff and M. Weller which has the merit of being clearer and more comprehensive since it conceives of autonomy as "the legally entrenched power of ethnic or territorial communities to exercise public functions (legislative, executive and adjudicative) independently of other sources of authority in the state, but subject to the overall legal order of the state."[49]

What is fundamentally the determining factor in territorial autonomy is the effective enjoyment of territorial democracy by a given ethnic group. This is because "territorial democracy" is central to the notion of territorial autonomy as

[46] Franck (1993, pp. 20–21). Unfortunately, there are also signs which clearly show that, as noted by Serge Sur, that "the international society has not, until now, been in a position to ensure the development of new states or regimes, certainly not in terms of economic development, but also institutional, legal, political and social terms. While international society has produced states, it has hardly known how to build them, neither the states it has manufactured nor those which have somehow formed themselves against it", Sur (1997, p. 3).

[47] Hannum and Lillich (1980, p. 859).

[48] "Autonomie, unité et démocratie" in Le Coadic (2003, p. 267).

[49] Wolff and Weller (2005, p. 13).

it is the only instrument which allows full and effective enjoyment of democracy at sub-state level as well as of human rights by the members of ethnic communities. On that basis, territorial autonomy can be defined as the enjoyment, by a human group, of legislative, executive and possibly judiciary powers granted by the state as part of the exercising of territorial democracy.

As we have seen earlier, territorial autonomy is as old as the state. It was born out of the inability of the traditional state, since its first appearance thousands of years ago, to complete the territorialization process. Since it could not exercise direct power over communities often conquered by force, the state found itself forced to tolerate these same communities running their own affairs. This was the case both for single states and whole empires. It was the modern state which, from the sixteenth century, has put an end to the autonomy of communities and local peculiarities as it was able to implement a systematic policy of unification and homogenization of society, a policy which was consolidated by the nation-state at the beginning of the nineteenth century. Nonetheless, territorial autonomy reappeared in the second half of the nineteenth century and the beginning of the twentieth century when it was applied to great effect in the Åland Islands issue following the recommendation made by the League of Nations to give pre-eminence to territorial integrity on the right to self-determination, while still taking the latter into account in order to allow the community involved to govern itself. It was applied in several regions in the world and has taken on great significance during recent decades where it seems to be associated with postmodernity.

The world is entering an era of postmodernity where the state, as a result of globalization and the advance of democracy, must share its sovereign power with new players, sub-national in the first case and transnational in the second. The centralized state, which manages all aspects of life in society and submits it to a process of homogenization which does not connect human potentialities with local cultures, is disappearing in favor of a state which associates and draws together national and regional synergies. Territorial autonomy is simultaneously the incarnation and the institutional channel for this profound change in the state without which it cannot survive. But the current autonomy, that is associated with the postmodern state, is different from the *de facto* autonomy which prevailed in the context of the traditional state because it became institutionalized and then confused with the right to self-determination with which it has a tendency to form a complement necessary to the principle of national sovereignty.

The revival of territorial autonomy[50] has, as we have seen earlier, started to take place decades ago within the European context when, in order to avoid disadvantaged regions falling further into poverty and missing out on the

[50] Territorial autonomy can be defined as the enjoyment, by a human group, of legislative, executive and possibly judiciary powers granted by the state as part of the exercising of territorial democracy. This is because "territorial democracy" is central to the notion of territorial autonomy as it allows effective enjoyment of human rights by the members of ethnic communities. For other different definitions of territorial autonomy, see Hannum and Lillich (1980); Lapidoth (2003, p. 267); Wolff and Weller (2005, p. 13).

phenomenon of globalization, the European Commission has encouraged decentralization in disadvantaged economic regions in agreement with the countries concerned who saw in that process a means of promoting development in these regions.

Outside Europe, countries like the United States and Canada, have long since strengthened their symmetrical federalism by adopting cultural pluralism, based on the respect and the enhancement of the cultural and ethnic identity of all sections of their societies. Other countries, often those moving towards democracy, have ended up putting in place structures of territorial autonomy to reorganize their societies in order to make them more viable.

The recourse to territorial autonomy – with the exception of Kosovo whose independence ended a process which started with the disintegration of Yugoslavia and the creation of Slovenia, Croatia, Montenegro – has also often been recommended by Western democracies as an alternative solution to self-determination-independence, which is perceived as an important factor of instability and insecurity. This policy has been particularly followed these last 20 years or so by the European Union, the CSCE (to which OSCE succeeded) and the Council of Europe, in order to stabilize the situation in Central and Eastern Europe following the collapse of Yugoslavia and the USSR.

In the European context, interest in autonomy has been shown since 1990 when the matter came up at the Commission on Security and Cooperation in Europe (CSCE). Hence, at the Commission's meeting at Copenhagen in June–July 1990, convened to work out the mechanics for the protection of human rights, the member states of the CSCE adopted the Copenhagen Document of the CSCE Conference on the Human Dimension (29 June 1990) which states that:

> "The participating states note the efforts undertaken to protect and create conditions for the promotion of the ethnic, cultural, linguistic and religious identity of certain national minorities by establishing, as one of the possible means to achieve these aims, appropriate local or autonomous administrations corresponding to the specific historical and territorial circumstances of such minorities and in accordance with the policies of the state concerned."

Similarly, in 1993, the Parliamentary Assembly of the Council of Europe, recommended, albeit more clearly, that:

> "In the regions where they are in a majority, the persons belonging to a national minority shall have the right to have at their disposal appropriate local or autonomous authorities or to have a special status, matching the specific historical and territorial situation and in accordance with the domestic legislation of the state."[51](Art.11)

The Framework Convention for the protection of national minorities in Europe adopted on 1 February 1995 by the Council of Europe also refers implicitly to autonomy when it lays down that states:

[51] Recommendation 1201 (1993) re an additional protocol to the European Convention on the Rights of Man regarding the rights of national minorities, Annex, Art. 11.

> "shall create the conditions necessary for the effective participation of persons belonging to national minorities in cultural, social and economic life and in public affairs, in particular those affecting them."(Art.15)

The 1999 Lund Recommendations on the effective participation of national minorities in public life (which, drawn up by a group of experts, served as a point of reference and inspiration for numerous governments within the CSCE) recommended that states accept territorial arrangements which "open up more opportunities for national minorities to exercise their authority on the affairs concerning them."

Within the United Nations, the Working Group on Minorities of the Sub-Committee on the Promotion and Protection of Human Rights, which comes under the umbrella of the Commission of Human Rights, came also to the conclusion, at the end of several studies carried out since 1995 on the right to self-determination and minorities, that it was appropriate to adopt a different approach to the exercise of the right to self-determination; one which does not necessarily cause the break-up of states and which can be very useful in this respect.[52] It also noted the emergence of a new states' practice which lent importance to autonomy, conceived as an appropriate means of dealing with secessionist movements which have appeared in the last few decades.

The Security Council has also, albeit indirectly, lent its support to federalism, which constitutes a broad form of autonomy, when it gave its blessing to the discussions between Georgia and Abkhazia with a view to adopting a new Constitution founded on federalist principles.[53]

Finally, the United Nations have also, every time the Settlement Plan for the Sahara came up against a new obstacle, ended up recommending that the parties involved take a close look at territorial autonomy.[54]

Thus, initiated decades ago by some Western democracies, the move towards sharing power with subnational entities has expanded to different parts of the world to the extent that at present there are two dozen countries encompassing over 40% of the world's population that exhibit the fundamental characteristics of a functioning federation[55] and in which there are more than 500 local governments.[56] The appeal of federation- meant here in its largest sense, that is the sharing of power between the state and local communities – has been increasing so strongly due to its success in allowing greater economic welfare, respect for the rights of local communities and quality of life that "the federal idea is now more popular internationally than at any time in history."[57]

---

[52] See the Working Note submitted by Weller (2005).

[53] UN Doc. S: Res. 993, 1995.

[54] See El Ouali (2008, pp. 127–143).

[55] See Watts (2008, p. 1).

[56] Colomer (2007, p. xi).

[57] Idem, p. 7.

The popularity acquired by territorial autonomy has led the latter, recalls H. Hannum,[58] to be adopted or proposed as a solution in countries as diverse as Finland, Norway, Sweden, Belgium, Spain, Denmark, Hungary, Romania, Yugoslavia, Bosnia and Herzegovina, Italy, United Kingdom, Turkey, Iraq, India, China, Sri Lanka, Papua New Guinea, Cyprus, the Philippines, Bangladesh, Russia, Georgia, Azerbaijan, Sudan, Sudan, Senegal, Canada, United States, Mexico, Brazil, Nicaragua, Panama and one can add Western Sahara. Such unprecedented move has pushed Daniel J. Elazar to admit "as the dust of the Cold War settles in the 1990s, we find more federal arrangements in the world than ever before, covering more people than ever before. These can be seen as the foundation stones of (a) new paradigm...Autonomy (which) must be seen as a form of federalism, not only is needed as a means to satisfy demands for self-determination that cannot be satisfied by independent statehood, it fits well into the new federalist paradigm..."[59]

The tendency to recommend the application of territorial autonomy as a definite status of a given territory must be distinguished from the policy imagined in recent years which aims of making of territorial autonomy only a transitory phase which can lead to independence or a more robust form of autonomy. This was the formula chosen to bring an end to a certain number of conflicts such as those which affected East Timor, the Southern Sudan, Bougainville, Montenegro, etc. But this formula, which seems to attract the sympathy of certain writers,[60] was based either on the unavowed intention of certain international players to indirectly favor secession and have it endorsed by referendum after a set period of time had elapsed, which is what in fact happened in both East Timor, Montenegro and Southern Sudan, or on a more or less ambiguous agreements between the warring factions where one of the two protagonists was seeking to gain time, whereas the definitive outcome of the status of the territory in question remained in the balance and there was no guarantee that war would not be resumed. Time will tell if such has been the case of the agreements recently signed in respect of Bougainville, New Caledonia, etc. It is within the framework of the first alternative that the Baker Plan II for the Sahara is to be found, in as much as the conditions planned for the holding of a referendum certainly seem to favor a given solution to the conflict.[61]

Leaving aside the controversial question of provisional autonomy while awaiting a definitive solution on the status of a given territory, it seems that an ever-growing number of states are now showing considerable interest in territorial

[58] "Territorial Autonomy: Permanent Solution or Step toward Secession ?", www.indonesiamission-ny.org/issuebaru/Mission/empwr/paper_hurstHannum_1.pdf.

[59] Daniel J. Elazar "Commentary" in W. Danspeckgruber and A. Watts (eds.) "Self-Determination and Self-Administration. A Sourcebook", op.cit., p. 92 and 93.

[60] See, for example, Williams and Pecci (2004, p. 347 et seq).

[61] See El Ouali (2008, pp. 137–140).

autonomy as a means of settling ethnic conflicts which pose a dangerous threat to the territorial integrity of these states. The concept of territorial autonomy has been rediscovered by a certain number of states which are expressing less apprehension about it, insofar as "it was no longer seen as the secessionist's stepping stone towards independence, but instead, in a 180 degree reversal of the previous position, autonomy was now considered as a possible tool in accommodating separatist movements without endangering the continued territorial integrity of an existing state."[62] Yet it is too early to deduce from this tendency, as certain writers have been hasty to do,[63] that an obligation to grant autonomy actually exists. It is true that autonomy has been recommended and applied in a growing number of cases, but the euphemistic drafting used in the aforementioned texts and declarations recommending vesting a certain interest in the formula for autonomy is sufficiently eloquent to show that it is difficult to speak of the existence, within the context of the law as it currently stands, of an obligation on the part of states to grant autonomy.[64] Similarly, as we shall see, a number of states continue to be skeptical about the relevance of territorial autonomy as a means of solving ethnic conflicts since it seems no more than a provisional compromise or a first stage in an overall process of re-territorialization which these same states reject because it works to the detriment of their territoriality.

Thus, we are today seeing the emergence of a new paradigm where self-determination means not so much independence as the right to democratic governance. But this is nothing more than a return to the original state of affairs, that is in other words, the genuine sense of the right to self-determination as proclaimed by the English, American and French Revolutions and meaning nothing other than the principle of national sovereignty and the right to democratic government. Certainly, independence has made it possible to put an end to colonial oppression, but the process of decolonization is, except in a few rare cases, a thing of the past. The new era is one of liberation, no longer national but democratic. Today, states are enjoined to become democratic whereas ethnonationalisms are called to explore the advantages offered by territorial autonomy.

Although territorial autonomy is generally considered to be a variation of the right to self-determination, its potential to respond to the identity aspirations of local communities has not until now been sufficiently exploited by the international community. It is to the advisability and timeliness of exploring this potential that certain states have sought to draw attention at debates within the United Nations General Assembly during 1993 on the question of "the effective implementation of the right to self-determination in the form of autonomy." Among the states taking a clear stance along these lines, Liechtenstein was prominent in stressing that "the

[62] Wolff and Weller (2005, p. 2).

[63] See, for example, Cardenas and Canas (2002, p. 103); Steven C. Roach "Minority Rights and an Emergent International Right to Autonomy: A Historical and Normative Assessment", op.cit. (2004), p. 418 et seq.

[64] See in this connection, Weller (2005, p. 13).

principle of self-determination, as enshrined in the United Nations Charter and other important international legal instruments, still has unexplored potential which offers the possibility that progress might be made in the directions we seek, and autonomy offers a particularly helpful practical device which could be developed within the broad scope of that principle. All this led us to suggest that the international community should explore the possibility of communities' having a degree of autonomy. This concept is very flexible and can be used constructively to cover different aspects of self-determination and thereby tailor the degree of self-expression enjoyed by communities to whatever is appropriate in their particular circumstances."[65] But with the ongoing paradigmatic change, territorial autonomy will have an increasing tendency to stop being a variation in the right to self-determination and will simply become confused with that right or at least constitute one of its most significant expressions. This is due not only to the fact that the international community is more and more reluctant to accept the emergence of new states which, apart from their unviable character, are increasingly perceived as a source of insecurity for foreign countries and breeding grounds of terrorism,[66] but also the fact that territorial autonomy constitutes the surest means of allowing the peoples concerned to enjoy effective democracy and good governance. Territorial autonomy offers a better guarantee than the right to self-determination-independence when it is a question of allowing a populace to determine freely for itself within a democratic system where there is no barrier to the enjoyment of human rights, collective or individual. Whereas the former colonies, which have become independent through the application of the right to self-determination-independence, have very often been left to their own devices and have seen their basic rights flouted by the oligarchs who have taken over from the colonizers, it has been different for the majority of populations who have had territorial autonomy. This is because there can be no territorial autonomy without democracy and a system which effectively protects human rights. Fundamentally linked to the effective existence of democracy at the level both of the central Administration of the state and the autonomous region, territorial autonomy has the function of allowing the right to democratic self-determination to express itself fully and, in so doing, allow the postmodern state to survive.

Thus, the present transformation in the understanding of self-determination marks a break with the hegemonic conception of self-determination which has prevailed since the 1960s and which, as we have seen above, has made of the right of self-determination a mechanical right to independence. True, the international doctrine has in the past decades sensed the existence of democratic self-determination by making the distinction between external self-determination, i.e. the right to political independence, and internal self-determination, that is the right of a people to choose its own system of government, but it has neglected the latter element or minimized its importance by confining it to the "manifestation

[65] Declaration by Prince Hans-Adam II of Liechtenstein, UN General Assembly, 25 October 1993, A/48/PV.36.

[66] For an edifying study of this question, cf. Rosecrance and Stein (2006).

of the totality of the (individual) rights embodied in the (1966) Covenant",[67] while it is fundamentally the right of the people as a group and not as individuals. More gravely, the same doctrine, while noticing the inconsistencies of self-determination-independence, amongst which the most important being, as we have seen above, the tacit agreement between great powers aiming at refusing to fix the criteria that can objectively help determine the people that qualify for self-determination, has argued that self-determination-independence was a legal right or, according to some authors, even more, a peremptory norm,[68] while the International Court of Justice saw it as "one of the essential principles of contemporary International Law" and made it clear that the right of peoples to self-determination is today a right *erga omnes*.[69] However, it is believed that these inconsistencies as well as the "Janus faces" of self-determination would have the tendency to belong to the past as a consensus is being increasingly reached on the issue that self-determination has only one meaning: popular sovereignty, and only one implication: the establishment of democracy within existing states. The manipulation of self-determination by great and regional powers all over the past two centuries has led all over the world to chaotic situations where disintegration has become a recurrent phenomenon. However, while disintegration used to affect only targeted foreign states, today it has become, as a result of the still prevalent effect of the ideology of self-determination-independence as well as the destructive impact of globalization on social and national homogeneity and the ensuing exacerbation of all types of ethnonationalism, a serious threat to the stability and survival of all states, including great and regional powers. The latter have also started to be aware of the backfire effect of disintegrating foreign states which, by leading to the emergence of failed states, generates civil wars, illegitimate use of violence as well as terrorist actions which affect not only the expansion and normal functioning of globalization as well as regional peace and stability but sometimes also directly the security of those states which have been at the origin of the implementation of self-determination. These are the reasons behind the emergence of a new doctrinal approach to self-determination in which democracy and territorial autonomy are the most important components.

Indeed, today a new doctrinal approach to self-determination seems on the rise. It aims at recognizing "the importance of, even the priority of, a specifically democratic interpretation of self-determination"[70] by putting a great emphasis on human rights and democratic participation and by seeking to "open up more possibilities to deal with self-determination claims in the context of alternative political arrangements, such as autonomy, federalism, multiculturalism or

[67] Cassese (1995, p. 53).

[68] See for instance Hector Gros Espiell, "Self-Determination and Jus Cogens A. Cassese (ed.) in "UN/Fundamental Rights", 1979, p. 167; Laing (1991–1992).

[69] Eastern Timor case (Portugal v Australia), ICJ Report, 1995, para 29. This position has been reiterated by the Court in its advisory opinion of 9 July 2004, ICJ Reports, 2004, para 88.

[70] Gould (2006, p. 48). See also Gould (1988); Plotke (2003); Mello (2004, p. 202 et seq).

overlapping sovereignties."[71] This approach, which is largely shared by an increasing number of scholars, has emerged in reaction to the conventional approach which has been prevalent since the 1960s and contributed in drawing up the ideology of self-determination-independence. It, first, critically examines the inconsistencies of self-determination in respect of its legal nature and content. Deborah D. Cass, recalling the catalyst role played by self-determination in the sudden disintegration of the Soviet Union and Yugoslavia, notes with perplexity that "One could expect therefore that a principle so readily utilized in the international arena would possess a definite meaning. This is not the case. Current international theory regarding self-determination is in a state of uncertainty and confusion. It is inconsistent within itself, and does not accord with state practice."[72] It is that lack of consistency, recognizes M. Koskennieni, which renders self-determination a legally unsustainable and useless norm and condemns it to be in a situation where "it cannot be kept apart from political priorities in particular situations."[73] The new approach stresses also that peace and justice can be established only through full compliance with democracy requirements and human rights as well as through greater tolerance between ethnic groups and communities as "the imposition of one nationalist discourse upon a (more) complex political reality often leads to tension."[74] Emilio J. Cardenas and Maria F. Canàs stress in this regard that the permanent search for roads towards independence through the window of self-determination has been the source of too much blood shedding and has made of the world an arena "filled with a variety of 'all-or-nothing patriots', unwilling to tolerate, or even compromise with, those people whose minds are entrenched in the past. They are only capable of further divisiveness, unable to understand that in order to be united, one must take the past into account and also be willing that there is a future. The future cannot simply repeat the past. Yet they lean towards isolationism, reject universal value, systematically refuse to find common ground, and disregard the liberties and dignity of others."[75] It was that intolerance, underlines A. Etzioni, which has, with rare exceptions, pushed "self-determination movements to undermine the potential for democratic development in nondemocratic countries and threaten the foundations of democracy in the democratic ones. It is time to withdraw moral approval from most of the movements and see them for what they mainly are-destructive."[76] Furthermore, intolerance, notes D. Plotke, never comes to an end, even when separation becomes a reality, as "separation creates new conflicts, each of which has the potential to be serious. One conflict is between the new states – and now they have armies! India and Pakistan come to

[71] Barnsley and Bleiker (2008, p. 121).

[72] Cass (1992, p. 21).

[73] Koskennieni (1994, p. 265).

[74] Barnsley and Bleiker (2008, p. 128).

[75] Cardenas and Canas (2002, p. 157).

[76] Etzioni (1992, p. 21).

mind. Another conflict is likely to happen, especially within the smaller of the two separated states. Fresh from its experience of having been dominated, the temptation to build and purify the new nation by harsh means often proves difficult to resist. After separation, moreover, the problem of diversity is apt to arise again (and soon) in both new states."[77] More gravely, the end of the Cold War has shown that intolerance was not limited to third world ethnonationalism as in Europe the disintegration of the Soviet Union and Yugoslavia has, recalls M. Freeman, "encouraged 'ethnic cleansing and generated massive refugee flows; provoked violence and gross violations of human rights; and threatened international peace and security by involving great powers in local ethno-nationalist conflicts."[78] Triggered by intolerance, self-determination claims have very frequently created a spiral of violence and a radicalization of insurgents and states' stands with no other alternative than war. "Overall" notes M. Weller,[79] "the all-or-nothing game of self-determination has helped to sustain conflicts, rather than resolve them. Self-styled self-determination movements see no alternative to armed struggle or to the use of terrorist strategies to achieve their aims. Central governments see little alternative to violent repression... (these are the reasons why) self-determination kills (and that) self-determination conflicts are among the most persistent and destructive forms of warfare". Sharing the view that self-determination has, because of its inner incoherence, been at the origin of a great number of intense conflicts and civil wars, Martin Griffiths reflects the arising understanding of self-determination when she stresses that "Saving it (i.e. self-determination) from a complete descent into incoherence will require a renewal of the links between autonomy, democracy, human rights and the right to self-determination. . .Self-determination does not have to mean irredentism, secession and the violent renegotiation of territorial frontiers. The promotion of minority rights, devolution, federalism and greater acknowledgment of the legitimacy of cultural self-expression are all expressions of self-determination."[80] These are some of the main reasons behind the present shift towards a new paradigm where self-determination becomes democratic and where territorial autonomy is conceived of as one of its most important expressions.[81] It is to take account of that paradigmatic shift that a new definition of self-determination is needed.

---

[77] Plotke (2003, p. 480).

[78] Freeman (1998, p. 357).

[79] Weller (2008, pp. 19 and 13).

[80] Griffiths (2003, pp. 46–47).

[81] On the conception that territorial autonomy is one of the most important expressions of self-determination, see Calogeropoulos-Stratis (1973, p. 199); Lapidoth (1981, pp. 379–389); Brownlie (1988, pp. 1–16); Eide (1990, pp. 15–32); Steiner (1991, p. 1539 et seq).; Hannum (1990, pp. 473–475) and Hannum (1993, p. 64); Chen (1991, p. 1288); Buchanan (1992, pp. 351–352); Heraclides (1992, p. 400); Halperin et al. (1992, p. 47); Binder (1993, p. 248 et seq.); Tomuschat (1993, pp. 13–17); A. Eide "In Search of Constructive Alternatives to Secession" in C. Tomuschat, idem, pp. 170–173; Cassese (1995, pp. 352–359); Cleveland (1995, p. 75); Freeman (1998, p. 370); Hannikainen (1998, p. 90); M. Suksi "On the Retrenchment of Autonomy" in M. Suksi (ed.)

The paradox is that, in spite of the plethora of the literature on the right to self-determination,[82] it is very rare to find definitions for it, as the doctrine generally prefers to focus on the beneficiaries of this right. But here, too, the paradox is no more than apparent because the doctrine has, by becoming impregnated with the paradigm that has prevailed since the Second World War, often made its own the idea that the right to self determination is nothing other than the right to independence. Thus, translating a general sentiment, Cobban was able to define the right to self-determination as the right of each nation "to constitute an independent state and determine its own government."[83] But by so doing, Cobban, like most other commentators on the subject, confuses the right to self-determination with break-away nationalism for which would-be nations must have their own states.[84] This confusion was comprehensible in an historical context where the international community was mobilized in favor of independence for colonial countries. It can no longer be justified today because, save for a few rare exceptions, there are no more peoples to liberate from the yoke of colonialism. However, one of the challenges faced by the international community is to allow these peoples to enjoy dignity and freedom in their own countries. A change in the overall paradigm regarding the conception and practice of self-determination is from then on a real necessity if these peoples are to be helped to regain their dignity, liberty and identity. But this change can come about only if the right to self-determination is once more vested with its authentic and original meaning.

The right to self-determination finds its origins, as we have seen earlier, in the principle of popular sovereignty proclaimed by the English, American and French Revolutions. It can also be recalled that Woodrow Wilson, who taught Political Science before becoming President of the United States and who, as we know, played an important part in the promotion of the right to self-determination, reminded delegates to the Paris Conference of 1919 that "the right to self-determination is the logical corollary to popular sovereignty; it is a synonym of the principle that government must be founded on the consent of those governed". The right to self-determination is therefore fundamentally associated with democracy. In this connection, J. Salmon also reminds us that the right to self-determination is a principle "of

"Autonomy: Applications and Implications", op.cit. (1998), p. 164; W. Danspeckgruber and A. Watts (eds.) Introduction of "Self-Determination and Self-Administration. A Sourcebook", op.cit., pp. 22–23; the contributions to the forgoing book: Falk (1997, p. 63); Ruth Lapidoth, "Commentary", p. 68; H. Owada, "Commentary", p. 77; Daniel J. Elazar, "Commentary", p. 91; Fred W. Riggs, "Commentary", p. 126; M. Walzer, "Commentary", p. 128; J. Cardenas and Canàs (2002, p. 159).

[82] See, inter alia, Cobban (1945); Johnson (1967); Ronen (1979); Calogeropoulos-Stratis (1973); Rigo-Sureda (1973); Guilhaudis (1976); Alexander and Frieflander (1980); Hector Gros Espiell "The Right to Self-Determination: Implementation of United Nations Resolutions", E/CN.4/Sub.2/405/Rev.1, 1980; Pomerance (1982); Crawford (1988); Tomuschat (1993); Cassese (1995); Batistich (1995, p. 7); Sellers (1996), Musgrave (1997); Dahbour (2003); M. Weller (2008) "Escaping the Self-determination Trap", op.cit.

[83] Cobban (1969, p. 39).

[84] See Gellner (1983, p. 1).

democratic inspiration which singles out the vocation of peoples to run their own affairs freely."[85] The problem is that democracy can sometimes produce a "tyranny by the majority" to the detriment of minority groups in society. That is why the right to self-determination must also be designed in a way that prevents any injustice or discrimination between different communities making up a society. Its objective should also be to allow minority groups to play a full part in political, economic and social activity, preserve and pass on their culture and have their common identity reflected in the institutions of the government under whose authority they live.[86]

From that point on, it can be affirmed that the right to self-determination is the right which enables every people, already constituted into a state, to posses effective power allowing it self-government through the free choice of its political system and the establishing of the principles and rules that ensure that all members of society can live in dignity, enjoy their rights and fundamental freedoms and that minority groups can maintain their identity and play a full part in the taking of decisions connected with the nation as a whole and the various ethnic groups to which they belong within it. Such a definition is not purely academic, because it actually reflects the right to self-determination currently in progress.[87] Finally, and more especially, such a definition has the merit of taking account the fact that territorial autonomy is, alongside national sovereignty, an essential ingredient in the right to self-determination without which the latter has no meaning. However, while, territorial autonomy appears to be a crucial element in the definition of postmodern self-determination which aims at helping states survive, yet it can sometimes play also a disintegrative role due to its ambivalent character.

6.2 The Ambivalent Character of Territorial Autonomy

The *raison d'être* of territorial autonomy is to be consensual insofar as it aims to establish a compromise between the right of the state to preserve its territorial integrity and the request from an ethnic group to determine its own affairs. This compromise rests in the recognition, within the right to democratic self-determination, of the right of self-government of an ethnic group territorially based in the state. However, although conceived of as a consensual principle, autonomy has also the tendency to become conflictual and frequently even to trigger a process of deterritorialization and reterritorialisation to the detriment of the state.

Territorial autonomy is thus a very complex instrument because, at the same time when it allows the state to survive in a world where various factors, the most prominent of which is globalization, threaten its territoriality, it also weakens it by

[85] Salmon (2001, p. 828).

[86] Brownlie (1988, p. 5).

[87] A definition close to our own but which leaves aside the question of the rights of national groups is given by Paust (1980, p. 13).

reinforcing its centrifugal tendencies. Hence, while it appears more and more as a factor for survival in the postmodern state, territorial autonomy can be also a factor of state's destabilization and disintegration. In reality what makes of territorial autonomy an ambivalent institution is the fact that its foundation is consensual while its implementation is very often, if not always, conflictual. That is why it is imperative for its application that territorial autonomy be submitted to a certain number of conditions in order to allow it to function properly.

6.2.1 The Consensual Character of Territorial Autonomy

As we have seen earlier, the problem of the congruence between the state and the nation seems to be becoming a general phenomenon, albeit one which varies in intensity depending on whether the countries concerned are old or new. This is the primary motivation for states, whose territoriality is under threat, to accept sharing their sovereignty within the framework of territorial autonomy, the aim of which is to reconcile the right of the state to maintain its territorial unity and the right of the ethnic group concerned to maintain its identity. To measure the sacrifice that the state accepts to make in order to maintain national cohesion, it is worth remembering what, under the provisions of International Law, constitutes the respective rights of the state and the ethnic groups which have the status of national minorities.

When one compares the respective rights of the state and the minorities, one realizes that, under current International Law, the right of the state to preserve its territorial unity is almost absolute because it corresponds to state territoriality as well as the rights deriving therefrom and that there is no international regulation which obliges the state to waive these rights. Conversely, the right of minorities to preserve their identity is relative and limited because it has no territorial basis and is reduced to the enjoyment by members of these minorities of individual and cultural rights.

Traditionally, as we have seen above, International Law does not accept the emergence of a new state unless separation is accepted by the concerned preexisting state. All that can be done is the recognition of individual and cultural rights when it is firmly established that a human community does constitute a national minority. A national minority is generally defined as a non-dominant group in the society possessing its own ethnic, religious, linguistic and other similar characteristics which clearly set it apart from the rest of the population and which the said group intends to preserve.[88]

Shortly after the First World War, some international agreements were signed to protect national minorities in the states which had arisen from the ashes of war. These agreements guaranteed certain rights, including the right to nationality, the

[88] See Koubi (1995, p. 254).

right to one's own language, the right to education in the mother tongue, the right of property, etc. These rights, were to be protected by the Council of the League of Nations, but the Council was reluctant to exercise the role attributed to it due to the condemnation of those countries whose system had been imposed upon them by the victorious nations (who, for their part, had made no similar international commitment in favor of the minorities living in their countries).

It was the failure of this system of international protection which was to persuade the United Nations, after the Second World War, not to repeat the same experience. Preference would be given rather, as we shall see later, to the recognition of individual and cultural rights to the members of national minorities and the proclamation that the best protection that can be given to them is the enjoyment of human rights and fundamental freedoms in the same way as the rest of the population in the state to which they belonged. I. Claude has given an excellent summary of the new philosophy championed by the international community when he wrote that:

> "The general tendency of the postwar movements for the promotion of human rights has been to subsume the problem of national minorities under the broader problem of ensuring basic individual rights to all human beings, without reference to membership in ethnic groups. The leading assumption has been that members of national minorities do not need, are not entitled to, or cannot be granted rights of a special character. The doctrine of human rights has been put forward as a substitute for the concept of minority rights, with the strong implication that minorities whose members enjoy individual equality of treatment cannot legitimately demand facilities for the maintenance of their ethnic particularism."[89]

Convinced that the enjoyment of human rights and fundamental freedoms "without distinction of any kind, such as race, colour, sex, language, religion, political or other opinion, national or social origin, property, birth or other status" [90] was sufficient to ensure the protection of all individuals, the international community did not, therefore, think it necessary to adopt specific legal instruments to protect minorities. The only stance taken by the international community in favour of minorities was to oblige states to allow them to keep their own identity and characteristics. This obligation was contained notably in the famous Art. 27 of the International Covenant on Civil and Political Rights which stipulated that:

> "In those states in which ethnic, religious or linguistic minorities exist, persons belonging to such minorities shall not be denied the right, in community with the other members of their group, to enjoy their own culture, to profess and practice their own religion, or to use their own language."

The obligation to ensure the respect of the identity of minorities was solemnly restated in the Declaration on the Rights of Persons Belonging to National or Ethnic, Religious and Linguistic Minorities.[91] The Declaration proclaimed that:

---

[89] Claude (1955, p. 211).

[90] Article 2, of the International Covenant on Civil and Political Rights (1966) Resolution 47/135 of 18 December 1992.

[91] Resolution 47/135 of 18 December 1992.

> "States shall protect the existence and the national or ethnic, cultural, religious and linguistic identity of minorities within their respective territories and shall encourage conditions for the promotion of that identity." (Article 1)

But, in the eyes of the United Nations, preserving the cultural identity of a given minority cannot in any way be detrimental to the territorial integrity of the country concerned. In the aforesaid Declaration, therefore, the General Assembly laid down that:

> "Nothing in the present Declaration may be construed as permitting any activity contrary to the purposes and principles of the United Nations, including sovereign equality, territorial integrity and political independence of states." (Article 8.4)

But the individualistic and cultural approach of the United Nations in favor of national minorities showed its limits when actually applied in practice by the various countries insofar as it did not always allow these same minorities to preserve their identity. The reason was that this approach disregarded "territorial democracy" which is crucial factor without which it would be impossible to guarantee effective enjoyment of the rights recognized by International Law to national minorities. It is, after all, on this basis that a fair compromise can be reached between the rights of the state and those of national minorities.

The individualistic and cultural approach limited to the application of human rights and fundamental freedoms is far from adequate to provide *ethnocultural justice*, in other words "the absence of relations of oppression and humiliation between different ethnocultural groups."[92] Thus, after analyzing this approach and its real impact on national minorities, W. Kymlicka concludes that the application of human rights to members of these minorities can leave the door open to many injustices, since it can be biased by the traditional rules of the democratic game, including, in particular, majority voting which can be oppressive – the famous "tyranny of the majority" – with regard to these same minorities.[93] He proposes that these rights can be complemented by rights proper to national minorities such as the right to use their languages, the right to self-government, the right to appropriate political representation, the right to autonomy within a federal context, etc. It would require, he goes on, a new conception of the rights of minorities which would lie between the right to self-determination conceived as a right to independence, which is deemed too strong, and the recognition of individual and cultural rights which is considered too weak and inadequate.[94] Some writers think this is already the case and that nowadays a fairly comprehensive legal regime exists in favor of minorities where the protection of their individual and cultural rights includes "a corollary principle [which] is the right of national peoples to exercise some degree of autonomy within existing states to govern their own affairs."[95] In fact, this regime

[92] Kymlicka (2001, p. 72 note 4).

[93] Idem, p. 69 et seq.

[94] Idem, p.123 et seq.

[95] Gurr (2000, p. 278).

does not exist yet because, as we have seen above, International Law still does not turn territorial autonomy into a legal obligation for the states. We can regret that, but this is the present state of positive law. Nonetheless, there is a growing interest among a certain number of states for the territorial autonomy formula.

The reason for this interest in territorial autonomy can be found in the fact that the exacerbation of ethnic conflicts can result in the individualistic and cultural approach to the rights of citizens belonging to a given national minority seeming out of date. This happens particularly when the ethnic group no longer recognizes itself in the state because it feels subject to discrimination or structural violence on the part of that same state which prevents it from leading a normal decent life. Structural violence exists particularly when "the institutional structures in place prevent (a given ethnic group) from satisfying its needs in terms of human development, such as security as well as effective, just and fair participation (in managing public issues)."[96] This possibly gives rise to ethno-nationalism when the "identity entrepreneurs"[97] succeed in mobilizing members of an ethnic group against the discrimination and domination of the state.[98] Such mobilization is never without ulterior motives, because it often finds its first expression in the search for power by local élites even if this can result (often thanks to the involvement of foreign players when this works to their advantage) in the disintegration of their own state. That search for power never stops, even when local population is granted territorial autonomy. That is why, as we shall see hereafter, many states continue to be skeptical about the relevance of territorial autonomy as a means of solving ethnic conflicts since it seems no more than a provisional compromise or a first stage in an overall process of re-territorialization which these same states reject because it works to the detriment of their territoriality.

6.2.2 The Conflictual Character of Territorial Autonomy

Since secession appears to be unacceptable to the international community, except in case of massive violations of human rights, the only reasonable prospect available to warring factions for resolving the possible contradiction between "a relationship of social domination which can be countered by a form of collective resistance"[99] is to introduce measures aimed at adjusting the exercise of power within the state. Today, this adjustment tends to take the form of territorial autonomy organized in such a way as to grant self-government to the minority

[96] Samarasinghe et al. (2001).

[97] Expression used more and more to describe local elites whose first motivation is the take over of power even if that supposes the destruction of their own state. See, for example, B. Badie (2002, p. 63).

[98] See Brass (1985, p. 28).

[99] Noreau and Vallet (2004).

concerned and allow it to enjoy territorial democracy. The only drawback is that this formula can in turn create another problem because it frequently, if not always, whets the appetite for power on the part of new autonomous entities that thirst for reterritorialization to the detriment of state territoriality. A new conflicting situation arises where the state finds itself on the defensive, facing assault from autonomous entities claiming more and more powers.[100] It is because they realized that this dynamic was full of dangers for their territoriality that certain states have put a brutal end to the experience of territorial autonomy, whereas others have tried to counter the assaults on their territoriality by making as few concessions as possible on the enlargement of the regime of autonomy. Such a situation, engaging the parties in a new spiral of tension and violence, is dangerous for the stability of states.[101] It requires the putting in place of conditions capable of breaking the vicious circle of conflictuality (by conflictuality it is meant here the tendency of territorial autonomy to become conflictual, i.e. to generate repetitive conflicts). It is worth pointing out the constituent elements in this resurgence of conflictuality before analyzing these conditions.

6.2.2.1 The Resurgence of Conflictuality

Apparently, the only time conflict seems to fade into the background is when the warring factions sign their agreement on territorial autonomy, because fairly often, the antagonism does not go away either before or after that time. This is partly due to illusions and perhaps also to misunderstandings or ulterior motives. "Offered reticently by the state and received ungratefully by the autonomous entities,"[102] territorial autonomy very quickly provokes antagonism, particularly on the level of power to be granted to the autonomous entities. This antagonism manifests itself at the stage of negotiations, where the choice is to be made between symmetrical and asymmetrical forms of autonomy. It arises after the autonomy has been put in place, because the autonomous entities, caught up in the whirlwind of power, are continually trying to increase this power to the detriment of the state.

The Opposition Between Symmetrical and Asymmetrical Autonomy

In general, States are firmly opposed to an asymmetrical form of territorial autonomy.[103] Autonomy is called asymmetrical when it grants a particular status to

---

[100] Another type of conflict also arises fairly frequently but this time within the new autonomous entity and not between the latter and the state. This conflict has been analyzed as benefiting the state insofar as territorial autonomy or, in a general way, federalism, causes hostility to deviate in respect of central government towards the new political institutions (the new autonomous entities) and also causes political competition to deviate towards local level, Levine (1999, p. 331).

[101] See the edifying study by Cornell (2002, pp. 245–276).

[102] Lapidoth (1994, p. 289).

[103] See McCray (2005).

a given region among the other regions within the country. In practice, states try, as far as possible, to avoid such a situation arising, and do so for three main reasons. The first is that such asymmetry potentially strengthens nationalism within the ethnic group in question and results in this group seeing itself more and more as a "nation", a nation which would be entitled to enjoy self-determination and thus acquire independence for itself. The second reason is that an asymmetric autonomy can in its turn, this time at the level of the newly autonomous region, create inequalities between the dominant ethnic group and any other smaller minorities. The third reason is that an asymmetric autonomy interferes with equality between all regions in the country, which, in time, can encourage the emergence or radicalization of other identity issues which thus might well cause the break-up of the whole country. It is particularly for this last reason that the French government, for instance, has constantly showed itself resolutely opposed to the granting of any significant degree of autonomy to Corsica for fear of provoking claims for similar status from the Bretons, Alsatians, Basques, etc., something which, in its eyes, could provoke the break-up of France. It is with a view to avoiding the drawbacks of asymmetric autonomy that certain states have tried to conceive systems of autonomy favoring all regions in the country and not one exclusively. This was, for example, the policy followed by the federal government in Canada which constantly took care, every time the province of Quebec managed to wrest additional powers from the Federation, to extend these same powers to all the other provinces. Spain also thought it necessary to extend autonomy to all regions in the country and not to reserve the status simply to Catalonia, the Basque country and Galicia. Expressing the same concern as states, regarding the possible destabilizing consequences of asymmetric autonomy, the OSCE also recommended using the formula of symmetric autonomy applicable in a general and similar way to all regions in a country.[104] Nevertheless, it can happen that the states concerned have no choice but to adopt asymmetric autonomy when a national minority has political backing from foreign states with sufficient power to help it impose that type of autonomy. It also happens where the ethnic minority is sufficiently strong to impose this type of autonomy. Finally, it might well be in the interest of a country not to insist on a symmetric form of autonomy as that can sometimes radicalize demands from ethnic groups who might even reach the point of seeking secession from the nation and no longer stay within its bosom.[105]

It has been established that asymmetry leads necessarily to resymmetrisation in so far as the state concerned is obliged to gradually and fatally grant similar and equal powers to all the regions without exception.[106] Resymmetrisation leads to the weakening of the state which finds itself dispossessed of a great amount of powers. Now, such weakening of the state may in the long run facilitate its own

[104] See W. Kymlicka "Reply and Conclusion", op.cit. (2001), p. 361.

[105] See J. McGray "Asymmetrical Federalism and the Plurinational State", op.cit. (2005), p. 12.

[106] See Requejo and Nagel (2011).

disintegration. But, certain writers consider states' apprehension about asymmetric autonomy, and its possible impact on the unity of the state, unfounded or exaggerated. They note that only very few instances of asymmetric autonomy have resulted in secession.[107] Other commentators are of the opinion that symmetric autonomy is not without dangers for the unity of the state either. Thus, according to W. Kymlicka, even the most perfected form of symmetric autonomy, namely federalism, can lead to the break-up of a state. The paradox is that it is the very success of the federation as a formula which can provoke an impulse to secede. On this subject, he writes that "the very success of federalism in accommodating self-government may simply encourage national minorities to seek secession. The more that federation succeeds in meeting the desire for self-government, the more it recognizes and affirms the sense of national identity amongst the minority group, and strengthens their political confidence. Where national minorities become more politically mobilized in this way, secession becomes more conceivable, and a more salient option, even with the best-designed federal institutions".[108] It is this same dynamic of strengthening group identity and the need for it to affirm itself as a "nation" which is very often behind the exacerbation of conflictuality and the tendency of autonomous entities to gain more powers.

The Exacerbation of Conflictuality: The Tendency for Autonomous Entities to Gain More Power

It is an established fact that, in general, agreements on power-sharing between governments and insurgents rarely produce a lasting peace. Thus, of the 61 such agreements concluded between 1944 and 1999, 27 were followed by civil war breaking out again when insurgents saw that the state was weak and that they had good chances of gaining the upper hand.[109] Since this involved the granting of territorial autonomy, it did not always result in a total end to armed conflict. Ted R. Gurr noted that of the 30 ethnic conflicts which were, in theory, meant to be brought to an end by the agreements on territorial autonomy, 13 continued or were resumed between the parties concerned.[110] This is because ethno-nationalists are often divided on the objectives to be attained and do not recognize each other under one leadership.[111] Here, a growing number of writers are of the opinion that the granting of territorial autonomy does not reduce the number of ethnic conflicts and the desire to secede, but, rather, it intensifies them insofar as it strengthens the ethnic identities of the populations concerned and provides the groups representing

---

[107] Idem and the doctrine cited, p. 14 et seq.

[108] Kymlicka (2001, p. 113).

[109] See Mukherjee (2006, p. 479 et seq).

[110] Gurr (2002, p. 203).

[111] Idem, p. 207.

them with additional tangible resources which allow them to bring increased pressure to bear on central government.[112] Thus, the granting of territorial autonomy does not necessarily put an end to the conflictuality which characterizes relations between the state and the ethnic groups opposed to it. But if war continues to prevail in a little under half the cases where territorial autonomy has been granted, conflict almost systematically continues to prevail in legal terms, the aim being on the part of the ethnic groups concerned to wrest the maximum degree of power possible from the state and to do so within a dynamic of re-territorialization aimed at calling into question the latter's territoriality.

Territorial autonomy is inspired by a dynamic which is quite particular to it: the quest for the continual extension of the powers of autonomous entities. This growth has been seen in some, if not all, territorial autonomy experiments seen around the world since the First World War. In the case of the Åland islands, for example, territorial autonomy, which was partially put in place as early as 1920, "has been expanded step by step to a point where it can be qualified as a 'state in the state', just short of independence."[113] In Belgium, enlargement of the regime of autonomy, which took the form of a federation, has gone so far and so quickly that "lucidity makes it necessary to admit that, in a federal state formed by disintegration (of former unitary state), the existence of autonomist pretensions weakens more than elsewhere the feeling of belonging to one single national community... In truth, weaknesses inexorably impinge on the sovereignty of the state. The scenario of the dislocation of the Belgian state structure is within the realm of possibility."[114] The increase of the power of autonomous entities is thus an open, dynamic and irreversible phenomenon,[115] but one which is often not peaceful because it is nearly always accompanied by virtually permanent state of conflictuality engendered by the desire of the state to preserve its prerogatives as circumscribed by the agreement on autonomy and the desire of the new sub-state entity to reduce these prerogatives to the maximum. Another striking example is that of regionalization within the European Union.

We have seen earlier how the European Commission has, with the view of avoiding disadvantaged economic regions falling further into poverty and missing out on the phenomenon of globalization, encouraged decentralization in disadvantaged regions in agreement with the countries concerned who saw that process as a

[112] See the bibliography cited by Brancati (2006, p. 652).

[113] T. Benedikter "The working autonomies in Europe: Territorial autonomy as a means of minority protection and conflict solution in the European experience – An overview and schematic comparison" www.gfbv.it/3dossier/eu-min/autonomy.html.

[114] M. Verdsussen "Le fédéralisme belge", www.unisi.it/ricerca/dip/dir_eco/COMPARATO/verdussen.doc.

[115] T. Benedikter "The working autonomies in Europe: Territorial autonomy as a means of minority protection and conflict solution in the European experience – An overview and schematic comparison", op.cit. See also the recent analysis of various cases made by the contributors to Ferran Requejo and Klaus-Jurgen Nagel (eds.) "Federalism Beyond Federations. Asymetry and Processes of Resymmetrisation", Burlington, Ashgate.

means of promoting development in these regions. Thus, some regions, certain of whom have traditionally constituted the territorial base of stateless nations (Catalonia, Scotland, Wales, etc.), have benefitted from progressive decentralization accompanied by financial aid from the European Regional Development Fund (since 1975) and the countries concerned. The policy of decentralization followed by the European Union has, while successfully and effectively promoting the development of certain regions, given a number of these regions the opportunity to emerge as more or less autonomous players on the international scene thanks notably to their involvement in the phenomenon of economic globalization. This has reinforced the regional and even nationalist sentiments of certain regional communities, thus creating a new dynamic which could in the future, were the European Union, for any reason, to withdraw its regional aid, strengthen the potential to cause a split between nation and state in the countries concerned.

It is undeniable that economic decentralization has, by encouraging the idea of territorial autonomy, created in the minds of a certain number of regional communities a strong desire to strengthen the situations newly acquired in terms of the powers to manage their own local affairs which they tend more and more to consider as being subnational or even downright national in character. Thus, to take the example of Catalonia, there have been constantly growing demands from local élites for greater autonomy and official recognition of what they think of as the Catalan "nation". As we know, the Spanish Constitution of 1978 has, while proclaiming the unity and indivisibility of the Spanish nation, recognized the right to autonomy of "nationalities and regions" and granted these areas (17 autonomous regions) fairly far-reaching legislative and executive powers. These powers have allowed the Catalans to manage their own affairs in matters of education, health, culture, housing, local transport, agriculture and local police; whereas central government has retained exclusive powers in the areas of defense, foreign policy, justice and general economic planning. As a result, Catalonia has made huge economic strides and, between 1987 and 1997, attained levels of economic growth in line with those of the *Länder* in Germany. Compared with other European regions, in terms of its GNP, it rose from 108th to 68th rank.[116] But although it has become, as the Catalans themselves avow, a "region with a democratic regime and enjoying the respect of its identity"[117]and has done so within a general Spanish context where "in many respects, autonomous governments act as *states* [our emphasis], at least they do so in respect of the powers at their disposal,"[118] Catalonia has not, however, ceased in recent years to be at loggerheads with central

[116] See Auberni (2003, p. 305).

[117] Idem.

[118] Montserrat Guicbernau "Entre autonomie et sécession : la prise en compte du nationalisme minoritaire en Catalogne" in Le Coadic (2003, p. 291).

government to claim the devolution of more powers.[119] Multiple concessions were made at the outset by the Spanish government, but the latter has often affirmed that it is even less prepared to grant new ones for fear of provoking a breakup of the Spanish state, particularly at a time when the number of Catalans in favor of secession is increasing.[120] But that has not prevented the Catalans from wrenching from the Spanish government a firmer statute of autonomy, adopted by referendum in July 2006.

Conceived at the outset solely as a means of economic development in the poor regions of the European Union, decentralization ended by becoming an opportunity for the rebirth of nationalist sentiments at all levels of society in the countries concerned. It was the possibility of such a situation actually occurring which traditionally encouraged certain states to show great reticence in accepting territorial autonomy.

6.2.2.2 The Reluctance of Certain States to Accept Territorial Autonomy

It is undeniable that many states are in principle very reticent, if not opposed, to the idea of applying territorial autonomy as a means of solving ethnic conflicts.[121] This is because territorial autonomy is seen as an institution which can weaken and call into question the sovereignty of states and also one which can pave the way for secession.[122] On this point H. Hannum thinks that, over recent decades, ethnic groups have started off by claiming protection of their identity through the preservation of their language, religion and culture, then gradually claiming greater political power through territorial autonomy and finally demanding secession with a view to creating their own state. When all is said and done, granting territorial autonomy to a particular ethnic group can encourage other ethnic groups within the same state or in neighbouring states to claim the same status, which can then lead to the break-up of the state. That is why the international community has always maintained that the most reasonable way of promoting the rights of national minorities is nothing other than respect for human rights and the fundamental freedoms of the people and the existence of a state respecting these rights. This has been eloquently set out by the Group of Experts on National Minorities set up

---

[119] This conflict was made worse by the complexity of Spanish constitutional provisions on autonomy. "The system (of Spanish autonomy), writes Carlos Flores Juberias, is very complex, a characteristic which has to a certain extent been behind the enormous conflict it generated", "Regionalization and Autonomy in Spain: The Making of the 'Estado delas Autonomias'" in Suksi (1998, p. 209).

[120] Idem, p. 296.

[121] Amongst the countries which are wildly opposed to the idea of autonomy, there are in particular the ex-communist countries who, having themselves just come out of a regime of territorial autonomy, are very well acquainted with the dynamic of reterritorialisation which inspires autonomous entities.

[122] Buchanan (1995, p. 54).

by the CSCE which, at its meeting in Geneva on 19 July 1991, emphasized in this regard that:

> "The participating states stress the continued importance of a thorough review of implementation of their CSCE commitments relating to persons belonging to national minorities. They [the participating states] emphasize that human rights and fundamental freedoms are the basis for the protection and promotion of rights of persons belonging to national minorities. They further recognize that questions relating to national minorities can only be satisfactorily resolved in a democratic political framework based on the rule of law, with a functioning independent judiciary. This framework guarantees full respect for human rights and fundamental freedoms, equal rights and status for all citizens, including persons belonging to national minorities, the free expression of all their legitimate interests and aspirations, political pluralism, social tolerance and the implementation of legal rules that place effective restraints on the abuse of governmental power."[123]

It is by starting from this basic assumption that the protection of the rights of a given minority was to be embodied in the application pure and simple of human rights and fundamental freedoms, as laid down in international instruments in favor of all men irrespective of origin or social or ethnic background and that for a long time the international community was very reticent to have recourse to territorial autonomy to resolve ethnic conflicts.

Thus, within the UN Human Rights Commission, the Working Group of the Sub-Committee on the Prevention of Discrimination and the Protection of Minorities has, as we saw above, paid particular attention in the last decade to the question of the relationship between the right to self-determination and autonomy. The amount of information the Working Group amassed on the various experiences, the reports and notes it produced and the debates and discussions these gave rise to have shown that there is a common perception of certain fundamental questions including in particular the fact that autonomy and integration must be conceived as complementary approaches, that autonomy does not necessarily have to be territorial in character and that, on the other hand, special attention must be paid to cultural autonomy.[124]

Similarly in Europe, the concern raised by the nature of territorial autonomy to be a force for disintegration encouraged the promotion of a policy essentially aimed at according priority to individual and functional autonomy. This policy was applied by the Council of Europe (CoE), the Organization for Security and Cooperation in Europe (OSCE) and the European Union (EU).

Thus, legal standards for the protection of minorities and the CoE Framework Convention for the protection of national minorities in Europe show a clear preference for individual rights. It is true that the Assembly of the CoE had in 1993 suggested adopting an additional protocol on the rights of minorities in the European Convention on Human Rights in which the draft of Art. 11 stipulated that

[123] Report of the meeting of Experts of the CSCE on national minorities, International Legal Materials, 1991.

[124] See Weller (2005, p. 2).

"In the regions where they are in a majority, the persons belonging to a national minority shall have the right to have at their disposal appropriate local or autonomous authorities or to have a special status, matching the specific historical and territorial situation and in accordance with the domestic legislation of the state." But this draft article was abandoned because of the vehement controversy it provoked in Europe.

The OSCE, for its part, constantly adhered to the principle of territorial integrity. This was reflected, first of all, in the Final Act of Helsinki of 1975 which, although affirming "the equal rights and self-determination of the people" (Principle VIII), nevertheless insisted on the obligation of states to respect the inviolability of borders (Principle III) and the territorial integrity of other states (Principle IV). This was subsequently reflected in the conservative and conciliatory role which the OSCE played, after the re-emergence of ethnic and minority conflicts in central and Eastern Europe following the break-up of the USSR and Yugoslavia. In this regard, Max van der Stoel, High Commissioner for National Minorities at the OSCE, a post created in 1992, played a crucial role in the calming of ethnic tensions and the promotion of a policy of minority integration. He was notably behind the launch of the meetings of experts which led to the adoption of the Lund Recommendations, the aim of which was to find a balance between the legitimate interests of states and minorities.[125] He was preoccupied with the exacerbation of ethnic identity issues which, in his eyes, risked in the long run pushing to disintegration of the states born out of the ruins of the USSR and Yugoslavia. This is why he will finally come down in favor of cultural autonomy to the detriment of territorial autonomy, arguing that even if the Copenhagen Document mentions territorial autonomy as a possible option, minorities must bear in mind that a demand of territorial autonomy will meet resistance and that they might achieve better results if they concentrated on legislation which enable them to have their say on questions as important as education and culture. More than this, he will not hesitate to declare that in his opinion, insufficient attention has been paid to the possibilities offered by non-territorial autonomy.[126]

Finally, the line followed by the EU consisted of endorsing the legal standards applicable to national minorities adopted by the OSCE and giving its backing to the moderate policy applied by the High Commissioner for National Minorities, to whom it delegated the task of checking whether the policies applied by central and Eastern Europe complied with the rights of minorities.[127] What determined this policy was the EU's need to provide very significant support to the efforts aiming at constructing nations in those countries. Clearly opposed to secession, the EU's policy on ethnic and minority conflicts in the countries of Central and Eastern Europe was aimed at facilitating access for minorities to the culture of the majority,

[125] See W.E. Kemp "Applying the Lund Recommendations: Challenges for the OSCE", www.isn.ethz.ch/4isf/Papers/ISF_WS_III_3_Kemp.pdf.

[126] "Reply and Conclusion" in W. Kymlicka and M. Opalski (2000, p. 361).

[127] Idem, p. 375.

rather than protecting the cultures of these minorities.[128] It was to this end that the EU adopted a Directive[129] on the respect of individual rights and the application of equal treatment of people irrespective of their ethnic or racial origin. Nevertheless, on occasion, its approach was geared more to the rights of groups while still recommending the adoption of arrangements based on power-sharing within a framework of culture and not territorial autonomy as was the case for Bulgaria, Romania and Slovakia.[130] The policy thus pursued by the EU was very effective thanks to the way it presented and implemented the social provisions it successfully applied as part of the process of Europeanization aimed at integrating new members to the Union. Nevertheless, an individualist and cultural approach can sometimes prove to be unsuitable and pave the way for a more ambitious formula, that of self-government as part of territorial democracy and to attain that by actually putting in place territorial autonomy, which can, depending on the circumstances and the various powers at force, be of either the symmetric or asymmetric variety. That is why it is advisable that some measures be taken in order to break the vicious circle of conflictuality.

6.2.3 Breaking the Vicious Circle of Conflictuality

To break the vicious circle of conflictuality, the state must firstly resume and strengthen its traditional role aiming at establishing congruence between it and the nation. This is a fundamental prerequisite in order for the state to ensure its own durability and continuity. But if the hyphen between the state and the nation is made difficult as a result of the persistence of ethnic antagonism and the state has no alternative other than accepting a regime of territorial autonomy, the latter has then to be conceived in a just and fair manner and in a way that prevents the exacerbation of this antagonism.

There are no magic recipes or pre-conditions for the consensual functioning of territorial autonomy, nor is it, incidentally, recommended for every situation.[131] It is even sometimes better not to put in place a system of autonomy than to have one which risks worsening relations between the state and the ethnic group or groups involved.[132] However, it remains a fact that among all the requisite conditions for territorial autonomy, there are two which are of a fundamental importance – effective democracy and regional integration.

[128] Noutcheva et al. (2004, p. 20).

[129] Council Directive 2000/43/EC of 29 June 2000.

[130] Cf. M. Brusis "The European Union and the Interethnic Power-Sharing Arrangements in Accession Countries", www.historyjournals.de/articles/hjg_eartic-j0005.html.

[131] On this, see the study by Mozaffar and Scarritt (2000, pp. 231–253).

[132] See Horowitz (2000, p. 601 et seq).

6.2.3.1 Effective Democracy

It might appear something of a paradox to bring up the question of democracy here when we know that often if not always, democracy has difficulty taking root and developing where there is ethnic heterogeneity. Did not John Stuart Mill in this regard show that democracy is almost impossible in a country made up of different nationalities?[133] Today, it is also proven that democracy has been able to take on concrete shape only in those countries where the process of building the state and nation is very old, in other words where the state has had sufficient time for its society to homogenize. Conversely, in societies where the state is a recent phenomenon, there are significant risks that these societies will remain heterogeneous and that "ethnic fragmentation may result in the break-up of the state or the change of regime, which may have serious repercussions on democracy".[134] For all that, it is nonetheless suggested that "democracy is the only regime that can handle ethnic cleavages in a manner that presents any hope of political stability in a country with strong ethnic fragmentation."[135]

Both the stability of states and international security as well as better protection of national minorities require preeminence to be given, in situations where ethnic conflicts seem irredeemably unsolvable, to local democracy by the establishing of a system of territorial autonomy. "It is this type of situation", B. Badie recalls, "which implies institutional arrangements favorable to the expansion of democracy (which in his eyes) supposes the reactivation of forms of local democracy, integrating communities nearby and the traditional structures of authority in the mobilization of citizens."[136] But the idea of calling on democracy to resolve ethnic problems is not new. Some 40 years ago, Arend Lijphart suggested such an approach within what he called "consociational democracy", which aimed to iron out the negative aspects of majority democracy[137] by allowing all sections of the population to share power and do so through four structures: a grand coalition between all ethnic groups to govern together, the provision to these groups of a right of veto in the decision-making process, the allocation of official positions and financial resources in the

---

[133] Mill "Considerations on Representative Government" in "Mill, Utilitarism, Liberty, and Representative Government "(1861), New York, E. P. Dutton, 1951, 486.

[134] Lane and Ersson (2003, p. 106).

[135] Idem.

[136] Badie (2002, pp. 69–70).

[137] Lijphart notes here that in plural societies, in other words, societies which are deeply divided depending on religious, ideological, linguistic, cultural, ethnic and racial allegiances and which virtually consist of separate subsocieties, with each one having its own political party, its interest group and means of communication, the flexibility needed for majority democracy is absent. In these conditions, the law of the majority is not only antidemocratic, but also dangerous, because the minorities to whom access to power is constantly denied will feel themselves excluded and that they are victims of discrimination. They will cease showing allegiance to the regime, Lijphart (1984, p. 22).

state based on ethnic proportionality and finally the granting of a federal type autonomy.[138]

Thus, there can be no territorial autonomy without democracy alongside a system which effectively protects human rights. In this regard it has been clearly shown how the lasting nature of territorial autonomy is linked to the effective existence of democracy at the level of both state and autonomous region.[139]

There can be no territorial autonomy without democracy and, in turn, a true democracy cannot be effective if it does not neutralize the negative aspects of majority democracy by granting the different sections of a plural society the right to govern themselves within consociational democracy based on a real sharing of power. This is because "there is an interaction between plural societies and consociational democracy: the former are a condition of the latter, the latter reinforces the former and makes it easy for them to pass into the public arena and the field of politics."[140] But more than that, the special nature of territorial autonomy, conceived within the framework of consociational democracy, is fundamentally to be a consensual means of allowing the effective enjoyment of the right to self-determination in order to ensure the preservation and respect of the identity of a given group and the participation of the latter in the exercising of power within a given society. Thus, it seems as well that if popular sovereignty has remained a fiction since it first appeared insofar as the people have never, except on rare exceptional occasions, been able to exercise such sovereignty, it is otherwise in the case of territorial autonomy because the latter's *raison d'être* is to allow the minority concerned not only to determine matters for itself by acquiring autonomous status, the terms of which it is authorized to negotiate, but also to govern itself effectively. We are thus a long way from the irrational human and territorial configurations and antidemocratic regimes which were created through the sham application of the right to self-determination to a number of colonial countries.

The relation between territorial autonomy and democracy is not one of speculation and theory. Indeed, it is a well-established fact that territorial autonomy has lasted only where democracy has prevailed. Thus, it has certainly been proved that territorial autonomy has failed where there is no democracy. After making such a comment, R. Lapidoth concludes that the condition *sine qua non* for territorial autonomy to succeed is that "the regime, both centrally and regionally, must be democratic."[141] Similarly, the Lund Recommendations are formal here when they affirm that "institutions of self-governance, whether non-territorial or territorial,

---

[138] Among his writings, see Lijphart (1969, pp. 205–225) and Lijphart (1977).

[139] See Kjell-Ake Nordquist "Autonomy as a Conflict-Solving Mechanism –An Overview" in M. Suksi (ed.) "Autonomy: Applications and Implications", op.cit. (1998), p. 69 et seq.

[140] Sindjoun (2000, p. 3).

[141] Lapidoth (2003, p. 277).

must be based on democratic principles to ensure that they genuinely reflect the views of the affected population."[142] Recent studies have also shown that where democracy is effective, the claims on identities and ethnic conflicts tend to fall off and become less intense.[143] Finally, it goes without saying that recourse to a form of autonomy based solely on democracy and ignoring human rights cannot be viable because "the democratic regulation of plural societies is not limited to the exercising of power, but is also related to the organization of the relationship between the governed and those governing them in terms of recognition and guarantee of human rights, the rights of the indigenous population, etc."[144]

But it is worth noting that the adoption pure and simple of democracy is not on its own sufficient to make territorial autonomy viable. Democracy needs, to fully exercise its positive effect on territorial autonomy, to be accompanied by the adoption of an electoral system which prevents the emergence of regional parties who tend to use the regime of territorial autonomy to separate the autonomous region from the rest of the country. In this respect it has been shown that the presence of regional parties (in other words, operating solely in the autonomous region) weakens the impact of territorial autonomy on the appeasement of ethnic conflicts and the prevention of secession. It is for that reason that the force of regional parties must be regulated by the putting in place of appropriate structures and decentralization mechanisms (i.e. territorial autonomy), such as some sort of electoral system.[145]

However, establishing an appropriate electoral system is not sufficient as well. In order to make of autonomy a viable institution, the latter has to take place in a political and economic system where there is a fair competition between all the concerned actors. Now, in order to be fair such competition requires the existence of an "open access order"[146] where violence is absent as a result of the creation of political, social and economic institutions that give individuals and social groups the possibility of having an open and competitive access to resources and social functions, and that simultaneously prevents their ability to solidify their advantage through rent-creation. Unfortunately, open access order remains limited to about 15% of the world's population[147] as the drive towards democracy which took place at the end of the Cold War, in different parts of the world, has very often given rise to hybrid regimes where democratic institutions are in practice reduced to pure

---

142 Recommendation No. 16.

143 See Gurr (2002, Second, p. 151 et seq).

144 Sindjoun (2000, p. 13).

145 Brancati (2006, p. 682). Also see Horowitz (2000), second edition in particular the section in Chapter 15 dealing with "Electoral systems and the reduction of conflicts".

146 This concept has been forged by North et al. (2009).

147 Idem, p. 13.

façade[148] mainly as a result of their manipulation by non elected or even elected tutelary authorities that limit elected officials' power to govern.

Effective democracy is therefore a crucial prerequisite for the good functioning of territorial autonomy. But democracy needs also as much as possible to be accompanied by regional integration in order to make of territorial autonomy a viable solution.

6.2.3.2 Regional Integration

Territoriality is, as we saw above, conditioned not only by the internal environment of the state, but also by its external environment. In effect, territoriality appears only when a group, having successfully established its control over a specific geographical area, has this control implicitly or explicitly admitted and recognized by the foreign group or groups who have successfully established similar control over neighbouring territories. Thus, the durability and stability of territoriality depend on internal factors as well as external ones. The latter have essentially been embodied in war which has always been a determining factor in what states subsequently become. But the impact of external factors was strengthened further when states understood, from the time of the French Revolution and the creation of the nation-state, the advantage gained by the manipulation of the right to self-determination. Secession has never materially come about simply from internal factors; it has always been the result of the conjunction of both internal and external factors. It is this reality which is cited by Donald D. Horowitz who recalls in this respect that "one fairly firm rule of thumb can be laid down at once. Whether and when a secessionist movement will emerge is determined mainly by domestic politics, by relations of groups and regions within the state. Whether a secessionist movement will achieve its aims, however, is determined largely by international politics, by the balance of interests and forces that extend beyond the state."[149] This is so because any question of territoriality or the conditions of its exercise, particularly those relating to territorial boundaries, can affect neighbouring territorialities and the regional balance determining them. This balance is conditioned by the level of congruence between states and existing nations within a given regional subsystem. Thus, if there is a significant level of congruence, there is little risk of the sub-region being destabilized by overlapping identity issues (which are cross-border and therefore affect two or more states at the same time) or regional wars.[150] Therefore, territorial autonomy is no exception to the rule insofar as it impacts, albeit in a special way, territoriality. It can also, as we have seen above, have destabilizing effects, not only within states but also on neighbouring states by the knock-on effect

[148] See Levitsky and Way (2010).

[149] Horowitz (2000, p. 230).

[150] See Miller (2005, p. 230 et seq).

of movements of identity and thus a possible destabilization of neighbouring countries. That is why regional integration seems to constitute a crucial condition for the success of any plan for territorial autonomy.

Among the virtues of regional integration is that of transcending and defusing territorial questions – and also settling them.[151] This is because successful regional integration often, if not always, embraces questions which are highly political and of common interest to those taking part in the integration process and also by bringing about a transfer of loyalties at both state and regional level[152] or at least by creating among the populations of the countries concerned the feeling of sharing the same destiny and constituting one and the same community. This feeling will be that much stronger if transnational links are established. This was eloquently shown by the experiment initiated in Europe in 1951 with the creation of the European Coal and Steel Community (ECSC) which would quickly make it possible to defuse territorial problems, notably between the traditional rivals, Germany and France.[153] The upshot was the return of the Saarland by the latter to the former and, especially since 1957, with the creating of the European Community, later to become the European Union. After the internecine wars that were a constant feature of their relations since they first emerged in the sixteenth century and were often triggered by territorial questions, countries in Europe and the West realized at the end of the Second World War that it had become necessary to conceive a new relationship – one based on cooperation and interdependence within a programme of regional integration. This made it possible not only to take the heat out of territorial problems but also, as we have seen above, to co-manage identity problems which have been very much part of the peripheral scene within the European Union since the end of the Cold War. But the capacity of the European Union to manage and settle territorial problems is clearly greater when these problems directly concern the member states of the European Union.[154]

6.3 The Self-Determination Changing Paradigm and the Western Sahara Conflict

Few would disagree that attempts to implement self-determination in the Western Sahara conflict over the past four decades have failed. But could it be otherwise in a situation where the right to self-determination has no place, as much because of the legal nature of the Saharan conflict, as because of its geopolitical complexity? Originally, the Sahara conflict was essentially a territorial conflict between

[151] See Diez et al. (2006, p. 563 et seq).

[152] Idem, p. 249.

[153] Cf. Cole (2001).

[154] Idem, p. 264.

Morocco and Spain, the former demanding that the latter return the Sahara provinces it had illegally occupied since the end of the nineteenth century. Spain, however, refused to return the territory and evoked first, sovereignty acquired under colonial law, and secondly, discovery of a *terra nullius*. Now, International Law dictates, as we have seen above, that a territorial conflict requires a solution based on a comparison of the legal rights, titles and evidence that each party to the dispute may claim to have.

The first mistake, therefore, lay in invoking the right to self-determination in a bilateral legal dispute the solution of which traditionally vests in the international law principles governing the settlement of territorial disputes either through negotiation between the parties, or through arbitration.

The second mistake lay in attempting to apply the inappropriate concept of self-determination to the Western Sahara conflict. Interpreted by Morocco's adversaries in the light of the controversial principle of the sanctity of colonial borders, self-determination was intended to achieve only one solution: the independence of Western Sahara. Morocco, in turn, claimed sovereignty over the territory; not on the basis of colonial law, but on titles and immemorial possession of a territory which had for centuries played a crucial role in its history, political configuration, and the making of its people.

The third mistake was the international community's failure to react in time to attempts by Morocco's adversaries to manipulate self-determination in order to facilitate the establishment of a puppet state in Western Sahara. Never in modern history has a principle of international law known such diverse and contradictory fortunes as the right to self-determination as reflected in the Western Saharan conflict. Referred to wittingly, or manipulatively by some, boycotted or attacked by others, the right to self-determination has never in four decades, ceased to be on the agenda and to see its implementation, whenever it seems imminent, come up against opposition from those who fear its consequences – opposition which has never been explicitly expressed, but the effectiveness of which has always been a deciding factor through the various subterfuges and delaying tactics which have been cleverly employed.

The fourth mistake was to continue claiming the implementation of self-determination/independence (that is self-determination necessarily leading to independence) while, as we have seen above, this concept has largely been abandoned by the international community in favor of democratic self-determination – and its current form at the sub-state level: territorial autonomy.

We know that the major factor in the failure of the 1990 Settlement Plan (SP) was the lack of agreement between the parties on the criteria by which to identify voters' eligible to take part in the referendum. This, too, is why the 2001 Framework Plan and the 2002 Peace Plan failed leading, in 2004, to the resignation of James Baker, the United Nations Secretary-General's Personal Envoy. Meanwhile, in April 2007 Morocco attempted to break this impasse through what has been termed 'the Moroccan Initiative' which proposed territorial autonomy for Western Sahara. It was in this light that the United Nations Security Council (SC) adopted resolution 1754 of 30 April 2007 calling for a compromise between Morocco's sovereignty over Western Sahara, on the one hand, and Polisario's claim to self-determination/independence, on the other. In real terms, all that this implies is a recognition of Moroccan sovereignty over Saharan territory, and the right of the Saharawi population to run its own affairs through territorial autonomy in a modern expression of democratic self-determination. There have been several rounds of negotiations and it is hoped that, although Polisario appears to be sticking to the old self-determination/independence rhetoric, the current round will usher in a new era for peace, stability and cooperation in the Maghreb region.

This section aims, first, to shown how self-determination/independence has failed to resolve the Western Sahara conflict, and second, that the United Nations (UN) has since 1991 tried to promote a compromise solution in the form of territorial autonomy.

6.3.1 The Failure of Self-Determination/Independence

Attempts since 1965 to apply the right to self-determination to the Sahara conflict have failed.

There was, first, the failure of Spain to create an artificial Saharan state under the cover of self-determination, then the failure of Algeria to achieve the same design, and finally the failure to implement self-determination under the UN 1990 SP.

After its independence in 1956, Morocco unsuccessfully demanded the restitution of the Sahara from Spain.[155] One year later Morocco invoked UN support in bringing Spain to the negotiating table. However, it was only in December 1965 that the United Nations General Assembly (GA) adopted a resolution echoing Morocco's request and inviting Spain to take immediate measures to liberate the territories of Ifni and the Spanish Sahara from colonial domination. Spain again refused to negotiate, forcing Morocco to demand that the right to self-determination be applied to the Sahara. After some procrastination, Spain finally accepted this proposal in the belief that it could manipulate the right to self-determination to create an artificial state in the Sahara. Spain changed its attitude for various reasons, three of which were central. First, it hoped to reduce the impact of Morocco's initiative in both the Organisation of African Unity (OAU) and the UN, favouring the right to self-determination as the vehicle for guaranteeing the liberation of territories occupied by Spain. This would be achieved, first by compelling Spain to negotiate, and second, by allowing a free expression of the will of the Saharawi people. Second, Spain believed that this would exacerbate the tensions which had arisen between the countries of the Maghreb. For the first time, Mauritania made claims akin to those of Morocco and Algeria so revealing its interest in the Sahara – albeit in the name of maintaining the geopolitical balance in the region. Lastly, and

[155] See on Morocco's claim to Sahara, El Ouali (2008, pp. 73–88).

most significantly, Spain hoped to manipulate the right to self-determination by creating an artificial state in Western Sahara so allowing it to exploit the phosphate deposits discovered in 1963 and viable from a production point of view since 1966.[156]

By playing on the international community's commitment to the right to self-determination and contradictions within the countries of the Maghreb, Spain succeeded on 20 December 1966 in moving the GA to adopt a resolution which distinguished the Ifni and Sahara questions, and applied two different processes for decolonisation – negotiation for the former, and the application of the right to self-determination for the latter – even though the two territories had been subjected to the same process and the same colonial regime.

Therefore, while Spain effectively agreed to enter into negotiations with Morocco over Ifni, which resulted in the latter's retrocession in 1969, it managed to delay the application of the right to self-determination in Western Sahara so as to establish the conditions for the organisation of a referendum which would allow it to carry through its neo-colonial policy. Of these conditions, the most important was the need to create from scratch a "Saharawi people" and political movements that could represent it. Prominent among these were PUNS and Polisario. In the meantime, Spain and Algeria agreed to create a puppet state in the Sahara over which they would exercise *de facto* condominium. Morocco and Mauritania, on the other hand, agreed to block the project.[157] On 3 July 1974 Spain proclaimed internal autonomy for Western Sahara, and on 20 August 1974 she informed the Secretary-General of the United Nations (S-G) of her unilateral decision to organise a referendum in Western Sahara in violation of various GA resolutions which had since 1966 consistently reiterated the necessity of involving all the parties concerned. Morocco's immediate reaction was to convince Mauritania to present a joint diplomatic front to thwart the Spanish attempts. Without substantial difficulty, it persuaded, as we have seen earlier, the GA to demand that Spain postpone the organisation of the referendum, and to call upon the International Court of Justice (ICJ) within the framework of a consultation process, to clarify the best policy to accelerate the decolonisation of Western Sahara. This policy would be based on whether the territory of the Sahara was, at the time of its colonisation by Spain, a *terra nullius*, and if not, what legal ties it had to the Kingdom of Morocco and Mauritania. In its advisory opinion of 16 October 1975, the Court concluded, on the one hand, that the Sahara territory had not been a *terra nullius,* and on the other, that before Spanish colonisation, legal ties existed between Morocco and Mauritania and the territory of the Sahara. But, the Court declared also in a terse and peremptory way, that it had not found legal ties of such a nature as might affect the application of resolution 1514 (XV) in the decolonisation of Western Sahara and, in particular, of the principle of self-determination through the free and

156 See Jacquier (1974, p. 691).

157 On the conditions of the Moroccan-Mauritanian reconciliation see Osman (1986, pp. 317–318).

genuine expression of the will of the peoples of the Territory. This statement contradicted the Court's fundamental position on the recognition of legal ties between the Sahara, and Morocco and Mauritania respectively. Having abandoned its legal role, the court delivered a political opinion which upset nobody in that the states involved could, taking one conclusion from the opinion rather than another, find reasons to be satisfied with it.

For Morocco, the Court supported its traditional legal claims, and it again tried to convince Spain to enter into negotiations for the handing back of the Sahara. This it did through the Green March which, thanks to its peaceful nature and the enthusiasm and passion it aroused among the public at large, had a decisive impact. So, on 18 October 1975, 2 days after plans for the Green March had been announced, Spain, caught unawares, tried to convince the Security Council (SC) to force Morocco to abandon its plan. Instead, the SC adopted a series of resolutions, starting on 22 October 1975, in which it at no time condemned the Green March, and at most, called upon the parties involved to demonstrate 'restraint and moderation'. Spain realized that it had no alternative but to agree to negotiations. These began on 24 October 1975 in Madrid. Mauritania joined on 27 October. However, Spain procrastinated and, under pressure from Algeria who delegated its Minister for the Interior to Madrid on 29 October as its ultimate betrayal of the Spanish government, terminated the negotiations.

Delayed to facilitate negotiations, the Green March set off on 6 November with its extraordinary procession of 3,50,000 volunteers. One day later, the SC adopted resolution 380 inviting the parties to open negotiations on the basis of article 33 of the Charter. By returning to the original solution advocated by the GA in 1965, this resolution had a decisive effect on Spain, prompting it to re-open negotiations. These began immediately between the three parties involved, despite Algeria's threat to attack Mauritania if President Ould Daddah refused to sign the Madrid Agreement.[158] On 14 November 1975 the Madrid Agreement was signed detailing the following decolonisation process for Western Sahara:

- Spain's responsibilities and powers over the territory of the Sahara would be transferred to an interim tri-partite administration; its presence in the territory was to terminate before 26 February 1976;
- The Saharawi population would be consulted through the General Assembly of the Sahrawi People (the *Djemaa*).

Less than 1 month later, the Madrid Agreement was adopted by the UN GA as resolution 3458 B of 10 December 1975. The Assembly acknowledged the tri-partite agreement between the governments of Spain, Morocco and Mauritania, and the text was submitted to the S-G on 18 November 1975 for registration.

Drawing the relevant conclusions from the court's opinion – recommended by the SC and supported by the GA – the practical aspects of the Madrid Agreement

[158] See Mokhtar Ould Daddah's memoirs (2003, p. 498 and 640).

were implemented even before it had been officially sanctioned by the *djemaa* on 26 February 1976. Algeria, however, despite its earlier stance on Spanish colonisation,[159] raised doubts as to the validity of the process for Morocco's recovery of the Sahara. No longer able to act under Spain's shadow, Algeria adopted the Spanish neo-colonial policy under the guise of the right to self-determination. Ironically, it was Morocco who again, advocated the application of the right to self-determination in the hope of ending any question as to the legitimacy of its repossession of the Sahara.

In the light of Algerian misgivings, Morocco again suggested resort to the right to self-determination. However, fearing the result of the self-determination referendum, Algeria called a halt to the process which was to have been led, initially within the framework of the OAU, and then within the UN. It was in this context that the S-G offered his good offices so resolving the situation. This meant that the idea of the right to self-determination could be reconsidered, and the UN plan to organise a self-determination referendum prepared.

Just when the Sahara conflict seemed to have been definitively resolved, Algeria tried to revive it. First, it armed Polisario to fight against the Morocco. It reinforced its military presence in various parts of Western Sahara, as emerged when units of the Moroccan army surprised units of the Algerian People's Army in February 1976 in Amgala, some 350 km from Tindouf, and inflicted heavy losses before capturing around one hundred Algerian officers and soldiers. It further pressured tens of thousands of Saharawi to flee Western Sahara so creating a refugee-like situation. In flagrant violation of international law, these refugees were held in military camps under the close control of armed Polisario militia and denied basic refugee rights including the right of movement and the possibility of enjoying lasting solutions, including the right to voluntary repatriation. Algeria then created, as we have seen above, the so-called "Sahrawi Arab Democratic Republic", territorially limited to Tindouf (outside the territory of the Sahara), and comprising the aforementioned refugees who continue to be held hostage in closed camps. It also managed to secure membership of the OAU for this imaginary republic in flagrant violation of international law. It finally tried to raise doubts in certain diplomatic circles about the validity of the process which allowed the liberation of Western Sahara and its reintegration into Morocco.

Algeria's hostile attitude and the withdrawal of Mauritania from the conflict following the agreement concluded on 5 August 1979 with the Polisario, induced Morocco to adopt a proactive policy within a global strategy comprising three objectives: to neutralise attacks by the Polisario by building a series walls of defence; to promote the development of the Sahara; and force its opponents to restrict the conflict to the diplomatic table by suggesting recourse to the right to self-determination in order to confirm its rights over the Sahara territory.

---

[159] See Zunes (1995).

The decisive military success achieved by Morocco, and the tremendous improvement in socio-economic conditions in the Sahara, induced Saharawi in the camps at Tindouf – including certain important leaders – to return home. It was against this background that Morocco proclaimed within the OAU its willingness to accept that its rights to the Saharan territory should be reaffirmed by recourse to the right to self-determination. The Moroccan initiative was welcomed by the OAU which at its 18th summit in Nairobi in June 1981, adopted resolution 103 giving an Implementation Committee (IC) full power to organise a self-determination referendum. The necessary procedures were established by the IC during its meetings in Nairobi between August 1981 and February 1982. However, the free expression of the Saharawi on their destiny would inevitably frustrate the vague hegemonic desires of Algeria, which did its best, first to block, and then to destroy, the conducting of the referendum in which the OAU was closely involved. First of all, it managed to persuade the OAU to call a halt to the process of organising the referendum by asking Morocco – contrary to the letter and spirit of the decisions of the IC – to enter into direct negotiations with Polisario. Secondly, it admitted the so-called SADR, so compelling Morocco to withdraw from the OAU in protest.

After Morocco's withdrawal from the OAU, King Hassan II appeared before the UN GA on 27 September 1983 to launch an appeal for the immediate organisation of a self-determination referendum under UN control. He further officially announced Morocco's commitment to be bound by the outcome. However, using the same methods which enabled it to bring the OAU to a complete standstill, Algeria pushed the GA to adopt resolution 3940 on 5 December 1984 in which it adopted resolution AHG 104 (XIC) of the OAU and, in turn, demanded direct negotiations between Morocco and Polisario and the continued involvement of the OAU in the Sahara question. In so doing, however, the GA in turn brought the Sahara conflict to a standstill, forcing the S-G to take on the role of mediator in order to resolve the situation. This led to the adoption of the Settlement Plan (SP), the implementation would also very quickly be deadlocked.

De Cuellar, the then UN S-G, had serious difficulties in convincing Algeria to accept his good offices, while Morocco agreed but on condition that the negotiations took place separately between the conflicting parties. While these indirect negotiations proceeded, an atmosphere of peace seemed to form in the Maghreb when, in May 1988, diplomatic relations between Morocco and Algeria were restored. This reflected on the mediation attempts by the United Nations Secretary-General which would lead to the UN's development, on 11 August 1988, of "Peace Settlement Proposals", with the aim of organising a self-determination referendum in the Sahara. These "Proposals" were accepted by the parties involved on 30 August and received the endorsement of the SC on 20 September. However, the S-G's plans for implementation were thwarted by the negative attitude adopted by Algeria within the Fourth Committee, where in October 1988 it reiterated its demand for "direct negotiations" between Morocco and Polisario on the basis of OAU resolution AHG 104, which Morocco rejected.

Despite the signing of the treaty creating the Arab Maghreb Union on 17 February 1989, Algeria's obstruction manifested itself in different ways, but in particular in the escalation of armed attacks by Polisario against the Moroccan territory. This did little to help the S-G resolve unresolved issues in his "Proposals" – notably voting criteria and the conditions for the implementation of the ceasefire. Voting criteria were also considered by the Identification Commission (IC) presided over by the Special Representative of the Secretary-General, Johanes Manz, and by chiefs of tribes in the Sahara. Following these meetings, the IC rejected the 1974 Spanish census as insufficiently representative, and called for comprehensive data to be made available. This notwithstanding, on 20 June 1990, the S-G's plan to organise a referendum on self-determination was ratified by the SC. However, the UN will very quickly fail to implement this plan.

One of the major factors contributing to the non-implementation of the SP was the lack of criteria by which to determine voter eligibility. There was no mention of how the 'Saharawi' were to be identified, and the complex reality, both in human terms and historically, was ignored. It was, in fact, based largely on the 1974 Spanish census which it envisaged updating through the IC. This led to insoluble difficulties, although the S-G amended the plan and this was ratified by the SC on 27 June 1990. The amendment required an examination of the 'requests by those who declare that they have the right to participate in the referendum because they are Saharawis and were not counted in the 1974 census' and called for 'renewed discussions [following those held in Geneva] with the tribal chiefs' on this matter after the decision to deploy MINURSO had been made. It also provided that after the discussions and the re-examination of the 1974 lists, the IC would publish 'instructions about the way Saharawis could individually submit a written request, before a certain deadline to be determined, to be included on the list because they were not counted in the 1974 census'.

However, serious difficulties surrounded eligibility to vote from the outset. In a letter to the S-G dated 30 July 1990, Morocco raised 'the difficulties which may arise in establishing an electoral roll' and insisted on the necessity of 'taking into account in establishing the electoral lists of Saharans who sought refuge in Morocco when the Territory was under the Spanish domination'.[160] Polisario, on the other hand, declared that 'the up-dating of the 1974 census cannot have any other meaning than the spelling correction of the names or the deletion of the names of those of deceased persons'.[161] In a first move aimed at easing these difficulties, the S-G in his report to the SC on 19 April 1991 highlighted that:

> "the Identification Commission's task will be to implement the proposals, agreed upon by the two parties, that all Western Saharans to whom the 1974 census undertaken by the Spanish authorities related and who are aged 18 years or over will have the right to vote, whether they are currently present in the Territory or living outside it as refugees of for other reasons. The Commission's mandate to update the 1974 census will include

[160] Moroccan Arab Press 19 October 1990.

[161] Press release 26 November 1990.

(a) removing from the lists the names of persons who have since died and (b) considering applications from persons who claim the right to participate in the referendum on the grounds that they are Western Saharans and were omitted from the 1974 census."[162]

However, seeing that the Identification Commission did not convene, and that the date for the start of referendum procedures was approaching, Morocco submitted two lists to the S-G, which included 1,20,000 Saharawi they felt should vote on the basis of their origin. Special Representative Johannes Manz objected claiming that the Moroccan claim had "nothing to do with the UN Plan"[163] and proposed very limited criteria for determining who qualified as 'Saharawi'. In reality, the position adopted by the Special Representative was unjustified, as the general practice when determining the electorate had been, whether before[164] or after the establishment of the UN,[165] to take into account the natives of the territory, whether they were resident, expatriate or in exile for whatever reason. This practice had even taken residents into account: that is people who had no connection with the territory concerned, but who had been asked to confirm that they had been resident there for varying periods.

A glimmer of hope emerged when the S-G admitted in his report to the SC on 19 December 1991, that the difficulties in the identification process should be resolved by recourse to objective factors such as the characteristics of the Saharan population – notably its nomadic tradition and the tribal structure; the fact that the conflicts in the territory over several decades had resulted in a large number of Saharans seeking refuge in neighbouring countries; and the fact that drought and the deteriorating economic situation had pushed other Saharans to seek employment in neighbouring countries. Taking these factors into consideration, the S-G concluded that the 1974 census could not on its own form the basis for establishing the list of eligible voters. His recommendations in this regard are so important that they deserve to be quoted *in extenso*:

"Firstly, it is considered that an appropriate link to the Territory exists when the applicant was born of a Saharan father born in the Territory. In that regard, consideration was given to the fact that, in 1974, Saharan tribal chiefs themselves developed a liberal norm, patterned after their own tradition. It is also appropriate to note that one of the main tasks of the United Nations has been to promote decolonisation around the world. In that context, people who fled colonial rule cannot be deprived of the right to decide on the future of the Territory to which they belong. Similarly, children, aged 18 years or more, should not be penalised just because their parents, owing to colonialism or other reasons mentioned above, chose or were obliged to leave their homes. However, in order not to widen excessively the scope of this provision, it has been restricted to one generation only. Secondly, taking into account current provisions regulating the acquisition of nationality in the countries of the region, it is considered that a member of a Saharan tribe belonging to the Territory is eligible to participate in the referendum if he or she has resided in the

[162] [19]S/22464, para 20.

[163] Statement, Le Monde 3 August 1991.

[164] See Wambaugh (1927, p. 153 et seq).

[165] See Vignes (1953, p. 316 et seq).

> Territory for a period of six consecutive years before 1 December 1974. That figure is not arbitrary: the period of six consecutive years represents the average period of residence required under the legal systems of the countries of the region as a condition for the acquisition of nationality. Lastly, as an uninterrupted period of 6 years might penalise those Saharans who, owing to a variety of circumstance, have had to move frequently across the border of the Territory, it was considered unnecessary to provide for a condition of an intermittent residence period of 12 years prior to 1 December 1974."[166]

These suggestions were welcomed by the SC on 31 December 1991.[167] They were accepted by Morocco, but rejected by Polisario. Deadlock ensued.

The implementation of the SP was entrusted to the United Nations Mission for the Organisation of a Referendum on Self-determination in the Western Sahara (MINURSO) created on 29 April 1991 by the SC in accordance with the SPs which Morocco and Polisario had accepted on 30 August 1988. To promote the implementation of the SP, MINURSO was tasked with: maintaining the ceasefire; freeing prisoners; overseeing the voluntary repatriation of refugees; determining the electoral body; and organising the referendum on self-determination. However, the only operation MINURSO managed to bring off more or less successfully, was the introduction of a ceasefire.[168]

The implementation of the SP floundered principally on the identification of voters. In his report to the SC on 28 February 1992, the new S-G, Boutros Boutros-Ghali, stressed that without agreement between the parties concerned on the criteria for identifying voters, the SP could not be implemented. He further stated that if this stalemate continued for the next 3 months, alternatives to resolve the issue would have to be explored. The S-G acknowledged the complexity of the task – one which had never before been undertaken by the UN. Differences appeared insurmountable. For Polisario, the only acceptable reference base was the 1974 Spanish census – with a possible 10% escalation to accommodate those who might inadvertently have been left off the original census. Furthermore, the identification of future voters could be done only on the basis of written documents issued by the Spanish colonial authorities. For Morocco, the 1974 census was unacceptable as large numbers of Saharawi had fled from Spanish repression and taken refuge in the north of Morocco. They could not be deprived of their right to decide the fate of a territory for which they had fought. It was inconceivable to Morocco that the Saharawis who had fled Spanish repression should be penalised by requiring them to present formal written identity papers issued by the coloniser decades after leaving the Sahara, and which did not reflect their nomadic structures and meant little when compared with oral evidence.

[166] Appendix to his report of 19 December 1991.

[167] Resolution 725 (1991).

[168] Concerning MINURSO, see Sola-Martin (2007) The United Nations Mission for the Referendum in Western Sahara. This study, which is the only monograph on the MINURSO, is unfortunately subjective because it seeks systematically to blame Morocco for the failure of the SP.

Nevertheless, despite continuing dissent on the criteria for determining voting rights, on 8 February 1994 the UN officially launched the identification operation by opening registration centres in Layoune and Tindouf. Despite continuing disagreement, the situation appeared to have been resolved on 30 April 1994 when Polisario accepted the de Cuellar criteria. The identification operation was launched in Layoune and Tindouf on 28 August 1994. On 15 October, the deadline for the submission of registration requests, 1,76,533 requests were submitted by Morocco, and 42,468 by Polisario. The identification work was carried out under chaotic conditions, essentially on the basis of the 1974 census and in disregard of the de Cuellar criteria. Oral proof was frequently rejected by the Chioukhs representing Polisario. Erik Jensen, the then head of MINURSO in charge of the identification operation, acknowledged that 'it was becoming increasingly apparent that not all sheikhs were independent nobles as heralded; their political instincts had been nurtured, and they had discovered the power of exercising a negative vote to veto unwanted applications'.[169] Hence the famous categories H, I and J suffered from the partiality of the identification process, in other words, the Saharawi who were members of the tribes who had fled to Morocco and Mauritania after opposing the Spanish occupiers. On 25 and 29 October 1995, Morocco complained about the discrimination facing the members of these tribes, It criticised the IC for establishing a hierarchy of criteria by for turning a blind eye to the actions of the Chioukhs representing Polisario who dismissed oral testimonies and thereby rejected the inclusion on the electoral lists of those who did not support them. The crisis in confidence between Morocco and the IC, seemed to be playing into the hands of Polisario. In informal SC discussions during December 1995, the S-G expressed his scepticism about the referendum, and made it clear that the only alternative was for the parties involved to negotiate a solution.[170] The crisis worsened because of Polisario'S opposition to the consideration of registration requests from Saharawis who had not been included in the 1974 census, in particular those tribal subdivisions belonging to categories H1, H61 and J51/52, as well as its refusal to accept oral testimonies. In January 1996 allegations of bias on the part of the IC led Under Secretary-General, Chinmaya Garekhan, to call for greater transparency on the part of the Commission.[171] On 31 January 1996, the SC, confirming doubts surrounding the IC's work, 'expresse[d] deep concern about the stalemate which has been hindering the identification process and the consequent lack of progress towards completion of the Settlement Plan'.[172] It also recommended that the two sides cooperate with the S-G and MINURSO in relaunching the identification process, overcoming the obstacles to this process, and implementing all the other elements of the SP in compliance with the relevant

[169] Jensen (2005, p. 79).

[170] Idem, p. 83.

[171] S-G Report S/1996/43 of 19 January 1996 paras 10, 15 and 16.

[172] Resolution 1042 (1996).

resolutions. This did not prevent the IC from adopting a new schedule in which priority was given to requests made by those who had been part of the 1974 census over those not included in the process. Morocco again condemned the discrimination which the IC had demonstrated and the process was again halted. According to Jensen, 77,058 requests had been processed at that time and 60,112 people had been identified. He acknowledged that given the revised census list numbered at 73,497, the hearings appeared to have been sufficient to reveal to an initiate which way the wind was blowing.[173]

The lack of agreement between the parties over the crucial question of the identification criteria made the SP impossible to implement[174] and the search for an alternative solution increased in intensity. This proved no easy task, but over time territorial autonomy emerged as the only viable alternative.

6.3.2 The United Nations Recommendation for Territorial Autonomy

The impossibility of agreement over the electoral criteria resulted in the UN effectively abandoning the SP in favour of an alternative solution. Interestingly, the majority of UN senior officials, including the Secretaries-General who had been involved in the implementation of the SP, recommended territorial autonomy as the only honourable and viable alternative solution to the Sahara question.[175]

Hence, the idea of granting autonomy to the Sahara was secretly contemplated when the first difficulties arose in the implementation of the SP. Perez de Cuellar considered it at the time.[176] He would later admit that he has never been convinced that independence would guarantee the best future for the people of Western Sahara.[177] The idea of granting autonomy to the Sahara was also implicitly raised by Boutros Boutros-Ghali when, in an attempt to end the deadlock, he proposed abandoning the SP as a third option to the SC on 26 January 1993. Erik Jensen expressed a view shared by many of his colleagues, when he said to Boutros Boutros-Ghali, during their first meeting at the end of November 1994 that:

> "My strategy [as head of MINURSO] was to get the process going but with no illusion that the parties would cooperate in implementing entirely the settlement plan as it stood.

[173] Jensen (2005, p. 85).

[174] F.Neisse observed other obstacles which, in his opinion, meant that the SP could not be implemented and which implied to him that 'it seems definite today that the self-determination referendum which should result in Western Sahara's independence or its incorporation into Morocco, will not take place'. See Neisse (2002, p. 702).

[175] See Messary (2001, p. 60); T.Shelley (2004) Endgame in the Western Sahara: What Future for Africa's Last Colony? 142–143; International Crisis Group (2007b, p. 6).

[176] Goulding (2002, pp. 211–212).

[177] de Cuellar (1997, p. 352).

> I hoped that engaging both Morocco and the Polisario for long enough and getting them to see where they were headed would induce them to talk. A realistic solution to the conflict would require a politically negotiated compromise to be endorsed in an act of self-determination'."[178]

He would later reveal that at that time S-G Boutros-Ghali, agreed to that solution. Furthermore, in 1996, in his discussions with Moroccan, Algerian and Polisario leaders after the identification operation had stalled, Jensen suggested they consider autonomy as a solution to the crisis as, he confessed, 'my proposal was an encounter at which everything could be discussed, but independence pure et simple et integration pure et simple'.[179] Exploratory discussions between Morocco and the Polisario in the same year resolved noting. However, after the election of Kofi Annan to the position of UN Secretary-General in 1997, the idea of autonomy was seen as a possible solution to the Sahara question.

In his first report to the SC on 27 February 1997, the new S-G outlined three options for breaking the deadlock: implementing the SP in its current form; introducing changes to the SP to make it acceptable to the parties involved; looking into other ways in which the international community could help the parties resolve their conflict. However, he believed that the only realistic solution was to explore the third option, which, in his view, could only be to grant autonomy to the Sahara under Moroccan sovereignty. It was with this aim in mind that he approached the former American Secretary of State, James Baker, to consider nomination as Special Envoy to negotiate a compromise between the conflicting parties; a compromise which would be based on granting advanced autonomy to Western Sahara in the context of the Kingdom of Morocco sovereignty.[180] He did this even though he was officially tasked to evaluate the SP's feasibility, examine how it could be taken up again in the near future, and recommend other ways for the peace process to proceed.[181]

After he accepted the position as Special Envoy to the S-G, it soon became clear to James Baker that the only realistic solution was to shift the emphasis to a negotiated solution in the form of autonomy. With this in mind he visited the region from 23 to 28 April 1997, only to learn that the parties involved still hoped to implement the SP.[182] Baker, therefore, decided to look at ways of implementing the SP.

Several meetings between the parties (in Lisbon 23 June and 23–30 August 1997; London 19–20 July 1997; and Houston 14–16 September 1997) mediated by Baker, led to a compromise over the disputed issues, in particular those relating to identification criteria.[183] In this regard, the parties agreed that they would not

---

[178] Jensen (2005, p. 75).

[179] Idem, p. 88.

[180] See Goulding (2002, p. 214).

[181] S-G Report S/1997/358 of May 1997 para 3.

[182] See on this Bolton (1998, pp. 6–7).

[183] See the Annex to the S-G Report of 24 September 1997.

support or present, directly or indirectly, for identification purposes, any members of the tribal groups H41, H61 and J51/52, except those included in the 1974 census and members of their immediate families. However, the parties would not actively prevent members of these tribal groups from putting themselves forward and would recognise the validity of reliable oral testimonies presented to the IC. The agreement between the parties seemed to satisfy Morocco in that it was finally officially admitted, on the one hand that members of the tribal groups H41, H61 and J51/52 had the right to request their inclusion on the register of electors, and on the other hand, that oral testimonies would be taken into consideration. After announcing the agreement between the parties, the S-G expressed his optimism about the implementation of the SP.[184] However, those in charge were under no illusion about how the situation would proceed, as 'the rocks likely to impede and endanger identification remained beneath the surface',[185] including the question of the selection of the Chioukhs in charge of identifying members of the tribal groups H41, H61 and J51/52, as well as determining how oral evidence should be evaluated.

Although the identification process re-started on 3 December 1997 it faced the same problems. The Moroccan press reported widely on the dysfunctions that the IC was experiencing and having observed the deadlock in the identification of members of tribal groups H41, H61 and J51/2, the S-G informed the Security Council on 11 September 1998 that his

> "Personal Envoy is pursuing his contacts with the parties so that he may assess whether the Settlement plan can be carried out in its present form or whether there may be adjustments to it. If he concludes that, even with such adjustments, the Plan cannot be carried out, he will advise me on other courses of action that could be pursued."[186]

The identification process for members of tribal groups H41, H61 and J51/52 eventually resumed on 15 June 1999 based on a "Protocol and Directives on Identification and Appeals Procedures" accepted by the parties.[187] It resulted in the identification of a limited number of people eligible to vote as confirmed by the S-G when he observed in his report to the SC on 6 December 1999, that "to date, a relatively small percentage of applicants from the above-mentioned the tribal groupings has been found eligible by the Identification Commission".[188] This was confirmed by the publication of the second provisional list on 17 January 1999, which showed that of the 51,220 people belonging to tribal groups H41, H61 and J51/52 interviewed, only 2,135 would be allowed to vote.[189] This caused great

[184] Idem, para 27.

[185] Jensen (2005, p. 95).

[186] S-G Report S/1998/849 of 11 September 1998.

[187] See the S-G Report S/1999/4831 of 13 May 1999 Addendum.

[188] S-G Report S/1999/1219 of 6 December 1999.

[189] The total number of people judged eligible to vote was 86 425, but 134 000 appeals are still to be examined.

concern in Morocco where the government and public opinion condemned the duplicity of the IC.

The identification process seemed to have come to a standstill yet again, even more so because of doubts raised, especially on the part of Morocco, about the transparency and reliability of the appeals process. This worried the S-G, who commented that 'the same underlying concerns are likely to pervade the appeal process as well'.[190] There was one problem in particular, which concerned the probity and impartiality of the Chioukhs' evidence, about which the S-G felt that "from the start, the single greatest obstacle to identification had been the issue of tribal leaders designed to testify, over which the two parties had markedly divergent views".[191] So, how to guarantee the right conditions for examining the 79,000 appeals resulting from the publication of the first part of the provisional list, and the 54,889 other appeals submitted after the publication of the second, when the appeals process was only launched on 15 July 1999? Many of those involved in the Sahara question at the UN were sceptical about how things would proceed, especially the S-G who brought the matter to the attention of the SC.[192]

After visiting the region between 8 and 11 April 2000, James Baker met with the parties involved in London on 14 May 2000 and 28 June 2000 in an attempt to resolve the situation, but to no avail.[193] A political solution also met with little support, Baker reporting that "neither party had shown any disposition to depart from the 'winner-take-all' mentality or appeared willing to discuss any possible solutions in which each would get some, but not all, of what it wanted and would allow the other side to do the same".[194] A month later, however, the S-G noted that

> "A political solution could be a number of things, but most importantly, it would not be a military solution. Such a solution could be: a negotiated agreement for full integration with Morocco; a negotiated agreement for full independence; or a negotiated agreement for something in between; or a negotiated agreement that would permit a successful implementation of the settlement plan."[195]

This was taken up by the SC which recommended that the parties enter into direct negotiations to resolve the problems facing the SP and to agree on a political solution to their dispute.[196] A meeting was consequently held in Berlin (28 September 2000) during which Baker again suggested that the parties consider a political solution. He said that "there were many ways to achieve self-determination. It could be achieved through war or revolution; it could be achieved through

---

[190] S-G Report S/2000/131 of 23 February 2000.

[191] Idem, para 21.

[192] Idem, para 32.

[193] S-G Report S/2000/683 of 18 July 2000 para 8.

[194] Technical meetings took place in Geneva on 20 and 21 July 2000, but failed to resolve the problems facing the SP, especially the appeals procedure.

[195] S-G Report S/2000/683 of 12 July 2000 para 29.

[196] Resolution 1309 (2000) 25 July 2000.

elections, but this required good will; or it could be achieved as had been done by parties to other disputes",[197] and asked the parties if they were prepared to try the last option without abandoning the SP. The Moroccan delegation reacted favourably to Baker's suggestion, agreeing to consider any way to come to a lasting and definitive solution that "would take account of Morocco's sovereignty and territorial integrity, and the specificities of the region, in compliance with the democratic and decentralisation principles that Morocco wished to develop and apply, beginning with the Sahara region".[198] In spite of this positive reaction, Baker remained sceptical, judging that "further meetings of the parties to seek a solution cannot succeed, and indeed could be counterproductive, unless the Government of Morocco ... is prepared to offer or support some devolution of governmental authority, for all inhabitants and former inhabitants of the Territory, that is genuine, substantial and in keeping with international norms".[199]

So, the situation remained at a standstill which meant that the IC could not start the appeals process. In spring 2001, Baker, seriously doubting that the SP could be implemented, put forward a "Framework Agreement", based on granting territorial autonomy to the Sahara.[200] The idea of autonomy, which had been latent since the first difficulties had appeared in the implementation of the SP, finally emerged officially from a diplomatic standpoint.

The system of autonomy proposed by the UN followed the normal pattern. The local population was to exercise exclusive jurisdiction, by means of legislative, executive and judicial powers in a number of areas including local government administration, territorial budget and taxes, internal security, social welfare, culture, education, commerce, transport, agriculture, mining, fishing, industry, the environment, housing, urban planning, water, electricity, roads and other basic infrastructures. Legislative power would vest in an Assembly elected by direct ballot for a 4-year term. To take part in the election for the Assembly, an individual had to be 18 years or older and either have been resident in the Sahara since 30 October 1998, or be on the repatriation list as at 31 October 2000. Members of the executive arm would be elected by those identified as eligible to vote by the IC, and whose names appeared on the provisional electoral registers drawn up on 30 December 1999. Judicial power would be given to judges originally from the Sahara and chosen from members of the National Institute for Judicial Studies. The Framework Agreement Project (FAP) highlighted the fact that all the laws promulgated by the Assembly, and all decisions taken by the tribunals were required to comply with the Moroccan Constitution.

---

[197] S-G Report S/2000/1029 of 25 October 2000 para 13.

[198] Idem, para 15.

[199] Idem, para 30.

[200] See Annex1 to the S-G Report S/2001/513 of 20 June 2001.

Finally, a referendum on the definitive status of the Sahara in which any voter who had been a permanent resident of the Sahara for the year prior to the referendum could take part, would be held after 5 years.

In his report to the SC, the S-G invited interested parties to meet

> "To discuss with specificity the elements of the proposed framework agreement, which aims at reaching an early, durable and agreed resolution of the conflict over Western Sahara in a way that does not foreclose self-determination, but indeed provides for it ... The proposed framework agreement is not unlike agreements used to address similar situations elsewhere a devolution of authority to the inhabitants of a non-self-governing territory is granted with the final status of the territory to be determined by a referendum."[201]

He further advocated that the SP be put on hold, and the IC's activities be suspended for the duration of the consultation process. This drew mixed reaction. Morocco announced that it was prepared to examine the Personal Envoy's proposal. Since King Hassan II famously raised the idea of one day applying the German *Länder* system to the Sahara,[202] opinions have changed significantly, moving on from the idea of regionalisation in the form of fairly advanced decentralisation, to the idea of true territorial autonomy which would allow the Saharawi population to govern themselves.

As for Algeria and the Polisario, they rejected the FAP. In Algeria's case, this project was not close enough to the approach which the UN had adopted until that time in that it "totally ignores the basic principles that have always founded the United Nations in the field of decolonisation in general and in that of Western Sahara in particular. In this regard, it is appropriate to recall that these principles are based on the self-determination and the free expression of the Saharawi people through a free, fair and impartial referendum for the self-determination of the people of Western Sahara".[203] It further allowed only for integrating the Sahara into Morocco. Algeria expressed surprise at the fact that this project no longer talked about the "Saharawi people", but simply the "population" of the Sahara, which implied that the right to self-determination had been abandoned. The Polisario reiterated its preference for the SP, and expressed its "total opposition to any solution that would ignore the inalienable right of the Saharawi people to self-determination and independence".[204] This was dismissed by Morocco for whom a return to the SP was unthinkable.

In its 1359 resolution of 29 June 2001, the SC invited all the parties to negotiate modifications to the FAP or suggestions for a political settlement through the Special Envoy. Accordingly, during the summer of 2001, James Baker tried, in vain, to convince Algeria and the Polisario to withdraw their objections to the FAP. However, in November 2001 at a meeting between Baker and President Abdelaziz

[201] S-G Report S/2001/613 of 20 June 2001 paras 54 and 55.

[202] Speech delivered on 24 October 1984 on the regionalisation of Morocco.

[203] Annex II of the S-G Report S/2001/613 of 20 June 2001 para 6.

[204] Idem, Annex IV.

Bouteflika the latter reiterated the fact that Algeria did not accept the FAP and, out of the blue, informed Baker that both his country and the Polisario would be prepared to look at or negotiate a division of the territory as a political solution to the Sahara conflict.[205] James Baker returned to Morocco gauge King Mohammed VI's reaction to this new development. The King rejected the suggestion of dividing the territory, and reiterated that Morocco was interested in looking into the FAP. Baker concluded that there was no point in discussing the FAP at that time as both the Algerian government and the Polisario were not prepared to participate in any discussions about it.

Observing that the outlook for the peace process in the Sahara was bleak, the S-G decided to relinquish his role as mediator in favour of leading the SC to impose a solution on the parties. In his opinion there were four possible solutions from which the SC could choose.[206] The options were:

- The compulsory implementation of the SP, i.e. without demanding the assent of the two parties before coming to a decision. This initiative would begin with the appeals process but, according to the S-G, even by adopting a non-consensual approach like this, the UN would face the same problems that had existed for the past 10 years.
- Revisions to the FAP taking into consideration the concerns expressed by the different parties and by other entities with experience to these kinds of documents. However, in this case, the Special Envoy would not seek the assent of the parties as had happened in the past with the SP and the FAP. The revised FAP would be submitted to the SC, and would then be presented to the parties as a non-negotiable agreement.
- Division of the territory, the political solution with the advantage of partially, if not entirely, satisfying all the parties, and inspired by previous territorial agreements, in terms of which in 1976 Morocco and Mauritania agreed on the division of land, without copying them. If the SC chose this option, and if the parties refused to accept it, or be ready for a division of the territory before 1 November 2002, the Personal Envoy would be asked to submit to the parties a proposal for the division of the territory which would also be submitted to the SC. This would be presented to the parties as a non-negotiable proposal.
- The withdrawal by the UN of its contribution to settling the Sahara question. In this case, the SC could decide to terminate MINURSO's activities, which, in the eyes of the S-G, would be an admission that, after trying for 11 years and after spending nearly 500 million dollars, the UN could not solve the Western Sahara problem without requiring that one or the other or both of the parties do something to which they did not voluntarily agree.

---

[205] This change in the Algerian position could be explained, according to H.Zoubir and Karima Benabdallah-Gambier, by the desire '"to serve American interests because the creation of partition of a Sahrawi state would allow Algeria to get rid of its petrol via Atlantic ports', see . "Western Sahara Deadlock", Middle East Report, Summer 2003, No 227, p. 11.

[206] S-G Report S/2002/178 of 19 February 2002.

The presentation of these options to the SC illustrated the difficult situation in which the UN had found itself as a result of its inability, clear from the outset, to adopt a satisfactory approach to the Sahara conflict. It is intellectually and morally difficult to admit that one could pass from one extreme solution (that of granting the right to self-determination and therefore following in the tradition of the UN's preference for independence) to another (division of the territory) which was the complete opposite of the right to self-determination, or another solution which was to accept the legitimacy of Morocco's reclamation of the Sahara, and give the Saharawi population a system of autonomy. Paradoxically, it was when the UN seemed finally to have understood the true nature of the conflict, that the S-G disappointed by the intransigence of the parties involved, chose to abandon his good offices role at the risk of putting the UN in an even more difficult position. The SC, however, did not really take the S-G's dangerous approach on board. It favoured none of the options raised, and asked him to 'consider' them 'actively'.[207] Nevertheless, there followed a period of hesitation and indecision within the UN about the best approach to adopt in seeking a solution to the conflict. In fact, the options proposed by the S-G put the SC in a difficult position in terms of how to proceed. The SC itself recognised its difficult position by "noting the fundamental differences with regard to the four options contained in the report of the Secretary-General of 19 February 2002"[208] and recommended that the Special Envoy continue his attempts at mediation. But the situation became even more complicated when, after a period of hiatus during which the organisation seemed not to know how to proceed, the S-G and his Special Envoy came back to recommend a 'fifth option'.[209]

According to the S-G, the fifth option, called "Peace Plan for Self-Determination of the People of Western Sahara" offered what

> "Could be an optimum political solution to the conflict over Western Sahara, providing the bona fide residents of Western Sahara, following an appropriate transitional period, the opportunity to determine their own future, which, in turn, would promote peace and stability in the region and would open the way to enhanced exchanges and cooperation between the countries of the Arab Maghreb Union. By combining elements of the framework agreement, favoured by Morocco, and the settlement plan, favoured by the Frente Polisario, it represents a fair and balanced approach, providing each side some, but perhaps not all, of what it wants. The peace plan, therefore, represents a compromise. And, unlike the Settlement Plan, it does not require the consent of both parties at each and every stage of implementation."[210]

The fifth option was not actually a combination of the SP and the FAP, as the autonomy regime was intended to be provisional, and its aim was to open the way for organising a referendum on self-determination which would result in the

[207] Security Council resolution 1394 (2002) 27 February 2002.

[208] Idem.

[209] Security Council resolution 1429 (2002), 30 July 2002.

[210] As defined by the Secretary-General. See his Report S/2003/565 of 2 May 2003.

Sahara's independence. It came within the framework of a policy that had recently been designed, as we have seen above, to resolve a number of conflicts, but in a way that would lead the territory concerned to independence gradually. So autonomy was simply a transitional phase in a process which must in principle lead towards independence. In this case, it was a round about way of implementing the SP, which had been rendered invalid because of the obstacles it had come up against which the UN thought could not be overcome and which led them, as we have seen, to seek mediation from the Special Envoy in order to find a compromise between the conflicting parties. And so the mediation efforts of the UN once again came to a standstill.

Thus, the autonomy status laid out by the Peace Plan seemed to be secondary to the crucial issue of determining the electorate who would be called upon, as a first step, to elect legislative and executive bodies, known as the 'Western Sahara Authority' and, as a second step, to determine the Sahara's definitive status. As for participation in the election of the legislative and executive powers, the Plan completely satisfied the Polisario, as it provided that

> "Those eligible to vote in the election for the Legislative Assembly and Chief Executive of the Western Sahara Authority are persons who are at least 18 years of age and whose names appear either on the provisional voter list of 30 December 1999 (without giving effect to any appeals or other objections) or on the repatriation list drawn up by UNHCR as at 31 October 2000. Those eligible to vote shall be determined by the United Nations, whose decision shall be final and without appeal."[211]

The Polisario could therefore establish its control over the Sahara and prepare for the referendum in their own time. As for participation in the vote on the definitive status of the Sahara, which had to take place 4 or 5 years after the Peace Plan was implemented, it seemed to benefit Morocco in that it was stated that

> "Those eligible to vote in the referendum are those persons who are at least 18 years of age and: (a) who have been identified as qualified to vote by the Identification Commission of the United Nations Mission for the Referendum in Western Sahara (MINURSO), as reflected on the provisional voter list of 30 December 1999 (without giving effect to any appeals or other objections); (b) whose names appear on the repatriation list drawn up by the United Nations High Commissioner for Refugees (UNHCR) as at 31 October 2000; or (c) who have resided continuously in Western Sahara since 30 December 1999. Those eligible to vote shall be determined by the United Nations, whose decision shall be final and without appeal."[212]

In fact, the Peace Plan here also benefited the Polisario as it reproduced, but in a way to aggravate them, the same insurmountable difficulties generated by the identification process which had stalled the SP. So it was laid out that

---

[211] Paragraph 16 of the 'Peace Plan for Self-Determination of the People of Western Sahara', Annex to Report S/2003/565 of 2 May 2003.

[212] Para. 16 of the "Peace Plan for Self-Determination of the People of Western Sahara", Annex of Report S/2003/565 2nd May 2003.

"The addition to the list of qualified voters of any person whose name does not appear either on the provisional voter list of 30 December 1999 or on the repatriation list drawn up by UNHCR as at 31 October 2000 can occur only if the status of that person as a continuous resident of Western Sahara since 30 December 1999 is supported by testimony from at least three credible persons and/or credible documentary evidence. The United Nations shall: (a) determine the credibility and legal sufficiency of all such testimony and other evidence; and (b) based on that testimony and other evidence, determine who is (and is not) entitled to be added to the list of qualified voters under this paragraph. These determinations by the United Nations shall be final and without appeal."[213]

The Peace Plan indeed represented a step backwards towards past problems. It was in fact a 'Settlement Plan II'. It is understandable in this case that Morocco[214] rejected it and the Polisario, after some delaying tactics, accepted it on 11 July 2003.[215] Paradoxically, the SC appearing to ignore these difficulties, had also given the impression of supporting the Peace Plan when, in a resolution adopted on 31 July 2003, it stated that it

"*continues to support* strongly the efforts of the Secretary-General and his Personal Envoy and similarly supports their Peace plan for self-determination of the people of Western Sahara as an optimum political solution on the basis of agreement between the two parties [and] *calls upon* the parties to work with the United Nations and with each other towards acceptance and implementation of the Peace plan."[216]

At the request of Morocco, there were several meetings with the Personal Envoy in an attempt to clarify the Moroccan position. This was explicitly formulated in a letter sent on 9 April 2004 from Morocco's Foreign Affairs Minister to the Personal Envoy. Morocco made it clear that it rejected the Peace Plan and was ready to negotiate an autonomy status which would allow the population of the Sahara to manage its own affairs while respecting Morocco's sovereignty and territorial integrity. Nevertheless, on the recommendation of the S-G, the SC reiterated "its support for the Peace Plan for Self-Determination of the People of Western Sahara as an optimum political solution on the basis of agreement between the two parties [and] also its strong support for the efforts of the Secretary-General and his Personal Envoy in order to achieve a mutually acceptable political solution to the dispute over Western Sahara".[217] However, despite the SC's appeal, the parties remained divided on the approach to resolve the Sahara conflict. Disenchanted, the S-G once again referred to the standstill, declaring: "When I last reported in April 2004, there was no agreement between the parties on the Peace Plan for Self- Determination of the People of Western Sahara. Such an agreement appears more distant today. Moreover, there is currently no agreement as to what can be done to overcome the

[213] Idem, para 5.

[214] Para 6.

[215] See Annex III of Report S/2003/565 2nd May 2003.

[216] Security Council Resolution 1495 (2003).

[217] Security Council resolution 1541 (2004) 29 April 2004.

existing deadlock".[218] This situation drove Baker to resign on 11 June 2004. Peter van Walsun was appointed new Special Envoy, but there was still no prospect of resolving the deadlock. The reports that the S-G made to the SC over the next 2 years became laconic. They expressed a general feeling of disenchantment with the UN whose inability to implement the right to self-determination was patent. But could the situation be any different where there was no place for the right to self-determination/independence, given that what was at stake was Morocco's sovereign right to recover a part of its national territory under colonial domination and the aspirations of the populations in this territory to enjoy their own particular culture within Moroccan society? Morocco seemed finally to have understood this when, on 6 November 2006, King Mohammed VI announced that his government was in the process of drafting a proposal for territorial autonomy allowing the local population to govern itself. The international community also seemed to be starting to appreciate the nature of the Sahara conflict, given the largely positive reactions to the announcement of this proposal.

After a major diplomatic campaign Morocco submitted a document to the new S-G, Ban Ki-moon, entitled "Moroccan Initiative to negotiate an autonomy statute for Western Sahara". The day before, the S-G had also received a letter from the Polisario in which it

> "Reiterates solemnly its acceptance of Baker Plan and declares its readiness to negotiate directly with the Kingdom of Morocco, under the auspices of the United Nations, the modalities for implementing it as well as those relating to the holding of a genuine referendum on self-determination in Western Sahara in strict conformity with the spirit and letter of the UN General Assembly resolution 1514 (XV) and within the format envisaged in the framework of Baker Plan, namely the choice between independence, integration into the Kingdom of Morocco and self-governance."

Although the content and message of the two letters were completely at odds, the S-G said at the time that he "welcome[s] every effort from the parties that can advance the possibility of achieving a just and mutually acceptable solution that will provide self-determination for the people of Western Sahara and encourage[s] the parties to enter into negotiations in good faith without preconditions",[219] and recommended to the SC that it "call upon the parties, Morocco and the Frente Polisario, to enter into negotiations without preconditions, with a view to achieving a just, lasting and mutually acceptable political solution that will provide for the self-determination of the people of Western Sahara".[220] The SC agreed with the S-G and, after taking both the Moroccan and the Polisario proposals into consideration, called upon the parties "to enter into negotiations without preconditions in good faith, taking into account the developments of the last months, with a view to achieving a just, lasting and mutually acceptable political solution, which will

---

[218] S/2004/827 20 October 2004.

[219] S/2007/202 13 April 2007 para 8.

[220] Idem, para 47.

provide for the self-determination of the people of Western Sahara' and requested 'the Secretary-General to set up these negotiations under his auspices".[221]

In accordance with SC resolution 1754, the UN, under Peter van Walsum, Personal Envoy to the S-G, was able to organise four meetings between the conflicting parties which allowed each party to put forward its position without really going into negotiations about it, while recognising that "the status quo is unacceptable".[222] In his report to the SC on 19 October 2007, the S-G deplored what he called the 'rigidity' in the positions of the parties "for it cannot really be maintained that the parties have entered into negotiations. This was not due to a lack of good faith on their part, but primarily ensued from predictable problems with the interpretation of the Council's call on them to enter into negotiations without preconditions".[223] For the S-G it seemed

> "Clear, however, that the negotiation process pursuant to resolution 1754 (2007) cannot be completely filled with discussions that do not touch on the proposals of the parties. It is also clear that the parties will not start negotiating without some further guidance from the Security Council. The Council could clarify that attendance at each round of the negotiation process is not equivalent to entering into negotiations. Paragraph 2 of resolution 1754 (2007) contains elements that cannot be separated. A political solution that does justice to all those elements will inevitably be of great complexity and will need to be negotiated with perseverance."[224]

It was true that SC resolution 1754 was, formally at least, slightly ambiguous in that it asked the parties to negotiate on the basis of two totally opposing positions. But fundamentally, this resolution implicitly invited the parties to enter into negotiations on the proposal for autonomy made by Morocco, as the context was all too clear: a pure and simple implementation of the right to self-determination was legally and practically impossible, as admitted by all the UN Secretaries-General who had dealt with the Sahara conflict since the 1980s. Resolution 1754 would be meaningless if it were to try to lead the parties to re-open discussions about the question of granting the right to self-determination, as, even supposing that Morocco were to accept that negotiations would deal with this right to self-determination, how could such a right be implemented when, as we have seen, all attempts made over the previous 40 years to implement it had failed? Especially when, in addition, the conditions under which the UN had tried to implement the SP, particularly in the way in which the voters would be determined, had rendered any referendum for self-determination irredeemably impossible. In other words, even going back to the beginning and again discussing the conditions under which a referendum for self-determination could be organised, was impossible because the basis on which the referendum could take place had been definitively destroyed, unless Algeria wanted, via Polisario, to prolong indefinitely a conflict whose cost

221 Security Council resolution 1754 (2007) 30 April 2007.

222 S-G Report to the SC S/2007/619 of 19 October 2007, para 8.

223 Idem, para 14.

224 Idem, para 10.

had already been too high for the refugees in Tindouf, the Maghreb, and the UN.[225] It was because they realised that the right to self-determination could not be implemented, that all the UN Secretaries-General, without exception, as well as their Personal Envoys, had come to the conclusion that the only viable and realistic solution was to set up a system of autonomy. The discussion on the conditions for applying the right to self-determination was all the more pointless in that it went against the customary rule of international law in terms of which, as has been confirmed by the ICJ, "the parties (in any international negotiation) are under an obligation to enter into negotiations with a view to arriving at an agreement, and not merely to go through a forma1 process of negotiation ... they are under an obligation so to conduct themselves in a way that the negotiations are meaningful, which will not be the case when either of them insists upon its own position without contemplating any modification of it".[226] In this instance, Morocco changed its position well before it went to the negotiating table and it was this change which led the SC to recommend that bona fide negotiations should commence. Therefore, good sense and good faith required that, if they were to be meaningful, negotiations then under way should deal essentially with Morocco's proposal to establish a system of autonomy in the Sahara to end a conflict which had gone on too long. We know that it was this solution to which, in a gesture of goodwill, Morocco finally agreed.

Drawing the conclusion that it was the stress on self-determination/independence that had led to the present deadlock, the international community has started to support a realistic approach to the Western Sahara conflict. Many states as well as the Security Council have come to see in the Moroccan Initiative a "serious" and "credible" proposal in order to definitely make an end to that conflict. Reflecting a general feeling among international actors, Peter van Walsum, the then Personal Envoy of the UN Secretary-General, has on 21 April 2008 declared to the Security Council that the independence of Western Sahara is not a realistic option and that genuine territorial autonomy under Moroccan sovereignty was the only feasible solution. We know that this has cost Peter van Walsum its post as Algeria was strongly opposed to the renewal of his mandate.

At present, the negotiations recommended by the Security Council in accordance to its Resolution 1754 seem to be stuck, despite the efforts deployed by Christopher Ross, the new Personal Envoy and the many informal meetings that he organized between the parties in the conflict. It is believed that these negotiations will reach a

[225] See International Crisis Group (2007a, p. 1). Since this involved the plight of the refugee Sahrawis in Tindouf, this report particularly points out that "The Sahrawis in the camps and more forgotten by the international community; they live in exile under the authority of a state which is only just democratic (Polisario and the Democratic Arab Sahrawi Republic), certain of whose leaders are suspected of adding to their personal wealth by embezzling funds from international aid. Polisario has also to face intensified rumblings from support whose morale and unity are weakening after years of paralysis and immobility", p 1. idem, para 47.

[226] North Sea Continental Shelf cases 1969 ICJ Reports 47.

tangible result only if Algeria changes its policy towards the Western Sahara conflict, accepts to renounce to its hegemonic policy and initiate real democratic changes in its own political system. Meanwhile, the dramatic situation prevailing in the Tindouf refugees camps calls out the international community to find an urgent solution to the Western Sahara conflict. It is unacceptable that the Sahrawi refugees are kept in military camps for now more than three decades in order to serve the political designs of Algeria and the Polisario.

Morocco's proposal to implement territory to the Western Sahara territory has since its inception gained an increasing support by the international community. I was so in reason of the advanced character of the suggested type of territorial autonomy. It appears indeed that the Moroccan Initiative is based on a far more progressive approach to territorial autonomy than that established by the Lund Recommendations. It also appears to bear comparison with the advanced experiences of autonomy in other nations. Besides, the Moroccan Initiative itself provides in this regard that "the Moroccan autonomy project draws inspiration from the relevant proposals of the United Nations Organisation and from the constitutional provisions in force in countries that are geographically and culturally close to Morocco. It is based on internationally recognised norms and standards".[227] In fact, the project put forward by the Moroccan Initiative suggested a model for autonomy which gave the Sahara Autonomous Region powers which it is difficult to find at once in any of the most advanced cases of autonomy, notably in Catalonia, the Åland Islands, the Faroe Islands, and Greenland.[228]

The Moroccan proposal to establish a system of territorial autonomy in Western Sahara has also gained momentum because of the failure of all attempts aimed at implementing self-determination/independence. It also reflects a general tendency that we find in different parts of the world where territorial autonomy is gaining precedence over self-determination/independence. In fact, such a move reflects, as we have seen earlier, the paradigmatic change that self-determination is undergoing and by which the latter becomes an instrument for establishing democracy instead of dismantling states and creating artificial entities in which poverty, instability, disorder and terrorism prevail.

References

Alexander Y, Frieflander RA (eds) (1980) Self- Determination: National, Regional, and Global Dimensions. Westview Press, Boulder

Auberni JAI (2003) Pour une Europe encourageant ses identités historiques et culturelles. In: Le Coadic R (ed) Identités et démocratie: diversité culturelle et mondialisation. Repenser la démocratie. Presses Universitaires de Rennes, Rennes

[227] "The Moroccan Initiative for negotiating an autonomy statute for the Sahara region", para 11.

[228] See the extensive comparision made by El Ouali (2008, p. 138 et seq).

Baillard J-F (2004) Le gouvernement du monde. Une critique politique de la globalisation, Fayard, Paris
Badie B (2002) La société plurielle entre mythes et réalités. Un essai d'identification politique de situations pluralistes in À la recherche de la démocratie, Mélanges offerts à Guy Hermet (ed.) Javier Santiso, Editions Karthala, Paris
Barnsley I, Bleiker R (2008) Self-determination: from decolonization to deterritorialization. Global Change Peace Security 20(2)
Batistich M (1995) The right to self- determination and international law. Auckland Univ Law Rev
Binder G (1993) The case for self-determination. Stanford J Int Law 29
Bolton J (1998) Resolving the Western Sahara conflict, transcript of the Congressional Defence and Foreign Policy Forum
Brancati D (2006) Decentralization: fuelling the fire or dampening the flames of ethnic conflicts and secessionism? Int Org 60
Brass P (1985) Ethnic groups and the state. In: Brass P (ed) Ethnic Groups and the State. Croom Helm, London
Brilmayer L (1991) Secession: a territorial reinterpretation. Yale J Int Law 16
Brownlie I (1988) The rights of peoples in modern international law. In: Crawford J (ed) The Rights of Peoples. Oxford University Press, Oxford
Buchanan A (1992) Self-determination and the right to secede. J Int Aff 45(2)
Buchanan A (1995) Federalism, secession, and the morality of inclusion. Arizona Law Rev 37
Buchheit LC (1978) Secession: The Legitimacy of Self-Determination. Yale University Press, New Haven
Burchill R (ed) (2006) Democracy and International Law. Ashgate, Aldershot
Calogeropoulos-Stratis S (1973) Le Droit des Peoples à Disposer D'eux-Mêmes. Bruylant, Bruxelles
Cardenas EJ, Canas MF (2002) The limits of self-determination. In: Danspeckgruber W (ed) The Self-Determination of Peoples: Community, Nation, and State in an Interdependent World. Lynne Rienner, Bouldner
Cass DZ (1992) Re-thinking self-determination: a critical analysis o current international law theories. Syracuse J Int'l Com 18
Casseese A (1995) Self-Determination: A Legal Reappraisal. Cambridge University Press, Cambridge
Cassese A (1995) Self-Determination of Peoples. A Legal Reappraisal. Cambridge University Press, Cambridge
Chevalier J (2004) L'Etat post-moderne, L.G.D.J, 2nd ed., Paris
Chen LC (1991) Self-determination and world public order. Notre Dame Law Rev 66
Christakis T (1999) Le droit à l'autodétermination en dehors des situations de décolonisation. La Documentation française, Paris
Claude I (1955) National Minorities: An International Problem, Harvard University Press, Cambridge
Cleveland H (1995) Birth of a New World. Basic Books, New York
Cobban A (1945) The Nation-State and National Self-Determination. Collins, The Fontana Library, London
Cole A (2001) Franco-German Relations. Longman, Harlow
Colomer JM (2007) Great Empires, Small Nations. The Uncertain Future of the Sovereign State. Routledge, London
Cornell SE (2002) Autonomy as a source of conflict. Caucasian conflicts in theoretical perspective. World Polit 54
Corten O (1999) A propos d'un désormais 'classique': le droit à l'autodétermination en dehors des situations de décolonisation de Théodore Christakis. RBDI 1
Crawford J (1979) The Creation of States in International Law. Clarendon University Press, Oxford
Crawford J (ed) (1988) The Rights of Peoples. Clarendon Press, Oxford

Crawford J (2000) State practice and international law in relation to unilateral secession. Bayefsky AF (ed) Self-Determination in International Law: Quebec and Lessons Learned. Available in http://canada.justice.gc/en/news/nr/1997/craw.html
Dahbour O (2003) Illusion of the Peoples. A Critique of National Self- Determination, Lexington Books, Lanham.
de Cuellar P (1997) Pilgrimage for Peace, St. Martin's, New York
Diez T, Stetter S, Alibert M (2006) The European Union and border conflicts: the transformative power of integration. Int Org 60
Eide A (1990) The universal declaration in space and time. In: Berting J et al (eds) Human Rights in a Pluralistic World: Individuals and Collectives. Roosevelt Study Center, Middelburg
Etzioni A (1992) The Evils of Self-Determination, Foreign Policy
Fabry M (2009) The right to democracy in international law: a classical liberal reassessment. Millennium J Int Stud 37(3)
Falk RA (1997) The Right of Self-Determination Under International Law: The Coherence of Doctrine Versus the Incoherence of Experience
Fox GH, Roth BR (eds) (2000) Democratic Governance and International Law. Cambridge University Press, Cambridge
Franck TR (1992) The emerging right to democratic governance. AJIL 86(1)
Franck TM (1993) Postmodern tribalism and the right to secession. In: Brolmann C, Lefeber R, Zieck M (eds) Peoples and Minorities in International Law. Martinus Nijhoff, London
Freeman M (1998) The Right to Self-Determination in International Politics: Six Theories in Search of a Policy, Review of International Studies 25
Gellner E (1983) Nations and Nationalism. Cornell University Press, Ithaca, NY
Gould CC (1988) Rethinking Democracy: Freedom and Social Cooperation in Politics, Economy, and Society. Cambridge University Press, Cambridge, chap.12
Gould CC (2006) Self-determination beyond sovereignty: relating transnational democracy to local autonomy. J Soc Philos 37(1)
Goulding M (2002) Peacemonger, John Murray, London
Griffiths M (2003) Self-Determination, International Society and World Order, Macquarie Law Journal 3
Guilhaudis JF (1976) Le droit des peuples à disposer d'eux-mêmes. Presses Universitaires de Grenoble, Grenoble
Gurr TR (2000) Peoples Versus States. Minorities at Risk in the New Century, 2nd edn. United States Institute of Peace Press, Washington
Gurr RR (2002) Peoples Versus States. Minorities at Risk in the New Century. United States Institute of Peace Press, Washington
Halperin M, Scheffer DJ et al (1992) Self-determination in the new world order: guidelines for us policy. Carnegie Endowment for International Peace, Washington
Hannikainen L (1998) Self-determination and autonomy in international law. In: Suksi M (ed) Autonomy: Applications and Implications. Kluwer Law International, The Hague
Hannum H (1990) Autonomy, Sovereignty and Self-Determination: The Accommodation of Conflicting Rights. University of Pennsylvania Press, Philadelphia
Hannum H (1993) Rethinking Self-Determination. Virginia J Int Law 34
Hannum H (1998a) The specter of secession: responding to claims for ethnic self-determination. Foreign Aff 77
Hannum H (1998b)The right to self-determination in the twenty-first century. Wash Lee Law Rev
Hannum H, Lillich RB (1980) The concept of autonomy in international law. AJIL 74
Heraclides A (1992) Secession and third-party intervention. J Int Aff 45(2)
Holsti KJ (2004) Taming the Sovereigns. Institutional Change in International Politics. Cambridge University Press, Cambridge
Horowitz DL (2000) Ethnic Groups in Conflict. University of California Press, Berkeley
International Crisis Group (2007a) Le Sahara Occidental: le coût humain, 11 June 2007, No 65

International Crisis Group (2007b) Western Sahara: Out of Impasse?, Middle/North Africa Report, 11 June 2007
Jacquier B (1974) L'autodétermination du Sahara espagnol, RGDIP
Jensen E (2005) Western Sahara. Anatomy of a stalemate, Lynne Rienner, Boulder London
Johnson HS (1967) Self-Determination Within the Community of Nations. Sijthoff, Leyden
Kamenka E (1988) Human rights, peoples' rights. In: Crawford J (ed) The Rights of Peoples. Clarendon Press, Oxford
Kirgis FL Jr (1998) The degree of self-determination in the United nations era. AJIL
Klabbers J, Lefeber R (1993) Africa: lost between self-determination and Uti Possidetis. In: Brolman C, Leber R, Zieck M (eds) Peoples and Minorities in International Law. Martinus Nijhoff, Dordrecht
Koskennieni M (1994) National Self-Determination Today: problems of Legal Theory and Practice, I.C.L.Q., 43
Koubi G (1995) Penser les minorités en droit. In: Fenet A (ed) Le Droit des Minorités. Bruylant, Brussels
Kymlicka W (2001) Politics in the Vernacular. Nationalism, Multiculturalism, and Citizenship. Oxford University Press, Oxford
Laing EA (1991–1992) The norm of self-determination 1941-1991. California WILJ 22
Lane J-E, Ersson S (2003) Democracy. A Comparative Approach. Routledge, London
Lapidoth R (1981) Some reflections on autonomy. In: Mélanges P. Reuter. A. Pédone, Paris
Lapidoth R (1994) Autonomy: potential and limitations. Int J Groups Rights 1
Lapidoth R (2003) Autonomie, unité et démocratie. In: Ronan Le Coadic (ed) Identités et démocratie: Diversité Culturelle et mondialisation. Presse Universitaires de Rennes, Rennes
League of Nations (1920) The Aalands Islands Question, Report of the International Committee of Jurists, Official Journal. Spec. Suppl. No 3
League of Nations (1921) Report by the Commission of Rapporteurs, LN Council Doc.B7:21/68/106
Levine A (1999) Political accommodation and the prevention of secessionist violence. Brown ME (ed) The International Dimensions of Internal Conflict. The MIT Press, London
Levitsky S, Way LA (2010) Competitive Authoritanianism. Hybrid Regimes After the Cold War. Cambridge University Press, New York
Lijphart A (1969) Consociational Democracy, World Politics 21
Lijphart A (1977) Democracy in Plural Societies, Yale University Press, New Haven
Lijphart A (1984) Democracies, Yale University Press, New Haven
McCray J (2005) Asymmetric federalism and the plurinational state. Contribution presented at the Third Conference on Federalism, Brussels, 3–5 March 2005
Mello B (2004) Recasting the right to self-determination: group rights and political participation. Soc Theory Pract 30
Messary N (2001) National security, the political space and citizenship: the case of Morocco and the Western Sahara, Journal of North African Studies 6/4
Miller B (2005) When and how regions become peaceful: potential theoretical pathways to peace. Int Stud Rev 7
Mokhtar Ould Daddah's memoirs (2003) La Mauritanie contre vents et marées
Mozaffar S, Scarritt JR (2000) Why territorial autonomy is not a viable option for managing ethnic conflict in african plural societies. In: Safran W, Maiz R (eds) Identity and Territorial Autonomy in Plural Societies. Frank Cass, London
Mukherjee B (2006) Why do political power-sharing agreements lead to enduring peaceful resolution of some civil wars, but not others? Int Stud Q 50
Musgrave ThD (1997) Self-Determination and national minorities. Clarendon Press, Oxford
Nanda V (1981) Self-determination under international law: validity of claims to secede. Case Western Reserve J Int Law 13
Neisse F (2002) Le règlement du conflit du Sahara occidental et l'ONU. Pour quelle "troisième voie"?, Annuaire Français de Relations Internationales

Noreau P, Vallet E (2004) Le droit comme ressource des minorités nationale :un modèle de mobilisation politique du droit. Université de Montréal, www.ie-ei.eu/bibliotheque/minorites.htm
North DC, Wallis JJ, Weingast BR (2009) Violence and Social Orders. A Conceptual Framework for Interpreting Recorded Human History. Cambridge University Press, Cambridge
Noutcheva G, Tocci N, Cppiers B, Kovziride T, Emerson M, Huysseune M (2004) Europeanization and secessionist conflicts: concepts and theories. J Ethnopolitics Issues in Europe I
Osman A (1986) La stratégie marocaine de la négociation et la récupération du Sahara in Edification d'un Etat moderne. Le Maroc de Hassan II
Paust JJ (1980) Self-determination: a definitional focus. In: Alexander Y, Riedlander RA (eds) Self- Determination: National, Regional, and Global Dimensions. Westview Press, Boulder
Plotke D (2003) Democracy and groups. Social Research 70:466–467
Pomerance M (1982) Self-Determination in Law and Practice. The New Doctrine in the United Nations. Nijhoff, The Hague
Requejo F, Nagel K-J (eds) (2011) Federalism Beyond Federations. Asymmetry and Processes of Resymmetrisation in Europe, Farnham/Burlington, Ashgate
Rigo-Sureda A (1973) "The Evolution" of the Right of Self-Determination. A Study of the United Nations Practice. Sijthoff, Leyden
Ronen D (1979) The Quest for Self-Determination. Yale University Press, New Haven
Rosecrance RN, Stein AA (2006) No More States? Globalization, National Self-Determination and Terrorism. Rowman & Littlefield Publishers Inc., New York
Salmon J (2001) Dictionnaire de Droit International, AUF
Samarasinghe S, Donaldson B, McGinn C (2001) Conflict vulnerability analysis. Issue, tools & responses. www.certi.org/publications/Manuals/CVA.pdf
Scharf MP (2003) Earned sovereignty: juridical underpinnings. Denv J Intl Law Policy 31(3):383
Sellers M (ed) (1996) The New World Order. Sovereignty, Human Rights and the Self-Determination of Peoples. Berg, Oxford
Shaw MN (1997) Peoples, territorialism and boundaries. Eur J Int Law 8(3)
Simpson GJ (1996) The diffusion of sovereignty: self-determination in the post-colonial age. In: Sellers M (ed) The New World Order Sovereignty, Human Rights and the Self-Determination of People. Berg, Oxford
Sindjoun L (2000) La dé mocratie est-elle soluble dans le pluralisme culturel?, Rapport Introductif, Colloque Commonwealth-Francophonie, Démocratie et sociétés plurielles, Yaounde
Sorensen G (2001) Changes in Statehood. The Transformation of International Relations. Palgrave, Houndmills
Steiner HJ (1991) Ideals and counter-ideals in the struggle over autonomy regimes for minorities. Notre Dame Law Rev 66
Suksi M (2005) Keeping the lid on the secession kettle-a review of legal interpretations concerning claims of self-determination by minority populations. Int J Minority Group Rights 12
Sur S (1997) The State between Fragmentation and Globalization, European Journal of International Law. 8(3)
Teson FR (1998) A Philosophy of International Law, Westview Press, Colorado
Tomuschat C (1993) Self-determination in a post-colonial world. In: Tomuschat C (ed) Modern Law of Self-Determination. Martinus Nijhoff, The Hague
Vignes G (1953) Les consultations populaires dans les territoires sous tutelle, RGDIP
Wambaugh S (1927) La pratique des plébiscites internationaux, RCADI 1927-IV
Watts RL (2008) Comparing Federal Systems. McGill-Queen's University Press, Montreal
Weller M (2005) Towards a General Comment on Self-Determination and Autonomy, Working Paper, Commission on Human Rights, Sub-Commission on the Promotion and Protection of Human Rights, Working Group on Minorities, Eleven session, 30 May–3 June 2005, E/CN.4/Sub.2/AC.5/2005/WP.5

Weller M (2008) Escaping the Self-determination Trap, Martinus Nijhoff Publishers, Leiden/Boston

Williams PR, Pecci FJ (2004) Earned sovereignty: bridging the gap between sovereignty and self-determination. Stanford J Int Law 40

Wolff S, Weller M (2005) Self-determination. A conceptual approach. In: Weller M, Wolff S (eds) Autonomy, Self-Government and Conflict Resolution. Innovative Approaches to Institutional Design in Divided Societies. Routledge, Oxon

Zunes S (1995) Algeria, the Maghreb Union, and the Western Sahara Stalemate, Arab Studies Quarterly:(28)

Conclusion

One of the major conclusions of this book is that the traditional reified approach of the principle of territorial integrity is not of great help if we want to capture the real nature, meaning and complexity of that principle. The use in an interactive manner of different scientific knowledge and disciplines has shown that territorial integrity is something more than the completeness/unity of state territory. Territorial integrity is in fact the elaborated and sophisticated legal expression of territoriality. It is intimately linked to the state as a legal entity the main objective of which is to ensure its perennial existence within a specific territory whose borders have been established in accordance with International Law. The heuristic capacity of the comprehensive approach adopted in this book has furthermore shown that territorial integrity is the cornerstone of International Law in that it is the foundational basis from which have emerged the legal principles that are the pillars of International Law.

Thus, territorial integrity has, first, given rise to major principles such as the principle of sovereignty and its corollary, the principle of nonintervention. Such conclusion is all the more important that International Law has witnessed a recurrent and never ended debate on the origin and basis of the principle of sovereignty. This debate, very often impregnated by ideological preoccupations and self-interest considerations, comes frequently into being when there is a crisis of the state institution, such as today with globalization, or when states in the periphery show a willingness to act in an independent manner in International Relations.

Territorial integrity has, second, given rise to legal principles which are directly related to territory such as the necessary consent of the state when delimiting its territory, a principle which has been obviously called into question by the proponents of the uti possidetis. Territory integrity has also given rise to the principle of the necessary consent of the state to territorial changes in compliance with the requirement of Constitutional law. Such requirement, which has been extensively discussed by traditional doctrine, has gained prominence in the past decades further to the development of self-determination and democracy.

A. El Ouali, *Territorial Integrity in a Globalizing World*,
DOI 10.1007/978-3-642-22869-8, © Springer-Verlag Berlin Heidelberg 2012

Looking in a new light at territorial integrity has also shown that the latter has undergone a major transformation when it integrated popular sovereignty, a fact without which the passage since the end of the eighteenth century from the patriarchal state to the nation-state would have been made impossible. It has also shown that territorial integrity has, by integrating popular sovereignty, that is self-determination, correlatively integrated a potential of self-destruction from which no state ethnically divided is immune.

One of the other important findings of our analysis of territorial integrity is also that the state has been able to survive for millenaries as the main form of the organization of human societies thanks to the flexibility of territoriality. It was indeed the latter that has enabled the state to adapt to changing situations either by sharing power through territorial autonomy or reinforcing the effectiveness of its territoriality or combining both under the federal system. Modern states have in particular shown a greater capacity to adapt to newly threatening situations than ancient states. This has been particularly the situation in Western countries where the states have never come to see the nation as something definitive and immutable. Quite the opposite, they have continued to apply homogenization policies and adjust them to the demands of modernization and liberal democracy. Reforms have often been adopted to strengthen the democratic base of the nation-state. The states have also continued to apply an inclusive policy by which people can integrate a common culture, irrespective of race or colour. Thus, to the Western mind, a nation is not a finished product, but rather, in the same way as a piece of Penelope canvas, a work in progress, not to be undone but constantly reworked, refined and adjusted with a view to maintaining the cohesion of society. However, globalization has led Western countries to forget the virtues of this constant work on preserving their homogeneity, which fact has caused the difficulty they are experiencing today in containing the emergence of the phenomenon of ethno-nationalism and maintaining intact the cohesion of their societies. But, the situation is clearly more serious in the rest of the world, particularly in the majority of Southern countries, where the states have rarely been able to homogenize the society and ensure the well being to their citizens and even sometimes to provide for the security of their people.

Because of globalization, the states today are indeed no longer sheltered against ethnic fragmentation. It is so because they are less able to provide for the welfare of their citizens. More serious is the fact that certain states are finding it difficult to provide even the minimum required to meet the first *raison d'être* of any state – the guarantee of security and public order within their own societies. If social, trades union and political protests were traditionally concerned with the economic and social policies applied by governments because they were considered anti-social and thus often aimed at the very existence of these governments, it is believed that popular protests will also increasingly tend to be directly aimed at the state and its very existence. Thus, the threat of traditional social unrest is now accompanied by the risk of states' fragmentation. This risk is all the greater when "any society is, in theory, plural, that is to say able to shape and re-shape itself depending on errors which, incidentally, could not be known about in advance and resulting from issues at stake, failed or successful enterprises, integration and political disintegration and counter mobilization."[1] European countries tried to lessen this risk by providing aid to the most impoverished European regions. Others, like the United States and Canada, have long since strengthened their symmetrical federalism by adopting cultural pluralism, based on the respect and the enhancement of the cultural and ethnic identity of all sections of their societies. Many states have also ended by putting in place structures of territorial autonomy meant to share power with local communities and therefore to prevent their own disintegration.

Territorial autonomy appears clearly to be necessary to the postmodern state because it can help it ensure its own survival. Broken up by globalization, the state must strengthen its foundations if it is to avoid paying the price of ethnic disintegration. At the end of the eighteenth century, the state realized that its survival depended on proclaiming national sovereignty, in other words, the consecration of the right to democratic self-determination. Today, the state must go further by strengthening democracy through the effective extension of local involvement in the form of territorial autonomy. A number of Northern countries have understood that their salvation rests in sharing their sovereignty with local communities. However, only few Southern countries have started to follow suit. We know that the ethnic conflicts and civil wars going on around the world primarily affect these countries. These conflicts will tend, because of globalization, to worsen and multiply. The risk of disintegration is therefore far greater for these countries. The latter can therefore no longer continue to indefinitely ignore what is today's foundation for the state – democratic self-determination and its necessary complement, territorial democracy.

However, the revival of territorial autonomy is not a panacea as it cannot alone help in addressing these challenges. The later can be met only if the states show a great sense of flexibility and adaptability. Obsessed by the challenges of economic globalization, the states have not so far shown that sense as they mostly tend to favor the market against society. By doing so, they are weakening if not destroying their "raison d'être" which is to provide the well being of those who make them exist, that is their own citizens. Therefore, the challenges posed by postmodernity require above all the "socialization" of globalization. A halt to the destructive potential of globalization, which is eloquently confirmed by the later present crisis, cannot be made unless the states revive what has been at the basis of their unprecedented strength: the conciliation between economic competition and social democracy. As for the Southern countries, they cannot survive without initiating a serious and credible process of good governance and effective democracy which are the only way to build from scratch viable societies and solid nation-states. However, meeting the challenges posed by globalization and its destabilizing impact is not an easy task in a situation where International Law does offer to states only a weak protection against external threats.

In the past decades, some states have disintegrated and disappeared from the world map. The international community has remained indifferent to that situation,

[1] B. Badie "La société plurielle entre mythes et réalités. Un essai d'identification politique de situations pluralistes", op.cit., p. 62.

although it did affect international peace and security. Such passive attitude reflects if any the biggest flaw of International Law: the lack of any obligation as well as a mechanism to protect the existence of the states members of the international community. Contemporary International Law remains therefore as primitive as did the old International Law. The latter, while recognizing states' right to use force in order to preserve their own existence, has concomitantly authorized the states to conquer other territories, that is to destroy other states and annex their territories. True, such situation has completely changed with the creation of the United Nations whose Charter has prohibited the use of force between states. However, the Charter did not put in place a system guaranteeing states' territorial integrity by the international community. It did not even consider establishing a system similar to the one created by the famous Article 10 of the League of Nations' Covenant, although it is true that the latter has very quickly lost its credibility as the League of Nations has never been able to make use of it. This may be considered as the biggest failure of the international community in establishing an international order guaranteeing the right of the existence of its members.

In internal law, the right of individuals to existence and security is protected by the state. This is the "raison d'être" of the state. It is that reason which justifies state's legitimate monopoly of violence. Such a situation does not exist in International Law. The latter has in fact been construed on an ambiguity as while it did proclaim the prohibition of the use of force, it has not established an international system by which it could guarantee the existence of the states and makes of this prohibition a reality. Although the UN Charter has established a system of collective security, the implementation of such a system has very often been blocked and neutralized by the rivalry between powerful states. The only progress made by International Law in protecting states' territories was the rise in states' practice of the obligation of non-recognition of territorial changes made by force, a practice which has emerged in order to make a balance to the inability of the international community to implement Article 10 of the League of Nations' Covenant. However, such a practice has not prevented territorial changes from continuing to happen through the unilateral use of force. Consequently, contemporary states will continue, as did ancient states, to count on the use of force as the ultimate way to protect their territorial integrity, that is their own existence. The international system will therefore remain unstable and anarchical as long as it does not give rise to a global governance possessing a legitimate monopoly of violence against the provision of protection to states' territorial integrity.

The unstable and anarchical character of the present international system, due to the lack of any international mechanism guaranteeing states' territorial integrity, may even more be aggravated by the fact that the world society is marked by "non-integration" and "multiplicity without unity"[2] as well as by a "disaggregated

[2] Beck (2000, p. 10).

world of governance"[3] as the latter is meant to protect the subjective interests of groups of individuals and not the supreme right to existence of the states which is nothing other than the right to existence of their peoples. A new world polity would emerge from the present unstable and chaotic situation only if a global system of governance is built in a way to provide to all the peoples across the world what only their states have so far been able to provide them with: the protection of their right to existence. Any attempt to conceive of the rise of a new international polity without taking into consideration such a fundamental prerequisite would remain chimerical.[4]

References

Beck U (2000) What is globalization? Polity Press, Cambridge

Keane J (2003) Global civil society? Cambridge University Press, Cambridge

Nye JS, Donahue JD (eds) (2000) Governance in a globalizing world. Brookings Institution Press, Washington

[3] Nye and Donahue (2000, p. 14).

[4] An example of a chimerical and an unrealistic approach to the emergence of new world polity is offered by Keane (2003, p. 96 and seq.).

Index

A. El Ouali, *Territorial Integrity in a Globalizing World*,
DOI 10.1007/978-3-642-22869-8,

MIX
Papier aus verantwortungsvollen Quellen
Paper from responsible sources
FSC® C105338

If you have any concerns about our products,
you can contact us on
ProductSafety@springernature.com

In case Publisher is established outside the EU,
the EU authorized representative is:
Springer Nature Customer Service Center GmbH
Europaplatz 3, 69115 Heidelberg, Germany

Printed by Libri Plureos GmbH
in Hamburg, Germany